GIVE ME A HOME AMONG THE GUMTREES

I've been around the world
A couple of times or maybe more
I've seen the sights and had delights
On every foreign shore
But when me (my) friends all ask me
The place that I adore
I tell them right away

Chorus

Give me a home among the gumtrees
With lots of plum trees
A dog or two and a barbecue
Flowers down the side
And vegies down the fence
All in Burke's Backyard!

Standing in the kitchen cooking up a roast
Or Vegemite on toast
You and me and a cup of tea
Then later on we'll settle down
And mull up on the porch
And watch the possums play

There's a Safeways on the corner
A Woolworths down the street
And a new place that just opened up
Where they regulate the heat
But I'd trade it all tomorrow
For a simple bush retreat
Where the kookaburras call

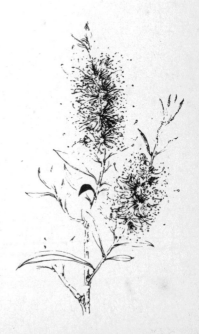

Some people build their houses
With fences all around
Others live in mansions
And some beneath the ground
But me I like the bush you know
With rabbits running 'round
And a pumpkin vine out the back

Lyrics printed by kind permission of Mushroom
Music Pty Ltd for the World.

Burke's Backyard

Burke's Backyard

Don Burke

HUTCHINSON AUSTRALIA

IN ASSOCIATION WITH MARGARET GEE

Hutchinson Australia,
an imprint of
Random Century Australia Pty Ltd
20 Alfred Street, Milsons Point, NSW 2061

Sydney Melbourne London
Auckland Johannesburg
and agencies throughout the world

First published in 1989
Reprinted December 1989

in association with MARGARET GEE
Suite 221, 1-12 Angel Place, Sydney, NSW 2000

Distributed by Random Century Australia Pty Ltd

National Library of Australia
Cataloguing-in-Publication Data

Burke, Don.
  Burke's backyard.

  Includes index.
  ISBN 0 09 169731 X

  1. Gardening—Australia. 2. Natural history—Australia.
  3. Dwellings—Maintenance and repair. I. Title. II. Title:
  Burke's backyard (Television program).

635.0994

Designed by Reno Visual Communications, Sydney
Typeset by Midland Typesetters, Victoria
Printed by Australian Print Group, Victoria
Production by Vantage Graphics, Sydney

Author's acknowledgements

An enormous amount of research went into this book. Whilst the blame for any and all errors rests with the bearded person on the cover, much of the credit for the good bits is due to others. Slaving away behind the scenes at 'Burke's Backyard' are a number of excellent researchers: Joanne Elliott, Lee Evans, Jenny James and Jan Stretton. Of course, Steve Wood our Executive Producer, and our presenters on the programme also contributed greatly: Densey Clyne, Harry Cooper, John Dengate, Fiona Fearon, Peter Harris, Karl Kruszelnicki, Reg Livermore, Jim Pike and Kay Stammers.

The organisation of this book was undertaken by Margaret Gee, who is simply one of the most impressive people I have ever met in the publishing industry, and Lee Evans. Lee's editing skills, combined with her attention to detail, bring great credit to all projects she undertakes and I am most grateful for her assistance.

My wife, Marea, must also be acknowledged. She constantly strives to make everything bearing the 'Burke's Backyard' name a success, and only a male ego and a desire not to disenchant those who believe I am responsible for all I utter prevents me from giving her more credit.

DENSEY CLYNE AND JIM FRAZIER

While Densey Clyne and Jim Frazier are known to viewers of 'Burke's Backyard' as the presenter and cameraman for many wildlife segments, their activities extend far beyond that.

Densey Clyne, naturalist, writer and photographer, is one of our best known communicators on natural history subjects. A keen and enthusiastic observer, she presents wildlife to viewers and readers alike with humour, sympathy and scientific accuracy. She has won numerous photographic and book awards including, on two occasions, the C.J.Dennis Award, and her books, articles and photographs are popular worldwide.

Jim Frazier, wildlife cameraman and photographer, has won a reputation for innovative photographic techniques. As Mantis Wildlife Films, he and Densey have travelled widely on filming trips for the BBC, ABC, Film Australia, National Geographic and other organisations. Their filming partnership has resulted in numerous awards. They contributed to the epic BBC TV series 'Life on Earth' and 'Living Planet', and more recently to the ABC's 'Nature of Australia'.

Publisher's acknowledgements

Margaret Gee would like to especially thank Anne Matthews, chief editor of the book, for her unstinting dedication to the accuracy and quality of the editorial content. Sincere thanks to Graham Rendoth for the cover design; Scott Cameron, the book's photographer; the production team at Vantage Graphics: Barry Smith, Marc Nolan, Louise Erratt, Yvonne Revenboer, Gatya Kelly; and Judith Barnard, Helen Carter and Dawn Collicoat of Midland Typesetters.

Many thanks also to Margo Lanagan, Christine Gee, Lisa Foulis and Isobel King for their editorial work.

Special thanks to Marea Burke, Lee Evans, Steve Wood, Trevor Eastment and the 'Burke's Backyard' team. Jackie Rothwell, Video Graphics Manager, and Pam Hose, Publicity Manager, TCN9 Sydney. Pat Cooper of the New South Wales Canine Council; and the illustrators of the dog breeds, Margaret and Marion Davidson. David and Charles, UK, publishers of 'The Big Book Of Cats' and Michael Lissmann, the illustrator of the cat breeds. Shirley Stackhouse for the illustrations of the plants. Pamela Polglase for the plant illustrations on pages 3, 8, 43, 117 and opposite the inside front cover.

Thanks also to Ernie Mason, Matthew Kelly, Alan Davidson, Simon Guthrie, Gayle Gray, Carmen Sin, Bruce Gee, Graeme Goldin, Alf Gates, Joan Webster, Doo-Mee the cover cat, and Kit Kat.

Finally, many thanks to Don Burke, who is the least 'lazy' person I have ever worked with.

CONTENTS

Chapter 12

IN THE GARDEN

PETS AND BACKYARD ANIMALS

HOME AMONG THE GUM TREES

NATIVE FAUNA

NATIVE FLORA

THE ENVIRONMENT

PEOPLE AND PLACES

CONTENTS

INTRODUCTION

There are vast numbers of Australians who are involved in backyard activities: breeding dogs, mowing lawns, or just swimming in a pool. Normal people doing normal things. The irony is that the media have largely ignored these people. Little is available in the electronic media about keeping and breeding dogs, cats, budgies or pigeons—yet over 60% of Australians are involved in these activities. Although gardening is covered in the media, it is normally all about winning the local gardening competition rather than how to enjoy your backyard: hard work rather than relaxation.

'Burke's Backyard' set out to service the Australian family by presenting the best possible information about their world in a digestible manner. Fascinating information about plants and animals, which is easy to understand but also scientifically correct and up to date. In an endeavour to support our television segments, it was decided to produce 'Fact Sheets' (i.e. background information) on most of the segments which are put to air. Herein we created a monster.

We receive up to 30,000 Fact Sheet requests per week and more of our staff are involved in processing these requests than are required for any other aspect of the show. Moreover, many people have written in asking for every Fact Sheet from every programme—past, present and future.

The sheer amount of information that we have processed since September, 1987 when 'Burke's Backyard' first went to air is amazing: ten segments per week for 80 weeks on air. We have covered a huge cross-section of subjects including dog breeds, cat breeds, budgies, horses, cows, canaries, how to grow native plants, camellias, azaleas, chrysanthemums, geraniums, numerous wildlife and ecological matters, how to build dog kennels, repair walls and broken windows, and so on.

Our team feels that we have brought a new scientific integrity and sheer honesty to our subject matter. We 'Road Test' dog and cat breeds and list more of their faults, strengths and veterinary problems than will be found anywhere else; despite the fact that many animal breeders don't want us to even know what the faults are. Where else could you discover that the much lauded Australian Cattle Dog has proved to be virtually useless with modern cattle and as a result is almost never used to work them? Where else could you find that Manx cats often produce kittens with an imperforate anus (no rear opening)?

We have set out to explode many of the old myths: many modern azaleas drop dead (no, it wasn't *your* fault!); top-dressing the lawn is often a useless or even harmful activity; placing drainage material in the bottom of a pot is pointless—and on the list goes.

Not every segment on the show generates a Fact Sheet. For example, the privacy of our Celebrity Gardeners is always respected. We have, however, collected most of what remains to form the basis of this book. A huge amount of research is contained herein and it has been extensively updated for publishing.

There has long been a need for a book like this—a treasure-trove of backyard information. We hope that it meets all of your needs and would welcome comments, criticisms or suggestions for future segments.

GARDEN SONG

Inch by inch, row by row
Going to make this garden grow
Going to make it deep and low
Going to make it fertile ground
Inch by inch, row by row
Please bless these seeds I sow
Please keep them safe below
Till the rain comes tumbling down

Pulling weeds and picking stones
We are made of dreams and bones
I need a place to call my own
Cause the time is close at hand
Grain for grain, sun and rain
Find my way in nature's chain
Tune my body and my brain
To the music of the land

Chorus—repeat first verse

Plant your rows straight and long
Season them with prayer and song
Mother Earth will make them strong
If you give them love and care.
An old crow watching from a tree
He's got his hungry eye on me
In my garden I'm as free
As that feathered thief up there

Chorus—repeat first verse

'Garden Song' (David Mallett)
© 1975 Cherry Lane Music Publishing Co Inc
for the World Warner Chappell Music Controls
all rights for Australia and New Zealand

IN THE GARDEN

CHAPTER 1
Garden Flowers and Shrubs

ANNUALS

Flowering annuals are available from nurseries and garden centres in fairly large sized pots, so that you can have instant colour in the garden. They are very good value; the recommended price of a 125mm (5″) pot being $3-$4. There is a wide range of plants and colours, for example, dianthus, dwarf snapdragon (*Antirrhinum kolibri*), verbena 'Flagship', polyanthus or primrose, pansies in many new varieties, and primulas.

Bloomers can be used as instant annuals in the garden for those people who do not want the fuss of planting seeds, the trouble of fending snails off young seedlings, or the delay of 10 weeks or more before flowering. They can also be used in containers on balconies or around green foliage pot plants for colour. If left in their pots outdoors, given plenty of water and fertilised every couple of weeks, they should last until October or November. They may also need to be trimmed back a little. If they are planted in the garden they should last even longer, that is, if planted in July or August they should last until January.

You may also consider using them indoors where they may last a week or two in an attractive pot—this is great value as an alternative to cut flowers.

Six-pack punnets are now widely available. These plants are stronger than seedlings and are already starting to flower. They will provide instant colour and will cost about $2.70 for the six plants.

ANTHURIUMS

One of the most curious and spectacular of all the tropical flowering plants is the Anthurium. This plant comes from the jungles of Central and South America, and its exotic, vivid, waxy blooms are popular in floral arrangements for weddings and restaurants.

The true flowers of the anthurium are actually tiny blooms which are massed over a spike or column (in the case of the form known as the Flamingo Flower the column is gracefully twisted). The spike projects from a bright, waxy shield or spathe, which is actually a specially developed leaf. There are 50-60 different varieties and colours range from pinks, white, reds and oranges to apricots, and also white with pink veins.

In ideal conditions anthuriums will flower virtually all year round, but numerous criteria must be met for that to occur. They require a stable temperature which does not drop below 16°C (61°F) at any time of the year. Often it is necessary to grow them in glasshouses.

Anthuriums need to be grown in a rich, moist compost with perfect drainage to avoid root disease problems. Pure peat moss or a very peaty open mix can be used.

Anthuriums also require lots of light and a heavily humid atmosphere. If grown in the home they need to be sprayed with water from an atomiser bottle at least twice a day.

Anthuriums detest strong fertilisers and grow best when dosed every couple of months with a liquid fertiliser at half strength.

Propagation is achieved by the division of older plants in early spring.

AZALEAS

There are many different types of azaleas and most people have had one that looked beautiful but eventually died, usually because it was not a hardy variety. Some azaleas are very difficult to grow and others are easy so it is very important to select your azalea carefully.

Don Burke has divided azaleas into four groups:

1 *Hardy, old-fashioned, tall-growing azaleas*. These are as hardy as Australian native plants and as quick growing. They are suitable for growing along roads, and similar areas, even in high pollution regions.

BURKE'S BACKYARD INFORMATION GUIDE

'Alba Magna'—white, green throat—grows to 2m (6½')
'Alphonse Anderson'—pink edged white, rosy blotch—grows to 2 metres
'Magnifica'—purple—grows to 2 metres
'Phoenicea'—deep mauve—grows to 2 metres
'Splendens'—rosy salmon pink—grows to 3m (10') or more
'Maves'—rich red—grows to 2 metres; not widely available
'Schryderii'—white flowers with mauve throat; somewhat scruffy bush—grows to 1-2m (3¼-6½')

2 *Smaller growing azaleas*, not as hardy as the first group but still very good performers in the ground. Dig plenty of compost into the soil prior to planting.

Reds: 'Advent Bells', 'Red Poppy', 'Avenir', 'Red Wing'
Whites: 'White Crane', 'White Prince' (deep pink throat), 'Snow Prince'
Pinks: 'Madame Auguste Haerens' (multi-colour), 'Dancer', 'Rose Queen', 'Sweet Nellie', 'Beverley Haerens' (very light pink to white), 'Pink Dream', 'My Fair Lady', 'Balsaminaeflorum'
Mauves: 'Bonnie McKee', 'James Belton', 'Phil Sherringham', 'Rosa Belton'
Purples: 'Happy Days', 'Violacea'

3 *Azaleas which are difficult to grow in the ground in many areas of Australia.* The further north, the more difficult they are to grow. They are, however, reasonably good in pots.

'Silver Anniversary'—silvery pink
'Comptesse de Kerchove'—light salmon, white edges
'Southern Aurora'—white with border of pink/red
'Elsa Karga'—the best red-coloured azalea
'Red Ruffles'—salmon red, ruffled petals

'Pink Ruffles'—two-tone pink, white edge, ruffled petals
'Leopold Astrid'—white with pink edge
'Searchlight'—white

4 Another group is *Kurumes*, which are generally 1-1.5m (3¼-5') tall and almost as wide. Virtually all Kurumes are easy to grow in the ground.

'Kirin'—bright silvery rose pink
'Christmas Cheer'—deep pink
'Princess Maude'—pink
'Kasane Kagaribi'—salmon pink
'Tancho'—pink, edged with rose
'Glowing Embers'—orange/red
'Osaraku'—white, edged with lavender
'Fred Colbert'—bright red
'Fairy Bells'—pale pink, flecked red

For those people who live in cooler areas of Australia, particularly in southern areas, there are deciduous azaleas, for example, Mollis azaleas. They come in a wide range of flower colours including yellow, apricot and orange/red. They do not grow well in middle to north Australia.

Care and drainage Azaleas insist on a well-drained, airy soil that is regularly watered. They demand a surface mulch (leaves, pinebark, compost) for peak performance and appreciate annual fertilising with Osmocote or cow manure.

From October to about April, you may need to spray with Lebaycid (spray again in 7-10 days for complete control) to control azalea lace bug and red spider, both of which cause the leaves to discolour to a silver or bronze tone. The flowers on most varieties are inclined to rot during humid periods—this disease is called petal blight. No spray will totally control this rot, but some success may be obtained by using Bayleton and/or Daconyl.

Drainage is at its very worst during winter. All too often drainage problems are caused by garden beds damming the natural runoff of water or by depressions being created at the time the house site was excavated. When it next rains, dress appropriately, take an umbrella and venture out into the garden. By standing in the rain you should be able to see where the water flows and where it is impeded. Place a marker at these positions and change the surface contours later on. If all else fails, dig a trench and install plastic agricultural pipe in a gravel bed leading water away from the moist areas.

BALSAM

Balsam, also known as Impatiens or Busy Lizzie, is an excellent plant for a shady spot that needs brightening up with some colour. Azaleas were once recommended for these areas but they are slow growing. The modern impatiens plant is colourful, hardy, fast growing, and easy to care for.

One of the plants that brought interest back to balsam was the New Guinea balsam. This is found in the wild with variegated leaves and a fairly wide colour range—red, pinks and orange. These plants are sterile, so if you hate impatiens because it seeds all over the backyard, then these are the ones for you. They do require a little more light than other varieties; they will grow in shade with fairly green leaves but need some sun for the variegations to show in the leaf.

The most useful of the balsams are those produced in North America, which are almost ground covers. These are the most modern variety which grow to only 10cm (4″) high and have a wide colour range—pink, flesh pink, reds, whites, even multicolours. They are the most popular bedding plant (annual) in the USA and we in Australia are only now realising how good they are. There are other types in this group—some very gaudy colours and some called 'ZigZag' with white through the red.

The most choice or showy varieties are the double flowering impatiens—they have miniature rose-like flowers in shell pink, red and white stripe, mid-pink, dark pink and many more. There is a very good range of the doubles—they are basically produced from the older type of balsam and therefore a little taller.

Balsam respond well to being cut back; they reshoot quickly and grow better for having been pruned.

My tip for using balsam is to grow the single white on the shady side of the house—it will lift the whole area.

Balsam can be bought in packets of seeds, or in pots, from most nurseries.

BANKSIAS

Banksias were named after Sir Joseph Banks, the English botanist who came to Australia with Captain Cook. He collected the first specimen, *Banksia serrata* at Botany Bay. There are more than sixty species of the banksia.

Banksias are grown for their foliage, for cut flowers, and to attract birds with their nectar. One of their best uses in the home garden is as a screening plant—the heath banksia, *Banksia ericifolia* is a suitable species.

The flower spikes of the banksia consist of hundreds of individual flowers on a conelike structure; some are spherical and others are like candles. After picking, they remain fresh for a long time and are popular for dried flower arrangements.

Banksia victoriae is a medium shrub growing to 7m (23′) high with woolly orange spikes; *Banksia ashbyi* grows to about 3m (10′) high with large orange spikes; *Banksia coccinea* is of varying size 1.5m-4m (5-13′), bearing bright red, short cylindrical spikes; *Banksia speciosa* is a large, round, dense shrub growing to about 6m (19½′) high with yellowish-green flower spikes; *Banksia baueri* is a small, round shrub less than 1m (3¼′) high with very large woolly brownish-grey flower spikes.

The contorted shape of the banksias provides good opportunities for wood turning. The following species lend themselves to wood turning:

Banksia spinulosa (hairpin banksia), a medium shrub up to 1.5m (5′) high with various forms of red to gold cylindrical flower spikes; *Banksia ericifolia* (heath banksia), a large, bushy shrub up to 5m (16½′) high with cylindrical orange flower spikes; *Banksia serrata* (old man banksia), a gnarled, large shrub up to 10m (33′) high with a cylindrical grey-green flower spike; *Banksia grandis*, variable from 1.5-10m (5-33′) high, with large yellow flower spikes.

The gnarled and twisted trunks of banksias are rather strange and are certainly not to everyone's liking—they are an acquired taste.

Banksias are easy to grow, but due to their sensitivity to phosphorous they are often killed by applications of superphosphate or lawn food.

Banksia ericifolia the heath banksia, is one of the most useful of all Australian native plants for its excellent screening qualities and its graceful and colourful appearance. It is a large, compact shrub with fine, mid-green leaves, which have a silvery-grey underside.

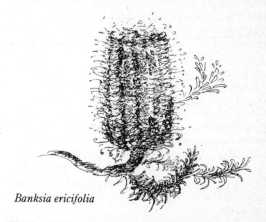

Banksia ericifolia

This banksia is common in sandstone and coastal areas and is hardy enough to grow well in seaside gardens. It tolerates a wide range of soil types but requires good drainage.

Banksia ericifolia bears large, bright, orange-red flower spikes 10-30cm (4-12″) long and 4-6cm (1½-2½″) wide. The long narrow cones that follow the flowers seed readily when they fall to the ground. In fact, natural plantings can easily be achieved by simply scattering cones around the garden. A number of seedlings can be expected to germinate from each cone but only one or two of the strongest will dominate and reach maturity. Observation of this process forms an excellent backyard biology lesson for school-age children.

The flowers are very attractive to honeyeaters and are useful for cut flower arrangements.

BEGONIAS

Hybrid begonia

Bedding or fibrous rooted Begonias are among the most hardworking and dependable of plants. Indeed, if it weren't for their ability to restrain themselves and their generous production of masses of flowers, they might have been classed as weeds, so able are they to flourish despite almost total neglect.

Grown singly, begonias can be a little bland and uninteresting. But as border or edging plants, or for massed displays of single colours, they can be quite eyecatching. If you wish to draw visitors' eyes to a special garden feature, flowers of the same colour can be planted in lines (straight or wavy) heading towards the feature.

Begonias flower over an extended period with some varieties continuing almost all year round. They can be grown from seed from spring to early summer. The seed is extremely fine, so may need to be started in punnets or seed boxes.

Bedding begonias can grow almost anywhere from heavy shade to full sun, although they do need regular watering in the latter position.

Colours range from white through pinks to dark red. Fortnightly applications of liquid fertiliser promote more rapid growth.

The bedding begonia is a trusty old-timer which deserves greater recognition, particularly as a useful element in garden design.

BERRIES

Berries produce colour for many months of the year and attract native birds, which feed on them through the cooler months. If care is taken not to plant a berry-bearing plant near a path, there will be no problems with them being squashed underfoot.

For a shady area there is *Ardisia crenata*, which grows to only about a metre (3¼') tall. It is mainly available in a red-berried form, but there is also a white form. It is very good in the ground and in pots. It can be brought inside for a month or two while in berry and then put back out in the garden.

Japanese sacred bamboo (*Nandina domestica*) is not true bamboo and will not take over the garden, but it does look a little like bamboo. It produces red berries, which often don't appear in warm climates; it needs a cooler climate to produce berries reliably. The leaves open as pink, become light green and in autumn turn to shades of red. They are very useful with their fine foliage and berries, which last for months when cut and placed in water. They are very hardy plants and there is also a dwarf variety, *Nandina domestica* 'Nana'.

A more common group of berry-bearing plants is the Cotoneasters. There are some attractive varieties within this group and their berries attract birds such as gang gang cockatoos. An attractive leaved variety is Cotoneaster horizontalis, which is almost prostrate with small, glossy, green leaves and a great number of red berries from late summer to mid-winter. Cotoneasters are very hardy and may end up as noxious weeds in some areas of Australia.

By far the most colourful and hardy berry plants for most areas are the Firethorns. However, they do have one fault—the thorns. *Pyracantha coccinea* 'Lalandei' has red, glossy berries. Pyracanthas also have two other coloured berries—orange and bright yellow, and they add a lot of colour to the garden in late autumn.

Both Cotoneasters and Pyracanthas can be pruned to grow as a hedge or espaliered against a wall.

If you live in a really cold area of Australia, Holly *(Ilex aquifolium)* will grow very well. Holly is slow growing, and a male plant must be present for the female to bear the red berries. There are many varieties with different leaf shapes and colours and some are more spiny than others.

BIRTHFLOWERS

The tradition of assigning a different birthflower to each month of the year originated in the northern hemisphere. A baby born in March could be presented with bunches or pots of jonquils and daffodils, which are in abundance at that time of the year. In the southern hemisphere, however, March babies would have to wait six months before catching their first glimpse of the designated birthflower, and so the custom has little relevance in countries south of the Equator.

For this reason we have chosen Australian birthflower alternatives which may be used to celebrate not only the birth of a new baby, but also the delicate beauty of our country's indigenous flora.

MONTH	AUSTRALIAN BIRTHFLOWERS	TRADITIONAL BIRTHFLOWERS
January	Blue-bell creeper (*Sollya heterophylla*)	Snowdrop, Carnation
February	Cut-leaf daisy (*Brachycome multifida*)	Violet, Primrose
March	Native rhododendron (*Rhododendron lochiae*)	Jonquil, Daffodil
April	Native violet (*Viola hederacea*)	Sweet pea, Daisy
May	Pink waxflower (*Crowea saligna*)	Lily-of-the-valley, Hawthorn
June	Payne's heath myrtle (*Thryptomene* 'Payne's Hybrid')	Rose, Honeysuckle
July	*Dampiera diversifolia*	Water lily, Larkspur
August	Grey spider flower (*Grevillea buxifolia*)	Poppy, Gladiolus
September	Brown boronia (*Boronia megastigma*)	Aster, Morning glory
October	Gawler bottlebrush (*Callistemon* 'Harkness')	Calendula, Cosmos
November	Flannel flower (*Actinotus helianthi*)	Chrysanthemum
December	Christmas bells (*Blandfordia grandiflora*)	Holly, Narcissus, Poinsettia

BLOSSOMS

Does your garden say it's spring? Nothing sings the song of spring more clearly than blossom trees.

If you have an older-style house, you can create a romantic springtime feeling with prunus—purple-leaved and with lovely flowers. But there are lots of flowering blossom trees to choose from. Flowering peaches are the most widely used. There are many colours, from deep reds to very pale pinks. They must be pruned immediately after flowering so that the fruit does not develop.

If you have a small backyard, there are dwarf peach trees that produce blossoms, and are small enough to be looked after easily. These don't take up too much space, and produce edible fruit as well.

Suggested blossom trees
Purple Prunus: Prunus cerasifera 'Nigra' (the best purple-leaved one) *Prunus x blireana*
Peaches: Prunus persica varieties
Blossom shrubs: Japonica—*Chaenomeles speciosa* has superb blossoms in late winter and spring in red, orange, pink and white.

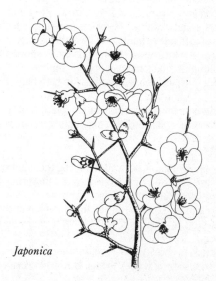

Japonica

BLUE AND WHITE FLOWERING PLANTS

According to the Chelsea Flower Show, blue and white are the most fashionable colours to use in the garden. They work well with just about everything.

For white flowers it is worthwhile thinking about daisies, for example, marguerites. Most varieties of daisy grow very well, and there are some blue varieties as well.

The bellflower, or campanula, with blue flowers, is very easy to grow in most areas of Australia. The small white flowering alyssum is an annual that will come up year after year, is easy to grow and is readily available at any nursery.

There are lots of other plants, for example, a variety of ardisia that has white berries instead of the usual red. It also has small white flowers.

Many standard garden allies come in a white variety, for example, azaleas, geraniums and pelargoniums, which are very hardy plants in most areas of Australia. Also available are blue-mauve varieties of verbena.

If you have a cottage-style or old-fashioned garden, you may like to try an aquilegia—a short-lived plant. Other hardy plants are the duranta and the New Zealand hebe, particularly 'Blue Gem'.

Probably the best white plant of all to have in the garden, if you are in a warm enough area, is a beautifully perfumed gardenia. If you do grow a gardenia, think of having a white oleander nearby. They go together very well, both having a lush, leafy look as well as the white flowers.

There are also lots of climbers that work well in the garden. Clematis is available in a blue-mauve range as well as white. One of the toughest of all the white flowering climbers for most areas is the white potato creeper or *Solanum jasminoides*. If you are a collector of plants, the blue and white variety of passionfruit, (which may be a little difficult to find) is well worth chasing.

There are also white roses, the various white snowball trees or viburnums, and a number of good annuals, for example, blue–purple lobelias, and violas in both blue and white.

For the ultimate in colour co-ordination, place your blue and white flowering plants in blue and white ceramic pots.

BONSAI

Bonsai are outdoor plants, but you can bring them indoors for two to three days at a time while they are flowering. In spring, many bonsai are in full flower, for example, wisteria and azaleas. It is possible to dig plants out of the garden in winter, pot them and prune them to shape for a spring display.

It's important to check your bonsai for new growth in spring and trim some of it back to stop the plant becoming rangy and large.

To shape branches, use copper wire hooked around the trunk of the plant and then wound around the branch you are intending to bend. Plants growing naturally in the ground have their branches weighed down with age, and grow almost horizontally, so this bending and shaping is done to make bonsai look as if they are very old—bonsai are not necessarily old trees at all. Keep winding the copper wire until the branch will stay in position. This will set after four to six weeks and then the copper wire should be removed to stop it cutting into the branch.

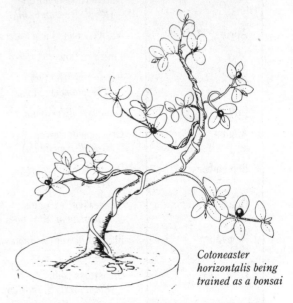

Cotoneaster horizontalis being trained as a bonsai

Bonsai should be watered regularly, especially in hot weather. They must never be allowed to completely dry out.

These plants need repotting about every two years. Lift them from their pots, remove one-third of the root system and put them back in the same pots with some new soil.

Bonsai need fertilising between early spring and late summer. If you are using a slow release fertiliser such as Nutricote or Osmocote, two applications will be enough. If you are using one of the liquid fertilisers, use it about once a month at half the recommended strength.

There are some plants that are not true bonsai but look very pretty in a small pot, for example, the golden form of melaleuca—'Revolution Gold'—and the dwarf prunus.

If you want to know more about bonsai, a particularly good book is *Bonsai: The Art, Science, History and Philosophy* by Deborah Koreshoff, published by Boolarong Publications, Brisbane.

For further information

Ray Nesci Bonsai Nursery Pty Ltd
26 Sagars Road
Kenthurst NSW 2156
Telephone (02) 654 1893

BORONIA

Australia's wildflowers are regarded as being the best in the world, and springtime is when they are at their most beautiful.

Boronias are related to the citrus family. People are often reluctant to plant them as they always seem to die in backyards: some are a little weak, but there is a lot of work being done to develop them by a select band of nurserymen in Australia.

The first of the boronias to be developed in cultivation was the brown boronia from Western Australia, *Boronia megastigma*, and there is now a huge range of colours available in this particular species. The wild variety of this boronia is brown, as the name suggests, but by the 1920s and 1930s such varieties as 'John McGuire's Red' which, like all of this group, has a stunning perfume, had been produced. There is also a yellow variety, 'Lutea', and a red and yellow striped version known as 'Harlequin'. There is even a blackish form that has curiously-turned petals and is almost jet black. The newest member of the group is 'Heaven Scent' which makes an excellent pot plant. It is a little more dense than most and does not have as strong a root system as some of the other varieties.

One of the best boronias is the 'Sydney Rose' (*Boronia serrulata*). It has the best perfume of the entire group, stunning flowers, and drops dead easily! There is a new variety that looks the same as the Sydney Rose but is called 'Aussie Rose'; it is a hybrid between the Sydney Rose and another species of boronia. One of the results of hybridising these plants is a vigorous root system. This particular plant is far less prone to dropping dead and to root rot than the original Sydney Rose. It has a number of other advantages, the main one being that flowers are produced all the way down the stem, not just at the tip as on the Sydney Rose.

This 'Aussie Rose' boronia may be a little difficult to obtain for a while but is well worth looking for.

If you have trouble growing boronias, you may find them easier to grow in a pot in a decent potting mix. Fongarid or Terrazole can be watered on the soil to stop root rot from killing the plants.

BOUGAINVILLEA

Bougainvilleas have to be one of the world's most colourful plants, often with variegated leaves and brightly coloured 'flowers'. Most people are aware of the pinks, reds and purples but there are also some gold, yellow and orange/tango shades as well. One of the problems with bougainvilleas is that they have nasty thorns, with the exception of the double-flower varieties. These have greatly reduced thorns, almost absent in some cases, and have wonderfully dense flowerheads. They are called 'doubles' because they have double the number of petals. One of the other difficulties with bougainvilleas is that their names are often confused. Also, the flowers can

bloom as one colour and then change over a week or so to a whole series of shades.

The most popular bougainvillea is 'Scarlett O'Hara', a brilliant red flower that fades to pink-purple as it ages. Another very popular red one is 'Mrs Butt'. It is slightly smaller in flower than 'Scarlett O'Hara' and not quite as red. Another that has become very popular in recent years is 'Sweetheart'. The old-fashioned purple variety is called 'Magnifica Traillii' and is possibly the most frost tolerant of all the bougainvilleas.

There are many other shades: 'Mrs Louis Wathen' is a tango shade, which opens a light orange and fades to pink. 'Temple Fire' has the unique characteristic of not being a climber. It is a low shrub 1–2m (3¼–6½') tall and is very useful on the coast as an alternative to a rose bush.

There are more gaudy bougainvilleas, for example, the multicoloured 'Mary Palmer' or 'Snowcap', which has white and pink flowers on the same plant at the same time. This is quite rare in the plant world. 'Raspberry Ice' has cherry-red flowers and variegated leaves. Another old-fashioned variety with variegated leaves is sold under many names, but is correctly called 'Harrisii Variegata'. It has purple-mauve flowers and looks wonderful in a hanging basket.

In many ways the double flowered varieties are the best, having fewer thorns, large clusters of flowerheads and less vigorous growth than the single varieties. There are only four varieties of doubles commonly available: double apricot/salmon (which may also throw a stem that flowers red), double red, double pink and double white (in the strong light this will show purple veins).

BOUVARDIAS

These medium-sized shrubs flower from late summer to late autumn. There is a single white flowering form, which is beautifully perfumed, and also a double white flowering form, which has only a faint scent. A red flowering form also exists but, although the flower colour is excellent, the perfume is barely perceptible.

Bouvardias are prone to fungal diseases and care needs to be taken with them in humid areas. They should grow well in elevated regions such as Melbourne's Dandenongs, and areas relatively free from fungal diseases, such as Perth. They require protection from heavy frosts.

Female trapdoor spiders can live for 20 years and never leave their burrows. In summer male trapdoors go door knocking in order to find a mate.

BROMELIADS

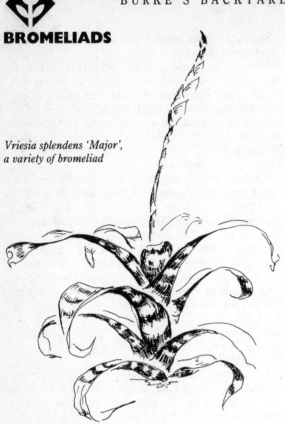

*Vriesia splendens 'Major',
a variety of bromeliad*

These weird, exotic plants come from central and
southern America, where they often live high in trees,
clinging to the trunk; or they may cling to a rock or even
grow in the ground in a forest or a desert. The Bromeliad
group includes pineapples (*Ananas comosus*). This large
fruit is actually composed of many separate smaller fruits
joined into one large structure. Pineapples, by the way,
were discovered by Columbus in 1493, and are a nutritious
fruit rich in vitamins A and C.

All bromeliads have minute scales on their leaves that
allow them to absorb water and nutrients directly into the
leaf. If there is no rainwater about, they can actually
absorb water straight from the air. These leaf scales often
form visible bands on the leaves. The leaves of many
species combine to form a vase shape, which holds a
continuous reservoir of water. Not only does the plant use
this water, but also various species of animals and plants
breed and live much of their lives in these little artificial
ponds. These organisms, through their excreta and dead
remains, contribute to a rich organic soup in the reservoir.

Most plants obtain their water and nourishment
through their roots. Not so bromeliads. Their roots do
little to provide water and chemicals for the plant.
Bromeliad roots mostly just enable the plant to cling to a
tree or rock. Some species such as Spanish Moss
(*Tillandsia usneoides*) have lost their roots completely.

This curious bromeliad lives on trees or even telegraph
poles, and looks like dead grey string.

The flowers of some species are spectacular and bizarre.
Some flowers look like bunches of grapes, others like
branched trees or fans, and some like feather dusters. In
certain species, the flower is underwater in the reservoir;
in this case the surrounding leaves usually colour
brilliantly.

Bromeliads are very easy to grow. They tolerate neglect,
low light intensity and even air conditioning. Grow them
in pots, on tree-fern trunks, on lumps of cork, or on tree
branches. They also thrive in terrariums or hanging
baskets.

They prefer an organic potting mix, composed of two
parts of a shop-bought mix and one part peat moss. Strong
fertilisers may burn them, so use either Fish Emulsion or
Nitrosol at about half the recommended strength, once or
twice a year.

Most bromeliads produce offshoots or 'pups' at the base
of the plant. Some species flower, produce pups and then
die, while others continue growing for years. The pups can
be twisted off when large enough and grown into new
plants. In this way one plant can be turned into many.

For further information

The Bromeliad Society of Australia, Inc, has clubs in
most states of Australia. Send enquiries to the Secretary,
PO Box 340, Ryde, NSW 2112.

BULBS

Autumn is bulb-planting time. Most bulbs can be planted
virtually all over Australia. However, refrigeration of tulip
bulbs during winter may be essential in the warmer areas.
They will probably flower once and not come up again.
This will not really matter, as they are fairly cheap to buy
and will look great growing in a pot.

There are many other bulbs: for example, freesias and
jonquils—the old-fashioned varieties of these are among
the world's best bulbs, because they can be planted in the
ground and left forever. They come up every year and not
only look good but are also perfumed. The flowers can be
cut and brought inside and the perfume will pervade the
whole house. Although there are many colours in these
bulbs, the old-fashioned creamy-white ones are more hardy
and easier to grow. There are many new and exciting
colours, for example, in freesias the 'Bergunden' variety,
which comes in a very wide range of colours.

Hyacinths are also perfumed and can be grown in
containers that can be brought inside. If you have a glass
container (the type with the waist in the centre) it is
important, after you have put the bulb in, to place the
container in a dark cupboard for a few weeks until the
bulb starts to grow.

Daffodils are also marvellous—there is now a wide

range of different varieties available, but note that the popular 'King Alfred' variety doesn't flower reliably in the warmer zones, that is, Sydney, Perth and areas north.

All of these bulbs can be grown in the ground.

Ranunculi (singular, Ranunculus)
Flowers—semi-double and double bowl-shaped flowers
Colours—reds, pink, orange, yellow, lemon, cream and white
Height—45-60cm (17¾-23½")
Uses—mass bedding, cut flowers
Planting—2-3cm (¾-1") deep, 15cm (6") apart

Daffodils and Jonquils
Flowers—variations on the cup and saucer or trumpet-shaped blooms on long stems
Colours—orange, gold, cream, white and numerous bi-colour combinations
Height—approximately 25cm (10")
Uses—plant in drifts, clumps or containers
Planting—7-12cm (2¾-4¾") deep, 15cm (6") apart

Hyacinths

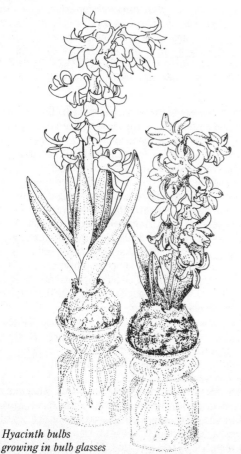

Hyacinth bulbs growing in bulb glasses

Flowers—tiny bell-shaped flowers clustered on large spikes, lovely fragrance
Colours—white, yellow, pink, red, light and dark blue
Height—30cm (12")
Uses—ideal for container growing but also grown in clumps in the garden
Planting—refrigerate in crisper for three or four weeks before planting, plant 10-15cm (4-6") deep and the same distance apart

Tulips
Flowers—large, bell or goblet-shaped blooms in a wide variety of forms
Colours—cream, yellow, orange, pink, scarlet, red, deep maroon and even black
Height—15-30cm (6-12")
Uses—in clumps and in containers
Planting—12-15cm (4¾-6") deep approximately 20cm (8") apart, refrigerate for up to eight weeks before planting; probably best regarded as an annual

There are also many types of containers in which any sort of bulb will grow. These include ceramic containers (reasonably expensive but worth the money), and a new type of plastic pot that looks like terracotta, and is often sold under the name of Terrapots (cheaper and harder-wearing than terracotta).

One interesting way of growing bulbs is to create a 'Roman candle' display in a pot. First, put in potting mix and daffodils, then more potting mix and hyacinths, more potting mix and jonquils. When they start to grow, the jonquils flower first, then the hyacinths and lastly the daffodils.

Bulbs are available from a number of places, for example, Yates bulbs from your local nursery.

For further information

Tesselaar's Padua Bulb Nurseries, Monbulk Road, Silvan, VIC 3795, Telephone (03) 737 9305, will post catalogues and bulbs all around Australia and may be contacted for further information about these and a wide range of other bulbs.

Some books with information on bulbs are *Yates Garden Guide: Growing Bulbs*, Kangaroo Press, and *Bulbs and Perennials* by Allan Seale.

CACTI

Cacti are spiny, succulent plants native to North and South America. They vary greatly in size and shape, but all are able to conserve moisture. They are perennials, and the stem of the plant produces the food as well as storing moisture. Their flowers are nearly always large and very brightly coloured, and those that flower at night are usually perfumed. Cacti are some of the most adaptable plants in the world, if their needs are understood.

Most cacti rest during the cold months and actively grow in spring and summer. A suitable potting mix can be made up of equal parts medium coarse river sand, peat moss, and loam or rich garden soil. This mixture is also excellent for in-ground planting. For white, hairy plants a small amount of horticultural lime or dolomite may be added. A nine-month slow release fertiliser, for example, Nutricote, should also be used.

Always remember to underpot a cactus. If the pot is too large, it is better to place two plants together in the pot. One small plant in a large pot may not have sufficient roots to absorb all of the available moisture, and this can lead to root disease.

There are no set rules for watering cacti, as it depends on the place and position of the plants. With desert-type cacti, water only when completely dry, probably once a week in the summer–autumn period, and often only once a month during winter.

Jungle-type cacti grow in natural habitats that are damp and steamy, and the plants need constant moisture. The soil should be kept just moist, but not wet. Jungle cacti do not like their roots to be disturbed, so do not repot them too frequently, but feed them regularly.

There are many different cacti, suitable for planting indoors, outdoors, in hanging baskets—in fact in just about any position in the house or garden.

Cacti Collectors' Corner specialises in rare and unusual cacti and other plants, which in many cases are not available anywhere else in Australia. The nursery's unique displays will fascinate any cactus lover, and a mail order service is available for specific requests. Other plants available from Cacti Collectors' Corner include bromeliads, orchids, bonsai and tillandsias.

For further information

Cacti Collectors' Corner
Gardenworld Nurseries
Springvale Road
Keysborough VIC 3173
Telephone (03) 798 5845

CAMELLIAS

Camellias, with their attractive, deep green foliage and exquisite blooms which last throughout our winter months, have become very popular plants both for gardens and tubs. There is a huge range of colours and many will be available at your local nursery, or at a specialist camellia outlet.

Varieties 'Lovelight', a large semi-double, is one of the best pure white camellias because it is a strong grower (some white camellias don't grow well). 'Margaret Davis' is a very attractive large, white informal double camellia with a cherry-red edge. 'Desire' is a large formal double white flower, flushed pink on the outer petals. 'Bob Hope' is a large, very deep red camellia. 'Mrs D. W. Davis Descanso' has large, frilly, pale pink blooms. 'D. Herzilia de Freitas Magalhaes' has medium-large, purple-mauve, frilly blooms and is an old Portuguese variety.

'Betty Ridley' is a formal double, slightly blue-toned pink, a vigorous early bloomer (April to September), and relatively sun hardy for a pink—it won't brown as much as other pale varieties. *Camellia chrysantha* bears lemon-yellow, miniature, single, 4cm (1½″) blooms. It has vigorous growth and huge, dark green leaves. Due to its colour this species is the latest sensation on the camellia scene. 'Erin Farmer' is a very reliable, large informal double, white with marginal pink blush. 'Frances Butler' is semi-double, and is of interest because it has a starlike shape due to straplike petals; it is a coral rose colour. 'Grand Slam' is a glowing deep red and extremely sun hardy which makes it great for new gardens lacking in shade-giving trees. 'Jeanette Cousin' is a semi-double pink with yellow stamens, also sun hardy. 'Marie Mackall' has a huge, light pink flower which may exceed 13cm (5″) in diameter, and is vigorous.

There is another group of camellias which are gaining in popularity: the *miniature camellias*, for example, 'Tinsie' a beautiful red variety. The most popular is 'Tiny Princess', with exquisite small pale pink flowers and a very dense attractive growth habit. Although the flowers are in miniature, the shrub itself will grow to the usual size. A number of miniature varieties have scented flowers.

Care In developing the wonderful camellia flowers, we have paid a price—some are not very vigorous in growth habit, for example, 'Elegans Supreme' which needs to be grafted to grow well. The usual technique used is a cutting graft. A piece is cut off two different camellias and joined together by slitting one and then striking it as a compound cutting. The reason for grafting is to put a really strong root system onto a modern variety.

Most people know that camellias need some shade, but they won't grow in full shade. Dappled light under gums or other tall trees is ideal. A slightly raised bed assists drainage and a good thick mulch improves the soil. Under these conditions camellias could grow to a maximum of 5–6 metres (16–20′), although it would take them at least 25 years to reach that size.

A white or light-coloured camellia should be planted in the shade, under trees, where it will be protected from the morning sun. If planted in a position where it gets morning sun, the blooms will brown off and look unattractive during winter.

Camellias also make excellent pot plants. They can be planted into either pure peat moss, or a mixture of two parts standard packaged potting mix and one part peat. The most appropriate fertiliser for camellias is one of the nine-month slow release forms. The bushes can be expected to flourish for a long period when grown in containers.

Reticulata camellias Reticulata camellias are the glamorous and elite members of their genus—and have a price tag to match. Many people unfamiliar with these camellias would be surprised to find them more expensive than others, but once viewed in full bloom these plants are unforgettable. The high price tag is due to the fact that they are grafted onto a hardy rootstock, rather than struck cheaply as cuttings.

Their bread-and-butter-plate-sized blooms, in a wide range of rich, glowing pinks and reds, surpass the flowers of all other species and forms. Most varieties produce blooms for at least two months during the cooler part of the year. The flowers are seen in their full brilliance if the plant is positioned where sunlight will strike the blooms at flowering time. These camellias require a little more light than the average and have a more open growth habit.

Reticulata camellias should be grown in a light, well drained soil with a high content of compost and organic matter.

Overwatering and overfertilising can result in defoliation—be sparing. Provide protection from strong winds.

Camellia sasanqua

Camellia sasanqua

The delicate flowers of the Sasanqua Camellia give no indication of the extreme hardiness of these plants, or their adaptability to a wide range of climatic and soil conditions. They are also excellent screen plants and can be used for formal hedges or topiary work, or left to grow naturally in the garden where they will last for many years. Because of their smaller leaves and delicate flowers they make very suitable bonsai subjects, and the more compact varieties make excellent tub specimens. Sasanquas are also the earliest camellias to bloom and as the flowers finish and the petals drop, a beautiful carpet of colour is formed underneath the tree, which later helps to mulch the roots of the plant.

A wide variety of colours is available and many new varieties are being developed, some with splashes or edging in another colour.

Some of the recommended sasanqua camellias are:

* 'Setsugekka', a white which will grow to 4.5m (15') or more—this is very useful as white flowers contrast well with other colours and a good white flower is often difficult to obtain
* 'Fuji-No-Mine', another excellent white
* 'Mine-No-Yuki', a beautiful, low growing variety, also with white flowers (Mine-No-Yuki, by the way, is Japanese for 'snow on the mountains')—has a rather sprawling open growth habit, but a lovely camellia
* 'Plantation Pink', 'Jennifer Susan' and 'Egao', all light pinks
* 'Bonanza', 'Lucinda' and 'Shishi Gashira', all deep pinks
* 'Crimson King', 'Crimson Tide' and 'Sparkling Burgundy', all red
* 'Yuletide' (a good strong clear red with very dense compact growth), 'Gwen Pike' (pink) and 'Little Pearl' (white), all good tub specimens
* 'Silver Dollar' (white) and 'Pure Silk' (pale pink)—new varieties
* 'Beatrice Emily' (white with burgundy outer petals—and an Australian variety, by the way) and 'Jane Morgan' (a white flower with a nice pink edge), good multicoloured varieties
* 'Something Special' is another new variety, a darker version of Jane Morgan—whiteish inside and pink towards the edges.

Sasanqua camellias are particularly versatile plants, which can be used for any purpose from intricate espalier against a wall, to topiary, tub planting or growing naturally in the garden. They will take any lighting conditions, from full sun right through to partial shade. Extremely beautiful and useful plants!

CARNIVOROUS PLANTS

Carnivorous plants attract and kill insects. They include pitcher plants, which trap insects; Venus fly traps which trap and kill insects; sundews and butterworts—insects

become stuck to their leaves—bladderworts; which suck insects inside, and tropical pitcher plants.

The most common mistake in growing these plants is keeping them as indoor plants and only watering them occasionally.

Carnivorous plants naturally grow in bogs and swamps, and therefore need full sun and to sit in water all the time, with lots of humidity around them.

A good idea is to create a bog garden around a fish pond, with peat moss, and plant carnivorous plants.

A mini bog garden can be created in a big ceramic bonsai pot. A big pot is best as it provides a large area from which moisture will evaporate and cause humidity. First, seal the drainage holes with silicone or put a plastic liner in so that the water doesn't drip out. Fill the pot with a mix of two parts peat moss and one part sand, and then plant.

Some carnivorous plants can go off in winter; a lot of the North American ones have a dormant time then and die right back. They will come up again in springtime.

Each leaf of the Venus fly trap (*Dionaea muscipula*) opens and closes only four or five times before it dies. If the leaves are stimulated to close all the time, they die off before new ones have a chance to grow.

Never fertilise carnivorous plants, repot only once a year into new mixture.

For further information

The Carnivorous Plant Society in each state can be contacted via the Carnivorous Plant Society of NSW, Lot 1 Taylors Arm Road, Collambatti, Kempsey, NSW 2440.

CHOOSING PLANTS

When you've decided you would like to buy a particular type of plant and have taken yourself off to the local nursery, one of the most perplexing activities is standing in front of half a dozen plants trying to work out which is the best. Is it the tall, stooping one; the short, squat one, the one with lots of new growth, even though it is rather yellow-looking; or the one with dark leaves but no new growth at all? There are some simple pointers which can help to make the decision easier.

Since nurseries are basically holding areas for produce on its way from the grower to the buyer, one of the commonest causes of distress to plants is a sudden change in temperature as they pass from the grower to the nursery to the home. Common victims of this sort of problem are indoor plants such as the happy plant, devil's ivy and the weeping fig (*Ficus benjamina*).

The symptoms that may appear on the first two plants are browning or yellowing along the sides of the leaves. These plants are usually grown in very hot glasshouses, and the change to nursery temperatures makes the plants sick. Once these plants have had time to acclimatise they usually grow normally again, so it is worth persevering with them. The reaction of the weeping fig to a sudden temperature and humidity change is to drop all or many of its leaves. A defoliated tree is certainly not very attractive and is not a good prospect, even though it will eventually come back into leaf. Before buying, check how long the plant has been in stock at the nursery: defoliation usually occurs within a fortnight of the change. One variety of *Ficus benjamina*, called 'Exotica', doesn't sulk as badly as its relatives.

One basic rule for making a rapid assessment as to whether a plant is growing well is to check whether the foliage occurs right from the bottom of the plant to the very top. This is a most important indicator of good, healthy growth. After the plant has passed that test you can check for lush, healthy-looking foliage, but remember that the colour and shininess of the foliage varies from species to species. Of course, some plants such as the golden diosma are supposed to have yellow leaves, but in this case just check that the foliage is not brown and dead instead of yellow and healthy.

The plant you want may be leaning over, instead of standing up straight, or it may have lost some of its potting mix and consequently have exposed roots. To determine whether these conditions represent problems, you will need to have some idea of the hardiness and general growth habit of the plant. Some plants, such as the lilly pilly, are hardy and tough, and some exposed roots will not hold them back as long as the rest of the plant looks healthy. Even so, if there is virtually no potting mix left in the pot give the plant a miss; it isn't worth taking the risk that it will fail to recover.

Similarly, plants which are leaning over should be assessed according to the nature of their species. Banksias, for example, always have distorted shapes, and as long as the plant looks healthy a lean probably adds to its charm. Grevilleas, on the other hand, are sometimes grown too fast, so that they end up tall and spindly and unable to stand without the support of a stake; if a grevillea can't hold itself upright without support don't buy it. You don't want to nurture it for a couple of years, only to find it topples as soon as it outgrows the stake.

When purchasing grevilleas, avoid buying plants which have been left in their pots too long. These plants can usually be distinguished by a slight blackening of the stems and the remains of dead flower spikes.

Pest or disease damage is not common in well-managed nurseries, but steer clear of plants with distorted or mottled and discoloured growth. Mild infestations of pests which may have chewed a few holes in the leaves can usually be controlled by manual or chemical means once you get them home, but you may be better off choosing some other species of plant less prone to attack if you want a hardy, low maintenance garden.

CHRISTMAS BUSHES

Would you like a plant that's extremely hardy in the

ground, that will grow in a pot for 20 years or so, and that will tolerate excessive wind, salt spray and the worst nature can throw at it? You need the New Zealand Christmas Bush or Pohutukawa.

There are many varieties of this plant, but the most popular is *Metrosideros thomasii* (an incorrect name—it should be *Metrosideros collina* var. *villosa*), which doesn't come from New Zealand but from Fiji. Another variety with a variegated leaf comes from the Kermadec Islands northeast of New Zealand. One has a creamy edge to the leaves and another has creamy-yellow centres. One curious member of the group is a climber, which has creamy flowers, but another (the Rata vine, *Metrosideros carminea*) has red flowers.

It is a very diverse group. There are a few Australian native members of the Metrosideros family. *M queenslandica*, for example, has golden-yellow flowers.

The fairly insignificant white flowers of the New South Wales Christmas Bush (*Ceratopetalum gummiferum*) are gone before the prized red Christmas 'flowers' appear. These 'flowers' are in fact the part that remains after the true flowers have died. They are the base of the flower or the calyx, which continues to grow and becomes quite large and red.

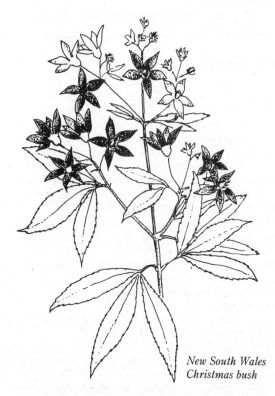

New South Wales Christmas bush

This part of the plant is not for pollination purposes, but acts as a little helicopter, which whirls away in the breeze and distributes the seed attached to it far and wide.

CHRYSANTHEMUMS

Whether you simply want to add late autumn colour to your garden beds or you wish to grow blooms for exhibition, or even cut flowers for Mother's Day, chrysanthemums are not difficult to grow and can become an inexpensive and absorbing hobby.

Chrysanthemums come in a wide range of shapes, sizes and colours. Those known as the Large Exhibition type can attain a breadth and depth of 22cm (8½") and more, with petals (or more correctly 'florets', for each petal is a complete flower in itself) being incurving, reflexing or a very pleasing combination of the two forms. The smallest chrysanthemum blooms are less than 2cm (¾") across and are displayed in masses over plants that grow no more than 20cm (8") high. These are very suitable for training as bonsai specimens.

In between the very largest and the very smallest comes a range of flower forms which growers describe as the fully double, tightly incurved form; the graceful fully reflexed type; and the intermediate form—a variation on the incurved or reflexed forms or a combination of the two. These types range from 12-16cm (4¾-6¼") across. Still other flower forms include the anemone-centred or pin-cushion type; the spidery or quilled variety with long narrow petals that open at the ends in a spoonlike fashion or flare out with hooks on the ends; the single types, with several rows of long, flattish petals radiating from a central, yellow, pollen-laden daisy eye; and the pompom types, which are, when fully developed, completely spherical. Bloom sizes for these kinds range from 3cm, (just over one inch), (on the plants of domed, 'charm' types) to 16cm (6¼").

Chrysanthemum colours include shades of red, purple, white, yellow, pink, mauve, bronze and cream. Some of them are bi-coloured, which adds to their appeal.

Growth habit and propagation Chrysanthemums are perennial plants, which means they can be propagated year after year from a parent plant. This is usually done in the spring, either by dividing the old plant or by taking cuttings from the basal shoots which develop during the growing cycle. Chrysanthemums die down over winter. Numerous named varieties are available, mainly through mail order suppliers. As they grow, most varieties need to be staked and tied.

All varieties are excellent for growing in borders, and many are well suited to pots. All varieties can be used for cut flowers. Most grow to less than a metre (3¼') in height although some can reach three metres (10') (usually when grown for exhibition blooms).

Plant chrysanthemums in full sun, in fertile soil rich in organic matter. Initial incorporation of a complete fertiliser should be followed by regular applications of liquid fertiliser to promote blooming.

Pests and diseases The most common problems in the backyard are caused by fungal diseases, caterpillars and aphids. The caterpillars can be controlled by spraying with Lebaycid or Dipel. Fungal problems are mostly caused by red rust and powdery mildew. These can be controlled using an all-purpose fungicide. Another fungal disease, white rust, has only recently arrived in Australia, and is characterised by lime green indented spots on the upper surface of the leaves, corresponding to pinkish to white spots on the underside. There is no cure for this disease; the entire infected plant should be removed immediately and burned.

Exhibition blooms To grow the magnificent blooms that are displayed at exhibitions of chrysanthemums, or in florist shops around Mother's Day, the number of blooms that each plant is permitted to carry is limited. Depending on the type of form you grow and what you wish to use them for, you can cultivate anything from two to twenty blooms. The greater the number, however, the smaller the bloom size, but even with smaller sizes the end result can be quite impressive.

'Autumn Glory' chrysanthemum Usually the first of the chrysanthemums you will see as Mother's Day draws near are the small, compact types with miniature flowers, normally sold under the name 'Autumn Glory'. They are members of a group of chrysanthemums known as the 'charm' varieties.

These chrysanthemums retail for between $3.50 and $4.50 per pot, and are basically indoor bloomers. They come in the same wide range of colours as the larger varieties. As an alternative to a bunch of flowers they will last for a number of weeks. After that you can either throw them out or plant them in the garden, which is worthwhile, as they grow well in all areas of Australia.

If you decide to plant them, prune them severely first, right back to just a small amount of stem. The remaining stumps will look rather terrible through winter, but below ground they will be developing their root systems and by spring will be ready to shoot again with great vigour.

Charm chrysanthemums need a good, loose soil with lots of organic matter—composted cow manure is ideal. They also need a position in full sun and are very frost hardy. They should be planted at the same level in the ground as they were in the pot—take care not to bury the stems. Use a complete fertiliser and water them regularly.

For further information

Each of the state groups holds regular meetings and exhibitions and publishes newsletters with articles of interest to enthusiasts.

The Chrysanthemum Society of NSW Inc
(Secretary, Mr Bruce Skeen)
8 Mountview Avenue
Doonside NSW 2767
Telephone (02) 622 9929

The Chrysanthemum Society of Victoria Inc
(Secretary, Mr John Longhurst)
38-40 Riverside Road
Warburton VIC 3799

The SA Chrysanthemum and Floral Art Society Inc
(Mr Frank Siddell)
Unit 1, 40 Heather Street
Windsor Gardens SA 5087

The WA Chrysanthemum Society Inc
(Secretary, Mrs Betty Eastlake)
50 Ogilvie Road
Mt Pleasant WA 6153

Hobart Horticultural Society (Chrysanthemum Section)
(Secretary, Mr Peter Brown)
Nubeena, Nubeena Crescent
Taroona TAS 7006

Recommended reading:
Growing Chrysanthemums by Bruce Skeen, Kangaroo Press, 1984, $12.95.

CLIMBERS
Climbing plants add tremendous charm to any garden. You can use these beautiful and useful plants to screen off unpleasant views, or to soften the rough, raw appearance of pergolas, balconies and masonry walls.

One of the best climbing plants is the native bower vine, *Pandorea jasminoides*, which displays light pink flowers for nine months of the year. In small, shady places try manettia, a small creeper with tiny cigar-shaped red and yellow flowers. The native bluebell creeper is an excellent but often forgotten climber. Wisteria is an excellent climbing plant but, like bougainvillea, it must be controlled so that it does not become invasive. There are, however, many climbers which will not become nuisances. Recommended for warmer areas is the potato creeper—a blue flowering climbing plant that likes a warm position. Also consider the dipladenia, which has light pink flowers and is also suited to warm climates.

For cooler climates, the banksia rose with its white or yellow flowers is highly recommended.

An ideal climbing plant for hard, dry, and inland areas is the pink trumpet creeper, *Podranea ricasoliana*. It may be grown over a shed or old fence to good effect and requires little care. It will survive frost, but looks somewhat rough and untidy during winter. This plant can be used effectively to beautify an ugly bank of soil.

For a more vibrant colour, the orange-red flowers of

black-eyed Susan, *Thunbergia alata*, may appeal. This species comes from South Africa and tolerates a dry position. The flowers usually have a black centre or 'eye', although many colour variations are now available through seed, including orange, yellow, cream and even a pure white version, often lacking the black eye. It is ideal for growing up or down walls, in a hanging basket or as a general groundcover. Black-eyed Susan flowers for most of the year, but is deciduous in cool areas and will suffer in heavy frosts. Nonetheless, it is a very attractive plant among the smaller, gentler climbers.

How climbing plants climb Climbing plants climb so that they can reach the sunlight, but instead of making their own wood to do this they save a lot of chemical energy by using something else for support. A climbing plant sends up a shoot which grows a little more each day and slowly spirals. When it touches some obstruction it starts to coil itself around that object and continues to climb up to the light. Most plants coil in the same direction, that is, anticlockwise; one of the exceptions to this rule is the hop plant which coils in a clockwise direction.

A very vigorous climbing plant like the beautiful wisteria can have a particularly harmful effect on a tree and eventually lead to its death. The climbing plant will strangle the life out of the branches, cutting into the living part of the tree and killing it. It may take years for this to happen but the tree will eventually die.

Growing wisteria on a native tree, or on any tree in many areas of Australia, can be in breach of a local council's Tree Preservation Ordinance.

Do think about what is going to happen to the tree when you put a climbing plant near one, and try to avoid the overly vigorous types of climbers like the wisteria.

CYCLAMEN

Native to Palestine, Asia Minor and the Eastern Mediterranean, cyclamen are brightly coloured, winter flowering plants for indoor use.

Standard cyclamen plants come in a wide range of pastel colours; some plain, others ruffled, striped or edged.

Miniature cyclamen have normal-sized leaves but smaller flowers. They come in a wide range of pastel pinks, purples and white. They tend to be hardier, longer flowering and more strongly scented than the larger varieties.

Cyclamen hederifolium, formerly *C. neopolitanum*, is a groundcover plant which flowers from late January until early June. It prefers cooler climates; it thrives in Tasmania but would be difficult, if not impossible, to find in Queensland. After five or six years each tuber can produce about 100 flowers and continue to do so for many years. The plant tolerates most conditions from a sunny rock garden to dense shade under trees. It will naturalise

from self-sown seed in mulch under deciduous trees or shrubs. The 15cm (6″) flower spikes range in colour from pale pink to deep rose and also white. They are very hardy but slow-growing in comparison with other varieties.

A large cyclamen will cost $9 per 125ml (5″) pot. Sometimes they are also available in punnets (two plants per punnet) for $2.50. Miniature cyclamens will cost $4.50–$6 for the same 125ml pot, but are less widely available. Neopolitans come in a 75ml (3″) pot and are quite hard to obtain.

When buying a cyclamen, check that stems, leaves and flowers are all fresh and upright and no leaves are drooping over the sides of the pot. Look among the leaves to make sure there are plenty of healthy flower buds. If the ends of leaves and flower stalks seem to be rotting, choose another plant.

Cyclamen flower from March to September. As the nights become warmer in late spring, flowering ceases, foliage yellows and the plants become dormant for a few months. From March to May keep your cyclamen out on a veranda, shaded patio or porch and bring it inside for only 2–3 days at a time, every 1–2 weeks. From May to September you can bring the plant indoors and place it in a position with plenty of light by day and a cool, dark period at night, for example, a kitchen windowsill with a northerly aspect. If you don't have a suitable window, you can put the plant outside each night. Being kept in a heated house at night is one of the main causes of non-flowering, even if the plant was already covered in buds when purchased. An hour or two of early morning sun helps to strengthen cyclamen plants.

As to watering, place the pot in a saucer and keep adding water to the saucer as required. You will know the plant has had all it needs for the time being when a little water remains in the saucer.

There is no need to fertilise while the plant is flowering—it will only tend to cause more leaf growth than bud formation. When planting your cyclamen out in the garden, add a complete fertiliser.

A cyclamen receiving too little light will develop yellow leaves and stretching of new leaves. If this occurs, either place the plant in a shady spot in your garden or put it outside on a veranda, patio or porch until new growth and flowers form. Cyclamen mite and caterpillars are lesser problems and should be treated with appropriate insecticides.

When it finishes flowering, throw your cyclamen away or plant it in a shady spot in the garden where it can survive for up to three years if watered in summer months. It should flower and enlarge every year.

Taronga is the Aboriginal name for "water view".

DAFFODILS

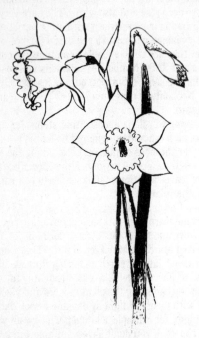

To many people Daffodils are simply daffodils, but in fact there is a huge range of these flowers in a variety of colours.

Tesselaar's Padua Bulb Nursery is one of the leading bulb nurseries in Australia. Anthony Tesselaar showed 'Burke's Backyard' a number of new daffodil varieties. These included:

* A miniature Campernelle, which is a particularly petite flower with a slight perfume, one of the few perfumed daffodils.
* A pretty creamy variety called 'New Moonshine'—a multi-flowering double.
* An exotic looking pink daffodil, 'Mrs Oscar Reynolds'. This flower has a white overlapping perianth with the long central cup being a deep shade of pink.
* An old daffodil variety coming back into fashion was 'Little Gentleman', which is great for rockeries and doesn't fall over as some other varieties are prone to.

Flowering People often complain that daffodils rarely flower much after the first year. Anthony Tesselaar recommends feeding twice a year to overcome the problem. Feed them once at planting time, and again when they are in flower, to give them food for the following year.

Some varieties perform a lot better than others and the key to success with daffodils seems to lie in selecting the right varieties for your area and purposes. The 'King Alfred' daffodil, for example, is not suited to warmer climates. It loves a cool climate and plenty of water.

'Golden Lion' was recommended as a particularly good yellow daffodil. The colour is said to be a very strong yellow and the plant itself is very free flowering. Great for the garden, for pots or for naturalising.

A daffodil that does well in all climates, even in the tropics, is 'Erlicheer', which carries clusters of up to 12 pointed, fully double, creamy white blooms on each stem. It is very vigorous, has solid deep green foliage and the flowers are highly perfumed.

Tesselaar's Nursery is open to the public between 14 September and 15 October. It is located at Monbulk Road, Silvan, VIC 3795. Telephone (03) 737 9305. Tesselaar's Nursery also specialises in mail order sales and will provide colourful, detailed catalogues on request.

DAPHNE

The Daphne is one of the world's loveliest perfumed plants and produces its marvellous scent in the middle of winter when everything else in the garden is huddled up against the cold. Unfortunately, the most common problem encountered with daphne plants is that they simply drop dead. In fact, many people who have tried in vain to grow them would probably be surprised to know that bushes can reach dimensions of 1.5m (5′) high by 1m (3′) wide.

The key to growing a beautiful daphne bush is to select a perfectly healthy young plant at the local nursery.

Daphnes are subject to a number of viral diseases. Fortunately, the symptoms of these are quite easy to distinguish. The first virus causes puckered, crinkled and distorted leaves. The base of the plant will tend to be lacking in foliage. This particular virus won't kill daphne directly but, being something like AIDS in human beings, it makes the plant weak and leaves it open to other infections such as root rot, which may eventually kill it.

The symptoms of the second viral disease are lots of small yellow blotches, spots and haloes on the leaves. This disease also leaves the plant open to attack from other pests and diseases.

An additional problem arising with these sorts of diseases is that they are transmitted by any of the sap sucking insects, such as aphids. If you have a healthy daphne plant close to an infected specimen, the viruses can easily move across with the aphids. So plants exhibiting these telltale signs in the nursery should definitely be avoided.

There is yet another trap for daphne buyers. Many plants originate from nurseries in Victoria's Dandenongs, where they are grown in the open ground in red clay soil. If the growers do not thoroughly wash this soil from the roots before potting the plants for sale, the red clay turns to suffocating mud in the pot and the plant is likely to die. Before buying a daphne plant it is advisable to scratch some of the potting mix away to look for any orange-red clay. If you are still desperate to buy the plant, make sure that you bare root it and wash all the red clay off before repotting it into a good quality potting mix. There is no need to avoid Dandenong-grown plants that have had their roots properly washed by the nursery before potting.

The ideal daphne to buy at a nursery has dark green foliage that is not distorted or discoloured, and which occurs from the very top of the plant right to the bottom. If you buy a healthy daphne you have a reasonable chance of growing it successfully.

The ideal climatic conditions for daphne are met in the cool, elevated areas of Australia, such as the Blue Mountains in New South Wales or the Dandenongs in Victoria. If you wish to grow them near the coast the trick is to give them perfect drainage; they are very susceptible to root rot. A container, such as a wine cask, filled with a good quality potting mix should result in good growth. Daphne plants prefer a partly shaded position—dappled light under trees is ideal.

If you want to grow daphne in the ground there are chemicals you can try to stop the root rot. Fongarid is readily available in a small, $6 container at the local nursery. A chemical called Ridomil is even better, but is available only in very large containers from large commercial produce stores for no less than $140, so it is quite impractical for most backyarders.

If you are careful to select a good plant from your nursery or garden centre, and you ensure that it is well drained, you too can have the privilege of sniffing the magnificent daphne perfume right through the winter.

DECORATOR PLANTS

Why not add a touch of imagination to your gardening and give your plants some new life with shape? Many different plants can be trained into standards. When choosing the plant, pick one with a good, strong straight shoot up the centre.

Clean the stem by clipping all the side shoots so that the growth can be centred in one area. It is important to leave the tip in the plant until it has grown to the height you desire.

Once the plant has reached the height you want, pinch out the tip and the plant will send out new shoots to the side. As the shoots mature, keep pinching out the tips to encourage growth in the one area. As the plant will be top heavy, it will always need to be staked. It is possible to work with a more mature plant, but the stem will remain nobbly from trimming.

Plants to make into standards
Azalea 'Alba Magna'
Bay tree
English box—slow growing
Japanese box—fast growing
Gardenia florida
Leptospermum scoparium

Fig—several types, which can be intertwined when growing
Bougainvillea
Wisteria

All standards need attention and require feeding every three months. A slow release fertiliser like Osmocote or Nutricote is recommended.

Plants can also be trained around wire shapes, which can be conical, hoops, or chicken wire shaped as animals. Choose a vigorous, dense plant like Solanum jasmine, which flowers most of the year. Put the wire shape in the pot over the plant and loosely wind around the wire before adding more soil.

'Burke's Backyard' gratefully acknowledges the assistance of:

Ron O'Shea
The Sydney Gardener Nursery
314 Willoughby Road,
Willoughby NSW 2068
Telephone (02) 438 3224

Camellia Grove Nursery
240 Mona Vale Road
St Ives NSW 2075
Telephone (02) 44 3402

ERIGERON

Erigeron or Summer Daisy is an herbaceous perennial with stems about 45-60cm (18-24″) tall and small daisy-like flowers about 1cm (½″) in diameter. They open as pink and fade to white with a yellow centre. They flower for most of the year and are very easy to grow. These plants will even grow in cracks in concrete paving, and are very good for softening a bare area of concrete or paving bricks, where they will seed themselves between cracks. They are inclined to spread, and can be cut back after summer and autumn flowering.

Summer daisies do not require much attention and are fast spreading. They will grow in a sunny or semi-shade position.

FERNS

Autumn is an ideal time to plant Ferns, as it allows them to settle in before winter and then establish themselves in spring before the onslaught of summer's drying temperatures. But, as with any group of plants, there are problems and pitfalls associated with growing ferns, and it helps to keep a few pointers in mind when setting out to choose one.

Choosing ferns The popular Fishbone Fern, for example, may look attractive in a pot, but will overrun and destroy your garden as efficiently as any weed. If you really want to grow this type of fern, buy a golden one—it will be less vigorous. Fishbones and Boston Ferns should be kept actively growing. They must be fertilised regularly and they need a fair amount of light and adequate water—don't let them dry out.

Maidenhair (*Adiantum*) varieties available from

nurseries are mostly unsuited to garden conditions and will often only flourish indoors. Many native species for outdoor growing do exist, but they are hard to find, which is unfortunate, as they can be used as a very effective ground cover, even in almost full sun and especially on uneven ground where mowing is a problem. When purchasing your maidenhair, or any other fern, quiz nursery or garden centre staff about its suitability for your climatic zone. The Giant Maidenhair Fern is one beautiful example, which is really suited only to the tropics.

Maidenhairs need to be kept in full, active growth. Use liquid food, such as Nitrosol, or slow release pellets, such as Nutricote. Cut out dead growth and occasionally cut the plants back well and fertilise for healthy new growth.

For a wonderful, lush, tropical rainforest atmosphere, prime choices would be the native ferns such as Staghorns and Elkhorns (*Platycerium*). Feed these with leaves, tea leaves and banana skins. Avoid attaching them to tree trunks, as the bark may rot and encourage pests and disease. Bird's-nest Ferns or Crow's Nest Ferns (*Asplenium australasicum*, often sold as *Asplenium nidus*) will grow up to 2m (6½′) across. There are many new varieties, some tasselled on the ends of their fronds. In middle and northern Australia, the Climbing Swamp Fern will climb up a gum tree. Also recommended is the curious-looking Holly Fern (*Cyrtomium falcatum*).

The Soft Tree Fern, Dicksonia, grows well in shade. Its trunk doesn't grow very high, but it bears soft green fronds. The trunk of the Rough Tree Fern, Cyathea, develops quite quickly, and this fern tolerates more sun than Dicksonia. It is usually sold in a pot with roots attached, whereas the Dicksonia is usually sold in the form of a rootless trunk.

If broad, shiny leaves don't appeal, there are many other ferns with lacy, divided fronds. The Rasp Fern grows in a very dense clump and does not take over the garden. This attractive fern is extremely hardy and produces bright, orange-red new growth. The Hen and Chicken Fern, *Asplenium bulbiferum*, is another appealing plant, which grows in a rosette of foliage and derives its name from the way it produces baby fern plants along its fronds. It will not tolerate full sun comfortably. The Blechnums, or Water Ferns, are another attractive group that grow in a rosette or circle of foliage and are not invasive. They look good all year round. *Blechnum nudum*, the Miniature Tree Fern, will grow in a pot. A good indoor-outdoor fern is *Davallia pyxidata*, or Hare's Foot Fern, which will spill out of a hanging pot.

The Mother Shield Fern is another variety that produces baby fern plants along its leaves. It will take almost full sun and is almost indestructible. The native King Fern, with its rosettes of foliage, also likes the sun.

Unfortunately, some of these lovely and versatile Australian native ferns are not readily available at all nurseries and garden centres. You may have to visit a specialist native plant nursery that sells ferns to obtain them.

To use ferns effectively, lots are needed. The soil must hold water, and therefore requires plenty of compost, which can be bought in bulk from a local landscaping company.

Using ferns Ferns are among the most useful of all garden plants, but most people seldom use them in the garden, or use them rather badly. Part of the problem with ferns is that many nurseries have never really been adventurous in displaying them and fail to give buyers ideas about how to use them. One nursery that has tackled this problem is King Country Nursery, of Redland Bay in Queensland. Their displays are imaginative and innovative demonstrations of how ferns can enhance any garden.

Techniques to take notice of include the ways in which natural forms can be incorporated into fern plantings. A section of a hollow log, for example, can be raised between trees or on poles and crammed with low growing and cascading ferns to create an archway with a tropical feel. Short lengths of hollow logs can be placed on end on the ground and used as planters for ferns—the wood and the ferns complement each other in a lovely natural way not attainable with plastic or terracotta containers. Such hollow log pots, spilling with ferns, can be attached to trees to replicate the epiphytic layers in rainforests.

Similarly, imagination should also be employed in the positioning of ferns—a single fern beside the rose bed will look decidedly odd, but a cluster of ferns of varying heights and complementary foliage patterns could transform a bland corner beside the garage, or an uninspiring side passage, into an appealing feature.

Growing No matter how appealing an arrangement of ferns is, it will not look good unless the ferns are growing well. One of the tricks is to provide the fern with a regular, reliable water supply—especially if it is in a hanging basket, where a quick flash of the hose once a week will amount to next to nothing (much of the water will run out of the basket before the plant has had time to absorb it). Trickle irrigation systems that slowly drip water for a certain period of time each day are ideal. When used with basket plants the tube runs up the hanger and along the top edge of the structure supporting the basket, and so is discreetly concealed.

The other major secret of successful fern growing is the potting mix. The mix needs to be highly organic. A particularly good recipe for fern potting mix is:

2 parts milled pine bark
2 parts hardwood sawdust
1 part coarse washed river sand
½ part granulated polystyrene
1 part spent mushroom compost

Ferns shown on 'Burke's Backyard'

* Hare's Foot Fern, *Davallia pyxidata* (shown growing in a log attached to a tree trunk)
* Basket Fern, *Drynaria rigidula* (shown in an overhead log trough)
* Bird's-nest Fern, *Asplenium australasicum* (also growing in overhead trough)
* Water Fern, *Blechnum* or *Lomaria gibbum*—a hardy fern, easy to grow in most areas of Australia
* Mother Shield Ferns, *Polystichums*—they often produce little baby ferns along the fronds
* Selaginella—not really a fern, just a relative
* Asparagus fern, *Asparagus densiflorus* 'Sprengeri'—not really a fern at all, but it goes well with a fern collection (shown in a hanging basket)
* Tassel ferns, Lycopodiums—(all shown in hanging baskets) distant relatives of ferns, and plants for the collector only, as they are very expensive and difficult to grow. Varieties include the Coarse Tassel Fern, the Rock Tassel Fern and the Black Stem Tassel Fern. These plants are suited to the warmer areas of Australia north of the Queensland border. They should be grown in a peaty mix, should not be watered in winter and should almost never be fertilised.

For further information

There are many other hardy ferns that will grow anywhere in Australia. Books written by Christopher J. Goudey and David L. Jones are excellent references for further information on this subject.

King Country Nursery
58 Dinwoodie Road
Thornlands QLD 4163
Telephone (07) 206 4051

Staghorns, Elkhorns and Bird's-nest ferns Among the

most spectacular of all garden plants are Staghorns and Elkhorns. But which is which? It's easy enough to remember that everything begins with an 's'; staghorns have a single set of antlers. Even their botanic name, *Platycerium superbum*, starts with an 's'.

Stags and elks need to be watered well every day during summer. Most people feed the plants with banana skins and tea leaves, but there is another technique that is a little more out of the ordinary.

Alec Blombery, one of Australia's leading authorities on native plants, and Director of the Stoney Range Flora Reserve in Sydney, has a particularly successful way of fertilising staghorns and elkhorns. He simply climbs up a ladder, puts two or three large handfuls of poultry manure into the back of the plant, then waters it in with copious amounts of water.

This technique also works well with other plants. For instance, if you have a Bird's-nest Fern, put a couple of large handfuls of poultry manure right in the centre and water in well to make sure the foliage doesn't burn.

Small brown spots that form under the leaves of staghorns and elkhorns contain the spores for reproductive purposes. If small white spots appear, however, these are probably scale insects. These suck the sap and lead to discolouration of the top of the leaves. They can be controlled by spraying with Lebaycid, with a little White Oil added. In time the leaves will improve, and as new leaves grow the plant will look much better.

If the foliage on your staghorn is peppered with small match-head-sized brown spots, as though somebody has machine-gunned the leaves, the damage is likely to have been caused by the staghorn beetle. These beetles are rarely seen as they feed at night. They can also be controlled with Lebaycid. Another problem is the appearance of brown, irregular 'fluffy' patches in the spore bearing area. This is likely to have been caused by something boring around the leaves, and will also respond to treatment with Lebaycid.

In summary, remember to keep your stags, elks and bird's-nest ferns regularly watered, particularly through the dry months; put lots of organic matter at the back of the plants and fertilise with poultry manure.

For further information

Stoney Range Flora Reserve
Pittwater Road
Dee Why NSW 2099

FREESIAS

Of all the bulbs you can grow in your garden, there is no doubt that the Freesia is one of the best. It is so vigorous in most areas of Australia that it can even establish itself as a roadside weed. The old creamy variety is the one most commonly seen.

These days there is a whole series of new varieties in magnificent colours that are definitely worth looking at. They have come a long way from the plain creamy one, but their perfume is not quite as good.

One of the early groups of very brightly coloured freesias was the super-giant strain, but now there is a variety called 'Burgunden'. These come in a really lovely range of colours—orange-yellow shades, creamy mauves, pink and whites, even into the purple range—but they also have a pretty good perfume.

Freesias are outstanding cut flowers; they last well and perfume the whole house.

If you want to grow freesias you will have to plant the bulbs in autumn, when they are available from nurseries.

If you are intending to grow freesias, there is a tremendous argument for considering the old-fashioned creamy varieties. The new colourful ones are wonderful, but nothing beats the tough, beautifully perfumed old varieties. They are so hardy, they will establish on your front nature strip, requiring no maintenance at all.

FUCHSIAS

Fuchsia gracilis

Fuchsias can be among the world's most difficult plants to grow. This is not necessarily the gardener's fault—there have been many magnificent varieties bred over recent years which look very attractive but do not grow well in many areas of Australia. Don't let a stunning flower on a plant lead you into buying it—it would be far better to ask your local nurseryman to recommend a good, hardy variety for your area.

Different varieties will appear to be the same in colour. A red and white fuchsia could be 'Cascade', a variety suitable for a hanging basket; 'Snowcap', prone to fungus disease and thus not suitable for a lot of areas; or 'Dainty Lady', a very hardy variety.

There is a wide range of colours available—mauves, purples, reds and multicolours, and the beautiful pendulous flowers appear through summer and last until autumn.

Fuchsias require specific good treatment. They will grow well in pots with good quality potting mix, and also perform well in the ground. However, if the soil is average and is not improved, the fuchsia may well not thrive. It is important to dig in plenty of compost, organic matter, and so on to improve the fluffiness or aeration of the soil to make them grow strongly. Keep the soil well watered.

Fuchsias will grow well in dappled light, in semi-shade or under a tree. Two or three hours of solid sun in the middle of the day will send the leaves purple, then brown, and the plant may well die, so protect it from strong light.

Fuchsias must be regularly fertilised with a liquid feed, such as Nitrosol or Fish Emulsion, or one of the four or five-month slow release granules, such as Osmocote or Nutricote.

There are a few other tricks worth remembering. Fuchsias grow particularly well in hanging baskets. They are a brittle plant and don't like wind or being knocked about. As well as being regularly fertilised, they need to be pruned frequently. As the flowers finish on the stem, just nip the stem back, and more new flowering growth will be produced. In warmer areas of Australia prune back hard in April. In cooler areas with frosts, wait until all the frosts are over—prune in early spring.

Basically, fuchsias will respond to good care. Be careful when selecting your variety—the old-fashioned hardier varieties will grow on forever.

Ten good upright varieties

'White King'—all white
'Sheryl Ann'—red and white
'Red Shadow'—red and purple
'Tuonella'—pink and mauve
'Bountiful'—pink and white
'Anna Marie'—red and violet
'Display'—all pink
'Tango Queen'—tangerine
'Applause'—coral-orange
'La Rosita'—all pink

Ten good basket varieties

'Troubador'—red and purple
'Wood Violet'—red and purple
'Hula Girl'—pink and white
'Marinka'—all red
'Blush of Dawn'—pink and mauve
'Pink Galore'—all pink
'Crimson Bedder'—red, variegated foliage
'Canary Bird'—yellow foliage, red and purple blooms
'La Campanella'—white and purple
'Enchanted'—red and purple

GARDENIAS

Gardenias are among the world's most exquisite plants, producing pure white flowers and balmy perfume through the warmer months of the year.

There are various types. One of the most interesting is *Gardenia augusta* 'Radicans', the prostrate variety—a great ground cover in most middle to northern areas of Australia. There are a number of more upright varieties, of which *Gardenia augusta* 'Florida' (the florist's gardenia) is probably the best.

Gardenias like almost full sunshine, rich, organic soil and regular fertilising.

It is typical for the leaves to yellow as the weather warms up in spring, so if this occurs there may be nothing to worry about.

The first thing to do is fertilise the plant. A cheap way is to get some sulphate of ammonia; put a dessertspoon in a watering can of water and use this as a liquid feed straight onto the plant. Aquasol can also be used—it will give a quick boost to a yellow gardenia.

If you do fertilise and it doesn't work, there may be a magnesium deficiency. What the plant needs is a good dose of salts—use a level dessertspoon of Epsom salts in a watering can of water and pour over the roots of the plant.

If it is still yellow, dig a hole beside the plant, or take the plant out of its pot, and check if there are any lumps on the roots. If there are, your gardenia has nematodes and will need treating with Nemacur.

Sometimes there may be other causes. For example, if a part of the plant has yellow leaves it is worth examining the roots for tunnelling—an ants' nest can weaken the plant and cause yellowing. Treat with ant insecticide from your local nursery—mix with water and soak it into the rootball.

Gardenias are tropical plants. They don't like the cold areas of Australia, but if you live in a cold area and grow them outside during the warm months and bring them into a very brightly lit sunroom during winter, they will do quite well.

Gardenias are one of the most rewarding shrubs to have; the flowers can be cut and brought inside and the perfume will pervade the whole house.

GERANIUMS

The humble garden Geranium has been grown for some hundreds of years, but many people are often confused about this plant's varieties.

There are a number of groups of geraniums. Possibly, the most useful is the Ivy-leaved geranium. Some of the new varieties have striped flowers, and they all come in a multitude of colours—lavenders through pinks to deep reds, some even a blackish red. They are climbing plants and are excellent when used on a mesh fence, or in hanging baskets.

The most spectacular of the geraniums are the Regal Pelargoniums. There is really no difference between Geraniums and Pelargoniums; the group is botanically known as Pelargoniums, but certain types are commonly referred to as geraniums. Whereas ivy-leaved geraniums grow best in full sun, regal pelargoniums grow best in part sun and part shade. Regal pelargoniums come in an astonishing variety of colours.

Zonal Geraniums are so called because of the zones of colour around their leaves—cream through greens to bronze. This is the group that home gardeners basically refer to as geraniums, and they are the variety most commonly found in our gardens. They come in beautiful colours—pinks, reds, mauves and whites, are hardy and can be grown in the average garden.

Some of the ivy-leaved geraniums have variegated leaves, and there is also a Miniature Ivy-leaved Geranium. They are strong growing and make an excellent display on an old mesh wire fence.

Scented geraniums Plants in flower are rather scarce in late autumn and through winter, but an interesting and varied garden relies on more than just colourful blooms for its charm and character. Scented foliage plants, grown close to paths or verandas where the brush of bodies and breezes releases their lovely fragrances, help to make gardens memorable.

Among the best of the scented foliage plants, and ones that soldier on all through winter, are the perfumed geraniums or pelargoniums. Not only do the crushed leaves exude powerful aromas, but they can also be used in the kitchen.

Cultivation Scented leaf geraniums are vigorous and hardy. They grow best in a good, friable, well-drained soil. They will suffer frost damage in unprotected situations, but can withstand remarkably low temperatures if not subjected to damp conditions at the same time. They prefer a warm, sunny but sheltered position. Don't overfertilise—a well balanced compost is adequate. Artificial fertilisers tend to promote rapid, weak growth. An autumn dressing of compost is advisable. Scented leaf geraniums are well suited to pot culture.

Varieties In most cases a fragrance is produced by a number of varieties or species, not just one. There are at least twelve varieties, for example, which have a rose scent.

Scented leaf geraniums are available in the following scents: rose, lemon, lime, citron (a cross between lemon and lime), apple, spicy-apple, nutmeg, orange, peppermint, coconut, nut, cinnamon, ginger, and 'aromatic'.

Uses Scented leaf geraniums can be used in potpourris, herbal pillows and sachets; in jellies, jams and confectionery; in pies, cakes and desserts, and even in savoury dishes and drinks. They can also be used in toiletries and cosmetics and the rose-scented geranium is grown commercially in many countries to provide most of the world's rose perfume.

For further information

Scented Leaf Pelargoniums by Diana O'Brien, published by Geraniums Galore in 1983, is available from some bookstores and nurseries or from Diana O'Brien, 98 Anzac Park, Campbell, ACT 2601, for $5, including postage. Telephone (062) 48 0649.

GREVILLEA CALEYI

Grevillea caleyi is a rare and endangered plant. There are less than 1000 plants of this species in the Ku-ring-gai National Park north of Sydney. It occurs only in a very small area in the vicinity of Mona Vale Road, in the National Park. Its habitat is restricted to iron-rich laterite soil (gravelly ironstone).

Size and growth habit: In a well-drained soil, *Grevillea caleyi* will form a beautiful foliage plant up to 2-4m (7-14') high and 3-5m (10-17') wide. Its leaves are reddish when young, grey-green when mature. The lacy foliage is covered by dense soft hair. Its flowers are pinky-red, toothbrush-shaped and about 5cm (2") long. They occur on new growth, mainly towards branch tips, and are attractive to birds. The fruits contain a single, heavy seed. The plant has a low seed output and the seeds are popular with predators, especially ants. More seedlings are found after bushfires, but 'cool' burns may not cause seed germination. The threats to the survival of *Grevillea caleyi* include pressure from habitat destruction, such as housing and other developments, roadworks, a new TAFE college, trails and tracks, weeds and rubbish.

Many people, and organisations such as the Royal Botanic Gardens, are interested in the preservation of *Grevillea caleyi*, and some plans for the area have been changed to save quite a large proportion of the plants, but the future for this species of grevillea is pretty grim.

Grevillea caleyi is difficult to propagate commercially in glasshouses watered by misting systems (the moisture trapped by the leaf hairs results in rotting) so many native plant nurseries are reluctant to grow this species. If you can find a nursery that stocks this rare plant you may care to try to grow one in your backyard. Even if the native populations are destroyed, it is not too late to ensure the survival of this species through cultivation.

HELICONIAS AND GINGERS

Heliconias are native to the jungles of South America, and come from the same family as tropical bananas, Musaceae.

They are used as cut flowers, in landscaping and as collectors' plants. Most of these plants require humid, tropical conditions to initiate flowering, so would need to be kept in a warm glasshouse or conservatory in temperate areas.

Some varieties can be grown as indoor plants, including Dwarf Heliconias and a form grown for its variegated leaves rather than its flowers.

The true flowers of heliconias are usually quite small and insignificant, but they grow inside showy, brilliantly coloured and beautifully shaped bracts. The bracts are frequently multicoloured and colours range from scarlet and orange to pink, yellow and green.

Heliconias should be planted in rich, peaty compost in a position which receives filtered sunlight. Occasional additions of decayed manure and regular watering, especially through summer, should be provided.

Gingers are native plants of tropical Asia, notably Indonesia, and also India.

They are used as cut flowers and for garden planting and landscaping. Many varieties are grown for their ornamental foliage, unusual both in form and colour. The spice ginger is prepared from the thick rhizomes of many members of this family of plants (Zingiberaceae).

The flowers of several forms of ginger are attractively perfumed. The flowers and coloured bracts come in a wide variety of colours and forms—the Torch Ginger, for example, bears an extraordinary resemblance to Australia's Waratah, although they are quite unrelated. Colours include red, pink, orange, yellow, green and white.

Gingers are hardy plants if provided with a forestlike environment with plenty of mulch and water. Several varieties are suitable for growing in temperate zones.

Some gingers can produce leaves to a height of 6m (20') in a tropical location.

Heliconias and gingers are tropical plants and they are only rarely available in the non-tropical areas of Australia such as Sydney, Perth and areas to the south of these cities.

HIBISCUS

Hibiscus 'El Capitolio Sport'

If you want to create the feeling of Tahiti in your garden, perhaps you should plant Hibiscus. However, if you live in a cooler climate, hibiscus often don't have a chance unless you know some tricks.

The Hawaiian hibiscus is the variety which produces huge flowers. Perhaps the most important thing to know when buying an Hawaiian hibiscus is that it needs to be a grafted plant. At local nurseries, the cheaper hibiscus would be cutting grown. If you live in middle to southern Australia they will never look as good as grafted hibiscus, and they may well die. At the stage that the grafted hibiscus are ready to be purchased, the graft will have nearly disappeared.

If you live in a really cold area with frosts, you cannot grow the Hawaiian hibiscus, but the Syrian hibiscus (*Hibiscus syriacus*) is a possibility. These are deciduous and come in a narrow but nice range of colours—whites through mauves and some pinks—singles and doubles.

There are two other cold climate groups: 'Rose of Sharon' (*Hibiscus mutablis*), which produces flowers that start white and change to pink, so that there is a range of colours on the plant at any one time; Hibiscus 'Southern Belle', which as possibly one of the world's largest flowers. It grows from a tuber, like a Dahlia, and can be bought in seed packets marketed by various companies.

In both the common varieties of hibiscus and the Hawaiian, spectacular colours are available. 'Red Robyn' is one of the best reds; 'Kinchen's Yellow' is a clear yellow; 'All Aglow', 'Coconut Ice' and 'Captain Charles Louis Hope' are multicoloured; 'Cindy' is deep pink; 'Rhinestone' is grey; 'Norma' is yellow with a pink centre; 'Freddie

Brubaker' is old gold with a red and white centre. Some unusual colours include 'Bill Stayton', coffee brown with an orange centre, and 'Stormy Days', which is grey-purple. There are also strangely shaped flowers, for example, 'El Capitolio Sport' and the 'Old Hawaiian' variety.

There are new varieties coming on to the market all the time. Hibiscus must be one of the world's most colourful flowers, and no matter where you live or what colour you prefer, there is a variety suitable for you.

IRIS

In recent years, the Tall Bearded Irises have been extensively developed to include a fabulous range of colours. If you plant Irises, they will still be blooming long after you have left the house, maybe two or three owners hence. They will flower every year without major pest or disease problems, and are extremely good plants to have in your garden.

The modern tall bearded irises not only rival Orchids, but in many cases surpass them in the range of colours available. Most people know the blues, mauves, purples and pinks available in irises, but there are now some astonishing colours—deep burgundy crowned with burnt yellow, lemon yellow, subtle blues and white, even purple with a white margin. There seems to be no end to the shades modern hybridists are able to produce. Certainly, the browns and so on are most unusual; perhaps only in Hibiscus do we see a similar range of colours.

Iris culture is very straightforward. When the clumps get too big, cut them apart with sharp secateurs, and plant a section of the rhizome and some leaves, cut back to about 12.5cm (5"). When planting, leave the top of the rhizome exposed above the soil (that is, don't completely bury it—it should float in the soil).

Tall bearded irises like to be fertilised a couple of times a year—in late winter and again after flowering in November-December. They also like a touch of lime (they need an alkaline soil), and do watch out for snails!

If you have a garden pond or a water feature, Louisiana Irises are perfect, and will grow either submerged or in dry soil around the pond. They are less spectacular than the tall bearded variety, and like an acid soil, but also come in good colours.

For further information

Irises are available from:

Rainbow Ridge Nursery
8 Taylors Rd
Dural NSW 2158
Telephone (02) 651 2857

Tempo-Two
(Barry and Leslie Blyth)
PO Box 60A
Pearcedale VIC 3912
Telephone (059) 78 6980

Iris Acres
PO Box 248
Meadows SA 5201
Telephone (08) 388 3299

JAPONICA

One of the first of the spring blossoms to come into flower is the Japonica or Japanese flowering quince, *Chaenomeles speciosa* (in fact the plant comes from China not Japan). It is available in a number of coloured varieties—white, pinky red, blood red, pink with white through it, and one variety with pink flowers and white flowers on the same bush. The pinky red is the most common and there are some double-flowering varieties.

Japonicas have never been really popular shrubs, probably because of their thorns, though they are not as thorny as a rose bush.

They are very useful plants because of their hardy qualities. Japonicas grow from Sydney to Perth and all areas south in any soil type. Even if not fertilised or regularly watered, they will probably survive.

A row of japonicas is very useful for planting in an area where you want to discourage people or dogs from walking.

They flower on fully mature bare stems and therefore are very attractive when cut and displayed in vases, particularly in Japanese-style arrangements.

Pruning is necessary to remove the oldest wood from the centre of the plant, to give space for new growth to develop. This pruning should be carried out after flowering in early spring.

Japonicas are called Japanese flowering quinces, because they produce small quinces which can be used for making jam.

Japonicas should be readily available at your local nursery, although many of the flowering varieties are quite rare.

KANGAROO PAW

Without doubt, the native Kangaroo Paw must be one of the best of all Australian plants. It will grow almost anywhere, will fit into any landscaping and is the single most attractive plant for Australian native birds, particularly the nectar-feeding ones.

Those who have been growing them at home over the past few years may have been disappointed in the muddy red colours of the flowers, and the black foliage disease. This has now been largely overcome with new hybrid varieties, which come in beautiful colours from clear yellow, apricot and orange, to clear red. There are even hybrid dwarf kangaroo paws, so if you want something smaller than a metre or so tall, you can try one of these. These new hybrids can be grown anywhere, from native rock gardens to suburban cottage gardens. One of their strengths is that they will grow in poor soil and, unlike many Australian native plants, they are not fussy about the exact type of fertiliser: for example, you can even use rose food. It might hurt your grevilleas, but it won't harm the kangaroo paw.

The best of the new hybrid kangaroo paws are the 'Bush Gems' range. The name of each of these varieties starts with the word 'bush', for instance, the yellow one is 'Bush Dawn'. There are also reds, oranges and other colours in the range. 'Dwarf Delight' is another good variety, as is the rare pink, called 'Pink Joey'.

LAVENDER

Lavender is one of the most versatile of all garden plants. It's practical—lavender can be used as a specimen plant, in herbaceous borders or as a hedge; it's colourful—forms include everything from deep to palest purple-blue and also pink and white; it's edible—lavender enriches both sweet and savoury dishes; it's reputed to have medicinal qualities—the oil is used as an inhalant, an antiseptic and for a soothing massage. Lavender is also scented—a delight when the dried flowers are placed in linen drawers, where they are also said to help repel moths; and, perhaps above all, it's so romantically evocative—the sort of old-world plant that reminds us of our grandmothers' time.

Varieties There are close to 30 species of lavender, but the needs of the average gardener are amply met by just a handful of varieties.

Common English Lavender, *Lavandula angustifolia* 'Vera', is probably the best choice if you have room for only one lavender bush. It can be used for craft or cooking, and bears tiny, deep mauve-blue flowers on long, stiff spikes. English lavender also comes in white, pink and dwarf forms. Dwarf forms are ideal for growing as low hedges because of their compact growth.

French lavender, *Lavandula dentata*, is a medium-sized variety (about a metre—3'—high) and is very hardy. As its name indicates, this variety has heavily toothed or serrated leaves. It bears soft mauve flowers almost all year, but the flower spikes are shorter and softer than those of the English lavender. This variety, like the English version, is often used for fresh bunches of flowers.

Italian lavender, *Lavandula stoechas*, is somewhat smaller, with a low, compact growth habit. The flowerheads are short, richly perfumed and deep purple in colour. It flowers for an extended period. This variety has been declared a noxious weed in Victoria—within the Melbourne metropolitan area it may be grown but not sold.

Spiked lavender, *Lavandula latifolia* 'Spica', is aptly named for its long flower spikes, which are ideal for craft purposes. It is a late flowering variety, which doesn't show colour until the end of summer.

Lavandula x *Allardi* (Allardi lavender) grows into a very large bush and must be pruned hard twice a year to retain its shape. It is the tallest lavender. It is ideal for cut flowers for floral art and in dried arrangements, but the dried blooms are unsuitable for use in potpourris.

Lavandula viridis is a variety with green flowers, also suitable for use as cut flowers.

Cultivation It is essential to *prune* lavender bushes hard, annually after flowering—one to two-thirds of the bush should be removed. Just trimming the flowers off cannot be regarded as adequate pruning if you want your lavenders to look shapely and compact next season. Cuttings may be taken at pruning time.

Excellent *drainage* is another key to successful lavender cultivation. All lavenders are susceptible to root rot.

Lavenders grow best in an alkaline soil so the addition of a handful of *lime* around the plants in the autumn is advisable. Water regularly and apply complete fertiliser in spring. Most lavenders tolerate dry conditions well and resent humid climates.

Harvesting Flowers are harvested in the summer after the dew has evaporated and before it becomes too hot. No part of the harvest need be wasted, as the stripped stalks can be used for firelighters or in the linen cupboard, and the leaves can be used in potpourri. This is because the volatile perfumed oils occur in all these parts of the plant, not just in the flowers. Flowers may be hung in bunches in an airy place or used as cut flowers and retained in the vase until they have dried completely.

Our story was filmed at Yuulong Lavender Estate, Yendon Road, Mt Egerton, VIC 3345. Telephone (053) 68 9453. The 16-hectare estate is open to the public from the second week in December until the end of February each summer, and sells a wide range of plants and lavender culinary and craft products during that period. The flowers of the 7000 plants grown at Yuulong are harvested by sickle.

LISIANTHUS

The Lisianthus is one of the newest plants to arrive on the Australian home garden and floristry scenes, but it has made a tremendous impact in a short time. Lisianthus are natives of the hot, dry areas of Mexico, Texas and other southern states of the USA, and were originally called Texas Blue Bonnets.

Uses Lisianthus are among the world's best and most popular cut flowers—bunches of blooms last for up to four weeks indoors. They can also be used as indoor potted colour, but flowers on indoor potted plants will last for only about two weeks, and the pot would need to be positioned in a very well-lit spot.

Colours The original blue colour has now been joined by white, pink, lilac, pink and white, and blue and white forms.

Flowering The main flowering period is in February and March. Nipping each branch back after the flower has finished may result in a second flush before winter. The bushes should be cut back quite hard to a neat, compact shape in early spring to encourage vigorous new growth, which should produce plentiful flowers the following year. However, many commercial growers treat the plant as an annual.

Growing Despite their delicate appearance, lisianthus are really quite hardy. They perform best when grown in a hot, dry position, either in pots or in the ground. They need full sun and dislike humidity and excess fertiliser. They need only a little water, and even less when they are ready to flower. Wetting the foliage should be avoided.

Availability Potted lisianthus are often hard to find, as supplies are not keeping up with the popularity of this plant. You may need to hunt around for lisianthus and you can expect to pay $3–$4 per pot. Look for a compact, multi-planted pot; these plants can tend to flop over, and if two to three plants are placed in the same pot they help to hold each other upright.

LUCULIAS

The Luculia is one of the loveliest of shrubs. Its hydrangea-like flowerheads come in rose pink or white and are highly fragrant.

The pink flowering form, which is the most popular, blooms from late autumn to midwinter, while the white luculia flowers in late spring and summer. The pink form is therefore generally more noticeable because it blooms when few other flowers are around to brighten winter gardens.

Luculias come from the Himalayas, so they grow best in cool, elevated zones (such as Toowoomba and the Blue

Luculia gratissima

Mountains, and perhaps the Dandenongs) but need some protection from severe frost. They may be hard to grow in humid coastal areas unless planted in a raised and well-drained bed. A light soil is best, with compost added prior to planting. They also appreciate a little lime. Mulch well to avoid the need to disturb the soil, as luculias resent interference with their roots. They require only light fertilising with animal manure in spring. If left well alone they can be quite long-lived.

Luculias grow to about 2.5m (8′) in height and width, if pruned lightly after flowering and grown in dappled light. They can grow much larger if unpruned and more heavily shaded.

MINIATURE ROSES

Miniature Roses are perhaps the best roses of all. They have dense foliage and most are hardy dwarf plants. They are good as a border in a sunny spot around the garden—maybe around some larger roses, or will create a mini-hedge, which should only rarely need trimming, because of its compact growth. Mini-roses are also outstanding tub plants for a sunny spot. They tend to get less foliage disease than normal roses and often there is less need to spray them.

In recent years a great range of new varieties has been produced in America. Mini-roses now come in a wide range of colours, from light red to deep red, mauve and orange-apricot, yellow and even white. They grow to around half a metre (18″) tall or even less.

Some of the best are white or cream with stripes of bright red in the middle. Miniature roses have been

grafted onto the stems of taller growing roses for a spectacular effect. Three different varieties can be grafted onto each stem, for instance, red, white and striped all on the one stock.

In the USA and France, many breeders are experimenting to produce an indoor rose, and also a variety which is between a miniature and full-grown rose in size. Some of these are called mini-floras, and we will hear more about them in years to come.

Few mini-roses are highly perfumed, so select yours carefully. An added bonus with the miniatures is that they are almost thornless.

Recommended varieties

'Baby Darling'—orange to salmon pink
'Beauty Secret'—deep red (fragrant)
'Cricket'—orange
'Green Ice'—white (excellent for hanging baskets)
'Holy Toledo'—apricot/yellow/orange
'Lavender Lace'—mauve
'Magic Carousel'—carmine and cream
'Mary Marshall'—pink (fragrant)
'Rise 'n' Shine'—deep yellow
'Starina'—cherry orange

MOONFLOWER

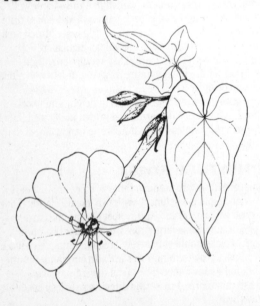

The Moonflower (*Ipomoea alba*) is aptly named as the flower opens when the moon is out. It opens just before dusk, is magnificent through the night, and by dawn is faded and dead. The moonflower is a climbing plant with a subtle and elusive perfume; it is hard to find. It grows in a temperate to warm climate, Sydney to Perth and north, but it may die down in winter.

Another fascinating plant is the Snail Flower (*Phaseolus caracalla*)—the flowers are coiled up and look like snails. It is another rare plant, with a beautiful perfume that smells best at night.

MORNING FLAG

The Morning Flag (*Orthrosanthus multiflorus*) is a very useful Australian native plant of the Iris family. It produces flower spikes bearing numerous rich blue flowers, which bloom continuously for many weeks during spring.

Morning flag grows hardily in most soils and conditions but is outstanding in damp areas. It makes an excellent tub specimen beside a swimming pool, and its straplike leaves blend particularly well with similar leaf forms, such as those of the Blackboy or Grass Tree (also suitable for tub culture).

This appealing plant is not very well known and may be difficult to obtain, but try your own local specialist Australian native plant nursery and you may be in luck.

NATIVE GROUND COVERS

Ground cover plants are extremely useful in the backyard, cascading over pots, covering areas where the grass won't grow, or just providing greenery in the garden.

Australian Native Daisy (*Brachycome multifida*) A small perennial plant with lilac-blue daisylike flowers. It grows well in most areas, and prefers a sunny position with good drainage. It is now available in various colours, mid blue, mauve, white, pink and a smaller flowered form.

Dampiera diversifolia Named after Sir William Dampier, this is another ground cover with dark blue–purple flowers which last for many months. Some forms spread by suckering. It is suited to dryer areas, such as Perth or Melbourne, and is not for humid areas. It prefers a sunny well-drained position.

Bush Maidenhair Fern (*Adiantum sp*) Grows readily in damp situations, shaded to partially sunny positions. It is very hardy and grows well in rock crevices.

Dusty Miller (*Spyridium cinereum*) Dark green, glossy foliage with silver-coloured leaves around fairly insignificant flowers. The contrast between silver and the glossy green foliage makes it a very attractive plant. It will cascade beautifully over the sides of a large pot.

Australian Native Violet (*Viola hederacea*) A small ivy-leafed violet, which will cascade over rocks, softening harsh appearances. It prefers a shady, moist position but will grow in full sun. It forms an extensive mat, and can be used in hanging baskets. There are a number of coloured varieties; the purple and white ones are the most common. The other varieties—white, blue, and so on—are not usually as hardy.

These violets can be crystallised to make an edible decoration for cakes and desserts. You will need:

Fresh violets
Egg white
Caster sugar
Purple food colouring (can be made by mixing red
                                    and blue together)
Small paint brush

Paint each violet thoroughly but lightly with egg white using the small paint brush. Mix a few drops of purple food colouring into the caster sugar and sprinkle the light purple coloured sugar evenly over all surfaces of each violet flower. Stand the flowers on a tray or wire rack in a warm dry place (for example beside a fire or heater, or in a very slow oven) until dry. Store the dried crystallised flowers in an airtight container between layers of tissue paper.

Hints: Pick violets with a length of stem attached and do not trim this off until after the violets have been placed on the tray or rack to dry. It is much easier to handle them by the stem during the painting process.

When mixing the food colouring into the caster sugar, put both ingredients inside a plastic bag—this saves mess and discoloured fingers.

A jar of crystallised violets decorated with purple ribbon makes a novel small gift.

ORANGE TRUMPET CREEPER

If you have an ugly garden shed or carport that needs camouflaging, a magnificent climber for this purpose is the Orange Trumpet Creeper or *Pyrostegia venusta*. Its best feature is its habit of clinging and draping itself over whatever you grow it on.

It is outstanding for any garden, because it will give many weeks of colour. The small tendrils it produces to cling on to fences and so on can be pulled off the fence very easily.

It is a reasonably vigorous grower, without being a weed. It will grow from Sydney to Perth and north, but it is not suitable for colder areas.

ORCHIDS

When most people think of orchids they visualise cymbidiums, but there is a great variety of orchids, for example, dendrobium hybrid (one of its parents is the Queensland floral emblem), and black orchids (*Catasetum tenebrosa*), originally from South America.

Also from South America comes a great indoor plant, the white pansy orchid or Miltonia. It produces up to 20 flowers on a couple of stems that can last as long as five weeks. This is much better value than buying orchids

from a florist; you can enjoy the beauty year after year.

From Thailand, the country of orchids, comes the slipper orchid or Paphiopedilum. Cattleya is an ideal orchid for cool climate areas of New South Wales and Victoria. Disa, a new collection of orchids from South Africa, grow in the ground in moss, and when the flower finishes the plant dies off. Don't destroy it; it will send up a new plant nearby, probably three or four from one plant.

The Stanhopea orchid is one of the world's weirdest plants—it comes from South America, and particularly from Peru. The flower originates from the base of the bulb and comes out of the bottom of the pot. Therefore the Stanhopea needs to be planted in a paperbark-lined wire basket or something similar.

Another unusual orchid comes from Western Australia: *Rhizanthella gardneri* grows completely underground. It has no green parts on it at all, and even flowers underground.

Australian natives In addition to the many imported varieties there is a whole range of Australian native orchids, and many of them are very charming, even if they do have dreadful names. For example, *Dendrobium gracilicaule*, which has pale yellow flowers with red-brown spots on the outside segments, or *Dendrobium kingianum* which is commonly known as the pink rock lily or orchid.

One of the most attractive orchids is *Dendrobium falcorostrum*, which has large snowy-white flowers and a sweet perfume. This is known as the beech orchid because it is found growing on beech trees (*Nothofagus spp*) along the coastal ranges from central New South Wales to southeast Queensland.

In the wild these orchids tend to hybridise a little, but extensive work by hobbyists has produced a whole new range of hybrid native orchids. Hybridisation is an extremely complex process. The first step is pollination, which is accomplished with a toothpick. The pollen from the male parent is carefully extracted and placed on the receptive part of the female parent. If fertilisation is successful, a seed pod should form within a few months. The seed pod is cut open under sterile conditions and the seeds spread on an agar jelly in a jar.

The seeds germinate quickly, and over the next six months the young hybrid plants are re-flasked twice more until they are perhaps 5cm (2") tall, at which stage they are hardened off and planted out into a community pot in a glasshouse. They will then take from two to seven years to flower.

One of the most spectacular new hybrids is *Dendrobium* 'Elegant Heart' which has the beautiful Cooktown orchid in its breeding as well as the rock lily and *D. tetragonum*; so it has two cool growing and one warm growing orchids in its make up.

Australian native orchids have a lot to offer. Many of them are exceptionally hardy plants, which can be left in their pots for many years. Pot them in a mix of equal parts of fine–medium pine bark, perlite and charcoal, and fertilise with Nitrosol or Aquasol.

In the wild many orchids grow on trees or rocks, so great use can be made of them in the backyard. To ensure pollination, some Australian orchids smell like gnats, mosquitoes, bees, spiders, birds, and other flowers.

Cymbidiums In recent years there have been some wonderful breeding advances with Cymbidium orchids. Gone are the days when the backyard orchid was simply white or a muted pastel pink. Breeders have worked to produce a broad range of colours, including green, red, yellow, purple, and even brown.

Miniature varieties have taken off as well, and these also exhibit an extensive range of colours. The current trend appears to be towards clear, bright colours such as golden yellow or lolly pink.

Despite their delicate appearance, cymbidium orchids can take quite rough treatment. Once they have finished flowering they can be repotted. Pull the plant out of the pot and examine the rootball. Usually you will find it is thickly matted and congested. The rootball can be banged against a hard surface to loosen the roots a little and then most of the roots should be trimmed off—in some cases it may be best to divide the orchid into two by cutting through the rootball with an old pair of secateurs.

Also take off back bulbs (dead-looking bulbs without leaves). If you don't, the new shoots don't have a chance to grow among all the dead wood. Clean the roots up properly; keep only the good roots with nice green points. Other dead roots are useless, so cut them off.

Pot the orchid into a good quality orchid potting mix. Planting into an inappropriate mix is one of the most common mistakes in orchid growing. Simply pour a little of the good quality orchid mix into the bottom of a pot, sit the orchid in it, and top the pot up with mix, making sure all the roots are covered.

Place bulbs at the rim of the pot so that the new bulbs can grow forward.

Fertilise your orchid with one of the nine-month slow release fertilisers, such as Osmocote, or a liquid fertiliser such as Nitrosol. After that, you can completely neglect your orchids and they will thrive in the backyard. Just be wary of placing them in too much shade, as this prevents flowering. If your orchids haven't flowered, try placing them in a sunnier position and they should recommence flowering next year. It should take orchids two years to flower after repotting.

Snail damage Winter is flowering time for cymbidium orchids, but vigilance is required to avoid missing out on blooms.

Check your orchids for flower spikes. On early-flowering cymbidiums brown marks may be visible on the petals and stems. These marks are caused by snails, which use their

rasp-like radulae to scrape up pieces of young plant tissue. If they happen to eat the end of the spike the flower buds will be lost.

Snail damage may be prevented by scattering pellets (take care to prevent pets and small children from reaching them) or by manual control.

Nurseries that specialise in growing cymbidium orchids can provide detailed information about varieties. Your local nursery or garden centre should be able to direct you to such nurseries.

Miniature cymbidiums Miniature cymbidiums have become very popular in recent years. The colour range is wide, from green/white through to deepest reds, burnt oranges, and lots more. They flower from May to August.

There are two main types of miniature cymbidiums, those whose flower spikes stand up clear of the foliage, and those with cascading flower spikes. These hang over the sides of the pot, and are particularly suitable for pots hanging from pergolas.

In the wild, these types of orchids never grow in soil, but high in the crutches of trees, and therefore the potting mix used for them should be very coarse and open, with lots of air in it. A good quality orchid potting mix is suitable.

The miniature cymbidiums are not difficult to grow. Throughout most of the middle of Australia, as long as it is not too cold or excessively hot, they will grow well. If they don't flower it is probably because they need more light—about 65-70% light—to flower consistently. Therefore the ideal position for them is in light shade under a gum tree, light shade cloth or a pergola.

Miniature cymbidiums produce more spikes of flowers per plant than do the larger varieties of orchids. They cost $15-$30 and are very easy to grow. If you keep them in good light you will have plenty of flowers that will last for many weeks indoors.

Phalaenopsis orchids The Phalaenopsis Orchid is a native of the warmer areas of Asia, where it grows on trees. With graceful arching flower spikes and soft green leaves, it is a very attractive plant, and at the moment it is very fashionable. There is a fairly good range of flower colours, mostly close to white or pink, and some with spots. They are quite expensive, the price ranging from $35 to $60 or more, but they should flower for about three or four months.

An individual flower will last about six weeks or more. Once the flowers start to fade, do not cut the whole spike off, just cut at the first 'notch' below the dead flowers. This will encourage a secondary flowering, providing more beautiful flowers to enjoy for another six to eight weeks.

These orchids are different from many others in that they do not have a bulb. Their roots are large and white or pale green, and are regarded as part of the overall beauty of the plant.

As the Phalaenopsis does not have a bulb or storage organ, it does not like to dry out. It grows best indoors and doesn't like cold temperatures. A room which is heated to a minimum of 16° or 17°C (61-63°F) with plenty of filtered light (direct sunlight can burn the leaves) would be the right environment.

Phalaenopsis orchids don't grow in normal orchid mix, but in a coarse redwood bark. This allows the roots to grow vigorously. It is also advisable to sit the pot above a tray containing some water and pebbles, or pine bark, to help increase the humidity. The plants may be misted with water from an atomiser.

Because the bark cannot hold nutrients, feed the orchids each month with a liquid fertiliser such as fish emulsion or Nitrosol; or four times a year with a three-month slow release fertiliser, such as Nutricote or Osmocote.

Importing orchids In centuries past the orchid was prized not only for its beauty but also as an aphrodisiac. They were collected by the wealthiest gardeners, who paid incredible prices for the plants at auctions.

At Mandai Gardens in Singapore, the landscaped orchid beds attract tourists all year round. Ninety percent of the blooms grown will be sold to the cut flower trade, but there is a million dollar market for plants in other countries like Australia, where the climate is suitable for orchid cultivation.

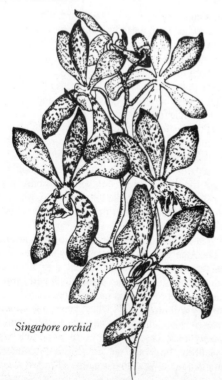

Singapore orchid

In a greenhouse, some beautiful hybrids can be grown. There are Vandas like the Josephine Van Brero hybrids, Arandas (Vandas crossed with Arachnis), a brilliant Renanthera hybrid, and so on. New hybrids are bred each year by transferring the pollen from one flower to the stigma of another. The resultant seedlings should combine the best features of each parent.

John Laycock started the nursery. His daughter Amy Ede's only interest in the blooms at the time was their use in corsages, but now she spends hours sorting the plants, which have been grown in sterile flasks on an agar jelly, and potting them in community pots.

Plants for export are washed in a mild solution of fungicide before being packed. When the plants arrive in Australia they have to be cleared through customs and then gassed with methyl bromide. Then they are quarantined for about three months.

Orchid Valley Nursery Orchid Valley Nursery (40km— 25 miles—south of Cairns in Queensland) was started three years ago by David and Susan Collier. They have developed the nursery as a tourist attraction which has its own railway line and station, and a number of other features to interest tourists. For her part in the development of the business, Susan was named Queensland Businesswoman of the Year two years ago.

The nursery is built amid 2.2ha (5.5 acres) of landscaped tropical gardens, which include many palm trees, including some from the Seychelles, Miami and South Africa.

The Colliers have two quarantine houses and run the largest privately owned quarantine station in Australia. They import their orchids from all over the world, including Hawaii, Thailand, South America and France.

The Colliers grow thousands of different varieties of orchids. They have bred 250 new ones, but have only named five. The orchids featured on 'Burke's Backyard' were:

Dendrobiums, which can be grown indoors or outdoors on a tree trunk, their natural habitat. Each flower spike can produce 20 flowers, and the plant will flower for several months. In size and shape the flowers show wide differences.

The Cattleya, known as the queen of orchids and probably the most loved orchid in the world, because of its huge showy blooms. This orchid is very hardy and grows vigorously. Many are suitable for temperate areas.

The Vanda The example we showed was grown in a basket, with its long roots dangling below. Fertiliser is sprayed onto the roots. Vanda orchids come in a diverse range of bloom sizes, shapes and colours.

Oncidiums, beautiful orchids, often with curiously formed flowers. These are generally reliable and hardy.

Epidendrums, which flower upside down in an extensive range of colours and grow beautifully indoors, and outdoors on rocks or trees.

The Colliers don't use soil but grow the orchids in pots of volcanic gravel. The plants receive a heavy watering once a week and the gravel stays wet for the rest of the week—the leaves are sometimes dampened between waterings.

Sales Orchids from Orchid Valley Nursery cost between $3.50 and $100. For an extra $10 they can be sent overnight almost anywhere in Australia. In fact, about 75% of the total production is sold via mail order. A catalogue and order form may be obtained by writing to the nursery.

Orchid Valley Nursery
Little Mulgrave Road
Little Mulgrave
(PO Box 196)
Gordonvale QLD 4865
Telephone (070) 56 1727

Orchids in Paradise Greg Dent, owner of Orchids of Paradise in Sydney has his own quarantine facility in the backyard so he can care for his plants during the required quarantine period. Government inspectors visit the greenhouse each month to check the progress of the plants, and to determine whether the orchids should be released. The orchids have to make a minimum of two leaves' growth and the inspector checks that the leaves are clear, with no virus or disease.

Imported orchids are not necessarily more expensive than those grown here; in fact, some can be cheaper.

Orchids in Paradise
8 Northbridge Plaza
Sailor's Bay Road
Northbridge NSW 2063
Telephone (02) 958 2122

For further information
To join an Orchid Society contact these secretaries:

Miss B. Oldfield
61 Mountford Avenue
Guildford NSW 2161
Telephone (02) 632 5712

Mrs I. Hutchins
37 Elliot Street
Mordialloc VIC 3195
Telephone (03) 580 4917

Mrs Noela Parsons
GPO Box 2002
Brisbane QLD 4001
Telephone (07) 273 1127

Mr Ivan May
7 Buchan Avenue
Beaumont SA 5066
Telephone (08) 79 4257

Mrs L. Manning
16 Cromer Road
Brentwood WA 6153
Telephone (09) 364 7968

The *Australian Orchid Review* is the official publication of the Orchid Society of NSW, Queensland Orchid Society, Victorian Orchid Club, Orchid Club of South Australia, and the Orchid Society of Western Australia.

ORNAMENTAL CHILLIES OR CAPSICUM

These perennials come in a wide variety of colours and shapes. Their fruits may be light green, yellow, purple, orange or red, and they can be elongated, pointed, round or oval in shape.

Ornamental chillies are grown as decorative plants in pots, garden borders or beds as an alternative to petunias or similar colourful plants. They are not recommended for eating: ordinary hot chillies are best for this purpose.

These are particularly hardy plants, tolerating most climates, but requiring full sun to do well.

PALMS

If you want something lush in the backyard, why not grow palm trees. Nowadays, you can buy huge palms, some up to 9m (30') tall, to drop into the ground and create an instant garden. There are dozens of varieties of palms—suitable for both indoor and outside growing.

The most popular in Australia is the cocos palm. It grows in full sun, is hardy and easy to grow, and particularly suitable for the middle of Australia.

The dwarf date palm grows to only about 2m (6') tall, is very tough and has fine fernlike foliage. Again, through the middle of Australia this is hardy and easy to grow.

The kentia palm is probably the world's most popular palm, but not the most hardy in outdoor conditions. It takes some shade but doesn't like too much cold. Another is the cabbage tree palm, from which Palm Beach in New South Wales got its name.

If you live in cold conditions, there are several suitable varieties. The American cotton palm will even cope with some snow, as will the tough windmill palm. Another cold climate palm is the European fan palm which will survive in the coldest weather Australia has to offer.

Your nursery will have plants which you can grow with your palms—New Zealand cordyline (red or green), bird's-nest fern, ponytail and asparagus meyerii. For a touch of class, try planting the dwarf tree fern (Blechnum nudum).

There are two main ways to use palms, either in a

formal row or in clumps. The latter will result in maximum privacy for your house and you can grow very colourful foliage plants as the understorey to the palms. Among those that have been used to good effect are: crotons, several different varieties of cordylines and impatiens (balsam), Japanese nandina, and Australian native violets.

Palms can be planted out from pots and as seedlings. Liberal use of fertiliser and good soil preparation— approximately 15cm (6″) of compost dug in and then covered by a mulch of compost—lead to rapid growth. Use fertiliser that is high in nitrogen during the growing season, (for example, Nitrophoska). Supplement this with Nitrosol.

Watch for caterpillars—if you see palm leaves stuck together and there is a grub inside when you pull them apart, just squash or remove it.

In general, indoor potted palms need a short spell outside in a sheltered position from time to time. Many palms make excellent outdoor tub specimens. In the garden, palms generally need some protection when young.

SOME PALMS TO GROW				
NAME	BOTANIC NAME	INDOORS	OUTDOORS	COMMENTS
Alexandra	*Archontophoenix alexandrae*	Short-lived (3-6 months) Not good indoors	Suits tropical and subtropical areas	Frost sensitive; a good tub plant
American Cotton	*Washingtonia filifera*	Not really suitable	Very tough; takes heavy frost	Fiendishly prickly
Atherton Tableland	*Laccospadix australasica*	Reasonably good in very bright light	Tolerates light frost	Very new—may tolerate less light indoors
Bamboo	*Chamaedorea microspadix*	Grows to around 2m (6½′); tolerates low light	Hardy when established; needs plenty of water in dry periods; shade in tropics, shelter in temperate	Looks like bamboo; forms dense clumps of suckers
Bangalow	*Archontophoenix cunninghamiana*	Disappointing—needs very bright light	Tolerates some cold (medium frost)	Suits middle Australia
Cabbage Tree	*Livistona australis*	Needs plenty of light, and spells outside	Takes some frost	Gives Palm Beach, Sydney, its name
Canary Island Date	*Phoenix canariensis*	Not suitable	Very heavy frost tolerated	Very popular in the past; takes inland dry heat
Chinese Fan	*Livistona chinensis*	Plenty of light	Tough indoors; takes medium frost	A bit prickly
Cocos	*Arecastrum romanzoffianum*	For a few months only	Tolerates heavy frost	Widely planted; very useful; very rapid grower

NAME	BOTANIC NAME	INDOORS	OUTDOORS	COMMENTS
Dwarf Date	*Phoenix roebelenii*	Plenty of light needed	Light—medium frost tolerated	Becoming popular; exceptionally hardy; grows to 2m (6½'); good at base of Cocos clump
European Fan	*Chamaerops humilis*	Needs sun outside, so not suitable indoors	Very heavy frost tolerated	Makes good clumps—hardy
European Windmill	*Trachycarpus fortunei*	Not really suitable	Takes snow	Wonderfully hardy in cooler areas
'Jade Empress'	*Rhapis multifida*	May be easy to grow indoors		Newly released
Kentia	*Howeia forsteriana*	Perhaps the world's best indoor palm; spreads out to fill up part of the room; hardy.	Does well in coastal districts	Good in groups, as far south as Melbourne; tolerates mild frost
Rhapis	*Rhapis excelsa*	Tolerates low light; lasts for years	Cold tolerant—may take light frost	Slow growing—can remain in same container for years

PELARGONIUMS

For many years Geraniums (known botanically as Pelargoniums) were out of vogue in Australian gardens—especially during the period in which Australian native plants were popular. Now the tide has turned and we're experiencing a huge move back to old-fashioned garden plants—and with it the rediscovery of the humble geranium. The geranium's position at the forefront of the old-fashioned garden revival is certainly well earned; few plants are as hardy and easy to grow anywhere in Australia as this. Geraniums also come in an astonishing range of flower colours, sizes, forms and shapes, as well as having an equally wide range of leaf colours, shapes and scents.

Some varieties *Common geraniums* or zonal pelargoniums.
* *Miniature varieties* of the common geranium, both single and double-flowered forms have been bred.
* The *tulip flowered variety*—each of the many individual flowers that make up a single flower head is shaped like a tulip bloom. This type of geranium was developed at Georyl Pelargonium Nursery in Victoria.
* *Coloured-leaved geraniums*—a form of zonal pelargonium grown for the attractive leaf colouring rather than for the blooms.

Regal pelargonium

* *Scented-leaved geraniums*, which produce peppermint, rose, nutmeg, lemon, apple and many other perfumes. These are best grown beside a frequently used path where the leaves will release romantic wafts of scent when brushed by passers-by.
* *Staph varieties*, which have frilly leaves and flowers.
* *Cactus varieties* with spiky flowers.
* *Ivy geraniums*, which are ideal for growing over trellises or fences (one plant will reach the top of a 2m (6') fence within two years).
* *Miniature ivy geraniums*, which are suited to hanging baskets and rock gardens.
* *Regal pelargoniums*, a broad group of elegant plants that produce very large heads of multicoloured flowers.

One of the most recent developments in regal pelargoniums has been the breeding of the first striped pelargonium, 'Tyabb Princess'. This plant is available from Mr G. Stockton, Georyl Pelargonium Nursery, 63 Graydens Road, Tyabb, VIC 3913. Telephone (059) 79 1349. This nursery is open to the public by appointment only, but will mail plants all over Australia. People in Victoria can send $2.20 to receive a catalogue, people in other states can receive one for $2.35.

Growing hints from Geoff Stockton of Georyl Pelargonium Nursery *Best aspect* Pelargoniums need a minimum of three hours of sunshine every day. The eastern side of the house is the best position.

Watering Don't over-water pelargoniums, and never plant them with azaleas or ferns, because these plants like a lot of water. Too much water will cause black stem rot in pelargoniums.

Pruning Cut plants back between December and March. Don't water them for one week before cutting back; this will prevent them from bleeding. If plants bleed, fungus spores will land in the juice and go down the stem to cause black stem rot.

Cut stems just above a node 20cm (8") above the ground. Leave plants that have been cut back for eight weeks before re-potting.

Cuttings Take cuttings 10cm (4") long. Cut from the stem just below a node. Plant cuttings in coarse river sand. Don't add peat moss; it will retain too much moisture. Plant 2.5cm (1") apart in a two-litre icecream container with holes punched in the bottom. Allow eight weeks for the cuttings to strike.

Fertilising Fertilise with Osmocote; 1 teaspoon per 15cm (6") pot, or 2 teaspoons per 20cm (8") pot. Don't over-fertilise.

Diseases Green virus—flowers open green. There is no cure. Pull out plants and burn them, or put them in the garbage.

Aphids and white flies—spray twice with a pyrethrin spray such as Zero Insect Killer or Mortein House and

Garden, three weeks apart to kill offspring as well as adults.

Rust on zonals—evidenced by brown spores on bottom of leaf. There is no cure, but prevent rust by pulling off and burning all leaves with spores on them, and then spraying fortnightly with Benlate.

Potted Pelargoniums Cut potted plants back to about 20cm (8") above the ground from February to March. Wait eight weeks, then repot. When new growth is 5cm (2") long, nip the tops out to create lovely rounded, bushy plants.

PERENNIALS

Among the first things to make an impact on the Australian environment when the white man began to settle here were his plants. Many plant varieties were brought from Europe, and most did not flower in winter. It has taken us a long time to realise that there are a lot of colourful plants that will not only keep their leaves in winter in most areas of Australia, but will flower as well. With the return to cottage-style gardens, the perennial is definitely back in fashion. There are many colourful plants that you can use in your backyard in winter.

Recommended plants
* *Adenandra fragrans*—pink scented flowers on a low growing bush.
* *Adenandra uniflora*—white flowers on a small bush
* *Hebe speciosa* 'Bouquet of Flowers'—Hebes are incredibly hardy, low growing shrubs.
* *Salvia rutilans* 'Pineapple Sage'—this can be used as a herb to make tea, but is best to grow in the garden for the red flowers.
* Linum (*Reinwardtia indica*)—flowers right through winter, with very clear bright yellow flowers. It is almost unkillable and is a low clumping plant less than a metre (3') tall, that will take some shade.
* Rosemary (*Rosmarinus officinalis* 'Blue Lagoon')—its aromatic leaves can be used for cooking, and it has light blue flowers through the cool months.
* Lachenalia—a bulbous plant that flowers for long periods through winter.
* Variegated saxifraga (*Saxifraga sarmentosa*) grows along the ground and has wonderful variegated coloured leaves.
* Dwarf white candytuft (*Iberis sempervirens* 'Little Gem') is a low growing plant with clear white flowers.

Many of these plants are not available at ordinary nurseries throughout Australia: it may be necessary to go to a cottage garden specialist nursery.

Some other plants to watch out for are: China rose 'Old Blush', that flowers on and off throughout the year; and also members of the daisy family, such as the marguerite daisy (*Chrysanthemum frutescens*), which will often flower all winter. Flowers can be white, pink or yellow. *Felicia echinata* flowers are in the mauve/blue colour range. There are also variegated felicia. *Aster frikarti* has daisylike flowers throughout winter.

PERENNIAL NURSERY

Perennials are plants that have a lifespan of three years or more and many remain in the garden permanently. Some perennials die down each year and remain dormant through winter before new shoots emerge in spring. In general perennials require very little attention, and it is their hardiness and reliability that have made them the backbone of cottage gardens over the years.

A resurgence of interest in cottage gardens has been paralleled by an increase in the number and size of nurseries specialising in these plants.

The nursery at which we filmed our segment for 'Burke's Backyard' was Lambley Nursery in Melbourne's Dandenongs. This nursery lists about 300 varieties in its catalogue and is currently trialling at least another 700 varieties, which have been imported from overseas. These imports are quarantined and then planted out at the nursery for two to three years to see how they perform under Australian conditions.

Plants that are for sale are also grown in the field. A mail order service to customers all over the country involves special preparation and packaging of plants prior to dispatch. The plants are dug out of the ground, the tops are trimmed to just a few centimetres above the crown of the plant, and then the roots are also trimmed. The soil is thoroughly washed away from the roots, because Dandenong soil is not generally compatible with other soils in the country and, while lovely and well drained in its place of origin, when lifted and planted in other people's gardens it can turn into pug.

Perennial plants in general tend to have more subtle, unobtrusive and harmonious flower colours than their sometimes gaudy annual cousins. Some of the varieties shown on our segment were: Astrantia, the foam flower, the horn poppy, red hot pokers (*Kniphofia*), monkshood, the cone flower, black-eyed Susan, and anthemis.

For further information

Lambley Nursery
PO Box 142
Olinda VIC 3788
Telephone (03) 751 1841

The nursery is situated at Fairhaven Street, Mt Dandenong, and can be inspected during February, March and April.

PERFUMED PLANTS

Luculia gratissima is not an easy plant to grow, but if you are successful it is very rewarding. It grows about 4–5m (12–15′) tall, and has large perfumed flowerheads. It needs a rich, well-drained soil and a sheltered position. It grows well in gardens below road level where it is well protected from wind. It can also be grown in tubs. The pink form is the most readily available, but there is a white flowering version as well. It flowers in winter and has a wonderful perfume.

Osmanthus fragrans flowers nearly all the year round. The flowers are small and white and not particularly attractive, but the perfume is excellent. It will grow over 3m (10′) tall and can be kept pruned. It is a hardy plant and likes a sunny, sheltered position. It also grows well in a pot.

Jonquils have a heady perfume and for this reason are probably a better choice than daffodils. They like an open sunny position, sheltered from wind.

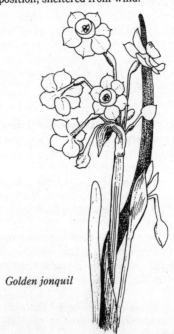

Golden jonquil

Winter honeysuckle (*Lonicera fragrantissima*) is a shrub form of honeysuckle. It produces white flowers right along the stems in winter, which have a very attractive perfume. It is an extremely hardy plant. It is quite difficult to obtain, but is available in New South Wales from Colonial Cottage Nursery, 62 Kenthurst Rd, Dural, NSW 2158. Telephone (02) 654 1340.

Daphne odora is a small evergreen shrub with sweetly scented flowers. It is very difficult to grow and dies very easily. It likes a well-drained, partly shaded and well-protected position. It may be easier to grow in a tub. When planting a daphne, it is a good idea to keep it slightly above the general level of the soil, to help reduce the possibility of collar rot. Treatment with Fongarid will help to prevent root rot.

In recent years a serious virus disease has affected daphnes. When buying a daphne, select carefully—the foliage should be evenly green, with no distorted new growth and no lighter green circles or patches on the leaves. There is no cure for the virus, which is probably spread by aphids.

French lavender (*Lavandula dentata*) has soft grey-green foliage and grows to about a metre (3-4'). It flowers almost all the year, but more abundantly in winter. It likes well-drained soil and an open, sunny position. The lilac flowers are lightly perfumed.

PLUMBAGO

Plumbago or Leadwort, *Plumbago auriculata* (syn P. *capensis*), originated in South Africa, and was introduced to Europe around 1818.

This evergreen shrub grows to about 2m (7') unsupported, but can climb to about 4m (14'). It bears sky-blue bunches of phlox-like flowers, borne throughout the warmer months and more prolifically during dry weather.

Any soil type is suitable for growing plumbago, but good drainage is preferred. The plant is frost tender and grows best in full sun or semi-shade. A heavy winter trimming will help to prevent straggling growth.

Plumbago is so hardy that it is virtually unkillable. It tolerates seaside, outback and polluted positions. Plumbago makes a beautiful informal hedge, smothered in blue flowers for much of the year. It also looks attractive in group plantings.

POINSETTIAS

The Poinsettia is one of the world's most colourful indoor and outdoor plants, and nowadays a good colour range is available; pink to red and a creamy colour that looks very subtle and effective indoors. They are extremely useful indoors, as they will provide from three to six months of colour for the same price as, or less than, a bunch of cut flowers.

Poinsettias can also be trained as standards, that is, having a long main stem or trunk with a ball of foliage on top, which can be attractive as an indoor feature or grown outdoors in a frost-free position.

The red parts of the poinsettia are really leaves or bracts, not flowers. The true flowers are in the centre of the red bracts, and are small and yellow-red in colour. The red bracts attract the pollinating insects to the flower in the centre.

Poinsettia belongs to the botanic family of Euphorbia, which means that it is closely related to the Crown of Thorns (*Euphorbia milii* var *splendens*), which grows along the ground, has spines and produces a caustic milky sap that flows from the cut stem. Other members of the euphorbia group that are not obviously related to the poinsettia, closely resemble cactus; some with small green leaves and others with no leaves at all, but many spines.

Membership of this family means that the poinsettia will tolerate fairly dry conditions. Indoors they will give three months or so of colour and then revert to a green plant—they will not colour up again indoors. Nurseries have induced flowering in the poinsettia by subjecting them to short day-lengths (ten hours of daylight or less) in glasshouses that are artificially darkened, but this cannot be done easily in the home. Either throw old plants away or, if you live in a frost-free area, plant them out in the garden.

There are some very good poinsettias for garden planting in frost-free areas, particularly the double growing variety *Euphorbia pulcherrima* 'Henriette Ecke', which looks like a waratah but is very hardy. After enjoying the flowers, cut back severely in late winter or early spring to about a metre (3') high. Poinsettias do especially well in a full sun position, protected from cold winter winds.

RARE PLANTS

One 'Burke's Backyard' programme featured a rare plant nursery, Yamina Rare Plants, which provides a mail order service. A list of their stock will be sent to you if you provide a stamped, addressed return envelope.

The unusual plants that Don showed were:

* Upright dissectum maple *Acer palmatum* 'Dissectum Seiryu'
* *Pieris japonica* 'Spring Candy'
* Golden monterey pine—*Pinus radiata* 'Aurea'
* *Illicium verum* 'Star Anise'
* Variegated liquidambar—*Liquidambar styraciflua* 'Golden Treasure'
* Variegated ginkgo or maidenhair—*Ginkgo biloba* 'Variegata'
* Monkey puzzle—*Araucaria araucana*
* Golden cryptomeria—*Cryptomeria japonica* 'Sekkan Sugi'
* *Garrya elliptica* 'James Roof'
* Golden variety of holly—*Ilex aquifolium* 'Golden King'
* Weeping form of giant redwood—*Sequoiadendron giganteum* 'Pendulum'
* Weeping larch—*Larix decidua* 'Julian's Weeper'
* Weeping *Nyssa sylvatica*—*Nyssa sylvatica* 'Autumn Cascades'
* Prostrate blue spruce—*Picea pungens* 'Glauca Prostrata'

For further information

Yamina Rare Plants
(Arnold Teese and Sons)
25 Moores Road
Monbulk VIC 3793
Telephone (03) 756 6335

RHODODENDRONS

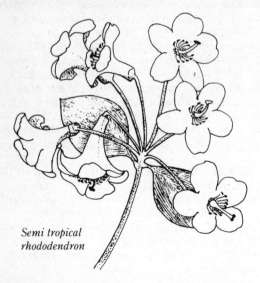

*Semi tropical
rhododendron*

Rhododendrons are among the world's most spectacular flowering plants. Varieties are available that grow to less than a metre (3′) high and others reach more than 10m (33′), although the most commonly sold types average around 2-3m (6-10′). All prefer an organic soil, so the addition of peat moss or compost to the soil is advisable. A surface mulch of leaf litter, compost or peat moss is essential for strong growth.

These plants prefer rather more sun than shade—ideally, they should have dappled light all day. In the mountains and higher regions most types happily grow in full sun, but in warmer coastal areas they like to be protected from the savage heat of midday and afternoons; under a gum tree is ideal.

Fertilising Rhododendrons are not gross feeders and may resent being over-fertilised. Nine-month Nutricote or Osmocote granules are ideal, but cow manure and Nitrosol are also excellent fertilisers. Do not let these plants dry out during the hot months as they are surface rooting, but also remember that they detest poor drainage.

Culture Most rhododendrons grow well in pots and any bagged potting mix is adequate. In areas where rhododendrons are less easy to grow (Sydney and the humid areas to the north), pot culture is the best method, although a sandy soil, well augmented with peat moss, is ideal. In the past, many rhododendrons were grown in Victoria's Dandenongs, then dug up, potted and sold through nurseries. Most of these plants died. While rhododendrons will grow in the red clay-like soil in the Dandenongs, this soil becomes a death warrant in other areas if it is left on the roots. When purchasing check that no red soil remains around the roots of your plant.

Colours Most yellow, and particularly the blue flowering varieties, are best confined to Australia's mountain zones, since they are rather more difficult to grow. Nonetheless, cream varieties such as 'Unique', or blueish varieties like 'Blue Peter', will grow almost anywhere in tubs, and sometimes in the ground.

Varieties such as 'Pink Pearl', 'Sir Robert Peel', and 'Elegans' are outstanding in most areas of Australia. The latter two are the tall, deep pink varieties seen growing around Sydney, Melbourne and other capital cities.

Pseudo-tropical rhododendrons The Malesian or Vireya group of rhododendrons are mostly epiphytic (a plant growing on another) plants from mountain areas of New Guinea, Borneo and Java. These plants are still rare, but some nurseries do sell them. Being ephiphytic in nature, most require a very peaty potting mix and will not grow well in the ground. They resent strong fertilisers and should be given half the recommended doses of Nitrosol or fish emulsion once or twice a year.

The Australian rhododendron, *R. lochiae*, has red flowers and is a superb pot plant for Sydney, Perth and Brisbane. It does less well in cooler areas.

ROSES

Roses have developed a reputation for being difficult, but half the battle is choosing the right type to suit your needs.

No plant better symbolises our mastery of nature than the rose. This most vicious of plants—originally a wild scrambling briar, similar to a blackberry—has been reduced in vigour, has had its perfume enhanced, its flowers beefed up and its flowering period lengthened; it has been grafted, pruned, bare-rooted and sprayed with chemicals. If ever a plant has been domesticated, it is the rose.

Today's more conservation-minded gardener tries to work with nature rather than subdue it. The older-style rose is seen as a plant needing constant applications of chemicals, regular pruning and heaps of fertiliser, but many modern roses are, in fact, relatively low maintenance plants, requiring little use, if any, of toxic chemicals.

For generations the public has been misled into believing that a rose is a rose is a rose: it most certainly is not. All roses differ in their resistance to disease, in their abundance of flowers, and other aspects: some roses are rubbish and others are diamonds. A good rose is arguably the most rewarding plant in the world.

More than two thirds of the world's palm species grow in rainforests.

Old-fashioned roses There are a number of reasons for
growing roses, but one is quite simple: your house might
demand it. Older-style houses are superbly complemented
by some of the older rambling roses. They have dense
foliage, are quite disease-resistant and have dainty,
abundant flowers. These are the varieties that billow over
pergolas and along fences, looking good even in long-
abandoned gardens. 'Cecile Brunner' and its climbing
varieties which are types of polyantha rose, are some of
the most sought after. This is a light pink with a delicious
perfume. 'Dorothy Perkins' is a true rambler with rose-
pink blooms. It is perfumed and cascades over banks and
so forth.

Many of the older roses flower for a very short period, so
do check before selecting a particular variety. All of those
listed in the table below flower for relatively long periods
and are worth growing. While many of the old-fashioned
roses are judged to be more attractive in their growth
habit than modern roses, they are not necessarily more
disease resistant, or as productive for cut flowers.

*Old-fashioned rose
variety, 'The Fairy'*

DON BURKE'S TOP TEN OLD-FASHIONED ROSES			
VARIETY	**TYPE**	**SCENT**	**DESCRIPTION**
'Duchesse de Brabant'	Tea Rose 1857	Good	Dense spreading bush 1 x 1m; mid-pink double flowers
'Francis Dubreuil'	Tea Rose 1894	Good	Sparse foliage, 1 x 0.4m; large dark crimson flowers
'Frau Dagmar Hartopp'	Rose rugosa 1914	Good	Bushy, 1 x 1.5m; lavender/pink flowers; prickly
'Honeyflow'	Australian Shrub Rose 1957	Fair	Medium-low bush, unusual panicles of single white flowers
'Jacques Cartier'	Portland 1868	Good	Dark green foliage, 1 x 0.6m; ruffled, deep pink flowers with light edge
'Mme Isaac Pereire'	Bourbon 1881	Superb	Strong bush, 2 x 1.5m; huge deep pink flowers
'Penelope'	Hybrid Musk 1924	Good	Dark green foliage; 1.5 x 1.5m; cream flowers
'Quatre Saisons'	Damask ancient	Superb	Sprawly shrub 1.5 x 1m; silky pink ruffled flower
'Reine des Violettes'	Hybrid Perpetual 1860	Superb	Upright shrub 1.5 x 1m; soft violet, very ruffled flowers
'The Fairy'	Polyantha 1932	Fair	Low growing 0.6 x 1.5m; small pink flowers

Miniature roses These really are good. No nasty thorns to cut you to pieces, just a few small prickles that you can ignore. Mini-roses grow to around half a metre (18″) tall or even less. The flower colour range is outstanding and they get few diseases. Along formal pathways, these create a mini-hedge which should only rarely need trimming, due to compact growth.

Few mini-roses are highly perfumed, so select yours carefully. Mini-roses are outstanding tub plants for a sunny spot, and in general are far hardier than most rose varieties. Needless to say, the smaller flowers are perfectly in proportion to the bush. Even if you have never grown roses, you should find a spot in your garden for one or more of these lovely plants.

Newer, small roses The Meillandina rose was recently introduced as an indoor variety, but these superb roses are better used outdoors as long-flowering, hardy miniatures. In the USA, there are many roses with group names like mini-floras—halfway between a floribunda rose and a true miniature. These would seem to have a huge future in Australia since they combine the best features of both types of rose. They should grow around 1-1.5m (3-5′) tall. Most specialist rose nurseries have at least a couple of mini-floras.

Climbing roses Many roses are promoted as good climbers but, of these, the banksia roses are the best of all. Only a yellow and a creamy white type are available in this variety. Some others worth considering are: 'Dorothy Perkins' (pink), 'Pascali' (white), 'Peter Frankenfeld' (pink), 'Queen Elizabeth' (pink), 'Iceberg' (white),

'Roundelay' (red), 'Sutter's Gold' (golden yellow), 'Cecile Brunner' (pink).

Make sure that each of these is marked as a climber, since many also occur as shrubs. For example, the name should read: 'Pascali' (climbing) or 'Pascali' (Clg).

Modern roses Many people prefer the older roses and miniatures to most of the more modern hybrid tea and floribunda groups. These modern varieties need more pruning and general care, and they tend to be upright, open bushes which may not suit many landscapes. Nonetheless, for cut flowers nothing can beat them.

Many varieties are excessively prone to fungal diseases such as powdery mildew and black spot, so you need to spray regularly with a fungicide if you want attractive plants. Many people do not want to use toxic chemicals in the garden, however, and this opinion does make sense.

If you don't want to spray, you might note that the following varieties are prone to fungal diseases in many areas and so might not suit you: 'Chicago Peace', 'Double Delight', 'Folklore', 'Friendship', 'Granada, 'Greg Chappell', 'Mercedes', 'Papa Meilland', 'Peace', 'Perfume Delight', 'Royal Highness', 'Sylvia', 'Tiffany', 'Virgo', 'Woburn Abbey'. There are, however, many roses that will perform quite well without regular spraying.

In Don Burke's opinion, the following are the ten best modern roses, when you balance perfume, disease resistance and beauty of flower. It is true that 'Double Delight' is a little fungus prone, but it is such a stunning rose, with such a superb perfume, that it is included anyway. There are more beautiful roses than some of those listed, but they are more difficult to grow and have other weaknesses.

DON BURKE'S TOP TEN MODERN ROSES			
VARIETY	**COLOUR**	**RESISTANCE TO FUNGAL DISEASE**	**SCENT**
'Blue Moon'	Mauve to blue	Good	Very good
'Double Delight'	Cream-edged red	Limited	Good
'Gold Medal'	Lemon yellow	Good	Good
'Helmut Schmidt'	Clear, soft yellow	Good	Good
'Iceberg'	White	Very good	Good
'Kentucky Derby'	Dark blackish-red	Good	Good
'Mister Lincoln'	Deep red	Very good	Excellent
'Peter Frankenfeld'	Rich deep pink	Very good	Good
'Queen Elizabeth'	Soft rose pink	Good	Good
'Red Gold'	Gold-edged orange-red	Good	None

Remember that roses need full sun all day to reach their best. The more shade, the more likely that fungal diseases will appear. Fertilise with rose food or citrus food in early spring, early summer and late summer. Mancozeb or Triforine should control most of the fungal disease problems. Prune annually during winter to open up the bush. Remove all old wood and generally tidy up the shape of the plant.

Selecting roses The time to buy roses is during winter, but at this time of year the plants are without leaves or flowers, and it is extremely difficult to work out which particular rose you would like. Even though the plants will have pictorial labels, the colours may not be exactly right and you cannot judge the perfume of the rose. This is why it is a good idea to go to a nursery when roses are in bloom, and write down which varieties you want.

Roses are sold in the following ways:

In bags—from a nursery they will cost $8 for an average rose. If you buy from one of the chain stores they will probably cost around $4. There is not much difference between them, it is just a matter of personal choice. However, nurseries do have more of the modern varieties. Many of the chain stores start to sell their roses from mid-May but this is too early—don't buy any roses until mid to late June or July, or later.

In pots—available from nurseries for approximately $5. It doesn't make any horticultural difference if they are bought in a bag or a pot—they will still grow in the same manner.

Bare rooted or from the open ground—available from nurseries. These are heeled into the open ground; you select your rose and it is dug out and wrapped for you.

If you are not in an area that sells a lot of roses, there are various nurseries, such as Swane's, 490 Glaston Road, Dural, NSW 2154, Telephone (02) 651 1322, that have mail-order catalogues. The price will vary, depending on whether or not it is a new variety of rose.

Roses are a great bargain; when you buy them they have been growing for two years since they were grafted—a fairly expensive process—and there was a year's growth of the understock before that.

Care of roses Though roses fill our gardens with their beautiful blooms and heady scents in spring, summer and autumn, the most demanding season for tending the rose bed is winter. Winter is the time for planting, pruning and spraying.

Pruning You will need a stout pair of gardening gloves (preferably leather), a pruning saw, a set of hand-held secateurs and, if you can afford them, a long handled set of secateurs as well.

Wear a glove on the hand you'll be using to remove the cut pieces of the stem. Most people prefer to hold secateurs in an ungloved hand.

The first thing to do when pruning a rose is to remove any old, woody, or dead material. This is where a pruning saw may be required. Then, with an ordinary pair of secateurs, simply shorten back most of the growth and remove any spindly branches. Removing dead wood at the base of the bush will expose any borers or problems. Roses should be pruned back to just under a metre (2½–3'). Try to leave younger branches that are strong and vigorous a little longer, and shorten older wood. In general try to remove growth from the centre of the plant, so that it forms an open, uncluttered vase shape that light and air can easily penetrate. Cut just above an outward facing bud, as this encourages growth outwards.

Spraying Roses are sprayed in winter to control scale insects (these appear as little silvery dots on the trunk and they sap the energy of the plant), and black spot (which is seen as black discolouration of the leaves), and to reduce pest and disease infestation around the plant. Not only the bush but the general area around it should be sprayed. Clean up any old leaves underneath the rose bush and put them in the garbage bin before spraying. Many people use lime-sulphur but you can also mix up Bordeaux powder or a little white oil. All of these sprays act to minimise the incidence of these problems. Triforine Rose Fungicide is best for keeping fungus away and your roses should be sprayed with this during the warmer months.

Planting Planting roses is, fortunately, not very difficult. If you bought your rose in a pot, it is simply a matter of tipping it out and planting it in the normal way.

If your rose has been bare rooted, there are a few simple steps to follow. The first thing is to take it out of its container and search for any odd-looking areas, such as dead wood or broken roots: snip them off with secateurs. Make a hole in the ground with a slight mound of earth in the centre. Place the plant on the mound and spread the roots out evenly over it. Position the plant so that the graft point (the line where the variety of rose you chose was joined to the understock plant) is 5–8cm (2–3") above the surrounding soil. Finally, fill in the hole.

Once you have covered the roots, it is best not to crush them by pressing the soil with your feet. Spread the soil around and firm it down gently with your hand. Don't compress the soil close to the base of the plant. Put some mulch over the freshly dug soil and water it in well.

Glossary of terms

Floribunda: Roses which produce flowers slightly smaller in size but grouped together in clusters.
Hybrid tea: Roses which produce large flowers ideal for floristry.

Miniature rose: Small bushes normally growing to 600mm (2') or less, unless grafted as standards.

Mini-floras: Hybrids between a miniature and a floribunda rose. Basically these are intermediate between the two, and grow to around 1–1.5m (3¼–5') tall.

Climbing rose: Usually a very vigorous mutant (or sport) from a bush rose. That is, it has returned to its briar growth habit.

SCHLUMBERGERA

Schlumbergera, which was formerly called Zygocactus, is a Brazilian epiphytic (a plant which grows on another) plant genus and a member of the cactus family. There is a wide range of colours available—white, pink, orange, purple, multicolours and even a very light yellow one called 'Gold Charm'. Unfortunately this colour often turns to pink.

Schlumbergeras are relatively easy plants to grow. They grow naturally in rainforests in the forks of trees, and so look best when cascading out of pots. Probably the best way to grow them is in a hanging basket, where they can weep down over the sides. In this situation they are very safe and will grow to perfection.

Potting Mix There should be *no soil* whatsoever in the mix. A good potting mix is:

75% bark fines, horticultural bark, and softwood and hardwood sawdust compost, in the ratio 1:1:4
20% peat
2–2½% perlite
2% very coarse sand

If you don't want to make the mix yourself, buy any brand of potting mix and combine it 50:50 with a good quality orchid potting mix. This will be a perfect mix for schlumbergeras.

Planting Plant into damp potting mixture, but *don't water the plant in*. This is very important. Just mist the plant until it settles in and then gradually start watering normally after two to three weeks.

The optimum repotting time is just after the plant has finished flowering, that is, August to September.

During the year keep the potting mix lightly moist at all times, increasing the water supply during flowering.

Situation Schlumbergeras like plenty of light but no direct sun. If they are in strong sun the leaves will turn purple and the plant may well die. They prefer 80% shade; a position in dappled light under a tree is ideal.

They are not an indoor plant. They can be brought indoors while in flower, but will not reflower indoors. After flowering they should be put back outside on a patio, pergola or in dappled light.

Fertiliser Fertilise with a nine-month slow release fertiliser, such as Nutricote, and a small amount of liquid fertiliser every two months throughout the year.

Best varieties by colour

Variety	Colour
'Can Can'	White with a fine magenta edge
'Cheryl'	pink
'Christmas Cheer'	orange
'Gold Charm'	yellow
'Kris Kringle'	mid-red
'Lavender Lady'	lavender
'Naomi'	tricolours
'Purple Thundercloud'	purple
'Tammy'	apricot
'White Christmas'	white

SCREENING PLANTS

It is possible to create garden privacy through dense screening plants within 18 months of planting—if you use fast-growing plants.

Grevillea x *hookeriana* and *Grevillea* 'Ivanhoe' are both rapid growing shrubs that will tolerate harsh conditions.

Banksia ericifolia will also be a successful screen—it is very dense and can be grown in 30cm (1') of soil with mulch.

For those who do not like Australian native plants, a screen of Shiny Xylosma (*Xylosma senticosa*) will grow very large and thick, and can also be pruned to a neat suburban hedge.

If you live on a very busy road, a privacy mound of soil will act as a sound barrier. Plants will not stop noise, but a mound of soil certainly will. This mound can be planted with Bottlebrush or Paperbarks—*Grevillea* 'Sandra Gordon' can be used but is easily blown over in strong winds. Ground covers, for example, *Grevillea* 'Poorinda Royal Mantle' can also be planted.

SNAPDRAGON 'CAMELOT'

Bedding Plants Australia chose an outstanding new dwarf snapdragon (*Antirrhinum majus* F1 hybrid), 'Camelot', as the 1989 Flower of the Year.

Growth habit This snapdragon has a supercompact plant habit—it grows to about 30cm (12″) in height—yet still maintains excellent vigour. It has multi-basal branching, which means that new shoots keep developing from the base of the plant. These produce new flowers, which cover the old flowers as they die off.

Colours Within the 'Camelot' range there are 11 different colours (the most extensive range ever developed in a dwarf snapdragon), ranging from bright yellows through rich reds to soft lilacs, and including bicolours.

Planting and flowering 'Camelot' can be grown in both autumn and spring in most states. Plant in early autumn for late autumn and early winter flower; in late autumn for late winter and spring flower; and in early summer for late summer flowers. Plants take about 14 weeks to flower—this is the earliest flowering snapdragon (by at least a week) available.

'Camelot' prefers full sun but will tolerate semi-shade. Seedlings should be planted about 20–25cm (8–10″) apart in a soil that is well drained, and with plenty of fertiliser and manure. They will withstand an occasional light frost. In hotter summer months the plants will grow to only 20–25cm (8–10″).

Rust resistance In trials conducted in different climatic areas at a wide range of locations, no rust was seen at any stage on this variety. It therefore appears to be more rust tolerant than other dwarf varieties; this has not been proven, however.

Availability Snapdragon 'Camelot' should now be available at most garden centres.

Cost Punnets retail for around $2 (the price range is $1.30–$1.80, but will vary between outlets).

SOUTH AFRICAN ORCHID BUSH

Originating in the Eastern Transvaal, the South African Orchid Bush (*Bauhinia galpinii*) is a fully evergreen shrub, 2–3m (6–10′) high by 3–4m (10–13′) wide. This bauhinia maintains an attractive appearance all year round, whereas most other members of this genus look thin and straggly at certain times of the year.

Its flowers are orange-red and orchidlike, and are produced from January to April or beyond.

Growing requirements *Bauhinia galpinii* is a sturdy shrub, despite its delicate appearance. It grows best in a reasonably frost-free area and is very hardy in Sydney, Perth and places to the north of these cities, where it can be grown as a magnificent freestanding shrub, or trained horizontally against a wall.

SWEET PEAS

There are many good reasons to consider growing Sweet Peas. Their delicate but profuse blooms herald the spring. They can transform a bare fence or shed wall into a soft wall of colour, and they also make attractive cut flowers and are highly perfumed.

Varieties Probably the best of the old fashioned, tall varieties (about 2m or 6′) is one called 'Tiffany'. It includes a broad range of strongly scented colours.

An unusual variety for people seeking a change from the usual colours, is 'Wiltshire Ripple'. This variety has white blooms edged and flecked with burgundy.

An excellent dwarf variety is 'Bijou', which grows to only 60cm (2′) in height. As a ground cover you could grow another variety, 'Snoopea'. Both of these are ideal for growing in tubs or in rockeries.

You will find an extensive range of sweet pea varieties on the seed shelves at nurseries and garden centres, so why not try out several of them until you find a favourite?

Trellising If you decide to grow the climbing varieties, you will need to provide them with some sort of support. Plastic mesh, nylon mesh or a piece of chook wire will do, but don't make the trellis too short—sweet pea plants twine together, and when they run out of something to hold onto they tend to topple in unison.

One simple, old-fashioned technique is to hammer some nails along a piece of wood, attach it to the top of a fence or wall, then run string up to the nails from wire pegs or a similar set of nails in wood placed at ground level. The sweet peas can easily be trained onto the strings.

For something a little more fancy, you can buy wooden frames, lattice or fan shaped, from garden centres. You can even grow tall, climbing varieties in pots if you set up a tripod frame in the pot. Plant a seedling at each corner of the frame. The same sort of frame can be constructed by using garden stakes tied together at the top—as a free-standing sweet pea pillar in the centre of the garden this could make quite an eye-catching feature.

Planting In most parts of Australia sweet peas can be sown from midsummer to late autumn but March and

April are usually the optimum months. You can buy punnets of seedlings as well as seed packets.

Seeds should be sown into moist soil and then left unwatered until either the soil dries out or the seedlings appear. Sweet peas react badly to overwet conditions. Do not pre-soak the seeds, and don't throw out any which may appear shrivelled or under-sized as these are often the darker colours.

Sweet peas should be grown in full sun in a well drained, slightly raised bed. They prefer a reasonably alkaline soil into which organic matter and a complete fertiliser have been incorporated.

Flowering Sweet peas take about 9–12 weeks from sowing to flowering. The more flowers you pick, the more will be produced. Remove spent blooms to prolong flowering. The sweet pea colour range is extensive—from pure white to cream, through many shades of pink to lavender and mauve, and on to light and dark reds, blue and purple.

A suggestion for children If you want to have some fun with the children, you could use sweet peas in a seed germinating project. Take some damp cotton wool and place a few seeds on it. Keep them indoors until they germinate, maybe in the kitchen, and then plant the little seedlings outside in the garden. Seedlings are delicate, so make sure you handle them very carefully.

THRYPTOMENE AND GREVILLEA LANIGERA

Thryptomene or Payne's Thryptomene is an Australian native plant with very pretty pink flowers, which attract butterflies, throughout autumn and winter. It will flower on and off right through the year and the Monarch, and Wanderer butterflies in particular are quite attracted to this plant.

It grows to a height of less than 1 metre (3') tall, and spreads well.

There are a number of other Australian native plants that flower throughout winter. One is *Grevillea lanigera*, which has really attractive foliage and pink flowers over a fairly long period. Sometimes it is called the woolly grevillea. *Grevillea lanigera* from Mt Tamboritha is a prostrate ground cover. Like most grevilleas, *Grevillea lanigera* is bird-attracting.

TIBOUCHINAS

The old-fashioned Lasiandra, also known as the Glory Tree but more correctly referred to as the tibouchina, is probably the most spectacular purple flowering shrub in the world—or, at least, it was. A stunning new range of smaller, more compact varieties has been produced in Australia, extending the range of colours and flowering seasons.

The old-fashioned version of the tibouchina is to be found soldiering on in many gardens throughout the warmer areas of Australia—Sydney, Perth, and areas north. Its large, deep purple, satiny flowers have a tropical, orchidlike quality about them, which is hardly surprising, since the plant comes originally from tropical South America.

Fortunately, tibouchinas are not tropical prima donnas, despite their origin. Provided their growing needs are attended to, they are among the hardiest and longest lived shrubs.

In general, tibouchinas are gross feeders, relishing regular doses of fertiliser (two or three times a year) and ample water. Soft, sappy growth is more prone to frost damage than harder wood, however, so don't overfertilise in cool areas.

Tibouchinas like a warm, sunny position, disliking frosts intensely. Most will positively enjoy being pruned. Savage pruning of old bushes of the varieties mentioned below yields excellent results. Despite all the above, tibouchinas will normally grow quite well in frost-free areas, even if you completely ignore them.

While the older tibouchina has outstanding 10cm (4") diameter flowers, it is rather inclined to become rangy and open in its growth habit. Unfortunately, it also grows to about 12m (39') tall and 4m (13') wide—simply too large for many gardens. The newer varieties are vastly improved in these respects.

During the 1950s, seed of many species of tibouchina was acquired from a seed collector in Brazil by the late Dr George Hewitt, MBE, of Bellingen, New South Wales. As Dr Hewitt cultivated and shared around his tibouchinas among nursery industry friends, interest in the new varieties increased, and a number have now become well established in the market place.

Varieties *Tibouchina* 'Jules' grows as a dense ball of foliage a metre (3') in diameter. If flowers so heavily from March to May that the foliage is obscured; the flower colour is a deep purple-blue. 'Jules' makes a superb tub plant, and is ideal for rockeries, small gardens, or even home unit balconies.

Tibouchina granulosa 'Kathleen' is a larger, pink flowering type with mid pink flowers, growing to about 5m (15'). The flowers appear from January to March.

Tibouchina mutabilis, sold as 'Noelene', bears mauve, deep pink, and white flowers all at the same time during its flowering period from October to November. It is an enchanting shrub growing 2–4m (6–13') tall.

Tibouchina clavata 'Alba', sold as 'Elsa', is a white flowering variety. Its flowers are a little smaller, 4–5cm (1½–2") across, pure white and graced with ten deep purple stamens. The foliage is silvery-green and complements the flower well. 'Elsa' has a flowering peak in spring, then flowers spasmodically throughout the year. Interestingly, it comes into full flower immediately after pruning and fertilising, at any time of the year. This variety has a tendency to become leggy, and the flowers are not spectacular when viewed from a distance, but it is still a charming garden plant and grows to about 2m (6').

Tibouchina lepidota 'Alstonville' grows 2.5–5m (8–15') tall, although it can be pruned to a smaller size. It also flowers from March to May, and is a smaller, denser version of the old-fashioned lasiandra. The flowers are deep purple.

Tibouchina 'Alstonville'

Tibouchina lepidota 'Alstonville Variegated' is identical to the above variety in all respects except for being slightly smaller and having variegated leaves. Like many other variegated plants it has a tendency to sunburn.

Tibouchina laxa, sold as 'Sky Lab', could be described as being three plants in one; a low shrub to 2m (6'), a graceful climber, or a spreading ground cover. It all depends on how you grow it, and is possibly best as a shrub, although it would need support. If left alone it grows as a ground cover. The flowers are rich purple.

TOPIARY AND PLAITED PLANTS

One of the latest garden trends—to trim, twist, plait and otherwise alter the shapes of plants—is a revival of an art form that dates back to Roman times and which had virtually disappeared from Australian gardens during the last half century. You can buy plants already shaped, or you can sharpen your shears and do it yourself.

Topiary Plants such as Box, Privet and Cypress, as well as other densely foliaged plants like the Box-leaved Honeysuckle, make good subjects for trimming and shaping into geometric designs or the forms of birds and animals. If purchased already shaped, these plants are expensive—$120 to $150 for even the most simple forms.

It is possible to make your own trimmed plants without too much difficulty. To make the traditional 'three balls on a stick' shape, we purchased an ordinary Golden Pencil Pine and simply clipped away the foliage until we had the beginnings of the design. With regular trimming as the new growth appears, the finished shape can be achieved within just a few months and at a saving of $70 to $80.

Animal shapes are easier to create if a chicken wire model of the finished design is fixed over the young plant, which is then threaded through the wire and trimmed into shape as it grows. Features such as beaks and eyes can be made of painted wood and fixed to the plant. A two-legged bird can be achieved by training two plants into one frame.

Privet is one of the worst weeds introduced into Australia and is a major threat to native plants in many bushland areas, but it has not been declared a noxious weed in any state. The very features which make it such a successful weed—its rapid, hardy growth, coupled with its fine, dense foliage—make it an ideal subject for topiary. A topiary work in privet may be started in a pot or in the ground. When the plant is about one and a half years old, the wire frame can be fitted around it, and a small shape under 60cm (2') high could be expected to take two or three years of regular maintenance before the leaves conceal the wire and the shape becomes recognisable.

Twisting and plaiting Where an ornamental stem shape (rather than a foliage shape) is required, *fig species* are ideal subjects. Standard figs with plaited stems are very fashionable and cost $25 to $50 ready-made. Again, it is quite possible to make your own, and you can buy the base plant for just $4 to $5, but it will take at least a year for the product to start looking reasonably good, and you may find it hard to achieve the even pattern of nursery grown ones.

Plants with two or three stems should be sought for twisting and plaiting. Figs grown by tissue culture are ideal, because they tend to produce more than one stem of fairly even thickness. Leaves and twigs should be trimmed from the lower section of each stem. Twisting involves winding two stems around each other and then securing them with tape to a small stake to stop them from unwinding. Budding tape is ideal—it is a soft, flexible, non-sticky tape used by nursery workers to join grafted plants together.

Plaiting requires three stems. Line the stems up side by side and taking the outside stem from one side, place it between the other two. Next take the outside stem from the other side and place it between the other two. Repeat the process and as you continue moving the outside stem from alternate sides into the centre, the plait will form. Initially the plait will be quite open, and slight tightening may be necessary after the stems begin to take shape. Eventually they will fuse together to form one trunk. If you prefer to keep the plait open, you can insert small rods into the gaps to hold them apart while the plant is taking shape. As for twisting, staking and tying is necessary initially.

TREE DAHLIAS

If you are a collector of rare plants, one variety that you might have is an old-fashioned Tree Dahlia. This is a true member of the dahlia family and grows 3.5–4.5m (12–15′) tall with huge underground tubers.

It is inclined to wind damage, and should be grown near the house in a protected position.

This is a fascinating mauve-flowering plant but it is not usually available at your local nursery. It is available at times from:

The Fragrant Garden
25 Portsmouth Road
Erina NSW 2250
Telephone (043) 67 7322

TUBEROSE

A charming flowering plant that has long been out of vogue but is now all set for a comeback is the Tuberose (*Polianthes tuberosa*). This tuberous-rooted perennial is not really a rose—in fact, it is not even remotely related to the rose. It has long, straplike leaves, which form a small clump at ground level.

The tuberose bears lovely white flowers on long spikes, each of which can last for three weeks or more. This is one of the world's best cut flowers, and the blooms are remarkable for the strength of their magnificent scent. The flowering period extends from summer to autumn.

A native of Mexico, the tuberose dislikes humidity and can suffer badly through the summer in very humid areas. The plant should be watered fairly frequently through the growing period and, if planted in full sun and in well-drained soil in a slightly protected position, this plant will generally be hardy and trouble-free. Tuberoses should be available in garden centres and nurseries during the flowering period.

VARIEGATED PLANTS

Variegated Pittosporum (*Pittosporum eugenioides* 'Variegatum') A good point about this plant is that it doesn't very often revert to a totally green leaf. If this does occur, cut the green leaves as soon as they appear.

Variegated Brush Box (*Lophostemon confertus*, previously *Tristania conferta*) This is an Australian native and is quite expensive to buy because it is grafted. You need to get rid of any reversion by cutting it out. If the reversion is high in the tree, long-handled loppers can be used.

Variegated Box Elder (Variegated *Acer negundo*) This is a smaller tree than the brush box, so if it reverts it is easier to cut out. The green leaves have more chlorophyll than the variegated ones, and therefore will grow more quickly and take over the plant.

It is not only plants with green and white leaves that will revert. The Purple Prunus (*Prunus cerasifera* 'Nigra', *Prunus* x *blireana*) is a grafted plant and if the rootstock is allowed to shoot and grow its green leaves you could soon have a fully green plant.

Variegated New Zealand Christmas Bush (*Metrosideros kermadecensis*) has very attractive variegated leaves that can revert to dull green leaves if they are not cut out. Citrus trees, for example, oranges and lemons, often shoot from the rootstock (for example, *Poncirus trifoliata*) below the graft. These shoots should be cut off as soon as they are seen.

A little judicious pruning will help keep variegated plants, prunus and citrus in good form.

VIOLETS

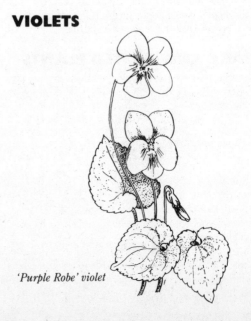

'Purple Robe' violet

If you have a shady area and you are looking for ground cover, consider violets. As well as cover, they produce perfumed cut flowers, are hardy and will grow even in cracks in the concrete.

Violets produce small seed pods, and these can be collected and scattered where you would like more plants. If you find you have too many leaves and not enough flowers, give the plant masses a good trim with cutters. Some people even mow them. This probably serves to let more light in. The more seed pods you remove, the more violets will flower.

There are many different varieties and colours of violets, and most nurseries have a selection. Nurseries specialising in cottage garden plants have the best range. Colours range from multicolours through violet shades to pinks and whites—some are spotted. Flowers can also be double or single, perfumed or not. The *Viola odorata* group are the perfumed ones, and the variety called 'Royal Robe' or 'Purple Robe' is arguably the best.

WARATAHS

Many people would like to grow a Waratah (*Telopea speciosissima*) but they are difficult to cultivate and often drop dead. This species is native to the area around Sydney and some other parts of New South Wales, while other species of waratahs grow in Victoria and Tasmania. The New South Wales waratah normally flowers red, but many produce pink or even white flowers.

The good news is that there has been a great deal of research into the cultivation of these plants recently. One expert suggests that you plant them on top of a brick in the following way:

* Choose a position away from large shrubs and trees from which water drains away well; weed this area.
* Place half a house brick in the position required. Turn the waratah out of its pot and place it carefully on top of the brick.
* Hill up around the plant with well-drained soil mix, making a soil 'saucer' to hold water. Reinforce the edge with stones, wood and so on. Mulch with well-rotted organic matter.
* For the first two to three weeks, if the plant is dry, water every few days to establish rooting by slowly dripping water into the saucer to thoroughly drench. *Do not* water by sprinkling daily.

It is essential to prune waratahs if you wish to keep them healthy. Most people take off a few centimetres of stem underneath the flower, but if the plant has grown lanky, the only thing to do is to trim it right back as near to ground level as possible.

It is a good idea to cut a waratah back when planting it; this makes it establish in the ground far more quickly. Waratahs can be fed in spring with a slow release complete fertiliser, such as Osmocote, or with blood-and-bone, poultry manure, or cow manure. They respond well to adequate fertilising.

Waratahs flower better in full sun, protected from strong, hot westerly winds.

WATERLILIES AND WATER PLANTS

There are two groups of Waterlilies: tropical waterlilies, the flowers of which stand a few inches clear of the surface of the water; and the hardy waterlilies, whose flowers actually float on the water.

Hardy waterlilies have a wide range of colours—yellow, through pink, red and white. The most useful of this group is the miniature hardy waterlily. These also come in a wide range of colours and have miniature leaves in proportion to their flowers, making them ideal to use in a small pond or in small containers. The hardy waterlilies flower from late spring through to February and March. The tropical varieties are at their peak of flowering in March and continue to flower into winter, so you can have flowering waterlilies for nine months of the year.

Hardy waterlilies need a minimum of four or five hours of sunshine each day and the tropicals need at least eight hours every day.

There are many other useful water plants, for example, the outstanding lotus, which has big flowers followed by curious seedheads—it is quite difficult to obtain. Water fringe has tiny little yellow flowers, while the iris family has some plants that will grow with their roots fully submerged in water. Pickerel rush has blue flowers; other alternatives are the green dwarf papyrus and the large variety of papyrus.

Fish also add interest to ponds and pools. In warmish areas, that is, Sydney to Perth and places north, tropical fish such as platy can be acclimatised to cool water and will do well; another variety is rosy barb. There are also Australian native fish, such as fire-tailed gudgeon and the Australian rainbow fish.

Waterlilies and water plants can also be grown in containers—terracotta or large glazed pots look very effective with colourful miniature waterlilies or water poppies in them.

WATTLES

The wattle is Australia's dominant plant group, with more than 900 species having been identified.

On 1 September 1988, the Federal government finally proclaimed the magnificent Golden Wattle, *Acacia pycnantha*, as our floral emblem. There is now a strong campaign in progress to have 1 September—when *Acacia pycnantha* is at its peak in most areas—declared National Wattle Day.

Acacia pycnantha is a very attractive plant about 4.5-6m (15-20') tall. Its distribution is restricted, being found naturally mostly in Victoria. It is quite attractive to native birds, with cockatoos in particular feeding on the seeds.

Although it is not available in many nurseries, *Acacia pycnantha* would be a delightful and patriotic addition to the average backyard.

History The first huts of our early settlers were made using a technique called 'wattle and daub' whereby branches were interwoven, then covered with mud to make walls and fences. Acacia branches were found to be the most suitable, and these trees came to be called wattles.

Flowers Each fluffy ball is a group of flowers (most easily seen at the bud stage). The shape and arrangements of these flower heads assist in identification.

Pollen Acacias are perfect for honey bees, which fill their pollen baskets in exchange for pollinating the flowers.

Nectar The leaves produce nectar in glands called nectaries. These attract ants, which may help in discouraging the attentions of predatory insects. In spite of the fact that many insects feed on acacias, this has not prevented them from becoming our most successful native plant.

Varieties Despite the fact that Australian native plants have been very popular over the past fifteen years, wattles have never been widespread in Australian gardens. People have avoided planting wattles because many of them are short-lived. The Cootamundra wattle for example, may live for only 7-12 years, and many people are terrified that when it finally dies they will be left with a large hole in the garden.

Black wattle (*Acacia decurrens*) is one of the tallest wattles and is particularly long-lived. *Acacia floribunda* is an attractive wattle with fine foliage, and because it doesn't grow too large it is good for screening purposes.

Another wattle that is great around the home is *Acacia cardiophylla*. It has beautiful grey-green foliage, which weeps like a willow's. It grows to only 2-3m (6-10') tall and so is a useful garden plant. It is spectacular when in flower.

A smaller, prostrate wattle is *Acacia amblygona prostrate*. It is very prickly and low growing, just a few inches tall. There are other prostrate wattles, for example, *Acacia lanuginosa*, a 'woolly' wattle that grows to just under 1 metre (3'). Another wattle, *Acacia ligulata prostrate*, will weep down a rock wall.

The best of all the prostrate wattles is *Acacia cultriformis*—the prostrate variety. It will cascade down the sides of pots and even looks great in the ground. An upright form of *Acacia cultriformis* is also available.

There is even a prostrate form of the Cootamundra Wattle (*Acacia baileyana*).

All these low-growing wattles are extremely hard to find—you will have to go to a specialist native plant nursery in your area.

Wattles don't necessarily cause hay fever—this is an old husbands' tale.

For further information on the campaign to have 1 September declared National Wattle Day, write to Maria Hitchcock, Old Inverell Road, Armidale, NSW 2350.

WHITE POTATO CREEPER

Nothing looks more ugly than a bare fence, particularly if it is made of metal or other assorted materials, and then neglected. To transform a fence like this and create something beautiful in an area of ugliness, a creeper could be planted near the fence and encouraged to cover it with flowers and greenery.

One suggestion is the White Potato Creeper, which is a strong, vigorous grower and a real survivor. In just 18 months this creeper can camouflage an ugly area, and it would also look lovely across a pergola or over an archway.

The white potato creeper, *Solanum jasminoides*, gets its name from solanum, which means potato (it really is related to the potato), and jasminoides, because someone thought it looked like a jasmine. It originally came from Brazil and prefers a warmish climate; in areas with cold winters or heavy frosts, it could be deciduous. It grows best in a sunny position with good drainage, but a warm position with wind protection will suit.

The white potato creeper has bright green, heart-shaped leaves and starry, white flowers that have a central cluster of yellow stamens. It flowers mainly in summer, but has occasional flowers through the year. The plant can become untidy and the older parts woody, but this can be corrected by pruning severely in late winter, and again later if necessary, to keep it under control and stimulate new growth. New plants can be propagated from cuttings.

Other varieties *Solanum seaforthianum* (blue potato creeper) has vivid blue starry flowers followed by small round, red fruit. It looks very effective when planted near the white potato creeper and grows to about 3m (10') in height.

There is also a variegated form of *Solanum jasminoides*, which is worth growing for its colourful foliage.

YELLOW BUTTON DAISY

The Yellow Button Daisy, *Helichrysum ramosissimum*, is an excellent ground cover. It is an Australian native plant that comes from central Queensland and New South Wales.

This plant spreads very quickly by suckering, and will

flower almost all the year round in a sunny, well-drained position. It is a good lawn substitute for a sloping area where it would be difficult to mow grass. It will not, however, withstand foot traffic.

The yellow button daisy is not easy to obtain, but should be available from specialist Australian native plant nurseries.

CHAPTER 2
Trees

AUTUMN FOLIAGE

Autumn is regarded by many people as the loveliest time of the year, when parks and gardens everywhere are filled with the fiery oranges, reds and yellows of deciduous trees. But the coloured leaves of autumn come at a price—bear in mind the hours spent on the end of a rake trying to clear the fallen leaves. While leaves make great mulch or compost for the garden, some of the very large trees, such as the pin oak (which doesn't colour terribly well anyway), may result in more work than you are able or prepared to handle.

Autumn foliage trees should be planted in full sun—lots of sun means lots of colour.

The relatively common Japanese maple is an outstanding autumn foliage plant. It comes in a tremendous range of colours and the mature trees are small enough to fit comfortably into the average garden. Japanese maples are hardy in Sydney and Perth and areas to the south of these cities. They vary enormously if grown from seed—some plants can still be quite green while others have almost completed their display.

The Tupelo, or *Nyssa sylvatica*, has beautifully layered branches and the glossy dark green oval leaves turn brilliant red in autumn. At maturity the tree can reach a height of 10m (33′) and a width of 6m (19½′) and it makes a good shade tree in summer. One of the great strengths of this useful tree is that it will grow in a very damp position in the garden.

One of the very rare varieties of autumn foliage tree is the Parrotia, a dense tree with oval foliage which first turns yellow and then bright scarlet. As a specimen tree for cooler areas this tree is ideal, but it is difficult to find at nurseries. In spring it is covered with clusters of small red flowers.

The Chinese tallow tree (*Sapium sebiferum*), is very popular with people who have small backyards, as its maximum height is around 6 metres (20′).

There are many varieties of ornamental grapes and these are very good for screening fences and so on. They are not difficult to control and will colour well in all areas of Australia.

If you like golden colours best, one of the outstanding

trees is the golden ash, which has large, somewhat fern-like leaves. The claret ash provides a deep red counterpart. Both trees are quick growing but only reach 10-13 metres (33-43′) in height, so do not overwhelm the garden.

Probably the best of the gold foliaged trees is the maidenhair tree, or Ginkgo, which has leaves shaped like giant maidenhair fern fronds. These leaves turn a clear bright yellow in autumn. This is a slow growing tree but it can eventually reach a height of 15 metres (49′) and a spread of 10 metres (33′) in an open, sunny position in deep, well-drained soil.

Much more commonly seen is the vibrant Liquidambar, with its leaves ranging from green through yellow and red to deep purple at the same time. It is a useful ornamental tree but it does have a very vigorous root system which can disturb paving and walls if planted too close to them. It grows to about 30 metres (100′).

BLACKBOYS

The Australian native Blackboy (*Xanthorrhoea*) or Grass Tree is one of the most peculiar plants in the world. It is the majestic bent and gnarled trunk that fascinates most people.

Probably the best blackboys in Australia are the ones found in Western Australia which are being commercially removed from the bush and sold. Blackboys may not be removed from their native habitats unless permission from a relevant authority, (such as the National Parks and Wildlife Service), has been obtained. Blackboys are quite easy to grow and each one is unique.

The rootball of a blackboy can weigh 180-227kg (400-500lb), so a special machine is needed to remove them from the soil without damaging the roots. They should be potted up for at least six months to a year before being available in a nursery—this potting period is essential for their stabilisation.

Blackboys are very expensive—$140-$200. If they have been dug out carefully and well looked after, they should not die. They are very, very slow growing—some specimens can be up to 400 years old.

These plants look attractive growing in containers, but very large tubs, for example, wine casks, are needed to take the very large rootball.

Use a top quality potting mix and mix equal parts with propagating sand so that there is excellent drainage. It is a good idea to put a spillover plant, for example, helichrysum at the base of the blackboy.

1000 year old lignotubers (the large storage roots of eucalyptus) have been found in the Australian desert.

CONIFERS

Conifers are usually cone-bearing, erect-growing evergreen shrubs or trees. Probably the most popular conifer in Australia today is Brunning's golden cypress (*Cupressus macrocarpa* 'Brunniana'). This conifer is susceptible to borer attack and often dies.

A good alternative to Brunning's golden cypress is the golden leyland cypress (*Cupressocyparis x leylandii* 'Castewallan Gold'). This is a very hardy plant; it is a rapid grower and is excellent for screening to provide privacy.

There are many conifers; some are dwarf and some produce foliage colour throughout the year. Probably the best of all the dwarf conifers is the golden bookleaf pine, sometimes called Biota (*Thuya orientalis* 'Aurea Nana'). It is a compact, rounded shrub, which grows to only about 1 metre (3'). It is excellent for small gardens, tubs or rock gardens.

Thuya occidentalis 'Rheingold' is another slow-growing dwarf conifer, reaching only about 1.5 metres (5'). The foliage is a greenish gold in summer, turning brown in winter, when it is often mistakenly thought to be dead.

One of the best performing ground covers is the shore juniper (*Juniperus conferta*). It is very hardy and long-lived and a good ground cover to beat the weeds.

The false cypress, *Chamaecyparis obtusa* 'Nana', is a dwarf conifer with dark green leaves. It is very long-lived and slow growing, taking about 100 years to reach a metre (3¼') in height. *Chamaecyparis obtusa* 'Nana Aurea' is the golden leaved form. It is particularly attractive in spring and summer, when the new golden growth appears.

Chamaecyparis pisifera 'Boulevard Curlytop' is a very attractive blue-grey conifer and is a fairly rapid grower to about two metres (6').

Cupressus macrocarpa 'Greenstead Magnifica' is a grafted conifer. The height of the plant will depend on the height of the graft. It can be grafted 45cm (18") above the ground or at ground level.

Most conifers are very hardy and will live for hundreds of years. They provide colour—blue, gold and various greens—throughout the year and look very attractive in the garden.

IRISH STRAWBERRY TREE

The Irish Strawberry Tree, *Arbutus unedo*, is an ideal plant for patriotic Irish people and their descendants to include in their gardens. It is suited to warm moist temperate and cool moist climatic zones.

The Irish strawberry tree comes from Ireland, Southern Europe and the Mediterranean. It is a domeshaped evergreen tree, which grows to a height of 5-6m (17-20') by 2-3m (6-10') wide. The foliage is dark green and glossy. The bark is reddish-brown and the branches tend to take on a twisted appearance with age.

In autumn the tree bears a profusion of white, pitcher-shaped flowers, which form in clusters. These are followed by small, rounded, red fruits that resemble strawberries and are edible but tasteless. It has been reported that consumption of large quantities of this fruit can cause drowsiness.

This plant grows best in a sunny position where it will receive direct sun for at least half the day, in light, well-drained preferably slightly acid soil. The foliage will burn if exposed to sea breezes in coastal gardens, but otherwise the tree is reasonably wind tolerant, although a slightly protected position may achieve better results.

Watering should be regular and thorough. Propagation is by seed in spring.

JAPANESE RAISIN TREE

Probably one of the weirdest plants in the world is the Japanese Raisin Tree, *Holvenia dulcis*, which actually comes from China, not Japan (although it is common in Japan).

It has strange woody-looking pieces—swollen twigs around the fruit. The fruit is delicious, and tastes just like raisins.

It is a deciduous tree and grows from the coldest areas right through to middle Australia, and will tolerate neglect. It fruits erratically, perhaps every second year.

The seeds are borne in the circular pieces on the end of the fruits and the tree is easy to propagate from seeds.

The Japanese raisin tree will probably be quite difficult to obtain. Two nurseries that currently have them are: Parr's Nursery, 65 Porters Road, Kenthurst, NSW 2156, Telephone (02) 654 1534, (this nursery is not open to the public but they do accept mail orders); and the Bonsai (Koreshoff) Nursery, Telfer Road, Castle Hill, NSW 2154, Telephone (02) 634 2410, which is open to the public seven days a week.

LILLY PILLY

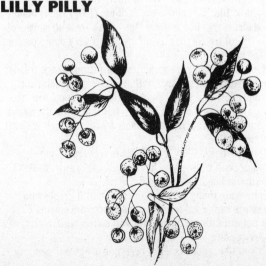

The Lilly Pilly is one of the loveliest of all Australian native plants, but most people have forgotten about it. Lilly pilly species are common in rainforests, coastal scrubs and moist eucalypt forests. They tolerate only light to moderate frosts. Only one species, *Acmena smithii*, extends naturally as far south as Victoria.

Lilly pillies have small but showy white or pale pink flowers, and bear small fruits in a wide range of colours—white, pink, red, purple, blue or black. Almost all the fruits are edible, though the palatability varies greatly from tasteless to delicious.

There are about 60 different species of lilly pilly, although only a small number are available from nurseries. Lilly pillies are suitable for shade, ornament, hedges, clipped specimen and tub plants. Many species form only small, compact, shrubby trees, about 6m (20') tall, at maturity. Others, such as the Giant Water Gum (*Syzygium francisii*), can grow into towering trees 25m tall and 20m wide (80' × 65'). There is even a variegated lilly pilly, *Acmena smithii* 'Elizabeth Isaacs', which was developed in Victoria, where it is a popular decorative plant in milder areas. Given the wide range available, there must surely be a lilly pilly to suit everyone.

Probably the best of the lilly pillies for the average backyard is *Syzygium luehmannii*—an awful name for a lovely tree. It normally grows to about 4.5–6m tall (15–20') in the average garden, a little taller if planted in a moist spot.

This species of lilly pilly has a lot to offer. It produces bright, pinkish-red, slightly conical berries, which are not large enough to be a squashy nuisance underfoot if they drop (that is, if you don't eat them, fresh or in jam, first). The lacy-looking new growth is a lovely, fresh, pinkish-red, which gradually turns bright lime green, providing several months of colour contrast with the dark, glossy mature leaves. The foliage has a soft, graceful appearance and grows densely and evenly over the full height of the tree, resulting in an elegant, almost weeping appearance; this species doubles as a useful screening plant. On top of all that, *Syzygium luehmannii* makes a fantastic pot plant, as well as an in-ground specimen.

MAGNOLIAS

Possibly the most elegant of all garden plants is the Magnolia—with its stunning flowers carried on a wonderful leafless framework of branches. Magnolias are among the world's oldest plants: five-million-year-old fossils occur over a wider territory than today's native habitat would suggest. These attractive plants present a very wide range of colours, all perfumed to some extent.

Name	Description
Magnolia x soulangeana	Deep pink outside, paler within; the most popular of all
Magnolia heptapeta (previously *M. denudata*)	White. Perfumed creamy flowers on dark branches
Magnolia quinquepeta 'Nigra'	Deep burgundy port wine
Magnolia stellata	White. Smaller, starry flowers, fragrant, and marginally hardier than other magnolias
Magnolia stellata 'Rosea'	A pink variety of the above.
Magnolia grandiflora	White. 'The White Magnolia Tree' of the familiar old Helen Hayes poem; huge, evergreen; gigantic, richly perfumed flowers

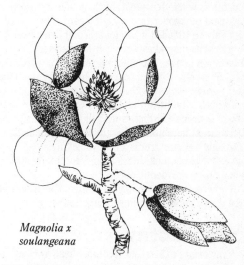

Magnolia x soulangeana

Growth habit Most magnolias do not develop a single trunk, so they are very broad at the base; they can grow very large (20–30m, 65–100') and therefore require lots of space.

Requirements Like huge gum trees, magnolias prefer rich, deep, well-drained soils and regular, even rainfall. Make sure the soil is well mulched. Magnolias are not for places with heavy frosts or shallow or sandy soils. A slightly raised area is an advantage, as is shelter from the wind.

Buying a magnolia Magnolias are rather expensive, never less than $20 at the local nursery. Potting mix old enough to grow weeds indicates a hardened off plant, which would be a better proposition than a freshly potted plant.

Michelias
Near relatives of the magnolias are Michelias.

Michelia figo is an evergreen shrub that grows to 3m (10′) and has very strongly perfumed, small, brown flowers that don't open wide.

Michelia champaca is an evergreen tree that grows to 10m (30′) with perfumed yellow flowers.

The deciduous magnolias are more spectacular than the evergreen michelias, because they produce their flowers when there are no leaves on the branches.

PEPPERCORN TREES

One of the most popular trees in Australia is the Peppercorn tree or Pepper tree, *Schinus areira*. It's a fantastic plant which withstands salt winds, will take really arid climates and grow to perfection in dry areas.

Perhaps because they can recognise and respect toughness when they see it, bush or country people have long held the pepper tree in high regard. They would probably be offended if you told them it came from South America, having taken it to their hearts as if it were an Australian native. You will find pepper trees growing over ancient sheepyards and next to homesteads on virtually every property west of the Great Divide.

The beautiful little white flowers among the weeping foliage bear male anthers with yellow pollen on them. The magnificent hot pink berries are borne on the female tree. Choosing a pepper tree is a bit like having a baby—you have to take pot luck. In all other respects, the male and female trees are identical.

If you have the space in your garden, this is definitely a tree worth hunting out in your local nursery.

TREE SURGERY

It is important to keep our trees in a healthy condition, even if it means that we have to spend money on qualified tree surgeons. If your tree has dead wood or dieback it is far better to call a qualified professional than to cut it back yourself and maybe cause irreparable damage. Many trees are badly damaged and even killed by having the top lopped off.

The cost of tree lopping varies depending on the height of the tree and what is underneath it, that is, an easily damaged roof or open ground. The cost of an average job could be anywhere between $150 and $900.

To remove branches without damaging the tree it is best to make a small cut on the bottom of the branch and then cut down from the top. Don't cut the branch off flush, but leave a 2.5cm (1″) collar and be careful not to tear fresh bark from the tree. If a hollow branch is opened up, it is best to fill it in; if moisture is let in, it creates an atmosphere for micro-organisms and other insects to breed, leading to further decay.

To fill the hole use butyl glaze (a type of putty) and paint with tree wound dressing to form a waterproof seal. A good wound dressing is called ATCS Tree Wound

Dressing and is distributed by Frenchs Forest Hardware, Shop 5, 7 Sorlie Road, Frenchs Forest, NSW 2086. Painting tree wound surfaces with Cuprinol wood preserver will also aid recovery.

WESTERN RED CEDAR

Thuya plicata is commonly known as Western Red Cedar. One specimen shown on 'Burke's Backyard' is 100 years old and grows in the garden at 'Yengo', Mount Wilson, New South Wales. This garden is open to the public in spring and autumn each year.

Thuya plicata is a native of coastal north-western America and California, and can grow to a height of 60m (200′) in cool, humid conditions. It features a symmetrical conical form and has rich, brown bark with vertical ridges, and large branches with deep green foliage that gives it a 'floppy' appearance. It makes an excellent specimen for a large lawn, and is an ideal windbreak, with foliage extending to the ground.

The western red cedar is not fast growing, taking about 10 years to reach 4m (13′). It is the source of a valuable, and highly durable timber.

CHAPTER 3
Vegetables

AFRICAN HORNED CUCUMBER

Cucumbers can be difficult to grow in your backyard. For example, when it rains, the cucumbers may become covered in powdery mildew, resulting in few leaves and poor fruit. However, the African Horned Cucumber (*Cucumis metuliferous*) is one variety of cucumber that is much easier to grow. When this cucumber is cut open it bleeds an orange fluid, which can be quite off-putting initially.

The African horned cucumber has been renamed by the New Zealanders as Kiwano and may be available in fruit shops under this name. It is a distinct species of cucumber, oval in shape, and carrying a number of thorny protuberances with horn-like ends. The vine is a free grower and climber, and requires the entire season to grow to perfection, making the fruit very late. When it does commence bearing, the little thorny 'cukes' are literally piled up on top of one another. When full grown, the fruits are leathery and useless, but when about half grown (approximately 5cm (2″) in diameter) they are the most delicious of all cucumbers, and may be eaten as freely as apples without fear of indigestion. When past this edible stage, they should be left to ripen. Then they become palatable again and the central portion, the pulp and seeds may be eaten with a spoon, like a passionfruit.

The seed can be sown from spring to mid-summer. If in

doubt, delay sowing for a couple of weeks.

Seed germination takes 10–14 days under favourable conditions. Sow two to four seeds to a depth of 0.5–1cm (¼–½") every 2m (6') apart, in well-prepared soil. An open sunny position is best, but plants can be trained up a trellis or fence where garden space is limited.

Edible fruit is usually harvested when they attain a length of 10–14cm (4–5½") or longer, depending on taste preference.

Seeds are not readily available from major seed companies, but they may be obtained by contacting Erica Vale (Aust) Pty Ltd, PO Box 50, Jannali, NSW 2226, Telephone (02) 533 3693, and enclosing $3 by cheque or money order, which will cover the cost of seeds (about 25), a jiffy bag and postage.

MUSHROOMS

An easy way to grow mushrooms at home is to buy a home mushroom kit, available from nurseries, garden centres and some hardware stores for $7–$9.

These kits comprise a bag of peat moss and the basic mushroom compost.

Before getting the mushrooms to grow, check that the colour of the mushroom compost is grey. This grey-looking compost is the actual mushroom fungus, and the white mushrooms that we eat are the fruiting bodies. The true mushroom fungus is what grows through the peat moss.

Easy-to-follow instructions, provided in the kit, explain how to level off the top of the compost, soak the peat, place it in a layer on top of the compost, and add a little more water. Once those steps are followed, the kit is ready to start growing mushrooms.

Simply put it away in some area where the temperature does not fluctuate too much; such as under the house, in the garden shed, or in a cupboard.

About six weeks later, tiny mushrooms will appear. A week after that, they are ready to eat. 'Button' mushrooms are the smallest edible mushrooms; 'cups' are larger but still fully closed; 'flats' are open and have more flavour, being more mature. The mushrooms form in 'flushes' seven to nine days apart, and the kit will crop for up to eight weeks if properly looked after.

For further information

Parramatta Mushroom Co Pty Ltd
12 River Road West
Parramatta NSW 2150
Telephone (02) 635 7477

ORIENTAL VEGETABLES

Yates has released a seed collection called 'Grow Your Own Oriental Vegetable Garden'. This is a kit of five individually-packed oriental vegetable seeds, which contains directions on how to grow them, as well as recipe

suggestions. The vegetables are Tatsoi, Chinese Cabbage Pak Choy, Long White Radish (also known as Daikon), Cabbage Michihili, and Turnip Hakurei. All varieties are suitable for autumn sowing. The seed kit is priced at $4.95 and is available wherever Yates seeds are sold, which means most hardware, gardening, supermarket, chain and department stores.

POTATOES

Potatoes (from Spanish 'patata'; 'spud', from a small spade used to dig potatoes; botanic name *Solanum tuberosum*) have been cultivated for about 8000 years and have the most spectacular history of any cultivated plant. They have been freeze-dried by the Peruvians for 2000 years.

Potatoes were carried from Peru to Europe by sixteenth century conquistadores, who subsisted on them during their plunderings of Inca gold and silver, and were long treated with suspicion and scorn. The scruffy-looking potato took a long time to reach popularity in Europe. Gaspar Bauhin (after whom Bauhinias were named) commented that 'the eating of them causes leprosy'. After official encouragement by King Charles II—who was paid a 'royalty' on the sale of potatoes in exchange for his support—they took off. By 1780 potatoes had become the major dietary component for the entire Irish peasant population.

After the potato was introduced to Ireland, the Irish population exploded and by 1845 exceeded eight million. This figure is more than double the present Irish population, and resulted in a density greater than that of modern-day China. It was not unusual for an adult in Ireland to eat up to 14 pounds (over 6kg) of potato a day.

From 1845–51, late potato blight, a fungal disease, wiped out entire crops, including stored potatoes. Both types of potato grown in Ireland were susceptible to the blight, and the resulting famine killed 12% of the population. More than 1.5 million Irish emigrated, mainly to America and Australia.

Nutritional value The potato is 99.9% fat free, contains one third of our daily vitamin C requirements (the best part is the skin), and can be prepared in many ways (up to 60 in some French cooking schools). Little else is needed in the human diet; one Scandinavian man lived healthily on nothing but potatoes and a little margarine for almost a year. Potatoes are also fed to livestock.

Crops With potatoes you can produce more nutrients on poor land and harvest sooner than any other crop; they grow from sea level to above 4000m (13 000').

The 13 000 different native strains of potato provide potato breeders with a goldmine of genetic material with which to improve varieties and ensure that 'King Potato' reigns supreme. There are varieties for every purpose.

A potato crop is as well suited to home gardening as it is to large-scale commercial production.

Solanine poisoning All potatoes contain a small amount of toxic glycoalkaloid called solanine. It is bitter and gives potatoes their flavour. Solanine does not accumulate in the body, so normal potatoes are quite safe. However, a large dose of solanine can cause vomiting, diarrhoea, neurological symptoms and even death. In pregnancy it can cause foetal death and resorption.

Increased solanine production in potatoes is induced by 24–48 hours of exposure to light, or by bruising, cutting or rotting. Fortunately, chlorophyll is produced along with the solanine, so the resulting green tinge is a warning sign of a dangerous potato. Shoots or sprouted 'eyes' contain even more solanine. It is very important that green or damaged potatoes are discarded. This is especially important if you are pregnant or likely to become pregnant.

Potatoes should be kept in a dark, airy place. Don't prepare them too far in advance, and never eat the shoots.

VEGETABLE GARDENS

The flavour of greens, picked fresh from your own garden just minutes before you eat them, is definitely hard to beat. Most people also find the idea of home-grown vegetables appealing for financial and health reasons. However, the task of actually setting up a new vegetable garden can be daunting because of the apparent technical complexities involved.

'Burke's Backyard' decided to simplify the process and put together a straightforward, practical recipe for a productive vegetable garden. At 33m² (355 sq ft), including paths, it's small enough to be incorporated into the average backyard, and plantings have been designed to supply the majority of vegetable requirements of a family of four, as economically as possible.

Planning Vegetables are sun lovers and ideally a vegetable garden should be situated where the plants will receive a minimum of four or five hours of direct sunlight every day. A north-to-northeast facing part of the garden is best, so we took a compass with us when choosing a site. We also took into account shade cast by trees, shrubs, walls or the house, as this would result in slower growth rates. We moved existing mesh to be used as support for climbing vegetables to the southern end of the garden, to prevent it shading the other vegetables.

Our chosen site was also protected from strong winds and was level—a sloping site would need to be terraced to avoid the erosion of loosened soil.

String was attached to short pegs to mark the outlines of the paths and beds. Bed and path width is a matter of personal choice. We made our paths 60cm (2') wide to allow plenty of room to move, and our beds 1.5m (5') wide to allow for several rows of vegetables across the bed, but still enabling the centre of the bed to be reached comfortably from the paths. This resulted in a bed area of 23m² (247½ sq ft) and a total area of 33m² (355 sq ft), including paths.

Preparation Lawn grasses can become terrible weeds when they appear in a vegetable garden. For this reason, the lawn where the garden was to be situated was removed with a spade, so that work could commence immediately on digging the garden beds. If time permits, the grass can be sprayed with Zero or Roundup and the beds dug after the grass has died.

Once the lawn had been removed from the garden area, the soil where the vegetable beds were to be formed was turned over to spade depth. Organic matter was incorporated to improve the soil—we used mushroom compost. This material is ideal and is available from local nurseries and landscape supply companies. The soil was a fairly heavy clay and the structure of this was improved by adding gypsum at the rate of one large handful per square metre (10 sq ft).

To prepare the soil for leaf crops, such as lettuce, add animal manure, for example, pelleted poultry manure.

Fertiliser is also needed to enrich the soil. Dynamic Lifter was used in the 'Burke's Backyard' garden but a good complete plant food, such as Hortico Gro-Plus, may also be used. The addition of these materials to the soil also adds bulk which raises the height of the beds, thereby improving drainage. After the organic matter and fertiliser was thoroughly dug into the garden beds, the whole area was watered (including the paths) to allow the area to settle.

The prepared beds should be left to settle for two to three weeks before planting commences.

We surfaced our paths with a layer of blue metal dust— the fine material left after blue metal gravel is made. This surface drains quickly and, unlike concrete or pavers, can simply be dug into the soil if the garden plan is altered at a later date. Lawn paths can result in high maintenance as, even when beds are edged (for example, with logs or bricks), there will be an increased risk of grass entering the beds and becoming a weed.

Costs

Item	Volume	Approxima Cost
Mushroom compost	2 cubic metres	$56
Metal dust	0.5 tonne	$15
Delivery of compost and dust		$20
Gypsum	2 × 25kg bags	$19
Dynamic Lifter fertiliser	1 × 20kg bag	$15
TOTAL		$125

Planting The weeks during which the freshly prepared garden is settling in can be put to good use by planting seeds into seed trays, or 'flats'. If you can't get flats from your local nursery, ordinary pots will do.

Fill the flats with seed raising mixture (also from the nursery) and level the surface. A handy tool for making neat rows of holes for the seeds to be planted into is a block of wood with nails hammered through it so that the points protrude about 6mm (¼"). The block is pressed onto the surface of the flat and rows of neat holes are left behind when it is removed. Two or three seeds should be placed in each hole and covered with a few millimetres of seed raising mix. The rows should be labelled, the surface smoothed, and the tray watered gently. A piece of flywire mesh can be placed across the surface of the tray to protect it from disturbance for the first five days or so, until the seedlings begin to emerge.

Make sure that the vegies are planted in the garden in straight rows so that it is easy to walk between them; you could perhaps put down stepping rounds so that your shoes don't get dirty.

The rows should be hilled up for good drainage—this stops the roots rotting and makes them easier to tend, hoe and weed.

Buying punnets of 30-50 seedlings is not necessarily a good idea; by the time they are separated there are hardly any roots left. When planted they will wilt fast on a hot day. It is better to buy the newer style of punnet that looks like an ice cube tray. Each seedling, with its own root system intact, can be easily lifted out. Even though there are fewer seedlings, there are probably more than enough for a family's use.

Particularly during summer, it is important to water in immediately and thoroughly with a trickling hose to give the seedlings a really good soak.

For an organic vegetable garden, crops should be rotated, for example, spinach one year and tomato the next. If you grow organically without using chemicals the produce is more healthy for the family.

There are many new varieties of plants, such as miniature varieties of corn (used in Chinese food) and tomatoes, that are very tasty.

It is important to get the timing right for vegetables—they can not be planted at just any time of the year.

BURKE'S BACKYARD SPRING VEGETABLE SELECTION			
VEGETABLE/HERB	**METHOD OF SOWING**	**QUANTITY**	**SPECIAL HINTS**
Basil	plants	2 plants	
Beans (climbing)	direct	1.5m row	Plant beans into moist soil—don't water until seedlings emerge
(dwarf)	direct	1.5m row	As above; successive sowings to be planted every month
Beetroot	seedtrays/direct	1.5m row seeds 1.5m row seedlings	Successive sowings every month
Capsicum	seedtrays/direct	2m row	
Chinese cabbage	direct	2 × 1.5m rows	
Chives	plants	1m row	
Cucumber	direct	1m row	Sow again in one month
Lettuce (two varieties)	seedtrays/direct	2 × 1.5m rows seedlings 2 × 1.5m rows seeds	Successive sowings every month
Mint	plants	4 varieties, 1 plant of each	
Oregano	plants	2 plants	
Parsley (Italian)	seedtrays/direct	3 plants	
(triple curled)	seedtrays/direct	4 × 1m rows	
Radish	seedtrays/direct	1m row	
Rhubarb	seedtrays/crowns	2 × crowns 4 × seedlings	Choose seedlings with red stems if preferred
Silverbeet	seedtrays/direct	2 × 1.5m rows	
Tomatoes (three varieties)	grafted seedtrays	1 plant 8 plants	Should feed a family of four Plant two per stake—prune to single leader
Zucchini	direct	1m row	Sow again in one month

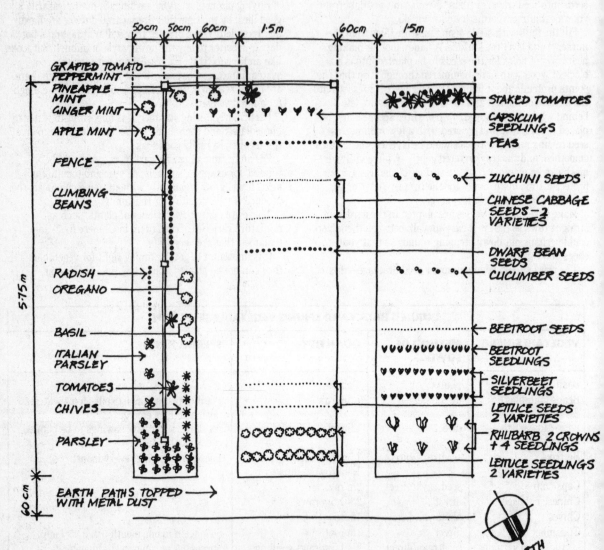

BURKE'S BACKYARD VEGETABLE GARDEN

Total area = 33 m² (355 ft²)
Bed area = 23 m² (247.5 ft²)

GARDEN MEASUREMENTS AND INITIAL PLANTING

Spaces beside beans, lettuce, zucchini, cucumber and beetroot allow for successive sowings of these crops at one month intervals.

The lettuce varieties we planted were 'Narromar' and 'Brown Mignonette'. The tomatoes were one 'Multi-Tom' grafted tomato, six 'Grosse Lisse', and two cocktail tomato plants, which are probably the hardiest of all tomatoes and require virtually no chemical pest and disease control.

You can scatter snail pellets around the vegetables, but be careful that local dogs don't have access to them because they are readily poisoned by the pellets.

A liquid fertiliser such as Nitrosol may be applied at monthly intervals.

Fireman's vegetable garden
One vegetable garden shown on 'Burke's Backyard' includes 40 different varieties of vegetables and a plot of show quality dahlias and gladioli. Growing extra-large produce for exhibition at local shows is one of the owner's hobbies.

Crop rotation, recycling of wastes and the use of animal manures as fertilisers are key principles involved in production of the vegetables. Horse manure is obtained from local stables but is not applied directly to the garden. Instead, it is tossed into the chookyard, where the chooks turn it over and add their own droppings to it—the result is a well-balanced mixture ideal for the garden.

The chooks also provide a source of droppings for use in making liquid fertiliser. The chook droppings are collected on bird wire placed under the perches where the birds roost at night. The droppings, bird wire and all are then immersed in a 44-gallon drum filled with water. After two or three weeks, during which the liquid is stirred frequently, the fertiliser is ready to be applied to the garden. The result is a liquid fertiliser high in nitrogen, which is especially good for leaf vegetables.

Chemicals are rarely used in the garden. Occasionally Defender is applied to reduce the slug and snail populations and Derris Dust is used to protect cabbages against the cabbage white butterfly.

For further information
The *Yates Garden Guide* is widely available for about $13 and provides detailed information for vegetable gardening in all parts of Australia. Your Department of Agriculture or Primary Industries will also have information on vegetable growing in your state.

WINTER VEGETABLES

By late autumn or early winter your vegie garden can be rather run down. It is therefore a good idea to improve the soil by adding manure or organic matter. Chicken manure is the best fertiliser for the vegetable garden, and leaves no chemical residue. Spread the manure over the soil and fork it in well. Ideally, the chicken manure should never be fresh—allow it to age or it might burn the roots of the plants. If you are in a hurry, use Dynamic Lifter, the pelleted poultry manure; it will not burn plants' roots.

Planting mixture, animal manures or compost could also be used.

After the manure is dug in, the garden can be left until spring, or you can plant it with vegetables that will grow through winter.

The onion family will now grow in most areas and includes shallots and leeks. There is a new onion distributed by Thompson & Morgan called the Sweet Sandwich F-1, which can be eaten like an apple.

In all but the coldest areas, cabbages can be planted. silver beet, commonly called spinach, can also be planted, as can some varieties of lettuce and broad beans.

After planting vegetables, it is important to put some Baysol or other snail killer around the plants. Make sure that dogs and cats don't go near snail killer, as it is poisonous to them.

Pumpkin leaves can often be covered with a white powder—powdery mildew. This can be sprayed with Benlate, but it is often unnecessary as even with this powdery mildew the pumpkins will still grow.

CHAPTER 4
Fruit and Nuts

CITRUS TREES
Citrus trees retain their shiny green leaves all year round. The fragrant white flowers are followed by attractive, edible, nutritious fruit. They are an excellent source of many vitamins, especially vitamin C, as well as mineral salts. Citrus can be planted in the front or back garden or in tubs on sunny balconies, and are by far the most practical fruit tree for home gardens. With relatively little care they produce lots of fruit over long periods.

Lemons
Eureka The best lemon for most home gardens and the most useful of all fruit trees. It fruits for most of the year with a heavy crop in summer, when lemons are expensive to buy. The fruit is juicy, has a rough orange-yellow skin, and is there for the picking all year. It is practically thornless and is the best lemon for coastal planting, although it is very prone to root rot in poorly drained positions.

Lisbon Produces lemons nearly all year, but is quite thorny. It is a very vigorous tree, suited to cooler areas. Seedless fruit peak in spring. 'Prior Lisbon' is less thorny and thus the better choice.

> *Being ground birds, partridges rarely, if ever, roost in pear trees.*

Meyer This variety bears earlier in the year and for a much shorter period than either Eureka or Lisbon and has a sweeter fruit. The main crop of fruit occurs in winter. The fruit has a smooth skin, with a rich yellow colour. It is more resistant to cold climates. This is a smaller tree and the best variety for growing in a tub.

Lemonade Tree This is a new lemon hybrid with a distinct lemonade flavour. It fruits for most of the year and the fruit is quite sweet. The tree is not as dense as other lemons, and the stems may blacken at certain times. The fruit is very good for juicing and cooking.

Oranges
Valencia This is the best orange for most home gardens. The main crop is in spring–summer, but fruit lasts for a long time on the tree. Fruit is medium-sized with a thin skin. This variety performs well on the coast. A seedless Valencia variety is sometimes available.

Washington Navel The fruit is seedless and very sweet. The main crop comes in winter–spring. It is an outstanding juicing orange, although the flavour deteriorates rapidly after juicing. This variety often doesn't produce as much fruit as Valencia, and is more difficult to grow.

Mandarins
Emperor This is probably the best variety of mandarin. The fruit has an excellent flavour, is very juicy and peels easily. It is large with a loose, orange-red skin, and lasts well on the tree. The main crop comes from May to September.

Thorny The best mandarin for the coast. The fruit has an excellent flavour and is very juicy. It has a tight, thin skin. The fruit are somewhat smaller than Emperor. The main crop comes in June–July.

Imperial An earlier fruiting Thorny variety. The main crop grows in May–June.

Kumquats
Calamondin A very decorative tub specimen, this is a prolific bearer two or three times a year. The main crop is in winter–spring. Use the fruit for superb marmalade or a tangy liqueur. A smaller growing citrus variety.

Calamondin Variegated A beautifully ornamental citrus featuring variegated leaves, this is an excellent tub plant, slightly smaller than Calamondin. The fruit are the same as Calamondin, but variegated.

Others The *Nagami* kumquat has a sweeter, more elongated fruit. *Chinoti* has a much larger fruit, which is also used for marmalades.

Limes
Tahiti Produces very juicy fruit, and is used in drinks or as a lemon substitute. The fruit is smaller than a lemon; the flesh is green and has no seeds. It fruits over a long period, with the main crop in winter. Pick while the fruit is still green.

West Indian This lime is not as good a grower as Tahiti. It has smaller fruit (10-cent coin size) but better flavour. It is better suited to tropical areas.

Grapefruit
Marsh This is the most popular grapefruit, a long fruiting seedless variety. The juicy fruit comes from May to July. It is a good inland or cooler climate variety.

Wheeny This is the best variety for coastal districts, good for jams or a healthy breakfast. It is a very heavy cropper with huge, juicy fruit; the main crop comes in spring. The fruit has seeds.

How to grow citrus All of the citrus group are easy to grow if a few basic rules are followed. Grow them in full sun, and don't grow anything on the ground underneath the foliage—especially not grass. Either keep the surrounding area well weeded or, better still, cover the soil with mulch. Do not cultivate the soil around citrus, as this causes root damage. Never plant citrus in a poorly drained position, and never allow soil to cover the root ball near the trunk (that is, don't plant too deeply).

Fertilise twice a year (February and September) with Citrus Food or poultry manure (Dynamic Lifter is recommended).

Ensure an adequate water supply, especially when fruit is growing.

DECIDUOUS FRUIT TREES
Winter is the traditional time of year to buy your deciduous fruit trees, as this is when they're in their dormant period. However, the prospective buyer can learn little about fruit trees just by looking at them at this time, as there is nothing to see but bare sticks.

To buy the first bunch of sticks you come to is not good enough. There is a wide range of varieties to suit different climates: early fruiting varieties usually escape the worst of the fruit fly attacks in semi-tropical areas; high-chill varieties will be productive only in areas with a cold winter; and so on. Some fruits take two to tango—two different varieties must be grown together before pollination takes place so that fruit formation can occur.

In general, your local nursery or garden centre can be expected to stock suitable varieties for your locality, but the following broad guidelines and information about specific varieties may help to determine what you will need to look for and what questions you should ask.

Peaches The 'Flordagold' variety of peach represents a breakthrough in peach breeding. This is one of a number of varieties bred in Florida, USA, to be productive in tropical areas. These peaches have a low chill requirement, which means they don't need extended periods of cold weather each winter to produce fruit the following season. Only one tree need be grown, as they don't need cross-pollination. Other varieties from this group are 'Maravilha', 'Blackburn' and 'Sherman's Red'.

Nectarines Nectarines are simply fuzzless varieties of true peaches. In cooler areas you can grow any variety you like, but for warmer zones there are several low-chill varieties which include 'Nectar Red', 'Sundowner' and 'Sun Red'.

Plums Nowadays plums come in a seemingly endless array of colours and range from the size of cherries to that of small apples. In the majority of cases, if you buy one plum tree you have to buy another variety as a pollinator. The most frequently used pollinator variety is 'Santa Rosa', but this variety, like the 'Satsuma' plum, actually pollinates itself and can be grown alone.

Apples Apples must also be grown in pairs, so if you want to grow a 'Granny Smith' you will need, say, a 'Jonathon', too, if you wish to harvest any fruit. One of the best new Australian varieties of apples is the 'Lady Williams', a red apple descended from the 'Granny Smith'; it has remarkable keeping qualities and a delicious flavour. This variety has a long flowering period and so is a useful pollinating variety.

Apricots and figs No pollinator is required—one tree is enough.

Almonds and pears Two trees are required for pollination to be achieved. Try the fruit of the crisp and refreshing 'Nashi' pear, which is increasing in popularity.

Persimmons If you like the flavour of persimmons but dislike the sticky texture of the ripe fruit, there are a number of new non-astringent varieties, which can be eaten while still crisp.

If your yard is simply too small or crowded to support two trees but you would like to grow fruits that need two for pollination, there is an answer. Simply plant the two trees in one hole in the ground. Provided you are careful to prune them so that both trees grow to the same size, you will get all the advantages of two trees for the size of one.

EXOTIC FRUIT

Custard apples (*Annona cherimola x squamosa*) It is possible to grow custard apples in most areas of Australia. If you can grow a citrus tree, you can probably manage a custard apple. In the cooler areas, the varieties to use are

the Cherimola types, as these are more hardy. Custard apples should fruit from when they are two years old.

Sweet persimmon (*Diospyros kaki*) These can be eaten when crisp, like an apple. They are part of the same family as the following fruit.

Black Sapoti or Chocolate Pudding Fruit (*Diospyros digyna*) These need to be softened at room temperature. They are usually dark brown or black inside, and with a few drops of brandy, cream or icecream they are delicious. They are very easy to grow in warmer climates, that is, Queensland, New South Wales as far south as Sydney, and north of Adelaide and Perth.

Dragon's eye or Longan (*Euphoria longan*) These are called dragon's eyes because of the small yellow fruit. They are very sweet, with brown skin that peels off, and the inside is similar to a lychee, to which it is related. Dragon's eyes are also sold as tinned fruit. This is a warm climate plant, suitable for the area north of Sydney to Perth.

To protect plants from cold, wet weather during winter, and to help them establish, put three stakes in the ground and pull a polythene bag or 'grow tube' over them like a sleeve. This will act as a mini-glasshouse and keep the plants warm.

Tropical guava (*Psidium guajava*) These have a very distinctive smell, are good to eat and very rich in vitamin C. They are very hardy trees that are untroubled by cool conditions and will grow in most areas of New South Wales, South Australia, Queensland and north of Perth in Western Australia.

There are many tropical fruits that are worth trying to grow. Since they are new to the market, you will have to hunt around to obtain them.

FRUIT TREES

Nothing tastes as good as the fruit you grow in your own backyard. But insufficient space can be a problem, especially since extra trees are often needed to ensure pollination. A possible solution to the problem is to plant more than one tree in the same hole, that is, multiple fruit tree planting.

Combinations There are a number of different possibilities. You could try three different apple varieties chosen so that you can have fruit for most of the year, that is, one that fruits in mid-January, one that fruits in late March, and a third that fruits late in June; three pear varieties; three cherry varieties; a peach and a nectarine tree seem to work well together; a combination of an apricot and a plum has also been tried, but, while it is generally successful, there have been some difficulties with fungal infections.

Sizes In four to five years the 'tree' can be expected to be 3m (10') tall and have a span of 2-2½m (6-8'), depending on pruning.

Pruning The trees are pruned as though they are just one tree, and by removing the limbs that come into the centre of the triangle. There is a dwarfing effect from growing three trees together and the result is that they grow collectively to about the size of one normal tree.

Root system Because each tree has its own root system, it is much better than a multigrafted tree that still has only one root system. Equally, it is much easier to identify and prune the branches belonging to each tree when you can trace them to a separate rootstock. In a multigrafted plant, confusion can lead to one variety taking over from the other two.

With multiple fruit tree planting you can have a longer fruiting period and a greater choice of fruit. Pollination is taken care of, and the overall plant is very compact—an ideal system for the backyard.

GRAPE CUTTINGS

The grape is the world's most popular fruit. For a few tips on growing them at home, Don visited the Wirra Wirra Vineyards in McLaren Vale, South Australia and sought advice from Greg Trott, caretaker of the Wirra Wirra Vineyards and Chairman of the McLaren Vale Wine Makers' Association.

Pruning The best time for pruning is from leaf fall—say, June to mid-August.

Cuttings When pruning, take your cuttings for next year's use. A base cut is taken from close in to the branch so that there are many nodes from which root growth will occur.

Trim the cuttings to about 35cm (14") in length. The cutting's thickness will go from about 15mm (⅝") to 3 or 4mm (⅛-³/₁₆").

Striking the cuttings Open ground near a vegetable garden is best, in case you forget to water your cuttings.

Dig a small trench from east to west, leaving a small hill of soil on the northern side. Place the cuttings so that their thick ends are 10cm (4") into the soil at the base of the trench, pointing towards the sun as they lie inclined on the small mound of soil. This ensures that the bark receives the correct amount of sunlight. Now back-fill the trench and water to exclude air.

Greg Trott has found his success rate with this method to be quite high.

Planting One year later, choose a healthy vine from your cuttings, trim the roots, and cut the shoot back to two or

three buds, so that when placed in the ground 10-15cm (4-6") of shoot protrudes. Back-fill, and water to seal the area firmly, as it is important that there is no air around the butts.

Training Attach a string to the shoot so that from September, when it starts to grow, it can wind its way up and grow straight.

Hardiness It is important that the plants be kept moist during the summer months. If this is done, the vines are quite hardy and can take hard pruning.

KIWI FRUIT

Kiwi fruit has become as familiar to most of us as strawberries and passionfruit through its use on the tops of pavlovas and in fruit salad, thanks in no small part to the marketing efforts of New Zealand growers. It was these farmers who changed the name from Chinese gooseberry to Kiwi fruit to help promote the fruit and make it identifiable with their country.

Kiwi fruit are more than just a garnish, however. The fruits are equally delicious when eaten as a fresh whole fruit—simply slice off the top and eat the flesh with a spoon. The fruit can also be juiced, dried, and made into an interesting jam.

Varieties 'Hayward' is best suited to Sydney, Perth and areas to the south of these cities. It has large fruit with good keeping quality and is very popular. 'Dexter' is better suited to the warmer areas to the north of Sydney and Perth. It is a vigorous vine, with large quantities of smaller fruit. It requires heavy pruning to keep it under control. 'Bruno' is another popular variety, which crops heavily and matures early. Other varieties are available, and advice about the best ones for your region may be obtained from state Departments of Agriculture and Primary Industries.

Buying Male and female flowers form on separate plants, so to produce fruit from a female vine you must grow a male as well. In a large backyard the ratio of males to females is generally 1:2; commercially it is 1:5 or 1:6.

Young male and female vines look the same, so you will need to rely on the labels when you buy potted, dormant plants from a nursery.

Multigrafting Sometimes vines are available on which both male and female plants have been grafted onto the same base. These plants are usually difficult to manage, because the male section is often too vigorous for the female and it is confusing to prune appropriately.

Position A pergola is an ideal structure over which to grow Kiwi fruit in the garden, although a ladder would be required for pruning. They can also be grown against fences or on other frames, but these must be strong, as mature vines in fruit are quite weighty. The position should also be sunny and not exposed to late frosts after mid-September. It is best to try to create an umbrella-like canopy of leaves, which will protect the fruit hanging beneath it from sunburn and desiccation. For this reason a horizontal frame works better than something vertical.

Wind protection is also important, for two reasons. The plants are highly prone to desiccation (overhead watering with a sprinkler or hose helps relieve this on a very bad windy day), and the new growth shoots are very brittle and snap easily in strong winds. To grow two vines along a fence you would need 9m (30') of space to stop them from overlapping.

Soil Good drainage is vital—Kiwi fruit do not like having wet feet. A rich loam is preferable and sandy soils should be enriched with large amounts of organic matter. Mulch the surface with more organic matter.

Animal manures and one of the nine-month slow release fertilisers should be applied in spring to maintain the vine through its growing months.

Kiwi fruit vines are fairly shallow-rooted so require regular watering in summer and a good thick mulch.

Pruning Kiwi fruit are deciduous and the main pruning takes place in the winter when the vines are bare. Pruning methods vary according to the structure on which the vine is growing and whether the vine is a male or a female.

Males are pruned heavily twice a year—first in winter and again after flowering. Females are pruned heavily in winter and lightly trimmed in summer to remove twining, non-productive growth.

Pruning for the first year involves nothing more than training a single central stem or trunk up to the top of the supporting structure by removing any branches that go off to the sides. If the vine is to grow along a fence, the top should be pinched out to encourage lateral stems to grow to form a T-shape. If the vine is to grow on a pergola, it is generally better to keep the main stem growing right up over the top. From the top of the trunk these main stems should be no more than 2.5m (8½') in length.

Once the basic shape (either a single stem or two arms) has been established, the fruit will form on the female vines on branches that grow from the sides of the main stems. Each winter these fruiting arms should be cut back to three or four buds in length. These buds will produce the next season's fruiting arms, and should in turn be trimmed to three or four buds in length. After about four years the fruiting arms should be removed back at the main stem to allow new ones to develop.

Fruit is produced only on new wood from the last season's growth. If a Kiwi fruit vine has been left unpruned for several years it should be pruned right back

to the basic framework so it can again start producing new wood closer to the main frame. Fruit produced nearer the centre of the plant is said to be better in all respects than that from towards the extremities of the plant.

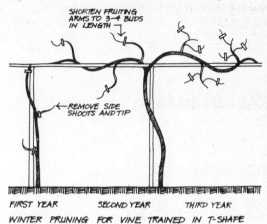

WINTER PRUNING FOR VINE TRAINED IN T-SHAPE

Harvesting Kiwi fruit take three to five years from planting to their first fruiting. The fruit are normally picked from April through to June but, like avocados, they don't ripen on the plant. This is an advantage; it makes them less attractive to birds and insects. They are much more resistant to fruit fly attack than most other garden fruits.

The harvested fruit can be frozen in polythene bags for keeping, or eaten fresh after being softened. You can soften the fruit by leaving them at room temperature for a few days or placing them in a plastic bag containing a ripe banana or apple.

Pests and diseases Kiwi fruit are reasonably hardy, provided they have good drainage so that the incidence of root diseases is reduced. Queensland fruit fly and leaf eating caterpillars should be controlled.

LADY WILLIAMS APPLES

In 1935, a natural apple seedling was found growing beside a tank stand at the home of Arthur and Maude Williams near Bunbury in Western Australia. It appears that this apple was a hybrid between a Granny Smith (Australia's famous apple) and a Yates—perhaps a Rokewood apple. The local children named the fruits 'Lady Williams apples'.

Only in the last 5–10 years has the potential of this apple been recognised.

The apple has an outstanding flavour. It crops late in the season; pick it around June. It doesn't sweeten up until two weeks before fruit drop. Its keeping qualities are particularly good up to six months without cold storage—June to December. The fruit is less prone to rot than other varieties; it suits areas with long, hot summers. It suits

the backyard grower; you don't have to prune it unless you want to alter its shape. It is somewhat susceptible to black spot or apple scab, which the backyard grower could control with Benlate or similar.

It has an extended blossom period. Because of this, it has no problems with crosspollination when grown with any other apple variety.

In Western Australia, the home of this apple, it sells very well and it is now becoming more readily available in other areas of Australia.

MACADAMIAS

It is very satisfying to grow your own nut trees in the backyard. However, in most areas of Australia, growing nuts is not a very practical proposition, certainly not through the centre of Australia. Macadamias are the exception; it is quite possible to grow a macadamia tree in your backyard. The macadamia is the only Australian native plant so far developed as a commercial food crop.

Macadamias need a frost-free area, and thus they will probably not grow south of a line from Sydney to Perth. They are native to the coastal areas of northern New South Wales and southern Queensland. They also prefer a rich soil and a good rainfall.

The best macadamia for a home garden is *Macadamia integrifolia*, which has three leaves to each node, and no prickles. It produces a much better fruit than *Macadamia tetraphylla*, which is very prickly and not suited for the home garden.

Another variety, 'Own Choice', is very good for our Australian conditions but it is not available in many areas. There are grafted varieties of *Macadamia integrifolia*, which are quite adequate, and readily available in most areas.

A light crop can be expected four to five years after planting. The macadamias are ready to pick when the husk pulls off easily and the inside of the husk starts to turn brown. The nuts can be cracked using a special tool or a hammer.

When the macadamias are harvested, they are left in a drying room for about two weeks and then de-husked and placed in a drying kiln, where the moisture content of the nut is reduced to around 2%. They are then graded, cracked open, packaged and sold.

PASSIONFRUIT

One of Australia's most popular fruiting plants is the passionfruit; a climbing evergreen plant which has its origins in South America.

The unusual flowers of the plant have given the fruit its name. Spanish priests who found the plant growing wild in Brazil used the flowers to explain the story of the Passion of Christ to the people they had come to convert. They showed how the three styles (female parts) of the plant represented the three nails in Christ; the filaments around the outside were said to represent the crown of thorns, or perhaps the Apostles.

Problems
No fruit   There are two things to remember if you have a passionfruit vine with no fruit. Don't use any fertiliser for a while or the plant won't fruit. Don't worry; the plant may simply be too young to fruit. It can take 6–18 months for a passionfruit vine to grow and settle in.

Woodiness virus   If the fruit is distorted, the growth itself is a bit mottled and the plant is looking woody and thin, it almost certainly has the woodiness virus and you should get rid of the plant. Plant a new one every few years, and you will have strong vines coming on all the time.

Fusarium wilt   This is a fungal disease. The leaves become pale green and then the whole vine wilts. The best way to avoid this is to plant a grafted passionfruit. A grafted passionfruit that has proved itself to be a success in Australia is the 'Nellie Kellie' variety.

Care   Passionfruit can be used in a variety of ways. Plant formally in a specific spot, or use informally, to cover an old tree stump, to grow over a wall, fence, and so on. The most vital factor is that they should be placed in a sunny position. A well-drained soil is also important. Fertilise between spring and February. If you already have citrus food or rose food on hand, they are fine for passionfruit, too.

Since passionfruit vines are often planted on a fence shared by neighbours, an important point to note is that the fruit usually occurs on the sunny side of the fence. If you are not careful, all the fruit could end up going to your neighbours.

Other varieties

Banana Passionfruit Vine The vine has attractive pink flowers and the fruit is yellowish, with much softer skin than that of the ordinary passionfruit. It is not difficult to crack the fruit open with your fingers. The flavour is not quite as acid as that of the ordinary passionfruit. The vine is reasonably cold hardy and is often used as the understock in grafting. It is also a long-lived variety, frequently lasting as long as twenty years.

Red Flowering Passionfruit This is probably the best of the ornamental passionfruits—that is, those with fruit that is not necessarily edible. It flowers over many months and covers large buildings or walls extremely well. These are slightly more tropical plants that don't handle frost well.

STRAWBERRIES

Strawberries are very popular with home gardeners. Strawberry plants are sold packaged in boxes labelled 'propagated from approved material', which means they are virus-free plants. When strawberries have been growing in the ground for one or two years they are infected by virus disease, usually transmitted by aphids, and become unhealthy and underproduce. If your strawberries are a couple of years old, throw them away (into the garbage bin, not the compost heap), buy new ones and start again.

The main varieties are Tioga and Torrey (and Red Gauntlet in colder areas) and these are available throughout Australia. The best time to plant strawberries is during April and May. Select a warm, well-drained spot in full sun. They will not grow in the shade and they hate frost.

Care Firstly, prepare the soil—dig in chook manure to improve the soil. Spread black plastic along the line where you intend to plant the strawberries. Remove the plants or runners, which are usually packed in peat moss, from the box, make a hole in the black plastic and plant the strawberry through the hole. The black plastic keeps the strawberry fruit off the ground and stops slaters, snails and so on from eating the fruit. *Everything* wants to eat strawberries, including birds, so it is advisable to put bird wire or mesh over the plants.

Fertilise the strawberries with rose or citrus food, any of the complete fertilisers or one of the various forms of poultry manure, such as Dynamic Lifter; use copper oxychloride if the strawberries get fungus disease in wet weather.

Strawberries can be grown in special strawberry pots or hydroponic containers, but it is just as effective to grow them in a large tub. If you want to grow them in containers, pick the one that suits you, but it is important to note that the bigger the container the better the results.

A cheap and practical container can be made simply by planting the strawberries into one of the polystyrene boxes often seen in greengrocers' shops—the type that usually contain peaches, mangoes and so on.

Wild strawberries are not edible, but are a good ground cover.

TOMATOES

If you buy tomatoes from the shops, the variety will most likely be 'Floradade'. This is a really tough tomato and has a good shelf life, but it's a variety to be avoided if you are growing your own, because it is not a good-tasting tomato. 'Grosse Lisse' is one of the best to plant.

Tomatoes are the best and most popular fruiting plant for backyards, and they produce 5–10kg (11–22lb) of fruit from one bush. If you live in the tropics, 'Scorpio' is possibly the best for you to try. If you do not like spraying, some of the smaller cherry tomatoes are excellent and very flavoursome. They resist fruit fly because of their tough skin.

Tomatoes can be grown from seed or as young seedlings: some are sold in cellular punnets. One of the most interesting ways to buy them is as grafted plants. They have two root systems. One grafted plant will feed the whole family, and these plants are particularly disease resistant.

There are two yellow varieties of tomato—one is the pear variety, which looks very attractive in salads. One of the greatest tomatoes ever is 'Oxheart'. It produces very large fruit, which are excellent stuffed and baked.

Gro-Plus is an excellent food for tomatoes, as is tomato food, citrus food or rose food. You will also need some tomato dust to protect your plants from insects and disease.

Yates Garden Guide gives very good detailed information about growing tomatoes.

Winter tomatoes Grafted tomatoes are available Australia-wide, but in Victoria and Tasmania they should be planted no later than early January, unless they can be grown inside a glasshouse, which permits year round growing. In climates such as those of Perth and Sydney, grafted tomatoes can be planted in March, while in subtropical to tropical areas garden planting is usually possible for most of the year. Prices vary from $4.50–$6 per plant.

The following information, *How to grow winter tomatoes*, was written by Neville Passmore for Blossoms Garden Centre, Gosnells, Western Australia, and is reprinted with kind permission of the author.

'You can plant tomatoes in early autumn (in frost-free or frost protected areas from Perth to Sydney and north of those cities) and if you follow this programme you should pick your first fruits nine weeks after planting.

'You should continue to pick fruits well into winter, thus saving a considerable amount of money on the family budget, as prices tend to climb the further we progress into the cooler weather.

'Winter rains reduce the amount of work required on vegie crops and there tends to be less insect pest infestation through the cooler months.

'The best varieties for planting out in late summer and early autumn are undoubtedly the grafted tomatoes, such as Maxitom, Whopper Cropper, Craigietom, Multitom, etc. Grafted varieties have proved to be very vigorous and produce vines well into the cooler months of winter.

'The wild tomato understock that supplies much of their strength is resistant to two of the main wilt diseases— verticillium and fusarium, and to nematodes. Nematodes are microscopic worms that invade the roots of tomatoes, causing swellings or galls which inhibit the ability of plants to draw up nutrients. Similarly, fungus diseases such as verticillium and fusarium will affect the ability of plants to transport nutrients and soil water through to their leaves and stems. When affected plants are subjected to stressful situations, such as hot weather or insect attacks, they very rapidly decline or wilt.

'However, grafted tomatoes are not resistant to tomato spotted virus, a wilt disease which can be transmitted from other plants in the garden by thrips. To keep tomato plants free from this wilt disease it is necessary to keep a regular Lanosan insecticide programme operating throughout the life of the plant.

'Grafted tomatoes are more resistant to cold weather and have significantly bigger crops compared to seedling varieties, bearing fruit much later in the cold season. (The largest vine Neville Passmore has seen was 9m (30′) wide by 6m (20′) high by 45cm (18″) deep, and carried 1000 tomatoes at the one time.) But frosts are a limiting factor and severe frosts will even kill a mature grafted tomato.

'For best results choose a sunny position, particularly one open to the north to maximise the hours of winter sunshine. Some gardeners in frost prone areas plant tomatoes under the eaves of their houses, in a north or west-facing position. Warmth radiated from a building will often protect plants from light frost.

'Prepare the soil by mixing in a bucket of chicken manure and a light dressing of lime—a tablespoon of lime is enough to treat a square metre (10 sq ft) of garden bed. Mix the manure and lime in to a depth of 15cm (6″). Plant your tomato with care to avoid any damage or disturbance to the root system.

'This is the ideal time to set a trellis or supporting system in place. Bamboo has proved to be a very useful trellis material for the past two winners of the Maxitom growing competition (held in WA).

'With grafted tomatoes it is not necessary to remove most of the early side shoots; rather, these can be trained into main trunks, as the plant has the vigour to support much more growth than the standard seedling.

'A microclimate can be created to enhance the growth of your winter tomato plants. Soil-warming mulches consisting of two separated layers of black and clear plastic will lift the soil temperature by a couple of degrees (celsius) and keep the soil fairly dry.

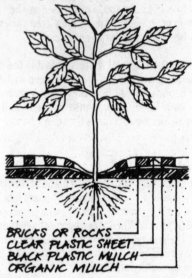

BRICKS OR ROCKS
CLEAR PLASTIC SHEET
BLACK PLASTIC MULCH
ORGANIC MULCH

'A sheltered place to protect the young tomato plant from cold winter winds will also help to get the plant moving.

'Tomatoes can be successfully grown in big tubs, and the advantage of this approach in the cooler months is that a pot full of soil will warm up much quicker when hit by the morning rays of the sun than a garden bed.

'The author recommends feeding young tomato plants with Potato E manure from the first week and every three or four weeks thereafter (Potato E manure is not available in all states—Yates Tomato Food or a complete vegetable fertiliser would also be suitable). This will help to overcome calcium deficiencies which lead to blossom end rot. Potato E manure is rich in phosphates, which also encourage strong root development.

'As soil temperatures start to drop, granular fertilisers become less available to the plant. It is recommended that you use a foliar application of a liquid fertiliser, in particular Phostrogen, to give the plant what is virtually an intravenous feed. Weekly applications of Phostrogen should begin from the day of planting and continue right through the life of the plant. Phostrogen is rich in potash, which is particularly important for flowering and fruiting plants, as it promotes flower setting and improves flavour in the fruits.

'Tomatoes are Australia's most popular home garden vegetable. You certainly can't beat the home-grown flavour of fruit picked off the bush and taken straight to the kitchen. With a bit of careful thought and some extra work it is possible to extend the tomato season well into our winter months.'

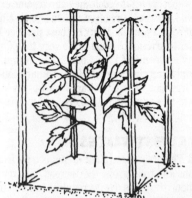

PROTECT YOUR MAXITOM WITH A HUT. CUT THE BOTTOM FROM A PLASTIC BAG, SUPPORT THE BAG WITH CANES AND BURY THE BOTTOM TO KEEP OUT DRAUGHTS. COVER (AT NIGHT) WITH PAPER WHEN FROST THREATENS

Neville Passmore is the General Manager of Blossoms Garden Centre, 2311 Albany Highway, Gosnells, WA 6110. Telephone (09) 398 2425, (09) 398 1315.

Handy hint In winter, tomatoes often produce many flowers but little fruit. Gently touch the flowers with a vibrating pillow or an electric toothbrush at about 10 am. This will shake the pollen over the flowers and improve pollination.

TROPICAL FRUITS

The new industry of Australian-grown exotic fruits promises to make Australians more adventurous in their fruit-eating habits. This table examines four of the new exotic fruits.

Fruit	Taste	Comments
Rambutan	Equal to the best lychees	Asian origin, related to lychees. Tree grows up to 15m (49'); suits Townsville to Cape York
Rollinia	Custardy	South American origin, related to the custard apple family; suitable for equatorial climates only
Cuban fibreless soursop	Magnificent acid flavour with a custardy texture	South American in origin; could be grown as far south as northern NSW; popular for blending in drinks and flavourings

Fruit	Taste	Comments
Miracle fruit	After eating this fruit, even lemons taste sweet	West African in origin; small tree

For further information

Rare Fruit Council of Australia Inc
PO Box 707
Cairns QLD 4870

CHAPTER 5
Lawns

COOL CLIMATE TURF

A lush, green magnificent lawn is the dream of many people, but one which few will ever achieve. In trying to save a few pennies by such measures as buying cheap varieties of lawn grasses and not preparing the ground properly, many people will find themselves spending perhaps hundreds of dollars over the next few years on extra fertiliser and water without ever really getting the lovely, lush result they seek. By buying a prestige, top quality lawn to begin with, and preparing the yard properly, the end result can be magnificent.

In the cooler climatic areas of Australia, grasses such as the common perennial ryegrass have been used in lawns for many years. This grass can look reasonably good, but bare areas often develop. The reason is that this is really a pasture grass and was developed for sheep fodder. It grows quite tall so the sheep can have their fill, but it doesn't spread enough to give dense coverage in a lawn.

More appropriate, high performance grass mixes for cool climate lawns contain ryegrasses, but these are varieties which have more suitable characteristics for this purpose.

In a 'Burke's Backyard' story we examined some of the lawn mixes marketed under the name of Jet Turf Lawn Seed. The high performance of these mixes is the result of the intensive research and development which goes into their production. Grass mixtures are deliberately grown under appalling conditions in low rainfall areas, in soils that set like concrete—all to see how much stress they can take. Some of the grass is mowed extremely closely in strips and then, to make things even worse, a wear machine is taken over the top of it. This machine has belts with studs poking through them that beat the grass. This subjects the lawn to the worst possible wear conditions imaginable. The mixes we examined were:

Mow Less lawn seed is made up of a mixture of different grasses, mainly based on a fine-leaved form of ryegrass, but it also contains some fine fescues. These grasses have a more horizontal growth habit, so bare patches between plants are less likely to occur. Additionally, since they do grow more horizontally, the mowing requirement is reduced by about 15–30%.

Water Less lawn seed creates a coarser type of lawn and is made up of a number of grasses, mainly fescues. It will tolerate fairly low amounts of moisture, and most of the dreadful things your dog might be able to do to it.

Oversow lawn seed is used to renovate worn out patchy lawns without removing the existing grass. All you need to do is rake your lawn, spread some of the seed mix over it, then rake it over again and water thoroughly and regularly. Six weeks later it should look lush and green.

These high quality grasses are also available as rolls of turf to make an instant lawn. The bottom line with lawns is that if you spend a little more money establishing a premium quality lawn you will be far better off in the long run.

LAWN BUYER'S GUIDE

A 'lawn buyer's guide' brochure is available from:

Valley Seeds Pty Ltd
RMB 1480
Alexandria VIC 3714
Telephone (057) 97 6203

LAWN MAINTENANCE

To maintain an attractive lawn without too much time and effort follow these simple steps.

Don't mow the lawn too closely; it is better to set the mower up a notch or two.

Spray bindii with Weedoben M or another special bindii spray.

Do not top-dress unless the lawn needs levelling; normally a lawn needs top-dressing once after it has been laid. Gently undulating lawns often add interest and drain better after rain.

Use a complete lawn food rather than sulphate of ammonia. The latter makes the lawn appear greener for a few weeks but can lead to problems in the long term. Complete lawn foods contain a balanced lawn diet, which already includes sulphate of ammonia. Apply lime every few years.

If the lawn has an untidy appearance it will often improve markedly if the edges are trimmed neatly. Struggling lawns are often an indication that the soil has become too compacted where cars frequently cross it, or where heavy equipment was moving around when the house was built. Once the soil has become compacted it will stay that way forever unless action is taken. A power aerator may be hired to aerate the soil, or you can do it by hand. Take an ordinary garden fork and work around the garden, digging it into the soil every 10 cm (4″) or so and rocking it backwards and forwards. This technique

requires a fit operator. Special hollow-tined aerating forks are sometimes available for the purpose.

In recent times, plant breeders have bred some exquisite types of lawns but these are often difficult to obtain, especially in country areas. Many of these prestige lawns are of different varieties of couch. One very tough, very green variety is Greenleaf Park Couch. This magnificent type needs only half the mowing of an ordinary couch lawn. Tiff Green and Tiff Dwarf are dwarf types best suited to frost-free areas. They hardly need mowing at all except to keep the weeds down.

LAWN SUBSTITUTES

Dichondra The great Australian dream is a perfect lawn. But as shrubs and trees grow, they spread out over the lawn and shade the grass. Grass requires full sun to grow well, so ugly dead patches soon appear in the shady areas.

An Australian native plant, dichondra, or kidney weed, can often save the situation. Although it grows best in sun, dichondra does extremely well in the shade. It is low growing; it can be walked on; it can be mown; it looks like a magnificent lawn; and it forms an automatic balance with the grass—that is, it grows less where grass thrives, but takes over where grass won't grow. As it is sold in seed form, it is easily sown, and being self-seeding, it spreads easily.

Dichondra is sold in various packaging methods, but will cost around $15–$20 for a quantity sufficient to cover an area of around 20m² (215 sq ft).

Other lawn substitutes Baby's Tears—this suits very moist, shady areas; it has dainty, light silvery green foliage and gives brilliant coverage. Unfortunately, it is too delicate to walk on.

Viola hederacea or Australian native violet—this has attractive leaves and beautiful purple and white flowers. It suits shady, moist areas, but again is not for walking on.

Paving—if nothing will grow, brick or other paving is far more attractive than bare earth or dead grass—don't fight nature!

TURF

The advantages of buying turf certainly outweigh the costs. Turf provides an instant lawn and there is no mud for the kids to grind into the carpet. Lawn grown from seed flowers more often, which reduces its attractiveness.

For the best results when laying turf, firstly loosen the soil surface and clear away all stones and rubbish.

Apply an even layer of quality soil and rotary hoe into the ground. Apply lime or dolomite at the rate of 2.5kg (5½lb) per 10m² (107sq ft). As lime and dolomite are insoluble, they must be worked into the soil. They contain calcium, which improves the structure of the soil, resulting in better drainage.

Next, broadcast a fertiliser like Banana Special, which

contains nitrogen, phosphorus and potassium. This will enable your lawn to develop good root and leaf growth. Nitrogen fertilisers may boost leaf growth, but too much will starve the turf if phosphorus and potassium are both absent.

Apart from Durban grass there are very few varieties of lawn that will be lush and green under a shady tree and still grow well in full sun. Durban grass is not suitable for frost areas.

If your couch grass is claggy it was probably a cheap variety originally. A variety like wintergreen couch (used on Parramatta stadium and Kerry Packer's polo fields) is excellent, as is Greenleaf park couch, sometimes called Greenlees park couch. These grasses can be neglected and still look reasonably good. It is completely false economy to buy cheap grass—the lawn will possibly contain nutgrass and create all sorts of maintenance problems. Buy the expensive grass and save money in the long term.

Kikuyu grass needs extra mowing in summer. Buffalo grass grows quite well in the shade, but it can irritate the skin.

Laying the turf is not difficult, but always order a little more than is needed, just in case. In summer lay the turf the day it arrives, as storing can damage or kill it.

A light rolling after laying will consolidate the ground, removing any high or low spots and thus help to avoid scalping the lawn later on when mowing.

Watering is essential—water the lawn well for two weeks after laying and water regularly thereafter.

It is advisable to fertilise three times per year. Chicken manure pellets are good—they will not burn the lawn—or use a complete lawn food.

It is important not to mow turf too closely, as this may weaken the grass. Some couch and kikuyu varieties may become thatched during their growth. To overcome this problem, reduce the mowing height gradually for a few weeks only. The end result will be a healthy, strong lawn.

WEEDS

Weeds grow in the lawn when the ground is uneven and is being scalped by the lawnmower. Try to level the lawn, and don't mow too closely. Use a complete lawn food (*not* sulphate of ammonia) two, three or even four times a year for a perfect lawn.

It is much better to encourage healthy lawn growth so that weeds do not grow, than to use chemicals to kill them.

Bindii To get rid of bindii, spray in autumn or winter before it sets prickles. Two good sprays are Weedoben M and Bin-Die. They will also kill broad-leaf weeds. Do not use bindii killers containing dicamba as they may kill nearby trees if used in a certain way.

Paspalum Spray with a paspalum killer, for example,

Lawn Paspalum Killer which will also kill summer grass. Summer grass produces seed heads which are useful for budgies and finches if you don't spray.

Winter grass This can be controlled chemically with Endothal or Poakil. These take two to eight weeks to work, so if the winter grass is setting seed it's too late. The seed heads are also good food for budgies and finches if you don't spray.

Clover can be left in a lawn to act as a natural lawn fertiliser, providing nitrogen for the soil. If you want to get rid of clover or creeping oxalis, use Clovoxal or another clover killer.

All of these chemicals kill the weeds but leave the lawn alive. They work differently on different types of lawns, so obtain the correct chemical for your lawn. If you are not sure what type of lawn you have, take a sample to your local nursery for identification.

Other weeds in the lawn can be killed with a Zero weeding wand, but be careful to touch just the weeds, not the grass.

CHAPTER 6
Gardening Tips and Techniques

ADELAIDE GARDENING

Soils are the basis of every good garden, and it pays to get some expert knowledge if you wish to achieve pleasing results. There is probably no area in Australia more peculiar in relation to its soil than the Adelaide region. Adelaide has three very distinct growing areas: the coastal foreshores, plains, and Adelaide hills.

Coastal foreshores

Problems Lack of good top soil—usually sand over limestone or sand over clay in sandy soils, the nutrients leach out easily; salt buildup in the soil; limestone ridges varying from a few centimetres thick to a few metres thick; yellowing and stunted growth due to lack of iron; strong, cold and salt-laden prevailing winds.

Solutions Build up a shelter belt, where possible, with indigenous plant material which has a proven track record. Build up sandy soil with plenty of leaf mulch or alternatives, with the addition of a complete mineral mixture. Break through the limestone ridge, using a pick if necessary. Add iron chelates as a foliar spray. Hose foliage weekly with fresh tap water. Maintain long, heavy, regular watering rather than frequent, short bursts.

Recommended plants Various species of westringia, correas, pimelea, pittosporum, metrosideros, myoporum, juniper, melaleuca, coastal tea-tree, eucalypt, callistemon, hebe.

Adelaide plains

Problems Generally clay silt soil with a high alkaline factor—soils can dry out and crack in summer and become sticky and boggy in winter; lack of iron resulting in yellowing of foliage and stunted growth; frosty, cold areas in winter—hot and dry in summer.

Solutions Improve the physical structure of the soil by adding gypsum. This helps to open up the soil, making it more porous, and to make iron more readily available to the plants. Iron chelates or manganese sulphate help the plants to receive an initial boost of iron. Use a well balanced fertiliser such as Osmocote.

Recommended plants Various species of hebe, sollya, anigozanthos, coleonema, callistemon, hardenbergia, felicia, juniper, eucalypt, ceanopthus, correa, euonymus, cassia, prunus, agonis, baeckea.

Adelaide hills

Problems Good top soil can vary from a depth of a few centimetres to a few metres over a shale–clay sub-base; cold and damp in winter with high rainfall; dense growth of stringybark gums, which leach the soil of precious nutrients and create shady areas, which in turn inhibit the growth of introduced species.

Solutions Introduce good soil where necessary and ensure there is sufficient drainage. Mulch heavily in summer. Avoid planting exotic species in close proximity to the base of gum trees. Select open, well-lit positions. Use a slow-release fertiliser.

Recommended plants Various species of azalea, camellia, rhododendron, pieris, erica, berberis, photinia, viburnum, grevillea, hydrangea, deciduous trees (birch, elm, maple, ash, magnolia), conifers, hebe, felicia, correa, leptospermum.

Obtain expert local advice from professional nursery staff in order to successfully deal with the specific problems relating to the various soils of the Adelaide region.

This article was prepared with the assistance of Mr Joe Sfarra of Lasscock's Garden Centre Pty Ltd, 334 Henley Beach Road, Lockleys, SA 5032. Telephone (08) 352 2004.

BOOKS

Don Burke recommends the following gardening books.

Yates Garden Guide for Australian Gardeners, published by Fontana/Collins. Available from bookstores and some nurseries and garden centres for about $12.95.

Creating Small Gardens, by Roy Strong, published by Conran Octopus, about $20.

What Garden Pest or Disease is That?, by Judy McMaugh, published by Lansdowne Press, about $40.

What Flower is That?, by Stirling Macoboy, published by Lansdowne Press, about $60.

Encyclopedia of Australian Gardening, published by Bay Books, available in weekly parts from newsagents. Back copies available, $2.50.

Library of Australian Gardening, published by Bay Books.

The Complete Australian Gardener, published by Bay Books.

Esther Dean's Gardening Book: Growing Without Digging, by Esther Dean, published by Harper & Rowe (Australasia) and available through major bookshops.

Colour Me A Garden, by Barbara O'Leary and Margaret Hanlon-Dunn, published by Golden Press, about $40.

COMPOST

Every gardener worth his or her salt has a compost heap and a personal recipe for composting. True garden lovers rave about compost and spend long hours tending, turning and topping up their heap.

The truth of the matter is that your garden soil needs a constant application of organic matter if it is to continue to work properly. Mulching and composting are excellent ways to administer the organic matter to ensure peak performance from your garden. It is a tragic waste to take grass clippings and plant prunings to the tip, and not use them to improve your garden. But if grass clippings are put onto gardens as a mulch while still fresh, they may form an impervious crust and slow down the growth of your plants.

Suggested brewing techniques for compost First, build your compost bin. Compostologists insist that not one, but two bins are needed; one for fresh organic matter and the other for material ready for use. There is a sound base of logic here; the second heap avoids the worst problem a composter has to face—no usable compost!

Compost bins can be made of brick, fibro or concrete blocks, or can be bought in various tumbler or bin designs. Which type you use is largely a matter of choice, but most purists use home-made bins. All compost bins must be bottomless—it is essential to have contact between compost and earth.

Alternate 15cm (6″) layers of grass clippings, leaves, and so on, with 2.5cm (1″) layers of garden soil. On top of each layer of clippings and leaves, spread some fertiliser: 250g (9oz) of sulphate of ammonia, a bucket of chook manure or whatever happens to be lying about. Continue building layers until the heap is full. Keep the heap moist but not wet.

Gardeners say 'Anything that has lived once can live

again', that is, anything organic can be composted. Nonetheless, I recommend that you avoid the following: trunks of trees greater than 30cm (12") in diameter; dead household pets such as dogs or cats (budgies compost well though); bulbous weeds such as onion weed, oxalis and nut grass, and also diseased plant parts.

The following items are excellent for composting: kitchen vegie scraps, leaves, fruit peelings, tea leaves, coffee grounds, animal manures and human hair. Human hair is regarded as the best of all compost ingredients; some gardeners recommend a good handful or two to be buried under rose bushes at planting time to help future growth. And hairdressers just sweep it up and throw it away!

Within seven days or so the heap will become quite hot, as decomposition starts. As it rots down, it is a good idea to turn the heap over every other week. The compost is ready when it is crumbly and dark brown, this stage being reached in about eight weeks in warm weather, but up to five months in the cold weather.

At this point, gardeners from all over your area will converge on your backyard to critically appraise your brew. Samples are taken from throughout the heap and tested for consistency, colour, odour and the number of worms present.

Having built and filled your compost bins, you can now send in your membership application to the Royal Horticultural Society—you are a qualified gardener!

Sewage sludge composts One solution to the sewage pollution problems of our cities not only takes the material right away from areas where it can result in pollution, but also recycles it into a usable, useful substance. The most heavily populated country on earth, China, has been practicing this for centuries. Sewage sludge is combined with sawdust and other materials to produce a composted substance which can be added to garden soil as a conditioner (similar in principle to mushroom compost).

The purpose of adding the sewage sludge to composting sawdust and other materials is to create a suitable environment for micro-organisms to break the sludge down—this works in a similar way to the backyard compost heap. As the material decomposes, heat (65–68°C) is generated within the heaps and this kills off pathogens, reducing them to an acceptable level. The Sydney Water Board, for example, takes samples which are tested by the Health Department in their laboratories before the material can be released for sale. Before composting begins, the sewage sludge from treatment plants has a strong odour and attracts a lot of flies, but after it has undergone the composting process the material has an acceptable organic odour, much like ordinary compost, and no longer attracts flies.

Horticulturally, the product has many uses; in potting mixes, in soil improvement, and as a mulching material. It can be used to replace traditional organic sources, such as manures, and works very well, although it should be regarded as a soil conditioner rather than a fertiliser.

The more of this compost you buy, the more sewage sludge is treated this way rather than being pumped into the sea or otherwise wasted.

One sewage sludge product, Biogrow, is available only in New South Wales and is produced by Amgrow Pty Ltd, Telephone (047) 29 0470. Top Australia in South Australia, Telephone (08) 47 5022, produce the Gro-wel range of products, also based on treated sewage and more widely available. Do support these products as they become available in your state.

CONCRETE POTS AND PLANT GROWTH

A commonly held belief, among nursery personnel and gardeners alike, is that plants that prefer acid soils should not be planted in concrete pots. The theory behind this belief is that lime leaches out of the pots and increases the alkalinity of the potting mix. On 'Burke's Backyard' we decided to put this belief to the test, and constructed a simple, small-scale experiment to see for ourselves how concrete pots affected the plants we grew in them.

For a period of four months we grew a range of supposedly lime-sensitive plants in a collection of pots of the same size and using the same standard potting mix. The plants included azaleas, silverbeet, hostas and ivy geraniums.

We divided the pots into four groups, making sure that every sort of plant was represented in each group. The groups were as follows: fresh-from-the-mould, unpainted concrete pots (weathered pots may lose much of the lime through leaching); terracotta pots; black plastic pots; black plastic pots to which half a cup of lime per pot was added to see what symptoms of lime intolerance could be observed in plant growth.

To assess the results of the experiment we examined the plants' size, health (to see whether increased lime resulted in noticeably increased disease susceptibility), and development, both of the upper portion of the plant and of the roots. At the end of the four month period there was no appreciable difference among the different groups of plants. In fact, the root systems of the plants in the concrete pots were growing in perfect health, right up against the sides of the pots.

We also monitored the pH (the level of acidity) of the potting mix throughout the experiment. Not only did we measure the potting mix at the sides of the pot and in the middle, but we also measured the water which leached through the pot and ran out through the drainage holes. We found the pH varied only slightly during the duration of the experiment, and even in the pots to which half a cup of lime had been added there was only a half of one pH point difference. The pH of the concrete pots varied even less than that.

In summary, this experiment provided absolutely no evidence to support the theory that concrete pots make any noticeable difference to the growth of lime-sensitive plants. So the next time somebody advises you not to grow plants in a concrete pot, go ahead and try it anyway.

CUTTINGS

Have you ever found a plant in a friend's garden, or even your own, which you would love to strike for yourself from a cutting, but discarded the idea because you didn't know how to go about it? Well it isn't really all that difficult, provided you follow a few simple guidelines.

The first thing to do is select a suitable piece of the plant to strike as a cutting. Take a look at the growing tips of the plant. Usually you will be able to notice differences in the stems—firm, hard, brown or greyish wood is usually last year's growth, while bright green or reddish stems terminating in growing tips are the new season's growth. It is the new season's growth which should be used for cuttings, but not when it is very fresh and soft and wilts rapidly when cut. The ideal stage to take cuttings is when the new growth is reasonably firm, and when its leaves have grown to their full size.

Preparing the cutting The length of stem suitable for using as a cutting varies from plant to plant. For the blue-flowered streptocarpus plant, for example, it is best to cut a piece about 7.5cm (3″) in length. Cut just below a leaf junction or node at the lower end and gently clip out the tip of the shoot just above a pair of mature leaves—this will cause the growing cutting to branch at the top rather than grow tall and spindly. If tiny buds cannot be seen where the leaves join the stem, you can leave the tip on the cutting if you prefer. Remove any flowers and all the leaves below the two at the top. Streptocarpus is particularly easy to strike from cuttings.

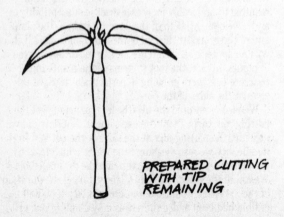

PREPARED CUTTING WITH TIP REMAINING

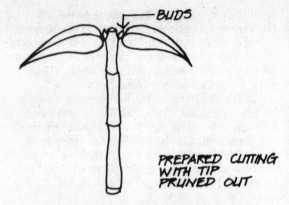

BUDS

PREPARED CUTTING WITH TIP PRUNED OUT

Planting the cutting Plant the cutting in a mixture of 50:50 sand and peat moss—*not dirt*. Don't use builders' sand—buy some propagating sand, or river sand, and wash it thoroughly to remove any fine particles. Disease organisms will not survive in this mixture, but the cutting certainly will. Put the mixture into either a brand new pot, or an old one cleaned out and washed in a solution of Dettol, or even some good old-fashioned household bleach. This will destroy any disease organisms.

Before planting the cutting, dip the bottom into a root promoting hormone powder. When you buy this hormone check the use-by date on the container carefully; it does not have a long shelf life. Make a hole in the potting mixture for each cutting. Even if you hope to end up with only one plant, put lots of cuttings in the one pot—maybe 20 streptocarpus in a 15cm (6″) pot. You can always choose the best one and throw the rest away or give them to friends. After planting the cuttings, water them in with a very fine spray, which won't dislodge them, until the potting mixture has settled.

Next place the pot in a glasshouse. If you don't have one you can make a mini-glasshouse using a clear plastic bag large enough to completely enclose the pot. Put the pot inside the bag and tie it tightly. An arch of wire can be pushed into the top of the pot to stop the bag from falling onto the plants. In six to eight weeks' time the cuttings should have developed rootballs, and at this time they can be hardened off gradually by opening the bag and leaving it for several days. The plants can then be planted out into larger individual containers. Take care to leave them in a protected, shady spot for a few weeks before exposing them to harsh sunlight.

FERTILISERS

Blood-and bone is a very safe and widely-used fertiliser for natives or other plants in your garden. Liquid fertilisers are also effective and quite safe. Nitrosol is possibly the best of these, closely followed by fish emulsion.

Aquasol is a very popular fertiliser. It is excellent but synthetic. It is crystalline in nature, but is applied mixed with water.

If you are really into natural processes, Maxicrop is a growth stimulant made from seaweed. Scientists are still debating whether it works or not, and if so, why. But some strawberry growers claim it not only makes the strawberries grow well, but makes them resistant to fungus. Vegimax is another new growth stimulant.

A garden fertiliser that everyone seems to forget is a trace element mix. Are your oranges a bit sour on the tree, your plants turning yellow, or the leaves somewhat spotted? Then you probably need to apply trace elements: they also help the plant to resist many diseases. It is best to apply fertiliser when it is raining.

FLORAL CLOCKS

While giant floral clocks are a common sight in Switzerland, they are rare in Australia. 'Burke's Backyard' observed the construction of a floral clock at the Resort Hotel Macquarie, in North Ryde, Sydney.

The land A slope of 15–30° or steeper is recommended to set the clock off. The diameter of the smallest ready-made floral clock is 3.5m (11½').

Setting up A central circular hole, lined with concrete or brick to provide waterproof housing and solid support for the 36kg (80lb) movement, is required. A lid is then fitted to cover this hole and the hands are fitted on top.

The mechanism This is two to three times stronger than a car gearbox, to withstand the pressures of strong winds, birds, and so on.

Controls The floral clock is connected underground to a master clock where adjustments can be made. Some have to be wound weekly, others have electronic controls. Accuracy is plus or minus one-tenth of a second per day.

Floral face The face is usually changed with the seasons; low growing plants with a tidy habit are recommended. For a low maintenance face, materials such as bark or gravel are recommended, with ceramic figures. If maintenance is not a problem, however, a larger number of flowering plants could be used and numbers could be made from hedged plants.

Cost A floral clock will cost $10 000 for materials, and about $10 000 more for installation and landscaping. There is also ongoing maintenance and replanting to consider.

For further information

Mechanisms for floral clocks can be obtained from Hertz Electronics, 539 Glenmore Road, Edgecliff, NSW 2027. Telephone (02) 32 3029.

FROST DAMAGE

If you understand the way that frost and cold air move, you can do a lot to minimise the damage that they cause.

Areas that are high up are less affected by cold air. Cold air accumulates in the lower areas of a garden because it is more dense than warm air. It rolls along the ground and collects in low spots. One of the first ways to reduce the danger of frosts is to plant in the higher parts of your backyard, and not in the low pockets that collect the cold air.

It is not advisable to form a barrier with a row of plants across the lowest area in the garden, as it will collect the cold air by damming it up.

To help keep plants alive, place them under eaves and trees, as frost doesn't form there as badly, if at all. Another good position is against a north-facing masonry wall, which will radiate heat at night, minimising frost.

It is not the freezing of the plant cells during the night that does the damage, it's the fast thaw in the morning when it warms up. One way of preventing extreme damage to plants is to put an automatic watering system on very early in the morning, maybe before dawn.

There are a number of products available to lessen the effect of winter on your plants. A new product is Agronet, a very fine netting which lets the air through but is claimed to reduce damage to your plants. It is available as a plastic sleeve that can be pulled down over your plants and tied at the top.

There is also a form of broad sheeting that is suitable for putting over gardens or vegetables. It is available in a home package for about $14.

It is also possible to make your own wire frame and put a plastic bag over it.

GARDEN ASTROLOGY

What we see through a telescope can certainly inform us about planetary movements and positions, but can stargazing actually tell us anything about gardening, and if so, how? Can the stars determine our suitability as gardeners? Will they tell us what and when to plant most successfully? When Reg Livermore consulted well-known and prominent astrologer Garry Wiseman on the subject, he provided the following observations:

'I have found that gardeners are very affectionate and caring sorts of people and I think that plants respond very well to love. A lot of gardeners seem to have become a bit cheesed off with people and they find plants much more honest, in a way. I've also found that gardeners are very intuitive and they can set up a kind of psychic communication with plants, so they can really understand them.

'A person from any of the 12 signs can be a gardener as long as they have that balance of a loving, affectionate nature. Sagittarians [Reg Livermore's star sign] aren't really patient enough for gardening but Sagittarius is an

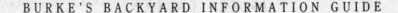
outdoor sign. There are more Cancerians and, especially, Taureans who are gardeners.

'Certain signs do appear to be more suited to growing particular plants than others. There seem to be a lot of Leo rose growers around and I think this is because the rose is a very Leo type of plant. It's like a king or a queen in its proud stance. Leo is the lion, which is the king or queen of beasts. Leo human beings prefer to be treated like aristocracy too. So when you're growing roses treat them nicely and they will reward you handsomely. But treat them roughly and you're going to get scratched on their thorns, which are like the lion's claws. The rose is the symbol of love, and no one loves love more than the Leos. So there are two connections between Leos and roses, love and aristocracy.

'It is possible to provide some astrological tips for growing roses, too. The sign of Leo is ruled by the sun, and roses just love the sun. They lap it up if you make sure they receive several hours of full sunlight a day. They don't like things to be too dark and damp. June is the usual time for planting roses, although in the colder climates the first week of July is probably better.

'Some other plants also relate to particular star signs. I think daffodils have a very strong Gemini quality, as they are so versatile and adaptable. Like Geminis they're here, there and everywhere like the Scarlet Pimpernel. As for poppies, we associate them with remembrance and Cancerians love to remember the past. So poppies are very Cancerian and they're one of the few flowers that seem to have an edible part (in this case, the seeds). Cancer people love their food and so that provides another very strong connection between the flower and the sign.

'Don Burke was born on July 16. His chart shows him to be a pretty fair gardener as you would imagine. He is a Cancerian, which is a maternal sign, so he is inclined to nurture and mother his plants. He's definitely one of the psychic gardeners and is very tuned in. He and I could actually swap places. We're both born on July 16. I could just grow a beard and he could shave his off. And if he ever needs another job he would be very good in my profession.'

GARDEN HOSE LEVEL

Water is an excellent measuring tool for finding levels; a continuous body of water always settles on a level surface. When the Egyptians built the pyramids they used a system of water-filled trenches to help them measure a level base on which to erect those mighty structures. You may not have contemplated something quite so grandiose in your backyard, but there are many purposes for which a level surface is required—such as when laying a patio, preparing a spot for a garden shed, or before planting a flat lawn.

The only tools you need are a couple of stakes about 1.5m (5') long, a measuring tape, water from a hose, and a length of clear plastic tube about 4-5m (13-16') long. The latter is quite inexpensive (just a few dollars) and can be purchased from hardware, pet or aquarium shops.

Procedure Decide which point of the yard is at the level you want the whole area to be. Hammer one stake into the ground at this point, and another stake at any other point.

Attach each end of the tube to the side of each of the stakes. Fill the tube with water by holding the hose over one end—keep running water through the tube until all air bubbles have been removed.

Measure the distance on the first stake from the top of the water to the soil surface. Go to the second stake and repeat the procedure. To make the soil around the second stake the same level as the soil around the first, you will need to either dig out or fill in the soil around the second stake until the measurement there equals the measurement at the first stake.

After equalling the two measurements, move the second stake to another position and repeat the procedure. Leave the first stake untouched. Eventually, when enough adjustments to levels around the second stake have been made, the site will have an even surface.

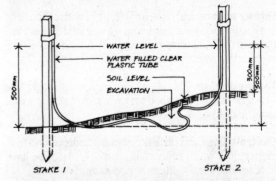

GARDEN PATHS—MOSS PROBLEMS

The first thing to do when trying to eradicate moss or algae from your garden path is to physically remove the substances already present. Scrub off with stiff bristled brushes or brooms, or a gerni, and then use one of the products available to kill off the moss or algae.

Household bleach in a bucket of water works well, but once the bleach is gone, the moss or algae is free to grow back in a few hours.

There is now a better way. One of the products on the market is Path-Free, a copper compound, which is applied to the area of paving to prevent algae or moss regrowing. Apply by putting 150ml into a 9-litre (2 gallon) bucket of water, stirring well and applying to the cleaned surface. This should keep the area clear for 2-3 months.

Another product on the market is Thompson's Water Seal. These products should be available at Mitre 10, BBC Hardware, McEwens, K-Mart stores, larger independent hardware stores and most nurseries.

GARDEN TOOLS

The tools you select to use in the garden determine how good a job you do, and also whether you damage your arms or back.

The most basic implement for use in the garden is a fork. If a good quality wooden handled fork is looked after well, for example, by regularly oiling the handle, it will last forever and perform well. It is important to care for your tools and not leave them out in the weather.

Spades It is preferable to buy a wooden handled one, as a metal handle will jar your arm and back each time you dig with it.

Trowels are very useful for smaller jobs. Some trowels bend at the junction of handle and blade. Check this before you buy.

Bow saw The best cutting implement for use in the backyard. The blades are extremely sharp and will cut through the boughs of trees very easily. When it starts to blunt, simply throw the blade away and insert a new one.

Secateurs Always buy the best; a more expensive pair will outlast a cheaper version. Some good brands are Wilkinson Sword, MBL or Felco. Try them out, and make sure they fit your hand before you buy them.

If you need to do fine pruning, a pair of bonsai pruners is excellent. These cost $70 or more.

The most useful cutting implement you can have in a backyard is an old kitchen knife that may have had the point broken off. It is great for weeding, as you can slip it under the crown of the weeds and lift them out.

GRAFTED PLANTS

If you select a grafted plant at your local nursery, there's one thing you can be certain of—it probably won't be very cheap. But there is a good reason for this, and it does make sense to invest the extra money. The labour intensive practice of grafting offers numerous advantages.

The *rose bush* is one of the best examples of the benefits of grafting, as it is probably the most commonly grafted plant anywhere in the world. Tough old briar plants, which would normally be awful weeds, are used as the 'understock'. The tops of the plants, just above the soil level, are removed and shoots of a pretty variety of rose are joined to the remaining stump. The reason is simple. Roses are highly bred plants and the price we have paid for this is a decline in vigour. The problem can be overcome by grafting them onto close relatives with strong, vigorous root systems. The end result is a combination of beauty and hardiness.

Citrus plants are also grafted, and again the plants chosen for the understock would otherwise be thorn covered weeds. Another part of the reason for grafting citrus is that they are difficult to propagate successfully by other means. And even if they are grown from seeds or cuttings they tend to have disease-prone roots. Understock plants are chosen for their resistance to root rot and other problems.

The grafted *passionfruit* demonstrates another of the reasons for grafting plants. It may seem strange to bother with grafting a plant as common and easy to grow as the passionfruit, but there are two benefits. Passionfruit are short-lived, and by grafting them onto longer-lived rootstocks they will last for several more years. Also, passionfruit are not well suited to cold climates, but a cold tolerant rootstock allows them to grow in cooler areas.

Grafted *avocados* offer many advantages over those grown from seed. Seedling avocados often grow into quite large trees, whereas grafted varieties are available that remain compact and low growing. Grafted varieties usually fruit within two to four years, whereas those grown from seed may take up to 20 years to bear fruit.

Grafting can also be used to create beautiful and unusual plants that don't occur naturally. Many *fruit trees* will not bear fruit unless they are within insect range of another variety with which they can crosspollinate. Grafting can produce a single tree with two or three different varieties on the one trunk. The result is a whole orchard on one tree. Lovely feature plants can be created by grafting weeping or groundcover plants onto tall stems or even sapling trees. Who has not admired the billowing cascade of a standard rose in full bloom? Several forms of groundcover grevillea can be grafted onto the tree form of the genus Grevillea, the silky oak, with stunning results. Similarly, weeping maples are grafted onto maple varieties that would have grown into trees. Grafted maples can cost about $85 each, but the time and work involved in growing beautiful specimens makes them worth every cent.

The approach graft Few home gardeners consider themselves sufficiently skilful or experienced to perform successful budding and grafting. The approach graft is so simple and straightforward that even the complete beginner with no background knowledge of plant propagation will be rewarded with a high success rate. The reason for this is that both plants remain attached to their own root systems until after the graft has formed and healed.

To perform the graft, place the understock plant and the scion (new top) close together. Using a razor blade or scalpel, cut a 2.5cm (1″) long strip of bark from both plants then tie the two stems firmly together with budding tape. It is not necessary to align the growth zones (cambial tissues) in each plant. As both plants are still supported by their own root systems, callus (repair) tissue forms quickly around the wounded area and some of this differentiates into cambium.

Kelpie means 'water spirit' and is a favourite word of Scottish shepherds.

Approach graft of two potted plants Approach grafts heal in about 6-12 weeks and can be performed at any time of the year. Healing and growth occur more rapidly from September to February, while response in winter tends to be poor. The two plants being grafted should be placed side by side. A sliver of bark 2½cm (1 inch) should be removed from each stem, and they then should be bound together tightly with budding tape. Removal of the budding tape, (6 to 12 weeks later), will reveal a white, cauliflower-like substance along the healed graft union.

After the graft union has healed, the top of the understock is removed flush with the top of the graft while the scion is severed immediately below the graft. The original base of the scion will continue to grow just as though pruned. The graft union should be re-taped for initial support and the newly grafted plant should be tightly tied to a stake at the union of scion and understock. Foliage should not be removed from the understock until the scion is growing vigorously.

The approach graft works for any plant that can be grafted.

1 WOUNDED PLANTS TAPED TOGETHER

2 AFTER HEALING TOP OF UNDERSTOCK AND BASE OF SCION ARE SEVERED

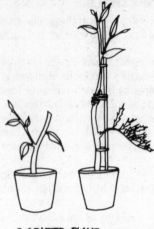

3 GRAFTED PLANT SUPPORTED FIRMLY BY STAKE

An example of grafting In one segment of 'Burke's Backyard', after pointing out the still-visible graft line on a 50-100 year old weeping beech tree grafted onto an ordinary beech trunk, Don gave some reasons for plant grafting and some pointers on purchasing grafted ornamental trees.

Why are plants grafted?
* For reliability—they may not be weeping if grown from seed.
* Because they may not grow from cuttings.
* For stronger root stocks—the example shown was a lilac grafted onto a privet rootstock for additional vigour.
* For ornamental purposes—a weeping tree can be created from a standard stock of some height. The weeping plant grows out and down.

Hints:
Choose the tallest possible grafted weeping standard tree. It is never going to grow beyond the height of the original graft. Remove suckers below the graft or they might take over from the tree on top.

GREEN MANURE

Green manure is a term used to describe plant crops grown by farmers, not for the purpose of harvesting seeds, fruits or vegetables, but simply for ploughing back into the ground, usually just before these plants reach maturity.

Like animal manures, the plant material adds vital organic matter to the soil. Once incorporated in the soil, the green manure breaks down and produces the same result as large scale composting. The green manure crop shown on 'Burke's Backyard' included millet and cow peas.

Of course, the same principle applies to backyard gardens. Regular additions of composted organic matter are vital for maintaining healthy, productive soils.

GROWING GIANT VEGIES

Jim Pike visited the spectacular vegetable garden of Mrs Eileen Chappel, world record holder for the largest cucumber (28.8kg—63½lb) and runner bean (6.8kg—15lb). At her Brisbane home giant pumpkins can also be found— she produced one of 210kg (463lb) for Expo.

Born and raised on the land, Mrs Chappel's interest in giant vegies was aroused by her membership of an organic gardening club. Her record-breaking hobby is just one aspect of her fascinating life; she lists tango dancing, ventriloquism, performing magic shows, visiting hospitals for the Red Cross and conducting occupational therapy classes among her interests.

Mrs Chappel's show-stopping vegies are a little tough by the time they are harvested, but make excellent pickles and relishes for charity fund-raising.

She attributes the secret of her success to horse manure, garden clippings, just the right amount of water and tender loving care. Mrs Chappel covers the vegies to protect them against storms, hail or too much sun, and does not grow the same vegetable in the same soil in successive years.

When told that a 30kg (66lb) cucumber would be a miracle, she made that her next goal. If vegies can be motivated by vitality and enthusiasm for hard work, Mrs Chappel is just the person to do it.

GROWING PLANTS FROM SEEDS

Growing plants from seeds is one of the most rewarding and pleasurable of garden activities. But while the enormous range of shapes, sizes and colours certainly makes seeds interesting, their complexity also leads to confusion over harvesting and planting techniques. Planting some seeds, such as beans, is simply a matter of poking them into the ground and waiting for a shoot to appear. But there are many others that require more substantial background knowledge to achieve results.

When growing many sorts of plants from seeds, even humble vegetables, there are a few tricks that will improve the chances of success. For example, if you grow a tomato plant that bears outstandingly well and tastes great, save an old fruit until it is completely ripe and fairly soft. Scoop out the seeds and throw them into a bottle, fill it up with water and ferment this mixture for two or three weeks. Pour off all the rotten liquid and the seeds will remain at the bottom. You can dry them out, store them in a cool dry place and sow them at your leisure.

Most vegetable seeds, and also those of some fruits, can be saved for following seasons. You can grow orange trees, for example, from orange pips, although they will take several years to fruit.

Mangoes Without question, the best fruit tree to grow from seed is the mango. The Bowen mango produces a cluster of seedlings from each seed, and as this plant is poly-embryonic (that is, the seed produces seedlings that are genetically identical to the parent plant) you grow Bowen mango seedlings from a Bowen mango seed—not some unidentified crossbred plant.

Avocados Avoid growing avocados from seed. They take seven to 20 years to bear fruit after the seeds are planted, and even then they may not bear good quality fruit and are likely to have grown into very large trees. A grafted avocado from a nursery is a much wiser choice.

Kentia palms can be grown from seed, but if you sow the green ones only about one in three will germinate. If you wait until the seeds are an orange-yellow-green colour you will find almost all of them will grow, but they do take from six months to two years to germinate.

Ferns will reward you with fantastic results if you pick the fronds that have little brown lumps on the back. Put them inside a paper bag, dry them out for a week, and the brown dust that remains is the spores. These are not actually seeds, as ferns reproduce differently to flowering plants, but they serve the same purpose. This technique can be used with all sorts of ferns, including staghorns.

Native plants Many native plants are very difficult to grow from seed. If you turn your back on a favourite grevillea you can guarantee that will be the moment when the seed capsules (which follow the flower after it has died away) will open and release their seeds, to be lost in the soil or mulch. The way to avoid this is to wait until the flower is starting to die off, then tie it up in the toe of an old nylon stocking with a little plant tie. Then when the seeds fall out they're caught, and you can sow them when you wish.

Another tip for growing native plants: if you're going to grow wattles from seeds, put your seeds in a pyrex dish, pour boiling water over them, leave them overnight, and sow the next day. The boiling water simulates the heat of a bushfire, which prompts wattle germination in the bush.

Sow all seeds into a simple 50:50 mixture of sand and peat moss. Cover them with the same mix by one or two times their own diameter. Very tiny seeds can be spread more evenly over the surface of the seed-raising mix if you mix them up with some ordinary sand and sprinkle the mixture over the pot.

After watering the pot, cover it with some sort of clinging plastic wrap, which will turn the pot into a miniature glasshouse. After the seeds have sprouted you can lift the plastic away and resume watering the seeds, regularly but lightly.

Lastly, if you decide to grow vegetables and flowers from seeds, do read the instructions on the packet—these will be your best guide to achieving good results. The *Yates Garden Guide* is an excellent reference source available to people who wish to grow plants from seed. It can be purchased from most bookstores for about $13.

HYDROPONICS AND HYDROCULTURE

Hydroponic plant growing techniques don't involve the use of soil. There are several different forms, but in all of them the plants receive their nutrients in solution. The roots of the plants either sit directly in the solution or are watered with it at intervals. In liquid culture the plants are supported above the solution, into which the roots grow directly. Media culture is where the roots grow into some sort of inert material such as gravel, sand, expanded clay, perlite, rockwool or wood shavings, to name but a few, and are watered with the nutrient solution.

The plant roots need oxygen, otherwise they will rot. This is achieved by such methods as keeping the nutrient solution shallow, aerating it, irrigating with it intermittently, spraying it onto the roots in a mist, and so on.

Several different hydroponics kits are available for indoor and backyard use. The kit that appeared in our story was manufactured by Luwasa Hydroculture.

Advantages Plants not grown in soil are free of soil-borne diseases. Hydroponics kits usually have regulatory gauges that indicate when and how much nutrient solution should be added. In commercial nurseries of the conventional kind, regulation of plant nutrient requirements and maintaining the correct chemical balance requires much technical skill and knowledge. Due to the design of hydroponics pots and the moisture retentive properties of the media used to fill them, most hydroponics kits may be left unattended for a number of weeks before extra solution needs to be added. This enables owners to take holidays without first arranging to have their plants watered constantly by a friend or relative. Greater uniformity of plant growth is made possible by controlled use of appropriately balanced nutrients. Quite large plants can be grown in relatively small pots, so you can grow large specimens without the expense and the cumbersome bulk of an equally large pot.

Disadvantages The initial cost is high, because of the specialised nature of the container, gauges and solution. Great accuracy is required in preparing the nutrient solution, as nutrient deficiencies and toxicities occur readily. Algae growth in the solution or on the media is not uncommon and this competes with the potted plant for air and nutrients.

For further information

Contact your local Department of Agriculture or Primary

Industries for information about the commercial and backyard hobby use of hydroponic systems. The New South Wales Department of Agriculture and Fisheries produces an informative sheet, *Hydroponics—Growing Plants Without Soil*, Agfact AC 13, second edition 1988, which may be purchased for $2.00 plus postage. Telephone (02) 217 6666 for details.

Luwasa Hydroculture (Australia) Pty Ltd
18 Rosebery Road
Kellyville NSW 2153
Telephone (02) 629 2311

Other Luwasa Hydroculture contact numbers are: Victoria (03) 466 2444, Queensland (07) 376 2744, South Australia (08) 354 0200, Western Australia (09) 446 5155.

LANDSCAPER

The work of Gary McLachlan, landscaper, was featured in an article in *Australian House and Garden*, in November 1987, as well as on 'Burke's Backyard'. You can contact him direct for further information about his work.

Gary McLachlan
The Orangery
62 Davies Road
Claremont WA 6008

LANDSCAPING

Once you have decided to landscape your backyard, the obvious decision to be made is whether to do it yourself or to employ a team of professional landscapers to do the job. One backyard which we looked at on 'Burke's Backyard' was originally estimated to cost $55 000 ($37 000 for the general landscaping work and $18 000 for a prestige swimming pool). The main elements involved were:

* existing sandstone pavers to be replaced with brick pavers
* existing pergola to be removed and replaced by a new, larger version
* existing barbecue to be replaced
* a swimming pool to be designed and constructed
* a grassy area for relaxation to be established around the pool
* the problems associated with the sloping block to be addressed, by terracing the backyard into two separate levels and installing a retaining wall
* creation of garden areas using brick edging and various other constructional features

The major impact on the backyard during the job was the installation of the swimming pool. Fortunately, in this case no major rock outcrops or other problems were discovered. Once the concrete shell of the pool was in place, it was the ideal time to install the essential drainage system, both around the pool and in the garden.

The paving around the pool was one of the most important aspects of the whole job. As a general rule, if bricks aren't laid correctly they may settle over the years and cause accidents, or even flooding, around the house. In this example—and in any instance where a swimming pool is surrounded by a large amount of paving—there will always be the problem of getting rid of water that is shed from the pool. A solution to this was shown in the form of an open drain, which has a specially designed cast iron grate that sits on the top of the drain. If the drain ever blocks, the relevant grate section can be lifted out and the blockage hosed away.

Lawns were installed—buffalo grass at the back where it is shady, and couch grass in the sun near the pool. The most important part of a lawn is the edge. The type of edging shown was brick. To lay the brick edging, a trench 150–200mm (6–7¾″) deep was dug, into which was laid 50mm (2″) of good stiff concrete. Some wire reinforcement was then placed in the concrete and the bricks were then mortared on top of it. It is important to note that mortar was used in the gaps between the bricks to avoid the possibility of jamming edging devices between them when the lawn was being cut and edged.

The final cost of the project was $64 000, that is, $9000 over the original budget. This additional cost was caused by the owners' decision to spend an extra $2000 on the pool and an extra $7000 to install an automatic sprinkler system.

The project was designed and constructed by Joanne Green Landscape Design Pty Ltd, 313 Barrenjoey Road, Newport, NSW 2106. Telephone (02) 979 5363.

LONG, NARROW BACKYARDS

A backyard 90m (300′) long by 6m (20′) wide, bare of anything but a few large trees, and well shaded by those and the trees in neighbouring yards, is hardly the stuff ideal backyards are made of. Yet it is possible to turn such an uninspiring, barren sliver of ground into an enticing garden of mystery; an idyllic retreat from the rush and bustle of city life.

A garden shown in one segment of 'Burke's Backyard' had undergone just such a transformation in only three years. The first step taken by the owners was to lay out a meandering path that snakes its way down the length of the yard to the compact vegetable garden, which was planted in the sunniest spot at the bottom of the garden. The path ends in a loop around a space-saving weeping mulberry tree, beside which a well-positioned garden seat entices the wanderer to pause and enjoy the peace and quiet of the garden for a few moments.

Another ingenious idea was to construct a gazebo halfway down the garden. The brightly painted gazebo has doorways on both sides and the central garden path runs straight through it. As a garden feature the gazebo is both eye-catching, with its carnival-like paintwork, and

functional, providing a convenient setting for outdoor meals.

Plants that thrive in the dappled shade created by the overhanging trees are hydrangeas, impatiens, plumbago, Japanese maples, May bush, pentas, murraya, and the softly perfumed native mint bush. However, this blend of plants was not providing much in the way of colour when we filmed the story in late summer. Without a splash of colour the abundance of dark foliage tends to give the garden a slightly closed, heavy atmosphere.

The plant we chose to brighten the garden was a dwarf variety of impatiens, 'Salmon Blush'. Use of large numbers of one type and colour of plant introduces a restful note of cohesion and continuity, simultaneously lightening the tone of the garden. Blobs of the chosen colour here and there among the other plants can work well, but an especially effective arrangement in a garden of this nature is to line the path with the plants to define its lazy twists and turns.

One last feature of the yard we showed was a mini-swimming pool, complete with continuous water jets, which make full scale swimming possible in an area only a few times larger than a bathtub.

Probably the most important lesson to be learned from this type of backyard is that you can work with and even emphasise the special character of the area available to you, rather than attempting to deal with it as if it were a standard garden. The second major lesson is that even if your backyard is of more conventional dimensions, it may be time to re-examine smaller narrow areas like the side passage or the strip beside the garage or drive, to see whether there might be something interesting and imaginative you can do with it after all.

MOSSING ROCKS

A rich emerald carpet of moss will enhance a rockery or stone-edging by softening and ageing even the freshest rocks. Moss adds character and charm, helps the rocks to blend in with their surroundings, lends definition to the contours of the rocks and, above all, provides that highly valued quality—a natural appearance.

The transformation of stark rocks and raw concrete begins with the collection of moss. Roadsides, ditches and areas around railway stations are likely sources, but take note of the aspect where the moss is growing and the amount of shade and moisture it receives each day. If there is too great a contrast between the microclimate of that location and your rockery, the moss may not survive. Don't try to grow moss in a dry, sunny, exposed position. Take a breadboard and a paint scraper or a kitchen knife with you, slide the scraper or knife under the moss and lift slabs of it onto the breadboard, on which it can be carried back to the garden.

Needless to say, moss should never be taken from forests or bushland areas, as this disturbs the ecosystem and may even endanger rare mosses.

Before applying the moss, soak it thoroughly with water and then squash it flat using the paint scraper. The moss should be squashed as flat as possible without fear of damaging it. This makes it easier to lift the moss and mould it to the shape of the rocks or across the concrete joins, and helps to prevent it from lifting away from those surfaces and drying out after a few days.

Water the moss regularly but very gently, so as not to disturb it, for several weeks. Some of the moss can be expected to die, but eventually most will take root on the rocks and should thrive if protected from extended exposure to direct sun and watered regularly.

Another trick for softening the appearance of stark, raw rocks is to paint them with some old, stale milk. This provides a food base for various sorts of algae to establish themselves, and within a matter of weeks the rocks will look as if they have been in position for years.

Potentially hazardous, unwanted moss and algae on paths can be removed using a copper-based product called Path-Free. Brush it onto the paths and they will remain clear of these plants for weeks at a time.

MULCHERS

Inevitably, if you have a backyard, you will have a few prunings to get rid of and there is no better way to do this than to mulch them and turn them into something useful. Large commercial mulchers do the job rapidly and efficiently, but the backyarder rarely has access to them. Fortunately, there is a series of domestic models for use in your own backyard. On 'Burke's Backyard' we tested some of them.

We tested the machines by feeding them gum tree material divided into different groups according to the thickness of the stems (the finest were less than pencil thickness, the thickest were 2.5cm (1″) in diameter). We also fed the machines some typical garden rubbish and leaves from a banana tree. Each of those types of material was put through each machine and the results were monitored.

It is critical when operating this sort of machinery to take safety precautions: wear a pair of goggles and a good solid pair of gloves.

The results of our test, with ratings out of 10, were as follows:

Tas Tanaka, two-stroke petrol engine
Price $695–$700
Availability Available nationally through various outlets.
Performance This machine was easy to start and very easy to clear when blocked; among its best features are the simple clips that secure the top of the machine in place. It did block when fed with moist material. It was very difficult to collect the mulch in a box under the outlet chute as it tended to spray everywhere. This machine has

no wheels, which makes moving it difficult, but it sits on the ground with a fair degree of stability. The chute for coarse material was awkwardly located.
Rating: 8

Black & Decker Shredder, electric motor
Price $339 upwards
Availability Available nationally through hardware and department stores.
Performance Being electrical, this machine was much quieter than the Tas Tanaka. Like the previous machine it lacked wheels, which reduced its manoeuvreability. It was resistant to stalling, but did eventually stall with moist material. The top chute is particularly well designed—the best of those we tried. The quality of the mulch it produced was excellent. Tools were provided with the machine, including the Allen key required for the bolt that fastens the top section.
Rating: 8½

Rover Muncher, electric motor
Price $279–$300
Availability Available nationally through mower dealers and major department stores.
Performance This machine demonstrated its excellence and outstanding value for money in our test. It was relatively quiet and was the only machine that did not clog when wet material was fed through it. The mulch was easily collected in a garbage bin fitted under the chute. The machine has wheels for easy moving, although there was no handle. The top of the machine was reasonably easy to open, but you could possibly lose the nuts after opening it.
Rating: 9½

Chipper Chopper, electric motor
Price $429–$509
Availability Available nationally through various outlets.
Performance This machine sprayed mulch everywhere, which made collection very difficult. It clogged frequently, particularly on wet material, and was difficult to clear once clogged. It does have wheels, although it is not easy to manoeuvre. Possibly the best feature of this mulcher is its very large input chute for coarse material.
Rating: 6

Moulin Mulcher, mower attachment
Price $240–$250
Availability Available nationally through mower dealers.
Performance This relatively new invention is a base plate that is clamped to your own lawnmower. The blades of your mower do the mulching. It is designed to fit either a Victa or a Rover mower but the manufacturers of these two brands do not endorse the product. The mulcher is secured to the mower using two bolts, which could cause

some rust on the frame of a pressed metal mower, and the wear and tear on the blades has not been assessed. Heavy woody material used in our test was only pushed through and scraped a little, but leafy material resulted in good quality mulch—although this mulcher was much slower to feed than the ordinary mulchers. A handy poker is supplied.

This is a clever concept, but for this amount of money it might be easier to simply rake garden leaves and rubbish together on the lawn and roar over the top of it with your mower. Most of the chopped material will be sucked up into the catcher and can simply be applied to the garden directly.

MULCHES

Mulch is the most important single ingredient of low maintenance gardening. The Almighty mulches all his forests with the natural leaf litter that falls—and you must admit He made some nice bits of greenery. Mulch suppresses weeds, keeps the soil warm in winter and cool in summer, insulates the soil against water loss, encourages myriads of beneficial soil organisms (worms, for example), improves soil structure and drainage, and adds nutrients to the soil.

What is mulch? It is simply a surface-covering for the soil. Normally, it is made up of pine bark, tanbark leaves, compost or shredded wood, although some people use gravel or even sawdust. A mulch should be around 7–10cm (3–4″) thick and it will probably need topping up once a year. This is because some of it rots away, some is blown about by the wind and the other 90% is usually buried by the dog, or used by the kids for mulch fights!

A properly mulched garden on an average suburban block should require only about four hours' weeding per year.

What about black plastic? In the dark ages (1970–78) gardeners and some landscapers used black plastic sheeting underneath the mulch to give total weed suppression. This plastic caused many problems. It starved the soil of oxygen, causing root dieback in the garden plants; the mulch slid off it in patches to reveal the ugly black plastic itself; and the plastic tore to permit weeds to grow through anyway. We now know that mulch alone stops most of the weeds, and the few that poke through can be squirted with Zero. See 'Glyphosate Herbicides'.

PEAT

When the Creature from the Black Lagoon looms up out of the water in a horror movie, the odds are it is bursting out of a peat bog. The peat moss that you use in your potting mix or in the garden comes from bogs, and once harvested it is a remarkably versatile and widely used product.

Peat is organic matter of geological origin (excluding coal), formed from dead plant-remains in water and in the absence of air. It occurs in bogs, swamplands and marshes.

Peat is a finite resource. In Australia we have peat supplies that will last a few hundred years. In Europe, countries such as Germany, Belgium, the Netherlands and Denmark have drained and cut away virtually all their commercial peatlands.

Imported peat generally comes from mosses. Australian varieties are mostly sedge peats, but a sphagnum moss peat farm is in operation in Tasmania.

Peat in history Peat mining in northern Europe has unearthed some grizzly discoveries. Humans were sacrificed in fertility rites and their bodies were thrown into peat bogs as long ago as 2400 years. Known as 'bog people', nearly 700 of those remains have now come to light. Peat moss has remarkable preservative qualities and the body tissues of these remains, including fine details of skin texture, veins and arteries, hair, and the contents of the stomach, appear virtually unchanged.

Cut and dried sods of peat moss have been used to insulate farmers' cottages and fuel hearths. American Indians used bog plants in food, medicine and for making tea, and they used dried sphagnum moss from peat bogs as nappies for their babies.

Dried sphagnum moss was used as a surgical dressing in the First World War because of its absorbency. Peat has also been used in this century as an alternative source of industrial energy. In the 1930s the Soviet Union introduced a process of milling peat that enabled them to run trains and factories on peat fuel during World War II.

Medical applications of peat go back to ancient times and in the nineteenth century mud baths of peat were used to treat rheumatic diseases in fashionable European spas.

In Scotland's Outer Hebrides the island's weavers have long used peat and bog plants to dye their famous tweeds.

Harvesting Traditional peat mining methods involve draining the swamp and drying the peat prior to harvesting. The sedge swamp where the 'Burke's Backyard' story was filmed is subject to various conservation requirements, stipulated by government departments and designed to ensure that the swamp is maintained as a viable wetland habitat for native birds and animals. Unique 'wet' mining methods have had to be developed.

The peat is dug from the deposit by a dredge floating on the swamp surface. The dredge cuts the peat from the deposit and mixes it with water to form a slurry, which is pumped from the swamp by the dredge via a pipeline. The peat slurry is pumped over a series of screens, which removes the peat fibre from the slurry and directs the water with silt contaminants into settling tanks. After the silt has settled, the clean water is returned to the swamp and the wet peat fibre is passed through a filter press to further reduce the water content. After drying, the peat passes through a mill, which reduces the fibre length to the desired range with minimal damage to its structure. The peat is then ready to be processed into the familiar products we see on our garden centre and nursery shelves.

Uses in the garden If potting mixes and soils are to work effectively, they need some sort of organic additive. Any form of organic additive will enable potting mixes and soils to hold moisture and air, both of which are essential. Peat moss is without question the best organic additive available.

Peat is dug into garden beds or before lawns are laid as a soil improver, used with soil to top-dress established lawns, incorporated in potting mixes, combined with sand to make an ideal cutting or seed-raising mix, and used as a surface mulch.

Australian peat moss is regarded as a particularly good variety although it may not last quite as long as some of the overseas types.

Commercial uses Peat is widely used in horticultural industries in plant production, landscaping, revegetation, mushroom production and vegetable production.

PERMACULTURE

Permaculture is the creation and the design of self-sustaining and productive landscapes.

An example of permaculture is fruit trees growing in a chook pen. The chooks' role is to manure the fruit trees and remove fruit-fly by eating the larvae and pupae. They shred all the waste, taking the seeds out and mixing it up with manure so that it can be put on the garden. The chooks clean up the whole area.

Newspaper can be used to cut down work in the garden. If there is a weed problem, lay newspaper down quite thickly, overlapping it well so that weeds like kikuyu can't creep through. As long as it is never disturbed, those weeds will not grow. On top of the newspaper put manure, worm castings, compost, straw, hay and lawn clippings and then it is ready to plant.

When harvesting lettuce, do not pick the best one. Let it go to seed and it will self-sow in the mulch.

By making good use of a small block you can reduce the chances of particular pest attacks on anything at all. Although you will have productive plants with their associated pests, other flowering plants will encourage the predators of those pests. An orange tree may harbour a praying mantis, a ladybird and a spider, all of which would be preying on the creatures that come to eat the orange tree.

Although most scientists would disagree, Bill Mollison

claimed in this interview that a commercial farm using heavy pesticides loses between 9% and 17% of its crop to pests. In a mixed system, using no pesticides, he claims that the expected loss is no more than 4%.

Companion planting is also very important. It can be very simple; for instance, planting lucerne between cotton will reduce the incidence of some pests. It can also be very complicated. If you grow an apple tree, you should choose all its friends to grow with it. Plant marigolds (only the dwarf variety has been shown to be effective) to reduce nematodes, and carrots or dill to attract specific wasps to the tree. Also grow lots of flowers under the tree, so that it is well pollinated. Six species, put together for distinct reasons, form a strong guild. If root rot is affecting avocados, planting bananas around the avocado may actually control the root rot by controlling soil moisture.

The above information was given to us by Bill Mollison, who has written a book entitled *Permaculture: A Designer's Manual*, published by Tagari Publications, PO Box 1, Tyalgum, NSW 2484. It costs about $70.

PLANTING SUCCESSFULLY

Remove the grass for a diameter of at least 2m (6') around the planting position and dig a large hole, turning all the soil over. The plant needs to be able to send its roots out into the surrounding soil to grow well. Try to maintain the 2m diameter so that grass doesn't grow right up to the plant, causing it to be damaged by the lawnmower.

Check the soil for beetles or beetle larvae, the white curl grubs, that could eat the roots of the plant. If they are present it may be necessary to use a lawn beetle spray after planting.

To prepare for planting, fork the soil over the area of the hole. It is advisable to wear shoes to protect your feet, not thongs, when using a garden fork.

Once the area is turned over, add organic matter (planting mixture, compost, potting mix or whatever). Spread it over the surface of the soil a few centimetres deep, and fork it in. This will improve the soil and it will hold moisture better, enabling the plant to establish itself quickly.

The soil in the hole should now be 2.5–5cm (1–2") above the surrounding ground. This is essential for good drainage, particularly if the surrounding ground is compacted.

Dig a hole for the plant in the centre of the pit. Take the plant out of the pot and look at the root system. The roots should be growing down so they will not tangle as the plant establishes. With a garden knife, make three vertical cuts, equally spaced about 1.25cm (½") deep down the sides of the rootball. This will cut any roots circling around the outside and stop knots forming as the roots grow.

Put the plant in the hole and push the soil up to it. Sculpt the soil by hilling it up around the plant and forming a depression close around the plant as well as at the base of the hill. These depressions will collect the water.

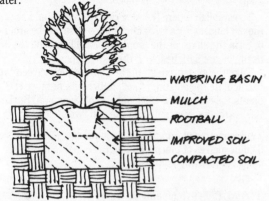

- WATERING BASIN
- MULCH
- ROOTBALL
- IMPROVED SOIL
- COMPACTED SOIL

New plants will require water every two or three days; more water than they were receiving in the pots before being planted. A really good soaking is essential.

Every plant that is put in the soil must be mulched. This stops moisture being lost and helps to prevent weed growth.

Do not fertilise at this stage, as it will burn the roots and do a lot of damage. Wait six to eight weeks before fertilising.

PLANTS FOR WET AREAS

Extended periods of wet weather can really show up the problem areas of your garden. Plants can keel over, sometimes months or even years later, because their roots, starved of oxygen, have rotted and died. In badly drained areas these plants may have coped but never really performed well. Continued rain was all they needed to finish them off.

The trick is to put in plants that revel in these situations. Many plants really do enjoy wet feet—for example, Canna lilies. These are available in shades of yellow, orange and red and there are even dwarf varieties.

For shady, moist positions any of the ferns will be happy. Blechnum and maidenhair are good examples; there are many types of each of these. Hen and chicken ferns also thrive and develop into big rosettes of beautiful foliage.

Don't overlook impatiens. Regarded by some people as weeds, they perform and flower for many months of the year. Many good varieties are available, dwarf or spreading, in a wide range of colours.

If you are a native plant enthusiast, you could try growing the good old-fashioned Australian native violet, which is a fabulous ground cover. It grows just as happily in sun or shade.

The best plant for a boggy situation is the bottlebrush. Any variety is suitable. Wild bottlebrushes live in swamps, as do the closely-related paperbarks. There are many paperbarks ranging from huge trees to small bushes. *Melaleuca linariifolia* 'Snowstorm' is a very showy one, which grows to about a metre (3–4′) tall.

Many rainforest plants are excellent for wet positions. One suggestion is blueberry ash, which has nice blue berries and either pink or white flowers. All of the lilly pillies, large and small, are fantastic in a wet position. One surprise is *Banksia robur*, as most banksias demand a well-drained position. The Morning Flag, *Orthrosanthus*, which has blue flowers just above the foliage, is another contender.

If you are not interested in native plants, there are many others that also perform very well. The following plants grow effectively in a moist position:

Pencil willow, a narrow variety of willow, which is evergreen and beautiful. This is useful, but does have a vigorous root system.
Tupelo (Nyssa sylvatica) is another beauty for a moist spot. A deciduous tree, its leaves turn to a rich blaze of colour in autumn before falling.

Agapanthus

Agapanthus is a reliable performer for any position, wet or dry.
New Zealand Christmas bush revels in wet conditions or by the sea and comes in plain green or variegated foliage.
Oleanders deserve much more acclaim—handsome, trouble-free and not caring whether it is wet or dry.

POLLINATING PHILODENDRONS

Philodendron selloum is a tough indoor plant, commonly found sitting unobtrusively in the corners of living-rooms across Australia. No one would suspect the complexity of its sex life and the unusual activities undertaken by commercial propagators to ensure continued production of this plant.

> *Balsa wood, which is one of the world's softest timbers, is classified as hardwood.*

This philodendron doesn't produce much in the way of stems that could be used to strike as cuttings, so it has to be grown from seed. In its native Central America, a night-flying moth assists in pollinating the plant as it flutters around the blooms. But in Australia, in the absence of this moth, human intervention is required to ensure that pollination takes place.

Each flower becomes heavily perfumed and sexually receptive on just one night in the year. Different flowers bloom on different nights over a period of about three months.

A philodendron flower is ready to be pollinated when it is open and the bottom part, the female portion, is hot. The flower warms to a temperature of about 35.5°C. The top part of the flower, a projection extending beyond the female section, is the male part. It produces pollen 24 hours after the flower has begun to close. This stops the plant from self-pollinating, but without the Brazilian moth that transports pollen from one bloom to another, pollination between plants would have little chance of occurring at all.

Philodendron seed growers simulate the actions of the moth and rub pollen collected from one flower onto another as required. From pollination to seed set takes about two months.

After producing pollen, the male part of the flower drops off, having served its useful purpose. Then the base of the flower, the female part, begins to swell. The seeds within it form in little capsules, about 30 seeds in each. The fruit that forms looks something like that of a monstera. After a couple of months the seed capsules break open and the seed is extracted in another process.

The ripe brown fruit, packed with seeds, is cut from the plant and stripped of its hard outer casing. The capsules within it are scraped out into a bucket. The tiny seeds must be removed from the capsules and cleaned of the sticky, mucilaginous matter that surrounds them. After washing, the seeds are dried on a screen and passed through a seed cleaning machine, which separates the dust and fibre from the seed. In the final step before marketing the seed to growers, a sample is taken for a germination test to ensure it is viable.

Nurseries grow the plant on to a height of 60cm-1m (2-3') and it is at this stage that the still immature plant is sold in nurseries.

PROBLEM CORNERS

Do you have a problem corner where the grass doesn't grow, most of the plants die and all the household junk is piled up? There is a solution.

The first thing to do is establish the direction of north. If your trouble corner is on the southern side of the house, there is little chance of the grass growing, as it will not grow in shade. Often garden beds along external walls of houses are less than 0.5m (18") wide, and this is not nearly enough for plants to grow well.

Tidy up any rubbish so that the area can be clearly seen.

To establish where the new garden edge should be, use the old landscaper's trick of placing a hose on the ground to form the shape of the proposed bed. Then bend the hose until you are satisfied with the new shape.

Take the measurement of the planned new garden bed to calculate the amount of soil, mulch and number of plants to be used. For the trouble spot shown on 'Burke's Backyard' (an area of 6×6m—20×20ft) we obtained:

2 cubic metres of organically enriched soil*	
3 cubic metres of pinebark mulch	$200
4 bags of planting mixture	
Plants	$450
TOTAL COST (including delivery)	$650

*It is critically important to get good quality soil, enriched with compost. Cheap soil costs more in the long run, because it never works well.

To choose a plant for a shady area, it is a good idea to look in the shade house at your local nursery.

Remove any existing grass (which can be replanted in bare areas to improve the lawn) and dig the soil thoroughly, particularly if it is compacted. Put soil over the area and contour it to make it interesting—a flat garden can be boring. Our mounds were placed to help hide an air-conditioning unit. Put in garden edging and mower strips. Larger stones were used for stepping stones to make a thoroughfare through the garden.

Position the plants in their pots, using the 'put and look' method, that is, place the pots in the position that you think is correct and then stand back to check the overall effect.

Plant, using the planting mixture, and then mulch with the pinebark to stop weeds growing and to encourage healthy growth. Water plants in gently.

All the numbered plants are new: existing plants are named on the diagram. Where more than one of a given plant was used, the number is included in brackets.

Plants used in the problem corner
1 *Camellia japonica* 'Dr Tinsley'
2 *Daphne odora*
3 *Viola hederacea* (8)
4 *Ardisia crenata* (3)
5 *Murraya paniculata* (2)
6 *Camellia japonica* 'Hikaru-Genji'
7 *Azalea indica* 'Mme Auguste Haerens'
8 *Azalea indica* 'Alphonse Anderson' (2)
9 *Camellia japonica* 'Tomorrow'
10 *Azalea indica* 'Jennifer Anne'
11 *Acanthus mollis* (2)
12 *Gardenia augusta* 'Radicans' (5)
13 *Primula malacoides* 'Gilham's White' (36)

PROBLEM CORNER AFTER PLANTING

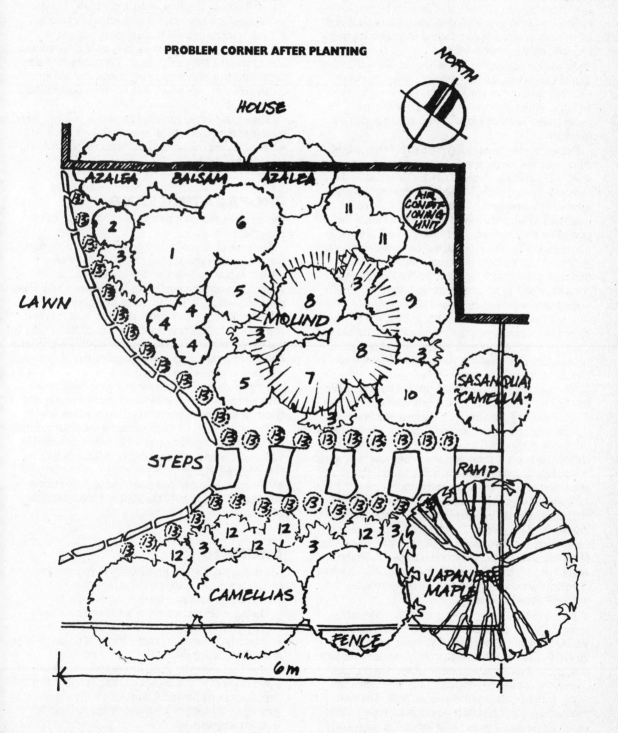

Sun/shade garden Virtually every garden has a problem
spot which presents all sorts of difficulties when it comes
to deciding how it should be used, and what to plant in it.
Often such spots can be transformed from embarrassing
eyesores into attractive features.

Obviously every garden is different but one of the ways
'Burke's Backyard' can help people discover the elusive
solutions to their own problem spots is to show how a
variety of difficult situations have been dealt with
successfully. The 'sun/shade' garden was just such an
example.

This garden was built in a typical 'out of sight, out of
mind' corner of the backyard. The construction of a garage
in front of a group of three citrus trees, bounded on the
other side by shed walls, blocked the trees from general
view, and the area swiftly became a weed infested
wasteland. When a studio was added to the rear of the
garage, the owners decided to tackle the weed problem,
but, as lack of time was the original cause of the trouble,
the garden that replaced the weeds would need to have a
minimum maintenance requirement. Work on the area
commenced just 18 months before we filmed it.

First to go were the weeds—and all the forgotten,
unwanted junk which was revealed in their wake. The
second step was to dig composted manure into the soil and
cover the entire surface with a couple of inches of pine
bark mulch. This prevented the millions of weed seeds
already in the soil from germinating.

We called this spot a sun/shade garden because, while
the high walls around the garden cast solid shadows over
it in the morning and afternoon, the area was exposed to
the full force of the sun's strongest rays for a few hours in
the middle of the day. This meant the garden could not be
regarded as either a shady spot or a sunny spot, and would
demand plants tough enough to withstand a little
discomfort at either end of the spectrum.

The initial planting was of vigorous climbers on wire
trellises against the ugly shed walls, to create a curtain of
green around the garden. The climbers used were: pink
trumpet creeper (*Podranea ricasoliana*), native bower vine
(*Pandorea jasminoides*), blue potato creeper (*Solanum
seaforthianum*), snail flower (*Phaseolus caracalla*), carolina
jasmine (*Gelsemium sempervirens*), banksia roses,
passionfruit and chokoes.

The plan for the rest of the garden was to use only
perennial plants or self-seeding annuals and to maximise
the use of ground cover plants that would cover
everything but the paths, and virtually eliminate the task
of weeding. A colour scheme for the flowers was also
chosen and adhered to—predominantly violet, blue and
white, with touches of yellow and soft pink. The most
successful group of ground covers have been the violets,
especially the native violet (*Viola hederacea*). The closely
related heartsease, with their delicate tricolour flowers,
have also proliferated.

The only large shrub added to the small garden was a
mauve flowering Buddleia, or butterfly bush. A pair of
yellow-faced honeyeaters, common suburban garden
visitors, were raising a nest of chicks in this bush.

The most prominent plant in the garden at the time of
filming was the Marguerite daisy. These delightful plants
form rounded bushes a metre (3') in diameter and are
densely covered with white, pink or yellow flowers from
late winter until early summer.

Maintenance of the sun/shade garden is now limited to
regular pruning and fertilising and only occasional
watering, as the thick mulch and sheltered position help to
conserve moisture.

PROPAGATING SAND

Do you make your own potting mix at home, or do you
propagate plants?

The basis of all good mixes, particularly for propagating,
is a good quality propagating sand. It is an expensive
product to buy ready-bagged and is often sold as 'double-
washed' propagating sand. Even this, however, will often
not work well at all, and may be of poor quality.

It doesn't matter how coarse the sand is, as long as
there are no fine particles in it. The fine particles must be
washed out of the mix, otherwise they will clog it up, and
if the sand is then used in a propagating mix, the cuttings
will die from lack of aeration.

If you place some of the sand in a bucket and rinse it
with water, you may find the water turns a murky clay
colour. If this occurs you must get rid of all the fine
rubbish that is in with the good coarse sand. Keep rinsing
the sand for up to 15 minutes with the hose on full. The
volume of material will probably be reduced by half.
However, the washed quality product that now remains
will be ready to add to peat moss, and so on to make a
propagating mix, or to be the basis of a potting mix for
growing plants.

PRUNING

There is nothing worse than having all your garden
shrubs hanging over the garden path, soaking you
whenever you walk past when it rains. But some
gardening books make pruning sound so difficult you
might prefer a soaking to attempting this task.
Fortunately, however, it is not difficult at all, provided you
know a few basic rules.

Grevilleas and many other native plants appreciate an
annual haircut after a major flowering. A light haircut all
over, taking care not to cut into older, leafless wood, is a
good idea. Anything that grows over the path can be
trimmed whenever you like.

To keep bottlebrush dense and attractive, prune back
just underneath the flower, as soon as the flowers begin to

fade. If this is not done, the plant may become loaded with seed capsules and look rather ugly.

Some non-native plants need a solid butchering every year. Tibouchina (lasiandra) and plants such as poinsettias are normally cut back about halfway immediately after flowering in tropical areas and at the end of winter in temperate zones.

Long-flowering plants such as roses need to have their dead flowers removed to prevent seeds from forming. This ensures many more flowers each year. The major pruning of roses and most other deciduous plants is done in winter when their leaves are absent; it is easier to see what you are doing at this stage. But if you don't care about losing potential flowers, you can prune any plant at any time of the year.

Method It is important to use a sharp pair of secateurs and make a clean, flat wound with no jagged projections; a rough wound rarely heals properly.

Scientists still dispute the value of tarry tree wound dressings. Don Burke is not inclined to use them, but would recommend you try a wood preserver such as Cuprinol or Pascol Wood Preserver. Any of the copper naphthanate wood preservers available at your local hardware store would do—but it is probably not necessary to use any dressing at all.

You are required by law to ensure that your trees and shrubs do not overhang the front of your property. If they do, your local council is entitled to prune them and charge you for the work they did, so do keep them trimmed back.

RAINFOREST GARDENS

One rainforest garden near Ipswich, Queensland, was established in an abandoned brick pit. All the soil and rocks for retaining walls were brought in. At the time this rainforest was planted, there were very few suitable plants available in nurseries and most of the planting was from specimens collected and grown from seeds.

The rainforest has now stabilised and is gradually spreading. It is all self-mulching. Many different birds have been attracted to this area by the rainforest. Two of the beautiful plants growing here are a palm called *Licuala ramsayi* and a Davidson's plum (*Davidsonia pruriens*), which has large attractive leaves and edible fruits. This is also a good indoor plant.

It is possible to establish a rainforest in your own backyard. These days, most nurseries carry a range of rainforest plants and there are many good books on suitable plants to grow, for example *Ornamental Rainforest Plants in Australia*, by David L. Jones, published by Reed Books Pty Ltd; or *Australian Rainforest Plants*, by Nan & Hugh Nicholson, published by Terania Rainforest Nursery, The Channon, via Lismore, NSW 2480.

Rainforest plants are available at most specialist Australian native nurseries, for example:

Hugh & Nan Nicholson, Terania Creek, NSW.
Telephone (066) 88 6204
Annangrove Grevilleas Native Nursery, Kenthurst, NSW.
Telephone (02) 654 1380
Austraflora Nursery, Montrose, VIC.
Telephone (03) 728 1222
Fairhill Nursery, Yandina, QLD.
Telephone (071) 46 7088
Wildflower Nursery, Wanneroo, WA.
Telephone (09) 409 9811
Zanthorrea Nursery, Maida Vale, WA.
Telephone (09) 454 6260

RAINY DAY GARDENING

Going out into the garden when it's raining may not be convenient, but you can learn a great deal more about your garden if you are prepared to get a bit wet.

Put indoor plants outside for a shower—remove the saucer so that the pot doesn't flood. Be careful the sun doesn't burn the plants when it reappears.

Plants that have been knocked over by wind should not be picked up until after the wind and rain have passed, as they may be knocked over yet again and suffer repeated damage.

The best time to fertilise is when it's raining. This stops the fertiliser from burning the plants. Rain also tends to wash fertiliser away, so you're replacing what the rain is removing. Recently applied weed and insect sprays will need to be applied again because they will be washed away.

Drainage problems can be spotted by feeling for waterlogged areas underfoot. These can result in plant root diseases if not alleviated.

Take a look at any downpipes or gutters that don't run into drains—the resultant flooding can be the start of lots of garden problems.

Don't dig a heavy clay soil during or soon after heavy rain; you may damage its structure permanently.

ROCK FACE GARDEN

The Rocks area in Sydney was once the rough, squalid end of the bustling harbour port. Now a beautifully restored slice of our history, it is a mecca for tourists and a heartland for artists and craftspeople like Anne Dybka, who works and lives in The Rocks.

Anne is probably the foremost glass engraver in Australia. Although the art goes back to Roman times, there are few glass engravers around these days because it takes so long to develop the necessary precision.

When Anne moved into her home seven years ago, she was confronted with a 21m (70') rock cliff as a backyard. Undaunted (after all, her craft involves bringing life to the inanimate), she turned it into a vertical jungle and then began working on the bare rock face at the end of her tiny street.

With the help of a friend who was happy to do the top-of-the-ladder work, and moral support from a neighbour, Anne has foliated the rock wall with a subtle variety of plants that, for the most part, require little soil. Those requiring more soil are planted inside shaped wiring and moulded to fit into the rock face as discreetly as possible. Sometimes they have to be secured by drilling into the rock. The wiring holding the plants to the rocks is disguised with trailing plants such as miniature Wandering Jew.

Among the plants used are many ferns and tree ferns, orchids, bromeliads, grevilleas, hoyas, lipstick plant, an umbrella tree, bougainvillea, crotons, a weeping mulberry tree, and above all of this, clinging to the top of the cliff, a fine old Moreton Bay fig tree.

Watering the upper part of the garden is achieved by hosing it from an upper window of Anne's house. The garden hose is hauled up the outside wall of the house by a piece of string hanging from the window.

As well as giving pleasure to the residents, Anne's rock wall garden delights tourists, who often stop to photograph this living wall hanging.

SOIL

To tell the difference between a sandy soil and a clay soil the following test can be carried out.

You will need a trowel, and a small board to work on. Take a small amount of soil, about a matchbox full. Moisten it just slightly and squeeze out any excess moisture, then work it together and roll into a snake. Put in on the board and try to bend it into a ring.

If it cracks when bent, it is a *sandy soil*.

If it bends easily to a doughnut shape without cracking, it is a *clay soil*.

If it bends halfway without cracking it is a *loam soil*.

Sandy soil To improve a sandy soil, dig in organic matter to fluff it up, so that it will hold moisture. Mushroom compost is a very good organic additive. Peat moss is excellent, as it will last longer in the soil than anything else, but it is expensive.

Most landscapers and nurseries use a composted sawdust and other waste materials, sometimes sold as 'Botany humus'—local landscape suppliers will have it under this name or similar.

Apply 5-7.5cm (2-3") of the organic matter over the soil to be improved. Spread it out and fork in well. It is a good idea to add a detergent, for example, Wetta Soil—15 ml (3 teaspoons) in a watering can full of water—and water it well into the area. This opens up the soil and allows rain to penetrate far better. Finally, cover with mulch on the surface to retain moisture.

Clay soil To improve clay soil, some form of calcium must be added. Garden lime or dolomite can be used, but the most common form of calcium is gypsum—it forces the clay soil to crack up internally. It should be applied at the rate of one handful to the square metre (11sq ft) over the area and then dug in, including with it some organic matter. Mulch the surface to retain moisture.

There are alternatives to gypsum—one is a liquid called Agrasol, and mushroom compost should be added along with this.

Adding sand to clay soils may not help. Unless vast amounts of sand are added, your soil will be little better off.

If you have a sandy or clay soil it is essential to prepare your soil properly before planting to ensure that plants grow as well as possible.

SUMMER GARDENING

The following hints and suggestions should help you to look after your plants during December, January and February.

Watering Summer is the toughest time of the year on newly planted vegetation, desiccation being the big killer at this time. Where regular, deep watering is difficult to arrange (such as when you go away on holidays) products such as the tree bag or trickle bag will water your plants automatically. These products are large bladders filled with water, which are placed at the base of a plant. An attached wick is buried in the ground beside the plant and this supplies water to the root zone for several weeks. Tree bags cost around $9 each, and are available from numberous outlets in all states—contact Tree Bag Australia, Box 944, Bathurst, NSW 2795. Telephone (063) 31 6040.

Mulching is vital for Australian gardens during summer; its water saving and soil improving effects cannot be overemphasised. The most commonly used, commercially available, form of mulch is pine bark, but another interesting one, which looks particularly good in a native garden, is leaf litter. It's basically just council prunings that have been chopped up in a machine. Leaf litter is more expensive than pine bark, however, because it rots down more quickly and so has to be replenished more often.

Soil conditioning If you are planting in the ground at this time of year, you may wish to use a soil conditioner. Many different brands are available around Australia, including Dig-it-in, Biogrow and Groganic. These products are commercial forms of compost (for example, composted sawdust). Dig a hole three or four times the size of the rootball of your plant, and dig the soil conditioner into the depression. This material acts as a moisture reserve as well as improving the soil. It costs about $5.25 a bag, and most garden centres stock it.

Potted plants should be checked to ensure that they are not too large for their pots. Plants that have outgrown their pots will dry out very quickly, and this will result in the leaves dying and dropping into the bottom of the pot. A plant displaying these symptoms should be urgently potted-on into a larger pot. If you decide to plant in the ground, be vigilant in keeping it watered.

Tropical plants This is the time of year to plant tropical plants, such as the beautiful climber, Alice Du Pont (*Mandevilla x amabilis*), frangipani, avocado, mango, and indeed any other tropical plant you would like to try growing.

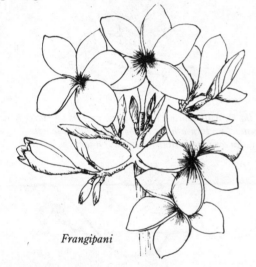

Frangipani

Indoor plants Early summer is the time to repot all your indoor plants. Choose the pots with care—those with a water reservoir from which the plant can draw moisture steadily over several days (for example, Décor Water Well pots, which come in a wide range of sizes and colours) are ideally suited to maidenhair ferns and African violets.

Scale insects Watch out for scale insects. These appear as small lumps (from pin-head to match-head in size) on the stems of maidenhair ferns, the trunks and branches of citrus, and on the leaves of many other plants. They can be anything from white or pale pink to dark brown in colour. When scratched off they come away easily and are soft and mushy underneath. Spray with Lebaycid to control scale insects. This is a good general insecticide which will also control sucking insects, which attack the leaves of indoor and outdoor plants, and fruit fly (in the areas where it is a problem).

Pruning during hot weather is not recommended because this can result in sunburn of exposed stems. Affected stems will turn grey on the upper surface but remain green on the underside.

Don't forget to water the garden regularly and deeply—oscillating sprinklers are well suited to this job. It's a myth that watering plants in the midday sun will burn them. You can water whenever you like, but watering in the hottest part of the day can result in greater water wastage through increased evaporation rates. Remember to stay informed about water restrictions which may apply in your area.

TRACE ELEMENTS

From time to time certain garden plants, particularly gardenias and citrus, show patterns of discolouration on the leaves. Sometimes the leaves appear to be mottled or spotted in light and dark green; in other cases the veins will turn yellow, or the rest of the leaf will fade and the veins will remain green; occasionally purplish colours and leaf distortion will occur. These abnormalities may appear first on the fresh, new growth in some plants but on the oldest leaves in others. Most people recognise these symptoms as a deficiency of some kind, but many become baffled when applications of fertiliser make no difference to the condition of the plant.

These symptoms usually indicate trace element deficiencies. The reason the plants may not respond to doses of fertiliser is that many fertilisers don't contain trace elements. The relationship between plants and trace elements is quite a delicate one and is not yet fully understood—research has been unable to determine exactly what many trace elements do for plants.

The consequences of trace element deficiency, however, are much easier to establish. Long before coloured patterns appear on the leaves, a deficient plant is likely to show retarded growth. This is often difficult to spot unless a well-fed plant is close by for comparison. Discoloured and distorted leaves indicate severe deficiencies.

Trace element deficiencies may also become apparent in a plant's reduced resistance to pests and diseases. This is because the deficiency disrupts the metabolism of the plant. A heavy population of leaf eating insects may be caused by the plant producing excessive amounts of sugars, which attract the insects. Woody parts of the plant are commonly weakened, and prone to attack from boring insects or snapping in the wind.

So what *are* trace elements? They are one of two groups of nutrient elements essential to plant growth; the major and the trace (or minor) nutrient elements. The major nutrient elements, which plants need in large amounts and which are supplied in the majority of fertilisers, are nitrogen, phosphorus, potassium, calcium, magnesium and sulphur. The minor or trace elements are needed in only small amounts and they include iron, manganese, copper, zinc, boron, molybdenum, cobalt, chlorine and sodium.

A deficiency in only one of these essential nutrient elements will result in poor growth. Sometimes a trace element will be in abundant supply in the soil, but the plant will still exhibit symptoms of a deficiency. This is because there are other factors, such as the pH of the soil, that determine whether the elements are available to the plants. Hence, even when the specific deficiency has been determined, additions of trace elements to the soil may not solve the problem—an alteration of the soil pH may be more important. The pH level at which all trace elements are most available to plants is pH 6.5-7.0.

There are a number of ways to find out what deficiencies your plants are suffering from. You can send a sample of the affected plant to one of the garden advisory services offered by state Departments of Agriculture or Primary Industries. You can have your soil tested by a private company (you can find them in the yellow pages of the telephone directory)—this costs about $70, but it does provide a detailed analysis which you can use to improve the whole garden. You can also buy information sheets from the Department of Agriculture or Primary Industries, or a book that covers trace elements (the CSIRO produces excellent and inexpensive small booklets entitled *Food for Plants and Soils*) and compare the leaves of your plant with those in the pictures.

Once you have established which trace element is deficient, you can buy a container of that specific trace element from your nursery or garden centre. If something wide-ranging is required, complete trace element mixtures are available. Alternatively, you can apply a complete fertiliser that lists trace elements in its contents. But one of the best sources of trace elements is simply organic material. This includes animal manure, treated human wastes, compost, liquid organic fertilisers (such as Nitrosol), and green manure.

TRANSPLANTING

During winter most large plants can be moved, although it is not advisable to move Australian native plants. Most deciduous plants, or evergreens from other countries, can be moved quite easily.

Firstly, check around under the plant and estimate the size of the root system. Dig a trench around the plant approximately as wide as the plant itself. For example, a 2m (6') tall Camellia that is 1m wide will probably have a 1m diameter rootball.

Also dig under the rootball until the plant can be rocked. When digging the hole, make a gently sloping ramp on one side. If it is a large plant it won't be easy to lift, so the trick is to get some sort of tarpaulin or mulch mat and slide it in under the front of the rootball. Rock the plant over and pull the tarpaulin out. Wrap the rootball in this material and it will be ready to slide up the ramp and over to its new location. Plant it at the same depth as it was before.

If it is to be put into a pot, hose most of the soil off the roots. If the main roots extend too far for the size of the

Moving large plants

Dig a trench around the rootball. Distance from trunk varies with size and species of plant.

Tilt the rootball, while a second person severs any large roots still intact underneath the rootball, and rolls a length of tarpaulin (or other suitable material) under the plant.

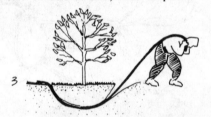

Drag the rootball, which now rests on the tarpaulin, out of the hole. One side of the hole has been sloped to facilitate this.

The relocated plant—mulched and watered.

pot, cut them off with secateurs. Place in the pot and add potting mixture. Take care to push the potting mix in around the roots, and then water well. Remove most flowers and flower buds if present. Put in a shady position for six to eight weeks or place shadecloth all over the plant and keep it well-watered.

To give the roots a chance to recover, use a liquid plant rooting hormone, for example, Hormone 20. This is essential whether or not the plant is put into the ground.

WATER FEATURES IN THE GARDEN

A small water feature in the backyard adds interest and atmosphere if designed and installed with care. Unfortunately, a poorly made water feature is unlikely to be worth the effort involved in constructing it, so close attention to planning is advisable.

Take care to select an appropriate setting for a water feature. If you plan to construct it in the form of a natural pool, it will look less artificial if it is nestled into an existing hollow or a lower spot in the yard.

Earth removed from the area where the pond is to be positioned may be used to form low, rounded hummocks in the surrounding lawn, or perhaps a bank which can be planted with ground covers. These features can add interest to an otherwise ordinary or monotonous garden.

An area of the garden that always seems to be damp and soggy may be a good spot to turn over to a more permanent and attractive water feature. However, try to avoid positioning the pond under trees that will drop large quantities of debris into it. Ponds that have goldfish in them should not be overhung by trees as the runoff can harm the fish.

The success or failure of any water feature is determined to a large extent by the way in which it is edged. Sometimes grass can be butted straight up to the edge of the water to good effect, but in most cases where a natural streamlike effect is sought, it is necessary to place rocks around the edge. If the rocks look too new or harsh, they can be softened and instantly 'aged' by laying moss in the crevices. Another edging alternative that often works well is to grow ground cover plants around the pond so that their foliage trails over the rim—the Australian native violet is an ever-useful example.

While water hyacinths, duckweed and bulrushes should be avoided because of their tendency to dominate the pond, there are a number of magnificent water plants that may be used. Water poppies, swamp iris, waterlilies—also available as miniatures—assorted rushes, and so on, will all give a most pleasant appearance.

If you decide to add a water feature to your garden be prepared to spend the time and money required to construct one that will work well, and lend charm and tranquillity to your garden for years to come.

WATER GARDEN

The house built over a dam which was featured in a story on 'Burke's Backyard' demonstrates an impressive solution to the problem of owning a block of land covered almost entirely by water. While such a block of land is a rarity, there are lessons to be learned from observing how an unusual feature can be worked with, rather than against, to create something unique and exciting.

The house was built on a large concrete platform standing on pillars in the dam, which has been stocked with edible fish.

While a conventional garden was not possible in these circumstances, there is a wide variety of water plants that produce foliage above the water surface, and these were used around the house to give it a garden in keeping with its setting. These plants are also suitable for inclusion in much smaller water features, such as backyard ponds or even large wine casks.

Suitable plants Tropical Waterlilies are available in a wide range of colours including blues, yellows and pinks. They will grow in most warmer areas of mainland Australia—certainly in Sydney, Perth and areas north of those cities.

Dwarf forms of Papyrus do very well both indoors and out, although some of them do die down in winter.

The Louisiana Iris grows in water and provides quite a wide range of decorative blooms.

Louisiana iris

Dwarf Variegated Rush, *Acorus gramineus*, adds a touch of colour of a different kind with its yellow and green striped leaves. The Pickerel Rush, *Pontederia cordata*, has blue flowers.

Nardoo, *Marsilea nutica*, has foliage which resembles the four leaf clover in shape. The leaves of this plant produce the seeds that were eaten by the explorers Burke and Wills in their desperate, unsuccessful attempt to ward off starvation in the desert.

Arum Lilies will grow in water or in a moist spot in the garden.

The Swamp Hibiscus produces red flowers and has unusual leaves shaped like those of a Japanese maple— quite different to those of most water plants.

These plants are available from many specialist water plant nurseries around Australia.

WETTING AGENTS

It is not uncommon to find plants in the garden that, although watered regularly, never seem to look terribly healthy. Sometimes, when plants are in pots, this can be caused by modern potting mixes, because they are often based on sawdust and can actually become water repellent. Although the potting mix can appear to have been watered on the surface, if you dig down a little you will find it is still quite dry.

Fortunately there are several Australian-developed products that solve this problem. The one we used is called Wetta Soil, a horticultural wetting agent. To an average 9-litre watering can, you add 15ml of this (about 3 teaspoons). If you put the Wetta Soil in first and then add the water, you get froth everywhere, so it is best to stir it in after you've added it to the water.

Then simply pour it onto the plant. It will soak into the potting mix really well, ridding it of the water repellency and opening it up, almost turning the potting mix into blotting paper.

Horticultural wetting agents are also good for watering lawn and garden areas. With lawn areas, it is important to aerate the soil with a fork, then water in a solution of Wetta Soil.

These products not only assist your plants in their growth, they also save a great deal of water since they allow it to penetrate easily and minimise runoff.

WINTER GARDEN JOBS

A good-looking garden generally results from attention to detail. The best way to find things that need attention is to take a stroll around the garden from time to time, particularly in winter, when the garden can tend to be forgotten, and simply take a good look around. Typical garden jobs likely to be encountered in the cooler months include the following.

Dead branch removal—check trees and shrubs for dead wood. When removing a branch, don't cut it quite flush with the trunk (the traditional method). Make your cut through dead rather than living tissue to avoid the risk of infection. Make a nick below the branch before sawing through from the top, to prevent the bark from tearing.

Control of weeds such as Bracken Fern, an incredibly tenacious weed but one that can be beaten. Don't cut it off; snap the stem and leave it lying down at ground level, so that the strong underground reserves of the plant are drained and weakened. This fern likes acid soil, so sprinkle some lime or dolomite around it.

Lichen often forms on the branches of garden plants, but it doesn't do any harm and often looks quite attractive. Don't worry about it.

Scale insects appear as pink or variously coloured raised dots along leaves. Spray with Malascale, but note that November to February is the best time to spray for scale.

Caterpillar webs—it is not uncommon to find one of your plants becoming choked with what looks like spider webs. In many cases the webs are actually produced by caterpillars. Remove them by hand—there is no need to spray.

Azalea lace bug—black spots under the leaves and bronzing on top are evidence that lace bugs have infested the azalea. It is too late to spray for this in winter, however. Spray from October through to April.

If you notice that some of your more touchy plant specimens are looking as though they are struggling to survive, it may be advisable to plant several more plants of that species, thereby increasing the chances of at least one surviving.

CHAPTER 7
Garden Pests and Problems

APHIDS

Aphids are often called black fly or greenfly, or sometimes plant lice, but aren't really flies, or lice either. They belong to a group of sap-sucking bugs, and their close relatives are the plant hoppers and cicadas.

An aphid's body has a tube that is used to suck the sap from the plant. This tube also injects enzymes, which break down the plant tissue. The damage aphids do to the growing tips of plants is caused by loss of sap and by the enzymes they inject. Some aphids also carry viruses that injure the plant.

Of the 100 or so kinds of aphids found in Australia, nearly half are foreign, which means that one way or another they have been introduced rather than developing here. In the early days plants were imported without being cleared for freeloading insects—quarantine regulations are now much more strict.

Most aphids don't lay eggs; they give birth to live young, and reproduce at an enormous rate. As female young are born they already have another female developing inside them. A single female is soon surrounded by a huge family of female offspring. So what happened to the males? Some kinds of aphids don't have males at all. Those that do only produce them at certain times of the year. The winged aphids which spread to new feeding grounds and start new colonies are usually females.

Aphids have many predators: they are a succulent seasonal food source, and some ladybirds feed on nothing else. They lay their eggs near the aphids so the wingless larvae have an immediate food source when they hatch. Large ladybirds can eat up to 50 aphids a day.

Hoverflies also prey on aphids and lay their eggs among them. Some wasps lay their eggs inside the bodies of aphids—when they hatch the larvae eat the aphids from the inside out. Small birds also eat aphids. Poison sprays are rarely necessary for control—they kill off the predators as well as the aphids. Nature will usually do the job without any help from you.

ARMYWORMS

Insect plagues have been a scourge upon farmers since agricultural practices began but it's not often that city dwellers suffer the impact of such disasters. But just such a plague recently devastated the lawns of parts of urban Australia, particularly along the east coast of New South Wales and Queensland.

Many people who take great pride in their lush, green lawns may find that within as little as 24 hours the grass appears to be turning brown and actually disappearing before their eyes. Degeneration of the lawn rapidly continues, often in a progressive 'front' across the lawn (much as a grassfire burns). Within a matter of days there may be not one blade of green to be seen.

The culprit is a little insect called the armyworm. It is not a worm at all, but the caterpillar of a moth, *Spodoptera mauritia*. Armyworms feed on lawns and other grasses and weeds. They tend to feed in large numbers, moving like an army (hence their name) from one area to the next, eating all the greenery they encounter. In severe infestations they eat the grass so completely that the lawn will be killed. In milder infestations the lawn will recover within two to three weeks.

Armyworms are difficult to see at first glance because they burrow into the lawn, or conceal themselves nearby during the daytime and come out to feed only at night. When feeding they are very active and can be spotted by torchlight. If you leave hessian bags lying on the lawn overnight, and lift them the next morning the armyworms may be revealed sheltering under them. Armyworms are up to 45mm (1¾") long with smooth brown to black bodies. Lengthwise stripes of a paler colour may be visible along the body.

If you are not prepared to let nature take its course and hope that your lawn will not be too severely damaged by armyworm invasion (remember, the lawn won't look much good anyway until active growth recommences in late spring), you will need to apply chemicals. There are a number of chemicals which can effect control, but check that armyworms are present before spraying; brown areas on the lawn could be symptoms of other pests or diseases requiring different treatments.

Caterpillar Killer, Lawn Grub Killer and Dipterex are three chemicals produced by Bayer, which all contain the active ingredient trichlorfon. These sprays must be used late in the day; the chemicals break down rapidly in sunlight. This is an advantage because the chemicals will kill the armyworms overnight but not harm other birds and animals that may occupy the lawn during the day—

some birds are likely to be attracted to infested lawns to eat the armyworms.

Another chemical which may be used, but which is not quite as effective as trichlorfon, is carbaryl. This spray (several forms are available) is relatively safe with birds but, like all chemicals, should be used with the utmost care and in accordance with the instructions printed on the packet.

If you can't find any caterpillars the problem may be due to a fungal disease. In that case Daconil or Mancozeb can be watered into the lawn with a watering can to kill the fungus.

BAMBOO

Bamboo is a truly amazing plant. It has been around for 150 million years. Contrary to popular belief, it is not actually a tree, but a grass. This grass has been measured as growing at the speed of up to 5cm (2") an hour. The ancient Chinese thought that the best place to sit, get drunk and write poetry was in a bamboo grove. A bamboo blowgun in the hands of a skilled operator is more accurate than a modern hand gun. Malaysian hunters can sink a dart seven or eight centimetres (3") into a deer at a range of 100 metres (328'). In Ecuador, the Jivaro tribe can hit hummingbirds at fifty metres (164').

Bamboo has been used to make furniture, paper, food, chopsticks, mats, shelter, baskets, skyscraper scaffolding in Asia and, until recently, record needles, polished jewellery and electric batteries. Of all the materials available on the planet, it was bamboo that Thomas Edison chose to use for a light bulb filament back in 1880. Now, a century later, that electric light bulb is burning today in the Smithsonian Institute in Washington, DC.

It is the unusual sex life of the bamboo that has led to the virtual extinction of the giant panda. Of the numerous types of eucalypts available in Australia, the koala can eat only a few, and similarly the panda can eat only four types of bamboo. In a bamboo grove all the bamboo is identical to each other. The plant reproduces by non-sexual reproduction—it puts out shoots which turn into new bamboo. You have probably seen bamboo shoots in a backyard, pushing their way through a concrete path or brick paving.

Somewhere between each 30 and 150 years, all bamboo of a particular type has a massive sex wave. The plants produce flowers, mix their pollen with each other, cast off

The Yulan or white magnolia tree has had three name changes. It was conspicua, then denudata, and now heptapeta.

their seeds—the bamboos of the next generation—and then they die. For the next 18 months, the giant panda will not be able to find any bamboo of that type. The advantage of this sex wave is that all the bamboo of the next generation is slightly different from its parents. This means that if there is a slight change in climate, some will be able to adapt to the new environment and survive.

Giant pandas should be meat-eaters, at least from the neck down; they have the short, complicated gut of a meat-eater, and will eat meat if they can catch it. From the neck up the giant panda is a vegetarian. It has the massive head and well-developed jaw and jaw muscles necessary to grind through its high fibre vegetarian diet.

Giant pandas eat bamboo leaves and shoots that are very low in nutrition. But, as they have the wrong type of gut, they obtain less than 20% of the food value of the food they eat (sheep, for comparison's sake, obtain 80%). The giant panda has to eat up to 40kg (88lb) of bamboo per day, and it doesn't have a lot of energy left over for fun—this is probably another reason why there are not many giant pandas.

Bamboo in the backyard The worst single problem in the backyard is when a neighbour plants bamboo right next to their fence. Bamboo very quickly sends out roots and young plants can come up as far as 6–9m (20–30') away.

In a recent Sydney court case, the owner of the property with the bamboo ended up having to pay court costs, as well as paying for the removal of the bamboo which had come up in a neighbour's backyard. The plant had grown under 6m (20') of paving, which had to be lifted for the roots to be removed. The neighbour had previously asked the owner to remove the bamboo.

If you are troubled by bamboo coming in from an adjacent property, make the owner aware of the fact that it is worrying you. Also, put the problem in writing, take photos and retain a record of the dates that you approach them about the removal of the bamboo. If the owner doesn't take responsibility for its removal, then it is the right of the neighbour to arrange for it to be removed, and to take court action for costs and compensation.

The best way to get rid of bamboo is to dig it out with a mattock.

To use chemicals to kill bamboo:
1 Cut bamboo down, leaving stalks.
2 Fertilise with sulphate of ammonia or any cheap nitrogenous fertiliser (about ½ cup to a watering can full of water). Water bamboo well with this. Bamboo is at its most vulnerable when it is actively growing.
3 Wait a few weeks until the bamboo is growing new foliage. Put diluted Zero or Roundup into a spraying device and thoroughly wet all stems and foliage.
4 Watch for any new growth and spray it again until it is all killed.

Great persistence is needed to completely rid your backyard of bamboo.

BINDII
Hand removal of the small, flat, fernlike bindii plant is extremely difficult; chemical sprays are considered advisable for use in controlling this weed. It is necessary to spray before summer—winter is an ideal time.

Generally, sprays labelled for control of this weed kill the bindii but leave the lawn grass unaffected. However, you will need to check that the spray you use is suitable for your particular lawn type.

Select a spray which does not contain Dicamba. It has recently been established that the use of bindii killers which contain this substance can kill nearby trees. If the Dicamba-based spray is applied heavily (for example, with a watering can) or if it is applied to shallow, sandy soils, and particularly if rain falls within 48 hours of application, nearby trees and shrubs are definitely at risk. There is at least one court case currently in progress in relation to this matter.

Weedoben M and Bin-Die are two examples of sprays which do not contain Dicamba.

CHICKWEED AND PETTY SPURGE
Chickweed and petty spurge are both widespread introduced weeds in Australia, but while chickweed is useful; highly palatable and nutritious to cage birds, chooks and even humans, petty spurge has been associated with cases of poisoning of domestic animals, and loss of appetite and egg-laying capacity in chooks. Unfortunately, the two are very similar in appearance, so it is important to learn the difference if you would like to take advantage of the value of chickweed and eradicate petty spurge from your backyard. Both weeds are easily removed by hand, and there is absolutely no need to spray them with chemicals.

Chickweed (*Stellaria media*) The first of many good things about chickweed is that its presence indicates that the soil in which it grows is in good condition. Chickweed prefers healthy soils, rich in trace elements, in moist areas.

Virtually all grass-eating domestic animals find chickweed highly palatable, but it is especially valuable in the diet of caged backyard pets (cockies, budgies, canaries, finches, chooks, rabbits and guinea pigs). In fact, the name derives from the pleasure with which chickens consume the foliage and seeds.

Chickweed spreads quickly; it grows flowers and sets seed all year round, so it is a good source of winter greens for your pets, although it does not withst d heavy frost.

You might like to try eating chickweed yourself. Clip the young stems with scissors—the leaves and stems are both edible. Chickweed can be washed and eaten raw in salads or chopped and boiled quickly for just two or three minutes, after which time it is said to taste like young English spinach.

Chickweed has also been used to make a variety of soothing and healing lotions and potions for everything from tired eyes, to itchy rashes and piles.

Chickweed

Petty spurge (*Euphorbia peplus*) The danger of petty spurge to animals lies in its milky white sap. This sap is highly caustic, but is also bitter, so fortunately the weed is generally not very palatable to animals. In previous centuries the sap was sometimes used to try to remove warts—thankfully, modern methods have made this remedy redundant.

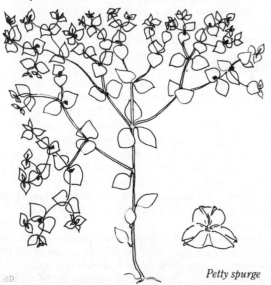

Petty spurge

Identifying chickweed and petty spurge The easiest way to tell the difference between these two plants is to snap one of the stems. Petty spurge immediately exudes a drop of milky sap while chickweed does not release any noticeable fluid.

There are also differences in the growth habits of the two plants. Petty spurge grows upright like a miniature tree, with a strong central stem, leafy on top and bare at the base. By contrast, chickweed has very soft, delicate foliage with several stems growing out from the base and sprawling along the ground.

Medicinal chickweed recipes

'Burke's Backyard' does not endorse these recipes: they have not been tested by us.

Chickweed Ointment
This recipe produces a balm or ointment which can be applied to skin ailments, including sores and piles.

30g (1oz) beeswax (buy from beekeepers)
175g (6oz) lanolin
250g (9oz) chickweed, chopped

Melt the beeswax and lanolin in a saucepan over a low heat. Don't allow it to boil. Stir in the chickweed. Put the mixture in an ovenproof dish, cover and cook in a low oven (95°C, 200°F, Gas 2) for four hours. Strain or sieve finely into a clean glass jar and set aside to cool before placing the lid on the jar.

Chickweed Poultice and Eye Lotion
This soothing poultice can be applied to various inflammations, external abscesses and ulcers. The water remaining after the poultice has been boiled can be used to soothe tired, sore eyes by moistening cotton balls in it and then placing them over the eyes.

To make the poultice and lotion, wrap a bunch of chickweed in a piece of fine cloth and boil for 10 minutes. Remove the bag from the water and apply as a poultice to affected area.

Edible chickweed recipes

Chickweed and Leek Soup (Chickaleeky)
1 litre (1¾ pints) chicken stock
4 leeks (or one large onion) sliced into rounds
2 potatoes, diced
250g (9oz) chickweed, washed and chopped
Salt and pepper to taste
3 tablespoons cream

Bring stock to boil, add leeks and potatoes and simmer for 10 minutes. Add chickweed, simmer 5-10 minutes more until vegetables are tender. Season with salt and pepper then puree in a blender or through a sieve. Return to the pot and reheat. Stir in cream just before serving. Garnish with fresh chickweed.

Chinese Chickweed
1 tablespoon cooking oil
1 clove garlic, chopped finely
Approx ½ teaspoon ginger, grated finely
2-3 shallots/spring onions, sliced finely
1 medium carrot, cut into fine strips
6 mushrooms, sliced finely
250g (9oz) chickweed, washed and chopped
125g (4½oz) mung bean sprouts
3 tablespoons water
1 tablespoon soy sauce or tamari
125g (4½oz) crispy noodles for garnish

In a wok or large frying pan, heat the cooking oil and sauté garlic, ginger and shallots for 3 minutes. Add carrot, cook 3 minutes. Add mushrooms, cook a further 3 minutes, stirring often. Add the remaining ingredients, except the noodles, and cover the pan. Reduce heat, simmer gently for a further 5 minutes. Use crispy noodles as garnish. Serve with rice and eat with chopsticks.

CITRUS BUD MITE

Citrus bud mite may attack all types of citrus, but it is mostly found on 'Eureka' lemons and 'Washington Navel' oranges.

The mite is so small that it can't be seen without a magnifying glass. It causes deformed leaves and buds as well as badly deformed fruit, which usually falls at an early stage.

To control this mite, spray with Kelthane in summer or early autumn.

CITRUS LEAF MINER

Probably the worst pest to hit Australian gardens in recent years is the citrus leaf miner. Heavily distorted new growth, and silvery scribble marks on the leaves like snail or slug tracks, are the telltale signs of citrus leaf miner attack. The marks are formed as a little caterpillar-like insect tunnels its way around inside the leaves. In severe cases the distortion of the leaves will almost destroy the plant.

Fortunately, citrus leaf miner affects only the secondary growth flush that occurs in late summer—early spring growth will not be damaged. If you wish to protect your citrus from this pest there are sprays that will do the job. Malathion is a registered spray for killing this insect. However, if you spray your citrus with Lebaycid (for fruit fly control) it will also control citrus leaf miner, even though it is not registered for this use in all areas. You should begin spraying at the onset of the summer growth flush, usually in January, and continue until that growth has matured.

With most plants, however, just trimming off the affected new growth during mid to late summer and putting it in the garbage bin is enough to control this pest.

If left unsprayed, the tree will produce normal growth again in spring.

Aphids on the growing tips of citrus are usually not a significant problem and do not require chemical control, especially when they are already being naturally controlled by predators such as ladybirds.

CYPRESS BARK WEEVIL

One of the most popular trees in the Australian garden is the Golden Cypress (*Cupressus macrocarpa* 'Brunniana'), which most people refer to as a Brunniana or Brunning's Golden Cypress.

It is a beautiful tree and often planted in rows, but this is not advisable, as it can cause problems. Golden cypresses will often die, starting from one area of the tree. If you look at the base of the tree you will see a resinous substance bleeding from the bark. This resin is produced by the tree to kill the borer attacking it. Pulling the bark away, you may find a young cypress bark weevil, which is attacking the lower metre or so of the tree. If you have a row of golden cypresses together they may all be destroyed by the weevil.

To determine whether your golden cypress is being attacked by cypress bark weevil, pull off some bark and look for a woven circular nest with a 6mm (¼") hole that the adult emerges through.

If under heavy attack, the cypress will probably die. There is no effective chemical to deal with the problem, and the only thing to do is to keep your tree in very healthy condition. Water during dry weather and fertilise twice a year in spring and autumn with a standard fertiliser; this will help your tree to repel the weevil.

In Sydney, Perth and areas north, the cypress bark weevil will always be a problem, and a row of golden cypresses is out of the question.

If your heart is set on a row of cypresses it would be better to use Golden Leyland Cypress (*Cupressocyparis x leylandii* 'Castewallan Gold').

FIREWEED

As you travel through many parts of Australia you pass mile after mile of gum trees, rolling hills and fields of wildflowers. However, many of the plants which flower beautifully right across the continent are not wildflowers at all. You can be sure almost anything with yellow flowers over a broad area is a weed.

The yellow-flowering Fireweed, which is a member of the daisy family, comes from South Africa and Madagascar. Its botanic name is *Senecio madagascariensis*. It is very pretty, but not the ideal plant to have growing around your house.

Fireweed is spreading rapidly throughout many areas of Australia. In the ten years from 1974-84 its spread along the coastal areas of New South Wales has been quite frightening. In 1974 it occurred in perhaps one-third of the coastal area; by 1984 it had spread across most of the coast. It is now recorded in Queensland and Western Australia and it probably won't be long before it occurs commonly in the other states.

Consideration is being given to making this plant a noxious weed in Queensland and we are sure that before long it will be classified as such in many other areas of Australia.

Fireweed spreads rapidly because of the form of the seedhead. It is similar to the 'Father Christmas' seedhead on the dandelion; the seeds blow in the wind and can spread over long distances on a windy day.

This weed can kill cows and horses. If they graze on it, fireweed causes major liver damage, which could lead to death. Fireweed grows strongly after drought when there is not much food for the cattle—hence the problem. Fortunately, sheep and goats are not as badly affected by this weed as cattle are.

Fireweed is not confined to grazing areas; it will certainly spread into any back or front yard.

Getting rid of fireweed If you are in a pastoral area, you can introduce sheep; they will graze it out without any significant risks to their health. Pasture improvement will also tend to get rid of it, we recommend adding superphosphate and maybe Nitram and some good pasture grasses.

The best method for your backyard or hobby farm is to simply pull it out. You must do this before it produces the white seedheads.

FUNGAL PLANT DISEASES

February and March tend to be the most humid months of the year, and high humidity means ideal conditions for fungus to attack garden plants.

Black spot The most common fungus problem in many Australian backyards would have to be black spot on rose bushes. The symptoms are black spots on the leaves, often surrounded by yellowish patches. Many people attempt to control this disease by removing infected leaves, wrapping them up and disposing of them in the garbage bin. This makes sense, since it reduces the incidence of re-infection of healthy leaves. In many areas however, spraying is also necessary. Triforine is possibly the best black spot spray available. Fortunately, some of the general rose sprays, such as the Defender brand, now contain Triforine as well as an insecticide to kill some of the pest insects that may be present on the roses.

Powdery mildew is another disease prevalent at this time of the year. It is frequently noticeable as a whiteish dusting or pale patches on the leaves of pumpkins, zucchinis and the like. Affected leaves gradually turn limp and yellow. Crepe myrtles and hydrangeas are among the

many other plants that commonly fall victim to this fungus. As with black spot, it is possible to remove affected leaves and dose the plant with fertiliser to help it along, but if you prefer spraying, any of the fungal sprays for roses, or even Benlate, will control summer powdery mildew.

Geranium rust, another fungus, is characterised by pinhead-sized brown dots covering the backs of the leaves, and yellow dots on the upper surface. Pruning and destroying the infected foliage and dosing with fertiliser to produce vigorous new growth may overcome the problem. Otherwise, spray with Zineb. Spraying will halt the spread of the disease to new leaves but it won't repair those already damaged.

Anthracnose Mangoes may be seen to have blackened areas of the fruits and leaves. These usually don't warrant concern if they appear in summer, but this disease does require attention if observed during the flowering period in spring. Infection at that time will prevent fruit from forming that season. If you wish to have your mango, and eat it too, you could spray with Mancozeb.

Peach leaf curl Puckered leaves on peaches or nectarines indicates this problem. Sprays are available—Peach Leaf Curl spray and Kocide are very effective—but there is nothing you can do once the problem is in evidence. The time to spray against this disease is in August, so a note on next year's calendar might help to remind you if you failed to control the disease this season.

Mould One disease which commonly appears on natives, such as tea-trees and gums, can't be ignored. A sooty black mould coating the leaves and stems is the most noticeable symptom of the problem but, in this case, the mould, which is a fungus, is not the cause of damage to the plant. Bugs, such as scale insects, suck sap from the plant, digest it and excrete copious quantities of sticky liquid over the stems and leaves. The black mould feeds on this liquid and so spreads over areas where the bugs have been. Once the bugs have gone the mould will die. A dose of Malascale will give good control, but so will pruning of the worst affected areas, followed by treatment with complete trace elements or a fertiliser rich in trace elements, such as Nitrosol.

Root rot is a fungal disease that strikes below the soil surface and causes the plant to wilt and die. Many plants will survive if treated early enough with Fongarid.

Some diseases that appear in late summer and early autumn are not worth spraying and are best ignored. Most magnolias, for example, will be looking fairly terrible almost everywhere in Australia at this time of the year— live with it and they'll pull through. In general, grow your plants in appropriate positions in the garden and fertilise them properly; their natural resistance will be such that most pests and diseases will either be absent or limited in extent.

GLYPHOSATE HERBICIDES

The war against the garden weed is probably the single greatest thing which unites gardeners. The activity of digging them out occupies hours upon hours of our leisure time. The best method of preventing weeds from getting a grip on the garden is to apply a good thick mulch to the soil surface, but even then a few weeds will be unstoppable, and this is when the question of whether or not to apply chemicals arises. As public awareness of our endangered environment increases, there is much confusion over whether, when, and how to use chemicals in the garden.

Chemical herbicides The most commonly used garden chemical in Australia today is Zero, a weed killer which contains the active ingredient glyphosate. On 'Burke's Backyard' we examined how effective glyphosate is, what forms of it are available, and how dangerous it is to the environment.

When you go to the local nursery or hardware store to buy this product you can rapidly become confused. Glyphosate is the basic ingredient in Zero, and Zero was the first form of this chemical to appear in the marketplace, although the extra-concentrated form of glyphosate has been sold under the name of Roundup for broadscale and commercial applications. Now glyphosate labelled as Roundup is also sold for backyard use, but in a form identical to Zero in concentration and every other aspect. The same chemical appears again under the label Wipeout, which has recently been released by Hortico.

Apart from differences in the names, the market has also been hit by a barrage of different concentrations of glyphosate and different forms of application. In one form, the chemical is diluted with water so that it is ready to spray, which makes it very convenient. Normally you should never mix garden chemicals with water and leave them, but with this particular product you can. The highly concentrated forms of the chemical are quite expensive, about $23 for 250ml (less than ½ pint), but are just as economical when diluted.

Yet another way of applying this chemical is with a type of weeding wand. Both large and small Zero wands are available but you may have to ask around for the smaller one. The wand is considered by many experts to be the best way of applying glyphosate.

You can make your own version of a wand if you want to apply the chemical to a specific plant close to others you want to keep. Just pour some of the concentrate into a container and use a 2.5cm (1") paintbrush to dab it on the leaves.

Glyphosate is a herbicide (a plant killer) so it effectively kills most plants, apart from some varieties like succulents. It works by disrupting the life process of the plant. This means that it is most effective on mature to older leaves during the growing season, when these leaves are manufacturing complex sugars by photosynthesis and exporting them to other parts of the plant. The chemical doesn't work well in the middle of the winter, when these processes are much reduced. The ideal time to use glyphosate is while the weather is warm, that is, from November to April. If you are using a paintbrush or a wick applicator you need only to touch a small percentage of the leaf area with the chemical for it to work effectively. This makes glyphosate an economical chemical to use. But you must be careful. When using it to kill weeds among good plants remember that this is not a selective herbicide. Whatever you apply it to, it will kill, although it works only on green parts of the plant (it is not taken in by brown bark).

Water and dust will neutralise glyphosate, so make sure the target weed is clean and dry, and that rain is not threatening. The advantage of this is that you can wash the chemical off a plant you touched accidentally if you do so within four hours of application.

Safety The most important question is, how safe is this particular chemical in the environment and what sort of risk does it pose to your own health? Glyphosate breaks down as soon as it touches the soil and according to current research it is non-residual, so it is relatively environmentally safe. As for human health, there is no evidence to suggest that it is anything other than a very safe garden chemical when used according to the directions on the container. There are very few chemicals on sale for use in Australian gardens that are as safe as glyphosate.

Nonetheless, if you are going to spend some time getting rid of the weeds in your garden it is always a good idea to first consider removing them by hand. Chemicals should always be a last resort, but you might use them on such things as bulbous weeds (for example, oxalis and onion weed) or plants with invasive runners (for example, couch grass and kikuyu).

KENTIA PALM SEED THEFT

You may think that in the privacy of your own backyard you are reasonably safe, and that the plants in your garden don't represent a security risk. This is usually the case but some plants can pose a very significant risk to the safety of your domain.

One such plant is the Kentia Palm (*Howeia forsteriana*)—the world's most popular palm and probably the hardiest of all indoor plants. When the seeds of this plant ripen each year they can definitely cause disruption of the tranquillity of the backyard.

One woman went out into her back garden to find some men gathering the palm seeds. When they saw her they dropped the bag of seeds, which she rushed over to retrieve. At that point the men fled; if they had decided to approach the lady to take the bag from her the outcome could have been more serious.

The reason for this peculiar intrusion is that over the last 10 years or so there has been a worldwide shortage of kentia palm seeds. The seeds are available only from the Australian region and this exclusiveness has meant that they have been worth as much as 10¢ each. The seeds are produced in large clusters, and a mature palm tree could be carrying over $1000 worth of seeds at any given time. This has attracted some very unpleasant types of people to the fringes of the nursery industry in the hope of making a quick dollar. The problem has become so serious in some suburbs that concerned residents have drawn their problem to the attention of the police and the media.

The police say they are concerned; people prepared to trespass and steal palm seeds are not likely to baulk at breaking into people's homes and stealing videos and televisions as well.

Understandably, the owners of kentia palms resent the invasion of their privacy, the threat to their security and the loss of income that is rightfully theirs. But they claim that nurseries, mindful of the popularity of these plants and fearful that seed vendors will simply go elsewhere if questioned, are contributing to the problem by buying seed from anyone who brings it to them. The owners say they want the nurseries to ask for receipts detailing the name of the person who sold the seed and the amount paid for them.

For their part nurseries and seed growers say they are concerned about their reputations and certainly don't want to be involved in anything unethical. They are trying to protect themselves from involvement by not associating with new pickers. The only advice the nurserymen say they can offer people is not to leave their properties; the obvious presence of the owners is probably the best deterrent to the thieves.

A decline in the demand for kentia palm seeds is likely to be the only thing that will curtail the activities of these thieves. In recent months the price of kentia palm seeds has slumped to a little under 8¢ each, and continues to drop. This is because the seeds simply aren't selling at the moment due to a normal, periodic decrease in demand and an improved supply of seed from Norfolk Island.

MEALY BUG

The worst indoor plant pest is the mealy bug. This is a small sap-sucking insect covered with white, mealy wax, with a fringe of wax around the edge. The plant under attack will be riddled with a white, flourlike substance that the mealy bug produces as camouflage. The mealy

bug is like a plant mosquito—it sucks sap and the plant develops an allergic reaction to chemicals from the bug. The end result is distorted new growth; the plant may become unhealthy and perhaps even die.

The main problem with the mealy bug is that it is almost impossible to get rid of, and it spreads very easily.

The surface under the plant which is being attacked by mealy bug becomes very sticky and stained, as the bug produces a sugary substance, which drips. Mealy bugs also attack the roots of the plant they are living on.

Cure Take the plant outside and remove any dead material on the stem. Mealy bugs live down in the sheaths that wrap around the stems and you will have to get rid of this so that the spray will reach the bug. The material from the plant must be put in the garbage, not on the compost heap, as it would infect other plants.

When the plant is cleaned up, spray it. The best spray is Lebaycid, and this should be measured accurately. It is important to spray when there is no wind, and to wear clothing that covers the skin. Spray the plant thoroughly, and pour any remaining spray into the soil to kill off the mealy bugs living among the roots. Wash your hands thoroughly and change your clothes immediately after spraying. Leave the plant to drain outside, at least overnight, and be careful not to leave it in the sun, as the leaves will burn.

If your plant is small, it is not necessary to mix up the spray. It would be preferable to use an aerosol, such as Folimat, which should be misted above the foliage, not sprayed directly onto it. Spray with White Oil as well, and this may give you some control of the mealy bug. Whichever technique you use, repeat the process in three weeks to kill off any newly hatched mealy bugs.

As mealy bug spreads so quickly to other plants, you may prefer to throw the plant in the garbage.

MOTH PLANT

The Moth plant (*Araujia hortorum*) is a common weed of coastal and tableland areas of eastern Australia. A native of Peru, this plant is widespread on better soils in wasteland areas and old orchards.

The moth plant grows as a tough, perennial climber with vigorous, twining, woody stems that exude a milky, sticky sap when broken. The leaves are dull green on the upper surface and greyish-white on the underside. The stems tangle themselves over any support, climbing through the tops of fences, trees and shrubs. The vine is

---

It's a myth that watering plants in the mid-day sun will burn them. Water whenever you like.

usually quite inconspicuous until a cloud of small white or pale pink flowers emerges in spring and summer. These are followed by green, fleshy, ridged, pear-shaped fruit up to 12cm (5″) long and about 6cm (2½″) in diameter. The fruits mature in late winter or spring, and split in half to release hundreds of seeds, each of which has a tuft of long, silky hairs attached to carry it on the breeze to a new location. In this way the weed spreads rapidly.

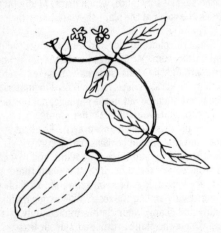

Control is by manual removal of the root system. If fruit have already formed, pick and dispose of them, as they are still capable of ripening and spreading seeds after the roots of the plant have been destroyed.

The moth plant is believed to be poisonous to poultry, dogs and possibly cattle.

NUISANCE PLANTS

When buying a plant from a nursery, make sure that the plant you choose is suitable for the position in which you want to plant it. Check how big it will grow and how extensive the root system will be. A *golden cypress* planted too near a fence will eventually push the fence over, for example. The *Queensland umbrella tree* will also move a fence if planted too close to it.

Ivy looks great covering either a paling or a brick fence. However, if the ivy covers a painted wall or roof and needs to be removed, the modified roots that attach it to the wall will leave unattractive marks.

Common jasmine can escape all over the garden and become a very annoying weed.

The *rhus tree* has beautiful crimson autumn foliage, but 98% of people can develop quite a severe allergy to this plant. In 10% of cases it may require hospitalisation. It is classified as a noxious weed in New South Wales and South Australia. There is a fine of $1000 for having the plant in your garden, and if it hangs over the fence or footpath and someone walking past or a neighbour develops an allergy, they are entitled to sue the owner of the land where the plant grows.

If you are planting a *camphor laurel*, make sure it is not near a masonry fence, unless it is a brick pier fence. This type of fence has brick piers at the corners and the rest of the fence is supported on an arch bar, so that it is suspended above the tree's roots. Therefore as the roots grow the fence should not be cracked.

A *cat's claw creeper* has pretty yellow flowers but has the potential to cover everything around it.

PEST CONTROL WITHOUT CHEMICALS

The following information was supplied by Judy McMaugh, Principal Horticulturist (Ornamentals), Department of Agriculture, NSW.

Insect numbers can often be kept down to a tolerable level in a home garden without the use of pesticides.

Aphids Hose off or squash with fingers. The few aphids not killed or removed will gradually build up into a new colony, and you may need to hose or squash them again.

Slugs and snails Use a beer trap. This can be made from a plastic container of about jam jar size, embedded in the soil at an angle so that the lip of the container is at ground level and the snails can crawl in easily. Put in about a cup of beer to attract the snails. From time to time remove dead snails and replenish the beer—as far as we know, they're not fussy about the brand!

Remove their hiding places. Get rid of the old bricks and pots and bits of wood you've left in a heap—snails love to lurk under such things.

Cutworms Make some traps. Use containers at least as deep as plastic drink cups, embedded in the soil so that the top is at ground level. Cutworms fall in when they are wandering around in the dark looking for your seedlings. Remove the trapped ones regularly.

Protect seedlings with a barrier. Cut the bottom from a large icecream container and push it about 5cm (2″) into the soil around seedlings. It should be at least 8cm (3¼″) above ground level so the cutworms can't vault over.

Whiteflies Make a trap from a piece of board painted bright yellow. About 30cm (12″) square would be a suitable size, but the shape doesn't really matter. Cover the board with a sticky substance like SAE 90 motor oil. The bright yellow attracts the insects and they stick to the board. Suspend the boards—at least four in every 12m² (40sq ft)—just above or between plants.

Steelblue sawfly grubs Try pruning. These insects gather together in bunches during the day and if they congregate on a small branch you can prune it off. Drop the grubs into a bucket of water with some household detergent.

Earwigs Make a trap. These insects like to hide in very small spaces where their bodies are in close contact with the surroundings. Try a flowerpot packed full of crumpled newspaper. The paper can be destroyed with the insects inside.

White cedar moth caterpillars Make a trap by tying a piece of sacking or similar material around the tree trunk. Use only one piece of rope or string across the middle of the sacking, and allow the top to drape down over the bottom half to form a fold. The caterpillars congregate in the fold during the day and can be removed and destroyed. Do not touch them with bare hands!

White-stemmed gum moth caterpillars Make a trap from sacking as described above. Locate it high on the trunk. These caterpillars fall for this trick only when young. Do not touch them with bare hands!

PESTS AND DISEASES

If your tree fern has brown fronds, it is a good idea to look underneath the leaf for insects. A hand lens or magnifying glass is very helpful in identifying pests or diseases on your plants.

The tree fern may have small black dots on it, which would be *thrips'* excreta, evidence that thrips (tiny insects) have been there even if there are none at the current time. If thrips are present they can be sprayed with pyrethrum. If there are none, fertilise with fish emulsion or Nitrosol, and water well.

Rhododendrons with silver on their leaves may also be suffering from thrips, but it could be *red spider* or *lace bug*. If these pests are present, spray with pyrethrum or Lebaycid.

A Kentia palm with chewed leaf ends and some leaves stuck together may be affected by *palm dart*, a little green caterpillar that lives between the leaves during the day and comes out at night to eat the ends of the leaves. There is no need to spray—just squash them.

Most *scale insects* can be sprayed with Malascale, a mixture of Malathion and White Oil, which is not overly toxic. You can mix the Malathion and White Oil together yourself and spray. If you would prefer to use an aerosol, spray with Folimat and immediately afterwards spray with White Oil. On ferns and delicate plants, these sprays should only be misted above the foliage.

Caterpillars Ignore, unless there are many of them. Spray if necessary with Dipel or Carbaryl.

Ants are harmless, but they may indicate scale insects. Spray scale with Malascale and leave the ants alone.

Aphids Spray with pyrethrum.

Borers Pour some methylated spirits down the borers' holes and give the tree or shrub some fertiliser and complete trace elements, and more water during dry periods.

Fruit fly Spray with Lebaycid or Chemspray Fruit Fly Kit.

Spiders Leave them alone; they devour many real pests.

Stink bugs can be controlled with Lebaycid.

Snails and slugs Unless they are doing damage to your seedlings, try to leave them alone. Remember, blue-tongue lizards live on snails, so no snails mean no blue-tongues.

Lawn beetles Ignore them, they do little harm.

Sudden dieback of plants Usually caused by root rot. Remove and destroy the plant. Try to improve the drainage in the area and replace the plant with a root rot resistant variety.

Bronze leaves on azaleas Spray between November and April with Lebaycid.

Any rose leaf problems Treat with rose fungicide, such as Triforine.

POISONOUS GARDEN PLANTS

Many garden plants can cause an unpleasant reaction if ingested and it is important that children are taught never to eat berries, seeds or any other plant parts before checking with an adult that they may do so. Fortunately, most poisonous plant parts have an unpleasant taste and, despite their abundance in our gardens, very few poisonings and deaths occur.

The *rhus or wax tree* is a serious problem in urban areas because, unlike most toxic plants, which must be consumed to produce an adverse reaction, mere contact with any part of this tree (the sap causes the worst symptoms) can cause very painful allergic reactions between 12 hours and seven days after contact. Although significant reactions are unlikely to occur the first time a person has contact with the tree, 98.5% of the population can develop an allergy to rhus. As rhus seeds freely, it has the potential to become a serious weed problem, and is already declared noxious in some parts of Australia. Contact your local Department of Agriculture for information on its status in your area.

The *yellow oleander or cook tree* is possibly Australia's most poisonous plant, and cardiac arrest caused by its consumption has claimed the lives of several children. Although the entire plant is poisonous, the fruits and seeds are the most dangerous parts, and the most attractive to children. Heart failure and respiratory paralysis can also result in death from eating as little as one leaf of the related oleander bush. The extremely unpleasant taste of this commonly cultivated plant has prevented many more poisonings from occuring.

The *angel's trumpet shrub* and other members of the genus Datura contain a mixture of poisonous substances in all plant parts which cause severe, and in some cases fatal, illness. The angel's trumpet shrub has large, slightly hairy leaves and large, pale, pendulous, trumpet-shaped flowers.

Surprisingly, perhaps the most dangerous garden plants are the edible ones, and many have caused fatalities.

PLANT	TOXIC PARTS
Apple	leaves and seeds in large amounts
Apricot	kernels in large amounts

Cherry	kernels
Loquat	seeds in large amounts
Peach	kernels, flowers, leaves and bark
Pear	seeds
Potato	leaves, shoots and green skin
Quince	seeds and fresh leaves
Rhubarb	leaf blades

ROOT ROT

If you have a section in your garden where your native plants are not growing as well as in other areas, check for root rot (Phytophthora) eating away at the roots of the plants. It may have come in a load of contaminated soil, and could be spread by running water so it's important not to have a leaking tap, a hose that is left running, or bad drainage.

Slightly damaged plants can be saved by watering the root zone well with Fongarid.

If the plants die, remove and replant with root rot resistant plants, for example, bottlebrush or paperbarks.

Improve drainage. Check your taps and hoses for leaking.

Phytophthora root rot is a very big problem affecting all kinds of plants, not just Australian natives.

SAWFLY LARVAE

Sawfly larvae are easily identified because they group in clusters on gum trees.

The eggs of the sawfly are deposited in slits in the leaves. After hatching, the larvae remain together in a group during the day, spread out over the tree to feed at night, and re-assemble the next day. They will defoliate the gum tree.

If you have a large gum tree, ignore them. If your gum tree is small and they are eating all the leaves, it's a simple matter to snip off the piece of branch they are on and destroy it.

SUMMER WEEDS

There are a number of common and very hardy summer weeds. Chief among the invasive grasses that readily wage war on rockeries and garden beds are *couch grass* and *kikuyu*, which both spread by sending out runners. Another tough-as-nails invader is *oxalis*. The white, pink and yellow flowers of the different forms can be quite appealing, but the underground stems with their many bulbs result in rapid infestation. The yellow form, *soursob*, is a particular problem in South Australia. *Onion weed* also produces bulbs and has an appearance similar to chives but should not be regarded as edible. *Wandering jew* will not only invade your garden but also presents a danger to dogs: it commonly causes dermatitis on the underparts of canines whey they lie on the weed in warm weather.

Control Most of these weeds can be effectively controlled with Zero, one of the glyphosate herbicides. A concentrated form of the same chemical can be bought in bulk under the name of Roundup. Zero is also available in weeding wand form. These chemicals work only through green tissues, not through the branches, trunk or soil, and when used to control grasses they should be applied to the mature leaves as well as the new growth.

Couch grass and kikuyu should be treated at the onset of warm weather and again in three weeks' time. Oxalis and onion weed will fall back on the resources of their dormant bulbs to resist spraying, so you may need to spray five or six times over the next 18 months to get effective control—be as persistent as the weeds.

Wandering jew is probably best removed by hand as it is not particularly well controlled by Zero. A much more toxic chemical, which does control the weed but which should be regarded as a last resort, is Tryquat. If you decide to use Tryquat, rake all the growth off the plant first and put all that material in a plastic bag in the sun for a few weeks to be sure you have killed it. Then fertilise the original patch of the weed to encourage healthy new growth before you spray—healthy growth will absorb the chemical more rapidly and result in a more complete kill.

Unfortunately, Tryquat is available only in large containers from rural produce stores.

CHAPTER 8
Garden Extras

ARTIFICIAL GRASS

Artificial grass originated in North America as a viable alternative to the tennis court surface. Potential was seen for the huge commercial market and artificial grass surfaces have been adapted and developed to suit any area in any weather condition.

Artificial grass is made from polypropylene, which is a by-product of oil. It is not affected by harsh sunlight, salt, chlorine, mildew or liquids. Your supplier of artificial grass will recommend if any special underlay is required: this may be necessary in wet areas where there is an inundation of salt water. Artificial grass is designed for use in the harsh climate of Australian summers, and is specially stabilised against ultraviolet radiation, which can cause rapid degradation of unstabilised surfaces.

Artificial grass is available in a range of modern colours. It will enhance your backyard landscaping, and is a practical surface around swimming pool or barbecue areas. The surface is kind to children's limbs in play areas, particularly if a rubber underlay is used. It is guaranteed for 5–10 years, although all the manufacturers claim it will last longer.

The cost of artificial grass will vary from $8.50 per metre to over $35.00 per metre, depending on the underlay you require, or if the grass needs to be specially treated.

Artificial grass can be used on tennis courts, pool and barbecue surrounds, stairs, bowling greens and child play areas, and is found in most sporting arenas.

For your nearest supplier, check the yellow pages telephone book, and ensure you specify your requirements so that the supplier can help you choose the correct surface.

For further information

Supergrasse Pty Ltd
65-75 Captain Cook Drive
(PO Box 427)
Caringbah NSW 2229
Telephone (02) 525 4366

ARTIFICIAL ROCKS

The following technique for creating lifelike artificial rocks was developed by Mr Bill Molyneux of Austraflora Nursery in Montrose, Victoria.

Once you have decided on the form which the fake rock is to take (such as a boulder, a rock pool, or an overhang to support a waterfall), the underlying shape should be formed using clay, old bricks, soil in bags or similar materials. It should then be covered with wire mesh for reinforcing. Small or low rocks can be shaped using only chicken wire mesh. The basic formwork is then coated in a mixture of:

4 parts gravel or very coarse sand
2 parts finer sand
1 part cement
½ a part of local soil

The soil is added to give the artificial rock a natural colour that will blend in with the environment and disguise the concrete.

A rough texture (for example, to simulate granite) can be created by waiting until the mixture has started to set, then lightly washing the surface with a hose and brushing it with a coarse wire brush. This action of the water and brush will expose the coarser particles in the mixture.

This simple recipe for making rocks can be used to re-create appealing rock formations you may have spotted in local bushland. Photographs of nature's originals may help to make copying easier.

The artificial rocks can be stained with tea leaves, gum leaves or even stale milk. Take care to match the sand or gravel in the mix with that which occurs locally.

Inlet and outlet pipes for rock pools and the like can easily be concealed beneath the artificial rocks.

AWNINGS

Have you considered dressing up your home with an awning? Awnings used to be terribly boring accessories, but today the market range is both spectacular and highly effective. Awnings will not only protect you and your family from the harsh rays of sun, but will lengthen the life of your furniture and curtains.

A variety of hardware is available to meet your needs. Spring loaded arms for greater strength are one of the options. Some companies offer a range of automatic wind and sun sensor attachments, which can be set to roll the awning in and out depending on the position of the sun. When a wind blows up, the wind sensor will activate the motor to put the awning safely away.

If you have a particular problem, such as the sun hitting your deck almost horizontally, why not look at a spring tensioned awning? These have two motors, one to roll the fabric out and the other to tighten it so that the awning will fit snugly around corners.

Advanced roller shutters may also be an option. These keep the heat out of the house in summer, and stop the cold from coming in during winter.

Just released on the market is the Vergola, a louvred roof system that opens and shuts either manually or electronically. A single sheet of metal will get very hot, but as the louvres are hollow, the air pockets inside help keep the roof cooler.

Fabric The modern trend in awnings seems to be towards acrylic fabrics that come in an incredible range of colours, rather than canvas, which wears and tears. Acrylic material is very durable; it won't rot or shrink, and will cut out 85% of the heat. If you have a large glass roof area in your home, a sun screen fabric is available that cuts out the heat but still lets the light through.

Guarantees All awning and installations we looked at in our programme are guaranteed for 12 months.

Stockists A complete range of awnings and attachments is available through most companies which sell awnings, or they should be able to recommend a reputable supplier.

We gratefully acknowledge the help given by the following companies:

Barter Blinds
167 Port Hacking Road
Miranda NSW 2228
Telephone (02) 522 6622

Aluxor Awnings
James Trading Co Pty Ltd
2 Paton Place
Manly Vale NSW 2093
Telephone (02) 949 6585

Vergola Pty Ltd
1391 Main North Road
Para Hill West SA 5096

Vergola Pty Ltd
14 Tepko Road
Terrey Hills NSW 2084
Telephone (02) 450 2700

CANVAS CLOTHESLINE COVER

The canvas cover shown in our programme segment was made by a tentmaker. The only commercially available covers that we know of come from Sungarden Clothesline Canopies, Factory 7, 8 Taronga Place, Mona Vale NSW 2103. Telephone (02) 997 7055. They take telephone enquiries and orders.

There are two different models available at the moment. 'Budget' is made from double coated polyethylene fabric, UV treated and water resistant, and is priced from $129 to $199.

'Deluxe' is made from 100% Australian cotton canvas, with air release vents, and is priced from $175 to $275. Both models have straight edges with a fringe. The smaller sizes are lightweight and easy to handle. Sizes to fit most hoists, old or new, are presently in stock. All covers come with full fitting instructions.

DECORATIVE GARDEN CHAIRS AND UMBRELLAS

Sandy De Beyer screen-prints outdoor umbrellas, deck chairs and directors' chairs. You can also buy just the covers for your chairs, without replacing the whole item. The cloth used is very strong and durable and is a 50% cotton-polyester mix. The cloth can be washed without removing it from the chair or umbrella. Scrub it with a warm cloth and soap powder, hose it down and leave it outdoors to dry, making sure that it is completely dry before folding it away.

All items can be purchased by mail, or from Sandy's shop at Mosman. The approximate current prices are:

Chairs—$69.95–$85
Chair covers—$29.95–$32.50
Tacks—$1
Umbrellas—$95

The products are all Australian made.

Sandy De Beyer may be contacted at 175 Avenue Road, Mosman, NSW 2088. Telephone (02) 968 1295.

GARDENESQUE

Period landscaping is now a popular area of home and garden restoration, and an exhibition called 'Gardenesque', which covered many aspects of garden ornamentation, was held at Parramatta's historic Elizabeth Farm in September 1988.

The following is a list of exhibitors and a guide to the gardenware they had on display.

Duane Norris & Associates Shop 8, Queens Court 118 Queen Street Woollahra NSW 2025 Telephone (02) 326 2160	Wide range of garden items, including edging tiles, sundials (about $85 for bronze) watering cans (old English with long spouts—$95–$175)
Linda Lehany 1 O'Hara Street Maryville NSW 2293 Telephone (049) 62 2337	Traditional wire garden ornaments
Paul Kenny Antiques 108 Hargrave Street Paddington NSW 2021 Telephone (02) 32 9392	Blue and white reproduction porcelain ware
The Restoration Centre (Barry Stewart) 276 Devonshire Street Surry Hills NSW 2010 Telephone (02) 698 5540	Edging tiles and furniture
Australian Hardwood Furniture (Toby Dupree) Methleigh Morley Street Millthorpe NSW 2798 Telephone (063) 66 3205	Squatters' chairs and hardwood furniture
Feature Cane (Helen Tindale) 641 Parramatta Road Leichhardt NSW 2040 Telephone (02) 569 7609	Seagrass, cane furniture

GARDEN LIGHTING

Garden lighting will change the mood of the area and bring out the magical beauty of the night garden. You can illuminate favourite trees and shrubs, or conceal those areas you would prefer not to see. Lighting can make a large garden seem warm and intimate, and a small area spacious and airy. Garden lights will deter intruders by eliminating shadows around your home, and will light entrances and paths to avoid accidents. They will also increase your entertaining area by creating another 'room' by the barbecue. When you are considering lighting your backyard, aspects of mood and fantasy, security and practicality must be taken into account.

Mood and fantasy The most effective method of achieving a fantasy look in your backyard is to use low voltage lights; kits are available. These lights are inexpensive, come in a variety of colours, and are easy to install. Low voltage garden lighting is essential in homes with children or a family of gardeners. Companies such as Arlec and Garden Glo offer a comprehensive range of mood lights at reasonable prices.

Installing fairy lights to create a magical fantasy in your backyard is certainly most attractive, but also very expensive. These lights are approximately $5.30 per metre and 200 metres (218 yards) is required to cover an average tree. You will also need a waterproof transformer and lead, at an additional cost. Your local lighting centre should be able to assist, or contact Bill Mitchell, Fairylights, 234 Sailors Bay Road, Northbridge, NSW 2063. Telephone (02) 958 1916. Bill will be able to assist you in contacting a distributor in your state.

Security Garden security lighting need not be obtrusive. It is possible to effectively light paths, garden areas, and walkways so that the lighting blends in well with your home. The most important requirement of security lighting is that the switches be close at hand. Many devices are available for this, including timers, sensor controls and other plug-in indoor switches.

Practicality Practical garden lighting will enhance your home and create another living space. By lighting an object or area from above, you will create a floodlit effect, which is ideal for barbecue and pool surrounds. When lighting the barbecue ensure that you shine two lights, one from each side, otherwise you will always be cooking in a shadow. The use of lights with amber or golden glass will reduce the number of insects attracted. GEC-Osram make the Perma-Flood and Porta-Flood, which are very popular and practical lights for entertainment areas. These will give you around 1500 hours of light and cost about 5¢ an hour to run. If you are considering these lights for a pool area, they must be used only for surrounds, as they are not bright enough to illuminate the pool for night swimming. The Super or Garden Flood lights are of quartz halogen, which will light up the backyard like a football oval. These sell for about $35–$40, with replacement bulbs at $15–$20, and should last about 2000 hours.

Installation Unless you are installing a Porta-Flood, which can be easily transferred around the garden on an extension lead, we recommend that a licensed electrician installs all garden lights. They will be able to run wiring to any part of the garden to be illuminated, and place lights at different angles in trees, and around paths, walkways and entertainment areas. A specialist in this field may be able to advise you on the placement of lights. You should discuss your requirements with a local outdoor garden lighting centre before making any unnecessary purchases.

Laws There are few legal problems connected with lighting any part of your backyard, although this does not apply to tennis court installations. Before installing your lights, check that the light source will not disturb your neighbours. Diffused lighting may be a viable alternative to a harsh glare. To achieve this, place the light source behind some translucent object such as frosted glass, or purchase a light with this type of fixture.

Costs The cost will vary depending on the size of your garden and the use you require from your garden lights. You may wish to seek advice from a landscape architect. You can spend anything from $20 for the Porta-Flood type, or $300 for a lighting kit, which will include eight lights, lead and a transformer, to hundreds of dollars if you want to illuminate most of your garden.

It is possible to light your garden with relative ease and only a reasonable amount of expense. Always seek advice from your local garden lighting centre or lighting manufacturers, many of whom have staff on hand to answer any queries. It is also essential to allow, in the budget, the cost of employing a qualified electrician to install your light, so you and your family can get pleasure out of the garden with safety.

GARDEN SOUND SYSTEMS

Imagine lazing by your pool in the balmy sunshine while the music of anyone from Mozart to Minnelli to Minogue wafts over you from every corner of the garden. Outdoor sound systems are a popular addition to the backyard—especially for people who regularly entertain outdoors—but the wide range available can be confusing to buyers. On 'Burke's Backyard' we took a look at the range, and asked Richard Wilkins, host of the Channel 9 television programme *MTV* for his comments on their relative merits.

A practical, if comic, new arrival on the market is The Rock, produced by Rockustics Inc. This is one of a range of weatherproof speakers now available that allow you to enjoy good quality sound outdoors on a permanent basis. The Rock is made of concrete, is fairly heavy, and is said to be very robust. The speaker is built into the rock and, yes, you do have to crack the bottom open if you want to get it serviced, and then re-cement it afterwards. Each speaker costs $600. The manufacturers say The Rock can even be placed in a landscaped waterfall, which is just as well; their height is perfect for attracting the attention of passing dogs.

There are numerous more conventional outdoor speakers. The weatherproof Omnispeaker (which, incidentally, is used in Disneyland) is readily portable; you can take it anywhere—by the pool or tennis court, or to the barbecue when you have guests.

If you prefer, you can put the Omnispeaker permanently in the ground, almost out of sight. It can be buried almost up to the foam collar near the top, which is where the sound comes from. All you do is dig a hole for the speaker and a narrow track to your house or wherever the stereo is, and bury the cable at least 10cm (4″) below the ground to make sure it doesn't become severed by lawnmowers or edgers. Hiding the cable also keeps the yard tidy. The cost is $300 per speaker. You can have any number of speakers, depending on the size of your backyard or your wallet. However, Richard Wilkins advises that if you are really serious about installing an outdoor sound system, you should make it permanent and have at least two speakers.

If you plan to have your speakers closer to the house or on a patio, you might try the BOSE speakers, which are a little cheaper at $225 each, and smaller, although not quite as flexible. The manufacturers say they will operate in rain, hail or snow. You can buy a monkey arm to clamp them to a post or a shelf, or an L-shaped bracket to fit them flush against the wall or under the eaves— inconspicuous and ideal for a patio or pool party.

If you want a speaker that is even more inconspicuous, try the Potted Sound model. The speakers are incorporated in a hanging plant basket, so the result is both decorative and practical. The speaker cable runs discreetly up through the top of the pot and then to your stereo system. This model radiates 360° of sound and costs $225 per speaker.

Yet another alternative is the speaker that can be immersed completely in water so you can listen to music while you are swimming around in your pool—ideal for aquarobics enthusiasts. They are quite expensive at $700 each, but the real catch is that, like pool lighting, you should have them installed while the pool is being built.

Outside the pool the music is barely audible but the water amplifies the signal 16 times. Richard Wilkins put this sound system to the test and found that the music needed to be turned up very loud to be heard over the noise of splashing arms and legs. The music is also necessarily interrupted constantly as the listener must keep surfacing for air. Otherwise the sound is surprisingly good.

Assessing the other speakers, Richard Wilkins rated the BOSE speaker as his personal favourite; it is a high technology well-weatherproofed speaker, which produces good quality sound. Richard said he felt the Potted Sound speaker was an amusing gimmick at the expense of sound quality, that the Omnispeaker produced good quality sound but was unattractive in appearance and, while it is portable, it should ideally be installed permanently. Richard felt that the Rock's greatest advantages are that it can blend with the environment and is likely to be overlooked by burglars.

GARGOYLES AND DRAGONS

A gargoyle is a decorated water spout, designed to throw water away from the footings of a building. The modern downpipe is not nearly as interesting!

The gargoyle of twelfth-century Gothic architecture is usually a grotesque crouching bird or beast, and may have been designed to ward off evil spirits.

In Australia, dragon ornaments were imported from Europe to decorate rooftops from 1890 to 1915. After Federation in 1901, new feelings of nationalism created a demand for Australian motifs such as kookaburras, kangaroos, and native flora, but ornaments were still European made. During the 1950s and 1960s many of these terracotta ornaments were discarded as kitsch.

The sole Australian manufacturer of hand-made terracotta gargoyles and dragons, Graeme Foote, reports a growing demand for his product, both for the restoration of Edwardian and Federation homes and as garden ornaments. People are particularly fond of dragons, which symbolise wealth and good luck in Asia.

For further information

Graeme or Angela Foote
Gargoyles and Dragons Pty Ltd
169 Canterbury Road
Canterbury VIC 3126
Telephone (03) 836 9555

GAZEBOS

The word gazebo means 'I gaze', and tradition dictates that a gazebo should always be positioned where it will command an impressive view. In the backyards of Australia that view may sometimes be of nothing more than a stretch of lawn or the passionfruit vine on the back fence, but in a garden corner thick with greenery and intersected with winding paths, a gazebo can become a tranquil bower from which to spy on garden birds and insects.

For perennial outdoor entertainers a gazebo will provide undercover seating during rain or strong heat. Gazebos can also be used as poolside or courtside pavilions or tea rooms. In one episode of 'Burke's Backyard' we saw how skilfully a walk-through gazebo had been used to add interest to a very long, narrow backyard.

Take care when choosing the size of your gazebo. It should be large enough to contain a table and enough chairs to seat the average number of people who will be using it, although an option is to have bench seats built into the structure. If you have a small yard, however, a large gazebo could dwarf it even more, or possibly make it look excessively cluttered. Also be aware of matching the colours of the gazebo with those of the house, just as you would with a garage.

Before purchasing your gazebo you must submit a building application to your local council and obtain permission to install the structure.

Most of the gazebos featured in the 'Burke's Backyard' story were made by Keith Cutting at the Gazebo Works, 3 Lytton Road, Moss Vale, NSW 2577. Telephone (048) 68 3653 or (048) 85 1328. This is a small family business where old fashioned craftsmanship is the order of the day, but it sells its gazebos nationally. There are two models: a hexagonal 2.9m (9') gazebo, which in its most basic kit form costs $1900, and an octagonal 3.8m (12') design, which starts at $2700. Numerous design variations are available; the most expensive design costs $5000. Delivery and installation costs $350 or more, and freight varies according to the destination.

The story also featured a square gazebo made of treated pine with a western red cedar roof, which is available nationally in kit form from Leisure Logs, PO Box 217, Round Corner, NSW 2158. Telephone (02) 651 2011. A 3m (9') design costs from $1875 to $2375, while a 4m (13') design costs $2500 to $3125, according to style variations. Some freight charges may be added.

GLASSHOUSES

Glasshouses are used to house collections of plants such as orchids, (to help keep them warm) and to propagate plants.

Glasshouses can be bought in kit form (glass, boxes of clips and the instructions for assembling). The cost of the basic glasshouse varies, depending on size, for example:
1.96m wide x 2.59m long (6½ x 8½')—$1200
2.98m wide x 3.82m long (10 x 12½')—$1600.

There are many extras to buy—shade kit, roof vents, and so on.

A shade kit contains shadecloth that sits over the glasshouse, held by brackets away from the glass. Shadecloth is needed to prevent too much sunlight from burning the plants. It is held away from the glass to stop any hail from hitting the glass.

If you are intending to display orchids and ferns, you will need benches; if propagating plants, you will need a propagation bench at a convenient height, heating cables, and an irrigation system. You could end up spending more money for these additional pieces than you did for the glasshouse itself. Therefore, it is necessary to plan carefully before you begin.

One of the newer innovations in glasshouse technology is the treated pine gardenhouse. You buy a pre-assembled wall and it's just a matter of putting some hex screws in, and the house is basically finished once you have inserted the glass.

If you are purchasing an aluminium glasshouse, a shade kit and so on, the assembly can be complex. For an extra $150–$200 it can be assembled for you, and this extra money would be well spent.

HAMMOCKS

There's something very restful about the motion of a hammock. But don't just hang it anywhere—it's important to create the right environment for your hammock if you want to enhance that feeling of serenity.

Placed in a corner of the backyard planted with shady trees and ferns, a hammock will transform that forgotten nook into a lovely, peaceful haven.

Erecting a hammock is not an entirely straightforward procedure. Even if you're lucky enough to have two trees conveniently spaced and just begging for a hammock, avoid the temptation to sling a rope around them. Over a long period this will cut into the bark and choke the tree. It is much better to drill a hole into the tree and screw in a galvanised eye bolt, or a sturdy coach screw with a ring head, and put the rope or the chain through that. This is much kinder to the tree.

The ideal distance between the two points is about 4m (13'). Don't worry if your trees are further apart; you can easily make up the distance with some strong rope or chain. Remember, the hammock should form an arch-like curve with the lowest part of it at least half a metre (2') from the ground.

It you don't have suitable trees you can use posts, or attach one end to a wall. You can even buy a hammock that comes with its own freestanding metal frame. There are also models with wooden spreaders at each end, which some people prefer; the spreaders help keep the hammock flat and stop it from cocooning the occupant.

Hammocks should not be limited to the garden. You can hang them in your sun or rumpus room and they're great on sundecks or verandas. This also saves you the worry of weathering; if an all-cotton material is left outside for long periods, it will naturally fade or rot.

Hammocks are not cheap. You can buy one for about $20 in an army disposal store, but usually they are about $80–$100. The top-of-the-range hammock, handwoven in Brazil, will set you back $260. (The first hammocks were made by Peruvian and Brazilian Indians from the bark of the Hamack tree.) These models are very decorative and also strong, holding 210kg (33 stone).

Once you have assembled your hammock it is advisable to practise getting into it correctly. First, take off your footwear, open up the hammock a little, and then sit right in the middle. Make sure that the fabric doesn't bunch up underneath you. Next, swing your legs diagonally into the hammock so that your head is facing towards one side and your legs towards the other. In this way you receive back support and the hammock will feel comfortable.

A point to remember: it is not a good idea to leave young children alone near a hammock. Do make sure they are supervised.

And a last word of warning: once you get into a hammock, you may never want to work again!

> *Few people are aware that Australia has about six species of deciduous gum trees.*

HAND-MADE TERRACOTTA POTS

Stephen Guildford has been making terracotta pots for about five years. They are a particular type of French provincial earthenware pot, which traditionally has been used to store olives, grain and liquids. They acted as refrigerators, keeping their contents cool by evaporation as the pot breathed.

Stephen began working in the traditional method after seeing it used by potters in the south of France. He uses clay, wood and lengths of rope, constructing a wooden framework and coiling the rope around it. He then smears the clay on as the pot is rotated against a template to give the smooth outside surface. The big advantage of this method is that the pot is made in one process, whereas earlier methods involved doing it in stages.

The whole process takes about half a day, and then the pot is allowed to dry out for seven or eight days before it is baked in the kiln. The firing takes 24 hours as the pots have to be heated up and cooled down slowly. It takes 40kg (88lb) of clay to make one pot. Depending on size, the pots cost between $125 and $295.

The range of pots allows them to be used for many different plants. They can also be used as decorative features inside, but remember to put a glazed dish underneath.

Stephen also makes a range of Portuguese-style lantern pots, which have a very strong Moorish influence, and terracotta ducks and pigeons.

For further information

Stephen Guildford
Promenade Pottery
145 Pacific Road
Palm Beach NSW 2108
Telephone (02) 919 5953

MOSAICS IN THE GARDEN

After cave painting, mosaic work is probably one of the oldest art forms. And, although expertise and artistry take time to develop, it is something that anyone can do at home.

Cynthia Turner is a mosaic artist who converts what most of us would regard as useless rubbish into garden works of art. Cynthia uses ceramic and other tiles, plates, pieces of mirror, shells, and even items such as knives and forks, to make her mosaics. In fact, absolutely anything that won't disintegrate in the weather can be used.

The basic structure on which the mosaic is to be laid, such as a garden lounge, is made out of concrete. A concrete mixer is not required—a trowel is adequate. The concrete is placed inside formwork, which establishes the shape of the lounge.

Next, the surface of the concrete is dampened, and a small section is covered with a cement based adhesive, available from any tiling company. Pieces of tile that have been broken using tile cutters or a hammer are simply pressed onto the adhesive at random. This part of the process is almost like putting together an enormous jigsaw puzzle. After the adhesive has set a little, the excess lumps can be removed to neaten the finished work.

For further information about techniques and commissioned works, contact Cynthia Turner, 46 Morris Street, Summer Hill, NSW 2130. Telephone (02) 798 5263.

MOSSY ANIMALS

If you have always wanted to own an animal but don't want the responsibility, the ongoing expenses or the exercise, there is one unusual alternative that requires nothing more than a regular spray of water to keep it alive and healthy.

A 'Fernery Friend', from the Dingley Fern Market in Melbourne, is a wire frame shaped like an animal and covered with a bush moss, *Thuidium furfurosum*, bound tightly to the frame with fishing line. For added interest, some of the animals have other plants, usually ivy or ficus, growing out of the frame as well. In the case of the 'bird in flight' model, elkhorn ferns are attached to the sides of the bird's body to form the wings.

The largest animal on display at the Dingley Fern Market is an elephant. It is 2m (7′) high and costs $795. The smallest mossy animals are 15cm (6″) high and cost $22. However, some suppliers in other states charge as much as twice the price.

The range of mossy animals includes four sizes of monkey, kangaroos, poodles, dancing bears, hanging bears, dachshunds, ducks, rabbits, flat ducks, dolphins jumping through hoops, turtles, cats, pigs, horse heads, snails, whales, seals, possums, koalas, swans, moose heads, deer and Bambis, giraffes and elephants.

'Fernery Friends' need to be kept out of direct sunlight, preferably in ferneries or under shady pergolas. They dislike windy conditions, which tend to dry them out. If they do dry up the Dingley Fern Market will take them back and inject new life into them.

For further information

Dingley Fern Market
233 Centre Dandenong Road
Dingley VIC 3172
Telephone (03) 551 1868

The Dingley Fern Market supplies a number of nurseries in other states with mossy animals. If you have difficulty in finding the products, however, contact the Dingley Fern market direct.

OUTDOOR COMMUNICATIONS

How many times have you found yourself out in the garden, unable to hear your telephone ringing at all? Or

you rush back inside to answer it, only to find it stops ringing just as you reach it. This is a frustrating experience, but one that is easy to remedy.

One of the cheapest and simplest methods is a telephone extension bell. This costs $25 to $30 and should come with a double adaptor. All you do is plug the bell and your telephone into the adaptor, put that into your wall socket and attach the other end under the eaves or to an exterior wall. Make sure it is protected from rain. It has an on-off switch, so you need to use it only when you are working outside.

For about $15 you can buy a 15m (50′) extension cord reel and take the telephone into the garden with you.

If you don't want to go to these lengths, the next step is the cordless phone. This consists of a battery operated handset linked by radio to a mains-powered base station, which means that you need a power point as well as a phone plug. The range of the phone is up to 250 metres (275 yards) from the base. There are many cordless phones on the market; the cheaper ones are around $180. But be warned, a 'Burke's Backyard' survey showed that many people who have bought phones under $200 have experienced problems, such as whirring sounds, or humming and whistling on the line, which often make it difficult to hear the person at the other end.

The great advantage of the cordless phone, of course, is that it means you are not tied to the house if you are expecting a call. Two hundred and fifty metres is quite a distance, but remember, they are only guaranteed to work this far if you have a direct line of vision from the base station. Any obstacles may decrease the range. If the obstacles are made of metal, such as a tin shed or fence mesh around a tennis court, you may lose the signal altogether.

The Tandy Electronics Duophone is the next in the price range, at about $330. Our survey indicated that it is probably well worth spending the extra money for a considerable improvement in reception and reliability.

The middle-of-the-range cordless phone, the Callmaster, is a little more expensive at between $395 and $450 and we have had some good reports about this one, too. It has dual channels, which means that if you get interference from a neighbour on the same channel, you can switch it over permanently to another. It also has a paging and intercom system, so you can talk to family members in other parts of the house or yard.

Telecom has recently launched a similar version, called the Nomad Plus which costs $449. This is too new to be tested, but Telecom claims to have looked at the problems cordless phones have had in the past and solved them all!

Many problems are caused by the user. It is no use dropping the phone on a hard surface or leaving it under the sprinkler all night and expecting it to be in perfect working order.

The top of the range is the Superphone CT 505 at between $595 and $650. This phone is used by nursery staff and workers in factories and on construction sites because of its ruggedness and reliability. It isn't as glamorous to look at or to hold as the other phones, and is heavier and bulkier. If you are using it only around your backyard, you may feel that you don't need to spend the extra couple of hundred dollars on a phone of this calibre. On the other hand, it has been proven to be the most reliable and powerful of the cordless phones, and it takes the most abuse.

If you have $3000 to $4500 to spare, you may like to invest in a cellular mobile phone. You don't need a base unit for these. They are self-contained phones that can be taken anywhere in Australia as long as there is a cellular network, and that means all capital cities and most regional centres. They are light; you can put them in your pocket, your handbag, or even your picnic basket. The one catch, of course, is the price tag. They cost $50 a month for the access fee and the calls are charged at STD rates; that's 39 cents a minute.

OUTDOOR FURNITURE

Outdoor furniture comes in a wide range of materials: these are some suggestions.

Timber 'Leisurecraft' California Redwood furniture is available in a large range of barbecue settings, chaises and accessories. Settings range from $350 to $1000 in price. 'Sturdiwood' Western Australian Jarrah outdoor furniture is also recommended.

Pine Pine Log Products manufacture a full range of outdoor furniture for domestic and other purposes, including planter boxes, benches, picnic settings, pergolas and ranch rail fencing. They will send you a brochure on request.

Pine Log Products
11 Bourke Street
North Parramatta NSW 2151
Telephone (02) 630 1258

Tubular PVC The genuine 'Polycane' range of patio and poolside settings is priced from $295; it includes a wide choice of settings, styles and accessories. The 'Sunray' range of poolside settings, recliners and accessories is also recommended.

Moulded plastic The 'Emu' Italia range of dining and patio furniture includes large extension tables, marquees and accessories. 'Allibert' garden and leisure furniture—the full range, and 'Plastex' moulded tables and chairs (sets) are also recommended. Prices range from $169 for a five-piece setting.

Tubular aluminium 'Mallin' of New Zealand produce an

exclusive range of entertainer settings in the latest fashion colours. The 'Casualife' easy living range includes settings and accessories.

Garden umbrellas The range of 'Shelta' and 'Casualife' umbrellas is recommended.

For further information

In New South Wales, these products are all available and on display at Alexander McDonalds Pty Ltd, Home and Garden Service Centre, 72-74 Cecil Avenue (corner Terminus St), Castle Hill, NSW 2154. Telephone (02) 634 4433.

PAVING

If you are considering paving around your home, swimming pool, barbecue area, garage or driveway, we have a few suggestions, but also recommend that you seek advice from your local building information service.

Probably the most inexpensive surface available is gravel at about $5 per metre. Another cheap alternative is the common house brick, at $7 per square metre, but it is fairly heavy to work with.

Concrete pavers, at $13 per square metre, are ideal for general purpose areas like pools, driveways and paths. They are not suitable for barbecue areas, as they will soak up the grease. They are a uniform size and thickness, and much easier to lay than the ordinary house brick.

Even clay pavers, at $20 per square metre, are still economical. They come in a variety of textures that are useful for various home applications. On the freshly laid clay pavers you will notice the salt coming to the surface. This is called efflorescence, and it will disappear in about six months. If you find the look too unattractive, a mild solution of hydrochloric acid washed over the surface will usually get rid of the problem.

At $42 per square metre, reconstituted sandstone is half the price of the real thing, and still looks terrific.

Quarry tiles are a popular type of paving. They can transform almost any area, but when using them in a garage or driveway, choose a glazed or semi-glazed finish, so oil and grease can be easily removed. The glazed surface is not wonderful for the pool area, however, as it can be very slippery. It will cost around $20 per metre.

It is important to choose a surface around the pool that won't cause accidents. A rough, almost uneven surface is recommended, such as uneven slate.

Remember, pavers tend to last forever, so take time to select the type that will be best for your needs.

For further information on the 'Claypave' range of Queensland-manufactured clay pavers (distributed throughout southeast Queensland and New South Wales), contact:

Amber (St George) Pty Ltd
110 Stoney Creek Road
Beverly Hills NSW 2209
Telephone (02) 570 6155

Amber (Blacktown) Pty Ltd
98 Richmond Road
Blacktown NSW 2148
Telephone (02) 671 3222

Amber (Gosford) Pty Ltd
293 Manns Road
Gosford NSW 2250
Telephone (043) 24 5366

Amber (Eastern Suburbs) Pty Ltd
12 Rainbow Street
Kingsford NSW 2032
Telephone (02) 663 3863

Amber (Liverpool) Pty Ltd
179 Elizabeth Drive
Liverpool NSW 2170
Telephone (02) 821 1133

Amber (Northern Beaches) Pty Ltd
42 Frenchs Forest Road
Seaforth NSW 2092
Telephone (02) 949 6600

Amber (Holdings) Pty Ltd
108 Pacific Highway
Waitara NSW 2077
Telephone (02) 487 2822

They will also provide information on Clark Brick pavers, or you can contact Clark Brick direct.

Clark Brick Ltd
Nuwarra Road
(PO Box 21)
Moorebank NSW 2170
Telephone (02) 602 0944

PONDS

There is something magnificent about water in the backyard, and many people have installed garden ponds, which often contain fish.

The first thing to do is to pick the location. Ideally it should be in a place that looks as if water would naturally accumulate in that position. Avoid tree roots that might upset the pond, and overhanging branches that might drop leaves in.

A pond constructed by digging a hole and placing a rubber or vinyl liner inside may be quick and simple, but it may also have a limited life, as some liners may become damaged and deteriorate. Construction of a more permanent pond generally takes more time and is more expensive, but it is worth the effort if you would like to

The following tips on pond installation were supplied by Garden Art Fountains.

Dos and don'ts

1 Do not install the pond in the lowest point of your garden. It will collect mud and rubbish every time it rains, and grass clippings when the lawn is mowed. There are two types of natural pools, the swamp at the lowest point of the terrain and the pond part-way down a slope, fed by a fresh mountain stream. The latter is the one to emulate.

2 Do not install the pond in full sun unless its only purpose is to grow waterlilies. It is better to have a shady end surrounded by trees and ferns and a sunny end for lilies.

3 Do not make a large shallow pond, particularly if it is to be in a sunny spot. Shallow water goes green much more readily than a deeper pond. Ideal depth is 460–600mm (1½–2′). This depth also suits waterlilies and fish.

4 Do not make a pond by cementing natural rocks together. It is most unlikely ever to hold water. Small soil movements cause cracks to open up between cement and rock and the water escapes. Use of a PVC liner will guarantee that a pond holds water.

5 Make sure that the garden at a higher point than the pond does not drain into the pond. Slope soil slightly to the side, so that water drains to either side of the pond. This makes an overflow unnecessary as the only rain going into pond is what actually lands there.

6 It is not true that waterlilies object to moving water— as long as no spray is landing on their leaves or flowers, they live quite happily in a stream. Books published in the UK advise against moving water because it lowers the temperature. In Sydney, Perth and areas north low temperatures are not a problem.

POOL LINERS

The attractive, heavy duty vinyl swimming pool liners made by Nylex are especially useful when restoring in-ground pools, as they can be installed over any surface, even if it is cracked.

The pool liners are pre-formed in the factory to fit pools of any shape, and then vacuum moulded on site for an exact fit and a wrinkle-free finish. The flexible qualities of the liner make it particularly suited to areas that are prone to ground movements.

The latest 'new season's prints' include Mediterranean Marble, Midnight Granite, Blue Splash Granite, Midnight Marble and Mudgee Slate, allowing you to create exactly the type of swimming pool to fit your lifestyle; cool and reflective, shimmering and inviting, or natural and relaxed.

Nylex pool liners have UV inhibitors to extend their life in the Aussie sun, and are Sanitized® to inhibit bacterial, algal and fungal growth. They are quick to install and are guaranteed for at least five years, although many last for well over 15 years.

It is possible to use these liners in above-ground pools, but this is an expensive option. However, liners developed especially for above-ground pools are available, mainly in plain colours and in one print called Palatine.

For an average-sized in-ground pool 4.5 × 9m (15 × 30′) that you wish to restore, the purchase and installation of a pool liner costs around $3100 if you choose the new season's prints, slightly less for plain colours. This cost depends of course on the shape of the pool and how easy the access is.

If you need to restore an in-ground pool, or are installing a new one, look at the range of Nylex new seasons prints as an alternative to conventional pool finishes. Enquire at your local swimming pool renovator or installer, or contact Nylex in your state.

POOL PREPARATION AND SAFETY

Backyard swimming pools must be maintained between the narrow range of acidity and alkalinity to avoid infections. If pools are not maintained correctly, children especially are at risk from infections of the ears, skin and eyes. There is also the potential for more serious infections like meningitis, hepatitis and gastroenteritis. When the pH level is too high, chlorine is not effective in killing off germs and bacteria. Chlorine is an oxidiser which burns out germs, forming chloramines, which are half-burned-out germs that smell of chlorine. While a pool is in regular use in summer, it is essential that you carry out regular chlorine checks.

Storage Always store chlorine in an airtight and childproof container. Use one container for one chemical, as different types of chlorine react violently to each other, and a serious accident may occur.

Fencing The biggest worry with pools is the danger that your child may drown. It is very hard to keep children away from water, but a fence will act as a deterrent. Council regulations vary, but a fence over 1.2m (4′) is advisable. There should be no footholds for climbing children, and a childproof lock should be checked regularly, as they can break. Check under the fence for gaps that may have been dug by a neighbourhood dog, and never leave pieces of furniture near the pool area, as they make wonderful ladders for adventurous children.

Drownings Death by drowning in children under five is the second commonest cause of death in that age group. It takes only three to four minutes from the time the child falls into the water and stops breathing, to the point at which they may be unable to recover. Children do not necessarily splash and make much noise when they fall; more frequently they just silently fall to the bottom.

Having your child taught to swim is advisable, but it may not prevent them from drowning. All children, under any circumstances, *must* be supervised when swimming and playing around the pool area.

SOLAR POOL HEATING

There is a good argument for heating your swimming pool—it can then be used for more months of the year. Solar heating is the most popular system; even in Melbourne it has approximately 60% of the pool heating market.

With solar heating, the house roof is used to heat the pool. Black strip absorbers made of EPDM (Ethyl propylene diene monomer), a synthetic rubber, are placed on the roof; the water is pumped up from the pool to the roof and back down to the pool. This system takes the heat out of the roof, thereby cooling the house, and puts it into the pool.

The Zane solar heating system which we looked at is a fully automatic, thermostatically controlled system, and is computer controlled through probes that register the temperature on the roof and the temperature in the pool. When the roof is significantly hotter than the pool, the system is automatically turned on. This is a drain on the pool's filtration system, so a second electric pump needs to be installed. The cost is usually between $900 and $1000 and is justifiable if it dramatically extends the use of the pool. There are many other solar systems available.

There are some trade offs with solar heating. The water has to be filtered for a number of extra hours per day, which can mean double the filtration costs per year—maybe $100 or so extra, if you do not have the second pump.

There is virtually no maintenance, but with a solar heated pool it is essential to keep the chlorine levels up to avoid the bacteria and algae problems that accompany warm water.

Comparative costs of pool heating methods

Solar (installation)	$3500
(ongoing—pump running costs)	$150 approx pa
Gas (installation)	$2500–$3500
(ongoing)	$1100 pa
Electrical (installation)	$4500
(ongoing)	$800 offpeak pa, or:
	$4000 mains pa

SUNDIALS

Dr Margaret Folkard and Mr John Ward come from careers as Defence Department physicists, although John has now retired and works full-time on making sundials. They started their hobby business, Sundials Australia, after making a sundial for a friend more than ten years ago. Since then they have toured the world researching sundials.

Uses Even though they can keep time precisely and are perfectly functional in fine weather, sundials are generally bought for ornamental purposes. People use them as a focal point in the garden, and their long term accuracy and durability make them suitable as family heirlooms. Sundials are very tactile objects and the larger Sundials Australia models, in particular, are designed for complete human involvement—you walk over them, climb over them, tell the time by your own shadow, and so on.

While the most common sundial is made up of a horizontal plate and a pointer, there is a different sundial for every location; some are vertical and can be fixed to walls; some are cylindrical (pillar sundials); some are shaped like books and crosses. Others are portable; or formed by stained glass windows (the shadow cast outside is read from inside the room); and there are spherical sundials, which are comprised of bronze bands and arrows (the armillary sphere with equatorial ring). Family names, emblems, coats-of-arms, drawings and inscriptions can be included in the designs.

Availability Sundials Australia makes standard models (each available in up to five different designs) for Brisbane, Sydney, Melbourne, Adelaide, Perth, Canberra, and Bowral (this last because of interest generated there by garden history societies). If you live more than 60km (38 miles) from these cities, Sundials Australia will make a suitable sundial and still charge the basic price.

Costs The basic capital city sundial, 30cm (12") in diameter, costs $250. The same model, custom-made with your picture or favourite piece of verse on it, costs $450. A larger, elaborately personalised sundial can cost about $1000. Large scale works are also commissioned for public gardens, shopping centres and schools.

Sundials Australia has resurrected the art of sundial making and married it with modern technology. The company's models are designed to keep accurate time to within a couple of minutes for 500–600 years, and are made from a bronze alloy not susceptible to 'bronze disease', so are highly durable.

Sundials available from garden centres tend to be inaccurate, because they are generally made to a single design regardless of where they are sold. In many cases the designs do not utilise modern technologies and the materials used are less durable. Prices range from $70–$120.

How sundials are made A correctly made sundial must have a time correction graph to compensate for the difference between solar time and clock time. The first step in making a sundial is to calculate these time corrections and the necessary angles of the sundial. These are drawn up into a design, of which a photographic negative is made in a darkroom. The prepared negative is then put in contact with a piece of material called a photopolymer. Ultraviolet light is beamed through the negative and this exposes the photopolymer underneath. The part which has been exposed hardens and the unexposed, softer material can be scrubbed away under running water. What is left is a series of hardened lines and numbers that can be used as a pattern on which the metal can be moulded. After the sundial has been cast in the bronze alloy, the plate and gnomon (the finger or pointer) are sanded, buffed and assembled, ready to mount on a pedestal in the backyard.

For further information

There are no distributors other than the Sundials Australia workshop. All enquiries should be directed to Sundials Australia, 3 Bedford Street, Kensington Park, SA 5068.

TENNIS COURTS

The cost of constructing or resurfacing a tennis court will depend on the company you deal with. The quoted price should include minimum excavation, base, fencing and surface. It will take about two months to install a court, as the asphalt and concrete require time to cure.

Surface	New court	Resurfacing
Wimbledon Grass	$35 000	$10 000
Tru-flex (Acrylic)	$26 000	$5 000
Supreme	$45-$50 000	$27 000
Rebound Ace	$65-$70 000	$40-$45 000

Council regulations Building codes and regulations change from council to council and state to state. We would strongly advise that anyone interested in installing a court should check first with the local council for any restrictions. Some councils have introduced a code which stipulates that your house, pool, court and paved area must not exceed 60% of your property.

Generally, lights are not permitted on residential courts, but you can apply to your council for special consideration. In Western Australia each court application is judged on its individual merit and this may include lighting.

Size The standard tennis court size is 23.75 x 11m (78 x 36'). Including court surrounds, an acceptable total size is 30.48 x 15.24m (100 x 50').

VICTORIAN GARDEN ORNAMENTS

In recent times garden ornaments have tended to be gaily coloured and frequently just a little too eye-catching, so that they tend to overshadow rather than complement and enhance the flowers and shrubs. Fortunately, the more subtle and elegant garden ornaments of the Victorian era

are once again available from many garden centres and nurseries.

The ornaments are mostly quite practical, as well as durable. Cast iron ornaments painted in the traditional Brunswick green team beautifully with the gleaming brass of others. Prices vary depending on the outlet, but the following list provides a rough guide.

Ornaments and approximate prices

Solid cast iron bird bath — $680
Foot scraper — $90
Lion's head fountain with pump, transformer and
  reservoir — $840
Brass garden tap plus gully trap — $740
Old-fashioned decorative garden edgers — $9 each
Hoop garden edgers — $17 for five
Ornate hose holder — $140
Hand operated, fully functional water pump — $395
Green garden frog sprinkler — $70
Wide variety of brass garden taps—$50-$80
Whimsical signs ('Bunnies Crossing', 'Ducks Crossing') —
  $50
Weather vanes—black, green or brass versions of roosters,
  ducks, kangaroos, golfers, and so on — $140-$200
Garden gates — $270-$1100
Garden arch—$200-$650
Ornamental garden stakes — $19 for three

An extensive range of hanging baskets and pot holders, coated in plastic coloured the same Brunswick green, makes it possible to match all your garden ornaments and accessories, both indoors and out.

Victorian garden ornaments are readily available in all states. Enquire at larger nurseries and garden centres, but remember, prices will vary.

CHAPTER 9
Gardens for Children

CUBBYHOUSES

The 'Burke's Backyard' story on cubbyhouses was filmed at:

The Cubby King
Rob (Wally) Wallington
49 Glanmire Road,
Baulkham Hills NSW 2153
Telephone (02) 624 8008.

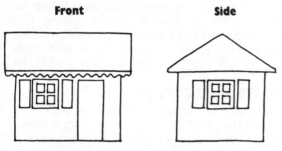

Front   Side

Cubby King cubbyhouses come in a variety of sizes; feature a lockable door, fixed or opening windows, and perspex window panes, and are fully weatherproof. For additional contacts, 'Cubby Houses' is listed in the index of yellow pages telephone books for each capital city.

DIRT HEAPS FOR CHILDREN

Most children will eventually need some backyard play equipment, and according to Don Burke, the most popular piece is the simple dirt heap.

If adults find dirt heaps boring it's only beause they've forgotten the power of childhood imagination. A dirt heap can be transformed into a mountain community complete with roads, tunnels, caves, farms, cities, mines, and lots more. Saucers sunk into the soil can form dams or lakes; sections of drainage pipe can become long tunnels.

From a child's point of view, a dirt heap has several advantages over a sand pit. A tunnel dug in sand will inevitably collapse while a dirt tunnel will stay put, and a dirt heap also allows one to indulge in the pleasure of making mud. Older children can use a dirt heap as a BMX bike jump, a fort or whatever takes their fancy.

Of course, parents derive some advantages from a dirt heap too—there will always be soil on hand for top dressing the lawn or for adding to garden beds.

Naturally, an afternoon on the dirt heap will result in some pretty filthy clothes, but usually not more than most modern laundry detergents can handle. Just make sure the children change into old clothes first and you should be able to minimise the upset of the odd stain mark.

The dirt heap shown in a 'Burke's Backyard' story was made up of approximately three tonnes of material. This amount would cost somewhere between $60 and $100 including delivery to your home—just look up a supplier in the Landscaping Supplies section of the yellow pages telephone book and ask for ordinary garden soil.

GARDEN MINI SAFARI

If you've run out of ideas or money for entertaining your younger children, a wildlife safari costs nothing at all; can be prepared within minutes in your own backyard; and will occupy the children for hours.

What you will need

* a ball of string
* a white bowl or container with a lid (an empty plastic icecream container is ideal)
* a kitchen strainer
* a pale-coloured pillow case
* a 'pooter', a tool which the environmental organisation, The Gould League, has designed for moving small animals from one container to another. Make your own by cutting a plastic straw in half; insert a piece of old nylon stocking between the two halves, and tape them together again. By pointing the straw at small animals and sucking air through it, the animal can be picked up by suction without fear of swallowing either it or any dirt; the stocking stops them from coming right through.
* a magnifying device such as a magnifying glass or a mini microscope. Educational toy shops sell the latter (some models allow both overhead and side viewing of the animal) for less than $15.

How to conduct the safari   Walk around the garden unrolling the ball of string behind you through as many different sorts of areas as are available. The string marks the safari route which your children will follow. All the children need to do is search for living things, such as insects, lizards, slugs and snails, spiders, millipedes and slaters along the path marked by the string.

There may often appear to be no obvious sign of living things, but the tiny inhabitants of leaf litter can be revealed by placing handfuls of litter in a kitchen strainer and shaking it over a white container. Watch closely for anything that moves against the white background, and use the pooter to transfer the little animals to your magnifying device.

If bushes at first appear to be uninhabited, place the pillow case under them and shake the branches vigorously so that small insects and spiders drop out onto the pale cloth.

If you don't know your insects very well, it is a good idea to have a book on hand for identification. One of numerous good books on Australian insects is *An*

Introduction to Australian Insects, by Hadlington and Johnston, New South Wales University Press, $14.95.

KIDS' PLAY

Mary Jeavons, a landscape architect and planner, recently completed a masters degree in which she examined kids' play. Ms Jeavons found that, disturbingly, modern playgrounds are generally inadequate in providing children with the stimulation and challenges they seek, both for pleasure and for learning experiences. This article summarises some of the research findings Ms Jeavons discussed with Don Burke on 'Burke's Backyard'.

'In a world where open space is at a premium, a child's search for adventure has become more difficult. The exciting bushland of yesterday has all too often been replaced by sterile concrete and barren grass.

'The sanitisation of urban creeks, by paving them with concrete to form stormwater drains, has removed all their associated life—yabbies, frogs, tadpoles, and so on. This has turned these areas into dead spaces with few interesting features.

'Children certainly need swings and slides to develop their gross motor skills, but they also need to be able to alter their playground environment. By changing things around and fiddling with them the children can exercise their creativity as well as their bodies. In this respect the adults who design playgrounds have already had all the fun. The designers, in most cases, are the people who get the most creative experience out of the playground—by the time it is accessible to children it is relatively static.

'Another dilemma arises where playgrounds are designed to be so safe that children are deprived of opportunities to learn to cope with challenges and danger. These experiences are a vital part of learning to respond to the demanding situations that confront all of us during our lives. However, parents tend to want all such risks to their children's wellbeing removed. The solution to this conflict is not clear.

'Children develop territories, which expand as they grow older. Boys' territories seem to be considerably larger than those of girls. There appears to be a widely held belief that boys will benefit from such exploration and the things they will encounter in the process, but girls will be safer if they stay at home. Girls are possibly being encouraged to think that they will not be interested in the things that boys will find further afield. Perhaps the desire to protect girls more than boys could deprive the girls of experiences and lessons vital to their development.

'Backyards vary enormously, but frequently these do not meet the needs of the children who occupy them. While some abound in pets of all sorts, which fascinate and provide great pleasure for the kids who own them, in others—particularly where guard dogs are kept—the pets actually frighten the children. This limits the kids' use of the backyard space, because they are unlikely to enter certain parts of it. It is also very important for backyards to be designed to allow kids to find little nooks and crannies where they can build cubbies or forts as backdrops for their imaginings. They need places to hide in and remove themselves from other people.

'Kids also appear to be generally much more aware of detail than adults. They tend to notice the things adults miss, such as textures and colours, or sunlight glinting on shiny surfaces. Area also seems to have a different significance for children—many adults remember spaces from childhood as being large but find them to be quite small when they revisit them later in life.

'In conclusion, it would appear that in modern planning we may be ignoring many of the fundamental things we enjoyed as kids, and which enriched our childhood. There is a greater need for us to examine the needs of children from a child's perspective. Many backyards are designed for adults, even though they are mostly occupied by kids.'

PLAY EQUIPMENT

Pine Log Products manufacture a 'domestic and kindergarten range' of play equipment, which includes tree houses, cubbyhouses, lookouts, swings, climbers, forts and sand pits. They will send you a brochure on request.

Pine Log Products
11 Bourke Street
North Parramatta NSW 2151
Telephone (02) 630 1258

TREE HOUSES

There are tree houses in backyards all over the world. Most children dream of building a house in a tree, be it a simple platform or a treetop mansion.

'Burke's Backyard' looked at the problems faced by one family whose neighbour objected to their tree house. The neighbour lodged an objection with the local council, who then ordered that the tree house be demolished. The family that had built the tree house appealed against the demolition order to the Land and Environment Court but, although the assessor was sympathetic to the children's aspirations, he supported the demolition order.

The Local Government Act states that anything that is a structure, made up of more than one part, requires approval. This need not necessarily involve a formal building application; a written request may suffice.

The council has to consider the effect the structure will have on neighbours, for example, overshadowing, overlooking, invasion of privacy, and so on.

So, *before* you set out to fulfil the kids' dreams of a tree house, contact your local council, explain the details, provide a plan and let them make an assessment—avoid the heartbreak of having to demolish the kids' castle.

CHAPTER 10
Indoor and Potted Plants

AFRICAN VIOLETS

African Violets (*Saintpaulia ionantha*) are wonderful plants. They are members of the Gesneriad family, which includes gloxinias and streptocarpus, and are possibly the world's most popular flowering indoor plants, with their interesting, hair covered foliage and 'spun sugar' flowers.

They originated in the higher elevations of tropical East Africa; the Usambara region, northeast Tanganyika (Tanzania) and South Kenya, and were collected in 1892 by Baron Walter von Saint Paul-Illaire. The plants were simple, with small blue flowers which gave little indication of the forms which would arise from them. Now there is a huge range of colours available and we are not too far away from having a true red African violet.

African violets have a natural tendency to mutate and give rise to new effects. These sports, and a century of hybridising have produced a wealth of possibilities. Flowers can be single, double and semi-double, with ruffles or fringes to different degrees. Flower colours can be blue, dark blue, purple, orchid, lavender, pale blue, pink, coral, peach, red, fuchsia, plum or white. As yet there are no yellow or orange African violets. Flower types can be 'Fantasy' (with a contrasting edge, spots or blotches), 'Geneva' (white-edged) or 'Chimera'—at the moment these are in vogue. They can have pale lavender stars on white backgrounds, white stars on 'Fantasy' backgrounds, pink speckled with blue, and many other variations.

Leaves can be plain, serrated, ruffled, scalloped, smooth, quilted or 'strawberry' in texture; and heart, oak or holly shaped.

There are standard, miniature, semi-miniature and trailing forms. The most exciting of the newer varieties of African violets are the miniature ones. Many of them are trailing varieties that will cascade over the side of the pot, and they are just as hardy as the larger sizes.

The most commonly encountered problem with African violets is that they won't flower. To promote flowering it is important to have the plant inside in a brightly lit position. If the plant is in a poorly lit position it will stop flowering and eventually die. Leaves should be kept dust-free with a soft brush.

African violets are relatively easy to grow. The potting mix is critical—it must be light and fluffy for excellent drainage. Add a little African violet fertiliser to promote growth and flowering.

Water only when the top of the soil is dry to the touch and always use tepid water. Wick pots are very good for African violets as the water is absorbed up the wick into the pot and the plant cannot be over or underwatered.

Ceramic self-watering pots are available at most craft shops. Overwatering probably kills more African violets than anything else. Remember, if in doubt about watering, *don't*. Once a week in summer and once a fortnight in winter is quite adequate.

If you have a sick African violet, you may have to be cruel to be kind! Remove it from the pot, pull the root system apart and trim off any dead roots; remove old leaves, leaving only the healthy young leaves; remove all flowers. Put a light and fluffy potting mix in the container (perlite and peat moss mix is typical of African violet potting mixtures) and repot the plant so that some of its elongated stem is buried, that is, quite deeply. This will grow into a healthy new plant with renewed vigour. The leaves that were removed can be trimmed so that the stem is 25–30mm (1–1½″) long and put into another little pot, pushed about 20mm (¾″) into a mixture of vermiculite and perlite and they will strike as cuttings in six to eight weeks.

If African violets are grown in too much shade they will suffer from a fungus disease (grey mould on leaves). Put them in a brightly lit position about 45cm (18″) from a sunny window with sheer curtains to filter strong sunlight. Use fluorescent lights if natural light is inadequate.

Prices for African violets range from $2–$10.

For further information

African Violet-Gesneriad Society of NSW Inc
(John Hodges)
PO Box 173
Homebush NSW 2140
Telephone (After Hours) (02) 674 4462

Early Morning African Violet Group Inc
12 Tarraleah Place
Boronia VIC 3155
Telephone (03) 800 2695

North West African Violet Group
17 Cohuna Street
West Brunswick VIC 3055

African Violet Society of Queensland
64 Armadale Street
St Lucia QLD 4067

African Violet-Gesneriad Society of SA
PO Box 261
Park Holme SA 5043

African Violet Society of WA
PO Box 3
South Perth WA 6151

African Violet-Gesneriad Society of Canberra Inc
Griffin Centre
Bunda Street
Canberra ACT 2601

BALCONY GARDENS

A great many people who live in flats or home units find themselves embarrassed by the state of the plants barely clinging to life out on their balconies. Even in cases where a special effort was made to make the area bright and attractive, all too often it ends up floundering.

The main reason for this is that balconies are extremely inhospitable environments for plants. They experience total shade for part of the day and the full blast of the sun for the remainder; they are exposed to wide temperature fluctuations; and they bear the full brunt of city pollution and windy weather.

Many balconies become crowded with indoor plants which are past their best and have been placed outside to recover. In such a harsh position their chances of survival, let alone recovery, are scant indeed. Not only do the plants look past their best, but also they are usually left in the containers in which they were purchased and the end result is a mess of mismatched containers of mostly drab colours and unimaginative shapes. Most balconies afford some sort of view, but too often the arrangement of plants actually detracts from rather than enhances it.

An effective balcony garden should form a link between the interior of the house and the outside environment. It should also suit the lifestyle of the occupants of the home (for example, it should be low maintenance for a busy family).

One 'Burke's Backyard' programme featured a 'makeover' of a city balcony garden. The following is a list of the plants that were growing on the balcony before our makeover, with comments on their suitability:

* Standard 'Iceberg' roses—exposed to too much shade and pollution to reach full potential.
* Azalea indica—position too hot and dry; prone to red spider mite; thrips and pollution.
* Recuperating indoor plants (*Dracaena marginata*, *Philodendron cordatum*, Maidenhair Fern)—not likely to recover for reasons mentioned previously.
* Petunias in terracotta disc—have performed well with a beautiful display for many months but now past their best and ready to be replaced.
* Cyclamen—appropriate plants but not used to their best advantage.
* Impatiens—not wind hardy; flowers well but needs constant watering.
* Lavender dentata (French)—an excellent choice; will cope with winds, loves the sun, fragrant, blooms all year round.

The containers on the balcony included a mixture of styles in black plastic, white metal and terracotta.

In the course of the makeover, the only plants retained from the original arrangement were the lavender and the cyclamen, but the containers used for the roses and petunias were suitable for recycling in the new design.

The refurbished balcony was based on a theme of simple, elegant lines and a cohesive colour scheme of white containers, dark green foliage and soft pink flowers.

The plants, and the reasons for using them, are as follows:

* Lavender—a second plant was purchased and the two were planted in the metal rose containers and moved forward into sunny corners.
* *Buxus sempervirens*—a hardy, low growing evergreen, used to border the front of the balcony between the lavenders and planted in matching, rectangular, metal troughs.
* Standard privet (*Ligustrum ovalifolium*)—the very qualities that make these plants unwanted weeds also make them superbly suited to growing on balconies. As evergreen plants, they only need an occasional haircut.
* *Primula obconica*—shade loving and long-flowering, these inexpensive plants provide a softening touch when planted under the privets and can be replaced seasonally.
* Coral Pink Cyclamen—echoes the colour of the primula and will take the cold of a Melbourne winter without flinching. The cyclamen were planted in the terracotta disc, but this was painted white to maintain the theme set for the other containers. The plant can be brought inside for indoor colour periodically.

A final touch chosen by the owners was a little bronze putti, which forms a link with some other pieces of statuary inside the home.

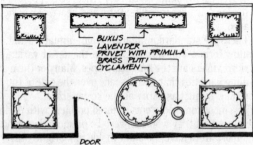

VIEW TO THE NORTH

Other common green plants that will resist wind, pollution and drying out in most areas are:

Pigface
Coprosma x kirkii
Agapanthus orientalis
Fishbone fern (*Nephrolepis* sp)
Ivy (*Hedera helix*)
New Zealand Christmas bush (*Metrosideros excelsa*)
Hebe x franciscana 'Blue Gem'
Russelia equisetiformis

Boston ivy (*Parthenocissus tricuspidata*)
Asparagus densiflorus 'Sprengeri'
Coprosma repens
Cissus rhombifolia
Philodendron selloum

BATHROOM PLANTS

Plants definitely add a nice touch to bathrooms. As you step out of the steamy mist of the shower and reach through some tangled greenery for your towel, visions of tropical island paradises are apt to drift around the fringes of your consciousness.

But what is it like for the plants? Are bathrooms really akin to equatorial jungles, and what plants are likely to perform best in this environment?

Unfortunately, bathrooms are actually quite inhospitable environments for most plants. For brief periods the plants are subjected to high humidity and blasts of hot air from heaters or hair dryers, while at other times the bathroom may become bitterly cold. Bathroom windows are often small, permitting minimal light entry. And, as if all that is not enough, bathroom plants are subjected to what, from their angle, could only be described as pollution from deodorants, hair sprays and talcum powder.

Plants commonly used in bathrooms include: *aspidistra*, the 'cast-iron plant'—very hardy, will survive virtually anywhere, including dimly-lit positions; *bamboo palm*, an elegant, hardy palm; *Cissus rhombifolia*—copes well and can be grown up a tall frame fixed in its pot, or can trail from a hanging basket; *devil's ivy*, another climber, which can be encouraged to outline the shower recess—virtually unkillable; *dieffenbachias*—much more touchy and disinclined to perform well under the stresses imposed by a bathroom; *fishbone fern*—needs a well-lit position and may not be a good long-term proposition; *happy plant*—a hardy survivor, even in only moderately lit conditions; *madonna lily* (*Spathiphyllum*)—reasonably hardy but may not flower unless placed close to a window.

Many people are convinced that the *maidenhair fern* will thrive in the humidity of the bathroom, but lots of light is its most important requirement. Place it close to a north-facing window. If this is not possible, grow one anyway, but just treat it as you would a bunch of flowers, and replace it when it starts to die.

Marantas are reasonably hardy and tolerant of quite low light intensity. *Parlour palms* are almost indestructible and one of the classic bathroom survivors. *Peperomias* are hardy little triers, well-suited to cramped bathrooms where something larger would get in the way. *Philodendrons* are very hardy, almost indestructible and able to survive even in dimly-lit positions.

Plants which begin to look a little worse for wear can be given a spell either in a more suitable indoor position (such as near a north-facing window admitting large amounts of light) or in a protected spot outside—except in winter.

Hanging baskets can be suspended over the bath or close to the window as required. Plastic pots are available in a range of colours to suit any decor. Lobster-pot style hanging baskets and containers, fitted with liners and topped with coconut fibre, can be used for a more earthy, natural effect. By placing odd pots inside matching containers you can simply and swiftly achieve a cohesive, co-ordinated look.

CUT FLOWERS

Cut flowers are best picked before they have fully matured so they will have a reasonable vase life. For this reason many flowers such as roses and gladioli are marketed in tight bud, while carnations are usually sold fully open, but could be opened by the consumer if purchased as half-open buds.

Others with a flowerhead comprising a number of flowers, such as freesias and alstroemeria, must have at least one flower fully coloured and developed or partly open. If picked tighter than this, the flowers will not open properly. The same is also true for daffodils, tulips and irises, which must be fully coloured and almost open when sold.

One reason for picking flowers in bud is that pollination usually starts the ageing process within the flower.

Avoid flowers that have:

* slimy stems (they must have been in water for some time)
* been standing in the sun
* been exposed to car exhaust fumes
* badly crushed or broken foliage
* dried or transparent petals, especially if there is some tip burn or browning
* shrivelled, unopened buds

Preserving cut flowers *Keep flowers cool.* As flowers are living, they respire (breathe and metabolise) at greater rates in higher temperatures thus depleting their energy resources much faster than they would at lower temperatures. Keep them away from heaters (especially kerosene) and draughts, which also tend to desiccate delicate petals.

Flowers are most often picked in the early morning, as they are cool and have not had a chance to wilt.

> *Backyard burning contributes approximately 30% of the brown haze pollution which hangs over our cities.*

According to leading horticultural lecturers, there are three main ways to extend the life of cut flowers:

* stop bacteria developing, for example, using bleach or Disprin
* feed the plants, for example, with sugar or lemonade
* encourage the flowers to drink, for example, with citric acid

There is a fourth way to control the life of cut flowers, and this involves ethylene. Ethylene is produced by plants as a trigger for the flower to die off and continue its reproductive cycle by going to seed.

If the ethylene trigger process can be interrupted the flower shouldn't wilt and die as quickly. Ethylene inhibitors used in laboratories include metal ions such as silver, nickel and copper. For the average person, however, activating metal ions at home is rather difficult. But there is one method which in a small way may inhibit ethylene. Use real copper pennies and activate the ions with a squeeze of acid such as lemon juice or vinegar. According to some horticulturists, this works well for carnations.

Ethylene is also made when gas heaters are burning, by car exhaust systems and by ripening fruit. So avoid these conditions when deciding where to place your arrangement.

Another major life-saving process is to cut flower stems underwater, thereby not allowing air bubbles to get inside the stems. While some people recommend bashing, splitting or shaving the stems ends, some horticulturists believe this only allows more room for bacteria to enter through the damaged tissue. They do, however, recommend re-cutting the stems with a sharp knife or secateurs.

Foliage that would be submerged in the vase should also be removed. Clean water is essential to prevent bacteria blocking the stems. Vases can be cleaned by washing in hot water (soap can also block flower stems) then filling with water and adding a few drops of bleach. Stand a few minutes to allow the bleach to work.

Preservative experiment 'Burke's Backyard' conducted a flower experiment that involved putting bunches of flowers—roses and daisies—into vases containing a variety of mixtures and additives, then recording their progress over two weeks.

Vase	Contents	Purpose
1	Plain tap water	Our control vase
2	Tap water and a few drops of Lanes Formula 20	Commercial hormone additive used by some florists

Vase	Contents	Purpose
3	Tap water and a twist of copper and a squeeze of lemon juice	Formula suggested by a leading horticulture lecturer—the acid in the lemon juice will activate the copper wire, which will give off an ethylene inhibitor—this interrupts the wilting process
4	Tap water and a dash of bleach	Bleach acts as a bactericide—bacteria can block water flow if it is sucked into the stem
5	Home-made floral preservative: 300ml lemonade (*not* diet), 300ml water and a teaspoon of sugar	Gives flowers sugar, while the acid in lemonade seems to encourage flowers to keep drinking
6	Tap water and a shot of gin	Possible antibacterial effect

Six bunches of roses ('Mercedes', 2m. Crimson to light red, cluster-flowered, fragrant) and six bunches of white shasta daisies (*Chrysanthemum maximum*, perennial, bush) were used in this experiment.

After two weeks only the daisies in Vase 5 were still alive, although not at their peak. The roses also fared best in Vase 5, but Vase 6 with the gin worked well until the eighth day. Vases 2, 3 and 4 lasted 2-3 days longer than the plain water.

This experiment was not conducted under laboratory conditions, but in a normal home environment, with ordinary heating and cooling systems operating.

EARTHWORMS IN POTS

The benefits to soil and plant health of a garden loaded with earthworms are numerous and well documented, but when these creatures extend their area of activity to include the potting mix around potted plants, a mysterious problem can result—disappearing potting mix.

When worms set up residence in pots, the level of potting mix can decline at a noticeable rate. If this is occurring, check the surface of the potting mix for crumbly chunks of material to confirm that worms are present—these are worm casts (faeces). The problem may of course result from other circumstances, for example, a broken pot. Then simply top the pot up with a little more potting mix. It is important not to bury the stem or trunk of the plant in the pot, but small additions of mix from time to time are unlikely to cause any damage in this regard.

Some people argue that worms in pots will damage the plant by interfering with such things as drainage or root growth. The best way to judge whether or not the plant is suffering is to examine its general appearance. If it appears to be doing well and has produced new growth or buds at appropriate times, you can be confident that the plant is not suffering from the presence of worms.

If you are really worried, you can pour a dilute solution of Condy's Crystals over the mix. Usually the worms will come to the surface to escape the solution; you can then wash them off and relocate them. Generally though, just keep topping up the potting mix and ignore the worms. If the plant is flourishing they could well be doing more good than harm.

HOYAS

Hoyas are one of the most unusual and collectable of all plants.

They do not like a dark indoor position, but will grow well on a patio, or in a bright sunroom where there is lots of glass and light. In many areas, such as coastal Sydney or coastal Perth, they will grow quite happily outdoors. They can be left in a pot undisturbed for years and do not mind being potbound. An ideal way to grow hoyas is in a hanging basket, where the plant can trail down and the lovely flowers can be seen to perfection.

The potting mix for hoyas needs to be light and fluffy and, as a general guide, should be 50% orchid compost and 50% ordinary potting mix. When they are being repotted, they should be handled gently, as the stems and branches are rather brittle and will break.

The most common hoya, *Hoya carnosa*, has a dark shiny leaf and starburst flowers, which look as if they have been dusted with icing sugar, but there are other varieties that are quite unlike each other. A variation of *Hoya carnosa*, for example, has crinkly leaves and is known as *Hoya carnosa* 'Krinkle'.

Some hoyas, such as *Hoya lacunosa*, have very tiny flowers, while an Australian native hoya, *Hoya macgillivrayi*, has huge flowers for a plant of this type and size.

The Indian Rope Hoya, *Hoya carnosa* 'Compacta', looks as though insects or mites have distorted the leaves. It is one of the many weird hoyas available. Another interesting one is Hoya 'Red Buttons', which has a flower so red that it is almost blackish, and yet another variety called Hoya 'Silver Pink' has silverish spotted leaves and a mid-pink flower.

Hoyas are ideal plants for a collector, or for someone who wants to specialise in unusual plants, and one of the first varieties to add to any collection is *Hoya imperialis*—if you can find a nursery that has it!

IKEBANA

Ikebana, one of the national arts of Japan, had its origins in the sixth century, with the introduction of Buddhism into Japan from China.

The Buddhist principle of destroying nothing, and living in harmony with nature led to the practice of gathering the branches and flowers blown off trees by the wind. These were put into water to prolong their life, and were used as offerings to Buddha. Buddhist priests developed a philosophy of spiritual discipline and humility, a heightened awareness of beauty and a respect for nature, and the offerings became more deliberately harmonised and formal.

By the fifteenth century the formal beginnings of ikebana as an art form were being practiced by noblemen and warriors, who regarded it as elegant and reflective of the transience of life. With the growing prosperity of the nobility, and the magnificence of the Buddhist temples, the simplicity of a single flowering branch in a vessel was developed into elaborate and lavish arrangements representing the grandeur and power of nature. The Japanese developed the art of ikebana, and rigid rules for combinations of materials and containers, balance and order in the arrangements were followed. Fashions in styles changed with social conditions and with the deliberate isolation of Japan from any outside influence for 300 years, the art remained uniquely Japanese, using only indigenous plants and flowers and following the strict rhythm of the seasons.

In 1868 Japan opened communications with the West, and Western flowers were brought in and cultivated. The modernisation of ikebana had begun. New schools and rules developed, with over 3000 schools operating today in Japan.

The study of ikebana develops an awareness of nature— the growth patterns of plants, the texture and symmetry of leaves, the fragility and strength of flowers, the character of the branches and space, and the power of the sun.

Three main schools of ikebana are taught in Australia. The school featured on 'Burke's Backyard' was Ohara.

Ohara was founded about 120 years ago after the restoration period of 1867. This is an extremely popular form of ikebana, as it emphasises the natural shape and colour of the plants and flowers used.

Ikenobo is the most traditional form, which dates back to the thirteenth century. These arrangements are very formal.

Sogetsu is an avant-garde movement introduced in the 1920s, and is a very individual form. This form can utilise plastic plants and silk flowers, emphasising forms and colours. The teachers listed below are all Sogetsu teachers with the highest qualifications. If, however, another school interests you, you may contact Ikebana International, which is listed in the white pages of each state telephone book.

For further information

Marge Hayes
3/40 View Street
Chatswood NSW 2067
Telephone (02) 411 6327

Elisabeth Angell
38 Ferdinand Avenue
North Balwyn VIC 3104
Telephone (03) 857 5657

Nora Dyer
Brisbane
Telephone (07) 371 4827

Marjorie Bromilow
Adelaide
Telephone (08) 296 8020

Akiko Chester
18b Casserley Avenue
Girrawheen WA 6064
Telephone (09) 343 2025

Sydney now has an Ikebana Centre which can provide information on courses and teaching:

Shop 5a, Edgecliff Centre
203 New South Head Road
Edgecliff NSW 2027
Telephone (02) 328 7566

INDOOR PLANTS

One of the first things to realise when you buy an indoor plant is that it will eventually die. Plants are not really designed to grow inside houses. The aim is to make them die as slowly as possible.

The hardiness of an indoor plant should be considered when making a selection—some are harder to kill than others.

Hardy indoor plants Spathiphyllum or madonna lily has glossy green leaves and a white flower. It will survive in

low light positions indoors, although it may never flower again.

The parlour palm (*Chamaedorea elegans*) is also very hardy indoors even in low light positions. It is cheap and almost indestructible.

Aspidistra elatior or cast iron plant is appropriately named because it too is virtually indestructible. It is also suitable for low light areas.

Kentia palms (*Howeia forsteriana*) are not cheap plants, but they are value for money because they are so hardy. Like most palms, they need regular watering and do best in a position where there is comfortable reading light.

Devil's ivy (*Epipremnum aureum*) is a very hardy indoor plant which suits low light positions. If the leaves are limp, it may be that it is getting too much water during the winter months.

Philodendrons are almost indestructible, but they do hate cold weather.

Temporary indoor plants There is a special group of plants which live for only a short time indoors. Anything that is colourful is probably very temporary indoors.

Cyclamens are magnificent flowering plants, but within a few weeks there will probably be one flower left and the options are then fairly clear. You can put it out in the garden and it may flower again next year, but in most areas of Australia you should put it in the garbage bin.

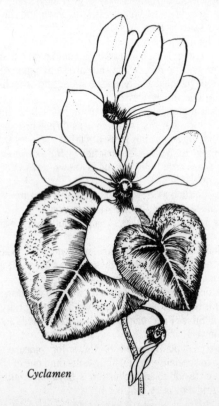

Cyclamen

Miniature African violets are very pretty but in about four weeks in an average indoor position they will probably look half dead. They can be revived and brought back to flower but the best option is to put them in the bin. An African violet that has been overwatered may recover if you let it dry out.

Poinsettias are great indoors. They give three to six months of colour, but then should be planted in the garden or thrown away.

Begonias are also suitable for a temporary stay indoors. The Rex Begonia is a tropical plant and doesn't like cold weather.

Unless you live in the tropics, Crotons are likely to die off during cold weather periods.

The ultimate in temporary plants is *Ardisia crenata* with its red or white berries. They can be brought in while the berries look good and then put back out in the garden two or three weeks later.

Indoor plants can be recycled. Maidenhairs will often die right down, but if put outside in a shady spot they will often grow again. If your red-edged dracaena is dying off, put it in a shady place in the garden and it will recover. The Asian belltree will look attractive inside for a few weeks, but then has to be put outdoors to recover.

Indoor plants hate cold weather. Do not put them outside until at least October.

Spring is a good time to get plants ready for summer. Indoor plants can be repotted in a good quality potting mix. Most indoor plants die from over-fertilising, so minimise this. Use a nine-month slow-release fertiliser, for example, Osmocote. If your indoor plants are in a well lit position and are growing rapidly then fertilising is important. However if growth is minimal, then fertilising should be minimal also.

Light Light is vital to the healthy growth of plants indoors. Plants use energy from sunlight to manufacture their own sugars through the process of photosynthesis. Adequate light is just as critical to plant survival as are adequate water, fertiliser and minerals.

A plant deprived of its light requirements will become elongated, lean towards the light and drop leaves it cannot support for lack of food—in effect it will starve to death from lack of light.

It is very difficult to assess how much or how little light is in a room since the human eye adjusts rapidly to low light intensities; that is, your eyes give a distorted impression. The following graph may give some idea of the dramatic decrease in light from outdoor to indoor positions. Note that a brightly lit outdoor position receives 12 000 foot candles (ft cd, a unit of illumination equivalent to 10.76 lux) of light, yet 1–2m (3-7') inside a window receives a mere 500 foot candles. A poorly lit position indoors receives about 50 foot candles (that is, 1/240 of outdoor light) or less.

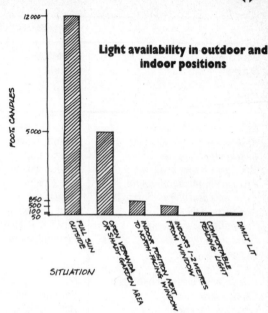

Light availability in outdoor and indoor positions

Estimating available light As a guide, a brightly lit indoor position next to a window receives 700-1000 ft cd; a plant 1–2 metres from a large window receives 200-750 ft cd; a plant positioned in comfortable reading light receives 75-200 ft cd; a plant in a dimly lit position receives 0-75 ft cd.

Determining light intensity using a camera Cameras with built-in light meters can be used to measure light intensity. Set the ASA film speed at 200, and the shutter speed at 1/125 of a second. Place a piece of plain white paper on the plant facing the main light source. Focus on the paper, centre the light meter needle, then read off the f stop (usually this is located on the section you have been turning to centre the needle). Calculate the foot candles as follows:

f stop	ft cd
2.8	32
4	64
5.6	125
8	250
11	500
16	1000

The male Platypus is one of the world's few venomous mammals. It has poisonous spurs on its hind legs, but a sting is not fatal.

MINIMUM LIGHT REQUIREMENTS		
BOTANIC NAME	COMMON NAME	MINIMUM LIGHT REQUIREMENTS* (ft cd)
Aglaonema commutatum	Chinese lucky plant	50-75
Anthurium species and cultivars	Flamingo plant	100-200
Aphelandra squarrosa	Zebra plant	Temporary only
Araucaria heterophylla	Norfolk Island pine	150
Arecastrum romanzoffianum	Cocos palm	250-300
Asparagus densiflorus 'Sprengeri'	Asparagus	200
Aspidistra elatior	Cast iron plant	50-75
Asplenium australasicum	Bird's-nest fern	75-150
Beaucarnea recurvata	Ponytail 'palm'	400-500
Bromeliads		150
Cacti		200
Caladium species and hybrids		100
Chamaedorea elegans	Parlour palm	50-100
Chamaedorea erumpens	Bamboo palm	100-150
Chlorophytum comosum	Ribbon grass	150-250
Chrysanthemums		
Cissus rhombifolia	Grape ivy	75-150
Codiaeum variegatum	Croton	150-250
Cycas revoluta	Sago palm	250-500
Dieffenbachia species and cultivars	Dumbcane	100-150
Dizygotheca elegantissima	False aralia	100-150
Dracaena deremensis		75-100
Dracaena fragrans	Chinese happy plant	50
Dracaena marginata		75-100
Epipremnum aureum	Devil's ivy	50-75 (over 75 preferred)
Euphorbia pulcherrima	Poinsettia	
Fatsia japonica	Aralia	150-250
Ficus benjamina	Weeping fig	150-200
Ficus elastica	Rubber tree	300-500
Ficus lyrata	Fiddle Leaf fig	200-250
Howeia forsteriana	Kentia palm	100-150
Livistona chinensis	Chinese fan palm	250-300
Maranta leuconeura	Prayer plant	75-100
Monstera deliciosa	Fruit salad plant	75-150
Nephrolepis exaltata	Boston fern	200-300
Philodendron cordatum	Heart-leaf philodendron	50-75
Philodendron selloum		75-150
Phoenix roebelenii	Pygmy date palm	100-150
Rhapis excelsa		100-150
Sansevieria trifasciata	Mother-in-law's tongue	50-75
Schefflera actinophylla	Umbrella tree	150
Schefflera arboricola	Dwarf umbrella tree	100-150
Spathiphyllum species and hybrids	Peace lily, madonna lily	75-100 (200-300 flowering)
Syngonium podophyllum	(example) 'White Butterfly'	100-150

* For active growth extra light is probably required

Indoor plant problems

No flowers on African violet
Move the plant to a bright position. Keep it quite dry—
about half the water required for normal plants. Use only
African violet fertiliser.

*Brown or sparse leaves on indoor plants, especially
dieffenbachias, aglaonemas and happy plants during winter*
This is cold damage. Keep plants away from rooms that
cool down excessively at night—sunrooms especially. Cut
down the watering during cold months, leaving the potting
mix quite dry. Recovery will follow in spring.

White, fluffy blobs of match-head size on foliage
This is mealy bug and it is very difficult to cure. Take
outside and spray with half-strength Lebaycid or the
aerosol Folimat. Keep in a shady area until dry, then
return the plant inside. Repeat treatment in 14–21 days.

Brown leaves on ferns
This is quite normal. Trim off the dead leaves with
scissors or, if the whole plant looks sad, snip it off near
ground level, then water and fertilise. It should recover in
a few weeks.

Lean, spindly plants
Starving to death from lack of sunshine, probably. Cut
back and put outside in shady spot for a month or two.

Tiny, silvery spots on leaves
This is caused by red spider or thrips. Place outside in a
shady area and water well for a few weeks, or spray with
Lebaycid at half the recommended strength.

Caring for indoor plants in winter Winter can be a
risky time for indoor plants. Home heating (and turning
off home heating) can cause plant damage, typically death
of leaf tip, purpling of leaf, leaf dieback, or leaf drop.

Things to watch for include:
Temperature fluctuation Measure this with a
maximum-minimum thermometer, which can be
purchased from medical and scientific supply companies.
Sudden temperature changes, such as those which occur
when home heating is turned off at night, can cause rapid
leaf drop. Plants near windows are more susceptible to
damage of this nature.
Low humidity Air conditioning can cause the tips and
edges of leaves to dehydrate and turn brown.
Overwatering This can cause dieback and increase the
risk of fungal disease. Without allowing them to dry out
badly, keep the plants a little bit low on water during
winter.
Too little light Indoor winter light may be insufficient

and can be supplemented with light from an ordinary light
globe or fluorescent lamp, provided you keep the lights on
for six to eight hours each day.

If all other indoor plants fail you, remember the old
Victorian favourite, the aspidistra, which managed to
grow in gas-lit rooms, surviving both the gas and the low
light.

MAIDENHAIR FERNS

Maidenhair Ferns can be among the most beautiful of
indoor plants, with their delicate, lacy fronds. But all too
often maidenhairs end up looking like untidy birds' nests,
with just the odd tinge of green here and there in a ragged
mass of shrivelled brown foliage. Don't despair if your
maidenhair is in this condition; these ferns are actually
very easy to grow once you're aware of the entirely
avoidable conditions that lead to miserable ferns.

One of the first things to consider is position. A common
assumption is that ferns like shady spots. This is true to
an extent; direct sun is too strong for the plants and
should be avoided. Maidenhairs require a very brightly lit
position indoors, so a spot beside a large window is ideal. A
window facing west may provide too harsh a light, but no
other directions should present problems.

If, however, you decide on a relatively dark spot, go
ahead and put it there. It won't last more than a month or
two, but for probably less than the price of a bunch of
flowers it will last a great deal longer. After a month or
two you may still be able to salvage what is left by
planting it out in the garden; otherwise, simply throw it
away. The position you choose depends on whether you
want a short-term or a long-term maidenhair.

The next point to consider is watering. Maidenhair
ferns can't tolerate drying out completely, nor do they like
being waterlogged or having their leaves wet. For these
reasons the ideal pot to grow your maidenhair in is one
that waters automatically, such as the Decor WaterWell
range. The bigger the pot, the better and larger your fern
will grow.

Plant your maidenhair in a good quality potting mix,
containing a high percentage of organic matter, such as
peat moss (two-thirds organic matter to one-third coarse
sand is ideal). Add some dolomite to the mix; maidenhair
ferns in the wild grow best in limestone areas. Fertilise
regularly with an organic fertiliser, such as fish emulsion
or Nitrosol (the latter is probably the best fertiliser for
ferns).

There is an enormous range of maidenhairs and it
includes large leafed, fine leafed, serrated and variegated
leafed forms. The varieties that grow best indoors do not
do well outdoors. Outdoor varieties are usually different
species and are not commonly available in nurseries.

If your maidenhair does go brown, it is usually possible
to save it by taking a pair of scissors and cutting off all the
leaves close to ground level. Don't be gentle, just clip

everything away. If you prefer, you can burn the foliage off by holding a lit piece of newspaper over it. The fern will usually regenerate within a few weeks.

If you are a keen maidenhair fan, a book is available on the subject: *Maidenhair Ferns in Cultivation*, by Christopher J. Goudey, Lothian Publishing Company Pty Ltd, 1985, is sold at good bookstores for about $60.

PIPES AS PLANTERS

Pipe sections make great pots—they can be arranged in groups so that there are some short and some tall, and all sorts of plants will grow well in them.

Place the pipe in the required position and raise it slightly off the ground on a little gravel or some chocks. Put about 5-7cm (2-3″) of gravel in the pot, then fill it with a very good quality potting mix that will drain well. It is then ready to plant with, for example, one taller plant and one spillover type.

As a final touch to make it look good, dress around the top of the pot with gravel of the same colour as, or contrasting to, the pipe section. Keep the level of the potting mix or gravel at about 2.5cm (1″) below the top of the container to facilitate watering. Water in well.

Pipe sections cost from $10 to $60 and are available from larger nurseries in many areas.

Tips on drainage It is important to put gravel in the bottom of the pipe and to sit it up a little on gravel or chocks to help with drainage—if the pipe sits flat on concrete, water will not drain.

These types of pots (pipe sections) are the only ones we recommend that gravel should be put into. In the usual type of pot all that is ever needed, top to bottom, is a good quality potting mix.

POTTING A PLANT

If a plant has just been purchased, do not leave it in a hot car but do water it every few days until you are ready to pot it up.

Potting mix In general, home-made potting mix grows poor quality plants. It is best to use a top-quality commercial potting mix, such as Rite-Gro or Debco.

Fertiliser The only safe type of fertiliser to use at planting time is the slow release type, such as Osmocote. Simply put the recommended amount under the rootball. Thereafter you could give your plants a boost with Nitrosol liquid fertiliser if necessary.

Procedure Do not fill the potting mix right to the top of the pot—leave about 2cm (1″) of space for watering. Never put any gravel or drainage material in the bottom of the pot; modern pots with adequate drainage holes require no material other than potting mix. Large tubs with wide

drainage holes may benefit from a piece of plastic flywire or broken crock over the hole to stop leakage of the potting mix. Make sure that you water the plant immediately after potting and at least once a week for the first month. Thereafter water as necessary.

Adding wetting agents to the potting mix helps substantially. Try Wetta Soil or Aqua Soil Wetter.

POTTING MIX

Growing plants in pots can be something of a hit and miss affair. Many of the potting mixtures that people make and use just don't quite work.

The CSIRO Division of Soils in South Australia is working towards establishing a standard for potting mixes so that everyone can be assured of a quality mix.

The problem with using garden soil in pots is that disease organisms, such as nematodes, may be brought in with the soil. Also, ordinary soil in a pot doesn't give enough air space for the plant's roots; they need oxygen.

There are many different components of potting mix, but balancing them out for the right physical properties can be difficult. You need the right amount of air, water and nutrient, so that there are no toxic amounts or deficiencies. Correct air porosity is essential. One important point to remember is that crocking or drainage gravel in pots is not necessary.

Modern professional potting mixes are made up of raw materials such as compost of pine bark, compost of sawdust and sands; nutrients are added, then the ingredients are mixed to get the larger pieces out and the correct air-filled porosity, and then packaged. Most modern potting mixes don't contain any soil.

The bottom line is that it is easier and better to buy a commercial potting mix, and a reasonably expensive one, if you want to obtain a degree of quality. Cheaper brands can be lacking in nutrient balance. Most nationally available brand names of potting mix are fairly good, some very good. During 1990 an Australian Standard for potting mixes will be set, after which the SAA will be able to license potting mix manufacturers.

If you want to make your own potting mix you must ensure that the air porosity and nutrient balance are correct. It can be difficult.

For further information

The CSIRO Publications Branch has several good booklets on this subject, in their *Discovering Soils* series:

Soils: An Outline of Their Properties and Management ($6.00), *Soil: Australia's Greatest Resource* ($5.00), *Composting* ($6.00), *What's wrong with my soil?* ($6.00), *Earthworms for Gardeners and Fishermen* ($6.00), *Food for Plants* ($6.00), *Organic Matter and Soils* ($6.00), *When should I water?* ($7.00), and *Potting Mixes and Care of Plants Growing in Them* ($6.00).

Write to CSIRO Publications, PO Box 89, East Melbourne, VIC 3002. Prices include posting and packaging.

PRUNING DEVIL'S IVY

Arguably the best of all indoor plants, and certainly the best survivor, would have to be Devil's Ivy. It grows for a long time indoors and the beautiful foliage (plain green or variegated in different patterns) will soon fill a corner. But what do you do when the foliage fills not only the corner but also climbs into cupboards, along shelves, and out across the floor towards your favourite chair? In these cases the plant will need to be pruned.

When pruning the devil's ivy it's always tempting to try to preserve as much foliage on the plant as possible, but this is the wrong thing to do. Stems near the base of the plant have fewer leaves and look awful—the plant will look and respond better if the stems are cut right back to the top of the totem or pole in the pot. If you can bear it you can even trim the stems right back to 10–15cm (4–6″) above the potting mix.

In two to three weeks the new growth will start to emerge, and the plant will rapidly thicken up. Devil's ivy will happily sit in the same pot for many years, so it may not be necessary to repot it. Fertilise with nine-month Osmocote or give it a liquid boost with Nitrosol.

The branches which have been severed need not be wasted, as every one of them can be used to make cuttings. Trim them back to a joint or node, dip the bottom end in hormone rooting powder and strike them in a small pot. Place the pot on a brightly lit window-ledge but not in direct sun, or put a mini-glasshouse over the pot by enclosing it completely in a clear plastic bag. The cuttings will produce roots within a week or two.

REPOTTING A PLANT

If you want to move a plant from one position to another, or if your plants have grown too big for their pots, winter is the best time to do something about it.

If you are removing a plant from a concrete pot, you may need to use a pruning saw with a flexible blade to get it out. If you can't get the plant's roots away from the edge of the pot, you can saw around the edge just to loosen it. With a plastic pot it is not usually necessary; the plant should come out easily when the container is tapped.

Once the plant is out of the container have a good look at the rootball to see if there has been damage from the tunnelling of worms and suchlike. Next, tease the roots out, so that when it is in the new pot the roots will establish quickly. A small hand fork or your fingers can be used to do this. The plant will now be ready to put into the new pot.

If using one of the new plastic terracotta pots with only one hole in the middle, it is a good idea to drill extra holes to improve drainage. To stop the soil leaking out, use a small piece of plastic flywire. There is no need to place any drainage material in the base of the pot, as a good potting mix will drain by itself. Put some potting mix in the bottom of the pot and insert the plant, checking that the height is correct and that it is in the middle of the pot. Fill up with potting mix, adding a nine-month slow release fertiliser, and water well.

Even if some of the roots were removed, it is not necessary to take leaves off as well. However, if there are any wayward branches, they should be trimmed off. Bonsai pruners are very good for this job.

WINDOW BOXES

One of the lovely sights in Mediterranean countries is the adornment of homes with flowers—pots of geraniums by the door, hanging baskets trailing blooms and foliage, and window boxes spilling over with colour. Our climate is not too dissimilar to that of the Mediterranean, and there are many Australian homes which could benefit from the same treatment. With the addition of window boxes, a house facade can be transformed from bland to beautiful virtually overnight.

Apart from being decorative, window boxes can also be quite practical. Imagine the pleasure of plucking a fresh herb from your windowsill or having the scent of fresh flowers wafting into your room. For those with tiny flats and no garden, this is one way in which you can grow something of your own.

Choosing window boxes Many people choose terracotta because of its lovely warm, earthy qualities although it is a little more expensive than most of the other types. Terracotta boxes can range from $14 for a tiny size (not very practical) to about $50 for a medium-sized one. They are very heavy, so are best suited to a wide, flat sill, although for safety reasons it is always advisable to place a couple of wedges underneath the box to slant it down towards the house.

If you are a little indecisive about the sorts of plants you want, you can always leave them in their separate pots. Place them, pot and all, into a large window box and change your blooms according to the season. This alternative can be expensive—a large steel window box could cost about $250.

Drainage is of the utmost importance. Some beautiful window boxes can be short on practical features, so keep an eye on this; if holes are too small, or absent altogether, you will find yourself with sick and dying plants, which make a most unattractive display. The holes should be very large and at least 30cm (12″) apart.

Beware, too, of small containers. They may look cute, but there is usually not enough space for most plants to live happily. The smaller the container the higher the maintenance. Larger containers have more capacity for root growth and moisture retention.

Wooden window boxes are attractive. They are much

lighter, and usually have reasonable drainage holes, although it is probably best to drill an extra one or two. A version made of marine ply to withstand the weather retails at about $40.

Lower down the scale you can buy a plastic box for $10 or a polystyrene one for $4.50. If you want to be really creative, you can buy a couple of little jars of paint from a craft shop (use acrylic, not turpentine-based paint) and transform a plain box into your own work of art. Polystyrene containers aren't as durable as the others, and many polystyrenes aren't ozone-friendly.

Making a window box If you can't find a window box to your liking or if you have a particular space you'd like it to fit, why not make one yourself in wood for about $30?

You will need some *wood*. Western red cedar or Californian redwoods are best for external use, as they are extremely durable, weatherproof, and may be left untreated if desired. You'll need 3 lengths 900×230×180mm (35½×9×7″), and 2 lengths 200×230×180mm (8×9×7″). *Other materials*: 32 brass countersunk screws 32mm (1¼″) long; a small bottle of PVA-type glue; mounting brackets, if necessary.

Method

1 Drill and countersink holes about 10cm (4″) apart along both edges of base.
2 Apply glue to the edge of each side, then assemble sides to base and screw in, making sure sides remain at right angles to base.
3 Fit in ends; glue and screw to sides and base.
4 Drill drain holes in base at least 2.5cm (1″) in diameter, and about 20cm (8″) apart.
5 Leave untreated, stain or paint.
6 Line with fibreglass flyscreen mesh to retain potting mix.
7 Ensure that the box is securely fitted to sill or brackets.

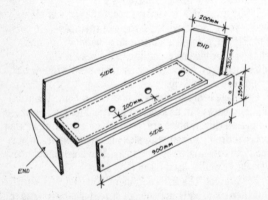

Support As mentioned, wedges help to hold a window box on a flat sill against the wall. If your windowsills are too narrow or sloping to support a window box, or your windows open outwards, your only solution is to get a

couple of strong brackets and fasten them to the outside of the wall to support the box. Obviously they have to be very secure, especially if they are a couple of storeys up; you wouldn't want the window box falling onto someone.

If you are attaching the brackets to masonry, it is best to drill holes and use Dynabolts rather than screws; these expand and lock into the wall. Rest the box on the brackets, but make sure you secure it to the brackets with a couple of nuts and bolts.

Filling the box It is a good idea to cover the drainage holes in the box with some fibreglass flywire mesh, which you can pick up very cheaply from any hardware shop. This means that you don't have dirty water dripping down the wall, or, worse still, onto people below. Fill the box with a good potting mix, not soil from the garden, then all you have to do is put in your favourite flowers and you'll have an instant garden.

In most areas you don't need council approval to put up a window box, but check anyway, especially to see if there is a heritage order on your street or suburb, which may limit alterations to the buildings.

Suitable plants *For shade:* impatiens or azaleas. *For sun:* bulbs, geraniums (especially ivy geraniums—very hardy), gerberas (for a hot and dry spot), daisies (especially erigeron and the native blue daisies, brachycome), herbs, ageratum, dianthus, begonias, climbers of all kinds, including 'Alice du Pont' and the white or blue potato creeper.

CHAPTER 11
Herbs and Sprouts

BASIL

Just when you thought you could impress your friends by confidently identifying Basil at first glance, both on your plate and in the garden, someone has gone and introduced an astonishing array of varieties that will throw even the most assiduous herb connoisseur. Basil, you thought, was always the one with bright, light green leaves—now they can be deep purple or red-stemmed. Well then, you could always try looking for the familiar medium-sized, slightly ridged leaves. Wrong again—now some have miniaturised leaves and others are so ruffled and dense they almost look like some sort of Chinese cabbage. If all else fails, you could turn to the sniff and taste test—powerfully aromatic basil certainly always used to be distinctive in the herb patch. Not any more: the new range includes the scents and flavours of cinnamon, licorice, lemon, ginger and Indian incense, of all things. If you think these new basils have got you beaten, why not try impressing your friends another way—simply grow the lot of them.

* Sweet Basil is the familiar old favourite with light green, 7-10cm (2½-4″) long leaves. It grows to about 60cm (2′) in height and bears small, white flowers.
* Bush Basil has also been around for a long time although it is not quite as common as sweet basil. It grows to 30cm (12″) high, has very small leaves and a compact growth habit. It can withstand harsher conditions than sweet basil and is better suited to confined spaces. It can last all winter indoors provided sufficient light is available.
* Opal Basil is similar to sweet basil but has slightly smaller, deep purple leaves.
* Basil Purple Ruffles has a sweet basil flavour with a hint of ginger. It has large, purple leaves with ruffled edges and makes an elegant garnishing herb and contrast plant in the herb garden. It colours herb vinegar red and has pink flowers on spikes 15cm (6″) long.
* Basil Green Ruffles again has the familiar flavour of cloves and spices and is used in the same way as sweet basil. It has large, frilly, decorative leaves.
* Cinnamon Basil has green leaves, purple stems and long, purple flower spikes. It can be used as an accompaniment to cooked apples and pears, and in fruit salad.
* Lemon Basil is delicious chopped into salads just before serving. It makes a refreshing tea and is useful in Asian cooking. It has a compact, bushy growth habit with white flowers.
* Licorice Basil makes a tasty addition to cooked carrots and fried fish fillets, or an unusual garnish for a cheese platter. It has purplish stems and flower spikes.
* Sacred Basil has a mildly intoxicating clove fragrance but is not as palatable as the other varieties. It is a bushy plant which grows to 70cm (28″) and bears long, mauve flower spikes. In India it is grown around temples by Hindu people.
* Spicy Globe Basil has tiny leaves, just 5mm (¼″) long, which are densely massed over the mounded, compact bush. With its clouds of white flowers, it makes an excellent edging plant. It has the same delicious flavour as sweet basil and can be used in the kitchen in just the same way.

These unusual basil varieties are not readily available in general nurseries as yet but should be sold at specialist herb nurseries. Alternatively you may be able to buy some in seed form—basils are annuals anyway. They grow through the warmer months and then usually die down over winter unless placed inside a glasshouse. So, while you could try growing some in autumn, particularly in warmer areas, the best time to buy plants is early in the spring to grow through the summer and autumn.

Basil is superb in any tomato dish and also combines deliciously with pasta, fish and eggs. Basil is easy to grow in a position in full sun. You can grow it in the garden or in pots—keep them somewhere near the kitchen so you can dash out and grab some for a meal whenever you feel like it. Basil prefers a rich soil with generous doses of fertiliser and regular, thorough watering.

At the end of a hot day, just after watering or when you brush past the bushes, the heady, spicy aroma of basil rapidly pervades the surrounding area. Even if you're not a keen cook, you will get great value out of basils just grown ornamentally and for sniffing as you walk past them.

HERB BASKETS

A herb basket is simple, practical and good to look at. It can be used to fill the kitchen with fragrance, to enhance your food and even to act as an unusual insect repellent.

Baskets can be wire-lined with coconut matting or of cane, lined with a weed mat to help with drainage. Herbs certainly don't like having their roots drowned.

Points to consider when choosing herb plants for the basket include the size of the plant—don't choose a very tall herb, for example fennel. A spillover type of plant will look attractive, and choose a plant that will adapt to dry conditions, for example, don't use watercress as it needs too much moisture.

Suggested plantings for a herb basket:
Place a weed mat and half the potting mix into the basket. Starting in the centre, plant basil (good for pasta and tomato dishes). Around the outside of the basket plant winter savory (for stuffings or sausages) and salad burnet (very tasty in salads). To complete the basket, plant thyme or oregano.

Suggested plantings for an insect repellent basket:
Pyrethrum—used to repel flies, and the flowers and leaves can be used to make a 'tea' which can be sprayed on other plants to help control caterpillars and other pests; tansy is also very good for repelling flies; cotton lavender—used to repel moths, a sprig can be hung in the wardrobe.

To keep your herb basket healthy, give it plenty of sun and water and a regular feeding of an organic fertiliser.

HERB BOOK

The New Honest Herbal: A sensible guide to herbs and related remedies, by Varro E. Tyler, PhD, is published by the George F. Stickley Company, 210 West Washington Square, Philadelphia, PA 19106, USA. (1987 edition, 254

> *The tradition of Ikebana was introduced to Japan by the Chinese in the 6th century.*

pages.) The book is available in Australia for $42.95 plus $4.00 for postage from Johima Books, PO Box C255, Cremorne, NSW 2090. Telephone (02) 953 8554.

The author's intention in writing this book was to provide a scientifically based perspective for people interested in herbal remedies. This book neither promotes nor rejects the use of herbs in self treatment, but rather it provides an objective evaluation of both the dangers and benefits of individual herbs in terms of the actions on the human body of their biochemical components. The book dispenses with the folklore with which this subject has always been tightly surrounded, and approaches it in a careful, factual way.

Despite its practical, scientific basis—which may suggest a dull, dry work—this book is interesting and enjoyable. After reading *The New Honest Herbal*, natural remedy enthusiasts will be able to prepare their own treatments with a greater degree of confidence in the outcome.

The book is very clearly set out with short chapters on each of the 108 herbs or herb groups covered. Additional chapters deal with evaluation of the arguments for and against herbal remedies (including a summarised table), and laws and regulations.

The author Dr Varro E. Tyler is the Executive Vice-President and Professor of Pharmacognosy (the science of medicines derived from natural sources) at Perdue University in the United States of America. Among his many honours and affiliations are Fellow of the Academy of Pharmaceutical Sciences and past President of the American College of Pharmacognosy and the American Association of Colleges of Pharmacy. Dr Tyler has travelled extensively in Europe, Asia and the Middle East as past of his first-hand studies (for more than 30 years) of the use of herbal medicines by people in many countries.

HERB GARDEN FERTILISER

Increasing public awareness of the influence of diet on health is leading growing numbers of people to adopt a more healthy diet—most probably won't give up eating red meat entirely, but will favour more chicken, fish and vegetables.

This trend, together with her own interest in healthy eating, has prompted freelance writer Carolyn Dunne to compile a collection of her own semi-vegetarian recipes, which involve the extensive use of herbs, in her book, *The Semi-Vegetarian Cookbook*, published by Bantam Books (1989), which is available in bookstores in all states for $19.95.

Regardless of whether or not you prefer a mostly vegetarian diet, there can be no doubt that any meal or recipe is enhanced by the use of herbs—especially those picked fresh from your own garden.

Carolyn Dunne considers herself to be a non-gardener, but as a keen and imaginative cook she was eager to establish a herb garden for culinary use. Carolyn has found she can grow thriving herbs by preparing the soil with a special mixture of ingredients. Her soil enriching recipe is as follows: Combine five kilos of cow manure, five handfuls of dolomite, and five handfuls of chicken poo. Dig this mixture thoroughly into the soil, and about once a week for three weeks turn the soil again. At the end of this period the manures will have aged sufficiently to prevent them from burning your plants. Plant the herbs of your choice, then stand back and admire them as they grow.

HERBS IN POTS

Herbs are extremely fashionable at the moment; they grow very rapidly and give a great return. If you like to entertain and to use herbs in cooking, there are many different varieties to try—see the following list for ideas.

To grow herbs you need to put them in full sun, preferably in the ground. You can also grow them in containers, but these must be large; wine casks for example. A group of pots together also looks attractive.

Before putting the potting mix in, place some plastic flywire offcuts over the holes to stop erosion. Then fill with a good quality potting mix. It's a good idea to enrich your potting mix with a little well-rotted animal manure such as Melcann Mixed Animal Manure.

Now it's planting time. Perhaps plant a bay tree first. This will grow into a reasonably large shrub in a pot, or into a tree in the garden. Bay leaves are great for curries and all meat dishes. You can then plant around the bay tree with another herb, for example, Italian parsley. This tastes much the same as ordinary parsley, but looks really dramatic on a plate.

One of the most fashionable herbs at the moment is sage. It is easy to grow, with attractive grey-green foliage. Mint is also good to grow, and there are lots of curious types, for example, apple mint. This has a slightly different flavour to ordinary mint, and is great in summer salads. Another suggestion is basil, which goes very well with tomato and many other dishes. It is an annual and dies off at the end of the season.

Ordinary mint is very good to grow in a pot, as it is not as invasive as it can be in the garden. Bronze fennel grows quite tall, looks very attractive and goes with both meat and salads.

Other herbs to plant are parsley, rosemary (which complements lamb so well), thyme (for adding to all savoury dishes) and chives (which will survive just about anywhere).

Maybe the last one to think about planting is an aloe vera plant, in case you cut your finger or burn yourself.

One last thing to do after planting seedlings is to sprinkle some snail pellets around them.

HERBS TO GROW

Angelica	For salads, vegetable and fish dishes and in desserts and preserves.
Anise	Flavouring for fish, soup, poultry and stews
Basil	Virtually all dishes except preserves, and especially good with tomatoes. A colourful, aromatic bush.
Bay	All dishes except dairy foods and sweet preserves.
Borage	Fresh young leaves used in soups, sauces, salads, rice, pasta and fish dishes, and in sweets and preserves. Rich in potassium and calcium.
Caraway	The seeds may be added to most foods to improve digestion, especially in baking, soups and cheese dishes.
Catnip	Soothing mint-flavoured drink for colds and fevers. Tonic for cats. Attracts bees.
Chamomile	Compost ingredient. Relieves flatulence, dyspepsia, nausea and vomiting.
Chervil	Used in soups, sauces, vegetable dishes and with all red and white meats. A tasty substitute for parsley.
Chives	For all but the sweet dishes. An onion-flavoured garnish.
Coriander	Both leaves and seeds are used in soups, salads, vegetable and savoury dishes, with dairy foods, red meat, baking and pickles.
Cumin	Flavouring for curries, meat, pickles and chutney.
Dill	Used in soups, sauces, salads, stews, with vegetables, red and white meats, and in pickles and chutneys. Dill water relieves indigestion.
Fennel	In soups and sauces, dairy, egg, and all meat dishes, especially fish. The seeds may be used in sweets and preserves.
Garlic	Enhances all but the sweet dishes and preserves.
Heartsease	Wild pansy. Decorative sprawling herb.
Hyssop	Reduces bruising. Attracts bees. Flavouring for pork and soup.
Lavender	Potpourri ingredient. Lavender oil repels insects (many varieties).
Lemon Balm	Potpourri ingredient. Flavouring for fish, soup and stews.
Lovage	Virtually all dishes, especially vegetarian fare. Has a yeasty celery aroma.
Marjoram	All but sweet dishes, excellent with egg, chicken and lamb.
Mint	Used in sauces, with vegetables and in fruit salad.
Oregano	Ideal for pasta and fish dishes, salads, vegetables and stews.
Parsley	Use the curled or French varieties for garnish and flavour in all but sweet dishes. Rich in vitamins, iron, magnesium and iodine.
Peppermint	Refreshing drink and useful flavouring agent.
Pot Marigold	Distinctive flavour in salads and omelettes.
Rocket	Cress-type salad herb. Excellent flavour.
Rosemary	Can be added to most savoury dishes, especially meats, but in small amounts due to its strong flavour and aroma.
Rue	Aromatic evergreen.
Sage	Used in all savoury dishes, especially with pork, poultry and fatty fish. Adds flavour to salads.
Salad Burnet	Flavouring for soups, cream cheese, herb butter.
Savory	Used in soups and sauces, salads and vegetable dishes, and with egg and all meat dishes.
Sorrel	Flavouring for soups, stews and omelettes.
Tarragon	All meats, especially chicken, and in soups, salads and vegetable dishes.
Thyme	A versatile group of herbs for use in all savoury dishes, especially stews, casseroles, vegetable dishes and with chicken. An aromatic evergreen.
Wormwood	Aromatic plant. Insect repellent.

For further information

Hemphill's Herbs: Their Cultivation and Usage
Lansdowne Press, $14.95 (distributed by Garry Allen—Telephone (02) 725 2933)
Herbs for Health
Landsdowne Press, $14.95

PRESERVING HERBS

While most herbs are best used fresh, this is sometimes not possible, and there are a few simple ways to preserve them.

The ideal way is to dry herbs; the main objective being to take the moisture out of the plant. The conventional method is to air-dry by picking the herbs early in the day, then tying them in bunches and hanging them in a cool, dry place. Alternatively, they may be spread out on a screen to dry. The herbs are ready to be stored when the leaves or stems snap.

Microwave drying Modern preserving methods include microwaving. The leaves should be quite dry before microwaving. Spread them out on paper towels, preferably not overlapping. If the leaves overlap it's possible that the centre may not dry completely.

You may need to experiment with the microwaving time, but start with two minutes and check regularly at 30-second intervals. The herbs are dry enough when they snap in your fingers with a clear snapping sound. If they don't, there is still too much moisture in them and they could go mouldy.

Bay leaves	Clean dry bay leaves; lay in a single layer on a kitchen towel, not overlapping each other. Microwave on 'high' for 10 minutes, then 45 seconds at a time until crisp.
Parsley	Wash, dry with paper towel, break into micro-stems or chop finely. Spread in a single layer on a paper towel. Microwave on 'high' for 2–3 minutes, turn and spread leaves, then cook a further 45 seconds at a time, taking out crisp leaves each time.
Marjoram	Wash, dry with a paper towel, strip individual leaves from stem. Lay in a single layer on a kitchen towel. Microwave on 'high' for 3–5 minutes. Take out leaves dry enough to snap in half, return others for 30 seconds at a time until all are done.
Dill or fennel	Break off tiny leaf groups from central stem. Microwave in a single layer on a paper towel for 1½ minutes on 'high', then 30 seconds at a time until crisp. Larger quantities take longer.
Chives	Chop into 1cm (¾″) lengths and shake free excess moisture in a sieve. Microwave on paper towel for 5 minutes on 'high', turning occasionally and separating any pieces clinging together. Replace paper towel if it becomes too damp. Continue with 45-second intervals on 'high' until completely dry.
Basil	Spread 3 or 4 large dry leaves at a time on a paper towel, not touching each other. Microwave on 'high' 1–2 minutes, then for 30-second intervals until crisp. If leaves go black, they will not crisp properly. Drying must be very swift to keep the colour, hence the use of very few leaves at a time. It is best to use basil that has been picked for some time so that the moisture content has already started to lessen.

Other methods Some herbs can be frozen successfully. Chop the herbs finely, add a little water then fill ice cube

segments. Chives, dill and parsley can be added straight from the freezer to cold soups. Herb flowers can also be frozen and added to iced drinks or punch for a fresh, interesting look.

Basil can be hard to dry, as it goes black when drying and in freezing. Try pureeing it in a little oil and keep it that way.

Herb vinegars are another use for garden herbs. Wash and dry the herb (for instance, rosemary), push it into a clean bottle, then fill with white or red wine vinegar. Put the bottle in a warm spot, such as a windowsill, for two to four weeks before use.

Easy, tasty uses of herbs include a summer herb dip, in which a cup of watercress and three-quarters of a cup of parsley and chives are mixed into a bowl of mayonnaise.

Make a tangy salad dressing with a cup of wine vinegar and a few tablespoons of chopped parsley and chives, mixed in a blender.

SPROUTS

When sprouted, certain seeds are delicious and provide vitamins, iron, minerals and an especially good type of fibre for reducing cholesterol levels. Protein is higher in the seed than in any other part of the plant. Sprouting seeds are fresh vegetables; they are still growing as you eat them. A whole range of seeds will sprout—alfalfa (lucerne), mung beans, lentils, mustard seeds and so on. The sprouting time varies from three to six days.

Growing sprouts at home is very easy. All you need is a large jar, some gauze or muslin and an elastic band. Put some seeds in the bottom of the jar, and rinse thoroughly two or three times by placing the gauze and elastic band over the top of the jar, and tipping upside down so the water drains out. Rinse well each day.

The colour of the sprouts can be controlled. If you want green sprouts, grow them on a bench in the sunlight, so that chlorophyll develops. If you want white sprouts, grow them in a dark cupboard or put the jar in a brown paper bag.

If you want the sprouts to grow curly, rotate the jar a little each day after rinsing.

Do not allow any variety to grow past six days, as this may spoil the flavour. To keep, rinse and place in the refrigerator in a sealed container or plastic bag.

All the varieties listed below can be cooked, or eaten fresh.

> *Because of their roof-top position, skylights provide more light than a conventional window of the same size.*

SPROUTING-AT-A-GLANCE					
Variety	Eating flavour	Rinses per day	Sprouting time	Approx yield	Length at harvest (cm)
Salad alfalfa	Fresh, sweet	2-3	4-6 days	8-10 times	3-5
Spicy fenugreek	Exotic, curry	2-3	3-6 days	6-8 times	1-5
Savoury party mix	Warm, spicy	2-3	4-6 days	6-8 times	3-5
Bean sprouts	Good-crisp	3-4	3-5 days	6-8 times	2-7
Sandwich mix	Sweet, piquant	2-3	3-6 days	6-8 times	3-5
Mixed salad sprouts	Superb	3-4	4-6 days	6-8 times	—
Snowbean sprouts	Sweet nutty	3-4	3-6 days	6-8 times	2-7

CHAPTER 12
Gardening Suppliers

AGRONET

Agronet is a light polypropylene and polyamide net for covering growing vegetable crops. It allows water, air and light, as well as herbicides and pesticides, to reach the plants, while keeping out birds, insects and frosts (down to -3°C, 27°F). The Australian and New Zealand distributors are:

Edward Keller (Australia) Pty Ltd
3 Walker Street
Braeside VIC 3195
Telephone (03) 580 1666

CIVIC TREES

Civic Trees are semi mature tree specialists, and a diverse nursery, growing trees from 1-7m tall. Their aim is to produce high quality trees, underpruned and with a full rootball to ensure a complete growth pattern with no root recovery trauma.

Being a wholesale outlet Civic Trees sell to other nurseries, civic groups and the local, state and federal government. Larger trees not available through retail outlets are sold to individuals.

Trees available

Acers	Jacaranda	Platanus
Araucarias	Liquidambar	Podocarpus
Cedrus	Lophostemon	Raphiolepis
Celtis	Magnolia	Sapium
Flindersia	Nyssa	Ulmus
Gleditsia		

For further information

Civic Trees
1 Harris Road
Dural NSW 2158
Telephone (02) 651 2833

FRUIT PICKER

The Ezy Pick fruit picker featured on 'Burke's Backyard' is available by mail order. Simply send a cheque or money order for $18 to:

Mr Frank Hamzsak
8 Codrington Street
Cranbourne VIC 3799

The $18 covers the cost of the Ezy Pick and all postage and handling charges.

GARDEN CLOTHING AND ACCESSORIES

All items featured in the 'Burke's Backyard Winter Gardening Collection' are available throughout Australia.

If you encounter any difficulty in obtaining an item call the relevant manufacturer on this list, who will be able to name your closest supplier.

Armour Driza-Bone Pty Ltd
Telephone (008) 773 800 (toll-free)

Riding coat, $130
Short coat, $115
Trousers, $80
Sou'wester, $25
Driza-Para riding coat, $140
Driza-Bone brumby jacket, $115

Available at major mens' country outfitters and department stores.

Agmer Drywear
Telephone (03) 791 4299

Short parka style jacket with hood, $62.40
PVC coated nylon jacket, $33
PVC coated nylon trousers, $20
PVA overall with Velcro and zip front, $61
Plastic bib-and-brace overall, $38.70

Available at disposal stores and camping shops as well as some department stores.

Bata Industrial Footwear

Telephone (02) 725 4797 or (03) 419 4655.

Range of gumboots in colours and black, $15-$30

Available in major department stores and all major footwear retail outlets.

Dunlop Footwear

Telephone (02) 790 4221

Prices start at $22 for ladies' gumboots.

Available at K-Mart and Woolworths.
Steel cap boots available through Protector Safety Pty Ltd.

Compleat Gardener

Sou'wester, $20
Waterproof kneeling cushion, $29
Organiser belt, $30
Carrybag, $20-$25
Log carrier, $27.50
Clipping collector, $30

The Compleat Gardener range is available from gift shops, some nurseries, Georges (Melbourne) and David Jones (Sydney).

Ezykneel

For $28, the Ezykneel is available from BBC, K-Mart, Target, Mitre 10, Big W and McEwans (Victoria).

Gardening gloves

The gardening gloves are available at Grace Bros, BBC, Target and most chain stores. They range in price from $1 to $4.

NARROMINE TRANSPLANTS

Narromine Transplants is the largest seedling production nursery in the Southern Hemisphere, and is adjacent to the Yates Seeds Research Station at Narromine, New South Wales. It doesn't, however, sell seedlings to backyard growers. In fact, all the seedlings it produces are sold to farmers and market gardeners.

Narromine Transplants produces 24 million seedlings a year and the whole process is fully automated. Specially designed trays have a separate, inverted, cone-shaped hole for each seedling. The hole is filled with peat moss and then a smaller hole is dibbled into it. Seed is sown into each hole through a vacuum powered drum, then topped off with vermiculite and the whole thing watered. The tray is then placed in a special chamber for a few days while germination takes place.

Five weeks after sowing, each seedling has developed a magnificent root system. The upside-down cone design makes extraction extremely easy; so easy that packers can just grab the seedlings out of the containers without doing them any damage at all, and pack them into boxes ready to be despatched to farmers or market gardeners all over the country.

These young plants are ideally suited for use with modern automatic planting machines. They are simply removed from the box and placed in the rotating cups of the machine, from which they drop like darts into the ground. This automation means that large areas can be planted with Narromine transplants very quickly.

This system is not used only for lettuce and other vegetables, but also for a number of other interesting types of plants. One such plant is saltbush, normally considered a weed, that grows in the outback. It is also a wonderful fodder plant for sheep and other animals, however, particularly in dry, arid, rough environments. So it is not just you and your family who enjoy eating the end product of this sort of modern propagation factory—the sheep get a good feed as well.

POWERJET

The Powerjet is a non-adjustable nozzle that fits onto a garden hose as an alternative to an ordinary nozzle. Its only purpose is as a cleaning tool and we found it to be effective in removing stains and algae from dirty bricks and paving, although the operator needs to be persistent. The Powerjet is made from solid brass and is available from hardware stores for about $10.

RETICULATION

Information about Oasis Watering Systems for residential and light commercial use can be obtained from:

Oasis Control Systems Pty Ltd
18 Hasler Road
Osborne Park WA 6017
Telephone (09) 446 9299

South Australian Branch

U12, 47 O.G. Road
Klemzig SA 5083
Telephone (08) 266 3655

ROCK AND MASONRY SPLITTER

Foseco Technik produce Splitter FA, a fast acting (in most materials, within 30 minutes) rock, concrete and masonry splitter for small-scale work. You can obtain their brochure by writing to or phoning them.

Foseco Technik
Stuart Street
Padstow NSW 2211
(PO Box 113
Revesby NSW 2212)
Telephone (02) 771 3111

YATES SEEDS

When buying a packet of seeds, it is hard to imagine the vast amount of research leading up to their production.

At the Yates Research Station in Narromine, New South Wales, a large number of vegetables are tested to determine if they are suitable for your backyard. Yates has a total of 40.5ha (100 acres) in an area that is ideal for growing vegetables, and they are involved in all aspects of seed research, transplants and seed production, producing more than 24 million seedlings every year.

Currently test trials are being carried out on 100 varieties of cabbages. Only one or two will be selected as suitable for marketing. The cabbages are assessed for all their characteristics; their appearance, internal characteristics, their compactness and ability to hold and not split and go to seed.

The whole process of breeding starts in the pollination houses, where the F1 hybrids are produced. F1 hybrids are produced from two different varieties of, say, cauliflowers, by taking the male stamen with pollen on it from one variety and rubbing it on the female stigma of a different variety of cauliflower. The same technique is used for producing many flowers and vegetables.

One of the most interesting new vegetables produced at the Yates testing station is a new variety of lettuce called Regency. This has red-edged leaves that look particularly attractive on a plate and was bred especially for the restaurant trade. Regency has an excellent flavour and is available to the home gardener.

If you are starting to grow vegetables in your home-garden, it would be a good idea to try some of the newer varieties that are currently available. Yates seeds are sold by most nurseries and gardening outlets.

PETS AND BACKYARD ANIMALS

CHAPTER I
Dog Breeds

CANINE CONTROL ASSOCIATIONS

Australian Capital Territory
The Canberra Kennel Association
PO Box 815
Dickson ACT 2602
Telephone (062) 41 4404

New South Wales
The New South Wales Canine Council
Locked Bag 27
Ashfield NSW 2131
Telephone (02) 716 7266

Northern Territory
The North Australian Canine Association
PO Box 37521
Winnellie NT 0821
Telephone (089) 84 3570

Queensland
The Canine Control Council of Queensland
PO Box 495
Fortitude Valley QLD 4006
Telephone (07) 252 2661

South Australia
The South Australian Canine Association
PO Box 844
Prospect East SA 5082
Telephone (08) 349 4797

Tasmania
The Kennel Control Council of Tasmania
The Rothman Building
Royal Showgrounds
Glenorchy TAS 7010
Telephone (002) 72 9443

Victoria
The Kennel Control Council of Victoria
Royal Showgrounds
Epsom Rd
Ascot Vale VIC 3032
Telephone (03) 376 3733

Western Australia
The Canine Association of Western Australia
PO Box 301
Gosnells WA 6110
Telephone (09) 455 1188

New Zealand
New Zealand Kennel Club Inc
Private Bag
Porirua
New Zealand
Telephone (4) 37 4489

DOG BREEDS REGISTERED IN AUSTRALIA

Group I (Toys)
Affenpinscher
Australian Silky Terrier
Bichon Frise
Cavalier King Charles Spaniel
Chihuahua (Long)
Chihuahua (Smooth)
Chinese Crested Dog
English Toy Terrier (Black and Tan)
Griffon Bruxellois
Italian Greyhound
Japanese Chin
King Charles Spaniel
Lowchen
Maltese
Miniature Pinscher

Papillon
Pekingese
Pomeranian
Pug
Tibetan Spaniel
Yorkshire Terrier

Group 2 (Terriers)
Airedale Terrier
American Staffordshire Terrier
Australian Terrier
Bedlington Terrier
Border Terrier
Bull Terrier
Bull Terrier (Miniature)
Cairn Terrier
Dandie Dinmont Terrier
Fox Terrier (Smooth)
Fox Terrier (Wire)
Glen of Imaal Terrier
Irish Terrier
Kerry Blue Terrier
Lakeland Terrier
Manchester Terrier
Norfolk Terrier
Norwich Terrier
Scottish Terrier
Sealyham Terrier
Skye Terrier
Soft Coated Wheaten Terrier
Staffordshire Bull Terrier
Welsh Terrier
West Highland White Terrier

Group 3 (Gundogs)
Brittany
Chesapeake Bay Retriever
Clumber Spaniel
Cocker Spaniel
Cocker Spaniel (American)
Curly Coated Retriever
English Setter
English Springer Spaniel
Flat Coated Retriever
German Shorthaired Pointer
German Wirehaired Pointer
Golden Retriever
Gordon Setter
Hungarian Vizsla
Irish Red and White Setter
Irish Setter
Irish Water Spaniel
Italian Spinone
Labrador Retriever
Large Munsterlander

Pointer
Sussex Spaniel
Weimaraner
Welsh Springer Spaniel

Group 4 (Hounds)
Afghan Hound
Basenji
Basset Hound
Beagle
Bloodhound
Borzoi
Dachshund (Long Haired)
Dachshund (Miniature Long Haired)
Dachshund (Smooth Haired)
Dachshund (Miniature Smooth Haired)
Dachshund (Wire Haired)
Dachshund (Miniature Wire Haired)
Deerhound
Elkhound
Finnish Spitz
Foxhound
Greyhound
Hamilton Stovare
Harrier
Ibizan Hound
Irish Wolfhound
Otterhound
Petit Basset Griffon Vendeen
Pharaoh Hound
Rhodesian Ridgeback
Saluki
Sloughi
Whippet

Group 5 (Working Dogs)
Anatolian Shepherd Dog
Australian Cattle Dog
Australian Kelpie
Bearded Collie
Belgian Shepherd Dog (Groenendael)
Belgian Shepherd Dog (Laekenois)
Belgian Shepherd Dog (Malinois)
Belgian Shepherd Dog (Tervueren)
Border Collie
Bouvier des Flandres
Briard
Collie (Rough)
Collie (Smooth)
German Shepherd Dog
Hungarian Puli
Maremma Sheepdog
Norwegian Buhund
Old English Sheepdog
Shetland Sheepdog

ROAD TEST

133

Stumpy Tail Cattle Dog
Swedish Vallhund
Welsh Corgi (Cardigan)
Welsh Corgi (Pembroke)

Group 6 (Utility)
Akita
Alaskan Malamute
Bernese Mountain Dog
Boxer
Bullmastiff
Dobermann
German Pinscher
Komondor
Mastiff
Newfoundland
Pyrenean Mountain Dog
Rottweiler
St Bernard
Samoyed
Schnauzer (Miniature)
Schnauzer
Schnauzer (Giant)
Shiba Inu
Siberian Husky
Tibetan Mastiff

Group 7 (Non Sporting)
Boston Terrier
British Bulldog
Chow Chow
Dalmatian
French Bulldog
German Spitz
Great Dane
Japanese Spitz
Keeshond
Lhasa Apso
Poodle (Standard)
Poodle (Miniature)
Poodle (Toy)
Schipperke
Shar Pei
Shih Tzu
Tibetan Terrier

ANATOLIAN KARABASH/ SHEPHERD

A wide range of large, strong dogs is used by the Turkish shepherds to protect their flocks. These dogs are known by the term 'coban kopegi'—shepherd's dog.

The Anatolian Karabash, however, is a distinct breed and is recognised as such by shepherds and many people throughout Turkey. The breed is renowned for its lion-like appearance, its strength and bravery, and for the faithful protection it gives, not only to the flocks, but to its master and the master's family.

The word karabash (kara bas) simply means 'black head' and is the colloquial name for this breed, which is also often called by the names 'Comar' and 'Samsun'. Both of these are translated as 'Mastiff'.

As a shepherd's dog the breed is greatly admired, and pockets of carefully bred dogs are to be found in all the sheep-rearing central-upland provinces.

Appearance The karabash is a large and handsome breed, the adult males standing 73–81cm (29–32″) at the shoulder. It is a whole-coloured dog with a short, dense coat which, like that of the old English Mastiff whose ancestry it probably shares, may be any shade of fawn from cream to red or (rarely) brindle, but always with black mask and ears. Black toenails are a mark of the purebred dog, as is a black tip to the tail, which is carried in an open curl over the back when the dog is alert.

Useful qualities Their owners take much pride in their size and bravery, their great stamina and their amazing speed, which enables them to run down wolves. With a heavy, well-set front and lighter but very powerful hindquarters, a karabash runs down a wolf by hurling his shoulder at the animal and smashing him to the ground.

In Turkey an Anatolian wins a wicked-looking spiked collar when it kills a wolf. Its ears are often cropped, supposedly to make it hear better and to stop other dogs or wolves grabbing it by the ear.

The karabash is not simply a shepherd's dog. It is widely used as a guard dog throughout Turkey by the military and many others.

A purebred karabash is greatly prized by his owner and considerable care is taken by some people in the production of strong, good-looking and typical dogs. The owner of a bitch may go to great lengths to purchase puppies from a particular breeder or from a special district such as Kangal. Thus, the strict selection for the type and working qualities over many centuries has ensured the conservation of large numbers of typical examples of the breed.

The process of natural selection has played an important part in the development of the karabash. Like all Turkish shepherds' dogs they lead an extremely hard-working life in tough conditions, and only the strongest survive. They must be able to work in all weathers, walking for many kilometres in the heat and dust of summer and sleeping on the hillsides in the thick snow of winter. Although their coats are short and close, they carry quite a heavy under-wool.

As a breed the karabash has a natural instinct to guard his own, whether it be his flocks, his master or his master's house and family. The male dogs, being larger and more efficient guards, are more often taken out with the flocks than are the bitches. Only a very few bitches are kept and these generally remain in the village or settlement and only occasionally accompany the shepherd and the flocks.

Karabash are not herders of sheep; their function is to stand apart from them and watch. Two or three dogs often run together with a big flock and they are trained to stay out on the hillside all night, if necessary, and without a shepherd.

Karabash have excellent hearing. They are noted, too, for their remarkable eyesight, and rely more on these two senses than on their sense of smell.

The shepherd is well aware of the fact that the bigger and stronger the dog the better the guard, so a chosen puppy is fed milk and plenty of scraps in the early months to give him a good start. Thereafter, however, the diet of the karabash is very poor. Shepherds' dogs are not fed meat in Turkey. Instead, a special paste of flour and water is made up for the dogs and each receives a handful or so of the paste each day. The flour is homeground and unpurified, and as such is far more nourishing than one might suppose, but even supplemented by household scraps and any small rodents the dogs are able to catch, it is a poor diet and only the hardiest of the species will survive on it.

For further information

Mrs Sue Freshwater
PO Box 104
Toodyay WA 6566

AUSTRALIAN CATTLE DOG

The Australian Cattle Dog was the result of many years of effort to breed a dog suitable for working cattle in this country's harsh conditions. The most popular dog used by early drovers and cattlemen after 1813 was the Smithfield, but its strength and endurance were questionable. Smithfields were also barkers, which suited sheep but not the semi-wild cattle herds of Australia.

Next came the Timmins biters, which employed Dingo-to-Smithfield crosses. Unfortunately, the biting of the dingo strain was too rough. Other crosses, such as a Rough Collie to a Bull Terrier, were unsuccessful with cattle.

Thomas Hall imported smooth-haired blue merle Highland Collies from Scotland in 1840. They too barked and headed, but once crossed with dingoes produced silent workers known as Hall's Heelers. They were very popular, and when some were sent to Sydney, they were purchased by the Baugust brothers in the 1880s.

These brothers aimed to improve on the dog, crossing it to Dalmatians (to instil a love of horses and faithfulness to their masters). This cross resulted in the loss of some working ability, so they looked to the black and tan Kelpie.

In 1893 a standard was written for the Australian Cattle Dog. This was endorsed in 1903 and only slightly varied in 1964.

Nowadays, Australian cattle dogs are rarely used to work cattle due to their aggressive nature and tendency to bite. While they are appropriate with semi-wild cattle, they are too rough with modern breeds. Their place has mainly been taken by the Australian Kelpie.

Appearance Cattle dogs are stocky, well-built and medium-set, and are compact and hard-muscled. They should have great agility, strength and endurance.

Dogs are 46–51cm (18–20″) high, bitches 45–48cm (17–19″). Dogs weigh 20–25kg (45–55lb), bitches 18–23kg (40–50lb).

These dogs have a double coat that is water resistant. The outer coat is harsh and keeps out chills and rain; the undercoat is thick and soft to insulate against temperature extremes.

Colours Australian cattle dogs come in two colours, blue and red. Different patterns and markings occur within these two colour groups.

The puppies are born white and don't develop their colours until they are about three or four weeks of age. The colour appears first at the feet and then moves up to the body.

Temperament Cattle dogs are said to be highly intelligent. They are suspicious, curious and wary of strangers. They are highly protective of and loyal to their 'pack' or family. They are amenable to discipline and learn quickly, but become bored with repetitive tasks.

Cattle dogs can be aloof, stubborn, strong-minded and in some cases excitable, but this last characteristic usually indicates a desire for stimulation. The dogs have active minds, and need exercise and activity to use up some of the energy they were bred to use behind cattle.

Some cattle dog characteristics that have served them well in the work for which they were bred—such as sneaky attacks from the rear and the tendency to bite if provoked—have given them a poor reputation as pets.

Useful qualities These dogs make good watch-dogs and are suitable as companions for active, outdoor people who are prepared to give the dog the time and attention it requires.

> *Due to their sensitivity to phosphorus, Banksias are often killed by applications of superphosphate or lawn food.*

ROAD TEST

Ideal owner Australian cattle dogs are not suitable for the elderly, for people living in flats or townhouses (they were bred to be kept outdoors), or for people interested in them only for fashion's sake.

The breed is well-suited to active people prepared to exercise and spend time with them. These dogs appear to enjoy battles of wits with their owners, so the owner needs to be someone who can respect and enjoy the dog's independent thinking—owning an Australian cattle dog can be something of a challenge. Cattle dogs are gregarious and enjoy the company of humans and animals, particularly other dogs, although male cattle dogs can be very aggressive towards one another. In many cases they should not be trusted with cats, however.

Training Australian cattle dogs are quick to learn if they wish to. They can also be very stubborn and single-minded, so a firm but patient hand is required.

Popularity Possibly reflecting the increased interest in things Australian during the last decade, Australian cattle dog registration figures have more than doubled in that time. Australian cattle dogs are part of the symbolism of the tough, macho Australian male, as well as being a popular advertising and fashion accessory.

Breeders believe that this dramatic rise in popularity is a regrettable thing. Similar cases in the past have resulted in backyard breeders producing poor quality animals in large quantities to cash in on the financial rewards from puppy sales. This leads to a decline in quality, which takes many years of careful breeding to rectify once the fashion fades.

Health Deafness is a congenital disease of the Australian cattle dog, and can affect any white or predominantly white puppies. These puppies are culled when the problem becomes apparent at three to four weeks, as the cattle dog club members are making a major effort to restrict and breed out this problem.

Otherwise, if the environmental requirements for exercise, attention and stimulation are met, Cattle dogs are very hardy. They are very long-lived; 12-15 years is average, 17 years not uncommon.

Exercise Suburban backyards are not really large enough for this breed unless the dog can be exercised daily (a morning jog twice around the block is sufficient). The exercise is important mentally as well as physically. If two dogs are kept together they will help to entertain and exercise each other.

Grooming Minimum maintenance is required; bathe the dog when it is dirty. The 'all-weather' coat should not be pampered, but a weekly brush is beneficial.

Feeding Like goats, Australian cattle dogs have a reputation for eating anything—even the washing at times. In general, however, a varied diet including dry food, mince, bones and canned dog food is suitable. The cost of food per week is $10-$15.

Cost A pet Australian cattle dog will cost $200 or more; show quality dogs cost $250-$400.

For further information

Australian Cattle Dog Society of New South Wales
(Secretary, Mrs D. Lawrence)
57 Ivy Street
Greenacre NSW 2190
Telephone (02) 642 4518

The Cattle Dog, Kelpie and Border Collie Club of Victoria
(Secretary, Mrs D. Haywood)
PO Box 175
Broadmeadows VIC 3407
Telephone (03) 305 4112

The Cattle Dog, Kelpie and Border Collie Club of Queensland
(Secretary, Mrs B. Scott)
Lot 43 Aberdeen Road
North Maclean QLD 4280
Telephone (07) 200 0585

In other states, contact the local canine councils.

AUSTRALIAN KELPIE

Kelpies were developed in Australia in the last century and are probably the world's most active and best working dogs. They come in a wide range of colours and separate strains have been developed for use as pets.

Working kelpies The kelpie in Australia has been developed as a working dog. It is very active, thrives on working and is capable of covering vast distances. The kelpie will run over the backs of huddled sheep. Working kelpies are not normally registered with kennel clubs. The working strain of kelpie does not adapt well to confined spaces.

Domestic kelpies The domestic or exhibition kelpie makes a far better pet. It is less hyperactive than the working strains, comes in a wide range of colours and is overall a more manageable domestic pet.

Domestic kelpies come in black, black and tan, red, red and tan, fawn, chocolate and smoke blue. Some but not all of these colours are available in working kelpies. At the withers dogs stand 46-51cm (18-20″) high, and bitches 43-48cm (17-19″). Working kelpies are slightly smaller.

Kelpies' coats are double, that is, having a short, dense undercoat with a close, hard, rain-resisting outer coat. The coats of both types of kelpies are similar, except that the domestic dog's is normally more luxuriant.

Problems There are very few genetic faults in the breed. The reddish colour that is sometimes seen around the eyelids of the red and brown kelpies is caused by a parasite (mange mite). It can be stopped easily with simple veterinary treatment. The tips of the ears can become fly bitten in the summer, but regular use of a repellent will help control this.

Temperament Kelpies are intelligent, dedicated (to work and owner), friendly, active, hardworking and tireless. Kelpies must be kept active, otherwise their boundless energy is likely to make them a frustrated nuisance to owners and neighbours.

Kelpies cost between $200 and $500. They will eat commercial dog foods and cost around $5 a week to feed. They live for 12–15 years.

For further information

When selecting the more domestic type of kelpie, it is advisable to seek guidance from the following.

Australian Kelpie Club of NSW
(Secretary, Mrs E. Park)
Lot 2 Western Road
Kemps Creek NSW 2171
Telephone (02) 826 1124

The Australian Cattle Dog and Kelpie Club of Victoria
(Secretary, Mr D. Hayward)
PO Box 175
Broadmeadows VIC 3047
Telephone (03) 305 4112

Cattle Dog, Kelpie and Border Collie Club of Queensland
(Secretary, Mrs B. Scott)
Lot 43 Aberdeen Rd
North Maclean QLD 4280
Telephone (07) 200 0585

The Australian Cattle Dog, Kelpie and Border Collie Club of SA Inc
(Secretary, Mrs S. Nicholson)
PO Summertown SA 5141
Telephone (08) 390 1417

Working Dog Club
(Secretary, Mrs H. Green)
Lot 106 Terrier Place
Gosnells WA 6110
Telephone (09) 398 4428

Tasmanian Working Sheepdog Association
c/- PO Box 94
Glenorchy TAS 7010
Telephone (002) 72 6812

North Australian Canine Association
PO Box 37521
Winnellie NT 0821
Telephone (089) 84 3570

Miss D. Smith
(Kelpie Breeder)
51 Gregory Street
Parap NT 0820
Telephone (089) 81 8569

AUSTRALIAN SILKY TERRIER

This is an Australian breed, which is not yet 100 years old. The breed began in about 1900–1901 when Australian Terriers were crossed with Yorkshire terriers. These black-and-tan terriers looked like odd Yorkshire terriers. Further crossing continued until the coat colour and silky texture were stabilised and the dogs bred as they are today.

The breed is known as the Australian Silky Terrier; it has been called the Sydney Silky and the Victorian Silky, but in 1959 it was changed to Australian silky terrier to clarify the situation. The dogs are very popular in the USA; there, they are known simply as silky terriers.

Character The dogs are described as being very alert, game, intelligent and active. They are good watch-dogs and friendly if introduced to strangers as friends. They are protective and some texts note that they will bite to protect their owners.

The dogs enjoy attention, and if ignored or left alone for long periods they can become yappy. If they are occupied and entertained this is not a problem.

ROAD TEST

Their behaviour towards children is good if they are reared with them. They can get excited and jump up at the children if they are noisy or boisterous. The dogs enjoy attention.

Suitability as a household pet Silkies are good household pets being small, non-destructive and not needing a lot of exercise. They are well-suited to life indoors. They dislike being wet and don't drop hair. They are ideal for the elderly or infirm.

Training Silkies are considered easy to train and they learn readily. They should be taught not to jump up at people.

Useful qualities The dogs were bred to chase rodents, and are very good watch-dogs.

Care The dogs need about 0.25kg daily of fresh or tinned meat and a good dry dog biscuit. Many seem partial to the occasional helping of Whiskettes. It is important that the dogs are groomed regularly to avoid knots and tangles.

Health The breed is very hardy, being bred from two tough terrier lines. Their major health risk could arise from their tendency to take on any interloper, be it Dobermann or Great Dane. It is not advisable to let silky terriers roam.

Cost Australian silky terriers cost about $150 for pet animals. They eat fresh or tinned meat and good dry biscuits, costing $5–$7 a week to feed. They live for approximately 14 years.

For further information

Australian Silky Terrier Club of NSW
(Secretary, Mrs Marie Watts)
Lot 3 The Northern Road
Bringelly NSW 2171
Telephone (047) 74 8750

Australian Silky Terrier Club of Queensland
(Secretary, Mrs Lorna Hinsch)
6 Stuart Street
Goodna QLD 4300

Australian Silky Terrier Club of Victoria
(Secretary, Mrs June Collins)
49 Sandford Avenue
North Sunshine VIC 3020

Australian Silky and Yorkshire Terrier Club (ACT)
(Secretary, Mrs K. Dean)
24 Canopus Crescent
Giralang ACT 2617

In other states, contact the Kennel Control Council or Canine Association.

BASENJI

The Basenji is a fascinating breed of dog. Like most wild varieties of dogs, it doesn't bark and comes into season only once a year. Basenjis were bred in Africa to hunt wild game and they are one of the hardiest types of dogs.

Ancient rock carvings of dogs similar to the basenji type have been dated at about 4000–5000 years old. None were thought to exist until comparatively recently, when the breed was rediscovered in Africa.

The native tribes called the dog 'watusi' which means 'wild thing'. As the dog doesn't bark, wooden bells were tied to the dog's neck or thighs so it could be followed when used to track down prey.

The fact that the dogs don't bark is possibly the breed's best-known feature. Instead they 'chortle' or whine. They are quiet, clean dogs and clean themselves like a cat.

Temperament Basenjis are considered protective, independent and intelligent, but can be stubborn when responding to owner's directions. More effort may be needed to train a basenji to obedience than to train other dog breeds. The breed retains a strong pack instinct, which can be seen as a plus when the family has children, but breeders often suggest that if the dog is to be left alone for long periods, two basenjis may be happier than one.

Exercise This is an active dog which benefits from exercise. Another surprise feature of the basenji is that it is an agile climber, and a high fence is essential for people considering buying a basenji. Breeders don't recommend this dog as being well-suited to flats, units or tiny backyards.

Appearance The standard for basenjis is 41cm (16") and 9.5kg (22lb) for bitches, while dogs are 43cm (17") and 11kg (24lb). There are three colours: red and white, black and white, and tan and white with melon pips (the eyebrow markings).

Health Basenjis have very few health problems. They don't like the cold and enjoy curling up in front of a fire or on the end of a bed. They live for approximately 12 years.

Cost Basenji pups cost $200–$250.

Popularity The breed is becoming more popular in Australia after being introduced to this country from Africa in 1939. There are clubs in NSW, Victoria and South Australia. In other states contact your local Canine Control Council.

For further information

The Basenji Hound Club of NSW
(Secretary, Miss H.P. Church)
53 Lisgar Street
Granville NSW 2142
Telephone (02) 637 4626

Basenji Club of Victoria Inc
(Secretary, Mrs J. Gregory)
18 Thompson Road
Upwey VIC 3158

Basenji Owners Club
(Secretary, Mrs D. Jolliffe)
9 Marlborough Street
Brighton SA 5048

BASSET HOUND

There is considerable disagreement about the origins of the Basset Hound. Some claim it is the result of a cross between the Bloodhound and the Beagle; others say it was a mutation found in a litter of French Staghounds. Yet others claim that the abbots of St Hubert of France were breeding them as early as the 1600s.

The basset was used by British landed gentry to hunt on foot. Due to its short legs and steady gait it was possible to keep pace with the Basset, where other hounds would need to be followed on horseback.

The basset hound has become an established and popular breed in Australia since it was introduced to this country during the earlier part of this century.

Appearance The basset hound is generally classed as a medium-sized dog. Despite its short legs, it has quite a heavy body and head. It has very long, floppy ears and a sad, droopy expression. The coat is short and smooth.

Its height is 33–38cm (13–15″), and its weight 25–32kg (55–70lb).

Colours The colours available are: tri-coloured (white, black and brown), lemon (pale lemon and white), red and white (deep red), and blank red (solid red with a speck of white on tail tip and feet).

Temperament Bassets are intelligent, quiet with children and eager to be part of the family. They can be stubborn and need discipline when young. They will bark at strangers and are wary of unfamiliar people.

Bassets are hounds, and when following a scent can disappear until they either find their quarry or are too hungry to bother. Bassets will also wander (usually following a scent) if unrestrained and unsupervised.

Exercise The basset is suitable for a townhouse or terrace but nothing smaller. When confined to a small yard, regular walks, even just around the block, are essential. Bassets are more than happy to spend the day just lying around, so they can easily grow fat if exercise is neglected.

Useful qualities The basset has a loud, deep bark which will often deter potential intruders.

The basset hound has a deep instinct for tracking and, if given the opportunity, its rabbiting skills can be aroused.

Bassets are considered to be one of the best companion dog breeds, suiting both young families and the elderly.

Grooming These dogs have a short, smooth coat which requires weekly brushing.

It is essential that the basset's long ears are wiped out weekly, using a soft cloth dampened with either warm water or one of the commercial preparations available from vets. Cotton buds should not be used as they can break and fall into the dog's ear canal, necessitating professional removal.

Health Bassets are not well suited to houses with steps, as they are prone to suffer from slipped discs, and constant climbing up and down stairs puts an added strain on the spine.

Owners should be strict with the ear cleaning regime. Dirt and wax can build up and present a perfect environment for bacterial infection.

Bassets will gorge themselves if allowed, and this can lead to a weight problem which places a further strain on the back.

Loose-lidded, weepy eyes can bring about infections from dirt and dust, particularly as the dog's head is so close to the ground.

Bassets must be picked up correctly, otherwise the added strain on their spines or front legs could permanently injure them. They should be picked up with one hand under the chest and the other supporting the rear end.

They live for 12–13 years.

Litters Bassets produce an average of 8–9 puppies per litter and have few whelping problems.

ROAD TEST

Cost of puppies Pets will be $300–$350, exhibition quality puppies cost $400.

Feeding Breeders recommend a varied diet of meat and vegetables. Calcium is essential for young dogs and pups to establish a strong frame to carry their weight as they mature. It will cost about $10 a week to feed a basset hound.

For further information

Basset Hound Club of NSW
(Secretary, Alan Stonehouse)
94 Elizabeth Street
Riverstone NSW 2765
Telephone (02) 627 3232

Basset Hound Club of Victoria
(c/- Jane Mountain)
McDonalds Road
Catani VIC 3981
Telephone (056) 29 4322

Basset Hound Club of Queensland
(c/- Mrs M Hewson)
PO Box 550
Woodridge QLD 4114
Telephone (07) 299 7743

Basset Hound Club of SA
(Mrs E A Moore)
PO Box 53
Old Noarlunga SA 5168
Telephone (08) 323 9163

There are no clubs in Western Australia, Tasmania or the Northern Territory.

BEAGLE

Beagles have been around for a long time, possibly five centuries. Queen Elizabeth I had a 'Pocket Beagle' (now extinct). Beagles are scent hounds and were used in packs to hunt rabbits and hares.

Appearance Beagles are very appealing, sturdy, compact dogs with gentle expressions and wonderful floppy ears. They are 33–40cm (13-16″) high. The males weigh 13kg (30lb), the females 11kg (25lb).

Colours They come in any recognised hound colour, except liver: tri-colour (black, tan and white); tan and white; badger (pied—black, tan and white on each hair); broken-tri (more white than the standard tri-colour); hare-pied (not found in Australia). The tip of the tail must be white, so that the dog can be easily seen while hunting.

Popularity Beagles do not suffer from bouts of being fashionable; they are consistently one of the most popular of the hounds.

Temperament Trustworthy and human-oriented, they are not excitable except when on a scent. They are full of fun and can be mischievous. The 'happy wanderer' of the dog world, the beagle has a wonderful personality.

Useful qualities The beagle is affectionate and therefore suitable for Pets as Therapy programmes. It is playful and makes a good companion dog, but is also useful as a guard dog, as it will bark at strangers. It also has a good sense of smell and is used in drug-sniffer work.

Training It is not easy to train beagles. They will join together in a group and track down a scent, so a lead is essential when on outings. Owners need patience and kindness to train a beagle, and even a trained beagle will not respond when on a scent trail.

Puppies Beagles average five puppies per litter. As with most dogs, some problems may arise with large litters. Puppies cost from $250–$300.

Feeding A beagle gains weight easily, as it will eat almost anything. A diet should be decided upon—for example, a good commercial canned food, mixed with vegetables and dog biscuits—and then adhered to fairly strictly.

Lifespan Most beagles have both a long and merry life, living for an average of 15 years.

Health Beagles may suffer from slipped discs in later life, but since they are a very robust dog, very few health problems develop.

Suitability as a household pet Beagles are neat and easy to groom; they need an enclosed backyard, but can dig their way out if lonely.

Ideal owner Beagles are ideal for a typical suburban family with kids and a backyard. They are not really suitable for working couples, nor for flats or units. They may be too enthusiastic for tiny children and the frail.

For further information

Beagle Club of NSW
(Secretary, Mrs E. Stoppard)
219 Eastern Road
Wahroonga NSW 2076
Telephone (02) 487 2931

Beagle Club of Victoria
(Secretary, Mr G. Morrissey)
2 Links Road
Bacchus Marsh VIC 3340
Telephone (053) 67 2068

Hound Club of Queensland
(Mrs V. Knopke)
6 Debenham Street
Sunnybank Hills QLD 4109
Telephone (075) 64 3942

Beagle Club of SA
(Secretary, Mrs B. Janssan)
Morris Road
Meadows SA 5201
Telephone (08) 388 3427

The WA Beagle Club Inc
(Secretary, Mrs Bailey)
15 Cadoc Street
Lynwood WA 6155
Telephone (09) 457 1437

Beagle Club of Tasmania
(Secretary, Miss E. Foster)
23 Illawarra Place
Glenorchy TAS 7010
Telephone (002) 72 3461

BEDLINGTON TERRIER

The Bedlington Terrier originated in the north of England around the Border country, where the gypsies favoured them because they were excellent chasers of small game. The name comes from the English village of Bedlington, where these dogs were bred from around 1820. They were used in the mines of Bedlington as ratters, and also as pit fighting dogs. The bedlington is a cross between a whippet and a terrier and is one of 22 breeds of terriers in Australia. Bedlingtons cost $300–$400 each.

Appearance An adult dog is about 41cm (16″) in height and weighs 8–10kg (18–23lb). Bedlingtons have what could be described as a 'mincing' gait and appear to dance or spring along, but they can run very fast when chasing game. All the areas of the dog's body that are likely to be exposed during a fight or while chasing game have longer hair on them, so game is likely to bite the hair rather than get hold of the skin of the dog. The ears, for example, feature a distinctive tassel at the ends, which is supposedly to protect the skin of the ear should a rat or similar animal jump at the dog and attach itself to the ear. The eyes are protected too; they are usually well sunk, and hair protects them.

Colours Bedlingtons are available in blue, liver, and blue and tan. There are also sandy, sandy and tan, and liver and tan varieties, but these colours are extremely rare.

Temperament They are intelligent, affectionate and adaptable dogs, although they can get a little excited at times.

Training They are relatively easy to train as they try hard to please their owners and respond well to discipline. They also travel well.

Suitability as a household pet Bedlingtons make excellent pets. They enjoy company, are neat and clean, and are easy-going in nature. As they do not shed their fur and are free from odour even when wet, they make good pets for households where there are allergy sufferers. They are also good watch-dogs and will alert the owner when strangers are around. As they have retained their terrier instinct, they will attack a stranger if threatened or provoked within their own environment.

Grooming The coat needs clipping every eight weeks and brushing thoroughly every week. If this is not done the coat will become badly matted. Grass seeds between the toes can cause severe irritation and have to be removed frequently. As with all hairy dogs, ticks can be a problem and bedlington's eyes should be checked regularly to see that they do not get clogged with 'sleep'.

For further information

Liz Wells
Bedlington Terrier Club
6 Annangrove Road
Kenthurst NSW 2156
Telephone (02) 654 1344

BORZOI

The Borzoi, sometimes referred to as the aristocrat of the dog world, was the exclusive pet of the czars of Russia for

ROAD TEST

many decades. The czars owned a huge kennel of these dogs and would present other royal families with a borzoi as a prestigious gift. The gift of a borzoi to Queen Victoria in 1842 marked the introduction of the breed to Britain.

The borzois were once known as Russian Wolfhounds but were renamed to avoid confusion with the Irish Wolfhound. Borzois were bred to hunt wolves and would flush out the prey and hold it by the throat until the hunters caught up and destroyed it.

Appearance These dogs weigh approximately 30–35kg (70–80lb). The standard height for dogs is more than 74cm (29"), while that for bitches is more than 69cm (27").

The borzoi's coat is silky, flat and wavy rather than thick and woolly. The borzoi has feathering (longer hairs) on its legs and chest and is shorthaired on the skull.

Colours Any coat colour is permissible but dark pigmentation on the nose, eyes and lips is favoured. The colours are loosely categorised as follows: red and white, black and white, cream and white, smoky-blue and white, black and tan and white, white, red, black, and brindle.

Temperament The borzoi is independent, cool and aloof, but enjoys human company and is affectionate without being overly demonstrative. These dogs are composed but wary of strangers and their characteristically swift movements are sometimes construed as nervousness.

Although borzois will tolerate and even protect children, they are not ideally suited to life with young families.

Borzois retain the hunting instinct they were bred to possess, so care should be taken to familiarise them with other animals, particularly small, fluffy ones.

Training Borzois do not generally excel at obedience, but like all dogs they should undergo basic training.

Grooming The borzoi needs regular care and should be bathed and groomed weekly. The silky quality of the coat prevents it from matting as rapidly as those of many other breeds (for example, the Afghan) and so the coat may be left for up to two weeks, but a daily brushing will keep it at its best. It will also help to remove the hairs which would otherwise be shed through the house.

Exercise The borzoi is not a dog for the lazy person. It requires lots of regular exercise—a daily walk with lots of free running is advisable.

Suitability as a household pet Due to its large size this is definitely not a dog for the flat or unit.

Borzois shed large quantities of hair at the start of summer and the end of winter and inevitably this ends up strewn all over furniture, carpets and clothing. A good vacuum cleaner is an essential accessory.

The dog should have access to a medium to large suburban backyard, otherwise its physical and mental well-being may suffer. A young dog can become frustrated if left alone for long periods without exercise and may develop nasty habits like digging up the garden.

Useful qualities The borzoi is a very good watch-dog and will attack a stranger if threatened or provoked.

Health Borzois live for approximately 10 years. They are generally a hardy, healthy breed but can have problems with their feet if the hair around the paws is not kept trimmed. If hair builds up between the toes the feet will become splayed and this makes running uncomfortable for the animal.

Compared with that of other longhaired breeds, the coat is relatively easy to care for. Tangles most often occur on the chest, under the tail and behind the ears, so special attention should be paid to grooming these areas.

Feeding Meat and 'complete' dog biscuits. It will cost $6–$8 a week to feed a borzoi.

Litters The average number of puppies per litter is five or six and there are very few whelping problems as the breed is long and slim. Puppies cost $150–$200 each, while show puppies start at $250.

For further information

The Borzoi Club of NSW
(Secretary, Mrs Claire O'Reilly)
29 Zambesi Road
Seven Hills NSW 2147
Telephone (02) 636 8087

The Borzoi Club of Victoria
(Secretary, Mrs D. Barclay)
346 Pound Road
Narre Warren VIC 3805
Telephone (03) 704 6823

The Borzoi Club of Queensland
(Secretary, Mrs Sandra Bibby)
Lot 42 Clifton Drive
Maclean via Jimboomba QLD 4280
Telephone (07) 297 5013

Borzoi clubs have not yet been established in other states but information about breeders can be obtained from state canine bodies. See 'Canine Control Associations'.

BOXER

The Boxer is so named because it throws its paws forward, like a boxer, when it wants to play. If you are looking for a large dog that isn't very aggressive and gets along well with kids, then the boxer could suit you. In Germany, boxers are used as attack and police dogs, but in Australia they are mainly guard dogs and companions. They are protective, playful and athletic.

There are two colours only in the boxers; brindle and red-and-white, but these colours have many varieties, particularly the brindle. There are inherent problems in the white gene: deafness and blindness both occur. In Australia boxers can have problems because of the strong sun; cancer can develop in old age.

Boxers are quite boisterous dogs, and if bored they can become barkers. Because they are so playful, young puppies are prone to swallowing toys and other small objects.

These dogs respond well to training, and because they are a large breed they should be well-disciplined. Training should start at a young age and the dogs can take 18 months before they mature.

Boxers are classed as a medium-sized dog, bitches being 53-58cm (21-23″) in height and weighing 28kg (62lb); dogs are 56-61cm (22-24″) high and weigh 30kg (66lb). The coat is short and shiny, lying smooth and tight across the skin. It is very easy to care for, only requiring brushing, and sheds very little.

All boxers in Australia have floppy ears; if a boxer has cropped ears it is imported. Cropping ears is an illegal operation in Australia.

Boxers require plenty of exercise, and enjoy chasing a ball and taking long walks. They are a popular family dog, totally trustworthy and loyal to their family and children.

Boxer pups cost $300-$350. Grown animals will cost about $12 a week to feed. Boxers live for 9-10 years.

For further information

The Boxer Club of NSW
(Secretary, Mrs R. Wagland)
16 Peel Road
Baulkham Hills NSW 2153
Telephone (02) 624 4104

Boxer Association of Victoria Inc
(Secretary, Mr A.C. Fry)
9 Leroux Street
East Oakleigh VIC 3166
Telephone (03) 569 9593

Queensland Boxer Club
(Secretary, Mrs D. Free)
71-81 Mount Cotton Road
Carbrook QLD 4130

Boxer Club of SA Inc
(Secretary, Mrs R. Rudd)
6 Fourth Street
Port Pirie SA 5540
Telephone (086) 32 6880

Boxer Club of WA
(Secretary, Mrs S. McKie)
7 Battersea Road
Canning Vale WA 6155

Boxer Club of Tasmania
(Secretary, Mrs B. Lampkin)
Telephone (002) 72 2046

BRITISH BULLDOG

The British Bulldog was originally bred from English Mastiffs. It is a man-made breed developed in the fifteenth and sixteenth centuries to bait bulls. The dogs would be put in a ring with a bull, which they would grab by the nose and hold until the bull gave in. Their owners would bet on which dog was best.

While bull-baiting was banned in most countries by the mid-nineteenth century, the physical characteristics of the bulldog had been set to gain maximum effect in the ring.

Appearance The undershot jaw and set-back nose of the bulldog allowed it to breathe without loosing its grip on the bull's nose, while the furrowed face may have been developed to prevent the dog's eyes being clogged by sweat or saliva from the unlucky victim. The dogs were bred small and short to be harder targets for the bulls.

The exhibiting standard for bulldogs puts males at about 25kg (55lb) while bitches should weigh about 23kg (50lb). The British bulldog should appear aloof and powerful.

The bulldog's coat is short and harsh to touch, but not bristly. It is easy to care for and is soft when brushed.

Colour Any coat colour is acceptable except pure black. Most dogs range from pure white to fawn, fawn and white, red and white as well as brindle. The dog's nose should be black.

ROAD TEST

Temperament Despite its rather awesome appearance, the British bulldog has one of the best personalities of all dog breeds. Breeders describe them as being 'tough, tender and terrific'. They are very affectionate dogs and sensitive to their owners. They are protective and gentle with children.

Training Bulldogs are described as being cunning rather than bright. They respond to training by trying to please their owners.

Suitability as a household pet Many bulldogs become house dogs, as they drop little hair, are not great barkers and are a small breed. They react positively to strangers if introduced by a family member, but can deter intruders more by their fierce appearance than any instinctive aggressiveness. They are extremely devoted to their family.

Exercise Bulldogs are suited to the backyard. A daily walk around the block is adequate. Walking in mid-summer heat, however, isn't recommended, as the dogs can overheat rapidly, which is dangerous to their health.

Feeding Breeders recommend 0.5kg–0.75kg (1¼–1¾lb) of fresh ground beef daily, supplemented with a handful of dog biscuits. Young dogs need calcium supplements while their bodies are growing. It takes about 12 months until a bulldog is fully mature physically. It will then cost $7 a week to feed.

Health One of the dog's most obvious features—its wrinkled nose—needs daily attention by cleaning under the fold with a solution of equal parts lanolin and boracic powder (available from chemists), mixed together and wiped under the fold with cottonwool or a clean tissue. Wipe dry with cottonwool or a tissue dampened with methylated spirits.

The bulldog can become short of breath when over-excited or taken on a long walk in heat, so owners should be careful not to over-tax their dogs. Breeders also suggest avoiding sugary sweets or foods, which seem to lift the dog's body temperature and can cause the 'slobbery' look some dogs are seen with.

Most breeders take pregnant bitches to a vet when whelping. Due to the large shoulders and head of the breed, some bitches can have difficulty presenting the pups, and unless you are serious about breeding bulldogs, this is best left to the experts.

Bulldogs cost $500–$600 each and live for 10–11 years.

For further information

The British Bulldog Club of NSW
(Secretary, Mrs Jean Turton)
29a Phyllis Street
Mt Pritchard NSW 2170
Telephone (02) 602 6985

The Northern British Bulldog Club of NSW
(Secretary, Miss Sue Butler)
55 Stevenson Avenue
Mayfield West NSW 2304
Telephone (02) 67 1465

The British Bulldog Club of Victoria
(Secretary, Mrs Wendy Boce)
4 Rochelle Court
Wheelers Hill VIC 3150

The British Bulldog Club of Queensland
(Mrs T. Hoddle)
13 Kamarin Street
Manly QLD 4179

British Bulldog of SA
(Mrs F. Barry)
PO Box 132
Smithfield SA 5114

The British Bulldog Club of Tasmania
(Mrs J. Ingles)
29 Beach Street
Bellerive TAS 7018

Western Australia (no club):
Mrs Betty Killerby
PO Box 1058
Bunbury WA 6230

Canberra (no club):
Mr John Cory
60 Bonython Street
Downer ACT 2602

New Zealand:
Mrs E. Halliday
25 Ferguson Street
Mangere East, New Zealand

BULLMASTIFF

The Bullmastiff is a man-made breed which originated in England, probably during the eighteenth century. Gamekeepers of large properties needed a dog to accompany them while patrolling their grounds at night; a dog which would protect the gamekeeper if he was attacked by poachers.

> *Pug faced dogs suffer from the heat in summer because their shortened mouth is an ineffective cooling device.*

A quote attributed to a Major A.J. Dawson says, 'The bullmastiff is as English as the cliffs of Dover. It is as harmful to children and honest people as a London policeman, but to the thievish and criminal fraternity is probably the most unpopular dog in the world—and proud of it.'

Bullmastiffs are a blend of 60% English Mastiff and 40% British Bulldog. The breed was first recognised by the Kennel Club of the United Kingdom in 1924.

Appearance Male bullmastiffs should stand about 63.5-68.5cm (25-27") and weigh 50-59kg (110-130lb). Bitches should stand 61-66cm (24-26") and weigh 41-50kg (90-110lb).

The bullmastiff coat is short and hard and lies flat to the body. The dog comes in any shade of brindle, fawn or red, but the most common in Australia seems to be fawn.

The dog's most obvious feature is its head, which is large and square with wrinkles when alert or at attention. The breed is powerfully built and should show strength.

Temperament The bullmastiff is extremely protective of its family. It is an alert, active dog and breeders claim that for such a large dog, it is rather quiet. Bullmastiffs aren't great barkers. They are not excitable dogs, but rather docile. They are not known to wander, preferring to stay with the family.

Due to its size and appearance the bullmastiff makes a good watch-dog, most intruders being scared off by the sight of such a large dog. Breeders say the dog can be relied upon to protect its territory. However, if strangers are introduced by the family they are accepted.

Exercise Despite being a large dog, bullmastiffs do not require a strict exercise regime. The dogs benefit more from a regular walk. Young dogs could be harmed if taken along on a long jog. This is due to the heavy frame of the immature pup.

Feeding Breeders of bullmastiffs recommend 60% fresh meat and 40% dog biscuits which have been slightly moistened. Pups need extra calcium to strengthen bones. It will cost $8-$10 a week to feed a bullmastiff.

Breeding Litters average eight or nine pups. As bullmastiffs have large heads, there can be problems in whelping; this is a breed to be left to experts. Caesarian births are common.

Health Bullmastiff breed clubs recommend that prospective owners buy from a reputable breeder. Most clubs have X-ray-cleared lines which means the parents have been X-rayed for hip dysplasia. Hip problems can also occur if the dog is allowed to become overweight. Bullmastiffs live for about 8½ years, up to 9 years. It is important that a close watch is kept on the dog's weight from about seven years.

Training As this is a large dog, new owners should become involved in obedience or similar classes. A large dog which will not obey its owner is a nuisance. Bullmastiffs respond to training and benefit from the teamwork.

They may take a little longer to train than, say, a German Shepherd or Dobermann, but many bullmastiffs have achieved obedience grades.

Suitability as a household pet Bullmastiffs are affectionate family dogs, which don't drop a lot of hair. The ideal owner would be an active person or family with a roomy backyard. It is definitely not for unit-dwellers.

Bullmastiffs respond well to children, and their protective nature is an advantage.

Cost Bullmastiff pets cost between $300 and $500, while showdogs range from $500-$1000 each.

For further information

Bullmastiff Club of NSW
(Secretary, Mrs N. Adela)
74 Goodacre Avenue
Fairfield West NSW 2165
Telephone (02) 604 3159

Bullmastiff Club of Victoria
(Secretary, Mrs B. Wright)
Lot 4 Mackelroy Road
Plenty VIC 3090
Telephone (03) 435 8201

Bullmastiff Club of Queensland
(Secretary, Mrs R. Spierenberg)
c/- 2 Dalmoral Road
Samford QLD 4520
Telephone (07) 289 1575

Bullmastiff Club of SA
c/- Mrs K. Marion
Lot 14 Sheoak Road
One Tree Hill SA 5114
Telephone (08) 280 7331

For Tasmania and Western Australia, contact the Victorian Bullmastiff Club.

BULL TERRIER

The Bull Terrier originated in England, where its ancestors were used for blood-sports such as dogfights and bull-baiting. The Bull terrier as we know it was developed in the second half of the nineteenth century by James Hinks of Birmingham, England, as a result of carefully controlled crosses between the original fighting dog, the

ROAD TEST

white English Terrier, and the Dalmatian. He called the resultant strain English Bull Terriers.

Initially, bull terriers were all white, but as many of these animals suffered deafness (which is genetically associated with white coat colour), breeders introduced coloured forms early this century.

Temperament   Bull terriers are extremely ferocious when provoked into a fight by another dog, and are capable of beating virtually any other dog of equal size except the Pit Bull Terrier. As fighting dogs, however, they were also bred to be highly responsive to their owners, and so the bull terrier is usually remarkably docile, affectionate, playful, reliable and protective with people.

Bull terriers make very good guard dogs, but will attack intruders. Bitches are usually markedly more docile and placid than dogs. One of the most obvious characteristics of the bull terrier is its toughness—the breed seems to be virtually impervious to pain.

The bull terrier owner who is prepared to give the dog the attention, devotion and companionship it needs will be rewarded with great loyalty, and those same qualities in return.

Appearance   There are no standard height or weight limits for the bull terrier. The coat is short, hard and flat and requires minimal care. The body is solid and muscular, without being fat. The bull terrier has a characteristic egg-shaped head with small eyes, pricked ears and a strong jaw.

Colour   There are two colour forms of the bull terrier; white (skin pigmentation and markings on the head are permitted), and coloured (any colour other than white, with or without white markings, as long as the white does not predominate). Brindle is preferred over other colours.

Exercise   These powerful dogs have seemingly unlimited energy reserves. The ideal home for a bull terrier will have a large backyard or, better still, will be in a rural area. In urban areas these dogs need regular exercise.

Training   Bull terriers should not be allowed to wander at will, as they are prone to becoming involved in scraps with other animals. They should be controlled at all times and disciplined when young. Teaching the dog to respond to basic commands requires time and patience.

Feeding   Bull terriers have large appetites and should be fed a balanced and varied diet.

Health   Bull terriers are relatively hardy but accident-prone dogs with few ailments. Pure white bull terriers often suffer from deafness. Eczema on the rump and tail is quite common.

Litters   The average litter size is six puppies. Assistance is sometimes required during the birth.

Lifespan   Bull terriers live for ten to twelve years.

Cost of puppies   Pets cost $300, registered animals $400–$500.

Ideal owner   Bull terriers are not well suited to inactive people or to inexperienced dog owners. They are said to be excellent family dogs, especially with children, but the temperaments of the parents of a puppy should be checked in this regard. Bull terriers are not suitable for families with toddlers, however, as these well-intentioned yobbos of the dog world can send young kids flying.

Suitability as a household pet   Bull terriers enjoy indoor life but, while many are kept successsfully in flats or apartments, they are much better suited to homes with backyards, where they can romp and tumble to use up some of their energy.

For further information

The Bull Terrier Club of NSW
(Secretary, Mrs L. Martin)
PO Box 379
Richmond NSW 2753
Telephone (045) 79 1231

The Bull Terrier Club of Victoria
(Secretary, Mr P. Oldridge)
PO Box 154
Fairfield VIC 3078
Telephone (054) 28 5287

The Bull Terrier Club of Queensland
(Secretary, Mrs E. Wilson)
31 Southey Street
Salisbury QLD 4107
Telephone (07) 277 1249

The Bull Terrier Club of SA
(Secretary, Mrs M. Green)
PO Box 105
Mt Agnes SA 5097
Telephone (08) 251 2148

The Bull Terrier Club of WA
(Secretary, Mrs S. Watkiss)
PO Box 451
Gosnells WA 6110
Telephone (09) 524 1056

The Tasmanian Bull Terrier Social Club
(Mrs J. Wiltshire)
Springdale Road
Collinvale TAS 7012
Telephone (002) 39 0291

CHIHUAHUA

This is the smallest breed of dog in the world and it is named after the state of Chihuahua in Mexico. While Mexico is accepted as the breed's place of immediate origin, there is evidence that its ancestors bear connections with China and Japan via the trade routes.

While the chihuahua is believed to have been a status symbol for the ruling classes of the Aztecs, it is also thought that those of lower social classes used them for food.

This breed is consistently highly popular in Australia, and even more so in the USA.

Appearance The height of the breed is not specified, but is usually less than 20cm (8"). Chihuahuas weigh up to 2.7kg (6lb), but 0.9–1.8kg (2–4lb) is preferred.

Coat There are two forms of chihuahua—the smooth-coated, with a soft, short, close coat; and the long-coated, with a long, soft, flat or slightly curly coat, fringed ears, feathered feet and legs, a ruff around the neck and a plumelike tail.

Colour Any colour or mixture of colours is allowed.

Grooming Both coat forms are easy to care for and should be brushed with a soft brush regularly.

Temperament The chihuahua makes an impact far greater than its small size would suggest. It is intensely loyal and affectionate, but can be temperamental, demanding and fussy, especially about food. Fortunately, this usually suits middle-aged to elderly people, to whom chihuahuas tend to appeal most. Chihuahuas have been described as the ultimate toy dog.

They are alert and intelligent, strong-willed, and ridiculously brave—they are generally prepared to fight dogs ten times their size. They make ideal miniature guard dogs. Chihuahuas may snap at children if teased, and they dislike strangers.

The breed is often described as being 'clannish'. This refers to its dislike of the company of other dog breeds and preference for its own.

Training Chihuahuas are moderately easy to train and have a reputation for being well-behaved in the show ring.

Exercise This breed is generally self-exercising but will enjoy regular walks.

Suitability as a household pet The chihuahua is an ideal housepet for town dwellers, as its exercise and space requirements can be met within the home.

Feeding Chihuahuas are obviously very small eaters and so are inexpensive to keep. Like all dogs, they need a varied diet, and two or three small meals a day will satisfy their tiny stomachs better than a large one. Chihuahuas which are spoiled by their devoted owners can readily develop fussy eating habits.

Health The chihuahua is hardier than is commonly believed, but it is prone to several ailments relating to the head and joints. The chihuahua's domed head makes it prone to hydrocephalus (water on the brain), and there is a soft spot on the top of the skull which should be handled with care to avoid injury. Several eye problems can occur. Luxating patella is an inherited condition, which causes a sideways swivelling action in the legs as the dog moves—dogs with this condition should not be used for breeding.

Litters Chihuahuas produce up to six puppies per litter. Size problems can occur, with puppies being too large for unassisted birth, so caesarian sections are common. Very small chihuahua bitches should not be used for breeding.

Ideal owner The ideal chihuahua owner is someone who is prepared to lavish attention and affection on the dog, and include it in everyday activities. This breed is also suitable for people with limited budgets and space. It is too delicate to be handled roughly by small children.

Puppies Puppies cost $150–$400. Chihuahuas will live for 10–14 years.

For further information

Chihuahua Club of NSW
(Secretary, Mrs Susan Jackson)
16 Ryan Road
Padstow NSW 2211
Telephone (02) 771 3989

Chihuahua Club of Victoria
(Secretary, Mrs Dorothy Fayer)
5 Lucas Court
West Sunshie VIC 3020
Telephone (03) 311 9953

Chihuahua Club of Queensland
(Secretary, Mrs J. Duncan)
15 McGahey Street
Rothwell QLD 4020
Telephone (07) 203 1413

> *To ensure pollination, some Australian orchids mimic and smell like gnats, mosquitoes, bees, spiders, birds and other flowers.*

ROAD TEST

Chihuahua Club of SA Inc
(Mrs B. Leonard)
Box 251
Greenacres SA 5086
Telephone (08) 261 2816

WA Chihuahua Club Inc
(Mrs G. Vine)
373 Burwick Street,
East Victoria Park WA 6101
Telephone (09) 361 7304

The Kennel Control Council of Tasmania
PO Box 116,
Glenorchy TAS 7010
Telephone (002) 72 9443

DACHSHUND

The following article was largely supplied by Sue Rose, Publicity Officer of the Dachshund Club of New South Wales, and breeder of standard smooth Dachshunds. She can be contacted by telephone on (02) 652 2346.

The origin of the Dachshund (pronounced 'daxund') has been lost in antiquity. It is thought that the dachshund came to prominence in Germany. The first recording of the breed was in Germany in the fourteenth century, but Germans call the dachshund a Teckel, as that was the inscription below a drawing of a long bodied, short legged dog on a tomb in ancient Egyptian times. German foresters perfected the breed to go to ground to hunt badger, fox and otter, and into dense forest where larger dogs weren't suitable. The miniatures were bred for rabbit hunting and were found to be particularly good for eradicating vermin. The long-hairs were suitable for water retrieving and the wire-hair's speciality was going for game in particularly dense scrub.

The first dachshunds were imported into England from Germany in the 1840s.

The early dachshunds differ a great deal from the present day specimens, and English breeders were very prominent in improving the breed. Early breeders noted that dachshunds had 'crooked front legs'.

The Dachshund Club of England was formed in 1881. The German Teckel Club was formed in 1887.

Dachshunds come in two sizes, standard and miniature. Standards weigh 9–11.5kg (20–26lb), miniatures weigh 4.5kg (11lb). The first imports to Australia were standard smooths in 1885. The other varieties were imported between 1945 and 1953. Miniature wires, as well as imported stock, were bred down from standard wires mated to miniature smooths (in Victoria only, where cross mating was allowed at the time).

From the Breed Standard 'First and foremost a sporting dog. The dachshund is versatile and adaptable and is at home in town or country, and as a house companion or working dog. It has the scenting powers of a Foxhound and unflinching courage, and will go to ground to fox, badger or otter.

'He is long, low, compact, well muscled and courageous and well suited to the work he was designed for—going to ground. He has a very penetrating bark which he must keep up for long periods for the hunters to locate him underground.

'The three coats—long, smooth and wire—and two sizes—standard and miniature—make the dachshund very versatile and well-suited to different game, for example, the long variety is very suited to water retrieving.

'Although the dachshund is not often used as a working dog in Australia, in Germany it must still pass a field trial before it can gain the title of champion.'

Coats
Smooth-hair Short and smooth but dense; impervious to mud and rain; thickest under the tail.

Long-hair Soft and straight with feathering on the outside of the ears, behind the front and rear legs, on the chest and along the body—at its longest under the tail, forming a flag. The coat should resemble that of an Irish Setter.

Wire-hair A short harsh coat over the body, with a thick undercoat. The wire-haired dog should have a beard and bushy eyebrows but the ears should be almost smooth. When viewed from a distance it should resemble a smooth-hair.

Colours Black and tan, red, shaded red, chocolate, chocolate dapple, silver dapple, fawn, tiger brindle, black brindle, red brindle and grizzle. The only colour not allowed is white, except for a small spot on the chest.

Health Prolapsed disc can occur, generally between the ages of five and seven years. This can usually be prevented by not allowing your dachshund to jump down too often, and so avoid jarring its back. A dog that is too fat is also a likely candidate for a prolapsed disc.

Administering two 500g vitamin C tablets regularly prevents this problem, but no one is sure why. Treatment is now available for a dog in this condition and it is not necessary to put the dog down.

Puppies The number of puppies in a litter varies according to the variety. For miniatures, four is about the norm, for standards, six.

Dachshunds do not whelp easily. Rather than breed a litter yourself, it is much less trouble to buy a puppy from an experienced breeder.

Cost The cost of puppies varies according to the variety. The following list is just a guide, and prices could be cheaper or dearer depending on the demand for puppies at the time. The Dachshund Club in your state will give you an idea of the price in your area.

Standard long	$200
Miniature long	$250
Standard smooth	$200
Miniature smooth	$350
Standard wire	$200
Miniature wire	$200

Breeders immunise and worm puppies before they are sold. Puppies should then be wormed every three months. They require a booster at 16 weeks and another parvo shot at about six months, and then once a year.

Lifespan Dachshunds live for 10–20 years.

Useful qualities Dachshunds are good at obedience training and are effective watch-dogs, as they have a very loud warning bark, but they are not yappy dogs. They are also great lapdogs, love a game of ball with the kids and also enjoy going for a jog.

Ideal owner There is a variety of dachshund suited to everyone. A longhair would suit asthma suffers; miniature smooths are great for the old or infirm; standards or miniatures are good for active people or kids, as they have plenty of energy.

Suitability as a household pet Dachshunds do not have a doggy odour, so are suitable indoor pets.

Feeding Dachshunds eat fresh meat and dog biscuits, 110–170g (4–6oz) per day for miniatures and 170–220g (6–8oz) per day for standards, depending on activity. Miniatures cost about $4 a week to feed, standards about $6.

Exercise The more exercise the better. Dachshunds get bored hanging around the yard and are enthusiastic eaters, so either exercise regularly or cut down the food.

Temperament Standard smooths are a bit standoffish, and are one-family dogs, but are at ease after being introduced to a friend and quite enjoy being patted and nursed. The other varieties are outgoing and friendly, but prefer their own family. A fully enclosed backyard is required. Dachshunds are hunters, and if they see something across the road they will hunt it. They have no road sense.

For further information

Books *Dachsunds in Australia*, by Jean Davis—gives details of all aspects of rearing a puppy. $27.50. The *National Dachshund Handbook*, compiled by Jean Davis

and Robin Hill. This has photos and pedigrees of show dogs in Australia, with the names and addresses of breeders. $29.50. Both books are available from the Dachshund Club of NSW.

Clubs

Dachshund Club of NSW Inc
(Mrs Valerie Palangas)
Valdachs Park
Treelands Close
Galston NSW 2159
Telephone (02) 653 1705

The Dachshund Club (Victoria)
(Mrs D Woodward)
2 Burdett Street
Frankston North VIC 3200
Telephone (03) 786 7880

Dachshund Club of Queensland
(Mrs C Dower)
64 Whitman Road
Cedarvale Via Beaudesert QLD 4285
Telephone (075) 43 1105

Dachshund Club of South Australia
(Mrs J Fuller)
PO Box 258
Two Wells SA 5501
Telephone (085) 20 2108

Dachshund Club of Western Australia
(Mrs E Bentley)
Lot 38 Passmore Road
Gosnells WA 6110
Telephone (09) 525 2250

Mrs Jean Taylor
2 Hymath Place
Norwood TAS 7250
Telephone (003) 44 2413

DALMATIAN

Dalmatians can be black-and-white or liver-and-white. This breed has everything to offer that a Labrador has and it is also a very stylish dog. Dalmatians are well-suited to Australian conditions—their coats are short, they don't mind the heat and they love to be in the water.

Temperament/appearance The dalmatian was developed as a coach dog, mainly during the nineteenth century. Later on they were used as fire dogs. The dalmatian learns very quickly and is eager to please its owner. It is powerful, muscular, outgoing, active and exuberant. Dalmatians shed their hair twice a year and because of their white coat they can get badly sunburnt,

ROAD TEST

so if you want one for a pet it is a good idea to get one with plenty of spots.

When selecting a puppy, watch for deafness and temperament. Dalmatians are very loving and loyal companions. If they are brought up with children they will be wonderful with them and are also good watch-dogs.

They are a powerful breed and so need discipline. They take a while to mature but with discipline they are very good dogs in obedience classes.

Dalmatians have few genetic faults and diseases and they are becoming more popular each year.

Cost Dalmatians eat dry food and meat, costing $7-$10 a week to feed. They cost $200 to $350 each for an unregistered pet, and $250 to $400 for a show quality animal. Dalmatians live for 12-15 years.

For further information

Dalmatian Club of NSW
(Secretary, Deborah Harbin)
PO Box 379
Mittagong NSW 2575
Telephone (048) 78 5253

Dalmatian Club of Victoria
(Secretary, Mrs J. Roisetter)
Lot 1 Koo Wee Rup Road
Koo Wee Rup VIC 3981
Telephone (059) 42 6320

Dalmatian Association of Queensland
(Secretary, Ms Marj Bloor)
57 Willard Road
Capalaba QLD 4157
Telephone (07) 390 1088

Dalmatian Club of SA Inc
(Secretary, Ms Raelene Evans)
PO Box 181
Two Wells SA 5501
Telephone (085) 20 2770

Dalmatian Club of ACT Inc
(Secretary, Jan Martin)
32 Sheehay Street
Evatt ACT 2617

There are no clubs in Western Australia, the Northern Territory or Tasmania.

DOBERMANN

The Dobermann was developed in Germany in the 1860s by Louis Dobermann, who used a variety of breeds (such as the old German Shepherd, Rottweiler, Black Greyhound and Manchester Terrier) to produce a companion-protector-guard dog. The first Dobermanns

came to Australia in the 1950s. 'Dobermann pinscher' means Dobermann terrier.

Popularity The popularity of dobermanns has increased steadily in the last seven years, perhaps because of the breed's guard-dog reputation, (and its exposure on the popular television program 'Magnum PI').

Appearance Dobermanns are of long, lean build, 65-69cm (25½-27″) at the shoulder. They weigh 30-40kg (66-88lb), and have clean-cut, agile and powerful bodies. Their ears are not cropped, as it is illegal here and in the UK. Their coats are short and smooth; and their tails are docked.

Colour Black is the most common colour, but brown, blue and fawn exist. All colours have rust markings.

Temperament Generally loyal, fearless and versatile, the dobermann is wary of strangers and very protective of its own. Not instinctively aggressive, it will 'hold' an intruder while seeming to assess the situation. Very responsible to its owners, it likes to be part of the family. Choose an outgoing pup from a reputable breeder.

Useful qualities Alert and watchful, dobermanns are a deterrent to intruders. They make loyal and affectionate family pets, and their fearlessness and intelligence makes them suitable for military, police, guard and guide work.

Training Start training early (four months). The dobermann learns quickly so teach it correctly from the outset. Go to classes—the owner needs training too—and continue training at home—the dog needs and thrives on stimulation.

Suitability as a household pet The dobermann is easily accommodated in the average, well-fenced backyard, but likes to come into the house too. Its short coat makes it clean and not smelly, but a wipe-over with a hot wet towel each week is beneficial. Its nails and ears need attention each week.

The dobermann needs daily exercise and exposure to normal neighbourhood happenings as much for mental well-being as physical health. It needs watching when children come to visit, as it is protective of the family's own children.

Ideal owner The ideal owner of a dobermann is a person of firm, cool temperament who is willing to spend time with the dog and allow it to share family outings. Dobermanns are fond of children and enjoy living with a family. The dobermann's threatening image is mainly caused by people who buy 'attack/guard' dogs and don't know how to handle them.

Puppies Dobermanns produce an average of six to nine puppies per litter, with as many as sixteen sometimes occurring. Caesarians are rare. Pet puppies cost $300 or more, show puppies $500 or more.

Feeding Dobermanns prefer a sensible diet. Don't overfeed them. A mixture of raw or cooked meat with a good dog kibble is ideal, with a calcium supplement up to the age of six to eight months.

Lifespan Dobermanns live for 8–10 years.

Health Eczema and dermatitis can occur in this breed, particularly in animals with fair coloured coats. Flies and mosquitoes can bite areas where the coat is thin or worn. 'Wobbles'— a skeletal problem in which vertebrae fuse, with the resultant nerve pressure mimicking hip dysplasia—can occur, usually after the age of five, by which time the dog may have already had offspring, making it a difficult problem to eradicate. Dobermanns' ears hang down, and therefore need regular cleaning.

For further information

The Dobermann Club of NSW
(Secretary, Charlene Middledorp)
1005 Anzac Parade
Maroubra NSW 2035
Telephone (02) 349 6482

Dobermann Club of Victoria
(Secretary, Eva Mooney)
50 Darlington Drive
Anakie VIC 3221
Telephone (052) 84 1265

Dobermann Club of Queensland
(Secretary, Mrs B. Eedy)
PO Box 2105
Marsden QLD 4132
Telephone (07) 297 5070 or 277 4636

Dobermann Club of SA
(Secretary, Christine Irvine)
12 Merriwa Road
Sheidow Park SA 5158
Telephone (08) 381 7894

Dobermann Club of WA Inc
(Secretary, Mrs D. Attard)
180 Sheperton Road
Victoria Park WA 6100
Telephone (09) 361 6963

Dobermann Club of Tasmania
(Secretary, Mrs H. Walker)
PO Box 477
Glenorchy TAS 7010

Dobermann Club of ACT Inc
(Secretary, Mrs S. Burns)
PO Box 17
Queanbeyan NSW 2620
Telephone (062) 97 6988

FOX TERRIER

Fox Terriers were used for centuries by gentlemen hunters chasing foxes in Britain. The dogs were small enough to be carried in saddle bags on horses. Once the foxhounds had flushed the prey, the fox terriers were released to chase it down the lair. Since then, the fox terrier has gained a reputation for its skill in ratting and generally being an all-purpose dog.

Popularity This breed is not nearly as popular as it was in the 1930s and 1940s. In those days there were more fox terriers as pets in Australia than in any other country. Fatty Finn and Ginger Meggs made them famous and popular, as they always had a 'foxie' by their sides.

Appearance In height the fox terrier is 38cm (15″); in weight, 8kg (18lb). It is white with patches of black or tan or both black and tan. It possesses good eyesight and a keen sense of smell.

Fox terriers are stylish, angular dogs with deep chests and long, chisel-shaped snouts. There are two basic varieties—smooth-haired and wire-haired.

The tail is docked so that it is level with the top of the head. When the dog stands, the tail should poke straight up. Tail docking was the custom during the time when the dogs went down burrows after foxes and rabbits. The docked tail provided an easy handle by which to pull out the dog.

ROAD TEST

Temperament Fox terriers are lively, outgoing, friendly and inquisitive, but they can be single-minded. Once on a chase there is little the owner can do to stop them. They can also be aggressive towards other dogs they do not know. They rarely initiate an incident, but they will finish it even with a Dobermann or Rottweiler. Given the opportunity, they will wander, purely on instinct, seeking out prey or chasing other animals.

They are terrific pets for kids and fun to play with, displaying incredible energy.

Training With a long history as working dogs, fox terriers respond very well to training and can be trained at a very early age in a very short time.

Useful qualities Fox terriers are good watch-dogs and will keep rodents under control. They make excellent family companions and are good with children. They are clean and their short hair is easy to care for. Generally they are long-lived and not prone to many illnesses.

The ideal owner of a fox terrier is anyone who has enough energy to give the dog the exercise it needs. Families with children are ideal, as the dog will happily join the children in all their activities. A mature fox terrier would make a good companion for an elderly person, but a puppy may be difficult to handle.

Grooming The fox terrier has a double coat and needs to be groomed when shedding in the case of the smooth-haired dogs. The wire-haired variety, however, is much more difficult to groom, which should be considered if the dog is bought to be shown. If the dog is kept only as a pet, the wire-haired coat can be neglected rather more without causing much harm. It will tend to lose its typical appearance, though.

Health Most health problems relate to the skin. Fox terriers are prone to eczema, and the ears should be watched for fly bite. Any other health problems usually stem from some incident involving another animal. The lively and excitable nature of fox terriers tends to make them more accident-prone than most other breeds, but their great hardiness and resilience means that they generally survive their accidents.

Cost Fox terriers cost $250 for a pet-quality animal and $5 a week to feed. They live for 14-15 years.

For further information

Fox Terrier Association of NSW
(Secretary, Mrs Proud)
Telephone (02) 625 0504

Smooth Haired Fox Terrier Association of NSW
(Miss E. Hall)
Telephone (063) 73 2213

Fox Terrier Club of Victoria
(Mrs E. Pearce)
44 Manningham Rd
Bulleen VIC 3015
Telephone (03) 850 1387

Kennel Association of Queensland
PO Box 524
Zillmere QLD 4034

Adelaide Kennel Club
PO Box 35
Semaphore SA 5019
Telephone (08) 248 1576

WA Kennel Control
PO Box 301
Gosnells WA 6110

Fox Terrier Club of Tasmania
(Mrs Barbara Attrill)
22 Jubilee Avenue
Brighton TAS 7030
Telephone (002) 68 1251

GERMAN SHEPHERD

The German Shepherd was developed in Germany in the late nineteenth and early twentieth centuries. The aim of fanciers was to improve on a native sheep-herding dog and develop its abilities as a guard and attack dog.

The breed has been known by several names. Originally it was named the Schaferhund. After the First World War, when any reference to Germany became unpopular, the breed became known as the Alsatian. The dogs themselves remained unchanged and are now known as German shepherds.

Despite the wolflike appearance of the breed, there is no involvement of the wolf in its ancestry.

Uses German shepherds are not used as herding dogs in Australia, but are ideally suited to being guard dogs, police dogs (performing sniffer and rescue work), guide dogs for the blind, and companion dogs. They excel at obedience work.

Popularity The German shepherd is the most popular breed of registered dog in Australia. Its popularity exceeds that of the next three most popular breeds (the Rottweiler, Australian Cattle Dog and Dobermann) put together.

Importation of German shepherds was banned from 1926 to 1975 after farmers and graziers claimed that the dogs were sheep killers and could cross with dingoes to produce super sheep killers. Breed groups eventually had the ban lifted when it became obvious that this fear was groundless and when new blood was sought to strengthen existing lines in Australia. The German shepherd is the only breed which has been banned in this way.

Temperament These dogs are extremely intelligent, trustworthy, loyal and of noble bearing. They are known for their strong protective instincts. They become excited when playing but are generally considered to be calm dogs. They are responsible for many acts of heroism.

It is claimed that German shepherds have a remarkable ability to discern between friend and foe when approached by strangers.

Training The German shepherd is a very intelligent dog which thrives on training and discipline. Clubs strongly recommend that new owners attend obedience classes with their animals, as a bored or uncontrollable dog is a liability.

Breeding German shepherd dog clubs in Australia have established an 'A-stamp' certificate system for breeding. The 'A' clearance stamp means that the puppy is of a quality acceptable for breeding. The system is designed to help reduce the incidence of hip dysplasia which has been common in the breed. The 'A-stamp' cannot guarantee that a puppy will not eventually suffer from hip dysplasia but it offers a good chance that it will be free of the problem.

Breeding controls Many dog breeds are subject to serious inherited problems resulting from incorrect breeding practices, where animals exhibiting such faults have not been rejected from breeding programmes. Some breeds have bone and joint problems, some have breeding problems, but the German Shepherd is prone to temperament problems.

This is a significant problem that cannot be ignored; the German shepherd is a large dog and can cause major injuries if it savages someone when frightened. This behaviour is called 'fear-biting' and was considered such a major problem that Australia banned the import of German shepherds for over 40 years. This ban was lifted only in the 1970s.

The German shepherd is now Australia's most popular dog and the German Shepherd League, through their various state councils, is tackling the temperament problem head-on by putting their dogs through breed surveys. This is the first breed society in this country to ever impose any sort of self-regulation.

The surveys were initiated as part of a responsible effort to improve the breed, maintain certain standards, and ensure that a breed ban was never again imposed. The principle behind the breed surveys is that the original qualities sought in the breeding of the German shepherd as a herding dog should be preserved (regardless of the fact that it is not used as a sheepdog in Australia). These ideals require that the dog be physically and constitutionally strong, sound and balanced, and this involves temperament as well.

The German Shepherd League stresses the importance of maintaining a minimum standard that can be readily identified by breeders, leading to a rapid advancement of the breed in this country.

Three tests are used to assess the temperament of each dog:

A one-on-one test, in which a dog, in the company of its owner, is approached by an unfamiliar person who stares at the dog's eyes and touches the animal. If the dog is intimidated by the assessor's stare, it will exhibit classic fear-biting behaviour and nip him or her.

A crowd test, in which a group of people surrounds the dog, with its owner, and everyone moves around each other to simulate typical conditions on a crowded footpath or in a shopping centre. A dog which lacks a 'firm' temperament will exhibit discomfort and nervousness.

A gun test requires that the dog exhibits tolerance to noise, as would be necessary in a herding dog. A starter's gun is fired overhead not far from the dog, and its reaction is assessed for signs of distress.

A dog that remains relaxed and unconcerned during these three tests is deemed to have passed. A German shepherd pet should be reliable enough to not only protect its master from danger, but also to behave itself in public.

Anyone considering purchasing a German shepherd pup should insist on seeing the certificates for the test results of both its parents. Breeding animals are also tested for the inherited bone disease, hip dysplasia (for which a certificate is also available), so the consumer has some evidence that the puppy for sale is sound in mind and body.

Litters The average size of a German shepherd litter is six puppies. Whelping problems are uncommon.

Colours There are two colour groups. The most popular is the gold and black, but sable (a rich golden brown) is becoming more popular.

Weight and height In weight, dogs are 34–35kg (75–77lb), bitches 30–32kg (66–70lb). In height, dogs are 65–66cm (25.5–26"), bitches 59–60cm (23–24").

Coat The coat should be no more than 5cm (2") long and should lie along the dog's body. The coat is 'feathered' at points such as the tail and parts of the lower legs. Daily brushing is recommended.

Longhaired German shepherds do occur occasionally but this is regarded as a fault in show dogs. Longhaired German shepherds are considered to be throwbacks to animals used in the early breeding programmes, and are sold as pets.

ROAD TEST

Suitability as a household pet German shepherds are relatively quiet dogs and tend not to bark unless alarmed or distressed.

They moult twice yearly but regular grooming will keep hair dropping under control.

Their protective instincts make them well suited to family life and they generally enjoy the attentions of children. They like to be in close contact with the family unit (which they adopt as their pack), so enjoy coming indoors.

Exercise An average backyard is adequate for keeping a German shepherd, but it is a large breed and daily exercise is very important.

Health Hip dysplasia is the most common health disorder in the breed. The socket and ball of the hip joint do not fit properly, with the result that arthritis sets in around the edges of the joint. The condition is mostly genetic but partly environmental. This and other health problems can largely be averted by buying a puppy from a recommended and reputable breeder who can provide the 'A-stamp'.

A healthy German shepherd will live for 10 years.

Breed Advisory Committees have been established by German shepherd clubs and these are designed to monitor breeding programmes so that dogs with poor health or unsatisfactory temperaments are not permitted to proliferate.

Feeding Breeders recommend 75% dry food, moistened with hot water, and 25% tinned or fresh meat or vegetables. It will cost $7-$9 a week to feed a German shepherd. Puppies cost $250 for a pet, $350 for a registered animal.

For further information

The German Shepherd Dog League of NSW
(President, Colin Spalding)
10 Berowra Road
Mt Colah NSW 2079
Telephone (02) 477 3067

Broken Hill German Shepherd Dog Club
(Secretary, Judi Simons)
274 Clarke Street
Broken Hill NSW 2880
Telephone (080) 3283

Newcastle and Hunter Region German Shepherd Dog Club
(Secretary, Gay Worthing)
4 Kahibah Street
Swansea NSW 2281
Telephone (049) 71 2710

The German Shepherd Dog Club of Victoria
(Secretary, Marilyn Wrigley)
PO Box 10
Ballarat VIC 3350
Telephone (053) 30 1578

German Shepherd Dog Club of Queensland
(Secretary, Lance Young)
PO Box 745
Kapalaba QLD 4157
Telephone (07) 390 1132

German Shepherd Dog Club of SA
(Secretary, Steve Collins)
PO Box 1421
Adelaide SA 5001
Telephone (085) 56 2340

German Shepherd Dog Club of WA
(Secretary, Sue Woollard)
34 Fraser Road
Canning Vale WA 6155
Telephone (09) 455 1071

German Shepherd Dog Club of Tasmania
(Secretary, Cathy Slot)
PO Box 217
New Norfolk TAS 7011

The German Shepherd Dog Club of NT
(Secretary, Dianne Jackman)
PO Box 1419
Darwin NT 0801
Telephone (089) 32 2255

ACT German Shepherd Dog Association
(Secretary, Eugene Nix)
PO Box 2
Fyshwick ACT 2600
Telephone (062) 38 2372

GREAT DANE

The Great Dane is not strictly from Denmark; the development of the breed took place in Germany, where it is known as the Deutsche Dogge. The ancestors of today's great dane were used to hunt wild boar, but the breed has since become much gentler in temperament, and taller and finer in structure.

The Second World War almost wiped the breed out, as the two major bases for the breeding of great danes, Germany and the UK, were involved in heavy bombing activities. Many top dogs and bloodlines were lost in bombings, and through kennel owners being unable to care for them adequately.

Great danes arrived in Australia in the 1930s. By the 1940s breeders around the world were consolidating and refining the breed once again.

Popularity Owning a great dane is a considerable responsibility, so the breed has never been subjected to fashion trends, and registration figures have remained fairly constant at a level of moderate popularity.

Appearance The great dane and the Irish wolfhound are the two tallest breeds of dog. The record for the tallest dog in the world was held by a British great dane, which died in 1984. He stood 105.4cm (41½″) tall and weighed 108kg (17 stone).

The minimum height for dogs is 76cm (30″); for bitches 71cm (28″). The minimum weight for dogs is 54kg (120lb); for bitches 45kg (100lb).

Coat Great danes have single coats, which are sleek but neither silky nor rough.

Colours There are five recognised colours in Australia: fawn, brindle, blue (Weimaraner colour; pale grey to slate), black (no white) and harlequin (white with black or blue 'torn' patches but not mixed blue/black).

There are many other variations, however, which can either be sold as pets or, if carrying certain genes, used to achieve particular colours or markings. The harlequins are known to exhibit 20 different variations.

Generally, completely white dogs are deaf or blind and so are culled at birth.

Temperament Great danes are swift, alert, courageous and friendly. They seem to be aware of their size and tend not to be timid, but are rather aloof with strangers. A great dane will bond strongly to its family and can be a very efficient guard dog.

Useful qualities Great danes make good companion dogs and are ideal jogging partners. They are instinctive guard dogs and their size makes them convincing in this role.

Training They are amiable but somewhat clumsy until 12 months old. Training is essential, as the breed is simply too large to manhandle. An early start to training, and perseverance, should result in an obedient animal attuned to your wishes.

Suitability as a household pet Great danes prefer indoor life and can fret if left outside. This breed drops very little hair, is not known for barking problems, and fleas and smelliness can be controlled with regular bathing.

Exercise Great danes can adapt to varying situations. If kept inside, where they would prefer to be, an average yard is adequate. A daily walk, two blocks in length, is probably adequate exercise, although great danes enjoy jogging.

Soft bedding is essential due to the weight of the dog and its lack of fur protection against callouses.

Ideal owner Great danes make very obvious and noticeable pets. They like to spend as much time as possible with people, and if no-one is at home during the working part of the day it is better to have two dogs to keep each other company. Great danes are said to be responsible with children. They are unsuitable for the aged or infirm due to their large size.

Litters The average number of puppies in a Great dane litter is 10, but the range extends from 2 to 22. Birthing problems are uncommon. Puppies cost $300 or more.

Feeding The average food requirement is 1.25kg (2¾lb) a day of a balanced and varied diet. The correct balance (dependent on the age and size of the dog) of calcium and phosphorus is necessary for good strong bone growth. Great danes cost about $15 a week to feed.

Lifespan Great danes live for eight or nine years. Unfortunately, there appears to be a negative correlation between size and longevity—the bigger the dog, the shorter the lifespan.

Health Like all large breeds, great danes are prone to a number of bone-related ailments. Pups should not be taken for long walks on hard surfaces before they are over six months old; over-exercise can cause shin-splints and joint damage. Hip dysplasia is another problem, but has almost been bred out of the breed. Cervical spondylopathy, a disease whose sufferers are known as 'wobblers', involves malformation of the cervical vertebrae, resulting in bruising of the spinal cord.

Pressure sores and callouses can develop if bedding is inadequate. Eyelid problems can be encountered and wall eyes occur occasionally in harlequins.

For further information

Great Dane Club of NSW
(Secretary, Miss C.A. Baker)
263 Spinks Road
Glossodia NSW 2756
Telephone (045) 76 5947

Great Dane Club of Victoria
(Secretary, Freda Greasley)
Lot 3, Connor Street
Lancefield VIC 3435

Great Dane Club of Queensland
(Secretary, Annette Findlay)
46 Larbonya Crescent
Capalaba QLD 4157
Telephone (07) 390 2342

ROAD TEST

Great Dane Club of WA
(c/- Mrs L. Gibbs)
10 Red Gum Avenue
Bellevue WA 6056
Telephone (09) 274 2288

Great Dane Club of SA
(Secretary, Sandra Nichols)
72 Penneys Hill Road
Hackham SA 5163
Telephone (08) 382 9381

GREYHOUND

Captain Cook had his Greyhound with him when he landed in Australia in 1770. The breed is reputed to be one of the oldest breeds of dogs in the world.

Uses Over the centuries greyhounds have been used for coursing a variety of game from leopards to hares, and they are generally considered the swiftest of all hounds.

In the public eye the greyhound is most often seen as a racing dog. However, they make excellent pets.

Many people will buy a greyhound and give it to a trainer to race it. Many go further and decide that greyhound training requires only a bit of common sense. A family can own a racing animal when a racehorse is out of their price range.

According to racing control boards, 95% of greyhounds are trained by hobby-trainers, usually families. Only 5% of greyhound trainers train for a living.

Exercise The greyhound must be muzzled when walking, and only four dogs can be walked by one person at a time. They require about 45 minutes' walking a day, so a prospective owner should be prepared to put in the effort.

Appearance Most greyhounds weigh 24–32kg (55–70lb). The breed has a slim, sleek body, narrow skull and long, strong legs. The greyhound comes in black, white, red, blue, fawn, or brindle. Any of these colours can be broken with white.

Temperament In temperament the greyhound is described as being one of the most even-tempered and gentle dogs. It is very sensitive to the family and needs affection and attention.

The dogs are known for their tendency to chase things. They enjoy long runs and have a strong pursuing instinct.

Health As regards health, racing greyhounds are more prone to leg and feet injuries. If their nails are left too long they can sink into the soft turf and 'spring' the toe (pull it out of its joint). Most racing dogs have their nails clipped monthly, pets six-weekly. Attention should be paid to the welfare of a racing greyhound to ensure its health is up to scratch.

In whelping the greyhound seems to have few problems. The pups are long and sleek and this is an advantage in whelping. Most litters average about seven, although litters of up to 16 have been known. Pups begin their training at about 18 months and will race until they are three or four years old.

Suitability as a household pet As housepets greyhounds shed little hair, but do benefit from a regular bath and brush. They are not known for barking habits, and have a positive reaction to strangers.

They do not make good guard dogs, being probably more likely to lick a burglar to death.

Training The dogs respond to a routine rather than a strict training pattern. They are not like German Shepherd dogs, which thrive on learning and training, but instead would prefer a half hour's playing with the children. They are active and affectionate dogs.

Greyhounds are also making a mark in the exhibition showring. While there are relatively few greyhounds being exhibited in Australia, in the United Kingdom and the United States, the breed enjoys great popularity.

Cost Greyhounds cost from $200 to $10 000. They eat fresh meat and dog biscuits, costing $30 a week to feed. They live for 12–14 years.

For further information

Greyhound Breeders, Owners and Trainers Association (NSW)
(Secretary, Mr T. Thompson)
PO Box 87
Five Dock NSW 2046
Telephone (02) 713 1955

The Greyhound Racing and Control Board (VIC)
3rd Floor Racing Industries Centre
1 Queens Road
Melbourne VIC 3004
Telephone (03) 267 3377

Greyhound Racing Control Board of Queensland
240 Sandgate Road
Albion QLD 4000
Telephone (07) 262 7800

The Gold Coast Greyhound Racing Club
PO Box 1090
Southport QLD 4215
Telephone (075) 32 2611

Greyhound Racing Control Board (SA)
153 Flinders Street
Adelaide SA 5000
Telephone (08) 268 1923

WA Greyhound Racing Association
Station Street
Cannington WA 6107
Telephone (09) 458 4600

For exhibition queries contact your state canine control or kennel control group—see 'Canine Control Associations'.

HUNGARIAN PULI

Research suggests that Pulis entered Hungary in ancient times from the area of Scythia, now southern Russia. Since the ninth century this breed has been used to work sheep on the plains of Hungary and, due to ruthless culling of poor quality animals over the centuries, the breed is considered to be physically and temperamentally outstanding for this work.

Pulis came to Australia in 1972. There are now about 300 in this country.

Appearance The distinctive feature of the Hungarian Puli is its amazing coat. Somewhat like a poodle's coat when young, the curly strands grow longer and longer, and as they lengthen they begin to intertwine and mat until the mature dog has cords of hair.

Genetics determine whether the cords are flat (ribbon) or round (pencil). It is possible to brush the coat out but this must commence before the cords begin to develop, and be continued thereafter to prevent them from developing. It can take up to five years for a Hungarian puli to achieve its full coat, which reaches the ground. Like the poodle, the puli doesn't shed or moult.

As the cords grow, it is necessary for the owner to separate them so that they don't begin to mat. This separating begins at skin level and should set the standard for the dog's full coat. The cords will grow evenly over the dog in layers, less so on the head and face, while the tummy is covered in fine curly ringlets.

Grooming Grooming of a corded coat means separating the cords and clearing it of burrs. As a corded coat can't be brushed, the burrs must be picked out by hand. A monthly washing is recommended, but excessive use of soap can dry out the coat and make it very brittle.

Breeders recommend that pulis kept as pets have their coats clipped shorter. This gives the dog greater freedom of movement and makes care of the coat easier.

Colours The Hungarian puli was originally a multicoloured breed but the attentions of breeders have changed the proportions of colours available.

Fifty years ago, for example, black pulis were a rarity but black is the only readily available colour in Australia today. White pulis have recently become popular in the USA, where grey and cream (or apricot) are also available.

The Australian standard allows for the following colours: black, rusty black, white and various shades of grey and apricot.

Weight and height Puli dogs are 40-44cm (16-17½") high and weigh 13-15kg (28½-33lb). Bitches are 37-41cm (14-16") high and 10-13kg (22-28½lb) in weight.

Temperament Hungarian pulis are considered to be willing, keen and intelligent dogs which respond rapidly to training. They have very strong herding instincts, and a puli raised as a pet will quickly pick up sheep working skills if returned to a rural environment.

Their loyalty and devotion helps to make pulis well suited to city life, and families with children. They also make good guard dogs.

Training Pulis respond readily to training, but need a firm hand. They appear to enjoy the mental stimulation of training.

Exercise As they were developed as working dogs, they need daily, vigorous exercise. A good run around a park, or a jog with their owner is ideal.

Suitability as a household pet As the puli doesn't shed hair it is considered a good indoor dog. However, this is not to say they are lapdogs—pulis are naturally quite lively and must have regular exercise if they are to remain contented indoors during the remainder of the day.

Hungarian pulis are reasonably adaptable, and don't smell or bark to any great extent, provided they are kept clean and comfortable.

Litters Litters are usually of four to six puppies. Pulis have no particular whelping problems.

Health Grass seeds are probably their major health problem as these become embedded in the thick coat and can cause irritation if they enter the ears. The ears need regular checking, and sometimes plucking, to keep them clear of overgrown hair. Vaseline rubbed between the toes helps keep the grass seeds out.

Feeding A diet of chicken mince, vegetables and dog biscuits is recommended, costing $5-$7 a week. A pet Hungarian puli will cost $350, a show dog $450.

Lifespan Pulis live for 10-12 years.

The Blue Mountains were named for the blueish haze which the fine drops of eucalyptus oil create.

ROAD TEST

Ideal owner This is not a dog for the lazy person; the coat requires care, and the breed's lively temperament and need for exercise demand attention and stimulation.

The puli is not a dog to be left alone. They adore families, but will often choose one person to become particularly attached to.

For further information

The Hungarian Puli Club of Victoria
(Secretary, Sue Huebner)
PO Box 31
Belgrave VIC 3160
Telephone (03) 751 1247

This is the only affiliated puli club in Australia. The Secretary can provide information about breeders in other states.

IRISH SETTER

The Irish Setter was developed as a working dog in Britain. By the late 1800s a type was set and adhered to by the majority of breeders, and an original red and white strain gave way to the solid red strain seen today.

Popularity Irish setters became extremely popular during the 1970s, but as trends have changed, numbers have stabilised at about half the number of last decade.

Nowadays only very serious breeders produce puppies, which enthusiasts say is a good thing because this maintains the quality of the breed, as well as the prices.

Appearance There is no set standard of height or weight for the Irish setter but the average bitch is 61-66cm (24-26″) in height, while the dogs are 66-71cm (26-28″). The coat is fine in texture; short on top with silky feathering on the tail, bib, ears and ankles. Though the hair is fine, it is very easy to care for.

Colour The coat should be a rich chestnut with no hint of black. White is allowable in minimal quantities on the chest, head and under the chin.

Temperament Irish setters have a reputation for being scatty and silly. This stems from their exuberance and endless energy, which can become a problem if owners fail to train and exercise their dogs properly.

They are loving but demanding dogs, requiring large amounts of stimulation. The natural liveliness of the breed needs to be channelled into positive areas such as obedience and agility trials. They must be involved with the family and its activities; if neglected, they will be inclined to try to escape, dig holes and be a general nuisance. Discipline during puppyhood is essential.

Training and exercise The Irish setter requires a firm but patient hand. Obedience classes are essential for young dogs with new owners. Irish setters may take a little longer to train than breeds such as the German Shepherd or Labrador, but patience and persistence will pay off and result in a happy and manageable dog. Several Irish setters have excelled at the very top levels of obedience in Australia in recent years.

It is essential to take the dog for a long walk each day, about 2km (1¼ miles), or at the very least, take it to a (council-approved) park for a daily run.

Useful qualities Irish setters were originally used for locating game. The dog would freeze like a pointer on scenting the quarry and then drop to the ground or 'set'. Some Irish setters will set on instinct but others need to be taught.

Companionship is the prime quality for which people purchase these dogs, as there is not much call nowadays for gundogs. Irish setters make reasonably good watchdogs as they are large and have a loud warning bark. It is unlikely that an Irish setter would attack an intruder.

Grooming Despite their elegant appearance Irish setters don't have demanding grooming requirements. Fortnightly bathing during summer, and possibly once a month during winter, will keep the dog clean, although a dog which is very active will require more frequent bathing, as it will tend to smell more strongly. A thorough brushing of 15-20 minutes once a week will keep the coat smooth and shiny. It is important to remove knots from the hair to avoid bad tangles.

Ideal owner The ideal owner of an Irish setter is someone with a lot of patience who is reasonably tolerant, especially when the dog is going through the fully-grown puppy stage. Families who will include the dog in their daily activities and lavish love and affection on it are ideal. Irish setters have a reputation for being good with children.

An Irish setter is also a suitable pet for a person living alone because of the company and devotion it provides. A puppy is not recommended for an aged person.

Suitability as a household pet Irish setters are not generally well suited to indoor life due to their lively temperament and boundless energy, although they can adapt to indoor life with training. They moult twice a year, producing large quantities of fine hair.

Health Some hereditary diseases affect the Irish setter, the major ones being hip dysplasia and progressive retinal atrophy. Neither of these is common.

Puppies can suffer from a deficiency (or an overdose) of

calcium during their early months, and it is essential that they receive the calcium amounts advised by a breeder or veterinarian.

Irish setters are also prone to a skin condition called demodex, which mostly affects puppies; and hepatitis, although the incidence of these diseases is rare.

Litters Litters usually comprise six to eight puppies and whelping is generally problem free.

Cost Pet Irish setters cost $200–$300; exhibition quality animals from $400.

Feeding Breeders recommend a varied diet of meat, dog biscuits and vegetables. A calcium supplement is important during the rapid growth period of puppies. It costs about $10 a week to feed an Irish setter.

For further information

Irish Setter Association (NSW)
(Miss P. Blamire)
1 Ash Street
Colo Vale NSW 2527
Telephone (048) 89 4321

Irish Setter Club Inc (Victoria)
(Mrs H. Allen)
7 Melton Grove
Croydon VIC 3136
Telephone (03) 725 8965

Irish Setter Association (Queensland)
(Ms J. Williams)
34 Kelvin Street
Woodridge QLD 4114
Telephone (07) 208 4919

Irish Setter Association (SA)
(Mrs B. Martin)
41 Lyons Road
Brooklyn Park SA 5032
Telephone (08) 43 6787

Irish Setter Association (WA)
(Sandra Peterka)
PO Box 44
York WA 6302
Telephone (096) 41 1231

Irish Setter Association (Tasmania)
(Lyn Ibbott)
Emu Plains
Cressy TAS 7302
Telephone (003) 97 6266

IRISH WATER SPANIEL

The Irish Water Spaniel is an ancient breed and doubt exists as to which breeds were involved in its lineage. It is believed to have been taken from Spain to Ireland, where the modern version was first bred by Justin McCarthy in 1850.

Popularity There are about 80 registered Irish water spaniels in Australia.

Temperament Said to be the clown of the spaniel family, this dog has a definite sense of humour. It is devoted to its master, yet affectionate and responsive to other members of the family. It has great stamina and endurance and is intelligent, obedient and eager to learn, as well as loyal and friendly. Despite numerous exceptions, in general it is not one of the best breeds for living with children, and is unsuitable for the aged and infirm.

This dog can be difficult with strangers, and prefers to remain reserved in the face of an unfamiliar situation. The dog must be correctly socialised as a puppy or it can become withdrawn and reserved. It needs obedience training early in life. If pushed too hard during training some dogs can become aggressive, so this is not a dog for beginners. The Irish water spaniel revels in human companionship and therefore requires an owner who is patient, tolerant and prepared to spend time with the dog.

Special qualities The Irish water spaniel has a superb record of performance in water retrieving and other gundog events. It is highly obedient if trained when young, and thrives on work and pleasing its owner. It has a highly developed scenting ability. It makes a reasonably good watch-dog, is clean, tidy and quiet as a house dog, but becomes boisterous once outside. Irish water spaniels have achieved recognition in obedience, tracking and field trials, but are not the easiest dog to work with in these fields because of their spontaneity and effervescence.

ROAD TEST

Exercise Irish water spaniels enjoy running free, and have a large exercise requirement. They can adapt to most situations if given regular exercise and plenty of human companionship.

Colours There is only one colour. It is a rich, dark liver with no white markings. The colour is called 'puce liver'.

Appearance This is the largest of the spaniel breeds. Dogs are 53–58cm (21–23″) high, bitches 51–56cm (20–22″).

The coat is the most distinctive feature of the breed. It is made up of dense, abundant, tight ringlets without any woolliness. It is a difficult coat to keep in show condition, but if the animal is kept only as a pet it requires moderate but regular (every three or four days) combing and brushing. The coat contains oil which picks up dust and will become matted if neglected. This oil helps to make the coat water resistant. The hair on the face, neck and tail is very short. The tail is referred to as a 'rat tail'. Both sexes have a little goatee beard.

Cost Puppies cost $300 each. Contact the Irish Water Spaniel Down Under Club for up-to-date information on the availability of puppies.

Health This is generally a hardy breed with no particular disease susceptibility.

Feeding It is a medium-sized dog with medium food requirements. One animal will probably eat $5–$7 worth of dry dog food and mince meat per week.

Lifespan A healthy Irish water spaniel will live for 14 years.

For further information

The Irish Water Spaniel Down Under Club
(Editor/Founder, Mrs Debbie Willett)
Lot 76 Wivenhoe Pocket Road
Fernvale QLD 4306
Telephone (075) 86 7350

This club regularly produces a large and informative magazine entitled *Rat Tail Tattler*.

JACK RUSSELL TERRIER

The Jack Russell Terrier has been around for a long time, over 100 years to be precise, yet it has never been officially recognised as a registered breed. This game little terrier takes its name from Parson John (Jack) Russell, a hunting parson who lived, worked and hunted in North Devon, England, until he died at the age of 88 in 1883.

A very keen foxhunter, he rode to hounds for most of his life, and as a young man at Oxford University he began to try to breed the ideal terrier to go to ground to flush out the fox for his hunts. He acquired the base dam for his hunt terriers while at Oxford, from a milkman at Marston. 'Trump' was a 'hard coated white bitch with tan head and a tan patch the size of a shilling at the base of her tail'. There is some dispute as to her size but 'she was the size of a full grown vixen and weighed approximately twelve pounds'.

Development The development of the Jack Russell terrier has been less than well documented chiefly because this redoubtable little dog has been bred for many different types of country and for different types of hunt. Thus the 'true' Jack Russell tends to vary according to where you get him or her. The current breed standards in the UK allow for several height variations, with one club having two height standards, one below 11 inches (28cm) and one above 11 inches. Yet another group will only admit dogs of 14 inches (36cm) and 14 pounds (7kg), stating that 'they are the only true Jack Russells that can trace their lines back to the original Trump'. This claim may be a little difficult to support due to the lack of records of breeding. Many dogs who come to us from England even now still suffer from this sad lack of anything vaguely representative of a pedigree.

A full description of the breed as it stands can be obtained from the breed standard as published in the Club's information sheet. This was compiled after several years of planning and referenda to members. It is still being developed, and should be used by all breeders as a yardstick. For this purpose the Club also provides a leaflet on breeding to help breeders understand the genetic possibilities of their stock.

Useful qualities All this aside, Jack Russells have a personality and a temperament that makes them not only incredibly brave for their size, but also both fun-loving and extremely loyal. They make brave, strong hunting dogs; in Australia they are used for such diverse game as rats, fox, kangaroo, wild pig and even venomous snakes, but they are also watch-dogs (not attack dogs) and some are now being trained as Hearing Dogs (they hear for the deaf as guide dogs see for the blind).

Appearance Basically the Jack Russell terrier is a 'strong, active, slimly-built terrier of great character, with a flexible body of medium length with very strong jaws. They should be smart movers with a keen expression; the tail may be natural length or docked; the coat may be rough, broken or smooth; the colour mainly white with markings from lemon through tans to black; temperament should be bold, fearless and quietly confident; they should be alert, lively and active in appearance'.

For further information

Jack Russell Terrier Club Inc
(Sarah Gaffikin)
PO Box 55
Katoomba NSW 2780

LABRADOR RETRIEVER

The Labrador is one of Australia's most consistently popular dogs. It has floppy ears, a waggy tail, a short hair coat, and is big enough to give an occasional ride to a toddler, yet small enough to fit into the family sedan. Some people say they are fabulous for kids because they are so playful; while others believe that they are great for old people because they are so quiet and gentle.

Originally bred as a hunting dog and still one of the most popular field trial dogs, the intelligent, friendly labrador is also known as the Guide Dog. An important reason for its success as a guide dog for the blind is the careful breeding and testing programme carried out by the World Guide Dogs of Australia. Only the most sensible and trainable dogs are selected to breed from and train. The Guide Dogs Association uses about 150 dogs a year. Labradors are gentle and can handle a lot of stress and anxiety, and most importantly, they will take to almost everybody. They can be bonded to a person in a matter of hours.

Labradors come in a range of personalities—the black ones are claimed to be more lively and boisterous than the yellow.

The lazier, calmer or more dignified labradors can be wonderful companions for the elderly or frail. The Pets As Therapy programme takes rejects from the Guide Dogs Association—dogs that may be unhappy in traffic, for example, and they become great companions and therapeutic aids. They can be placed with quadriplegics, paraplegics or multiple sclerosis sufferers in wheelchairs, and will accept a wheelchair as part of the person.

Labradors, like many other large dogs, are often born with hip or elbow diseases such as hip dysplasia, which can become crippling. Make sure the vet thoroughly checks the dog's joints, and check that the parents of any pup you look at have been X-rayed to make sure they have normal hips.

Take your labrador to the vet every six months for a checkup. Keep it fit and active, and not too fat. Train it early by taking it to a training school. Not all labradors are suitable for Guide Dogs or children's pets, so choose carefully.

Labradors eat 50% canned and 50% dry dog food, costing about $10 a week to feed. They cost $300-$400 to buy and live for 12-13 years.

For further information

The Labrador Retriever Club of NSW
(Secretary, J. Ellem)
1116 Fifth Avenue
Austral NSW 2171
Telephone (02) 606 9454

Victorian Labrador Retriever Club
(Secretary, Mr G. Toner)
45 Constantine Drive
Lara VIC 3212
Telephone (052) 82 2241

Labrador Retriever Club of Queensland
(Secretary, Mrs P. Cameron)
100 Graham Road
Strathpine QLD 4500
Telephone (07) 205 4667

Labrador Retriever Club of SA Inc
(Mrs C. Waters)
PO Box 604
Virginia SA 5120
Telephone (085) 20 2312

Labrador Retriever Club of WA
(Secretary, Mrs L.M. Malcolm)
41 Wendouree Road
Wilson WA 6107
Telephone (09) 458 4450

OLD ENGLISH SHEEPDOG

Old English Sheepdogs were bred in England as working dogs to herd and guard sheep. The long hair gave the dog protection from the weather.

Popularity Old English sheepdogs became very trendy in the 1970s, which resulted in large numbers of unwanted dogs when their owners did not have enough interest in the breed to look after their pets. Their popularity has since declined and now the people who buy old English sheepdogs are usually genuine buyers, aware of the work required in keeping the dogs. The clubs run a welfare scheme, which finds new homes for dogs that are unwanted or not cared for.

ROAD TEST

Appearance Old English sheepdogs are 56-61cm (22-24") in height, and weigh 30-40kg (70-90lb). They have docked tails and very long and shaggy coats. They are able to see slightly through the hair over their eyes, but owners should pin this hair back except when the dogs are in the show ring as it obstructs their vision.

Colours Old English sheepdogs come in grey, grey-grizzle, blue, and blue-merle. Puppies are born black and white. Quite a few dogs are born with one blue eye and one brown eye—this is not regarded as a fault and does not impair vision.

Temperament Loving and friendly but not placid, old English sheepdogs are big clowns, and full of personality. They love to entertain the family. They are very good and protective with children. They will not wander, but should be confined to their own backyard—their lack of road sense can make them a hazard to traffic and endanger their own safety.

Useful qualities Old English sheepdogs make marvellous companions. In some cases they make quite good domestic guard dogs, partly because they have an unusual, deep, rolling bark, known as a potcasse bark.

Training Though they appear quite goofy, old English sheepdogs respond well to training. Like virtually all breeds, they should be trained as pups and should not be allowed to develop bad habits.

Ideal owner The ideal owner of an old English sheepdog is a completely dedicated person who is prepared to devote *at least* three hours every week to grooming. The owner will need to wipe the sleep out of the dog's eyes, check the pads of its feet, remove every knot and burr from its coat, and check its bottom. The long coat can result in faeces getting caught in the fur, which starts to mat and can become flyblown, so a good hose down is needed once a week.

Clubs strongly advise potential owners to really look into the breed thoroughly by attending shows, talking to other owners and reading as much literature as possible—clubs are happy to provide assistance in this regard.

When puppies are 12-18 months old they lose their puppy fur and start growing a new coat. This results in fur being dropped everywhere, which is dreadful indoors, especially on dark carpets and furniture. At this time the puppy needs constant grooming and attention.

At all ages old English sheepdogs need an enclosed backyard and must be exercised by walking every day.

Feeding A grown animal will require one meal daily, consisting of 300-400g mince meat, 700g canned dog food, and a cup of dried dog food. Regular multivitamins and

heartworm control should also be included. It costs approximately $20 a week to feed an old English sheepdog.

Lifespan Old English sheepdogs live for 11-12 years.

Health Old English sheepdogs' ears must be checked and cleaned twice a week, as they are long and dangly and get dirty and foul-smelling very easily. Many breeders pluck the hairs from the ears to assist in keeping them clean. Hair also grows between the pads of the feet and can collect burrs, which can make the dog lame. It is necessary to cut the hair from the pads each month, and they need to be checked every few days by running a finger around each foot.

Puppies The average litter contains about seven puppies. Birthing problems are rarely encountered. Old English sheepdog puppies cost $300 for a pet, and $700 or more for a showdog.

For further information

The Old English Sheepdog by Anne Davis ($26.00 approximately) is a good book on the breed.

Gail Lovett
27 Harrisons Lane
Glenorie NSW 2157
Telephone (02) 652 1021

Mrs June Soderstrom
Lot 14 Soblue Chase
Carroll Lane
Greenvale VIC 3047
Telephone (03) 333 1354

Mrs Pat McLeod
PO Box 117
Aspley QLD 4034
Telephone (07) 263 1436

Edith Thew
PO Box 1108
Bridgewater SA 5155
Telephone (08) 339 1266

Mrs Donna Kennington
26 Caluna Way
Forestfield WA 6058
Telephone (09) 453 1005

Lynette Bailey
22 Leyland Road
Claremont TAS 7011
Telephone (002) 49 2398

PEKINGESE

The Pekingese was exclusively bred by Chinese royalty until the Boxer Rebellion in the nineteenth century. The pekingese of the Chinese royal courts were so spoiled that human wet nurses were provided for the pups. British troops stormed the Imperial Palace in 1860, and while most of the Chinese Imperial family had retreated to the hills, two elderly aunts remained at the palace, committing suicide before the troops arrived. Five pekingese were found guarding the bodies of their mistresses.

These dogs were taken back to England by Lord John Hay. Most were used for breeding purposes, but one, named Looty, was presented to Queen Victoria and lived with her for 13 years (a very old dog for the breed).

The pekingese are surrounded by myth and legend, the most common stories concern the breed's origin. It is said that a lion fell in love with a marmoset monkey. The lion went to Buddha and pleaded to be made small to marry the monkey. Buddha agreed, and the pekingese was the offspring of this liaison. This is why the breed is known as the lion-dog.

Temperament According to breeders, you don't own a peke; it owns you. They are intelligent dogs but, like many toy breeds, their manipulative skills have been honed by centuries of pampering. Pekingese adore attention, are very self-assured and have an inbuilt sense of dignity. They are well-suited in size and temperament to the elderly, frail or handicapped. Pekingese can be very aggressive and will bluff much larger dogs. If spoilt, they can be aggressively protective of their owners.

Appearance Dogs weigh 3.5-5.5kg (7½-12lb), bitches 3.5-6kg (7½-13lb). The pekingese is one of the very few breeds whose standard allows, indeed encourages, bitches to be larger than dogs. There is no set height standard but pekingese are approximately 25cm (10″) tall. They have flat, square faces with a roll over the nose; large, dark eyes; thick, heart-shaped, fluffy ears, and a long, stocky body.

Colour Ninety percent of pekingese have brindle in the coat, that is, a base colour with black markings, usually on the face and to varying degrees in the coat.

Colours include fawn brindle, grey brindle, black, red brindle, clear colours (very uncommon) and parti-colours (more than one colour on the same dog).

Grooming Pekingese have a double coat: a very soft, fragile undercoat and a coarse top coat. Show pekingese are groomed extremely carefully to avoid damaging or stripping-out the undercoat. Pets are probably better off without the undercoat, however.

As the coat is fragile, pekingese are rarely bathed. Coats are kept clean and fresh by spraying with a mixture of hair conditioner and water; then powdered with talc and well brushed. This keeps the hair and skin healthy and fresh. Pekingese must be brushed every day to avoid hours of untangling knots. It is essential that pekes have their faces, eyes and bottoms washed daily.

Feeding Pekingese will eat almost anything, including canned dog food, dog biscuits, chops, chicken, fish and vegetables. They cost $4–$5 to feed per week.

Useful qualities The pekingese is essentially a highly domesticated companion dog. It can be a good watch-dog and will bark to alert its owner.

Suitability as a household pet Pekingese are house dogs and are not at all suited to being tied up in the backyard. They do drop some hair, but correct and frequent grooming will minimise this problem. Regular grooming and attention to hygiene also minimises odour.

Pekingese are not recommended for families with children under the age of two or three years, as the dogs will snap if poked and prodded.

Exercise Pekingese require minimal exercise and this makes them well suited to the elderly, infirm or handicapped person wanting company. They do not like getting dirty, but enjoy a quick tramp around the block.

Training Pekes are stubborn, and the trick is often to convince them that they are doing what they, rather than you, want. Pekingese can't bear being dirty and are consequently easy to house-train at an early age.

Popularity Pekingese require lots of time and devotion if they are to be exhibited with success, so many potential breeders turn to low maintenance alternatives.

Pekingese are moderately popular, but as with all pure breeds enthusiasts prefer numbers to remain stable. Trendiness carries the price of backyard breeders exploiting the fashion and breeding substandard animals in large quantities.

Health Fleas are bad news for peke breeders; scratching dogs get tangles and knots. Vigilance is required. Bone problems can occur in dwarfed breeds like the pekingese. The flat face does not provide much protection against accidental facial injuries. Despite these dogs being inclined to make snuffling noises, breeders claim that breathing problems are uncommon. However, the roll of skin above the nose must be washed and dried daily.

Pekingese are prone to eye problems. The eyes should be washed daily, and any sign of irritation should be checked immediately. The ears should be checked weekly to see that they are clean and dry.

ROAD TEST

Breeding Breeding is definitely a problem area for pekingese and not a potential income earner for the amateur breeder. The average litter size is three puppies, but due to the shape of the breed's head, bitches cannot birth unassisted, and a large percentage of births are by caesarian.

Puppies cost $300–$400, and the dogs live for 10–12 years.

For further information

Pekingese Club of NSW
(Mrs S. O'Cass)
42 Balmoral Road
Kellyville NSW 2153
Telephone (02) 62 9303

Pekingese Club of Victoria
(Mrs G. Pateman)
1 Liston Street
Burwood VIC 3125
Telephone (03) 889 5096

Pekingese Club of SA
(Mrs G. Cope)
48 Doradus Avenue
Hope Valley SA 5090
Telephone (08) 264 0602

Mrs V. Chivers
Valvista Kennels
4 Crufts Way
Canning Vale WA 6155

PEMBROKE WELSH CORGI

As with most long-established breeds there are numerous theories concerning the origin of the Pembroke Welsh Corgi. One of the most common claims is that the breed dates back to the reign of Henry III in the thirteenth century. Henry brought Flemish weavers to England to establish their weaving mills around Wales. The weavers brought with them their sheep, cattle and their tailless working dogs, which were bred with the local working dogs.

The Cardigan Corgi is traced back through the group of dogs which also gave rise to the Dachshund and Basset Hound. The Pembrokes were bred to be more fleet of foot than the Cardigans and were used mostly in the lowland areas, while the broader-footed Cardigans were used in the higher areas.

The two forms were frequently bred together until they were separated into two distinct groups after the intervention of the UK Kennel Club in 1934. The first Pembrokes were brought to Australia in the same year.

The Pembrokes soared past the Cardigans in popularity when the seven-year-old Princess Elizabeth (now Queen

Elizabeth II) was given a Pembroke pup called Dookie by her father in 1933.

Temperament The Pembroke corgi is highly intelligent, companionable, biddable, inquisitive, independent and faithful to its owners. It loves and needs company, is discerning with strangers, and is not easily intimidated. It is a bold, outgoing and workmanlike dog. Corgis often seem to appeal to and suit older people, fulfilling a mutual need for company.

During the 1970s the breed suffered from being too popular; many Pembrokes ended up in pounds and shelters due to indiscriminate breeding and subsequent problems with the dogs.

The Pembroke corgi isn't a dog which will accept teasing or bad treatment, and will snap if annoyed. Owners need to exert control over their dogs to avoid them becoming nuisances.

Appearance Pembrokes should be 25–30cm (10–12″) at the shoulder. Dogs should weigh 10–12kg (22–26lb) and bitches 10–11kg (22–24lb).

They have a double coat, mid-length, straight and with a dense undercoat—never soft, wavy or wiry. The coat sheds dirt relatively easily.

There is a known mutation within the breed which produces dogs known as 'fluffies'. In the UK they are usually culled, but this is not the case in Australia. Fluffies have very long coats but almost no undercoat. This means they get dirty very easily; they have lost the natural waterproofing of the coats of most working dogs, and they also shed far more hair than normal coated corgis.

Colours Pembrokes come in self-coloured red, sable (black tipped), fawn, and black and tan. All colours are permissible, with or without white markings. Other colours such as blue and cream occur rarely. Pembrokes are whelped greyish and develop their colour as they age.

Puppies Litters average six puppies, commonly six to ten. Whelping problems are rare.

Health Corgis can have problems with their weight, as they usually manage to twist their owners around their paws and receive regular tidbits. This is not a good policy and should be avoided, as it often leads to trouble later in life, such as hip or shoulder stresses, usually after the dog has been put on an exercise and diet regime and then over-exercised.

Corgis can also have a problem with flies biting their soft ears. Repellent creams may be needed when the dogs are outside.

The rare cream-coloured corgis are often afflicted with congenital abnormalities and are more susceptible to disease.

Suitability as a household pet Pembrokes make very good pets. They are easy to toilet train, and they don't take up a lot of room. Barking can become a problem if the dog is not disciplined when it barks unnecessarily.

Ideal owner Pembrokes are ideally suited to older, mature people, particularly the elderly as they thrive on attention and constant company. They are ideal for suburban backyards and can live in a flat or unit, but do need regular exercise to avoid getting too fat. As these dogs were used for working, they are happy inside or outside but most pet owners keep them inside.

A working couple away for long periods may find their corgi will fret and bark and make a nuisance of itself. In such cases, breeders strongly recommend that two corgis be kept together to keep each other company.

Useful qualities Enthusiasts say Pembroke corgis are the ideal suburban Australian dog, as they are hardy, small and compact, and utterly devoted to their owners. They are primarily a companion dog nowadays, but their protective instincts seem to reassure many older owners living alone. The dogs will bark if anyone approaches.

Grooming A brush once or twice a week will suffice to keep control of the hair, especially during the twice yearly shedding for bitches and yearly shedding for dogs.

Training As Pembrokes were bred as working dogs, they respond well to training. A firm hand and sensible attitude are required, but the dogs enjoy the stimulation of training and obedience work.

Feeding A balanced diet of good dog biscuits, canned food and/or fresh meat is ideal for Pembroke corgis, and will cost $3-$4 per week.

Puppies Pembroke corgi puppies cost $300 or more, and live for 12-14 years.

For further information

The Welsh Corgi Club of NSW
20 Mansfield Road
Galston NSW 2159
Telephone (02) 653 1389

The Welsh Corgi Club of Victoria
22 Greenhills Avenue
Montrose VIC 3765
Telephone (03) 728 1750

The Welsh Corgi Club of Queensland
11 Wolcott Street
Wishart QLD 4122
Telephone (07) 343 1444

The Welsh Corgi Club of SA
8 Paradise Grove
Highbury SA 5089

The Welsh Corgi Club of WA
59 Frederic Street
Helena Valley WA 6056

The Welsh Corgi Club of Tasmania
126 Riawena Road
Rose Bay TAS 7015
Telephone (002) 43 7153

PIT BULL TERRIER

Much controversy surrounds the American Pit Bull Terrier. It is a true fighting dog, unregistered by kennel clubs but said to be the true descendant of the original English Bulldog.

Following recent importation of examples of this breed into Australia, concerns have been raised over whether there is a place for the breed in this country and, if so, how potential dangers to the public can be averted.

In America these dogs are reported to have killed more people in one year (1987) than funnel web spiders have killed in Australia in the last 200 years. The American pit bull terrier has a reputation for being the meanest creature (when fighting) ever bred by man. In the USA, where there may be as many as a million of the breed, some people have suggested that these dogs be outlawed because of vicious attacks that have resulted in numerous deaths.

Through selective breeding the pit bulls have been engineered for fighting. Some are reputed to attack without provocation (small children are common targets) with jaws that can bite with the force of 1800lbs per square inch. The dogs can bite for hours, until complete exhaustion or death results.

In New York City, fights between these dogs are being used as a kind of warfare between rival gangs from different areas. This has led to confiscation of dogs used

ROAD TEST

for fighting, in an effort to stop the fights and protect the neighbourhood.

US officials say that the American pit bull terrier is nothing short of a lethal weapon in the wrong hands. Animal advocates say that unless pit bulls can be kept away from irresponsible owners, dogfights and attacks on people will continue. The ultimate losers may be the dogs.

The owners of the American pit bull terriers imported into Australia say they became interested in the breed after reading that they were good family dogs, great athletes and suitable for protection and hunting. Breeders say that in a society where violence is becoming increasingly prevalent, many people are seeking good protection dogs—a role at which the American pit bull terrier is said to excel.

Australian breeders claim that the problems in the USA have resulted from the dogs falling into the hands of the wrong people—people involved with drugs and other illegal activities—who have mistrained the animals. They claim that by taking due care to match puppies to owners they deem responsible, it is unlikely that the breed will fall into the wrong hands and become a problem in this country.

POODLE

Originally, Poodles had a very thick coat which was matted and oiled to keep out the cold when the dogs were retrieving water birds. The face, legs and other parts of the body were clipped so that the dogs could get out of freezing rivers once the coat was soaked and heavy.

Nowadays, the coat is clipped into a variety of special trims, such as the Continental clip, the Lion clip, the Puppy clip, and so on. Poodles are the ultimate show dog. The coat never stops growing; it is almost like a type of wool. It is rarely troublesome to allergic people, but needs to be groomed constantly, as it doesn't shed. Grooming is an ongoing expense for the life of the dog. It is a good idea to teach the puppy to enjoy being groomed daily.

Poodles come in three sizes: toys, under 28cm (11"); miniatures, under 38cm (15") and standards, over 63.5cm (25").

In Europe, poodles are talented circus performers and they perform well in obedience trials.

These dogs are judged on their short compact back, straight legs, clean chiselled face with lustrous dark eyes, angulation of the hind leg, and healthy coat.

Poodles are bright, intelligent and adaptable, with delightful sparkling, occasionally neurotic, personalities; they are easy to live with, and to train. Choose a pup carefully from happy parents, not necessarily show animals. Prices vary from state to state, but a toy poodle should cost approximately $300, a miniature about $200 and a standard $350–$500. Poodles cost about $10 a week to feed and live for 12–15 years.

For further information

Poodle Club of NSW
10 O'Connors Road
Beacon Hill NSW 2100
Telephone (02) 45 1456

Poodle Club of Victoria
(Mr N. Price)
33 Weir Street
Balwyn VIC 3103
Telephone (03) 836 8784

Poodle Club of Queensland
(Mrs P.C. Hogg)
41 Harlen Road
Salisbury QLD 4107
Telephone (07) 275 2000

Poodle Club of SA
(Secretary, Mrs J. Geschmay)
Box 716
Victor Harbor SA 5211
Telephone (085) 52 4477

RHODESIAN RIDGEBACK

The Rhodesian Ridgeback as it appears today was established as a breed in the 1950s in what was formerly Rhodesia and is now Zimbabwe. Known also as the African Lion Dog, the Rhodesian ridgeback is a mixture of many breeds including the Hottentot (from which the ridge originated).

The Rhodesian ridgeback was bred for two purposes: to protect the farm and the farmer's family when settlers went off to fight in the many colonial wars, and as a hunting dog in groups of three or four when farmers hunted large animals, such as lions. The dogs would bay the prey (hold the lion) until the hunter caught up.

Popularity Registration figures for Rhodesian ridgebacks have increased rapidly in Australia in recent years. Their popularity may be attributed to their distinctive appearance, easy-to-care-for coat, pleasant temperament and rarity of health problems.

Appearance In height, dogs are 63–67cm (25–27") high, bitches 61–66cm (24–26"). Dogs weigh about 38kg (80lb), bitches about 33kg (70lb).

Colours There are two colour definitions for the Rhodesian ridgeback: liver-nosed and black-nosed.

The soft, short coat is a wheaten colour. A little white on the chest and toes is acceptable. If a hair is plucked from the coat it should be coloured light to dark; a solid-coloured hair is a fault.

The most obvious characteristic of the Rhodesian

ridgeback is its ridge, which can extend from the shoulders to the tail. This is a strip of hair which grows in the opposite direction to the surrounding coat. In exhibition dogs the ridge must run from immediately between the shoulders to the haunch. The ridge must be clearly defined and tapering to a point. There must be two identical crowns (swirls of hair), which are opposite each other and do not extend more than one-third down the ridge. Some ridgebacks, often as many as 50% of the litter, are born with only part, or no ridge and these are usually sold as pets.

Health Because the appearance of the ridge is highly variable, most faults are associated with it. Pups can be born with only part or no ridge at all, and with one to four crowns anywhere over the back. The ridge can also stop part of the way and begin again further down the back.

A small percentage of Rhodesian ridgebacks are born with an inherited fault called a dermoid sinus. This is a pucker in the back ridge which extends into the spine and can damage the vertebrae to the extent that the dog may be crippled. It is a tube from a hairless follicle and can be seen if the hair is shaved away. The veterinary profession regards this problem as being genetically associated with the ridge as, although dermoid sinus can occur in other animals, there is no breed consistency as there is with Rhodesian ridgebacks. Reputable breeders cull pups with this fault but a veterinary checkup would be advisable if you suspect your ridgeback has a dermoid sinus.

Hip dysplasia is a reasonably common problem in this breed—affected animals should not be used for breeding.

Temperament Rhodesian ridgebacks are described as being powerful and elegant, have a reputation for bravery, and are friendly but wary of strangers. They make very good guard dogs, are not overly excitable and, despite being classed as a hound, rarely bark or howl.

Ridgebacks tend to be very protective of the family, but will probably have one favourite. They are good with the family children but will not usually allow other children to treat them in the same way.

Training The ridgeback is easily bored by repetitious work. It will take to basic obedience, but if a command or sequence is repeated too often the dog will probably lose interest and become irritable.

Puppies The average litter size ranges from eight to 12 puppies and, while most are easy whelpers, some bitches do have problems. Pet ridgeback puppies sell for $200, show animals for $350 or more.

Feeding Ridgebacks are not fussy eaters. Feed with normal rations of canned and dried foods. Ridgebacks cost approximately $5.50 a week to feed.

Lifespan Ridgebacks live for an average of 11 years.

Suitability as a household pet The Rhodesian ridgeback can be kept as a house pet and enjoys living with a family. It sheds its coat twice yearly but not much hair is lost and a good brush will keep that under control. Regular maintenance such as washing and brushing and controlling parasites is essential for all dogs and presents few problems with the ridgeback.

However, ridgebacks kept in a confined area should be exercised regularly. They love running and chasing and benefit greatly from a long run. They are said to be sight hounds and so chase things by sight and not scent.

For further information

The Rhodesian Ridgeback Club was formed in Sydney in the early 1970s and now has a membership of over 300 people. A magazine is sent to members bi-monthly. It contains news from other states, obedience news, photographs, general items of interest and details of forthcoming social events.

The Rhodesian Ridgeback Club
(Secretary, Miss K. Nieuwenhuis)
PO Box 101
Douglas Park NSW 2569
Telephone (046) 30 9071

Ridgeback clubs have been formed in other states but the list below comprises representatives of the Rhodesian Ridgeback Club in each state.

Colleen Aitchison
13 Churchill Street
Ringwood VIC 3134
Telephone (03) 870 7776

> *In a recent survey, barking dogs were rated as the most annoying source of noise pollution.*

ROAD TEST

Rosemary Marshall
c/- Post Office
Highfields QLD 4352
Telephone (076) 96 6227

Robyn Geraghty
25 Marriott Avenue
Modbury North SA 5092
Telephone (08) 264 6227

Jan Benson
88 Lyall Street
Redcliffe WA 6104
Telephone (09) 277 5872

Lyn Young
PO Box 340
Glenorchy TAS 7101
Telephone (002) 72 9245

Helen Mosslar
51 Wakelin Court
Weston ACT 2611
Telephone (062) 88 6332

ROTTWEILER

The Rottweiler originated in Germany, but its ancestors are believed to have accompanied the invading Roman forces across the Alpine passes from Italy.

The rottweiler was originally used as a skilful cattle dog, and continued to perform this function around the small German town of Rottweil until numbers dwindled almost to the point of extinction around the turn of this century. Enthusiasts began to revive and improve the breed in about 1910. The uses of this working breed have been expanded to include draught, guard, police, and rescue work.

Popularity During the late 1980s, the rottweiler has become one of Australia's canine fashions. Between 1985 and 1987 the number of rottweilers registered in Australia doubled, making the breed second only to the German Shepherd in popularity.

Appearance In height, dogs are 63.5-68.5cm (25-27"), bitches 58.5-63.5cm (23-25"). The coat is short and flat, the body compact and heavily muscled.

Colour All animals are black with tan markings on face, chest, and legs.

Temperament Rottweilers are cautious with strangers but tend to be easy-going, affectionate, devoted and loyal with their families. They are intelligent, strong, active, purposeful and single-minded, and have a great capacity to learn.

Some rottweilers are good with children, but this cannot be said for the breed as a whole. The aggressiveness of the breed is currently being reassessed due to a number of recent attacks on children in the UK and USA. Rottweilers will tolerate, rather than enjoy, the company of other pets.

Training Rottweilers, like other breeds intended to be working dogs, can become terrible nuisances and even dangerous if uncontrolled, untrained and indulged. Training is vital if the best qualities of the breed—its strength, toughness and single-mindedness—are to be enjoyed and put to good use. Training should commence at six weeks and continue, every day, until the dog is six years old. A rottweiler that does not respond to verbal commands can be strong enough to pull an adult off his or her feet.

Exercise Rottweilers need daily, vigorous, strenuous exercise (that is, running, jumping, and climbing) for their physical and mental wellbeing. In rural areas or on large blocks, and especially where two or more dogs are kept together, rottweilers will exercise themselves to some extent. But in confined areas rottweiler owners will need to be prepared to work up a sweat.

Health Rottweilers are prone to inherited bone diseases such as hip dysplasia, which serious breeders are attempting to reduce by selective breeding. Skin and eye problems also occur. It is possible for purchasers to insist on, and obtain, a guarantee of replacement if a puppy develops any serious genetic abnormality before two years of age. The rise in popularity of the breed has led to some indiscriminate breeding, and such a written guarantee provides the purchaser with some form of safeguard.

Suitability as a household pet The rottweiler is happy to share family life indoors, but needs daily, strenuous exercise. It is not suited to living in flats or units.

Ideal owner A desire to follow fashion is the worst reason for buying a dog of any breed and, in the case of the rottweiler, you could be buying a large bundle of trouble.

If you are fit and active, and tough yet fair; if you are accustomed to large dogs and are keen on training, and if you want a strong, confident dog that will protect you, then the rottweiler could well be the dog for you.

Feeding Rottweilers present no special problems or requirements.

Litters Litters usually comprise eight or more puppies and birthing problems are uncommon.

Cost of puppies Pet rottweilers cost $250, registered animals $500 or more.

Lifespan 10 years.

For further information

Rottweiler Club of NSW
(Secretary, Mr P. Gray)
13 Kilmorey Street
Busby NSW 2168

Rottweiler Club of Victoria
(Secretary, Mrs Reid)
57 Coppards Road
Newcomb VIC 3219
Telephone (052) 48 4889

Rottweiler Club of Queensland
(Secretary, Mrs D. Hansen)
PO Box 872
Beenleigh QLD 4207
Telephone (07) 379 9190

Rottweiler Club of SA
(Secretary, Mr C. Pearson)
PO Box 59
Bridgewater SA 5155
Telephone (08) 370 9472

Rottweiler Club of WA
(Secretary, Ms Y. Jeffrey)
8 Orchard Road
South Lake WA 6164
Telephone (09) 417 1455

Rottweiler Social Club of Tasmania
(Secretary, Mrs K. Lethbridge)
Telephone (002) 72 4157

SAMOYED

The Samoyed is an extremely ancient breed. It has been a companion to the nomadic peoples of northern Russia and Siberia for thousands of years. They use the dog to herd reindeer, pull sleds, carry packs and guard people. The samoyed has been widely used in Arctic and Antarctic sled expeditions.

Around 1890 several animals were imported into England from Siberia, and all the stock in the western world stems from these few animals. Only white and creamy colours were imported, although other colours exist in the land of origin. The samoyed is said to be the purest breed of dog in the world, because in the western world there hasn't been any infusion of blood from other breeds.

The samoyed is slowly increasing in popularity; there are 250-300 club members in Australia.

Appearance Samoyeds weigh 20-40kg (45-90lb). The dogs are 51-56cm (20-22") high; the bitches 46-51cm (18-20").

The samoyed comes in only two colours—pure white, or white and cream or biscuit. Its lips, nose and the rims of its eyes are black. It is sometimes called 'the smiling dog' because of its characteristic upturned lips. It has a soft, thick, short undercoat. Its outer coat is long, harsh and glistening with 'silver tips'. A wire comb is recommended for getting through the undercoat once a week. Dog books often say that samoyeds, like all Arctic dogs, don't shed their hair, but the breeders we interviewed said they shed at least once a year, and should be brushed daily at that time; large amounts of undercoat will come away. Samoyeds can be bathed and blow dried (which can take up to 2½ hours) or 'dry cleaned' by brushing talcum powder or boracic acid through the coat.

Hair shed by samoyed dogs can be spun and knitted or crocheted into garments.

Temperament The Samoyed is very affectionate and friendly and loves to hang around people. It is so friendly it will hop into a car with a complete stranger. Samoyeds seem to have retained some nomadic tendencies and a dog can wander off fossicking around and then forget where it is. The breed is fabulous with children, highly tolerant and makes a reasonable guard dog, but is not guaranteed in this capacity. These dogs can be yappy but this is usually just a sign of boredom.

Health This breed is generally very hardy but can have problems with ticks due to the difficulty of locating them in the thick coat.

In hot weather the thick coat insulates the dog against heat and actually keeps its skin cooler, but if the dog is exercised vigorously its body temperature rises and the coat prevents excess heat from dissipating, which results in heat stress.

Some hip dysplasia has been encountered but breeders are taking steps to wipe this out.

Litters Samoyeds produce 1-10 puppies per litter, but five or six is average. Litters and births are normally trouble free. Puppies cost from $350 to $500 each and will live for 12-15 years.

Ideal owner The ideal samoyed owner needs to be able and prepared to regularly exercise and groom the dog. These are wonderful companion dogs well suited to children and older (but not aged or infirm) people.

This breed is popular because it doesn't have a doggy odour. It is great with kids and is non-aggressive. It loves car travel and can be kept in small areas as long as it receives daily walks.

Untrained dogs can be 'ratty' and as training takes a bit of effort it is highly recommended that dog and owner attend obedience classes from an early age. Some samoyeds are competing successfully in obedience work.

ROAD TEST

Feeding Samoyeds enjoy a combination of raw meat, canned and dry food. They utilise their food very well and eat surprisingly little for their size. If overfed they will rapidly run to fat. Food per adult dog would probably cost $4–$6 each week.

For further information

This is the Samoyed by Joan McDonald Brearley, TFH Publications. Usually available from pet shops.
The New Complete Samoyed by Robert H. and Dolly Ward, Howell Book House.
The Samoyed by The Samoyed Association of UK, c/- The Kennel Club, 1 Clarges Street, Piccadilly, London, WIY 8AB, UK

The various state Samoyed Club Secretaries are as follows:

Mr R. Grubb
PO Box 330
Fairy Meadow NSW 2519
Telephone (042) 83 1045

Mrs H. Hill
PO Box 35
Diamond Creek VIC 3039
Telephone (03) 438 1110

Mrs J. McCulloch
26-30 Second Avenue
Marsden QLD 4132
Telephone (07) 200 8532

Mrs A. Grose
Lot 9 Aunger Road
Two Wells SA 5501
Telephone (085) 24 3271

Mrs M. Gould
Lot 6 Furley Road
Southern River WA 6110
Telephone (09) 490 1410

Mrs T. Pittman (ACT)
17 Euroka Avenue
Murrumbateman NSW 2582
Telephone (062) 27 5640

SHAR-PEI

The name 'Shar-pei' is Chinese for 'sandy' and refers to the gritty feel of the dog's coat. Shar-peis were first recorded as tomb guard dogs in 202 BC and were later used as hunting and fighting dogs.

The first pair of shar-peis came to Australia in 1979, and it wasn't until 1985 that they were recognised as a pedigree and allowed to be shown. There are approximately 36 registered shar-peis in Australia.

Appearance They are the world's wrinkliest dogs. They do grow into their skins when fully grown, but their wrinkles are still a feature.

The breed is mostly trouble free but there can be a problem with wrinkles turning their eyelashes into their eyes, causing irritation and tear-staining.

As pups, shar-peis make a snuffling noise. Their bark is quite low-pitched. There is a variety of fur types: velvety, coarse, wire-brush and brush. Shar-peis come in black, fawn, red, chocolate, red-fawn, cream-fawn, lighter fawn with red streak and ears and brick-shaded markings.

Ideal owner These dogs are bought for their uniqueness. They are a very devoted dog and need the company of someone who loves animals. An owner would have to be prepared to put a lot of time into their care and include them in the family.

Cost Shar-peis cost $1500–$2500. They eat 0.5–1kg of mince and dry food every day, costing $20 a week to feed. They live for 12–14 years.

For further information

Barbara Trevare
PO Box 57
Rouse Hill NSW 2153
Telephone (02) 679 1086

STUMPY-TAIL CATTLE DOG

Stumpy-tail cattle dogs are the world's rarest breed of dog. There is only one registered breeder in the world.

The breed's origins go back to the early 1800s when two Australians, Smithfield and Hall, saw bob-tailed dogs working cattle in the United Kingdom. The men were so impressed by the working abilities of these dogs that they brought two bitches back to Australia. In the development of the stumpy-tail cattle dog crosses were made with the dingo and various other dog breeds. Unfortunately, no reliable records were kept of these breeds.

Appearance The stumpy-tail cattle dog can be all blue or all red (flecked with white) but never the two colours on one dog. Blue dogs can have a dark eye patch but no red colouring, and red flecked dogs can have red patches.

Tails can be non-existent or 10cm (4″) in length. Stumpy-tail cattle dogs have finer features than Australian cattle dogs, and longer legs and a narrower head.

Pups are born white and develop their colour and markings at about three weeks of age. As with many tailless breeds, stumpy-tail cattle dogs are occasionally born without an anus. These dogs are culled.

While there may be unregistered stumpy-tailed cattle dogs around, unless the dogs came from Mrs Iris Heale of Brisbane they are not a true, registered stumpy-tail cattle dog.

Popularity Early this century the 'stumpy' was more popular than the long-tails. However, the breed became mixed when the stumpy-tail was crossed with other breeds. Subsequently stumpy-tail pups were being born in litters of long-tail bitches. When stumpy and long-tail dogs were found to be registered out of the same bitch, the Canine Control Council de-registered all stumpy-tail cattle dogs.

Cost Stumpies sell for approximately $500, but the waiting list is very long. Only four or five dogs are bred each year. However, many owners of stumpy-tail cattle dogs say they are better workers than their long-tail cousins.

Since the 'Burke's Backyard' programme was screened, a number of breeders have begun breeding programmes to develop stumpy-tail cattle dogs, and eventual registration by Kennel Clubs is likely.

For further information

Iris and Les Heale
37 Park Road
Wooloowin QLD 4030
Telephone (07) 857 4374

Details of New South Wales dog breed clubs and associations contacts have been supplied with the kind permission of the NSW Canine Council.

CHAPTER 2
Dog Care

ANAL GLANDS

On either side of a dog's anus is the anal gland. Unfortunately, a lot of little dogs (for example, poodles), develop an accumulation in these sacs, which can sometimes rupture or form an abscess.

This problem often causes discomfort to dogs. They will drag their bottoms on the ground, as they do with tapeworm. If your dog is doing this and there are no tapeworms present, you should think about cleaning out the anal glands.

To clean the sacs out, take a swab and, aiming the dog away from yourself, squeeze either side from slightly below the anus upwards. If you are unsure about doing this, then take your dog to your local vet.

BARKING

Why do dogs bark? The dog is a pack animal and the family unit becomes the pack to the domesticated dog. A dog needs to be with its family to feel comfortable and secure. If a dog is restricted to a small backyard, it may have become bored. If a dog sees other dogs passing, it will bark at them for something to do.

The key to stopping dogs barking is training—a dog needs some training every day, if only for 10 minutes. You can learn to train your dog by going to a private instructor or an obedience class. A small amount of daily training gives your dog mental exercise and it will not be so inclined to expend energy on barking.

Install a doggy door or some form of access to the house, so that the dog feels secure and not isolated. Make sure the dog is fed before you go to bed so that it is contented and relaxed and more likely to sleep rather than prowl about the house.

These three things will greatly reduce the stress on the dog that causes it to bark day and night.

If you are worried by a neighbour's dog barking during the night, there are a number of things you might like to try. Contact the local council by phone, in writing or in person and lodge a complaint about the dog barking. Obtain literature on dog training and obedience classes and put it in the neighbours' letterbox. Find out the phone number of the neighbours and ring them at night when the dog is barking.

If you own a barking dog, it is your responsibility to shut it up. Keeping it inside the house or a shed at night may help. The dog can be surgically debarked by a vet if the only other choice is putting the animal down.

CARSICKNESS

Carsickness in pets is a very common problem. Carsickness or motion sickness is due to a disturbance of the semi-circular canal within the middle ear. This is treated mainly with antihistamine tranquillisers. As with people, it is advisable to obtain tablets for your dog.

The usual medication for dogs is Aceprome (ACP), a tranquilliser and antihistamine. It will work well, stop the sickness and sedate the dog.

There are a few home-made remedies to help your dog.

Take the dog on very short trips—perhaps to the shops and back—and gradually lengthen the trips. Pups will often get over their carsickness if you get them accustomed to the movement of the car.

Some people like to give the dog apple cider vinegar in its dinner the night before. Other people give their dog a junket tablet before they leave.

DOG BEDS

The canine hammock is an excellent value-for-money dog bed. It consists of a rectangular, tubular metal frame on legs and a hessian or canvas cover, which fits over the top of the frame.

This type of bed will not give the dog bed sores, which can become a nasty problem with some sorts of bedding.

Canine hammocks are available from most of the larger pet and department stores. They come in a range of sizes and prices range from about $20 to $60. When you purchase one, it is a good idea to buy an extra cover or two. These are inexpensive and you can replace the original when it starts to show wear and tear although, depending on the dog, covers can last for several years.

A similar product, called the Weatherbed, is a strong frame bed which can be left outside in all weathers. It is also wonderfully comfortable for the dog. The Weatherbed comes in four sizes, ranges in price from about $47–$65, and is available from pet shops all around Australia.

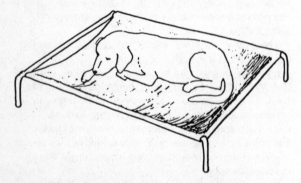

DOG DROPPINGS ON LAWNS

While many home gardeners swear by the use of water-filled bottles as a way of keeping dogs from defecating on the lawn, a New Zealand study indicates that they may actually encourage dogs.

Dr Louis Leland, a Doctor of Philosophy and Psychology at the University of Otago, presented a paper at the National Psychological Society conference in August 1988. In it he detailed a study by his students in a New Zealand town.

Twenty-seven known dog-dropped-on lawns were monitored daily for 28 days and the findings recorded. Of the lawns monitored, 14 had water-filled bottles while 13 did not. The bottles were plastic PET bottles with the lids facing the street, labels face down.

The results revealed that lawns with the bottles were 3.6 times more likely to have dogs defecate on them than the lawns without bottles.

The study was carried out over a month to combat the 'novelty' effect on animals. When farmers put scarecrows out to scare birds, the 'novelty' or scare-ability wears off after two weeks, and the birds even perch on the scarecrows.

After two weeks in the dog v bottle trial, Dr Leland says the effectiveness remained the same—very little. He says dogs tend to mark a conspicuous object with urine as a territorial boundary. The bottles on the lawns became marked, and therefore attracted more attention and investigation by other dogs.

Apparently, while the dog is marking its territory, it also takes the opportunity to complete its 'business'.

DOG FOOD RECIPE

If your female dog is creating circular dead patches in the lawn when she urinates this may be due to a dietary imbalance. The following diet has been found to cure this problem in most bitches.

> 40% meat
> 40% beans and pumpkin or carrots
> 20% rice

As soon as the meat content of the dog's diet is reduced, the bare patches in the lawn should start to disappear.

DOG PSYCHOLOGY

If your dog has developed bad habits like chewing clothes, digging holes, constant barking or just being over-protective, all is not lost.

Any dog can be retrained and disciplined to suit your household. As every dog is an individual, different methods of training must be applied. This article covers only a few problems, and the treatment for these animals may not work for you. In all difficult cases you should seek advice from a dog training expert in your own state.

A small squirt or bucket of water will often be a useful deterrent if your dog tends to chase cars, or jumps up to the wirescreen door. If a dog in your street does race out each time a car drives by, you will need a passenger with you to throw the water.

Often a barking dog can be disciplined with the use of the word 'Bah'. Many dogs seem to understand this word, as it's like a growl and they respond to it easily. It can be used in many instances, even when the dog jumps all over you and your guests; as the owner, put your knee up between you and the dog and sternly say 'Bah'.

If your dog will not settle happily on a chain, provide him with a running wire so he can run up and down. He then has a lot more yard to cover and he will be happier.

Dogs digging holes in the garden are a big problem and it is difficult to stop them. The first thing to do is to shoo the dog away and fill the hole in. To ensure that the dog doesn't dig in the same spot again, put some of its droppings in the hole and cover them with a couple of inches of dirt. This method may not necessarily stop the dog from digging in other areas.

Most importantly, keep your dog entertained. Throw a ball for it, take it for a walk to keep it interested. A happy and active dog will make a much better pet.

For further information

Silvia Wilson
c/- RSPCA
Montague Street
Fairy Meadow NSW 2519
Telephone (042) 28 9495 (business), (042) 71 2309 (home)

DOG SHOWS

For information about dog shows in your state contact your state kennel control body, see 'Canine Control Associations'. They will also be able to provide names of club secretaries and breeders of show-winning animals of the breed in which you are interested. These people will be able to give an indication of the work involved in preparing that particular breed for exhibition.

DOG TRACKING

If you would like information on dog tracking or are interested in joining a dog tracking club, please contact:

Tracking and Rescue Dog Club of NSW
(Secretary, Mrs Elvina Brodie)
36a Graham Street
Auburn NSW 2144
Telephone (02) 649 6231

Miss I. Cant
4/18 First Avenue
St Peters SA 5069
Telephone (08) 42 1238

Each year, 1 million umbrellas are sold in Australia and about 8,000 are left on the country's transport system.

DOG WALKING SERVICE

The dog walking service featured on 'Burke's Backyard' is available only in Sydney, as far as we know. For further information telephone:

Amanda Croft
Walk Easy Walkabout
Queen Street
Woollahra NSW 2025
Telephone (02) 32 4568

Amanda is a trained veterinary nurse and offers a range of pet services.

DOG WASTE DISPOSAL

Petclean products, including Supa Scoopers and Petclean Disposer units, in which waste is bacteriologically decomposed, are manufactured in Australia and distributed by:

Western Pacific Distribution Co
8 Beaconsfield Road
Briar Hill VIC 3088
Telephone (03) 435 2980

They will send out an informative brochure on request.

DOG WORMS

Puppies can carry a lethal weapon—the roundworm. If a child picks up a roundworm egg from a pup's manure and it hatches in the body, there is a chance that the larva from that egg could lodge at the back of the eye, damaging the retina and causing blindness.

Roundworm is diagnosed by looking for the eggs in the pup's manure under the microscope. To understand the problem we need to know the life cycle of the roundworm.

The dog swallows an egg. Once in the dog's intestines, it hatches into a larva, which migrates through the wall of the intestine and into the liver. It spends some time feeding and enlarging and then travels via the bloodstream to the dog's lung. It spends more time there enlarging and feeding, and finally is coughed up and swallowed and develops into an adult worm in the dog's intestine, capable of producing its own egg.

The larva does not undergo the same life cycle in your child's body; it gets lost, and occasionally ends up in the eye.

It is very important to control this problem by worming your dog. Worming your child will not prevent the problem, but worming the dog will. As a young pup it should be wormed every 14 days until it is four months old and then regularly every three months.

EAR CARE

Many dogs suffer from ear problems. Dogs with floppy ears, for example, Dobermanns, have particular problems in the wintertime as well as the summertime. In the wintertime the major problem is the crustiness that occurs on the ends of their ears. This is in fact chilblains, and it can be treated with Pergalen. This can be bought over the counter at most pharmacies. All you have to do is apply this a couple of times a day to the tips of the dog's ears and after a week or ten days you will find the lesions will disappear.

Summer problems are very different. A lot of Blue Cattle dogs and some German Shepherds actually attract flies. These flies will bite the dog, often around the tip of the ear, but sometimes around the base of the ear canal as well. It creates irritation and blood loss. The dogs flick their ears, shake their heads and splatter blood all over the place. It is pretty nasty, and often the area becomes infected. This can be controlled fairly easily by several products which you can buy over the counter or from your local vet. Repel-X is a spray that is good not only for the ears but for the body as a whole. Fly Repella is a cream, which is preferable because it lasts longer. Smear it on the dog's ear tips at the beginning of the day and it will give it day long protection. Fly repellent cream is also quite good.

Dogs with long hair and floppy ears have a different problem. Grass seeds often penetrate their skin and cause abscesses and infection. If you live in an area where ticks occur, be careful; they are often hard to find in dogs with long hair on their ears.

If your dog injures its ear, maybe by running past a rose bush or under a barbed wire fence, and ends up with a cut on the end, Elastoplast can be put right around the whole ear, that is, the ear can be 'sandwiched' between the Elastoplast, and then the Elastoplast can be trimmed off to approximately a quarter of an inch around the ear. It can be left on for two to three weeks and will stop the bleeding.

Because the ear canal of a dog runs vertically and then horizontally, you must be very careful not to place anything in a dog's ear, as it will be impossible to retrieve.

Your fingers are the safest means of gently removing excess hair from the ear canal. Use a little talcum powder on your fingertips, so that you can grasp and gently tease out the hair to free the canal and allow air circulation. After this procedure, a little methylated spirits on a cotton bud can be used to complete the cleaning.

Dogs with ear discharge or smelly ears may not respond to these simple treatments and may need to visit the vet. It could be an infection or a grass seed, but remember, whatever goes into your dog's ear canal has to defy gravity to get out again!

MEDICATION

Ear and eye drops for dogs From time to time your dog may need to be given ear or eye drops or ointment. Sounds simple, but it can be a bit difficult if you haven't done it

before. As with most tricky jobs, there are a few pointers which can make the job easier.

Some tubes come with a metal tip, which can damage the eye if not used with care. The ideal way is to squeeze a little ointment onto the tip of your finger and wipe that into the eye. The two lids should then be rolled together to spread the ointment around.

Other tubes come with a plastic tip, which will not damage the eye if it should touch the surface. The ointment can be applied directly to the eye by pulling the lower lid down and running the tube along it. The two lids should then be massaged together. Your vet may be able to give you a little plastic piece to fit over the end of the tube.

To apply drops to the eye and make them stay there, get the dog to look skyward so that the eye is as level as possible. Then apply the prescribed dosage onto the surface of the eye and give it a chance to spread.

When applying ear drops, you have to be careful not to create an air lock in the canal. There is a vertical part and a horizontal part of the canal, shaped something like an L. It is difficult to count the number of drops to apply, so just give the applicator a good squirt into the ear canal. Then close the flap of the ear over and give it a rub, massaging the ear thoroughly. The dog enjoys this and the movement will get rid of any air lock that forms in the ear canal.

Liquids Sometimes a visit to the vet results in the dog's owner being handed a bottle of some sort of liquid medication and instructions to give the dog perhaps 10ml per day. Trying to get two teaspoons of medicine into a dog is very difficult and likely to result in at least half the medication being wasted. Fortunately, there is a simple and straightforward trick that makes dosing dogs with liquid medicine easy.

Ask the vet for a syringe (without a needle) that is large enough to contain the required dose. You can fill the syringe with medicine with great accuracy.

All dogs have a ready-made funnel into which you can administer the medication; down the side of the mouth between the teeth and the fold of the lip. Slip the syringe gently inside this fold and express the medicine.

Using this technique you will find that even the worst tasting medicines will be a great deal easier to administer.

Tablets Three strategies for getting tablets into your dog:
1 Taking advantage of the fact that a dog won't bite its own skin, use your left hand (over the top of the dog's jaw) to push the skin between the two jaws and over the large canine teeth. With the other hand, put the tablet slightly to one side, over the back of the tongue. Give the throat a gentle rub.
2 Sausage meat is much stickier than mince. Roll the tablet into a ball of meat, or use a whole sausage or frankfurter. If you have a large amount of sausage mince, you can roll up a series of tablets and freeze them until they are needed.

3 Cheese is hard for a dog to resist. Press the tablet into a chunk of soft cheese, such as Kraft cheddar, and the dog is likely to gulp it down.

NAIL CARE

Cutting If dogs are running around on the lawn and don't have a good solid surface like concrete to wear down their nails, you will occasionally need to trim their nails, paying attention to the dew claw. Be careful to avoid cutting the bloodline—this will be seen as a pink area down the centre of the nail. Just cut the hook off the tip of the nail; don't clip back too far.

If you do cut your dog's toenails too far back and draw blood, you might try the following techniques to stem the flow.
Cornflour Coat the foot; the cornflour makes a matrix on which the blood can clot.
Hydrogen peroxide (neat) A good clotting agent; dab it on with a tissue or cotton bud.
Styptic pencil Wet it under the tap and dab it on to the nail.
Cautery Smokers can use the lighted tip of a cigarette to seal the nail.
If none of these methods work, it will be necessary to take the dog to the vet for treatment.

Filing You can avoid the problem altogether by filing the dog's nails instead of clipping them. Give the dog a manicure by following this procedure: using a bastard file from the tool box, file underneath the nail first, then up and down. Then finish off neatly with an emery board (made from a piece of emery tape glued onto five-ply).

With the dog's co-operation and a little experience you can become an accomplished canine nail artist!

RAT CATCHER DOGS

Over 50 years ago Brisbane City Council devised an unusual solution to the problem of rat location and control, and it is still in operation today. They trained a team of rat catcher dogs. These dogs are used mostly as sniffer dogs to pinpoint where rats are hiding, but digging for the rats and destroying them when they appear is also part of their work.

The team currently comprises seven men and nine dogs. Seven of the dogs are either Fox Terriers or Miniature Fox Terriers and the other two are Jack Russell Terriers. Each man owns his own dog or dogs, which are usually rescued from the pound. The men try to obtain young dogs and start training them at about 12-14 months.

The dogs and handlers work every day. At 7.30 am they gather at the council depot to receive their assignments for the day and then they head off, mostly in pairs, in the four complaints vehicles at their disposal.

Daily and yearly tallies of rat kills are recorded. In 1988 the dogs caught over 1100 rats. Kills are declining as rural activities are pushed further out of town, and as baiting and refuse disposal operations become more effective. Some of the most disruptive cases of rat damage about which the council receives complaints include chewed telephone lines, which knock out telephones, and chewed wiring of washing machines and dishwashers.

For further information

Brisbane City Council
69 Ann Street
Brisbane QLD 4000
Telephone: Complaints (Rats and Mice) (07) 225 4352, or Health (Mosquitoes and Rodents) (07) 225 4351.

REMOVING DOGS' TEAR STAINS

Tear staining of fur on dogs' faces is caused by excessive tear production, and is generally more prevalent in toy breeds. There are two problems which require a trip to the vet: entropion (in-growing hairs on the eyelids) and tear duct blockage (the tears cannot drain down the nasal passages).

If the dog has neither of these problems, tear staining may be caused by hair falling into the dog's eyes. To avoid this it is best to have the hair around the eyes clipped closely. Another solution is to keep the hair above the dog's eyes pulled back in a bow or clip. Also, a little Vaseline smeared under the eye will prevent the tears from sticking.

To remove brown tear stains from white fur, mix either boracic acid or cornflour with a little water and a couple of drops of peroxide. Work the paste into the hair, allow it to dry, then brush it out.

SELECTING A PUPPY

It is very important, when selecting a puppy from an Animal Rescue Centre, to know exactly what you want your dog to be like.

The best age for a dog to adapt to a new family is under four months because this is when a dog bonds to its pack (the new family)—later is often too late. Older dogs may have been left at a Rescue Centre because of their problems, for example, wandering or bad temperament.

If you wish to get a young pup that will be friendly with visitors, there is a simple test that you can do. Gently hold the pup on its back for 30 seconds—a normal friendly dog will just lie there and you will know it is ideal for a family pet. If this action frightens the dog and it pulls away, then it is probably best left for someone who is skilled at handling such behaviour.

If the puppy bites at your hand when under stress while it is little, it will probably bite a lot harder when it is big.

Another simple test to carry out on a pup, if you have a young family, is the stress test. Gently grab the pup from behind, just as kids do, and watch the reaction. A sensible pup will not be disturbed by this, but be careful of one that snaps at your hand or shrieks.

ROAD TEST

Make sure the pup is healthy, with bright eyes, a soft shiny coat, and no diarrhoea. Beware of the listless one that hangs over the water bowl or lies in the corner.

It can be a gamble buying a dog from an animal shelter if you don't know what you are looking for, but if you like surprises and choose carefully, you will end up with a great pet that has been immunised and desexed, for $65–$90. Don't forget to join a dog obedience class.

TAIL DOCKING

Tail docking has been an emotive issue for many years. Of 156 pure breeds of dog, about 50 have their tails docked. The cases for and against tail docking are as follows:

For docking

There is no legal prohibition of docking and most vets perform the operation.

Against docking

Ear cropping is illegal. Other operations considered cruel such as debarking and de-clawing have to be performed as an alternative to euthanasia. Many vets perform docking only to forestall amateur operations.

De-sexing is more painful and debilitating than docking. Young puppies (three to five days old) have only gristlelike tails and don't experience much pain. The pain is only transitory (as in circumcision in humans). Pups resume suckling as soon as the operation is over. Evidence of the degree of pain suffered has never been produced.

Sharp scissors, blood loss and extreme pain make for quite a gruesome operation. Pups are too young for anaesthesia; no pain relief is given.

To preserve tradition some man-made pure breeds have to be docked. They would look ugly with tails and would not conform to worldwide standards.

Docking is only a fashion. All dogs are born with tails which 'set them off'.

Breeders don't know which dogs will be pets and which will be working dogs, so they dock them all early on when it is a simpler operation.

Most dogs are pets which don't experience the perils of bygone hunting days. Dogs *use* their tails as organs of communication and

Hunting and working dogs used to be rescued by their stumpy 'handle'. It is difficult to heal an injured tail.

Many farm animals are docked—it is mandatory for sheep in Australia. By leaving the tail on, infection risk is increased. Fly strike can occur.

Breeders and exhibitors are not prepared for change, out of loyalty to their breed standards. There are no judging guidelines for the 'correct' tail if left on.

balance and to swat flies. Bull Terriers often damage their tails and yet they are not docked. Nature hasn't docked the dingo's tail and it is a working dog.

Normal attention to a pet's well-being negates the risk of fly strike. Many fluffy dogs such as Huskies and Samoyeds do not have their tails docked and don't experience particular problems as a result.

Governing bodies say docking is optional. In the UK more and more dogs are shown with tails *on*. If judges gave points *for* tails the practice could be expected to disappear more rapidly.

Ultimately, the decision whether or not to dock is up to the individual breeder. It is a personal decision.

WEANING PUPPIES

Once puppies reach 4½ weeks of age the mother can be removed for short periods, increasing daily, until at six weeks there is total removal.

The mother's milk will dry up by itself, but if mastitis develops veterinary attention is necessary. Check the mammary glands for lumps (without rubbing and thereby stimulating further milk production).

After having removed the puppies' source of milk, you must supply food. The following can be tried: commercial foods—for example, Pal Puppy Food; fussy eaters might eat children's canned foods—for example, creamed chicken; a home-made mixture (thick soup consistency) of high protein baby cereal, egg yolk (not the egg white as this will block the absorption of vitamin B), milk, calcium supplement; meat: steak shredded from cheap stewing steak is less sticky than mince and easier for pups to pick up; add calcium supplement.

Worm the puppies with Drontal Allwormer at three to four weeks, then fortnightly; at 10 weeks the pups should be worm free. Thereafter check instructions for dosage and frequency.

Make sure the puppies get their initial temporary vaccination at six weeks, a repeat at 12 weeks, and a booster at 16 weeks.

Very fit, healthy puppies should result from following these suggestions.

WET WEATHER SKIN DISEASES

Fungi may attack dogs' skin during wet weather.

One of these diseases is a *fungal dermatitis* or *ringworm*. It is not the same ringworm that is transmissible from animals to man. In this case it is picked up from the soil and creates lesions. These lesions are not painful, and are easy to treat. Dab on a topical iodine with a sponge and cover the area well. Do this once a day for about ten days.

Another disease is *wet dermatitis* or *eczema*, which spreads very quickly and is very painful and dangerous to the dog. The dog will need immediate veterinary treatment, antibiotics and topical preparations.

WHELPING PUPS

You will know when the bitch is about to have pups—the day before, she will start to get quite agitated, and a discharge will start from her vulva. You should then be organised for the pups' arrival—you will have known the approximate date in advance as the normal gestation period is 63 days.

The first thing to do if your bitch is about to whelp is to prepare a whelping box. It should be big enough to give the bitch room to turn around, and for the pups. Line it with shredded newspaper; this is much better than straw or cloth, which the pups can get underneath and the bitch may then lie on them.

The bitch will start to puff and pant and you will know that the time is not far off. She will start to strain and after approximately two hours should produce the first puppy. Most pups come out head first, but some may come backwards, so don't be alarmed. The bitch will clean the pups up fairly quickly herself. She will lick the membranes away from their heads, noses and mouths, gradually stripping it over the rest of the pups' bodies so that all that it is attached to is the cord. She will then bite it off close to the pups' abdomens, leaving a short stump.

If it is her first litter she may need some help to get the membranes away from the head area. If she goes for more than two hours without producing a pup, or if she develops an abnormal discharge, you will need to take her to your local vet to be checked.

> *The strawberry is composed of over 250 different fruits fused together, none of which is a berry.*

CHAPTER 3
Cat Breeds

FELINE CONTROL ASSOCIATIONS
Australian Capital Territory
RNCAS Cat Club
PO Box 404
Dickson ACT 2602
Telephone (062) 41 2478

New South Wales
RAS Cat Control
PO Box 4317
Sydney NSW 2001
Telephone (02) 331 9135/6

Northern Territory
Cat Association of the NT
GPO Box 3870
Darwin NT 0801

Queensland
Queensland Feline Administration
180 Sherbrooke Road
Willawong QLD 4110
Telephone (07) 372 1346

South Australia
Feline Association of SA
(Secretary, Lee Caldwell)
21 Poole Street
Osborne SA 5017
Telephone (08) 248 2106

Tasmania
Cat Control Council of Tasmania
PO Box 116
Glenorchy TAS 7010
Telephone (002) 72 9443

Victoria
Feline Control Council
c/- Showgrounds
Epsom Road
Ascot Vale VIC 3032
Telephone (03) 376 3733

Western Australia
Feline Control Council
PO Box 135
Claremont WA 6010
Telephone (09) 384 1933

ROAD TEST

ABYSSINIAN AND SOMALI

In 1868 a British military expedition returned from Abyssinia, and brought with them a cat reputed to be the first Abyssinian to reach Britain. The breed was being listed by 1882, and by 1970 was recognised as a true breed throughout the world. The cats bear a remarkable resemblance to the sacred cats of ancient Egypt. The Somalis were bred from the late 1960s, using a recessive longhaired gene in the Abyssinians. They are very popular in North America, and have become even more popular in recent years.

General appearance The cats are medium-sized, slender, firm, muscular and lithe; they stand on 'tiptoe' and have tufted ears and large eyes coloured green, gold or hazel.

Colours The Abyssinian's distinctive coat is agouti, that is, each hair is 'ticked' with darker colour bands (two or three in the Abyssinian, 10–12 on the longer-haired Somali). It is sometimes called a 'bunny coat'. Coat colours are tawny, cinnamon, blue, fawn, tawny-silver, cinnamon-silver, fawn-silver and blue-silver.

Temperament In addition to irresistible good looks, Abyssinians and Somalis are blessed with appealing personalities. They are intelligent and doglike and are frequently one-person cats.

Useful qualities Independent and individual, they don't have a noisy cry; they are a good companion, whose loyalty makes them a good cat for people who think they don't like cats!

Training With some patience on the owner's part, the cat can learn some tricks and games, but it is strong-natured and spirited.

Kittens Abyssinians are not prolific breeders. They produce three to four kittens at most, so they can be hard to obtain. Kittens cost from $150 for pets, and $250 upwards for show cats. The cats live for about nine years.

Health problems/faults Abyssinians are susceptible to kidney and gum problems, and the cinnamon-silver variety is vulnerable to skin complaints. Feline leukaemia has taken its toll on the breed in the past.

Suitability as a household pet Weekly brushing with a soft brush and wet hands is necessary, as they shed some hair, but they are not especially prone to furballs; most seem to dislike car trips. These cats are not fussy eaters.

Ideal owner Abyssinians are not for apartment dwellers or families with children less than eight or nine years old.

The kitten must like you and it would be best to select another if it doesn't settle down after the first two weeks.

For further information

Abyssinian Cat Club of Australasia
(Secretary, Mrs Matthews)
GPO Box 2323
Sydney NSW 2001
Telephone (02) 412 3125

Mrs S. Weaver-Hall
Obanya
Wellington Road
Clematis VIC 3782
Telephone (059) 68 4275

As there are no specialist Abyssinian clubs in other states, we recommend contacting feline control councils for breeder contacts. See 'Feline Control Associations'.

BRITISH SHORTHAIR

These cats were originally found in the alleys of nineteenth-century British cities. A man called Harrison Weir loved the British street cat so much that he selected some of the hardiest and strongest, bred them, and almost single-handedly created the British Shorthair. It became an officially acknowledged breed by 1889, and went on to become one of the most popular breeds in cat shows at that time. Today they are not as popular, as it can be difficult for the average person to tell the difference between a British shorthair and an everyday moggy. Generally, the public sees British shorthairs as expensive moggies, but the British Blue *is* appreciated.

General appearance British shorthairs have a solid, muscular build, a round head and large, round eyes. Males weigh up to about 6.5kg (14lb) and females to 5.5kg (12lb). They are the heaviest cat breed.

Colours Seventeen different colours are recognised in the UK. Australian breeders usually aim for solid colours, including blue, white, black and cream. Tabbies and spotted varieties also exist. The eyes of a shorthair are orange or copper in colour.

Temperament Placid, not demanding, tolerant, docile and respectful; they are home-loving.
British shorthairs are not vocal cats and can cope with being alone without fretting. They are not inclined to wander and will tolerate children.
They are not suitable for leash training, but will respond to calling, and may be taught simple tricks such as rolling over.
British shorthairs are not destructive with furniture and are quite happy in flats and townhouses, as well as

suburban homes. A pot of grass is desirable for the high-rise-flat-dwelling cat. They do shed, but stroking removes excess fur. They suit most people from children to the elderly. While they enjoy company, they would also suit a working couple, and are recommended for all cat lovers.

Three to four kittens per litter is average; sometimes there is only one: these cats are not big breeders. Kittens cost $200 or more. The cats live for 12–15 years.

British shorthairs should be given fresh meat daily, chicken or rabbit occasionally, rice as an extra, and cheese from time to time. Calcium supplements should be given to kittens and queens. Cows' milk is unsuitable for this breed. Food costs around $5–$6 a week.

Health   There are no hereditary defects, as British shorthairs are out-crossed to Persians every five or six generations. They are very vigorous, strong and healthy. Like most cats, they get furballs.

For further information   There is only one specialist British shorthair cat club in Australia. There are breeders throughout the country, however, details of whom can be obtained by contacting the Feline Control Association in your state.

The British Shorthair Cat Society
(Secretary, Gillian Hurle)
PO Box 434
Artarmon NSW 2064
Telephone (02) 879 6008

BURMESE

The Burmese cat has been bred since about 1930 from a little cat called Womnow that was found in Burma by a ship's doctor. The doctor took the cat back to America, crossbred it with a Siamese cat and kept only the darker offspring. The breed has increased since then to include lighter coloured cats and is now one of the most popular breeds in Australia. Burmese can live for between 12 and 18 years. They are friendly and will allow themselves to be picked up and taken away so they need to be watched when they are outside.

Appearance Burmese are much like Siamese in their general appearance and build. They are sleek cats with finely defined features and have a particularly graceful way of walking and moving.

Colours A range of ten colours is available: brown, blue, chocolate, lilac, red, cream, brown tortie, blue cream, chocolate tortie, and lilac cream.

Feeding Burmese will eat meat and tinned food and need access to a patch of grass to aid their digestion. The cost of feeding a Burmese is between $8 and $10 a week, depending on the variety of food given.

Temperament The Burmese is a lovable, affectionate cat, which likes to be around its owner and involved in the happenings around the house. Individual cats have different personalities but they are generally good companions and thrive on affection. They like a scratching post and will stretch and scratch on this if one is available.

Cost Prices for Burmese kittens range from $130 to $200, depending on the colour chosen.

For further information

The Burmese Cat Society of Australasia
(Secretary, Mrs H. Rossiter)
28 The Crescent
Marayong NSW 2148
Telephone (02) 671 4158.

HIMALAYAN OR COLOURPOINT LONGHAIR

The Himalayan breed came about when two English breeders decided to combine the beauty of the Persian with the colourpoints and blue eyes of the Siamese in the 1940s. Himalayans were brought to Australia during the late 1960s to early 1970s and they have quickly become a popular breed.

Appearance The Himalayan takes after the Persian in body type, being quite a 'chunky'-looking cat with solid, short legs and a round pressed-in face. Most weigh about 5kg (11lb).

Coat Exhibition Himalayans have a softer coat than those usually sold as pets. The pet Himalayans tend to have a silky coat, which is not as heavy as that of the exhibition cats. The cats with the heavier coats are usually chosen by exhibitors, who then sell the silky-coated kittens for pets. Silky-coated kittens and adults are usually far easier to care for, as their coats are easier to groom.

Pet Himalayans should be groomed three times a week. Exhibition cats are groomed daily. Grooming involves brushing or combing talcum powder through the coat. The coat sheds in summer and if the cat is not groomed on a regular basis, this can be a problem in the home.

ROAD TEST

Himalayans should be bathed fortnightly—this is not difficult, as kittens are used to being bathed by the time they are sold and as long as this practice is continued regularly, the cats will remain quite accepting.

Colours A wide range of colours has been developed in this breed, including seal point, blue point, chocolate point, lilac point, red point, tortie point, blue-cream point, lilac-cream point, and lynx point (a tabby-like pattern to the points in a variety of colours).

Breeding Himalayans are still mated with Persians every two or three generations to retain the Persian body type. About four kittens are produced in each litter and kittening problems are rare. Kittens are born white and begin to show their colour points at 12 days.

Temperament This breed is very affectionate, quite tolerant of children, and capable of being trained at an early age to act on command. Himalayans are placid and adaptable and not aggressive, as Siamese often are. However, they are not as lazy as Persians and enjoy a little more activity.

Suitability as a household pet Himalayans will live quite happily indoors all their lives and are well suited to apartments and units. They are not hunters and prefer to keep clean and stay inside as long as a litter tray and scratching pole are provided. It is also important that if the cat does live in an apartment, the owner plants a pot of grass (for example, lawn seed or kikuyu) to be kept indoors for the cat. Cats eat grass to aid their digestion or to regurgitate furballs.

Health The Himalayan is generally a very healthy breed of cat. Their major problem is furballs due to their long fur. Some breeders recommend feeding the cats sardines in oil in preference to trying to make the cat swallow liquid paraffin. Ticks are another threat to long-haired breeds and thorough checking and supervision is required in tick zones.

Feeding The diet should comprise raw beef and tinned fish alternately, vitamin supplements, grated cheese, and a little dry food. Calcium is important for kittens and lactating queens but this should be supplied in a low-lactose milk powder solution, as the Himalayans have inherited the intolerance to milk typical of oriental breeds. The cost of feeding will be $7–$8 per week.

Lifespan Himalayans are quite long-lived cats, with an average lifespan of 15 years.

Cost Himalayans from a reputable breeder will cost about $120-$200 for a pet-quality kitten without papers. These kittens are sold at about 10 weeks, wormed and vaccinated. Vaccinated and wormed exhibition-quality kittens will cost about $350–$500 with papers.

For further information

These cats are known as Himalayans in some states and as Colourpoint Longhairs in others, although they are all the same breed. New South Wales has a Himalayan Cat Club and several other states are planning to start clubs. People in all states other than New South Wales should contact their state feline council for information about breeders of these cats. See 'Feline Control Associations'.

The Himalayan Cat Club of NSW
(Secretary, Mrs C. Bourne)
PO Box 3
Canterbury NSW 2193
Telephone (02) 78 5672

MANX

There are a number of theories as to why the Manx cat doesn't have a tail. One suggests that when Noah was stocking the ark with animals, the Manx was out playing; it was the last to board the ark and had its tail slammed off in the door. The scientific theory is that a mutant dominant gene is responsible for the cat being born without a tail. Why this gene is only found in the Manx cat is not fully understood.

The Manx and the long-haired Cymric are the only tailless cat breeds. At the point where the tail should begin, there is a small hollow, sometimes covered with a tuft of hair.

Manx are very intelligent cats; they are placid and loyal and a good show pet for those who like something different.

Appearance Manx can be virtually any colour or pattern—tortoiseshell, white, red and black, silver, white, cameo, and so on. Another distinctive feature is their double coat; a soft undercoat and a coarse and glossy top coat.

The cat often gives the impression of permanently walking downhill. The reason for this is that their hind-quarters are raised, supposedly to give them a better sense of balance to compensate for their lack of tail.

Breeding There are a number of breeding difficulties with the Manx cat. Some kittens are born with no anus, and others with part of a tail, or even with a longer tail than a normal cat.

The Manx is quite rare, there are only ten or twelve breeders in Australia. The rare long-haired variety, the Cymric, looks like a Persian but has a definite advantage in that its coat is virtually tangle-free.

Cost Manx cats cost $100-$180. They eat tinned or fresh meat and biscuits, costing $3-$4 a week to feed.

Lifespan Manx cats live for around 13 years.

For further information

Contact Feline Control Associations.

PERSIAN/LONGHAIR

This breed is known as the Persian in North America but is called the Longhair in Britain and Europe. Australian clubs tend to follow British terminology, but both names are used.

The long coat of this breed appears to have its genetic origins in Asia Minor, but the development of the large head and heavy, compact body took place in Europe—initially in Italy, but mostly in France and England. In Britain the different colour forms are actually classified as separate breeds, because very slight differences can be detected in the body type from one colour to another.

Appearance The Persian/longhair has a large head with a distinctive flattened face, large, round eyes and a very short nose. The body is compact, solid and stocky, with a short bushy tail, short muscular legs, and large feet.

The coat is dense, thick, silky and particularly bulky around the neck and tail. In this breed the undercoat (or down hair) is sometimes as long as the guard hairs, and this helps to make the coat so full and dense.

Colours Persians/longhairs come in an enormous range of colours. These include solid colours, tabbies,

tortoiseshells, bi-colours, and several shaded or patterned variations.

Grooming Adult Persian/longhair cats require daily grooming; their fine hair tangles readily. The area around the tail is particularly prone to becoming dirty and matted.

Temperament Despite their frowning expressions, these cats are placid, gentle and quick to adapt to changes in their environment. They are usually undemonstrative, but sociable, even towards other cats. These characteristics, combined with an affectionate nature, give the Persian/longhair a most appealing temperament.

Suitability as a household pet This breed is tranquil, sedate and home-loving, and so is well suited to indoor life. Furballs, however, can become an unpleasant problem if not alleviated by daily grooming.

Ideal owner Persians/longhairs enjoy the company of people who are calm and gentle with cats, and who are prepared to accept and return the cat's affection. The prospective owner of a Persian/longhair must be prepared to remain dedicated to the task of daily grooming.

Health This breed suffers from a number of inherited diseases, which relate to the eyelids, eyeballs and tear drainage.

White cats with blue eyes are often deaf from birth, but an increased sharpness of the other senses compensates to some extent for the lack of hearing. White-coated cats are also prone to solar dermatitis around the ears (which can become cancerous), and their coat often becomes stained around the face and tail areas.

Cats with very short noses can sometimes suffer from breathing problems. A pronounced fold of skin above the nose can interfere with the tear ducts, and cause blockages that result in infection.

As cats groom themselves with their tongues, they lick loose hairs and dirt from the coat. The hairs that are swallowed can form a hard lump in the intestine—this is called a furball. Furballs are a common problem with this

ROAD TEST

breed, and if they remain inside the cat can cause illness and even death. Daily brushing helps to reduce the incidence of furballs, and breeders or veterinarians should be consulted for other control recommendations.

Feeding   Persians/longhairs require a balanced and varied diet. Overfeeding can eventually result in cardiac problems.

Litters   Litters are generally small—usually about four kittens. Problems are rare and these cats tend to make good mothers.

Lifespan   Persians/longhairs live for ten to twelve years.

Cost of kittens   Pets cost $200, show quality animals $450–$500.

For further information

NSW RAS Cat Control
PO Box 4317
Sydney NSW 2001
Telephone (02) 331 9135, or (02) 331 9136

Pedigreed Persian Cat Club of Victoria
(Secretary, Mr David Dedman)
10 Cooks Crescent
Warrandyte VIC 3113
Telephone (03) 844 2350

Federated Longhair Breeders' Association of Queensland
(Mrs Meg Christianson)
38 Amherst Street
Acacia Ridge QLD 4110
Telephone (07) 277 6331

Persian Breeders' Cat Club of South Australia
(Mrs Cheryl Ross)
10 Mason Avenue
Happy Valley SA 5159
Telephone (08) 381 6470

Feline Control Council of Western Australia
PO Box 135
Claremont WA 6010
Telephone (09) 384 1933

Tasmanian Longhair Cat Society
(Secretary, Mr Menzies)
13 Jackson Street
Glenorchy TAS 7010
Telephone (002) 72 3507

REX

The Rex was a spontaneous mutation of the domestic cat. The rex gene eliminates the long guard hairs and most of the 'awn' hairs that form the top layer of fur in normal cats.

Although such mutations had occurred previously, it was only in 1950 when a curly-coated cat was born in an otherwise normal litter in Cornwall, England, that it was taken seriously and bred back to its mother to produce more curly-coated kittens. Ten years later another curly-coated kitten was found in Devon, England and bred to the Cornish line, but they could not produce curly-coated kittens together. So the Devon Rex and Cornish Rex became effectively different breeds.

Appearance   The Cornish rex has a curly or wavy undercoat that is very fine, silky and close-fitting with no top coat or longer guard hairs. The Devon rex also has the fine, silky, curly undercoat, but in addition has a few guard hairs. Even the whiskers are curly on these cats.

Both types have essentially foreign (Siamese) bodies that are medium length, lean, light, but solidly muscular, with an arched back and long, straight legs.

The Cornish has a medium-length triangular head, a long straight nose and large ears blending into the triangular shape of the head. The Devon has a triangular head, too, but fuller cheeks, a shorter nose with a stop (a dip or break in the line), and extremely large, wide-set ears.

Originally available only in brown tabby colour, the Rex is now available in virtually all colours. Most popular are black, smoke, white, white with blue, chocolate or seal points.

Its call is more of a chirrup than a meow, and its tail wags slowly when the cat is happy.

Temperament   Very determined—the rex will continue to jump up on your lap or shoulder no matter how many times you remove it. It constantly seeks out company, therefore it is a good lap pet. It is very playful, even when quite old, and is therefore a good kids' pet. It is difficult to train.

Since rexes love company, two cats should be purchased if owners will be away most of the time.

'Cheeky' is a word often used to describe the rexes' personality. They are very athletic and agile. They are also outgoing. They will 'front' a dog and often make the dog back off.

Coat Although they do moult, rexes' coats are so fine that you will find virtually no fur around the house. Because of their thin coats, they have proved to be excellent for people who are otherwise allergic to cats. They are not totally allergy-free but certainly greatly allergy-reduced. Many people who have these allergies are irritated by cats' skin, not just by their fur; obviously they would still find problems with a rex.

The coat tends to thicken up a little in winter and thin down in summer. It may take up to 18 months for a rex's coat to settle; you can still show a cat up to the age of 18 months even if the coat is patchy, and not lose points. If it is no better after that age, then the coat is going to be unacceptable for showing. Whiskers are curly, very bristly, and break easily.

Care Rexes are hardy cats. However, since their coats are thinner it is recommended that they are not moved from a very warm environment beside a heater in the home straight out into a cold backyard. Chills are not a major problem, but this is probably because care is always taken to ensure they are not put into an environment likely to cause problems. They are not susceptible to cat flu or chills, and being originally farm cats are very hardy. The ears can be a problem, especially those of the Devon rex. Because they are so large, they collect dust and need to be cleaned.

Rexes' eyes, too, are large and need to be well cared for. Curly eyelash is a problem which has been experienced overseas, but has not appeared in Australia yet.

Grooming Because of their thin coats, virtually no grooming is involved in keeping a rex. Claws may be trimmed, as in most breeds. To avoid curly eyelash (where lashes curl up and grow into the eye and cause irritation) be vigilant in keeping such eyelashes trimmed.

Feeding A good quality tinned cat food is recommended, as is semi-lean mince, in preference to 'lean' mince; some fat in the diet may help ward off the possibility of chills. Dried food is recommended in small quantities only. Egg yolk and cheese are added to the meat or tinned cat food. Rexes cost $7–$10 a week to feed.

Breeding Rexes have little trouble giving birth, but usually have a litter of only 3–4 kittens. Rexes live for about 15 years.

Cost Rexes cost $150–$350.

Ideal owner Breeders say that these cats are good with everyone. They state that they react to the people around them. They will race around the house with 6–10 year olds, yet be very quiet with elderly people or infants.

For further information

The Rex Club of New South Wales has members from all states as well as from overseas. They will be pleased to handle enquiries from all states.

Rex Club of NSW
(Publicity Officer, Colleen Walters)
22 Dolans Road
Cronulla NSW 2230
Telephone (02) 523 2962

RUSSIAN BLUE

The Russian Blue is thought to have originated in the Russian port of Archangel, and sailors are believed to have brought the cats to England in the last century.

There were some problems with breeding during the early part of this century. During the First and Second World Wars the cats were unable to be imported from Russia for breeding, and British breeders compromised by breeding their cats out to British shorthairs and Siamese, which had somewhat similar colouring.

This backfired when the features of a typical Russian blue became blurred and more Siamese in type. This type is now considered to be a fault in exhibiting. The cats became long and svelte, their normally plush coat roughened and their soft voices became harsh. The eye colour was also affected, with a blue tinge becoming apparent; yellow was also detected.

After the Second World War British breeders of Russian blues made an effort to restore the cats' original shape and temperament. The breeders imported fresh Russian lines and used these in their breeding programmes.

ROAD TEST

Appearance Nowadays the cats would be described as being big, solid cats, well-muscled and powerful. They have long legs and are described as being elegant. When the ears are held back the skull should have a snake-like appearance.

Russian blues have distinctive whisker pads, which fluff up when they are excited or alarmed. They have almond-shaped eyes of a vivid green. Another distinctive feature is their shoulder blades, which are quite close together and very prominent.

The legs and muzzle are silvery; each whisker should be silver-tipped. The cats have a long tapering tail, small oval feet and large ears, which are set straight up, not slanted. The ears are also translucent.

The cat has a short, thick, plush coat. The undercoat protects the cat from the cold and gives the coat the silvery lustre of mink. This is the distinctive character of the breed.

Russian blues come in all shades of grey up to blue-grey, evenly distributed.

Care Russian blues are very hardy cats, sensibly built without any particular health problems.

Kittens Their litters are usually of about four kittens, and there are no problems to speak of with kittening. Kittens cost $200 each. The cats live for 14–15 years.

Feeding Russian blues eat meat, mostly beef, sometimes rabbit and roast chicken. Breakfast can be a brand food with grated cheese and cat biscuits. Fresh beef, rabbit or chicken in the evening, with brown rice and grated carrot twice weekly. They cost $10 a week to feed.

Character Russian blues are known to be shy with strangers; they are family cats but can become attached to one person if they get most attention from that family member. They are very quiet cats which don't like loud noises or noisy people. They are said to be the gentlest of all cat breeds, and are extremely tranquil.

They are the ideal apartment cat, being very house-loving and rarely known to wander. They chatter to their owners, particularly around feed time. The cat spends many winter hours near the stove or radiator, but if necessary, it can stand the cold as its Russian ancestors did.

The cats suit a family with children, as long as they aren't too rowdy. They tend to shy away from noisy children.

Faults White spots or white hairs are faults in this breed. Obesity may occur with a quiet lifestyle. Breeders have mentioned the occasional kinked tail, which may be a remnant of the Siamese influence of early this century.

For further information

Federal Cat Club of Australasia
(President, Mrs Brenda Hornibrook)
Telephone (02) 810 7663

SCOTTISH FOLD

The Scottish Fold breed has been listed for exhibition in New South Wales and Victoria, while in Queensland it is recognised by three independent bodies, and in Western Australia it is registered as an Experimental Breed. The Cat and Feline Control Council of Australia see the breed as passing on mutations, and like to keep the registered cats 'pure'.

Appearance The Scottish fold was introduced into Australia in 1972. The cat has a natural mutation which has been preserved by breeding to the British Shorthair and domestic cats in Scotland and England. The head is round and well set on a short, thick neck. There is considerable breadth between the ears. The ear is distinguished by a definite fold line, the degree of which will vary from a small, tightly folded ear to a somewhat larger, less tightly folded ear. The body is short, cobby and broad across the shoulders and rump. The tail is in proportion to the body and less flexible than that of other cats.

The peculiar characteristic of the breed is that many of the litter will have ear cartilages which do not mature. This becomes evident after the twentieth day. Some have normal pricked ears, and others look like dogs' ears. This does not affect their hearing, but some vets say the cats are prone to ear infections.

Temperament The Scottish fold is very good with children, being gentle and affectionate, and will take lots of rough treatment. It does well as a companion, hence is very good for the elderly, and it lives quite happily in small areas such as home units.

Cost Scottish folds cost $200–$450. They eat domestic cat food, chicken and fresh meat, and cost $12 a week to feed.

Lifespan They live for 10–15 years.

For further information

Gabrielle Kaufman
PO Box 40
Macedon VIC 3440
Telephone (054) 26 1255.

Cheryl Hearn
16 Killeen Street
Sunshine VIC 3020
Telephone (03) 311 4343.

SIAMESE

Siamese are probably the most recognisable breed of cat, with their coloured mask, ears, stockings and tail (the points), and their piercing blue eyes.

The cats have a cream-coloured slender body with points in four different shades: seal (beige coat, dark brown, almost black points); blue (white coat, light to mid grey points); chocolate (ivory coat, milk-chocolate points); lilac (glacial white coat, grey-pink points, lavender-pink nose).

The modern Siamese has a wedge-shaped head, elongated ears that are wide at the base, and almond-shaped blue eyes. Squints are definitely a fault, as are kinked tails.

The ideal owner for a Siamese is someone who will give it the attention it demands. The cats are very human-oriented and can fret if neglected. They can be trained to the leash and are described as being the most doglike of the cat breeds.

Siamese are known for being vocal (that is, they meow loudly) and owners talk to their pets. According to breeders this is their way of communicating with humans. They are ideal for household people who want a pet to talk to. The cats prefer life indoors, and as they have a short, fine coat, they tend to feel the cold more than most breeds.

Siamese females tend to reach puberty earlier than other breeds; females can become pregnant at five months and litters can be large. Kittens are born white; the points develop as they grow.

Diet Breeders recommend raw mince and tinned cat food for Siamese cats. Kittens need calcium supplements until they are nine months old to prevent rickets.

Faults Siamese can be prone to respiratory problems. Common faults are weak legs, white feet or wide cheeks and a short muzzle. Their fine body and pelvis can occasionally cause problems when kittening.

Cost It will cost approximately $150 upwards for a kitten from a breeder. They usually live for 16–17 years.

For further information

Siamese and Shorthaired Cat Club
(Secretary, Mrs B. Jackson)
51 Calool Crescent
Belrose NSW 2085
Telephone (02) 452 4371.

Siamese Cat Society of NSW
(Secretary, Mrs M. Sherwood)
89a Grosvenor Street
Wahroonga NSW 2076
Telephone (02) 487 1381.

SPOTTED MIST

The Spotted Mist is the only breed which has originated entirely in Australia—from the idea stage through the establishment of breeding programmes and rules to the emergence of the finished product. In 1977 Dr Truda Straede applied for and was granted 'provisional permission to experiment' in developing the spotted mist as a new breed, by the NSW Royal Agricultural Society Cat Control Consultative Committee.

The breeds used in the development of the spotted mist were the domestic and Burmese—from which the spotting (a version of the tabby pattern) was obtained—and the Abyssinian, which provided the ticking for the background of the coat. The ticking must be present to enhance the spotted pattern.

In 1987 the spotted mist was accepted by the RAS Cat Control and fully registered spotted mists now have their own breed class at shows.

Popularity As the breed is still new, the numbers of spotted mists are not large. There are around 50 breeding cats and about 200 pets—neutered animals are not considered to be of value to the breeding programme.

New South Wales is the only state to have registered the spotted mist, but the ACT has applied to obtain the rules and standard, and enquiries have been received from New Zealand. United States judges who saw the breed at this year's Sydney Royal Easter Show expressed great interest in them.

Appearance This is a cat of no extremes—its general shape is like that of a nice, well-balanced domestic. The coat is short, but dense and soft like that of a Burmese.

Colours The spotted mist colouration is very subtle. The pattern is made up of darker spots on a lighter, 'misted' ground. The colour of the spots determines the name of the colour of the cat; the background colour is in every case a creamy, mushroom shade.

The colours which have already been named are brown, blue, chocolate, and lilac. Another colour which has not yet been named is gold or caramel, and pink is theoretically possible, but there are no examples of it yet.

ROAD TEST

Temperament Spotted mists are said to be outstandingly affectionate and gentle. Adult males can live together in groups, which is evidence that they are not very aggressive even under conditions that bring out the most extreme aggressive behaviour.

Spotted mists are said to be excellent with children and are very obliging when called upon to participate in games. They remain very kittenish all their lives, but are trainable from 9–10 weeks without undue difficulty. One of the specially endearing characteristics of the breed is that they adore their owners so much they drool!

Spotted mists are so affectionate that they are prone to becoming very spoilt and this can create problems if you are planning to board them from time to time. Dr Straede recommends they be kept with a domestic (an ordinary cat) to remind them that they are cats.

Useful qualities Spotted mists are good mousers and are great with children, the latter quality being one of the original purposes of the breed.

Grooming They require general hand grooming, but no special requirements.

Feeding They will eat cheap raw meat and good quality biscuits, costing as little as $1.80 per cat per week to feed.

Health They have no special health problems but the lighter colours (like all light coloured cats) are more prone to allergies and skin cancers than the darker ones.

Lifespan It is too early to tell just how long-lived the cats will be on average. However, some of the original kittens are still in fine condition at 12 years of age.

Breeding There are no apparent breeding problems. Spotted mists have been selected during the breeding programme for ease of breeding and small litters of four or five kittens.

Cost Kittens cost $200 for a pet; $300 for a fully vaccinated, fully registered, 12-week-old breeding female.

For further information

Dr T.M. Straede
PO Box 384
Epping NSW 2121
Telephone (045) 75 0227

There is no spotted mist club or society as yet, but enthusiasts produce an informative newsletter, *On the Spot*, every two months.

TURKISH VAN

The Turkish Van cat has been known in its homeland of Turkey for centuries. It appears to have its origin around the Lake Van area of Turkey, an area known for its bitterly cold, snowy winters. The first Turkish vans were brought to Australia in 1985.

Popularity This breed is so new to Australia that it is not at all well-known. There are currently less than 100 Turkish vans in the country.

Special characteristics The most obvious peculiarity of this breed is its fascination with water. In fact, when brought up near water, Turkish vans are known to enjoy swimming.

Indoors, their love of water can leave owners with the occasional headache when they tip over their waterbowls to play in the resultant puddle, or even climb into the sink. Running water trickling from a hose or tap holds an even greater fascination for these cats.

Although Turkish vans are reputed to have been domesticated for centuries, they appear to have been left to fend for themselves to a large extent, and this could be why these cats are very protective of their kittens. They also seem to have a strong attraction to containers into which they can climb or squeeze. This too could reflect a closer association with the wild than most other breeds.

Appearance Turkish vans have a white body with auburn markings around the ears, and an auburn tail. This pattern is very rare in cats, but highly consistent in this breed. Kittens are born with their markings, whereas in some breeds they appear only after 12 days.

The body of the Turkish van is large and muscular, and the head is a short wedge with a long nose and amber eyes. Turkish vans are classed as longhaired cats, but in the warmer areas of Australia the coat will not develop its full length and density. The Turkish van coat is smooth, soft and silky, with no woolly undercoat.

Grooming A twice-weekly brushing with a short-bristled brush is adequate, although a daily brushing is best when the cat is shedding heavily in November. As there is no woolly undercoat, tangles are rare. Regular washing in lukewarm water is generally enjoyed by the cats.

Temperament Turkish vans are strong, adaptable cats that don't require much pampering. They are active and inquisitive cats and can frequently get into mischief. Turkish vans are more doggish in character than most felines.

Suitability as a household pet Turkish vans take well to house life but enjoy a ramble in the garden. They will choose the softest, warmest beds and regard them as their own. They will shed white hairs at the start of summer, but daily brushing at this time will help save dark clothes and furnishings from collecting a dusting of white.

Ideal owner Turkish vans are likely to appeal to any cat lover because they have a strong character and are hardy and independent. They will stand and assess strangers rather than scuttle away and hide.

Turkish vans are companionable and their fondness for water can make them entertaining as long as the owner is prepared to wipe the floors after them. They do not appear to be troubled by being left inside all day while working couples are away.

Litters Turkish van kittens are very robust and breeding problems are generally not encountered, although litters are usually small—only three to five kittens each time. Kittens cost $250 or more, and will cost $4-$5 per week to feed per cat for a varied diet. They live for 12-15 years.

Health Turkish vans have not been in Australia long enough for owners to discover whether they are prone to any particular health problems, but according to UK journals the breed is trouble free if kept vaccinated and clean. No problems have as yet been encountered by Australian owners.

For further information
Send a stamped, self-addressed, A4 envelope to:

Marilyn Brown
5 Sirius Court
Whittington VIC 3219
Telephone (052) 48 3989

Pauline Halpin
119 Inkerman Street
Maryborough VIC 3465
Telephone (054) 61 2602

CHAPTER 4
Cat Care

CAT MAT

The Cat Mat is simply a plastic mat with a cat food dish built into the centre of it. This means that the cat can eat its food without making a mess all over the floor, and without knocking its dish over. The Cat Mat is available from pet shops for about $5.

CRICKET, THE OLDEST CAT IN AUSTRALIA

The oldest living cat in Australia is believed to be 'Cricket', who turned 35 in April 1989.

Cricket was found in his owners' backyard in Melbourne as a tiny kitten which had been dumped over their fence. They moved to Queensland eight years ago,

but despite their concerns the change in climate appears not to have disturbed Cricket.

Until recently Cricket's owners had another cat two years older than Cricket, but he died when a car accidentally backed over him.

Cricket eats large quantities of a varied diet of mostly cooked meats, and he lives outdoors. His owners can think of no explanation for the longevity of their cats.

The Guinness Book of Records lists the oldest cat ever recorded as a tabby, 'Puss', owned by Mrs T. Holway of Clayhidon, Devon, UK. Puss celebrated his 36th birthday on 28 November 1939 and died the next day.

EAR CARE

Cats can have problems with their ears in the summertime. White cats often suffer from sunburn on the tips of their ears and this can develop into cancer. Sunscreen should be applied to the tips of the ears a couple of times a day, or better still keep cats with white ears inside, out of the sun.

FELINE AIDS

The following article, 'An AIDS-like Disease in Cats', by Margaret Sabine, Associate Professor in Veterinary Virology, Department of Veterinary Pathology, University of Sydney, is reproduced with kind permission of the author.

'The feline immunodeficiency virus (FIV), which causes a disease in cats called feline AIDS, or FAIDS, was first isolated in the USA in 1987. The virus is similar to HIV (human immunodeficiency virus) which causes human AIDS. However the feline virus does not cause disease in humans and the human virus does not cause disease in cats.

'The viruses concerned are called lentiviruses or 'slow viruses' because they cause diseases with long incubation periods. Lentivirus diseases of many species have been recognised for a long time, for example equine infectious anaemia (1840s), visna/maedi of sheep (1930s), goat arthritis/encephalitis (1970s) and human AIDS (1981). The viruses do not cross the species barrier and they infect only the species named. None of the animal viruses show great antigenic similarity to HIV or to each other.

'FIV and HIV are quite similar in the diseases they produce, which are often due to 'opportunistic infections', namely, infections caused by normally harmless organisms which do damage only when the immune system is depressed.

'Test-kits for detecting FIV antibody analogous to those used for AIDS were developed soon after the discovery of the virus. Presence of the antibody means that there has been contact with the virus. In the case of HIV, the virus persists in the presence of antibody.

'Coopers Veterinary Products donated some imported test-kits to the Department of Veterinary Pathology. Feline serum and plasma samples which had been collected and stored between 1970 and 1988 were tested for the presence of FIV antibody. The first serum shown to be antibody-positive was collected in 1972. Fresh samples from clinical cases have since been tested. Clinical conditions associated with presence of FIV antibodies have been skin ulceration, gingivitis, chronic respiratory infections and weight loss. Anaemia, lymphadenopathy, fever, neurological abnormalities and abortion have been described by others.

'Surveys carried out in the USA, Europe and Japan have shown the virus to be present in a low percentage (1-2%) of healthy cats but in up to 30% of 'sick' cats. Like all lentiviruses, FIV is extremely difficult to spread. The exact method is not known but is probably through bites. Outdoor roaming male cats showed the highest rate of infection. Venereal and in utero transmission of virus have not been observed nor has transmission through milk. Cats in close contact with FIV positive cats have remained uninfected over periods as long as 14 months.

'The length of the incubation period between infection and development of the disease is not known. It is not known whether disease necessarily develops or whether recovery from viral infection is possible.

'What does this mean now for the cat, the owner and the veterinarian? There is clearly no need for panic, as the virus has been in this country for at least 16 years. As with feline leukaemia virus, there is now a test available to enable diagnosis of some difficult disease syndromes. An FIV positive cat with an opportunistic infection because of immunosuppression may not survive. A healthy FIV positive cat may live for many years and evidently poses little risk even to its housemates.

'Thus, in the light of present knowledge, there is no justification for euthanasia of FIV positive healthy cats. Such cats pose no threat to humans, and remarkably little to other cats. Even the outcome for themselves is unknown. The FIV antibody test should be used as a diagnostic tool in suspected cases of immunosuppressive disease.'

FLEA CONTROL IN CATS

Flea control in dogs is fairly straightforward—most dogs are bathed regularly and also wear flea collars. However, since cats have a natural aversion to water they cannot be washed once a week with an insecticidal wash. We therefore have to try other measures to get rid of fleas on cats.

One treatment we can use is a spray. The trouble is that generally cats do not like sprays either, so the best remedy to get rid of fleas is a flea powder especially designed for cats.

When putting the powder on cats there are a few tricks to doing it successfully. Sprinkle the powder all over the cat's body, then brush the powder against the lie of the coat, stroking the fur with your hand. The cat will like the stroking and will more easily tolerate the application of flea powder because it is being stroked while the treatment is being applied.

Because cats groom themselves with their tongues, the loose powder on the surface of the coat has to be removed and this can be done with a damp sponge. Just wipe the cat all over to remove the excess powder and it won't have any problems when it grooms itself.

And don't forget to wash the powder dust off yourself when you've finished treating the cat.

FURBALLS

Long-haired cats like Persians, Persian crosses, Himalayans and Birmans lose a lot more hair than moggie cats and Siamese cats. The hair gets into the cat's stomach via its tongue, which is covered by fine barbs; as it licks its fur these barbs collect all the dead hair and the cat swallows it.

The cat has its own solution for getting rid of this hair. It will go out and eat some nice fresh grass and make itself sick. If you own a cat and live in a home unit or flat, and the cat can't get outside to eat grass, it will need a laxative. Laxatives come in various forms. There are commercial brands, which you can buy from your veterinarian or the pet shop, and there is old-fashioned liquid paraffin.

The cat will need a dose of liquid paraffin of between 2.5 and 5mls. An old syringe is the easiest thing to use. Be careful, *don't squirt in too quickly*. Give the cat a chance to swallow in between each squirt. It's a good idea just to stroke its chin, to prompt it to swallow the medication.

ORPHAN KITTENS

If you have an orphan kitten, you have to be its mother, that is, generally look after the kitten as you would a baby.

You will need to teach the kitten how to urinate and defecate. To do this, use a swab or tissue and gently stroke around the vulva and the kitten will perform. You will also need to gently clean any discharge from around the nostrils or face.

There are a number of proprietary products on the market with which you can feed your kittens, for example, Animalac, made by Troy. Make up the formula by accurately following the directions on the pack, and have it warm or at body temperature. If the kitten is very small and weak you will need to use an infant feeding tube. Work out how far to push it down by measuring it on the outside of the kitten from the last rib to the tip of the kitten's nose. If you push the tube down that far you know it has to be in the stomach—if it doesn't go down that far it is in the lungs and the cat will drown if you put food in the tube. Suck up some formula into the tube, push it over the back of the kitten's tongue right down into the stomach and then squirt the food in with the syringe. The kitten will take three syringes full three times each day. If the kitten is stronger, just use the syringe to feed it. There are also special dropper bottles available from your vet or pet shop.

If you are unsure about feeding your orphan cat, seek advice from your local vet.

PLAQUE ON CATS' TEETH

Plaque is the brown material that builds up on cats' molars. Basically it is just a secretion from saliva but it also leads to redness around the gumline, called gingivitis. It can be treated on a co-operative cat by using your thumbnail and just flaking this brown material off the tooth. However, if the cat isn't co-operative a general anaesthetic has to be used and the tartar scraped off using a metal instrument.

Cats do not get cavities, but the tartar causes a gap between the gumline and the tooth and infection can get into the gum and under the tooth causing it to rot and fall out.

We can prevent this problem by stopping the breakdown in the tooth-gum junction. Give your cat something hard to chew on, bones, for example. Too much canned cat food helps to create this problem, so give your cat a bone occasionally to help flake the tartar off.

RODENT ULCERS

In some cats, a rodent ulcer forms where the point of one of the long canine teeth sticks into the cat's lip.

The name of the ailment may suggest that the cat has been bitten by some sort of rodent (for example, a mouse or rat), but it is more likely to have derived in some way from the word 'eroding'.

In serious cases the ailment is treated by removing the offending tooth under general anaesthesia. The task is not an easy one, as the canine tooth, which is adapted for ripping and tearing, is very strong and is embedded for about two-thirds of its length in the animal's gum. Loss of the canine teeth does not make eating any more difficult for the cat.

Each case requires individual assessment. Consult your veterinarian for further advice.

CHAPTER 5
Bird Breeds

BACKYARD CHOOKS

Like the lemon tree and vegetable patch, the sight of a handful of chooks assiduously working over the lawn

clippings is bound to evoke memories of the backyard of yesteryear—a time in which the economic climate demanded practical, productive use of garden space.

Economics It *is* economically viable to produce your own eggs. In fact, if your family consumes 18 eggs a week you will save 50¢-$1 each week. This calculation takes into account costs of $14 for a 40kg (90lb) bag of food plus $300 for the purchase of a new zincalume shed, averaged out over an appropriate period.

Regulations While some urban councils discourage and restrict the keeping of chooks, you are allowed to keep them in most urban areas as long as you comply with the regulations set down by your local council.

Some councils do not permit the keeping of roosters, and many stipulate that the poultry yard must be located a certain distance away from boundaries, be fully enclosed and have a concrete floor. Contact your local council for full details before you proceed with your chook-keeping plans.

In each state there is also an organisation which issues licences for commercial egg production. Currently, in all states except South Australia and Victoria, if you have 21 laying hens or more you must obtain a Poultry Farmer Licence. In South Australia and Victoria you may keep up to 50 birds without a licence.

Choosing chooks Essentially there are three broad categories of chooks bred in Australia: table birds bred for meat, layers bred to produce eggs, and pure breeds of fancy poultry which come in all shapes and sizes and are bred to a standard just like the different breeds of cats and dogs.

Table birds are of little value to the average family seeking a regular supply of eggs.

Pure breeds of fancy poultry are generally more attractive in appearance than crossbreds, but are likely to be slightly less productive in terms of egg laying.

Crossbred laying chooks are usually reliable egg layers and are readily available from hatcheries. They are usually available as day old chickens for about $19 a dozen, and at 'point of lay' (ready to commence laying), about 20 weeks old, for about $45 a dozen.

A family using 18 eggs a week would need five to seven hens.

Hatcheries cross different breeds of chooks to produce more vigorous and productive laying strains. White birds are a White Leghorn cross, black ones are Australorp crosses and reddish brown ones are predominantly Rhode Island Reds.

Unless you wish to breed your own chickens, it is not necessary to keep a rooster, and in most cases he is simply an extra (and frequently noisy) mouth to feed.

Raising chickens You can usually buy day old chickens which have been sexed as females, but buy one or two more than you need, both because the odd male can still appear and also to allow for occasional losses.

Day old chickens will need to be provided with warmth for the first five or six weeks. A 75W light globe positioned about 20cm (8″) above the floor of a large box should provide ample heat for the first two weeks. After that the globe should be raised in height, or the strength of the globe reduced gradually. Make sure the chickens have an area where they can escape from the heat if necessary. Overheated chickens will pant and move as far away from the light as possible. Chickens that are too cold will crowd together, standing up directly under the light. Contented chickens usually sleep quietly and evenly spaced under and around the lamp.

Point of lay pullets (young females) require much less work and are usually the best option. They are just as easy to tame as day old chickens. Try to buy birds with untrimmed beaks as this practice is of no advantage for backyard birds.

For the first 10–12 weeks the chickens should be fed a commercial medicated chick starter crumbles ration followed by medicated grower crumbles until they commence laying. From that time onwards they should be fed a layer ration. Six hens will eat about 5.5kg (13lb) of layer feed every week. Commercially prepared rations are specially balanced, so it is best not to supplement them with other grains. Kitchen scraps provide the chooks with an interesting diversion but remember, the less balanced the diet, the fewer eggs the chooks will lay. If soft shelled eggs become a problem, provide the chooks with shell grit.

Housing Ideally a chook pen should be comprised of a shed, covered and enclosed on three sides, with the fourth side facing north and opening into a small yard fully enclosed with chicken wire. The mesh should extend down below ground level for at least 15cm (6″) to minimise the risk of dogs or foxes digging under the fence to enter the yard. The back wall of the shed should have a ventilation window in it.

Metal bird aviaries can be purchased for $200–$300 and will cost $50 to erect. They can be adapted to include a small run.

There is a range of designs and materials suitable for building chook pens. The less wood used in the structure the better. Wood can harbour pests such as mites—piping is a better option.

Chook yard design (See diagram). Vary dimensions to suit space available. Each hen requires at least 0.35 square metres of floor space.

Accessories Dishes for food and water usually result in much wastage through soiling and overturning. It is far

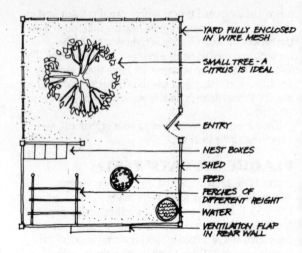

YARD FULLY ENCLOSED IN WIRE MESH

SMALL TREE – A CITRUS IS IDEAL

ENTRY

NEST BOXES
SHED
FEED
PERCHES OF DIFFERENT HEIGHT
WATER
VENTILATION FLAP IN REAR WALL

better to use automatic feeders and waterers.

An automatic waterer, comprising a plastic tank connected to a gravity-fed drinking attachment, will provide 10 chooks with water for 10 days and costs about $50 (the tank holds 20 litres—5¼ gallons).

An automatic galvanised feeder with a capacity of 50kg (110lb) costs about $38, while one of 7kg (15lb) costs about $19. Plastic automatic feeders tend to become brittle and fall apart after about 18 months to two years of exposure to the sun.

Health Chickens bred at hatcheries are normally vaccinated when they are a day old against the highly contagious Mareks disease. Medicated chick starter crumbles and medicated grower crumbles will help to protect the growing chickens against other illnesses.

External lice and mites are probably the worst problems suffered by adult birds. Products such as Pestene (active ingredient Rotenone) and Coopex (active ingredient Permethrin) provide good control.

Usually when a chook becomes seriously ill veterinary treatment is not economically viable and it is best to destroy the bird humanely.

BANTAM CHOOKS
Bantams are miniature chooks usually about one-quarter of the weight of their large counterparts (ordinary large sized chooks are referred to as 'standards'). There is doubt about the origin of bantams but it is thought the first breeds may have developed in the Orient.

Breeds and colours There are many different breeds of bantams, and within each breed there is usually a wide range of colours and, occasionally, differences in the formation of the comb.

For example, there are 23 recognised varieties of the Leghorn breed of bantams (SC = Single Comb, RC = Rose Comb):

SC Barred, SC Black, SC Black Tailed Red, SC Blue, RC and SC Buff, RC and SC Buff Columbian, RC and SC Columbian, RC Dominique, RC and SC Dark Brown, RC and SC Exchequer, SC Golden, RC and SC Light Brown, SC Mille Fleur, SC Red, SC Silver and RC and SC White.

Not all breeds and colours of bantams have been bred down from standard sized chooks. Some have developed from selective breeding between other bantams.

Varieties of bantams include White Leghorns, Rhode Island Reds, Rhode Island Whites, Columbian Wyandottes, White Wyandottes, Australorps, Old English Game (originally bred for cockfights), and Black Pekins. Some breeds have been developed more for ornamental than productive purposes and are not likely to produce enough eggs for even a small family. Ask breeders about productivity before you buy.

A warning to prospective bantam keepers: always check with your local council first to see what regulations apply to keeping chooks in your area. Numerous restrictions apply in some areas.

Comparison of bantams with standard chooks

Temperament Bantams are alert and friendly. They have the same basic temperaments as larger breeds but generally are easier to handle and better as children's pets because of their smaller size. However, bantam roosters, particularly the hard (tight) feathered, or game, breeds— for example, Old English Game—can be very aggressive although this varies with the different strains. Soft feathered (fluffy) breeds tend to be generally more docile. Because of their smaller size bantams do less damage to gardens when scratching around than do standard chooks.

Housing Bantams require about one-third of the space necessary for standard chooks. However, 0.2 square metres (about a square foot) of floor space per bantam should be regarded as the minimum.

Feeding Bantams eat exactly the same sorts of food as standards but require less than half as much. That is, bantams eat less than 500g (1lb) a week per bird of commercial poultry feed plus household scraps. It costs about 50¢ a week per bird to feed bantams.

Laying ability In general, each bantam will lay as many eggs per week and per year as each standard chook of the same breed. However, this varies widely with the particular strain of chook, that is, within the one breed and size some strains or breeding lines will lay very much better than others. Four to five eggs a week per hen in the first two years (except during moult) is a good average level of production. Bantams will live for four to eight years.

Size of eggs Once again, this varies enormously, even between individual birds within the same breed. The ratios, in cooking, of 2:1 and 3:2 bantam to standard eggs are widely accepted. This means that when compared with the size of the birds, bantam eggs are proportionally larger than standard eggs. There is no discernible taste difference between bantam and standard eggs.

Weight of birds According to the American Poultry Standards book, bantams are one-fourth to one-fifth the weight of their large counterparts.

Price per bird Ordinary, non-show quality, $2–$5; proven show quality, $30–$50; top quality, $100.

For further information

British Poultry Standards, $85 from Bantam Club of NSW. Edited by C.G. May, Newnes-Butterworths, 3rd edition, 1971.

This book provides a brief history, a detailed description and a judging standard for each breed. It is of great value to anyone wishing to show their poultry.

American Standard of Perfection, published periodically by the American Poultry Association, New York. $60 from Bantam Club of NSW.

Less widely used in Australia than the British book.

Pure Breed Poultry Raising by Rick Kemp, Kangaroo Press, 1985. $10.95 from most bookstores.

Written primarily about standard chooks but a good general guide to the husbandry and showing of fancy breeds. Written for Australian conditions.

Bantam Club of NSW
291 Galston Road
Galston NSW 2159

This club produces a monthly magazine, *The Fancier's Gazette*. The club has members in all states and will readily supply information about bantam husbandry, breeds and their availability, showing and so on upon request. They will redirect enquiries to appropriate clubs and breed societies in other states.

> *Fifteenth century topiarists in Italy shaped box trees into giants, ships, apes, donkeys, the Pope, cardinals and various philosophers.*

ROAD TEST

BIRMINGHAM ROLLER PIGEON

The Birmingham Roller was developed in England, in and around the vicinity of Birmingham, from which the breed derives its name. It is thought to have been developed from the Dutch Tumbler and/or the Oriental Roller, more than 100 years ago. The Birmingham roller was selected for its spinning ability and birds failing to so perform were eliminated in the course of breeding, to give us the acrobat of today.

The first flying competitions generally matched individual birds. The bird which met all the requirements of the judges as regards style and regularity of performance and flew in the best style was the winner. Modern competition originated in Birmingham and became organised in about 1920, with the introduction of the marking ring. A kit of about 20 birds was flown, which had to fly for 20 minutes. They were judged on the number of turns they performed that included every bird in the kit, and the quality of performance was also taken into account.

The first Birmingham rollers were imported into Australia just before the Second World War and it is from these few pairs of birds that all of the Birmingham rollers in Australia originate. For the last 30 years it has been illegal to import any birds into Australia. A quarantine station has been built in Melbourne to enable bird fanciers to import birds. This quarantine station should be operating shortly, and if the roller fanciers can organise a shipment, there will be a real injection of new blood into Australian Birmingham rollers.

As well as being valued for its flying qualities, this bird also has a keen following from fanciers interested in exhibiting it at pigeon shows. It has a quiet, steady temperament.

The *flying* Birmingham roller fancier breeds rollers for their acrobatic qualities in the air. The ideal is a roller which does backward somersaults in the air; from the side it looks like a small ball, with a hole appearing in the centre, speeding downwards. A good roller must be able to control its rolling, otherwise it will become what is termed a 'roll down' and will kill itself by rolling too far and hitting the ground. Performing rollers can cost up to $700 a pair.

The *show* Birmingham roller fancier breeds rollers for their looks. The ideal show roller has the correct shaped head, neck and body. It has the correct coloured eyes, correct feathering, beak setting, leg position, and so on. Show birds cost about $15 a pair.

In Australia the Birmingham roller pigeon is exhibited both as a show bird and as a performing bird. While show rollers can still fly and roll, performing birds usually are too lean and muscular to be successfully exhibited.

Each state has its favourite activity; in New South Wales show Birmingham rollers are most popular, while in Western Australia performing rollers are favoured.

There is still confusion as to why Birmingham rollers tumble. Some think it may be an epileptic fit, while others think the birds enjoy the tumbling, or it could be a nervous reaction to predators such as hawks.

About 10 to 20 birds fly in a kit, and it may take a long time before the kit flies neatly and tumbles well. Many breeders fly their birds for 20 minutes to an hour each day, usually in the early morning or late afternoon. The birds are affected by the weather, temperature, and most importantly the wind. Birds can easily get blown out of their range in strong winds and most breeders avoid flying them in these conditions.

For 20 birds a loft of about 1.2 x 1.2m (4 x 4') is recommended and this should be checked daily, water refreshed and fresh food provided. When you are cleaning the loft you should wear a dust mask, as dust from the feathers can damage your lungs if you are exposed to it for long periods.

Birmingham rollers eat pigeon mix, and will cost about 15¢ a week per bird to feed. They live for 8–15 years.

Birmingham Rollers come in the most common pigeon colours: black, blue, red and mixes of these colours and markings.

For further information There are a number of clubs throughout Australia, catering for the Birmingham roller fancier. In New South Wales there is the National Show Birmingham Roller Club, which has members through New South Wales, Victoria, the ACT and Queensland. The NSBRC was formed as a national club for fanciers who are mainly interested in flying their Birmingham rollers, and in the near future will be organising flying competitions and other activities. At present the NSBRC is organising an annual show, which is to be held in Moss Vale, New South Wales, and is supporting four regional shows in Albury, the Hunter Valley, Melbourne and Sydney. For information on the NSBRC please contact:

Dave Willans
PO Box 45
Mittagong NSW 2575.
Telephone (048) 89 4319 (home)

Other contacts:

Sydney Performing Roller Club
(Secretary, George Witenko)
95 Magoware Road
Girraween NSW 2145
Telephone (02) 636 7706

Australian Birmingham Roller Club
(Secretary, C. Attard)
2 Menzie St
Braybrook VIC 3019

Performing Roller Club
(Secretary, K. Coppin)
52 Links Road
Ardeer VIC 3022

Chevy Walker
M/S 183, 3 Burgess Rd
Calico Creek
Gympie QLD 4570
Telephone (071) 83 2909

Birmingham Roller Club of WA
(Secretary, D. Mannion)
22 Kitchener Street
North Beach WA 6020

EXHIBITION BUDGIES

Exhibiting the modern budgie is a highly organised affair.
These days the very best representatives from each state
in Australia compete in national championships. It is very
competitive to breed exhibition budgies. More than
300 000 registered budgies are bred in Australia every
year, and many more unregistered birds. The number of
thoroughbred horses registered each year is a mere 18 000.

There is a very big difference in size between the large
exhibition budgie and a budgie bred from wild budgie
stock. Selective breeding over 140 years has developed the
large exhibition budgerigar.

Features to look for in exhibition budgies are:
size—about 22.2cm (8¾″) long; a large well-rounded head; a
deep and wide mask (clear area under beak)—yellow in a
green series bird or white in a blue series; six evenly
spaced large spots on the mask; good colour—the colour of
every part of the budgie is specified by standard—and good
deportment; good behaviour—the bird has to be trained at
a young age to show itself. It needs to be able to sit on the
perch so the judge can examine it, and it must move from
perch to perch so that you can see both sides of the bird.
Exhibition budgies are bright and companionable. They
eat seed, shellgrit and cuttlefish and cost 50–60¢ to feed a
week. The birds cost $20–$100, although prices up to
$5000 have been paid for exceptional birds. They live, on
average, for seven years.

For further information

Budgerigar Society of Australia Inc
(Information Officer, Barry Ryan)
25 Lyton Street
Blacktown NSW 2148.
Telephone (02) 671 5380

Barry is available to answer any enquiries about
budgies and, as many vets are not keen on treating pet
budgies, he can recommend vets who will be helpful.

The Australian National Budgerigar Council
(Secretary, Mr B.R. West)
38 Acheron Avenue North
Cranbrook QLD 4814
Telephone (077) 79 1138

Budgerigar Council of Australia
(Harry Eady—The Trill Budgie Hotline)
20 Walter Street
Bulleen VIC 3105
Telephone (03) 850 2664

The Budgerigar Society of Australasia
(Secretary, Mr Bill Williams)
21 Ryan Place
Beacon Hill NSW 2100
Telephone (02) 905 3065

Budgerigar Society of South Australia
(Hon. Secretary, Mr K. Murphy)
9 Raymond Avenue
North Plympton SA 5037
Telephone (08) 297 9362

The Western Australia Budgerigar Council
(Secretary, Mrs C. Pearce)
16 Bannerman Avenue
Marangaroo WA 6064
Telephone (09) 342 8237

The South Queensland Budgerigar Breeders Association
(Secretary, Mr John Glynn)
36 Sloane Street
Stafford Heights QLD 4053
Telephone (07) 359 8050

The Tasmanian Budgerigar Council
(Secretary, Mr J.H. Burn)
RMB 723
New Norfolk TAS 7140
Telephone (002) 61 1497

GOULDIAN FINCH

Australia is renowned for having the best collection of
wild birds for its land size of any country on earth.
Finches are among the most colourful of all its birds.

The Gouldian Finch was named after Elizabeth, wife of
ornithologist John Gould (1804–1881). In the wild there are
some problems with them and their numbers. However,
they breed extremely well in captivity. The Gouldian finch
and the Zebra finch are probably the most domesticated of
all the Australian finches, and they do not mind if you
inspect their nesting boxes regularly. They emerge from
the nest at about six weeks.

From the time they hatch they have a number of purple-
blue spots at the corners of their beak. Inside a nesting
box (or in a nest inside a tree limb, where they breed in the
wild), it is very dark and these iridescent spots enable the

parent to find them in the dark. Gouldian finches are rare in that they come in a range of colours in the wild. The predominant variety in the wild is the black-headed form. There is also a deep blood red variety. One form that is rare in the wild but quite common in captivity is the yellow-headed finch (in fact, a light orange). Chicks are a very dull green-brown colour and are very inconspicuous. Eggs are approximately 1.6cm in length.

Gouldian finches are docile birds, easy to breed and to keep in captivity, and their basic care is quite simple. They are bred in flocks, maybe 3–5 pairs in an average-sized aviary. They are prone to a few diseases in captivity, so it's a good idea to put 5cm (2″) or more of coarse shellgrit on the floor of the cage to stop parasitic worms from building up. AWS3 (crystalline Anchor cordial) can be added to their drinking water to stop a lot of the diseases of birds in captivity, but it is very difficult to buy. Feed Gouldian finches plain canary seed with just a touch of millet. They will cost 10¢ a week per bird to feed.

Gouldian finches are normally sold from October to February by pet shops or bird dealers. In areas south of Queensland they require a very protected aviary to shield them from winter cold. They cost approximately $65 a pair and live for five years. Uncoloured juvenile Gouldian finches may breed within six weeks of leaving the nest. To help Gouldian finches breed really well in captivity, they should be given seed heads, for example, summer grass. Apparently in the wild they eat only a variety of sorghum called *Sorghum intrans*.

For further information
AWS3 is available from:

Feathered Friend
695 Forest Road
Bexley NSW 2207
Telephone (02) 588 6364

GRASS PARROT

Most Australian Grass Parrots (Neophemas and Psephotus) are native to arid inland areas; some come from rocky coastal fringes. Although not native to Europe, they are extremely popular there in captivity and many mutations of these parrots have been bred overseas.

Appearance Australian grass parrots are only a little larger than a budgerigar, about 20cm (7–8″) in length; Neophemas weigh 45–50g (1¾oz), but some Psephotus, such as the Blue Bonnet, can weigh up to 140g (5oz). They have an elegant body shape and are some of the world's most beautiful birds.

Colours Some are spectacularly coloured, for example, the Scarlet-chested parrot (*Neophema splendida*). Others such as Bourke's parrot (*Neophema bourkii*) are more subtle in the wild, with tones of pink, blue and brown, but in captivity a superb rose colour has been bred, and a cream Bourke.

The Torquoisine parrot (*Neophema pulchella*) has a yellow mutation which is very striking, as well as red-fronted and red-fronted yellow varieties.

Popularity The popularity of these birds will tend to increase due to additional improvements which will make them outstandingly beautiful birds.

Temperament Generally non-aggressive and peaceful birds, grass parrots are easy to keep and usually willing to breed; their small size does not demand a huge aviary (2.1m x 80cm x 1.8m/7′ x 31.5″ x 6′ high) is sufficient room per pair. They cost $70 or more per pair. Cost increases with rarity. Grass parrots live for about 12 years (some are still breeding at 10 years), and a lifespan up to 17 years has been noted. Up to seven young may be produced at a time.

Feeding Grass parrots like a diet of mainly canary mix, millets, small sunflower seeds and hulled oats. They like greens—sprouted seeds, dandelions, silver beet. Shellgrit, cuttlefish, rock salt lick and arrowroot biscuits and seeding grasses and thistles will also please them.

Water is best given in dishes 30 x 30 x 5cm deep (12 x 12 x 12″), on the ground on bricks; freshen it daily.

Health Examine and quarantine new birds for six weeks. A worming programme is essential. Sick birds should be isolated and taken to a vet who specialises in birds.

Captive breeding programmes may help to re-establish in the wild the very rare Orange-bellied parrot (*Neophema chrysogaster*). The same programme may be used for ground parrots. If a captive breeding programme had been established in the 1920s, the Paradise parrot (*Psephotus pulcherrimus*), last sighted in 1927, could be flourishing today.

For further information

A guide to Neophema and Psephotus—Grass Parrots, published by *Australian Birdkeeper Magazine*, PO Box 579, Coolangatta, QLD 4225, Telephone (075) 54 4669, is available at leading pet shops or may be purchased directly from *Australian Birdkeeper Magazine*. The price is $19.95, and this includes postage within Australia if purchased from the magazine. This company also distributes the following:
   A Guide to Rosellas ($11.95 including postage)
   Australian Birdkeeper ($4.95 per issue, 6 pa).

The Neophema and Grass Parrot Society of Australia
PO Box 425
Guildford NSW 2161

This is the only known grass parrot club in Australia.

MUSCOVY DUCK

The Muscovy (*Cairina moschata*) is a native South American duck and appears to be the only domestic duck breed which is not a descendant of the Mallard. Muscovy drakes lack the curly tail feathers characteristic of drakes of all other breeds. The name muscovy is said to be derived from an odour of musk which pervades the duck's skin but which disappears when cooked.

The muscovy belongs to a different species from other domestic ducks and geese. Consequently the progeny that result from crosses between the two groups are sterile. Muscovies live for seven to eight years.

Temperament Muscovies are docile, placid and slow moving if unthreatened. They do not enjoy being caught and picked up, and will claw and squirt their droppings as a form of defence.

The drakes can be bad tempered and aggressive and are not suitable as pets. Drakes will fight together and have been known to kill, and even eat, ducklings.

Flight Muscovy drakes are too heavy to fly but the ducks, unlike other domestic breeds, are perfectly capable of flying short distances and perching. You can confine them to your backyard either by keeping them in a fully enclosed pen or by clipping the flight feathers on one wing.

Impact on the garden Muscovies are not noticeably enthusiastic about searching for snails but are quite proficient at snapping up insects that come near them.

Muscovies will graze the lawn a little and will sample succulent greens, but two or three ducks in the average backyard are unlikely to cause much damage. Small barriers can be used to protect plants if necessary.

Laying ability A muscovy duck will lay a clutch of 15-18 eggs, one per day, and then sit, if allowed. Otherwise she will take a break and lay another clutch. The eggs are about 1½ times the size of hen's eggs and are equally edible—duck eggs are said to make perfect pavlovas.

Muscovies make excellent mothers if allowed to hatch their eggs. Muscovy eggs take five weeks to hatch whereas other ducks' eggs take four.

Health Muscovies have very few ailments and are hardier than other domestic duck breeds.

Care must be taken to provide ducklings with water troughs shallow enough to allow them to climb out easily—otherwise they will lose strength and drown. Ducklings must also be warm and dry before nightfall or in very cold weather, as they have limited ability to restore lost body heat.

Housing Predators such as foxes and dogs will often make a meal of a duck, so some form of protective fencing or night-time housing is essential. If the ducks muddy their pen it may be necessary to place the drinker on wire over a shallow pit.

Appearance Muscovies are easily distinguished from other breeds by their faces which are devoid of feathers, bright red, fleshy and carunculated (lumpy). The male, when alarmed, excited or angry, will erect the feathers on the top of his head and appear quite leery and wicked.

Male muscovies are considerably larger than females. Large males weigh as much as 8kg (17½lb) and females approximately half as much.

Colours Muscovies come in white, black and white, blue (a light grey colour) and white, and bronze and white. A fawn and white colour also occurs but is much less common.

Feeding Ducks should have access to a high quality, well balanced feed, specifically formulated for ducks. Their nutrient requirements differ significantly from those of chickens. Duck feed is available from produce stores. Muscovies will cost about 50¢ a week per bird to feed.

Kitchen scraps and grass clippings should also be included in the diet. Drinking water should be cool and clean—the ducks will quickly muddy their water and, if uncleaned, it can be a source of infection.

Muscovies cost $5-$50 for mature birds; ducklings are $2.

For further information

Contact the Royal Agricultural Society in your state for the names of breeders who exhibited birds in recent shows.

RED FACTOR CANARY

The modern Red Factor Canary was just a fantasy until about 30 years ago. The clear red bird of today is the spectacular result of very sophisticated breeding techniques.

Initially canary breeders attempted to produce an orange or red bird by crossing the canary with various species of finch. The end result was inevitably a sterile cross. But they found that when they crossed the canary with a Red Siskin, a red and black bird of the finch family and a close relative of the canary, some of the offspring were fertile. From that point on it was a process of refinement; mating the clearest of the birds with the least black year after year, until the black markings finally disappeared.

Popularity Ten years ago, red factor canaries were extremely popular. Since then, their popularity has waned a little, the Border Fancy probably being the most popular

ROAD TEST

on the show bench at present, but the red factor is still a frequent choice for pet owners.

General appearance Red factor canaries are slightly smaller than other exhibition canary types, such as Border Fancy or Norwich. Many people regard red factor canaries as being much prettier than the yellows.

Colourfeeding The red colour is not entirely inherited, but the true red can only be achieved in birds which have the red factor. An intensifier, Canthaxanthin, is used to intensify the colour. Feeding the colour intensifier to a yellow–brown canary that does not have the red factor results in an orange or burnt orange bird.

If you buy a red factor canary and don't colourfeed it, it will lose its red plumage at the annual moult time— around December. The new feathers will be peachy apricot in colour.

It is important to note that you colourfeed your canary only when it is moulting. Start in late August to early September, and continue through to March; this is when the feathers are forming and the colour is determined. Exhibitors usually keep their birds on a weak solution through the show season, in case the bird drops a feather, which could grow back uncoloured.

Before commercial preparations were available, canary breeders fed their birds yellow–red vegetables such as red peppers or carrots to achieve the colours. Some birds were fed carrot juice and grated carrot almost exclusively to intensify the colour.

New colour canaries From the development of the red factor canary has come a whole range of new mutations which are referred to as 'New Colour' canaries. The group as a whole therefore now covers quite a range of colour variations.

Red Factor Lipochromes These are probably the most readily recognised of the breed. They are bright red and apricot.

Red Factor Melanins These are the dark red-bronze and red-cinnamon birds.

Red Agates and Isabels (dilutes) These are similar to the Red Factor Melanins but are basically a diluted version— that is, where a red-bronze has black striations, a red agate has grey striations.

Ino Inos can be red, silver or gold with brown markings. The markings form a beaten copper effect over the bird's wings and mantle. All Inos have a bright ruby eye.

Satinette This is a similar type of bird to the Ino, but its markings are in the form of striations. Again, the bird can be red, silver or gold. The Satinette also has a red eye.

Opal A most attractive bird with dark silvery-grey markings. There are red, silver or gold varieties. The Opal factor removes all traces of brown from the bird.

Pastel Again, available in red, silver or gold. Exhibits a suffusion of brown over the bird, giving a true pastel effect. The feather quality of these birds is outstanding.

Ivory This mutation is the only factor which changes the lipochrome colouring of the bird (the above-mentioned mutations affect the melanin colouring). The ivory factor changes red to soft rose and yellow to ivory or pale lemon.

Temperament The birds can be extremely aggressive towards each other, possibly because of the Siskin influence in their development. They are generally more active than the larger canaries. The males particularly, can brawl in the aviary when the breeding season nears.

Canaries are not gregarious, and you should be careful if choosing two. Two males will fight, and while a male and female rarely fight, they will effectively ignore each other except during the mating season.

Canaries don't interact with people in the way that budgerigars do.

Suitability as a household pet Apart from their lack of interaction with their owners, most of the character-istics of these birds make them ideal housepets. They are not expensive to buy or maintain; they are not demanding; they are happy if left on their own; they entertain with their whistling (see below). As they do not enjoy being handled, they are not recommended as pets for young children.

Whistling If you are buying only one bird, make sure you get a male; telling males and females apart can be difficult, so you should wait until you hear the canary in action before purchasing. Canaries have their own song, but it is possible to teach them a series of notes (they have been known to imitate owners who whistle up their dogs). The risk is, however, that in learning these new notes, they may forget their own song.

Care Canaries need space to jump around in. A cage with minimum dimensions of 45×30×30cm (18×12×12″) is recommended for one bird. You will need a larger cage if you have more than one bird.

Dry shell grit should be on the floor of the cage and its location should be draught-free. A cover for the birdcage is also an essential requirement for a bedtime routine.

Feeding A quality seed mix from a good pet produce store is recommended. Cuttlefish should be given as well as greens, such as endive, chicory, silverbeet, and so on. (Remember that small amounts of sprayed chemicals would be enough to adversely affect a canary, so wash vegetables carefully.) Wheatgerm, breadcrumbs and sprouts can also be offered.

Cost   Red factor canaries cost $25–$30, although a top exhibition bird could sell for more than $40. You can expect the birds to live for an average of five years. A non-removable breeder's ring is placed on birds at 7–8 days; it identifies the canary's ancestry and breeder.

Health problems   Proper care is the key to good health. For example, stale food can be a killer, as bacteria can build up in it, and a bird with a bacterial infection is very difficult to deal with. It should be kept out of draughts, which seem to lower birds' resistance to infection.

The bird should be covered at the same time each evening, as a confused routine causes disruption and stress. Light affects the bird's metabolism.

For further information

Mr W.J. Van Hoboken
(President)
Australian New Colour Canary Research Association and
Canary Breeders' Association of Australia Inc
96A Plymouth Road
Ringwood VIC 3134
Telephone (03) 876 3637

CHAPTER 6
Bird Care

BEAK AND FEATHER DISEASE OF PARROTS

In Australia, and probably other countries, Psittacine Beak and Feather Disease (PBFD) and French Moult in budgerigars are the same disease. PBFD is caused by an infectious virus. It is not a new disease—it has been around for several decades, at least.

The PBFD virus causes death of the epidermal cells of the feathers and beak, which upsets the normal pattern of growth of these structures, and causes reduced function of the immune system.

Cockatoos commonly suffer severe feather loss, beak rot and impaired immunity, so that they are likely to contract other infections. The smaller parrots' beaks are rarely affected; commonly they lose only flight feathers and don't seem to be affected by immunosuppression. Mildly affected parrots may recover clinically but they could still transmit the virus to other birds.

Many species of Australasian psittacine birds and several species of African and South American psittacines are known to be susceptible, and there is no reason to believe that all species aren't likely to contract the virus.

The disease is common in captive cockatoos of the genus Cacatua including the sulphur-crested cockatoo, galah, pink cockatoo, little corella, long-billed corella, lesser sulphur-crested cockatoo, triton cockatoo, and Goffin's cockatoo. PBFD occurs uncommonly in the cockatiel and has been diagnosed in the gang-gang cockatoo. The disease is also extremely common in aviary collections of budgerigars and lovebirds.

PBFD occurs in wild psittacine birds in Australia, including reports of 10–20% in sulphur-crested cockatoos in south-eastern Australia. PBFD also occurs in wild galahs and little corellas, rainbow lorikeets, king parrots, 28 varieties of parrots and in red-capped parrots.

This disease also limits the success of breeding of endangered species, such as the orange-bellied parrot, in captivity . A breeding programme in Tasmania has been very successful but now that PBFD has appeared in the captive birds they won't be returned to the wild as originally intended, for fear of wiping out what is left of the wild population.

PBFD is probably transmitted orally, but carriage of the virus on the eggshell is a distinct possibility. In aviaries the incidence of disease increases as the breeding season progresses and the same nests are used for successive clutches of eggs—this appears to be because the amount of virus, which is shed in faeces and feather dander, builds up in the nest. The younger a bird is when exposed to the virus, the greater is the chance that it will develop the disease and the more severe the problem is likely to be; as birds get older they become more resistant. Species in the genus Cacatua are more likely to develop severe disease than other genera of psittacine birds.

The prognosis for recovery of feather growth is poor. Some birds live for long periods with poor feathering, whereas others suddenly or progressively lose their appetite, become depressed, lose weight and die. In some cases degeneration of the beak impairs eating and leads to starvation.

There is no treatment or vaccine available for the control of PBFD. The current recommendation to vets is that infected birds be destroyed, but in the case of pet birds this can be avoided until the bird begins to experience obvious pain and discomfort. In aviaries some control is achieved by strict attention to hygiene (cleaning and disinfecting nests between clutches) and culling affected birds. When purchasing a bird, pay particular attention to the plumage, and have any feather abnormalities, such as a dirty or greasy appearance, examined by a veterinarian to obtain an accurate diagnosis.

Research into this disease is being conducted in Western Australia, and if the work is to continue donations will be required. You can send your donation to Beak and Feather Disease Research, School of Veterinary Studies, Murdoch University, Murdoch, WA 6150. Telephone (09) 332 2211.

BIRD FEEDER

The Bird Haven bird feeder is a wooden bird house with open sides. It may be either suspended from a chain or fixed to the top of a freestanding pole. The base of the Bird Haven is approximately 50×33cm (20×13″) and is shaped as a tray to hold birdseed or other sorts of bird food, which is protected from the weather by the overhanging roof.

The feeder comes in kit form and must be assembled by the purchaser. The optional pole is 2m (6½′) long. All bolts are plated so that they won't rust. There are two versions available—a green-painted pine model with a western red cedar roof, and one made completely of western red cedar. If not varnished or given a clear finish, the cedar parts will age to grey.

Prices

Item	Price	Postage VIC, TAS, SA, NSW	Postage WA, NT, QLD
Bird Haven Kit (western red cedar)	$42.45	$8.50	$10.50
Bird Haven Kit (green pine with western red cedar roof)	$37.45	$8.50	$10.50
Pole	$12.50	$3.50	$3.50

Bird Haven bird feeders are available from:

Bush Haven Pet Products
467 Broadgully Road
(PO Box 8)
Diamond Creek VIC 3089
Telephone (03) 718 1368

BUDGERIGAR BEAKS

A reasonably common problem for caged budgerigars is an undershot or overshot beak. The bottom part of the beak normally fits inside the upper part, which overlaps it by 3mm. In the case of an overgrown beak one part grows too long—either the top beak extends well over the bottom one or the bottom beak grows out over the top beak. Surprisingly, the bird can still eat, which is why many cases remain untreated for some time.

The problem results from an infection around the beak caused by a little parasitic mite. Veterinarians know this mite as *Cnemidocoptes pilae*, but most people call it fungus or scaly face.

Before treating the parasite the overgrown beak must be trimmed back so that the two beaks fit together properly. Elaborate equipment is not required, just use ordinary clippers for human nails. But take care, the beak tissue is actual living tissue. There is a major blood vessel in the upper beak and a lot of little ones in the bottom beak so just trim back very carefully, taking a small piece at a time. You may need to trim the beak back again every 10–14 days to keep the overgrowth under control.

Now you can turn your attention to treating the little parasite, which is living in tiny burrows it has dug around the beak. Smear a little liquid paraffin around the whole area, using a cotton bud. This will suffocate the parasites in their holes. Use a little on the bird's feet as well, because the parasite also attacks the feet, and a touch on the vent is also advisable. You will have to repeat the treatment once a week for a month to eliminate the problem.

It is a good idea to add a little liquid calcium to the drinking water—Calcium Sandoz Syrup at the rate of about one part in a hundred is ideal. A crystal of gelatine added to the drinking water is also beneficial. These additives will help to strengthen the bird's beak as it regrows.

An overgrown beak indicates the bird is in a generally run-down condition, usually caused by incorrect diet and unsatisfactory environment. To rectify this, expose the bird to sunshine for a minimum of an hour or two every day. This will facilitate vitamin D production. Give the bird a plentiful supply of cuttlefish bone and shellgrit as well as daily treats of one or more of these items: apple, carrot, raw silver beet, corn, wintergrass, summergrass, chickweed or any sprouting or seeding varieties of seed. Persist if the bird fails to eat these at first.

Ensure that at least one of the perches is made from a fresh gum tree branch approximately 1cm (³/₈″) in diameter. The branch should ideally be irregular in diameter, forked, and replaced every week or two. It will provide something to chew on to exercise and shape the beak, as well as foot exercise.

CLIPPING BIRDS' WINGS

If you need to clip your bird's wings to stop it flying away from your yard, it is essential to clip only the correct feathers. *Do not cut all the wing feathers*—you only need to unbalance the wings so that the bird can still fly safely (for example, from a height to the ground), but not a long distance.

A bird's feathers when fully grown are dead and there is no pain for the bird in having them clipped.

Spread out one of the bird's wings and cut off the seven outer primary flight feathers (the first seven large feathers on the wing) at the base. If you are in doubt as to the correct feathers to cut, please take your bird along to the local vet for advice.

COCKATOO SCHOOL

The bird taming policy at Cocka-2000 Cockatoo School in Beverly Hills, New South Wales, is as follows.

'Our skilled staff are well qualified to tame wild or naughty birds.

'The normal procedure is for the owner to bring the bird to the Cockatoo School for taming, and then pick up the bird after taming has been completed. Pick up and delivery by Cocka-2000 can be arranged at a nominal cost to the owner.

'Wild birds require varying amounts of time to tame. The average requirement for a bird from the bush is two weeks. If a wild bird has been in a home for some period of time the taming time may be reduced. Some birds require more than two weeks to tame and some are untameable.

'If we accept a bird in the Cockatoo School we guarantee the taming or there is no charge to the owner.

'The cost to the owner for taming is based on the time required to tame the bird. This cost is $12 per day or $60 per week, which is based upon a five day per week training schedule. The minimum charge for taming a bird is $60.'

Cocka-2000 sells tamed birds for $150 upwards, and also offers a bird care and bird accessories service.

For further information

Richard Hendrickson
Cocka-2000
2c Edgbaston Road
Beverly Hills NSW 2209
Telephone (02) 579 2277

FREE RANGE HOUSE BIRDS

Jim Pike visited a home where the owners love their pet birds so much they give them the run of the house.

The birds shown were:

2 Major Mitchell cockatoos, Major and Maria
1 cockatoo, Sam
1 galah, Buster
3 cockatiels, Mark, Emma and Thomas
2 hybrids (between galah and corella), Moppet and Mister

Also inside, but caged, are Fred and Mother, two canaries that have been retired from the backyard breeding aviaries.

The birds that are allowed to free range still have cages, to which they can retire when they feel the need. They are given plenty of branches to chew on as a means of protecting the furniture from attack.

You should be aware that diseases can be transmitted both ways when you kiss birds. This practice should generally be avoided.

RINGS ON BIRDS

Many birds have rings on their legs for identification, and these can provide a great deal of information about the bird.

If you find a pigeon with a ring on its leg it is probably a racing pigeon. If you ring the Pigeon Fanciers' Union they will be able to put you in contact with the person who lost the bird. Very often pigeons are caught in big storms and lose their way.

The ring on the pigeon's leg will have letters on it, for example, 'HD', which probably stands for Hills District, where the bird comes from; '1987', which indicates that the bird was bred in that season; and a ring number, for example, '1203'. The breeder has a record of the birth and the parents of the particular bird.

If you find a budgerigar with a ring on its leg, you should ring Barry Ryan of the Budgerigar Society (02) 671 5380. He'll be able to trace the bird for you.

Budgerigars and canaries run into problems with the rings on their legs, due mainly to a buildup of scale underneath the ring. You can help by lubricating the area under the ring with liquid paraffin so that the ring can move freely. In some circumstances the leg becomes very swollen as a result of having been bitten or injured, and the ring needs to be removed. This is something a vet should do.

The big problem is keeping the leg still while the ring is cut off. Birds' legs, particularly canaries', are like little matches and it is easy to break one while trying to cut through the band. A vet will give the bird an anaesthetic to avoid this happening.

SELF-MUTILATION IN BIRDS

Budgerigars, South African lovebirds and galahs can sometimes pull the feathers off their lower abdomen area and also off their wings, leaving bald patches.

You will need to see your local vet if this problem occurs. The vet will treat the condition, probably using hormone therapy—one injection a month for 3-4 months. This injection is given in the breast.

A barrier should be put on the bird to stop it plucking the area while it is healing. Cut a circle of stiff paper and staple it around the neck. The bird will still be able to eat and drink.

CHAPTER 7
Beekeeping

The easiest way to start keeping bees as a backyard hobby is to join a beekeepers' association. In these associations the more experienced beekeepers will show beginners how to set up and maintain a hive, and provide advice and assistance on all aspects of this interesting hobby.

All hives must be registered with the Department of Agriculture or Primary Industries in each state. Small registration fees must be paid every one to three years. Registration procedures enable these government departments to keep a check on hives for disease control purposes.

ROAD TEST

Beginners can start either by purchasing an operating hive complete with bees for about $70–$80, or by purchasing a brand new empty hive with frames and wax foundation (this needs to be assembled and painted) for about $80 and stocking it with a nucleus hive of bees for $35–$45. Operating hives are considerably cheaper but should be purchased only from a reputable breeder, as they do carry a risk that the bees may be diseased or have unfavourable temperaments resulting from crossbreeding with feral male bees (drones). The queen bee should be replaced every one to two years—queens cost about $8 each—but if properly maintained, the hive can continue indefinitely.

Other basic equipment includes a smoker (smoke keeps the bees quiet during inspection of the hive), a hive tool to open the hive, and some protective clothing (a veil and gloves). These items will cost approximately $95. Depending on the season, husbandry, and a number of other variable factors, each hive can be expected to produce about 18kg (40lb) honey per year, although it is possible to produce 45kg (100lb) or more.

Bees require a nectar source, and urban areas usually abound with a wide range of flowers. A tub of damp sand near the hive will provide the bees with a suitable water source and keep them away from neighbours' pools and taps.

Complaints from neighbours are one of the biggest problems encountered with beekeeping. Therefore, if the hobby is to be enjoyed it is best to warn neighbours of your intentions (and maybe offer them a jar of honey after the harvest) and try to deal with their concerns before you start. Bees fly over obstacles such as backyard fences and shrubs, so in urban areas they are usually flying over, rather than through, other people's gardens. Obstacles can be used to alter the flight path of the bees if necessary. Hives should be placed in a warm sunny position and *not* close to houses or paths.

Children and bees are compatible, but if a member of the family is allergic to bee stings, it is unwise to expose them to increased risks. If this is the case, you may be able to keep your hives in the gardens of friends. Bee stings usually claim one or two lives each year.

Beekeepers who wear protective clothing and disturb their hives only when necessary are rarely stung by their bees. Different strains of bees vary in temperament—this should be taken into consideration when the colony is purchased. When working near the bees or opening the hive, move quietly and calmly, and don't wear cosmetics such as perfumes, deodorants, aftershave, and so on, as these may upset and annoy the bees.

The way in which a bee sting is removed can make the difference between minor irritation, and intense pain and severe reaction. Correct removal involves gently scraping the sting out of the skin using a knife or sharp fingernail. Rubbing or squeezing should be avoided as this will distribute the venom more widely and rapidly.

Apart from the initial outlay involved in establishing a hive, beekeeping is an economical hobby. Home-made honey can be produced for one half to two-thirds the price of shop-bought honey.

For further information and the location of your nearest beekeepers' association, contact the editor of *The Australasian Beekeeper*, Mr Bill Winner, Pender Beekeeping Supplies Pty Ltd, Private Mail Bag 19, Maitland, NSW 2320. Telephone (049) 32 7244.

CHAPTER 8
Cavies

Modern cavies originated in Peru, South America. The ancient Incas domesticated the cavy in prehistoric times.

Early Dutch navigators were probably the first to bring cavies or 'guinea pigs' to Europe via their territory of Guiana on the northeast tip of South America. The 'guinea' part of the popular name is probably a mispronunciation of their original port of embarkation.

These little animals are not really pigs at all, even though they are known as 'boars' and 'sows'. They are, in fact, rodents and more closely related to porcupines than anything else.

Their gestation period is more than two months and they bear large, fully furred, *very* quickly active babies, which are suckled for about three weeks—unlike rabbits, which have many tiny, unfurred, blind and helpless babies. Cavies can bear three litters a year (not a good idea, as the sow becomes very run-down). Their litters are not usually large. Since the mother cavy has only two teats, she is kept very busy if she has more than two babies.

Feeding Rabbit or guinea pig pellets should be on offer at all times, in either a well-shaped dish or a heavy container. Seed containers used for cage birds are available in different sizes and make excellent, inexpensive well dishes. *Never* use poultry pellets as they contain meatmeal, which will damage your pet's liver and kill it.

Water should always be available, and gravity feed bottles are useful. These can be placed on the front door of the hutch, on the outside. Use a piece of wire or elastic threaded through the wire to hold the top of the bottle. The drinking tube through the wire will ensure that the bottle stays in position.

Cavies need fresh grass daily. A handful is sufficient, but the more the better, as it supplies their daily vitamin C requirement. Please make sure that no chemicals or fertilisers have been used on the grass you feed to your pet.

Apart from the above, your cavy should be fed twice daily—morning and evening—with any, or a mixture, of the following.

Cabbage (small amounts if it likes it)	Plantain
Cauliflower leaves	Apples, pears, (cores or peelings)
Celery tops or stalks, washed	Lucerne hay or chaff
Carrots, tops and peelings	Pea shells and peas
Lettuce (small amounts)	Banana peels and strips of leaves
Parsley	Watermelon and rockmelon
Beans (runner type)	Cucumber
Sweet corn and husks with silk	Tomatoes
Spinach	Silverbeet
Dandelions	Chicory
Milk thistles (not prickly ones)	Mint (occasional piece)
	Young dock leaves

If he has a good grazing patch all day, it should be adequate to feed him in the evening with other vegetables to balance his diet, and keep him going through the night.

Make sure that there are no toxic weeds in the grass you feed your pet, or in the patch of lawn where it grazes. Such things as oxtails, oleander, rhubarb leaves and many others can kill a cavy within minutes. If in doubt, *don't* feed it the leaves.

Wholemeal bread, dried hard, makes a change in diet, and is good for a cavy's teeth. He can have rolled oats, mixed in with his pellets, or instead of pellets for a day or two, if you run out. He will also appreciate the occasional treat of hulled oats. *Never* feed cavies dry bran; if followed by water (and cavies invariably drink after dry foods) it can be fatal.

Housing A cavy needs strong protection against dogs and cats and even some people. It can easily die of fright even if untouched. If the backyard is secure, with high gates and fences, a cage on the ground is ideal. It can have a detachable run that can be moved around on the grass, and a box for sleeping and shelter, with its base a few inches off the ground for dryness during nasty weather. The box should be light enough to carry into a garage or under cover for additional safety at night.

To keep your pet's hutch dry, line the bottom of the box with contact adhesive paper before putting down newspaper. Alternatively, apply several coats of non-toxic gloss paint. Place straw, hay, shavings or chaff on top of the newspaper and your pet has a soft, clean, comfortable and edible bed. When cleaning, simply pull out the newspaper, and the soiled bedding will slide out with it. Brush any leftover bits and pieces out of the hutch, and reline with paper as before. To overcome any unpleasant odours (which usually develop only when hutches are not cleaned frequently enough, or are too small for the animal's requirements), sprinkle common garden lime before placing newspaper in the hutch.

The soiled bedding makes a marvellous mulch for your garden. When cleaning the hutch, keep the chaff for the compost heap, and bag the newspaper for council rubbish collection.

The cage needs protection from wind, rain and sun. Some winter sun is good for cavies, but they can't take much summer sun. Insulation paper will help reflect the heat away.

Don't keep your cavy in a wire-bottomed hutch. It may appear to keep clean, but this is not really the case. It will also hurt the cavy's tender feet and make it miserable. If it is in an outside run, make sure that your cavy cannot squeeze through what may seem to you to be a tiny space!

Health A cavy is a very clean and healthy animal when cared for. Cavies do not smell, but uneaten greens left in the cage will develop a whiff and should be removed. A cavy exposed to draughts and damp conditions can easily catch cold and develop pneumonia, so keep its bed clean and dry, and ensure that it has protection from rain and night dew.

In summer, a cavy which gets too hot will appreciate a dish of tepid water to paddle, or even to lie in, to cool itself. Since it will probably tip the dish over, it is a good idea to have a heavy clay saucer of the type used for the base of plant pots. A cavy prostrate with heat exhaustion may sometimes be revived, if you are quick enough, if it is placed for a few minutes in a bowl of tepid water. Do not dry it, but let it drip-dry out of the heat.

Occasionally, toenails need clipping—do be careful to cut only the dead nail beyond the vein that can be seen in the claw.

If you notice that the cavy's 'personal pellets' are not pellets but loose motions, cut down on the amount of green food until things improve. This is usually all the treatment needed for diarrhoea. Be sure to store his food pellets and bedding where mice cannot run through them, as these rodents bring lice and infestations to cavies. If you notice any insect nasties such as lice, mites, and so on, use an insect powder or wash designed for cats (*not* dogs).

If your cavy is not well, it will appear huddled and not its usual lively self. Its eyes may be runny, it may sneeze or just look miserable. Put it in a clean box (a cardboard box with high sides will do), clean the hutch out and keep

> *Contrary to popular belief, spiders are not insects. They are arachnids. An insect has 6 legs and a spider has 8.*

ROAD TEST

the cavy in the box, preferably inside, until it is better. It will probably be bouncing again in a day or two. *Never allow penicillin to be used for any illness your pet may suffer, as cavies are allergic to it and it will kill them without exception.*

An only cavy is a lonely cavy. Give him company, cuddles and lots of attention and he will whistle and whicker whenever he hears or sees you. Two sows (females) can live together quite happily, but two boars will be peaceful only if they have been raised together from babyhood, and then only if they never see, hear or smell a sow. Never put adult boars together, as they fight quite dreadfully and can inflict severe injuries on each other and you, if you should get between them during an argument.

For further information

NSW Cavy Club
(Secretary, Karen Parsons)
12 Lawson Avenue
South Camden NSW 2570
Telephone (046) 55 1083

CHAPTER 9
Cows

DEXTER COW

The Dexter breed originated in southern Ireland, apparently through a process of deliberate selection for creating smaller animals. The breed became very popular as a house cow in England in the late 1800s, but numbers declined during the middle part of this century; the breed was in danger of extinction 20 years ago. There has been a recent resurgence of interest in the breed and numbers are gradually increasing again.

Dexters were imported to Australia around the turn of the century but died out in this country before or during the 1920s.

Uses and characteristics The dexter is a hardy and adaptable breed of cow, described as being able to 'scavenge' on poor country and thrive on a miscellaneous diet.

The dexter is a dual purpose breed, that is, suitable for milk and meat production. It needs only about half the food required by large breeds such as the Friesian. The dexter is said to be capable of producing up to 20 litres (about 5 gallons) of milk per day with a high butterfat level (4%). The small joints of the dexter carcase make them ideal for a family deep freeze. Dexter cows make excellent mothers and take readily to the multiple suckling of calves. Some cows have been used to suckle orphaned

lambs and even piglets. Longevity is another characteristic of the breed.

Appearance The dexter is the smallest British cattle breed. There are two forms of these cattle; short-legged and long-legged. The short-legged form results from a dwarfing gene, which is also associated with a deformity. When two short-legged animals are mated together, up to 25% of their progeny are born with a squashed 'bulldog' face, and these have to be destroyed. The deformity does not appear in the progeny of matings where one or both parents are of the long-legged form.

Most dexters reach no more than 1.1m (44″) at the withers although some long-legged animals reach 1.2m (47″).

There are three colours—black, red and dun. Most of the animals in Australia (both pure and from upgrading programmes) are black.

Getting started There are three ways to obtain dexter cattle in Australia:
1 Upgrading from another breed by inseminating cows of other breeds with imported dexter semen. The offspring are then inseminated with dexter semen, and so on, until after four generations the progeny can be classed as purebred dexters.
2 Embryo transfer; which involves implanting imported dexter embryos into cows of other breeds.
3 Importing live animals. By mid-1989 a total of four dexters had been imported to Australia. Two of these have since calved and one has died, leaving a total of five purebred animals in this country.

Regulations While dexters are certainly smaller than other breeds, they are subject to exactly the same council regulations. Council by-laws generally restrict the keeping of cattle to areas which are zoned rural; it is generally not permissible to keep cattle in areas zoned urban or residential. Check with your council before proceeding with plans to keep a dexter.

For further information

The Australasian Dexter Association
(Secretary, Ms Marie Fromholtz)
Royal Showgrounds
Epsom Road
Ascot Vale VIC 3032
Telephone (03) 376 3733

HOUSE COW

The most common dairy cattle breeds in Australia are:
Jersey Cream or tan with black nose. This is the smallest breed—it eats and produces smaller amounts but generally gives the creamiest milk. It is a popular house cow breed.
Guernsey Caramel and white. These are small cows, with

creamy milk. They are not as common as the Jersey but are ideally suited to house cow purposes.

Ayrshire Dark red and white. These cows are of medium size and milk production.

Illawarra Mostly red but often with some white markings. These cows are an Australian breed of medium size and productivity.

Holstein Friesian Black and white. Commonly known as the Friesian, this large cow can be expected to eat more than the other breeds, and is likely to produce far more milk than the average family could possibly need.

Despite these generalisations, excellent house cows can be obtained from any breed (and just as often from crossbred animals) if selected and looked after with care.

Regulations Before you consider buying a cow, check with your local council to see whether you are permitted to keep one on your property. In general, council by-laws decree that cows may not be kept in areas zoned residential, but may be kept in areas zoned rural, as long as they do not represent a nuisance to neighbours (for example, in terms of smell or effluent).

Brucellosis and tuberculosis eradication schemes have been undertaken on a national basis for many years, and these diseases have been all but eliminated from the national dairy herd. However, it is wise to contact your local branch of the Pastures Protection Board as soon as you decide to buy a cow. They can advise you of the status of herds in the area.

According to Dairy Industry Acts, it is illegal to sell or give away milk if you are not registered as a dairy. This means that milk from a house cow may be used only by the owners of the cow. All milk for sale must undergo pasteurisation, but if your cow is free of tuberculosis and brucellosis her untreated milk does not represent a threat to your health.

Selecting a cow Provided the cow can produce milk, the most important criterion for selection is temperament. A dairy cow selected as a house cow needs to have a quiet, calm, obliging temperament. A cow which is aggressive, or nervous and timid is likely to be far more trouble than she is worth.

Approach the cow quietly but firmly from the front and give her a scratch on the head to test her reaction before running your hand along her to the other end. Put one hand on her back so that you can feel if she is going to kick, then run your other hand down over her udder. If there is any evidence of soreness, tenderness or lumps, start looking for another cow or you will be facing an instant vet bill. When assessing the teats, a good rule is that they be at least the length of your own thumb for comfortable milking. The udder should be tight, firm and well suspended above the ground; the risk of infection or injury will be increased if the udder is sagging close to mud, dust or obstacles.

Temperament Apart from the calm and placid characteristics already mentioned, cows tend to be compulsive spectators and they like to have a very close look at things. So, if you try to mend the fence or prune a tree in the paddock you will usually find yourself reaching over or around the cow to work. They generally find grooming irresistible, although their grooming requirements are negligible.

Care In general terms, 0.4ha (1 acre) of well watered permanent pasture on fertile soils will easily support one small cow, if managed with care.

A small shed adjoining the cow bails will keep the cow comfortable and dry in wet or hot weather, and stop her from using and dirtying the cow bails shed.

Plain fencing of three strand barbed wire, tightly strained, is recommended. Many cows will lean over plain wire fences until they sag and fall.

Electric fencing is really worth considering; it can be moved around, one large paddock can be simply subdivided, and cows learn to respect fences. A Power unit will cost about $150, and every 200m (700′) of fencing about $100.

Cows can be tethered, but should be watched until accustomed to it. Use a leather collar and a broad link chain with swivel clips at both ends. It is a good idea to thread the chain through a length of hose for at least one and a half times the cow's length to prevent the cow from catching its feet.

Feeding Correct nutrition is very important and a paddock deep in grass may not necessarily be highly nutritive. It is a good idea to consult your local veterinarian, Department of Agriculture or Primary Industries, or dairy farmer for advice. In general terms a permanent pasture that can be irrigated when necessary will supply most of the cow's food requirements. This can be supplemented with lucerne hay or chaff, which is highly nutritious and supplies necessary roughage. Milk production can be boosted by feeding concentrates such as dairy meal or dairy pellets. Your vet may advise calcium supplements, especially for older cows.

The cost of food per week varies greatly, according to the quality of the pasture, the area available, the number of cows, and so on. A very general estimate is $4-$7 per cow (where most of the cow's needs are met by the pasture).

Health Cows should be wormed, usually every three to six months. It is a good idea to ask your local vet for advice about an annual health routine appropriate for your area. A healthy cow will live for 14 years.

Some plants are toxic to cattle. If in doubt, especially if cows have not been kept on your property before, consult the agronomist at the local Department of Agriculture or Primary Industries—it's a good idea to take samples along.

ROAD TEST

Mating You can take the cow to a nearby bull for mating, but most house cows are artificially inseminated. Your Department of Agriculture or Primary Industries can give you the name of the local technician who will come to your property and artificially inseminate the cow with semen from the bull of your choice.

Breeding and milking Cows normally have one calf at a time. Veterinarians say calving difficulties are one of the major problems with house cows due to such circumstances as cows being put in calf when they are too young or too undernourished, and little cows being mated to bulls of large breeds so they end up trying unsuccessfully to give birth to enormous calves. If a cow has been straining to have a calf for a couple of hours without the birth progressing, it is advisable to seek the advice of a vet or experienced dairy farmer.

Cows do not produce an equal amount of milk all year round. In fact, for about two months they produce no milk at all, so it is possible to go away for a holiday, as long as someone can feed and water your cow for you.

For efficiency, productivity and economy the cow should ideally calve on the same day every year. The gestation period is nine months, so she should conceive three months after she calves. Her milk production will rise to a peak about six to ten weeks after calving and then gradually decline. For the last two months before her new calf is due, milking should cease so that the milk-producing tissue in the udder is allowed to regenerate. The cow also regains body condition in readiness for the start of the next lactation. If the cow is not dried off, she will not produce as well in the subsequent lactation.

Observe strict hygiene at all times when milking. Many cows are quiet enough to milk unrestrained in the paddock, but a covered area makes for greater comfort in all weathers, a sealed floor keeps the dust down, and a restraining head bail means the cow can't walk away halfway through the milking.

Cows are creatures of habit, so follow a regular routine and milk at regular times to get the best response from the cow. Once you have established a routine, each milking will probably take about 15 minutes.

The milking procedure:
Feed the cow and lock her head in the bail, if you have one. Wash the udder with warm, soapy water. Massaging with warm water stimulates milk let-down. Squirt the first milk from each teat onto the ground. It is higher in bacteria and you can see if there are any clots which would indicate an infection. Sit on a stool and hold the bucket between your knees or your feet.

Grasp a teat in each hand. The teat is an open chamber with a narrow canal at each end, so the idea is to clamp the top of the teat between thumb and forefinger and then squeeze the milk out through the bottom of the teat. Then relax the hand to allow the teat to fill again before

repeating the action. If you don't clamp the top, you'll find you squeeze most of the milk back into the udder.

To remove the last of the milk it may be necessary to lubricate the teat with petroleum jelly or milk froth and 'strip' the milk out by running the thumb and forefinger down the teat repeatedly.

Strain the milk, through a piece of cheesecloth placed in a strainer, into a large bowl or saucepan. Place in the refrigerator for 24–48 hours to allow the cream to rise to the top. Skim off the cream with a large spoon and pour the milk into jugs for use.

A good method of productively disposing of excess milk is to rear dairy or beef calves, which can be sold when convenient.

Financial analysis Keeping a cow per annum:	$
Purchase of milking cow $550, over 10 years	55
Artificial insemination	40
Bucket, strainer, cloths, etc. $10, over 2 years	5
Shed, bails $500, over 10 years	50
Feed $6 per week	312
Fencing (electric) $350, over 10 years	35
Dairy products bought when cow is dry	96
(A) Total expenses for one cow for one year	593
(B) Income from one cow for one year	
One calf sold at 6–12 months	200
(C = A–B) NET EXPENSES PER ANNUM FOR KEEPING A COW	$393

Buying dairy products per annum:	$
8 litres milk per week @ 92¢/per litre	383
1kg margarine or butter per week @ $3.00/kg	150
300ml cream per week @ 80¢/300ml	40
(D) NET EXPENSES PER ANNUM FOR BUYING DAIRY PRODUCTS	$573

In highly generalised terms, you will save $180 (D–C) per year if you have a house cow and produce some of your own dairy products instead of buying them. However, this calculation does not include the cost of water for the cow or the cost of your own labour in milking and tending, which can be expected to involve 30 minutes (2 x 15 minutes) per day for 300 days, which equals 150 hours per year.

For further information

An excellent book on all aspects of buying and owning a house cow in Australia is *Keeping a Cow* by Jim Wilson, published by Kangaroo Press, 1983. It is available for $12.95 from most bookstores.

Contact the Royal Agricultural Society in your capital city for breed society contacts, or the local Department of Agriculture or Primary Industries. A local dairy farmer can often be another good source of information.

CHAPTER 10
Donkeys

The correct name for the donkey is *Equus asinus*. A female donkey is called a 'jenny', a male a 'jack', a baby a 'foal' and a desexed male a 'gelding'.

While all donkeys in Australia are regarded as being of the one breed, there are three distinct types.

Australian These donkeys have developed from animals brought to Australia from North Africa and India for use in donkey trains, which carried wool across Australia. They are exactly the same as feral donkeys: typically dun, grey or black with the characteristic dark cross over the withers. They have very long ears, a longer, horsey head, and are 10½–12 hands high.

English There were no pure English or Irish donkeys in Australia until 10 years ago, when enthusiasts began to import jacks. Importation can cost up to $18 000. As a result English and Irish breeders want to keep their bloodlines separate from the common Australian lines. English donkeys have shorter ears and thicker, rounder heads. They are usually 9½–10½ hands high and tend to exhibit broken colours, piebalds and skewbalds. They are the most placid of the three types.

Irish These have the same shape as English donkeys but are smaller still, 8½–9½ hands high. They exhibit all colour types but tend to be solid in colour rather than patterned. They are a lot livelier and spunkier than the English donkeys.

In addition to these three main types *Mammoth* donkeys were once used at sugar mills in Queensland, but there are thought to be none left in this country. They originated in Spain and went from there to the USA. They are said to reach 16 hands. There is much interest in them here, and some enthusiasts are considering trying to import them from the US.

Colours Donkeys come in white, grey (many variations), black-chocolate, roan, dun, tan, chestnut (a rusty colour), brown, piebald and skewbald. All donkeys bear the characteristic dark stripe over the withers, but in some colours it is not very apparent.

There are 1600–2000 donkeys currently registered in Australia. This includes 250–300 English/Irish donkeys, of which 30–40 are pure bred imported jacks.

Temperament Donkeys are highly individual. They are patient and wise, the gentlest and most placid of equines. When a donkey is frightened or confused, its natural instinct is to stand still and look carefully at whatever is frightening it. This trait makes donkeys safer riding animals for children than ponies and horses, which tend to rear or bolt when alarmed. Over the centuries this trait has also caused donkeys to be labelled 'stubborn' but

according to one expert, they would never have become such willing, successful and widely used work animals if they were truly stubborn or reluctant. If forced when afraid, donkeys will resist by refusing to move, and may even squat, sit or lie down flat if not given time to come to terms with what is frightening them.

When feeling threatened by an unfamiliar animal a donkey tends to attack—it runs forward braying, ears back, kicking and biting. Donkeys are especially protective of their young.

Donkeys can learn their names and come when called; they are creatures of habit and like an established routine.

Breeding Jacks can be dangerous, especially to small animals, and should be kept only by studs. Jacks bray almost continuously when without company. They have an amazingly strong breeding instinct and are very hard to contain when they sense a jenny in season.

Jennies can be put in foal between the ages of three and 30 years. They come into season every three weeks for five to seven days. Their gestation period is 12½ months (old timers used to say 'a year and a day') but varies from 11½ to 13½ months. They produce one foal per pregnancy. Twins are very, very rare and the survival of both is even less likely. At birth 99% of cases require no interference. In bad weather new foals seem quite susceptible to pneumonia.

Registration The NSW Donkey Breed Society Ltd opened its stud book in 1985. It is open for all donkeys and includes a section for non-pedigreed pets. A donkey of unknown parentage can be registered as a 1st Generation donkey, its progeny as 2nd Generation, its 'grand' progeny as 3rd Generation, and its 'great-grand' progeny as 4th Generation, or Stud donkeys.

The English Donkey Society of Australia also has a stud book. Their aim is to breed pure English/Irish donkeys by starting with a cross between an Australian donkey and a pure English/Irish jack and thereafter mating each generation back to a pure English/Irish animal. The results can be registered as Half Breds, Three Quarter Breds, and Pure Breds.

Branding provides permanent identification of the animal and is usually necessary when breeding. Consult your Department of Agriculture or Primary Industries for details.

Care Check with your local council to see if you are permitted to keep a horse or donkey in your area.

One acre (about 0.5ha) is really the minimum manageable area. Divide into two paddocks with a strong shelter shed accessible from both paddocks.

Straw bedding is best but must be changed frequently. Sawdust or wood shavings are not suitable because they stick in the donkey's hair (especially when damp) and can cause hair to fall out. Also donkeys will eat sawdust and

ROAD TEST

wood shavings, and if they're from treated wood there is a high risk of poisoning.

The ideal owner of a donkey is patient, understanding, and gentle but firm. A donkey will take advantage of an owner who lacks confidence and most problems with donkeys result from owners' inexperience. Time and patience are required to train donkeys, and immediate results should not be expected. Frequent short sessions (daily for a few weeks) bring best results. Some degree of training is essential so that the animal can be handled with safety and control for basic husbandry tasks (vet work, grooming, and so on).

Health Donkey's hooves must be cleaned weekly and trimmed regularly (about every eight weeks). If kept on wet ground, donkeys are prone to a hoof infection called 'seedy toe'.

Vaccinate against tetanus and strangles (a bacterial disease). Donkeys are vulnerable to internal parasites (red worms, white worms, lungworms, bot fly larvae—drench for control), and external parasites (lice, ticks, fleas and mites—various treatments available).

Donkeys commonly live for 30–40 years. Donkeys living for 50 years have been recorded in England.

Uses Donkeys are traditionally beasts of burden, but they can be used for snigging (pulling an object without wheels along the ground), riding, including jumping (usually only the Australian type), harness work, teaching other animals to lead (usually young show bulls), and as nannies for other stock, for example, young horses. A donkey has a quietening influence. If a donkey comes when called, other animals will follow it.

Donkeys are also used as riding animals for disabled children—they have proved superior to ponies in terms of reliability and capacity to respond to verbal commands.

Feeding Donkeys' natural food is coarse grass. Paddocks must be rotated. Most donkeys (especially working, riding, or pregnant ones) need a daily supplement; primarily hay, with some commercially manufactured horse concentrates. Always put out a mineral salt lick.

Equipment Basic equipment needed to keep a donkey is: a headstall and lead rope *or* a rope halter, a hoof pick, a feed bucket, a source of fresh water, and a grooming brush (a scrubbing brush will do at first).

Costs To buy *Australian* donkeys: Feral, approximately $100. Handled, $200–$300. Educated for harness or riding, $500 or more.
English/Irish donkeys: Foal as pet, $250–$300. Half Bred, $300–$600. Three Quarter Bred, $800–$900. Pure Bred, $1000–$6000.

For further information

Books
Donkey Business: A Guide for Raising and Training Donkeys, by Christine Berry and Jinny Robinson, published by the authors, 1981. Available from the NSW Donkey Breed Society.
Donkey Business Two, published by Christine Berry, Jinny Robinson and Jo-Anne Kokos, $15.99.
To Own a Donkey, by Jenifer Simpson, Angus & Robertson Publishers, 1985, $12.95.
Australian Donkeys, and *Donkeys, Ponies and Mules*, both by Anne Walker, Humphrey & Formula Publishers, 1970s, under $5.00 each.

Societies
NSW Donkey Breed Society Ltd
(President, John Vaughan)
4 Roughley Road
Kenthurst NSW 2154
Telephone (02) 654 1564

(Secretary, Peg Cleary)
Blind Road
Nelson NSW 2175

Donkey Society of Australia
(President)
PO Box 128
Kenilworth QLD 4574
Telephone (071) 46 0127

(Secretary, Bev Dubber)
PO Box 438
Morwell VIC 3840

The English Donkey Society of Australia
(Secretary, Mrs Kerry Wailes)
PO Box 132
Exeter NSW 2579

CHAPTER 11
Fish

GOLDFISH

Buying some goldfish and setting up a tank is an exciting and enjoyable activity for the whole family. But it can also be a distressing and unrewarding disaster if inadequate equipment and the more delicate varieties of goldfish are purchased.

The fish It is important to select a goldfish variety that is appropriate for beginners. In general, goldfish with single tail fins are hardiest and easiest to keep alive. Plain, orange or red goldfish with single tail fins (such as the Comet variety) are probably the hardiest of all, but the speckled or mottled Shubunkins are also quite resilient.

Fish with double tail fins, rounder and more compact bodies, and a wriggling swimming action, (such as the Fantails and Veiltails) are slightly more susceptible to a number of internal complaints than the slimmer, straight-swimming varieties. Keeping fish with double tail fins should preferably be attempted after the ordinary goldfish have been kept successfully for some time.

For the more experienced goldfish keeper, there are several fancy varieties, such as the Lionhead (with a warty crest on its head and no dorsal fin) and the Oranda (similar but with a dorsal fin). Fancy varieties can cost more than $40 each.

The appealing, bubble-eyed, Black Moor goldfish is also a little too delicate for the beginner.

The equipment   The golden rule when purchasing a tank is to buy the biggest one you can afford. A 22 litre (5 gallon) tank is probably the minimum size for successful goldfish keeping—tiny tanks are not at all suitable.

The next purchase should be a pump and a filtering unit, which will circulate the water and enable you to keep more fish in a healthier condition for a longer time. Tubing is needed to connect the pump and filter.

Gravel and weeds will beautify the tank and make it more interesting to look at. It is a popular misconception that the weeds will oxygenate the water—in fact, the air bubbling through the filter system performs that task.

You will need commercially prepared goldfish food and, to prepare the tank water for your fish, you'll need some water purifying liquid.

If you spend a little more money and purchase the right equipment when you begin, you will vastly increase the enjoyment and pleasure of your new hobby.

Goldfish starter kit

	$
Two goldfish	5.00
Tank	35.00
Pump	14.50
Filter	15.00
Tube	.50
Gravel and weeds	8.00
Water purifying liquid	4.00
Food	4.50
TOTAL Approximately	$ 86.50

KOI CARP

Converting a swimming pool to a fish pond can be done by using the existing swimming pool equipment. However, the pool filter needs to be run 24 hours per day to aerate the water and give the fish oxygen, and to keep the water clean so that the fish are easily seen.

Koi Carp can be fed with 'Go Cat', which is very low in

fat. It will float, and this brings the fish to the surface so they can be seen.

It is a good idea to have a special pond for breeding. At breeding time (November) put a female koi carp and two or three males in the special pond. When they spawn over the plants remove these and put them in another pond so that the fish can't eat the eggs.

If you can bring yourself to do it, you can even eat your koi carp—they are perfectly edible and this was one of the original purposes for which they were kept in ancient China and Japan.

Koi carp can't be legally kept in all states of Australia. If in doubt about your own state, please contact your local Fisheries Department.

For further information

Australian Koi Association
829 Punchbowl Road
Punchbowl NSW 2196
Telephone (02) 709 3981

MAKING AN AQUARIUM

Aquarium fish make great indoor pets because they occupy a very small space, don't shed hair on the furniture, and don't need to be let in and out, exercised or trained. You can be certain you'll never have complaints from the neighbours about the noise they make either. Moreover, a well constructed aquarium can be as eyecatching and interesting as any work of art you might hang on the wall.

The following information was written by John West, Aquarium Supervisor at Taronga Zoo in Sydney, New South Wales, and is reprinted with kind permission of the author.

'Today's technology and advanced materials and equipment make it much easier to develop a more elaborate water quality control system. These can include the addition or replacement of the internally based biological filter with a high capacity mechanical, wet/dry biological type filter, chemical filters such as ozone or UV steriliser, protein skimmer and charcoal filters. They all, to varying degrees, help to maintain a stable environment.

'This simple design is a proven water quality control system which, when properly maintained, will provide a healthy environment for keeping aquatic animals in good condition for a long period of time.

Babies having babies—uncoloured juvenile Gouldian Finches may breed within 6 weeks of leaving the nest.

207

Basic equipment

1. An inert container, preferably an all glass or acrylic tank with a capacity in excess of 90 litres (20 gallons). The tank should have a transparent, tight-fitting lid.
2. A sturdy metal or wooden stand. Remember, water weighs approximately 1kg (2¼lb) per litre.
3. Good quality fresh water (let stand in a plastic container overnight before use).
4. A subgravel filter plate with air lift tubes. The plate must be large enough to cover the tank bottom completely.
5. Sufficient river gravel (particle size 1-2mm), enough to cover the subgravel plate to an even depth of 10cm (4").
6. A reliable air compressor/pump to supply enough air to run the required number of air lifts.
7. A reliable external power filter with filter medium (this piece of equipment is optional).
8. An adjustable, thermostatically controlled, submersible heater (for tropical animals only).
9. Air line tubing, gang valve and several air stones/diffusers.
10. Overhead lighting for the tank (fluorescent tube with reflector).
11. A hydrometer and a thermometer.
12. A selection of rocks, plants, etc for decoration and hiding places for animals.
13. A sheet of polystyrene foam, 1.5-2.5cm (½-1") thick, the size of the tank base.

Points to consider

Having obtained the equipment, there are several points to consider before setting up the tank.

* Make absolutely sure that the floor will support the combined weight of the tank, stand, water and accessories.
* Choose a position for the tank which is frequented by people. This will ensure that the fish do not hide each time someone enters the area.
* Keep the tank away from direct draughts.
* Do not allow fats or oils to enter the tank in any way. Keep it away from the kitchen areas.
* Do not position the tank in areas which might be sprayed by insecticides or near overhanging cupboards or shelves containing insecticides, etc.
* If possible, place the tank near a window to gain some indirect sunlight.

Setting up the tank

1. Clean the tank with fresh water and check for leaks.
2. Place the sheet of polystyrene foam between the tank and the stand. This will even out any roughness and provide a cushion for the tank.
3. Ensure the tank is level on the stand before filling.
4. Assemble the subgravel plate and airlifts and place it into the tank. Make sure the entire bottom of the tank is covered by the plate. A subgravel plate must allow water to pass through it via holes or saw cuts in the plate. The plate must be off the bottom of the tank by at least 8-10mm (³/₈"). This can be done by placing several blocks under the plate. Airlift tubes can be any PVC pipe greater than 2.5cm (1") in diameter and cut to the level of the water level in the tank. For large tanks the airlifts should be at least 30cm (12") apart.
5. Wash the river gravel thoroughly and place it evenly over the subgravel plate to a depth of 10cm (4").
6. If an external power filter is to be added, do so at this point (as per manufacturer's instructions).
7. Place the air compressor/pump in a suitable position, away from areas which might contaminate the air (carpet spray, insecticide sprays, household cleaners, smoke, etc).
8. Cut the air line to suit, and place the air stones on the ends which go to the bottom of the airlifts. If an air stone lifts during the operation add a small piece of lead weight near the air stone to keep it down (paint the lead piece with nail varnish). Alternatively, silicone the air tubing to the back wall of the tank to stop it moving.
9. Hook up all airlift tubes to the gang valve and from the valve to the air compressor.
10. Add the water to the tank to a level approximately 10cm (4") from the required level or to the top of the airlifts.
11. Start the air compressor/pump and external power filter (if fitted). Adjust the air to give a medium size air flow from the airlifts. Too strong or too weak an air flow will result in inefficient operation of the subgravel filter.
12. If tropical species are to be kept, the heater should be placed in the tank and turned on.
13. Add rocks, decor and plants to give plenty of secure hiding places for the new arrivals.
14. Allow the system to operate for 24 hours to attain physical equilibrium.

Introduce a few hardy fish to the aquarium to ensure they suffer no adverse affects before adding more expensive or sensitive fish.'

Aquarium plants

When choosing plants for your aquarium, there is no need to limit yourself to the range available at the aquarium store, and thereby find yourself with an aquarium virtually identical to those of all your neighbours. You can create a theme for your aquarium, such as a reedy creek bed, and choose plants and fish that match the theme.

Unusual plant sources to be considered are the local creek and the local nursery. If you do take any plants out of a local waterway, you must be very careful not to damage the environment. While you should be able to find some interesting plants in the local creek, it should be remembered that these may last only three to six months in your aquarium. You will then need to replace them when you clean out the aquarium.

From the nursery you can make a selection from the water-based plants available (such as dwarf papyrus). Whether you buy a plant at the nursery or dig it up from a waterway, it is critically important that both stems and roots be thoroughly washed of any soil or other debris before the plant is positioned in the aquarium gravel.

These unusual plants—especially those which grow above the water level—will need quite a strong light for healthy growth. You may need to suspend a light from the ceiling so that the plant parts above water level are not in shadow.

MARINE FISH

Most marine fish sold in Australia come from the Great Barrier Reef, although a few are imported from Hawaii and Indonesia. It has only been in the past 15 years or so that tanks and filtration systems enabling the keeping of marine fish have been developed.

Tank Allow about 120cm² of water surface area for every 1cm of fish body length (1 sq ft of water for every 3″ of fish). Marine fish shouldn't be kept in any tank measuring less than 900 x 300 x 380mm (36 x 12 x 15″), and holding about 104 litres (23 gallons) of water when set up.

Tanks with painted metal frames and putty-glazed panels are unsuitable for marine fish. The corrosive salt water will attack the metal and putty and release toxic materials into the water. Silicone-sealed, bonded all-glass tanks are eminently suitable for use as saltwater aquariums, as they are impervious to saltwater damage.

Take care to choose a location which can support the weight of the aquarium when it is filled with water. A tank of 900mm (36″) will weigh at least 150kg (330lb) when fully furnished. A firm, level support is essential for all aquariums.

Light and heat The tank needs to be kept at a constant 24°C (75°F). A good heater and thermometer are essential. Most people use fluorescent tubes but high-tech globes are available for specialist uses. The size of the water heater will depend on the size of the tank. It must be almost fully submerged. The aerators operate the undergravel filters as well as providing oxygen to undergravel bacteria, which act as the biological filter.

Filtration It is critical that the marine aquarium water is kept in top condition, and that the harmful effects of the fishes' waste products (visible and invisible) are reduced to a minimum. Water conditions are so critical that filtration *must* be used.

Two types of filtration are used in marine aquariums: power or mechanical filtration, and biological filtration. When using power filters pumps are used to pump water through a medium to strain out impurities. Biological filters use living organisms to cleanse the water: the bacteria live in shellgrit on the base of tank.

Water Most aquariums sell seawater or synthetic seawater mixes. Natural seawater has too much potential for pollution and impurities, which can kill your fish. If mixing synthetic salts, don't use a metal container.

Water may need to be changed in parts, *not all at once,* usually about 25–33% every month or so. Ensure the replacement water is of similar salinity and temperature to the original. You will need a hydrometer to test salinity, a nitrite test to check that the bacterial action is correct, and a pH tester to determine whether the water is too acid or alkaline.

What to keep It is advisable to keep only one species, as most fish are territorial and in the confines of a small tank it is difficult for a fish to swim away or hide if threatened. The most commonly kept marine fish are clowns and damsel fish. They are relatively hardy and cheap. You can also keep a range of invertebrates including crabs, marine snails, clams, sponges, anemones and even octopus. Octopus tend to be rather difficult to keep, so it's best to start with an easier marine creature.

Clown fish will cost $10 or more, damsels about $5, large lionfish $70, corals from $25. Seahorses cost approximately $12. The prices vary enormously depending on the fish, its size, its rarity and the difficulty in keeping it.

Clown fish will live about 4–10 years. Anemones ($10–$20) have been known to live for 80 years, but 4–10 years is more realistic. Clown fish benefit particularly from an accompanying anemone, as they live in anemones in their natural habitat.

Feeding Marine fish eat plankton, shrimp and fish flakes. A wide variety of commercially-prepared fish flakes is available from most aquarium shops, as is frozen, dried and even live food. Predatory animals need to be fed live food.

Breeding Fish will not often breed in tanks. The confined area means that there is rarely enough room to establish territorial boundaries. Fish live for 3-10 years.

Diseases Parasites tend to be the major problem facing marine fish, mostly due, say aquarium-owners, to poor maintenance. Commercial treatments are available from aquarium shops, but first check if water balances, temperature, nitrite and pH are correct. Blistering, growths and loss of balance need closer attention.

For further information

A Fishkeeper's Guide to Marine Fishes, by Dick Mills, Salamander Books Ltd. Approximately $17.
Practical Encyclopedia of the Marine Aquarium, by Dick Mills, Salamander Books Ltd. Approximately $49.95.
Keeping Marine Fish, by Graham Lundegaard, Blandford Press. Approximately $15.

CHAPTER 12
Horses and Ponies

ARABIAN HORSE

The following article is reproduced courtesy of Val Males of Ralvon Arab Stud.

'Fact and fantasy have become so intermingled in the many writings about the Arabian that it is almost impossible to give an accurate account of its origin. Suffice it to say that the Arabian is one of the oldest, purest and supposedly most beautiful breeds of horses in existence. It is recognised worldwide for its contribution to almost every other light breed of horse. Throughout its known history of over four thousand years, the Arabian has always been renowned for the ability to pass on its soundness of wind and limb, as well as its ability to survive and breed under all conditions in any country.

'The Arabian has always been an extremely popular working horse. Tales of his inherent capacity for incredible endurance and thriftiness have been passed from generation to generation through the centuries.

'Thriving under modern conditions of good care and attention, the Arabian serves mankind in a doglike manner, that is, his superior intelligence, docile disposition and eagerness to please make him the ideal choice in such diverse specialist fields as endurance riding, trail riding, dressage and cutting competitions. The same horse may be called upon to be a working horse, a show or pleasure horse and a child's pony club mount. Its proud bearing, curvaceous form and unique 'floating' action have led to the Arabian being registered as the ultimate in horseflesh.

Derivatives of the Arabian
The Anglo Arabian

'The Anglo Arabian should combine the best qualities of the Arabian and the thoroughbred (racehorse). Generally speaking, these horses are larger than the average purebred Arabian and more placid than the thoroughbred.

'The Anglo Arabian is derived from pure Arabian and pure thoroughbred blood exclusively. Although Anglo Arabians may carry a combination of Arabian and thoroughbred blood in many different proportions, the original sources must be from the pure Arabian and the stud book thoroughbred. Many people think that because a thoroughbred is registered as a racehorse, (for example with the Australian Jockey Club), it is automatically included in a stud book for thoroughbreds. This is not necessarily so, and careful investigation should be undertaken before using any thoroughbred for breeding Anglo Arabians. Provided the thoroughbred is recorded in the stud book and has a page and volume number, it may be used to breed Anglo Arabians.

'For many hundreds of years, different countries have produced Anglo Arabians from various combinations of matings between Arabian and thoroughbred horses, particularly for purposes where speed and endurance have been requirements. Recent research has revealed that a very high proportion of early Australian horses, known as 'Whalers', which were exported as war remounts, were in fact Anglo Arabians, and even under today's requirements many would have been eligible for registration as such.

'Because of the stringent requirements for registration and some natural reluctance for owners to mate their best Arabian mares with thoroughbred stallions and vice versa, registered Anglo Arabians have always been bred in relatively small numbers. Despite this, owners of Anglo Arabians tend to covet these horses because of their inherent ability to excel under the stress of the most difficult and exacting competition.

The Arabian Pony

'The Arabian Pony Register was started recently when the Arabian Horse Society of Australia Limited recognised the need for a special register for horses that are the result of a cross or subsequent recrossings between pure Arabians and Australian Stud Book Ponies (or other such ponies recognised by the Australian Pony Stud Book Society for inclusion in its Stud Book). Prior to the formation of the Arabian Horse Society of Australia Limited, and during the formative years of the Australian Pony Stud Book Society, horses of this cross were often registered as Australian Ponies. When pony numbers grew and a definite type of Australian pony evolved, the Australian Pony Stud Book was closed to the Arabian crossed with the pony. This was understandable and a necessary part of growth. Although these horses were technically part-bred Arabians and were later able to be registered as such, they were, because of their smaller size, often outclassed and discriminated against in 'open' competition with other part-bred Arabians.

'The Arabian pony offers a great deal as a small horse that can safely be used for a young child, but which is not so small as to be quickly outgrown. The addition of Arabian blood generally increased the length of shoulder, added lightness of forehead and thus created a small riding horse rather than a pony—in type rather than height, that is.

'Apart from their relative sizes, both the Arabian and the pony have many similar points in their standards of excellence and so are very compatible. This combination of breeds has brought about a lovely little horse, which brings a lot of pleasure to its owners.

The Part-bred Arabian

Part-bred Arabians are required to carry a minimum of 50% pure Arabian blood. Though other crossings may be made, the most common mating is between a pure Arabian stallion and an unregistered mare. (Sometimes an Arabian stallion is used with a mare of another breed, or which is registered in another register such as a Palomino or an Australian Stockhorse. This still results in a horse with 50% Arabian blood, which may then be crossed with another of similar breeding, colour or type as required.)

'Part-bred Arabians invariably inherit a large proportion of Arabian characteristics, particularly docility, toughness and the ability to be good 'all-rounders'. As a result of this versatility, the better part-bred Arabians are constantly sought after for use in most fields of open equine competition, sport and pleasure.

'The usually low cost of the part-bred Arabian, when compared to that of the pure Arabian, makes him the obvious choice for those who want to try the widely acclaimed qualities of the Arabian without going in boots and all. Many noted breeders of pure Arabians began to breed them because after first owning a part-bred Arabian, they became eager to buy a pure one.

'Subsequent recrossings of part-bred Arabians with pure Arabians to produce horses with 75% and upwards of pure Arabian blood often result in beautiful individuals that are outwardly indistinguishable from the pure Arabian. Notwithstanding this quality, no upgrading to a pure Arabian is possible. This is one reason why most prominent Arabian breed societies, worldwide, provide a separate register for part-bred Arabians and other Arabian derivatives, which can thus rightly be recorded and preserved as valued ambassadors for the Arabian breed.'

The above article was written by an Arabian horse owner. While, in general, it is quite accurate, many horse experts would not agree with the statements about the breed's temperament. Many Arabian horses are judged to have a less than docile nature, and to be suited for advanced riders only.

HORSE RESCUE

Horse Rescue is a non-profit group operated by Sally and Rex Davies and a handful of volunteers. The organisation receives no funding from any organisation or government.

The purpose of the group is to rescue abandoned and ill-treated horses from people's properties. Other horses come from organisations such as the RSPCA and Animal Welfare, who are unable to place them with caring people, and from individuals who, due to disability or ill health, are unable to care for their horses any longer.

By the time Sally Davies is notified, usually by concerned neighbours, that a horse needs to be rescued, the animal is severely emaciated and often injured or ill. Sally takes the horse to her own property and rehabilitates it at an initial cost of about $50 per week.

Sally Davies believes there is a need for prospective, first-time horse owners to be better informed about the responsibilities involved before buying an animal. Among the worst offenders are people who decide to breed horses to make money from a small piece of land. They start with inferior stock and continue to breed the horses without thorough attention to training and care, and consequently are unable to sell the young stock. The overstocked property becomes a drain on the owner's income, interest in the venture dissipates, and the horses are neglected. Outgrown children's ponies are also common victims of neglect.

The future of the Horse Rescue service is uncertain; the rehabilitation of neglected horses is financially demanding and the group relies solely on donations and the assistance of volunteers.

If you would like to assist in reducing the suffering of animals, please send your donation to:

The Horse Rescue Centre
PO Box 17
Rouse Hill NSW 2153
Telephone (02) 627 1267

The International League for the Protection of Horses
PO Box C616
Clarence Street
NSW 2001
Telephone (02) 360 3646

HORSE TETANUS AND STRANGLES

These are two preventable diseases in horses.

Tetanus The main problem is that there are two types of tetanus injections. One that gives permanent protection; Tetanus vaccination, and the other that gives temporary protection and is called Tetanus antitoxin. The latter is given if the vet is called to an injured horse; it is quick acting, gives short term protection and the horse doesn't react to it at all.

Tetanus vaccination causes the body to react but it gives protection for five years.

Strangles This is caused by a simple bacteria, which affects the glands under the horse's neck, causing huge swellings in these glands. It can actually strangle the horse by putting so much pressure on the larynx that the animal finds it impossible to breathe. Vaccination prevents

ROAD TEST

this and should be performed annually.

Remember, long term protection means vaccination.

MINIATURE PONY

The Australian Miniature Pony Society was formed in 1974. It caters for all miniature ponies in this country, providing pony meets with the society's requirements, which briefly means that the pony is 87cm (34¼") or less in height, and free from hereditary unsoundness.

There are three recognised breeds of miniature ponies: the *Australian Miniature Pony*, a small, well proportioned pony with a gentle and affectionate nature, showing refinement and femininity in mares, and boldness and masculinity in stallions. The pony should look just like a typical pony, in miniature; the *American Miniature Horse*, which is finer and leggier than the Australian miniature pony; the *Fallabella*, originally developed by the Fallabella family in Argentina. This breed is the result of crossing the Shetland Pony with the Argentine Prairie Pony. In recent years the Fallabella has taken on the appearance of a very fine and leggy pony; in some countries it is referred to as a horse, rather than a pony.

It is certain that all miniature breeds owe their real origin to the English Shetland, crossed with one of a large number of either horse or pony breeds.

It is also possible for a Shetland pony to be registered as an Australian miniature pony if it meets with the Society's requirements.

Popularity The breed has been officially established for 14 years and ponies are registered from all states of Australia. There are over 500 adults and twice as many foals at present, and numbers are definitely on the increase. Their popularity is such that demand far exceeds availability.

Registration Foals must have at least one registered Australian miniature pony parent to be eligible for registration. However, ponies over two years of age with unregistered parents may be 'Adult Registered'. The Foundation Stud Book will remain open until at least 1994—after that time only foals with both parents registered will be eligible for registration. In order to register ponies it is necessary to become a member of the Society.

The height measurement is taken from the high point of the withers. The height of the pony must be re-checked at four years of age to ensure continued registration.

Colours All colours are acceptable. Typically they include black, grey, chestnut, bay, red and white pinto, black and white pinto, palomino, grey palomino, buckskin, and taffy.

Temperament Miniature ponies are gentle and generally well behaved as long as they are treated intelligently.

They are ideal for handicapped people: the Society has two members in wheelchairs who own Australian miniature ponies and can manage them quite well.

Uses and abilities The main uses of miniature ponies are as show animals and harness ponies. They are particularly useful for people with small yards, who love horses but cannot keep a full-sized animal. They are hardy, friendly and to many people, irresistible. They are easier to transport and load onto horse floats than larger horses and are also cheaper to feed.

Care The main requirements for keeping a miniature pony are: adequate fencing—they can find even tiny openings—and careful attention to diet. Miniature ponies do not need much concentrated food (such as Stud Mix) and they can get very fat on grass alone. Fatness can lead to problems such as founder.

Problems An undershot or overshot jaw constitutes disqualification from registration. Other problems can include the nervous reactions of larger horses to miniature varieties, and the limited availability of gear to fit miniature ponies.

Cost The cost of a miniature pony varies according to age, sex and quality. A foal or pet will cost about $500–$700, a good mare or stallion $1500–$2000, and a top of the range animal (best 2%) $5000–$7000.

Shows Shows are conducted in every state with classes for Australian miniature ponies. Contact your state delegate or the society secretary for the details of such shows. Frequently the Society's magazine *Small Talk* lists upcoming shows.

The main classes are halter classes, where the judge should be looking for type and conformity to the Standard of Excellence (available from the society). In addition, some shows will have harness classes. Here the judge should be looking for the performance of the animal as a harness pony.

For further information

The best book on the breed is the Society's *Information and Guidelines Booklet*, 1st edition, 1988, ($4.00) available from the Secretary.

Australian Miniature Pony Society
(Secretary, Mrs Margaret Rowe)
30 Hanckel Road
Oakville NSW 2765
Telephone (02) 627 1729

Mr Robert J. Edwards
(Victorian Delegate)
64 English Street
Seville VIC 3139
Telephone (059) 64 3075

Mrs Marion Goodwin
(North Queensland Delegate)
M/S 763 Vanderwolf Road
Pialba QLD 4655
Telephone (071) 28 2409

Mr John McKenzie
(South Queensland Delegate)
Cranbrook
M/S 612 McKenzie Road
Kingaroy QLD 4610
Telephone (071) 64 1157

Mrs Betty Wales
(South Australian Delegate)
'Fair Isle'
Martins Road
Oakbank SA 5243
Telephone (08) 388 4576

Mrs Sue Lane
(Western Australian Delegate)
c/- Betty's Cattery
Welsh Pool Road
Wattlegrove WA 6107
Telephone (09) 453 6416 (BH), (09) 459 4977 (AH)

Mr Kenneth F. Williams
(Tasmanian Delegate)
RSD 1410 West Pine
Penguin TAS 7316
Telephone (004) 37 5287

PONY PURCHASING

Many children have longed to own a pony, but buying a pony is a major undertaking, and an awareness of what sorts of items will be needed and what they're likely to cost is most important.

Where do you go to buy your horse? A good starting place is the local pony club, where you should ask questions, listen carefully and observe keenly. This is where you can learn about differences between breeds and where they can be purchased.

The single most important quality to look for in a pony is a good temperament. You must be able to catch it easily, and remember, that once you put your child on the horse, it is going to teach the child to ride for at least the first year or two. You should be able to pick up the horse's feet in order to clean them, and make sure the animal is not frightened or irritable when handled around the head. The need for a problem-free temperament cannot be overstated.

Have the horse examined by a veterinarian to make sure it is sound. The vet will be able to detect problems, with the legs and hooves, for example, which are unnoticeable to the untrained eye.

A good, sound pony can be expected to cost in excess of $800. But that is only part of the full expense.

Equipment Opt for quality—that is, strength and safety—rather than economy or appearance.

A good quality bridle, bit and reins will cost about $150.

Don't buy a new saddle until you and your child are more experienced. Buy something second-hand, but make sure it is of good quality, with the leather and stitching in good order and no breaks in the saddle tree (the spine and ribs of the saddle). Together with mounts, the saddle is likely to cost $350–$400.

Make sure the saddle has safety stirrups—lifesaving devices. These stirrups have rubber sides which will allow the child's feet to slip out of them should he or she become partly dismounted when riding.

Accessories are never-ending and include such items as head collars, leads, saddle cloths, a grooming kit, hood picks, fly veils, and so on. $80 will not be adequate.

Last but by no means least, buy a crash hat—it could save your child's life. You can buy a new pony any day of the week but children are impossible to replace. An approved crash hat will cost about $50.

Feeding At last you have your child mounted on his or her most precious possession, but that's not the end of the story. The ongoing cost of feeding the animal will need to be considered, but there is no need to buy the most expensive feed available. A mixture of lucerne and oaten chaff, with a little linseed and peanut meal added to it, is perfectly adequate. Leave out the oats in this sort of ration. You're only going riding once or twice a week, not trying to win a Melbourne Cup. Folactin Red is a good reliable vitamin supplement, and Thrive P is a good mineral supplement. Combine this with a biscuit of lucerne hay and the ration is balanced and complete. This will cost about $15 a week for the average pony.

Transport A horse float for transporting the horse will cost about $3500–$4000.

RACEHORSES

You may be able to own a racehorse regardless of the size of your backyard, but the size of your bank balance will be critical; this is one of the most expensive 'pets' you can buy and there is no guarantee that your outlay (which is continuous) will ever be recovered.

Racehorses are commonly bought by trainers at yearling sales and then syndicated to between four and twenty people. This means that if a horse costs $10 000 (which is at the lower end of the price scale) you could buy a share for between $500 to $2500. The horse remains at the

ROAD TEST

trainer's stables in his or her care for the duration of its racing life.

After this initial cost you can expect to pay $20–$60 in weekly costs, which covers feeding, stabling and training. Having a young horse correctly broken in and educated could mean the difference between success and failure.

Money spent on a racehorse probably needs to be regarded as disposable income. If the owner of a horse in training is to break even over a twelve month period, the horse would need to win a Saturday metropolitan race worth at least $13 000 during the year. Unfortunately the reality is that only a tiny proportion of all the horses in training ever goes on to win such a race.

One of the best things about owning a racehorse is that you don't have to be involved in the 5 am starts which must be kept by the trainer, jockey and strapper. Apart from dropping in to the stable from time to time, you will only need to be present on race days, and when the bills arrive!

A racehorse in training is fed a high energy diet (it will eat about $20 worth of food per day), which tends to increase the liveliness of the horse. This characteristic, of course, is ideal for racing, but could result in the odd nip if your horse is feeling excitable when you come to say hello. Retired or out of work racehorses fed normal rations are generally not so highly strung, and often make excellent hacks for pleasure riding, dressage events and other more gentle activities.

The racing life of a horse is four to five years, but if there is an early indication that the horse is not realising its potential (or, worse still, lacks potential altogether) it is best to sell it immediately to avoid incurring the high costs of keeping it.

CHAPTER 13
Insects

ANTS

The social organisation of ants is similar to that of human society, each individual having his own special task.

Ants produce antibiotics as protection against soil fungi. To research ant antibiotics at Macquarie University, ant farms are kept in the laboratory.

Housing While commercial ant farms are fine for small ants, the larger ones require perspex boxes or vegetable containers. Ventilation, moisture and artificial tunnels are required.

For backyard ant keeping, small ants in hollow timber are the easiest to collect; place the log in your container. Children should always check with parents before venturing into ant farming.

Around April most ants tend to swarm, and it is quite easy to catch males and females. Ants as big as Australian

Bull Ants can survive without a queen, but only male ants will hatch out. The males do not work as well as the female workers; they feed and mate. A mated queen ant can lay eggs and be the source of an entire colony.

Ants grasp with their pincers and sting with their tail. When first collected, the bull ants are ferocious, but they calm down after a few months. Some people are allergic to their stings, so the ants need to be treated with respect.

Food Feed ants a mixture of agar powder, multivitamins, honey and eggs.

STICK INSECTS

Stick insects (phasmids) make excellent pets and are almost certainly the best of the entire insect group for keeping in captivity.

They are relatively long lived—up to three or four years—are completely harmless, and possess neither the desire nor the ability to escape. They will happily breed in captivity. The females will drop eggs at random without ever having mated with a male of the species, a phenomenon rare in animals. Even more curiously, these eggs can produce both male and female offspring. Normally, unfertilised females can produce only female offspring.

Your pet stick insects will happily live out their lives on a collection of sticks in a vase, but you can also keep them in a disused fish tank or similar structure.

They require fresh leaves each day from almost any garden plant. Some suitable plants are the Sydney peppermint (*Eucalyptus piperita*), the red bloodwood (*Eucalyptus gummifera*), the Sydney red gum (*Angophora costata*), the tea trees *Leptospermum juniperinum* and *Leptospermum myrtifolium*, and the black wattle (*Callicoma serratifolia*).

Probably any gum tree, tea tree, brush box, turpentine or even she-oaks would suffice.

These insects also appreciate an occasional drink of water from an eye-dropper.

The Regal stick insect from Queensland, at 30cm (11¾"), is the world's longest insect.

CHAPTER 14
Mice

The most common pet mice sold in Australia are pink-eyed whites, piebalds, caramels, golds, skewbalds and occasionally blues (grey).

Mice are cheap (50–70¢ each), and easy to look after as long as a few important points are kept in mind: they need daily food and water; they become smelly if neglected; they can be easy to lose.

Mice need about 100 cubic cm (6 cubic ") of space per

animal. Commercial mouse cages begin at about $13 for a single-storey-plus-treadmill cage for two mice. You can buy mouse toys such as treadmills, play boots and plastic 'houses' for a few dollars, and can make your own mouse cages with plywood, plastic, glass or wire netting. Aquariums are also good mouse cages, but they can be heavy to lift and clean. The cage floor should be covered to a depth of 2.5cm (1″) with absorbent material such as sawdust, wood shavings or kitty litter.

Maintenance Cage hygiene seems to be the key to mouse health and wellbeing. Keep the cage out of direct sunlight and draughts. Draughts can lead to respiratory problems, while overheating will distress the mice.

Clean the cage and replace the floor covering at least every second day. As mice are naturally clean animals—they will use the furthest corner of the cage for their toilet—bedding can be changed less frequently. While cleaning the cage with hot, soapy water and household bleach put mice into a bucket, with a toy to keep them amused. Make sure the cage and bedding are dry before replacing the mice. This is also a good time to check if there are any mass escape plans in progress with holes being gnawed through the plywood.

Feeding Mice must be one of the cheapest animals to feed, costing about 20¢ a week each. They eat almost everything. Mouse cubes, fruit and vegetable scraps and even birdseed are said to be acceptable mouse fodder. It is very important that fresh water is constantly available.

Allied Feeds produce Rat and Mouse Kubes, which they say are suitable for breeding and growing rats and mice. While some pet shop owners have said that chicken pellets are also acceptable, some warn against them, as they contain high concentrations of calcium for eggshell strength. This can exacerbate the mouse's teeth-growing process. Mice, as rodents, have teeth which constantly grow, and overgrowth can be a problem in mice with a diet lacking hard substances.

Problems Male mice are quite aggressive and fights can result in severe cuts and bites. These can sometimes turn into ulcers or abcesses, which should be treated with antiseptics, or even antibiotics.

Diarrhoea can be caused by many diseases, worms, bacteria, infections or simply too much fruit and vegetables in the diet. Cut down on these, clean the cage and disinfect it. If the problem persists, take the mouse and a sample of its droppings to the vet for further diagnosis. If the opposite problem, constipation, occurs, a good dose of fruit and vegies should clear things up.

Head tilt, caused by a middle-ear infection, can be treated with antibiotics.

Mice are prone to respiratory disorders which are often called 'snuffles' by pet shop owners. Sneezing, breathing problems and sniffly noses indicate that the mouse needs to see a vet, or pneumonia can easily develop.

Asthma is fairly common, usually due to an allergy to the floor covering in the cage. Try changing the bedding.

Mouse pox can lead to sudden death after very few symptoms. Sometimes a scabby lump appears on the skin. There is no cure and the disease is highly contagious. It may mean culling the entire herd, but a vet's diagnosis is recommended.

Foot and tail rot starts as a sore and increases in size. It can be controlled if caught early.

If your mouse dribbles and is not old enough to be senile, it could have teeth problems. The mouse can starve to death if these are not cured. Overgrown teeth can be cut or trimmed.

Mice can have fits. Experts recommend culling.

Cannibalism is rife among mice. Adults often eat their young and keeping the babies apart from the adults is advised. Adult mice can also eat other, weaker adults.

Mice can be born without tails, and this is usually an inherited trait. It does not affect the mouse. Mice can also develop gangrene of the tail, which is cured by amputation.

Handling Mice bite when frightened or in self-defence, so correct handling will keep both the owner and the mouse happy. Catch a mouse by the base of its tail then gently lift it onto your palm. If mice are handled regularly, they should overcome their instinctive nervousness of humans. They are inquisitive and excitable animals.

Mice are nocturnal animals so are busiest at night, but they do need several hours of light during which to sleep. They are gregarious and while it's said that a single pet mouse can fret, a long-time breeder says it's more likely the mouse is miserable because of the cold than because of a lack of company. So it appears two mice work best, and herein lies the next big decision: to breed or not to breed.

Breeding If you don't want a mouse population crisis, buy two females. Males get along well as long as there are no females. Fights between males can end in nasty injuries.

Mice have a gestation period of 21 days and can give birth to up to 15 young per litter, although in captivity litters of seven to ten are more likely. Pups are born hairless and blind. Cottonwool makes an ideal nesting material. Pups are weaned at about four weeks, and at

Orchids represent the pinnacle of plant evolution—one seventh of all plant species in the world are orchids.

ROAD TEST

this age they are sexually mature. The fast breeding rate of mice means that the potential for severe overcrowding is very high. Overcrowding brings out the worst in mice—cannibalism is common. Mice live for two to three years.

CHAPTER 15
Native Animals

Although baby native animals are very appealing and it is tempting to keep them, many of them are not suitable as pets at all. As soon as they start to grow out of their baby stage many problems will arise.

Wombats are particularly cute as babies, but as they grow they begin to exhibit aggressive behaviour. In the wild, the mother would simply retaliate by 'beating the stuffing' out of the youngster and sending him packing once his behaviour became unacceptable. In captivity, however, this does not happen and the irritating behaviour will continue. Another difficulty with wombats is that they like to burrow and dig holes in the ground, and they also start chewing holes in doors to try to get inside.

Kangaroos and *wallabies* cause problems too as they grow older. It is important to realise how kangaroo society works and that these animals live in herds. It is the natural instinct of the males, for example, to try to dominate all the other males and to mate with the females. If there are no other kangaroos or wallabies around towards whom these activities can be directed, their natural instincts will be directed towards people.

So, although baby native animals can be really cute and cuddly, as adults they can cause all sorts of problems if people have made pets of them.

The best thing to do is to contact your local National Parks and Wildlife Service and get advice on releasing the baby animals as soon as it is possible to do so with safety. It is, in many instances, illegal to keep native animals so it is important to check with the National Parks and Wildlife Service in your state.

CHAPTER 16
Rabbits

Rabbits make very good pets. There are thirty or more different varieties, and some suggestions are:

Chinchilla giganta grows to 9-10kg (20-22lb). It is one of the biggest varieties available.

Netherlands Dwarfs and *Ruby-eyed White Dwarf* (albino). Dwarfs are not really suitable pets for children under six or seven years of age—they are temperamental and therefore not as easy to handle as the larger ones. These are more suitable for breeders or for shows.

Dwarf Lops have floppy ears that lie vertically down the side of the face. They have a good temperament and these rabbits are most suitable for pets.

Rabbits are easy to look after. They need a well-balanced diet, for example, pellets, endives, carrots, parsley, celery and clover. They also need a well-ventilated area, and a good sized cage so they can move around. They are suitable indoor pets because it is possible to housetrain them. If a small tray with newspaper and a few droppings, or urine impregnated paper, is placed in a confined area they will usually go back to it.

Dwarf rabbits cost $40–$60, good breeding stock a lot more.

Rabbits can be kept in all states (except Queensland, unless you are a magician), although there are restrictions as to the number you may have. It is best to check with the Department of Agriculture or Primary Industries in your own state.

CHAPTER 17
Rats

Mention rats, and most people think of plagues—the Black Death in particular, which was carried by the fleas of the black rat (*Rattus rattus*) and killed up to 25 million people in the 1300s.

Today's fancy rats come from docile strains of the brown rat (*Rattus norvegicus*) and have been domesticated, coloured and selected for use as pets and laboratory animals.

Popularity Rat owners say that rats are misunderstood and their bad reputation is undeserved. In the UK rat and mouse breeding is popular, especially among children.

In Australia rats are becoming popular pets for teenagers, probably for their shock value as much as for any other aspect.

General appearance Most pet rats have a body length of 25-30cm (10-12") and a tail length of 25cm (10"), although length at maturity can vary from 16-50cm (6¼-20"). Weight ranges from 250 to 600g (½-1½lb).

The colours available are: black with a white belly; white (albino); black and white; black hooded/capped; agouti (grey hairs with paler tips); agouti hooded/capped; and gold/caramel.

Temperament Rats are inquisitive, active and agile creatures and they enjoy a run around the room. If just one rat is kept, it can become quite devoted to its owner.

Rats can be alarmed if handled roughly. Fights are rare, but rats don't enjoy the company of other rodent species, and it is best not to keep them with guinea pigs, rabbits, hamsters, and so on. Wild rats are a bad influence, so every effort should be made to prevent contact with your domestic rat.

Pet rats should be allowed outside only under close supervision, because they tend to wander away.

Surprisingly, rats can be compatible with cats and dogs, provided they have been brought up together, and depending on the temperament of the animal concerned.

Useful qualities Being largely nocturnal, rats are great pets for insomniacs. Rats are quick learners, create minimal noise, and are small and easily carried. They make a good, small, cheap pet, costing no more than $5 each.

Training It is possible to train a rat to perch on your shoulder and come to your call. Toilet training is not a problem, as rats will tend to use one corner of their cage consistently. Handy people might enjoy making mazes for the rat to roam in and solve. A food reward is usually given, although some rats can be taught a 'no' command if it is followed by a loud handclap.

Litters Litters usually comprise 6–12 baby rats and birthing problems are extremely rare.

Housing A large bird cage with bars spaced too closely for a rat to squeeze through makes an airy and easy-to-clean rat pen. The minimum space per rat should be 40 x 25 x 25cm (16 x 10 x 10″). Kitty litter makes the best floor covering and the pen should be disinfected twice weekly. Traditional glass tanks are heavy and have inadequate ventilation and exercise facilities.

A heavy water dish will enable the rat to wash its paws as well as take a drink. Uneaten food should be removed after a few hours. Rats like to sleep in mini-hammocks, and a beanie makes a good winter bed. A padded milk carton is a suitable nesting box. Exercise is best catered for by allowing the rat out into the room, although climbing around the perches of the bird cage also provides exercise and stimulation. Exercise wheels are not generally necessary.

Feeding A varied diet is preferable to rat pellets, and the following items can be included: Weet Bix, wholemeal bread, fruit, vegetables, marrow bone, peanut butter, dampened dog food, and bones to gnaw. Fish, and sugary or salty items should be excluded from the diet. Birdseed can be given as a treat. Feeding costs are minimal.

Health Rats are generally healthy and old age—they live for three to five years—is the main cause of death. Hygiene is crucial to their wellbeing. Fleas are not usually a problem, but a cat flea spray can be used if necessary. Rats are easily poisoned, as they cannot vomit. Be careful

when handling rats, they should be supported at both ends and not held by the sensitive tail.

Suitability as a household pet Rats are great for confined areas such as home units. They do not have the strong scent gland possessed by mice. They are very clean and groom constantly, but shed hair only in small quantities.

Ideal owner A rat is a great pet for a flat dweller who keeps late hours and wants a small, cheap, clean and affectionate furry pet. Rats are *not* suitable for small children, as they need to be handled gently and carefully.

CHAPTER 18
Sheep

To shrug yourself into the warmth of a woollen jumper knitted, spun and even *grown* by your own efforts can hardly be surpassed as a rewarding and satisfying experience.

It can be a practical proposition for the average backyarder, but only if he or she is prepared to make the effort required to keep a sheep healthy and happy, and to sacrifice a few shrubs and garden beds to make room for an outdoor, mobile deep-pile carpet.

Colours Sheep come in black, white, grey, and mottled or piebald combinations of all three mixed together. Many sheep with black or grey wool appear brown in colour because the ends of the fleece bleach in the sun. True brown pigmented sheep do exist, but are much less common. These sheep are known as 'moorits' and are distinguished from bleached sheep by a complete absence of any black fibres on the body. They may be champagne, through to dark rust or chocolate, in colour.

As black fleeces contaminate white fleeces commercially, (500g of coloured wool, whether pigmented or stained, can reduce the value of 550 tonnes of wool by as much as 15%) they are frowned upon by the Australian Wool Corporation and are rarely farmed on a large scale. People who keep sheep as pets, however, commonly have an interest in spinning the wool and making garments, so they tend to prefer black, grey and coloured animals for interest and variety.

Care There are two major problems with keeping sheep as pets in urban or semi-rural areas. High rainfall in coastal areas promotes health problems, for example, intestinal worm burdens, footrot or fly strike. Dog attacks are the second problem—dogs would have to be the biggest killer of urban and semi-rural sheep. Sheep instinctively take fright at the sight of dogs and even a small dog can chase a

ROAD TEST

sheep until it drops dead. Sheep should be locked in a dog-proof enclosure at night (a chook pen, for example). Daytime fencing should be of special sheep wire or some other structure sturdy enough to prevent sheep from escaping. Electric fencing is ineffective for sheep because their wool insulates them from the shock.

Rams are potentially dangerous animals, especially if tame; once they've lost their fear of humans they'll always choose to butt you over instead of running away. Rams are definitely not suitable as backyard pets. Wethers (castrated rams), however, are usually very quiet and docile.

Temperament While there is some predictable variation in the temperaments of different breeds, all sheep are for the most part warily friendly. The exercise of hand feeding the animals once or twice a day quickly familiarises them with human contact, and results in the sheep becoming calm and easy to handle.

Health and diet Sheep are subject to a wide variety of health problems and diseases and must undergo an annual programme of vaccinations, drenches, hoof trimming, crutching (cutting wool from around the rear end to prevent fly strike—flies lay their eggs in the putrid wool and the maggots enter the skin and eat the sheep), shearing, and so on.

Sheep without wool on the face and legs are slightly lower maintenance animals than those with wool that can grow across their vision and must be clipped away at intervals.

People with just one or two sheep and an aversion to giving injections and suchlike can arrange to have a vet carry out these activities. New owners would be well advised to ask their vet to prepare an annual programme of activities for them.

Sheep can live on a diet of grass alone but supplementing it with grain, such as crushed oats and bran, and lucerne hay is highly recommended for correct nutrition. Plenty of grass in the paddock is not necessarily a sign that all is well. Sheep will enjoy defoliating and ring-barking garden shrubs and trees, and seem to have a special ability to detect which plant is your favourite and attack that one first. Fine mesh bird wire and other materials can be used to protect the plants.

Sheep can be expected to live for eight to twelve years, but many well-cared-for animals exceed this age.

Shearing Shearers who will shear small numbers of sheep can be located in newspaper advertisements and by questioning other sheep owners. Normally sheep are shorn once a year with electric shears. It is quite possible for any able-bodied person to shear sheep, but it is time-consuming and back-breaking work for the inexperienced, and requires great care to avoid damaging the sheep or the fleece.

Wool products Hand-spinning using a spinning wheel is not difficult to learn. Usually wool from the fleece is combed to remove debris caught in it before it is spun. The spun wool is then washed and made up into the typically rich, earthy, warm and durable garments which are so popular today. Basic spinning wheels cost about $180 but the widest range of models occupies the $200–$300 price range.

Cost A young sheep will cost $20–$100, and the cost of its food per week will be $1–$2.

For further information

Black and Coloured Sheep Breeders Association of NSW (Secretary, Mrs Marlene Taylor)
'Quambatook'
Quandialla NSW 2721
Telephone (063) 47 2160

Black and Coloured Sheep Breeders of Victoria (Secretary, Mrs Marree Vinnicombe)
'Rochford Park'
RMB 1040
Mitiamo VIC 3573
Telephone (054) 36 6274

Queensland Coloured Sheep Owners Association (Secretary, Ruth Thompson)
PO Box 89
Red Hill QLD 4059
Telephone (075) 46 2358

South Australian Coloured Sheep Owners Society Inc (Secretary, Verle Wood)
Box 110
Eastwood SA 5063
Telephone (08) 254 6739

Melanian Sheep Breeders Society (Secretary, Jenny Donaldson)
40 Lefroy Street
Gingin WA 6503
Telephone (095) 75 2008

CHAPTER 19
Pet Care

ANIMAL CHIROPRACTOR

For information about chiropractic care for animals, contact:

George Schofield
1530 Mickleham Road
Yuroke VIC 3063
Telephone (03) 333 1602

The story we showed on 'Burke's Backyard' featured George Schofield, and he will assist in any direct questions you may have. He may also be able to tell you of an animal chiropractor in your area.

PETS IN SUMMER

If you are going away and leaving your dog unattended at home over the summer, make sure you leave plenty of water in a suitable container that can't be knocked over. It is a good idea to put a brick in a bucket of water to overcome this problem.

If you are leaving a caged bird at home, make sure it is not placed too close to a window as it will become overheated.

Never leave an animal inside a car, as the temperature can rise as high as 60°C (140°F).

Summer is the time for fleas and ticks. For those areas that have tick problems, a two-month tick collar is available which will help to remedy the situation.

Five-month flea control collars, which are very good, are also available and there are a couple of natural herb collars on the market. Fleas can also be controlled by ProBan, which is given by mouth.

There is a wide range of flea washes on the market. A couple are based on diazinon, one based on malathion and the highly recommended Asuntol, based on coumaphos. Washes cannot be used if ProBan is being given.

A range of sprays and powders are also sold, which all work well on animals.

As fleas breed in dust and dirt, it is important to control this in and around the home. Products such as Flea Proof (available from supermarkets, chemists and pet shops) and Siphotrol (available from your vet) for use indoors, are suggested. Baytex 550, based on fenthion, is fairly safe to use outside in the yard. The advantage of these products is that they stop the fleas breeding.

For effective control you really need to use a combination of different treatments for the environment and the animal.

TRANSPORTING PETS

There comes a time in everyone's life when they decide to move from one home to another. If the move is interstate, special arrangements need to be made for transporting pets, but if you are moving locally you should be able to manage transporting the budgie, the cat or the dog by car, with the help of the following tips.

Small caged birds You don't want your pet to escape during the journey, so the first step is to make sure the cage door doesn't shake open, by securing it with a tie, or wire.

The second step is to stop drinking water from spilling all over the cage on the trip. If you think the journey will be too long or hot for the bird to go without water, place a piece of cotton wool in the drinker.

The third step is to cover the bird up. If you are travelling at night the lights from oncoming cars will alarm the bird and place it under more stress than is necessary.

Cats The biggest problem with transporting cats is trying to find and catch them when you're ready to leave. They seem to know when something is going on, and make themselves scarce.

Most cats dislike car travel, so be sure to enclose the cat securely in a cage. It could cause an accident if it interferes with your driving. Cardboard cages just don't have enough structural strength for a big adult cat. They can rip through the holes in the sides and escape. Use a cage with a strong plastic base and a wire top. If you don't own one you can probably rent or borrow from your local vet.

When you get the cat to the other end, just lock it up inside for three or four days to teach it to stay at the new house.

There is an old wives' tale about putting butter on the feet of the cat so that when it licks the butter off it will get rid of the smells of the old house. It might be worthwhile but also messy.

Dogs Many dogs appear to enjoy car travel, but for your own safety and that of the dog make sure your pet stays in the passenger-side footwell—an airborne dog in a car accident becomes a lethal weapon. If your dog is averse to, or unfamiliar with, car travel, give it an ACP tablet, which you can obtain from your veterinarian. This is a tranquilliser and also stops your pet from getting sick in the car.

If this sounds like too much trouble on top of all the other hassles of moving, there are a few companies who will move your animals for you. If you are moving interstate, it is certainly advisable to use a specialist company to transport your animals.

CHAPTER 20
Pets as Therapy

Most people are familiar with the purpose of guide dogs, but not too many are aware of Pets as Therapy (PAT) dogs.

They're trained as companion dogs for the disabled, or for people who live in institutions. Scientists have proved that having a dog to caress makes you feel good and lowers your blood pressure. Pets as Therapy dogs also give some people the will to live and enjoy life.

Potential Pets as Therapy dogs are fostered by volunteer

ROAD TEST

families for 12 months as part of the Puppy Walking Scheme, during which time they are acclimatised to family life, and their temperament and character are assessed. They then return to the Pets as Therapy Centre for intensive training.

Committed, professional staff, quality dogs, and the generosity of the public through donations and volunteer work make the Australian PAT scheme the most successful in the world.

Three types of dogs are trained by PAT centres. *Companion dogs* cost $2500 to train, and are great antidotes to loneliness. *Social dogs* cost $2500 to train, and provide wonderful company for people in institutions. *Support dogs* are an exciting new development, designed to enable disabled people to have a greater opportunity to move around their environment. The dogs are strong, calm and dependable enough to act as a firm support for disabled people as they attempt to leave their wheelchairs and achieve greater mobility. Special harnesses are used to protect the dogs.

The costs of training these animals may seem prohibitive, but dogs are often generously sponsored by community organisations. This gives financially disadvantaged, disabled people a chance to own one of these very special dogs.

Plans are underway to establish the scheme in other states apart from New South Wales; and South Australian and Victorian branches now operate small-scale schemes.

For further information

Pets as Therapy
77 Deepfields Road
Catherine Field NSW 2171
Telephone (02) 606 5600

CHAPTER 21
Animal Agent

If you have an unusual pet, or think that your pet may be suitable for television work, please contact:

Rhonda Hall
Animals All
90 Arcadia Road
Arcadia NSW 2159
Telephone (02) 653 1279

CHAPTER 22
Pet Cemeteries

What do you do when the beloved family pet has passed on? The traditional option has been a backyard burial, but some councils prohibit this, and many pet owners feel they would like to see Rover or Felix given a more dignified send-off. Perhaps the fit and proper place for our little mates is the pet cemetery.

There are a number of pet cemeteries around Australia. Generally they can be located in the yellow pages of the telephone directory under Pet Cemeteries.

At the Animal Memorial Cemetery and Crematorium in New South Wales about 40 cremations and six burials are performed each month. Cremation costs from $110—depending on the size of the animal—and burials cost from $220 in the pet's blanket, to $670 in a lined casket.

It is not unusual for many pet owners who have taken advantage of this service to will that their own ashes be placed beside those of their pet.

For further information

The Animal Memorial Cemetery and Crematorium
St Mary's Road
Berkshire Park NSW 2765
Telephone (045) 72 5333

CHAPTER 23
Taxidermy

Having an animal stuffed by a taxidermist is one lasting way to remember your favourite pet. Taxidermy is also a means by which bird breeders can retain particular specimens that may be rare or unusual. And, of course, an animal can start its life (as a favourite pet, that is) at the taxidermist—how else could you keep a pet pig, or maybe even a tiger, in a flat?

Bird keepers and loving pet owners provide much of the taxidermist's work. Animals that are to be preserved should be placed in the freezer, if possible, until they can be taken to the taxidermist. A photograph of the pet helps the taxidermist to give the finished product proportion and character.

The process of stuffing the animal involves making an incision from the tail to the breastbone and from there working the skin away so that the body comes out complete. An incision under the neck allows the same to be done for the head. The skin is then treated and soaked in a preserving formula for a number of days. Wires are placed in the wings and legs to give them shape. The skin is then fitted over a body frame, which is padded in the appropriate places with wood wool, sown up and made to stand in an upright position. Various poses can be requested.

Basic prices range from $280 for cats, $350 for small dogs, $180 for rabbits, and $85 for budgerigars. Large dogs can represent a problem due to difficulties in fitting the big frame into the skin.

For further information

Animal Fetish
62 Flinders Street
Darlinghurst NSW 2010
Telephone (02) 361 0808

HOME AMONG THE GUM TREES

CHAPTER I
Around the Home

ACOUSTICS

If you live on a busy road, you will know how stressful the noise from traffic can be. Environmental acoustics involves the control of noise pollution created by road traffic, aircraft, factories and construction equipment.

There are a number of things you can do to minimise noise coming into your property. There is also some very good research being done by the various Departments of Main Roads as well as by the State Pollution Control Commissions.

We carried out a test on a particularly noisy road by placing a noise level analyser adjacent to the road. The reading was 83 decibels. A reading was then taken on the other side of a mound of soil that had been placed near a dwelling to reduce noise. The reading was 68.8 decibels. Thus a mound, which can be shaped and planted to look like a natural feature, can provide noise protection.

The results of traffic noise can be stress and loss of sleep. There is very little that the Department of Main Roads can suggest to people who live on major roads but the following may help.

A good front fence of brick, stone or timber (brush fences are not nearly as good for noise reduction) will reduce noise, as will a solid gate that fits neatly at ground level. It is useless to have a solid fence and wrought iron gates.

Inside the fence itself it is better to have softer cultivated soil, rather than heavy paving on which the noise would bounce around.

A row of plants will give a good psychological effect in that the traffic cannot be seen, but it isn't really effective—you would need a thick depth of plants (17m or 56′) to reduce noise.

Double-glazing on windows is certainly effective. It is fairly expensive, however and essential to have it fitted properly with no air gaps. It is important to have seals on doors and windows and not to have ventilators in the wall that faces the traffic noise.

If you live on a busy road it will always be noisy. Therefore try to live at the back of your house, away from the noise. If you are looking at houses to buy, don't forget to inspect the house during weekdays at peak hours, since there may be less noise on weekends.

The Department of Main Roads is trying to improve noise levels by putting up barriers such as mounds, fences and fences on top of mounds.

For further information on noise pollution, contact the State Pollution Control Commission, the Department of Main Roads or the Road Construction Authority in your state. Booklets and information sheets have been printed by the government to assist you in this matter.

BIRD CONTROL

The Hot Foot Bird Control is a kit designed to stop birds from perching in the garden. It retails for $29.95, and includes a tube of gel and Crystal Coat spray coating, which is applied to the surfaces of objects to deter the birds. It is available through: Hot Foot International, 104 Porters Road, Kenthurst, NSW 2156. The factory is:

ICCI (Australia) Pty Ltd
13 Turbo Road
Marong VIC 3515
Telephone (054) 654 2133

BOX TRAILERS

The 'Burke's Backyard' story about box trailers was shot at:

Classic Trailers
126 Taren Point Road
Taren Point NSW 2229
Telephone (02) 525 7599

We suggest that you contact either Jeff Bernard or Graham Jones at Classic Trailers, with any questions you may have about box trailers. They can advise you on available sizes and prices.

BUSHFIRES

The following are suggestions made by bushfire safety expert Joan Webster to assist in protecting yourself and your house against a bushfire.

Roof area A continuous metal sheeting roof is safer than tiles. A rubble drain instead of gutters will help prevent the roof from catching fire. Ends of rafters should be painted.

Windows Use metal flywire on the outside of windows or preferably roll down tightly fitting, metal shutters.

Ensure that there are no gaps to the *sub-floor area* where embers could get in and ignite from under the floor. Put metal flywire over vents.

If a bushfire is threatening your house wear *protective clothing*, for example, pure wool or strong cotton, to completely cover the skin. Wet a cloth to put over your nose and protect your eyes.

Take your *hose* inside the house as intense heat can melt it. Bring a *ladder* inside so that you can gain access to the ceiling hatch.

Place a bucket of water in the roof through the *access hole (manhole)* in the ceiling in case an ember gets into the roof void. This area should be checked frequently.

Bring the *doormat* inside; if embers land on it they will burn very quickly and set fire to the outside of the house.

Plug the *keyhole* with a piece of Blu-tack or plasticine so no draughts can enter. Seal the house as well as possible. Place wet towels by the door to stop sparks blowing in underneath.

If your *curtains* are flammable, take them down. If not, put a wet blanket up in case the window breaks.

Think ahead and have as big a *reserve water supply* as you possibly can. Have buckets placed strategically all around your house: fill up everything you can before a fire comes to your area, because when the fire comes the water pressure will go off.

For further information Joan Webster has written a book on the subject: *The Complete Australian Bushfire Book*, published by Thomas Nelson, Australia. It costs approximately $22.95, and is available at most bookshops. If you find that you are having trouble getting the book, simply ask your bookseller to order it in from the publisher. The book is excellent and has been officially endorsed by bushfire authorities and fire brigades all over this country.

CHANDELIERS

'Burke's Backyard' filmed a story about chandelier cleaning and restoration with Mr Fabian Russell, who is a licensed restorer and cleaner of crystal chandeliers—a very unusual occupation, and almost a dying trade. He trained as a chandelier assembler at Mark Foys, who were the biggest importers of chandeliers in the 1950s. The imported chandeliers were all European, mainly from Czechoslovakia with some from Sweden and Italy.

Mr Russell can be contacted for professional chandelier cleaning and restoration requirements, but has a few tips to offer those who wish to clean their own crystal chandeliers. Chandeliers are great dust collectors and should be cleaned regularly so the intricate shapes don't dull. The average home chandelier need not be taken down for cleaning, but the floor underneath it should be covered with a sheet or towel. Take care not to wet the actual light holder during the cleaning process. Mr Russell recommends using Trix detergent, bleach and Domestos— apply this with a soft rag and then just wipe it off with a linen serviette to give it an extra bright sparkle.

For further information
Mr Fabian Russell
134 Excelsior Street
Merrylands NSW 2160
Telephone (02) 632 7574

CHIMNEY-POTS

'Burke's Backyard' filmed a story about chimney-pot making at the family business of Fred A. Mashman, which has been making chimney-pots for over 100 years. Mashmans have been at their present site in Kingsgrove, Sydney for 80 years.

Chimney-pots have been part of the range since the business began, with over 20 different styles being made today. Many styles are not standard but designed to the particular specifications of homeowners and their existing chimney-pots.

The pots are made from terracotta clay and are either hand moulded or hand thrown. They are then left to dry and baked in down-draught kilns. After this process they are cooled and sold.

The price range varies from $47 to $170. Mashmans sell direct to the public and supply large chain hardware stores.

Chimney-pots can also be used as garden lights or for storing brooms, rakes, and so on.

Fred A. Mashman also make many other products using terracotta clay: agricultural pipes, quarry tiles, paving tiles, ventilator bricks, channel pipes for surface drainage, pipes used for wine racks, letter box bricks, roofing finials and crests.

For further information
Fred A. Mashman
Mashman Avenue
Kingsgrove NSW 2208
Telephone (02) 502 2344

CHIMNEY-SWEEPS

All chimneys need regular cleaning, even those of the modern pot-bellied and slow-combustion stoves. Soot can build up to the extent where the chimney can catch fire, or cause the wallpaper to become combustible through excessive heat.

If a fire is used two or three nights a week on a regular basis or as the main source of heating and cooking, the chimney needs to be swept each year. Some insurance companies can require that a chimney be kept in a clean condition and regularly swept.

Some chimney-sweeping jobs can be difficult; for instance the chimneys of homes 70–80 years old, which have had their fireplaces boarded over. During renovations the chimneys are often rediscovered, and may take a little longer to sweep than the usual hour or so needed to clean a regularly treated stack. In older terraced homes the chimneys can be a real danger if not properly cleaned before being used.

Possums can be a problem, as they will persist in occupying the chimney even when a smoky fire has been lit under them. Apparently they like the warmth of the chimney.

The cost of chimney-sweeping is around the $55 mark, depending on how dirty or difficult the chimney is. This includes an inspection and report on the condition of the chimney, and an assessment as to whether any work is needed. Occasionally a chimney-sweep is asked to repair damage caused by people who try to do it themselves by throwing a bag tied to a brick down the chimney. This often results in knocked-out bricks and other internal damage to the chimney.

The chimney-sweep used in the 'Burke's Backyard' segment was Noel Moore of Carmel's Chimney Sweep Co (incorporating Sweep-A-Gram), 432A Old Northern Road, Glenhaven, NSW 2154. Telephone (02) 634 7710.

Noel's great-grandfather was one of the last of London's climbing boys, who were sent onto the roofs of the city to clean the chimneys.

CRIME PREVENTION

To return home and discover that your house has been broken into and your personal belongings have been stolen is a shocking experience. In the light of current crime statistics, it is in everyone's interests to do whatever is possible to ensure the security of their possessions.

Bars on windows and doors, and a good burglar alarm, make for a fairly good guarantee that you won't have any unwelcome guests. But if you don't want to go to that extreme, or if you just can't afford it, there are a number of simple yet effective things you can do around your own home that don't cost any money, and will help dissuade a would-be burglar from picking on your place.

According to security consultants, the best way to work out how to safeguard your home is to think like a thief.

Imagine that you are a burglar and you are trying to break into your own home. What would you do?

Obviously the first thing is to look for a point of entry. Most people will secure the main entrance in some way, but don't forget side gates—these should be equally strong and locked with good quality locks. A determined thief may still decide to climb over the back fence, but this will take longer and there is a much greater likelihood that he or she will be seen. Your aim should be to create a deterrent by making entry as difficult as possible.

The next thing a thief would do is to look for something to use to break into the house. Don't leave tools or garden implements lying around, as these are ideal for a thief to make use of when trying to break into your house. These implements can not only be used to smash through or prise open the windows; worse still, they can be used against you if you happen to be in the house.

Once the tools and garden implements have been placed inside a garage or garden shed, the door should be locked with a good quality padlock. Recent research undertaken by insurance companies has shown that over 25% of goods stolen are taken from either a garden shed or from a garage.

When you examine items in your shed or garage you will realize the extent of their cumulative worth. Power tools, whipper snippers, bikes and so on can easily add up to $3000 or $4000 worth of goods. And again, tools make breaking into the house a breeze. Lawnmowers are now considered to be a prime target for theft. Worth about $400 to $500, they are just as big a target as videos or televisions.

One of the best ways to protect your garden tools and your valuables is to engrave your driving licence number on to all items, because that makes it very difficult for a thief to dispose of the property. You can buy engraving tools at most hardware stores for a few dollars, or you can borrow one from your local Neighbourhood Watch.

Watch-dogs are a popular security investment but, unfortunately, all they do in many situations is simply watch. They are, however, good deterrents and their presence stops many break-and-enter crimes. Nevertheless, they should not be relied upon totally.

Don't put garden rubbish in boxes that have obviously contained computer equipment, videos or other electrical goods. If you put garden rubbish out for the council to collect in containers of this nature you are simply advertising the items that the thief can expect to find inside your home.

One of the best deterrents against criminal activity in any neighbourhood is for people to be involved in Neighbourhood Watch. If the scheme is not operating in your particular area make sure that you at least follow the basic principles, and that simply means being vigilant— vigilance is the best deterrent of all.

It is important to have your house number clearly

displayed on the letterbox or on the house; if an emergency service (such as the police or an ambulance) is trying to find you quickly, they need to know exactly where you are.

If you are going away for a holiday, arrange to have a friend collect your mail or have it held at the post office. Stop paper and milk deliveries too. Never leave a key hidden somewhere near the door, and never leave notes advertising your absence. Don't make things easy for thieves.

EARTH-COVERED HOUSES

These are energy-efficient homes which are designed to blend in with the surrounding natural environment.

'Ecaspace 1' is an earth-covered demonstration home located at Castle Hill in New South Wales. Its landscape architects were ECA Space Design Pty Ltd, 4 De Villiers Avenue, Chatswood, NSW 2067. The interior design consultant was Sue Klimpsch, 69 Annesley Street, Leichhardt, NSW 2040; and the engineers were Painter, Merryfull, Griffith & Associates Pty Ltd, 214 Parramatta Road, Homebush, NSW 2140.

FIRST AID: CHOKING

Choking can happen to anyone, in any age group.

It may be due to a spasm of the larynx; this occurs sometimes when a liquid contacts this area of the throat, and the larynx closes to prevent the liquid from entering the lungs. Unfortunately this spasm also prevents or restricts the flow of air into the lungs. Or it may be caused by a blockage, partial or complete, of the airway.

Choking is preventable. It is most commonly caused by:

* a sudden laugh or cry while something is in the mouth (particularly in children)
* a child running and stumbling while something is in the mouth
* inadequate chewing of food
* swallowing splinters of bone
* inhaling while eating

An acute obstruction of the upper airway by an impacted foreign body is a rare and life-threatening emergency. Lodgment of such an object in or just above the victim's windpipe is a problem of the senile, the weak, those with diseases of the central nervous system and the intoxicated. This may in part be due to the reduced ability of these groups of people to swallow efficiently and attempt to clear, or partially clear, their own airway by coughing.

The choking victim may be conscious or unconscious. The conscious victim should be encouraged to breathe deeply and to remove the object by coughing. Use gravity to assist this wherever possible. Adults can lean over with their head near their knees; an infant or child can be positioned across your lap with the head down. Check the airway and remove any visible obstruction with your fingers.

If the conscious victim continues to show signs of partial airway obstruction, such as wheezing, laboured, difficult or noisy breathing, he or she should be transported to hospital or medical aid, preferably by ambulance.

The unconscious victim (breathing or not) should also be positioned with the head low to maximise the effect of gravity. Check the airway and remove any visible obstruction with your fingers. Give three or four sharp blows between the shoulder-blades (sharp smacks for children and infants). If needed, give up to four chest thrusts (short, sharp squeezing of the rib cage, both sides, lower half). The breathing must then be re-assessed.

If the victim is not breathing, Expired Air Resuscitation (EAR) and, if necessary, maintenance of circulation by External Cardiac Compression (ECC) must be carried out as basic life support. Medical aid and ambulance transport is essential and a matter of urgency.

Do yourself and your family a favour—enrol in a St John Ambulance Association First Aid Course.

References
Australian First Aid, the authorised manual of St John Ambulance Australia, pp. 250–252; Australian Resuscitation Council, '*The management of choking due to suspected impaction of foreign material in or just above the windpipe*', Interim Policy Statement No 4.3.6., November 1985.

FLAGS

You may be interested in adding a decorative flag to your home or garden.

Australiana Flags make a full range, from the Eureka Flag to the United Nations Flag, all printed or sewn in a range of sizes. They are specialists in national, historical, corporate, maritime and personal flags; flagpoles; research and etiquette advice; and vexillology (the study of flags). Their current price list is available on request.

Australiana Flags
PO Box 38
Northbridge NSW 2063
Telephone (02) 958 3246

GARAGE SALES

As we are deciding whether or not to dispose of a particular item, there are very few of us who are able to recognise that it won't be used again. The result is that garages and garden sheds across Australia are bursting at the seams with items their owners don't really need or want.

But one person's junk is another's bargain; the answer to the problem is to hold a garage sale. Here are some of the basic ground rules you should stick to if you want to make some cash.

Pick the right day. Make sure your garage sale is not competing with a sporting grand final or some other major event.

Advertise. Take out an ad in the major local paper and in the suburban papers as an extra backup. Make sure you mention what you think could be the big sellers at your sale, such as plants, trailers, a canoe, bikes, and bric-a-brac (bric-a-brac is always good; no one really knows exactly what it is). Put an ad in your local supermarket and in the milk bar window, but while you're doing this make sure you aren't breaking any council regulations.

Make up some signs. Place them on street corners and, of course, right outside, so everyone will know which house is yours. Again, check council regulations regarding where you can place signs.

A little *bunting* is a good idea—perhaps some streamers to catch the eye of passers-by.

Make *parking* as easy as possible. Ask your neighbours if they would park their cars a little away from your house on the day, so that potential buyers have access.

Present your goods appealingly. Separate what you are selling into groups of similar items, such as plants, car parts, toys. Place knick-knacks up high where they can be seen, rather than burying them on the ground where people have to dig through them.

Have all your goods *labelled with a price.* You can use chalk, a felt-tipped pen or even the little stickers you can buy from a stationery shop.

Have an extension lead on hand so people can see for themselves that electrical appliances do or don't work.

Have lots of change ready. If you can't change larger notes, you may lose sales.

For a professional touch supply plastic bags, boxes or paper in which to pack purchases.

Keep an eye on the house and don't leave things that are not for sale lying around where they could mysteriously disappear.

Make sure there is only one entrance/exit for the garage, and position yourself where you can see as much of the area as possible.

Have a tarpaulin or ground sheet on hand in case of rain or too much sun.

Be prepared to drop your prices as the day goes on, unless, of course, you really enjoy the haggling.

A few toys will help to entertain and occupy small children while their parents are perusing the items for sale.

Cups of coffee, tea or cordial for sale might be a means of making a few extra dollars.

One final point to remember with regard to garage sales is that the rule is 'caveat emptor'—let the buyer beware.

Once a sale has been made, that's the end of the story. There is no reason why you should give the money back once the transaction has been completed.

HOME BUYING

The Royal Australian Institute of Architects (RAIA) runs low cost advisory services in each capital city and many regional cities throughout Australia. The services provide Australian homeowners with detailed advice on every aspect of buying, renovating and building homes.

The following free technical information sheets are available by sending a request and a stamped self-addressed envelope to Archicentre Melbourne, 530 Glenferrie Road, Hawthorn, VIC 3122.

* Do it yourself home buyer checklist
* Do it yourself renovator guide
* Home maintenance guide
* Cracking in brickwork and block masonry
* Termites and borers
* Treatment of damp walls
* Re-blocking
* Roofing and guttering

RAIA Information Centre telephone numbers are listed below:

Victoria	(Archicentre)	
	Melbourne	(03) 819 4577
	Geelong	(052) 21 8029
	Albury/Wodonga	(060) 21 6410
	Country areas	(008) 13 3038
South Australia	(Archicentre)	
	Adelaide	(08) 272 7044
New South Wales	(Architects Advisory Service)	
	Sydney	(02) 356 3122
Queensland	(Architects Advisory Service)	
	Brisbane	(07) 229 6244
West Australia	(Architects Advisory Service)	
	Perth	(09) 328 8861
ACT	(Architects Advisory Service)	
	Canberra	(062) 73 2353
Tasmania	(RAIA)	(002) 34 5464
Northern Territory	(RAIA)	(089) 81 2288

HOUSEHOLD AND BACKYARD CHEMICALS

Chemicals stored in the home and backyard can pose a real threat to both people and the environment if not used or disposed of correctly. The average Australian household contains 10–30 litres (2–6½ gallons) of chemicals that are potentially dangerous to the environment and humans.

The most important thing to remember with household and garden chemicals is to keep them safely locked away from children and pets. Chemicals should never be transferred from their original packaging. Never pour any type of chemical into a drink bottle, even if it is clearly labelled. In most states it is illegal to present chemicals in any packaging other than its original and/or registered packaging.

If you have any queries about household chemicals that you wish to dispose of, or would like some advice, these organisations should be able to help.

State Pollution Control Commission
GPO Box 4036
Sydney NSW 2001
Telephone (02) 265 8888

Waste Advisory Service
The Melbourne and Metropolitan Board of Works
601 Little Collins Street
Melbourne VIC 3000
Telephone (03) 615 5547

Chief Inspector of Drugs and Poisons
Queensland Health Department
GPO Box 48
Brisbane QLD 4001
Telephone (07) 234 0960

Department of Environment and Planning Information
Centre
Lower Ground Floor
55 Grenfell Street
Adelaide SA 5000
Telephone (08) 216 7860

Sven Hansen
Health Inspection Services
WA Health Department
189 Royal Street
East Perth WA 6000
Telephone (09) 222 4222

LAND ASSESSMENT

Choosing a block of land is one of those highly complicated tasks involving dozens of things to think about; you can never be sure if you have remembered them all. Even after major considerations, such as price range and proximity to employment and schools, have narrowed the choice to just a few localities, attempting to determine the merits of any particular block over those around it can be a bewildering exercise. While many of the activities involved in the purchase of land are best dealt with by the appropriate professional people, the more you find out about the land yourself, the more aware you will be of exactly what you are getting.

Take a trip to the *local council* and examine maps of the region. Examination of zoning, land use, contour maps and so on will give you a really good feel for the area. Look for existing and proposed zoning and the proximity of other zones which may affect yours; for example, rural, industrial, tourism. Escarpment or foreshore protection zoned areas can be bought but not built on or interfered with in any way. Thus they can greatly reduce the usable area of a block of land.

Look for the 100 year flood contour, which is a number of metres above sea level. The level was raised in many areas in 1978, which means that houses built above the line before 1978, but which are now below the line, are subject to special building restrictions. In general, councils will refuse plans to build dwellings below this level.

Look for power transmission lines and substations. Power lines crossing a property will deter 90% of buyers.

Look for proposed resumption of land in the region for water, energy, health, council and roads authorities.

Look for proximity to bushland such as national parks to assess bushfire risks.

Go to the *building inspectors' department* at the local council and look at plans and restrictions on buildings in the area. Check whether any covenants apply on building developments.

Check proximity to *public transport* and amenities.

Check for possible sources of excessive *noise*, such as aircraft flight paths, railways, major roads, playing fields, and so on.

Ask the nearest established neighbours about the quality of *local services* (they may be more honest than a real estate agent). While you are there, ask about pleasant and unpleasant *weather* conditions likely to be experienced at different times of the year, the standard of *television reception*; and taste a glass of local *water*.

Once you believe you have located a suitable block, pack a picnic and go and camp on it for a day. This will enable you to get to know your block and get a feel for the *neighbourhood*.

Take a compass to determine the *aspect* of the block. Depending on the design and placement of your house, the aspect could place definite limitations on the sorts of plants that will grow comfortably in your garden.

Take a close look at any *vegetation* present. Certain native species can indicate climatic or environmental features; for example, melaleucas tend to occur naturally on soils that may become periodically waterlogged. Trees on a block may make it look more appealing, but they often suffer irreparable damage from earthmoving equipment both above and below ground (from sideswiping and soil compaction). They may also have to be removed for house construction to take place, or council regulations may prevent them from being removed at all, and may ultimately represent nothing more than an additional expense.

Take a bucket, a spade, and some plastic bags and collect a few *soil* samples. For around $75 you can have the soil tested (commercial services are listed in the yellow pages of the telephone directory). The resultant analysis may save you hundreds of dollars in lost plants in the long term because it will identify, and tell you how to correct, deficiencies and structural problems.

A spirit level, preferably placed on a long plank, will help to give you a rough idea of the degree of *slope* on the block and indicate possible fill requirements and drainage difficulties.

If you have your heart set on a particular house design, make a cardboard scale model with the windows and doors marked on it. By placing the model in a level spot and watching the play of *light and shadow* across it during the day, you will gain a remarkably accurate picture of how light and shade will affect the house (that is, through cooling, heating, glare, and so on). You will also be able to see which rooms will take advantage of any views. It is much easier to make adjustments to a cardboard design than to rectify the problems after the house is built.

LETTERBOXES

If you are concerned about whether your letterbox comes up to scratch, you can ring your local post office and they will be able to tell you, but here are the basics.

The main requirement is that the postie is able to deliver your mail without having to get off his bike or moped. If you have a rose bush, for instance, which obscures the box, the postie doesn't have to deliver if he does not have easy access to the box. Your mail could be left at the post office for collection.

Letterboxes can be of any design, but Australia Post has guidelines:

1 The letterbox should be large enough to accept all mail regularly received.

2 Minimum internal dimensions of a box should be 230mm (9″) wide across the front, 160mm (6¼″) deep top to bottom, and 330mm (13″) long front to back.

3 The slot should be horizontal and a minimum of 230mm (9″) wide by 30mm (1¼″) high.

4 A second slot, for daily newspapers and magazines only, is recommended.

Siting The letterbox should be on the footpath or the roadway boundary of your property. If your property has a driveway, the box should be at the crossing of the driveway with the property boundary or footpath. If you share a driveway with next door's property, the box has to be placed at a common point where the property boundaries join at the footpath.

Letterboxes should be positioned between 0.9–1.2m (3–4′) off the ground.

Police and ambulance officers also emphasise that it is a good idea to have the house number clearly marked on your letterbox, as it saves a lot of searching time when an emergency occurs.

Clean out your letterbox regularly so that it doesn't get invaded by spiders, or full of leaves and twigs. A secure door latch or lock on the box is also a good idea for security.

New letterboxes are available from most large hardware stores, including:

Velox Engineering
48 Waratah Street
Kirrawee NSW 2232
Telephone (02) 542 1700

Valleycraft Pty Ltd
7 Hereford Street
Berkeley Vale NSW 2259
Telephone (02) 88 2533

NIGGERHEAD TERMITES

It is important to know a few basic facts about termites: there are many species, and not all of them attack houses.

One commonly seen species, particularly in bushland areas, is the *Nasutitermes walkeri*, or niggerhead termite. It is called a niggerhead termite because its nest, which forms a mound on the trunk or branch of a tree, looks like a tightly curled afro hairstyle. The mound is connected to a colony in the root of the tree.

Although the niggerhead termite can damage trees, it does not attack houses. It will nest in debilitated or dying trees and by eating the timber it returns minerals needed for the next generation of trees to the soil.

The nests of niggerhead termites are often used by native animals and birdlife as nests or refuges. As the termite nests are 'air-conditioned', with high humidity and an even 25°C (77°F) temperature throughout the year, they make ideal homes for other animals.

Lorikeets often take advantage of tree crutches softened by termites to build their nests, as do native and honey bees.

Termites will travel underground through channels up to 50m (164′) from the nest. The termite queen lives in the root crown of the tree.

It is important that homeowners identify the termite nesting near their homes before chemical barrier treatments are performed, to prevent the unnecessary spraying of chemicals.

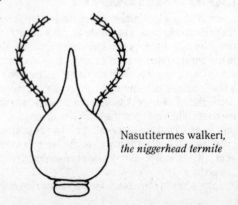

Nasutitermes walkeri,
the niggerhead termite

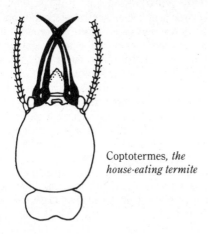

Coptotermes, *the house-eating termite*

PEST CONTROL

Quassia chips have been used for centuries as a pesticide. The advantage is that they break down in 24 hours—in other words, there is no residual effect after this period. The chips are boiled, then the liquid strained and used as a spray. Quassia chips are also used to repel possums and make a good all-round garden spray for aphids and caterpillars. The chips are available in packs of 100g from The Fragrant Garden, Portsmouth Road, Erina, NSW 2210, for $3 direct, or $4 posted. Quassia is toxic to fish, dogs and rabbits, so ensure these are not near the area to be sprayed.

Coopex Spider, Cockroach and Ant Dust is a low toxicity permethrin-based dust manufactured by Defender and can be used both outdoors and indoors to control a wide range of insects for up to four months. Other insects controlled by Coopex are fleas, carpet beetles, clothes moths, bedbugs, silverfish, houseflies and mosquitoes. The dust has little or no odour and is non-staining and stable when used on inert surfaces. Coopex is a relatively safe alternative to using more toxic substances in and around the home. It is available in 500g resealable packs for around $6.25 from garden centres, nurseries and hardware stores throughout Australia.

Mortein Nostalgic Atomiser A reminder of times past is now available from major supermarkets for around $4. The product, a simple atomiser with a 'bike pump' handle, uses your muscle-power, and not propellants such as chlorofluorocarbons, to spray Liquid Mortein Plus ($2.60 for 500ml).

Just remember that this product is not designed to be used on plants.

Flea Proof is an insecticidal mist (fogger) used to control fleas in homes. It works by killing adult insects and preventing the maturity of eggs and larvae. Used correctly, Flea Proof should provide protection for up to nine months. Manufacturers also recommend that pets are treated with proper pet shampoo/rinses and flea collars to limit reinfestation. Flea Proof is available from pet shops, pharmacies, and some hardware stores for about $20. It is manufactured by Zoecon Australia Ltd, PO Box 101, North Ryde, NSW 2113. Telephone (02) 805 3558.

Hortico Ant and Roach Gun retails for $8.70. *Defender Spider, Cockroach and Ant Insecticide* retails for $4.60. Both products contain permethrin, which is a highly effective surface spray. They are available at garden centres, hardware stores, larger supermarkets and department stores.

POLLEN ALLERGIES

While most of us associate springtime with warm sunshine, gentle breezes and the colourful splash of blossoms as nature spills its paints over the landscape; there are thousands of people for whom springtime represents the miserable discomfort of watery eyes, a runny nose, an itchy face and bouts of sneezing. Symptoms such as these that occur only in spring or summer tend to indicate an allergy to pollen—allergic rhinitis or 'hay fever'.

Naturally, many people attribute their symptoms to plants, which flower conspicuously at this time of the year—the massed blooms of wattle and heavy scent of privet have earned these plants bad reputations as hay fever culprits. The pollen from these plants *is* allergenic but only to a small proportion of people. For example, when people who complain of allergy to wattle are tested, an average of only three out of ten test positive.

The prime offenders in almost every case are actually the pollens from inconspicuous imported grasses, weeds and trees.

Perennial rye grass produces commonly allergenic pollen, and because of its widespread use as a pasture plant and the extent to which pollen grains can travel in the wind, this plant represents a major problem for hay fever sufferers.

The pollen from winter grass is allergenic, and as this plant flowers during winter it extends the hay fever season for many people.

Other plants that can cause pollen allergies in spring are plane trees, birch trees (a problem encountered increasingly in Canberra, where these trees are popular), casuarinas, chrysanthemums and other members of the daisy family, plantain weed and couch grass.

Most people with seasonal hay fever can get 90% relief within two to three days with appropriate treatment. Tablets such as non-sedating antihistamines are very good. In more severe cases topical sprays through the nose are used. If these give no relief a specialist can start the patient on injection treatment before the season begins. Consult your doctor for further information.

PREPARING YOUR HOUSE FOR PAINTING

If the wall you wish to paint is peeling and has cracked plaster, the first thing to do is to remove all the old paint with a good, sharp scraper. The wall should then be washed with a sugar soap solution and left to dry. (Sugar soap can be bought at local hardware stores—it removes mould and dirt.)

Clean out the cracks and holes you intend to fill and dampen them with a solution of Bondcrete or Bondseal. This helps the filler to stick to the wall.

Patch the cracks or holes with a cellulose filler and smooth it off with a spatula. For a clean, professional finish on large holes, it is worth investing in a broad bladed filling knife. Make the filler really stiff, so that the scraper can actually stand up in it. This will mean that a minimum of sanding is needed when the filler is dry. Very large holes should first be filled with a stiff sand and cement mix to fill up the bulk of the gap, then finished over the top with the filler mix. When the filler has dried, it can be sanded back flush with the wall and dusted off. It is then ready to paint.

Before you paint, fill the cracks around the window frames or skirting boards with a flexible filler.

External walls usually require tougher treatment. To achieve a high quality finish it may be necessary to burn off the old paint. You can do this with a hired blowtorch.

RATS AS VERMIN

To discover that you are sharing your house with rats is a disturbing and upsetting experience. They are noisy, scrabbling around in the roof cavity; they smell; and they're destructive and wasteful, as they chew their way through absolutely anything they can get their teeth into. But dwarfing every other factor, of course, is the spectre of disease, hauntingly linked with rats in the pages of our history books. Earlier this century both Sydney and Adelaide suffered outbreaks of bubonic plague carried by rats. In fact, Sydney was the first place where the link between rats and plagues was scientifically proven.

There are two sorts of introduced rats that may enter houses, black and brown. Despite their names, the two species can be very similar in colour—shape is the primary means of differentiating between them. Brown rats are the sumo wrestlers of the rat world; they have large, bulky bodies with shorter tails and ears. Black rats are much slimmer, with tails longer than their bodies and large, thin ears. Brown rats are usually paler, have scruffier fur and their tails are often scabby. Brown rats can be domesticated, and it is from them that the coloured and docile strains kept as pets or for laboratory use have been bred.

Black rats prefer high places and tend to live in ceilings, walls and hollow trees. Brown rats prefer an underground environment and inhabit sewers, cellars and the like. Black rats will cower if cornered; brown rats are much more aggressive and will come out fighting. Fortunately, brown rats are not very common and are limited to some coastal areas and the Riverina.

There are also numerous native rats and mice, and these species are protected. Introduced rats are rodents and have the typical long, chisel-shaped teeth of all rodents. Incidentally, it is because their teeth grow continuously and need to be worn down that rodent rats are such unstoppable gnawers. Most of the native rats and mice are marsupials and have small pointed teeth. While this is a reliable guide to telling the difference, there are few people with any inclination to get close enough to examine the mouths of rats. Additionally, there are some native rodent species which are very difficult to distinguish from introduced rats. Native rats do not live in houses in urban areas, but if you live away from the suburbs it is a good idea to try to trap one of the rats and have it identified at a museum or by a park ranger before you put baits or destructive traps in place.

If you have problems with rats, there is a range of ways to remove them. As a preventative measure it's advisable to clean up piles of palings, long grass and so on around the yard, which may make attractive nesting sites. Clean up any crumbs of food and try to eliminate or cover (for example, with tough fly screen) entry points around the house. This includes doors, windows, and especially the roof cavity, but rats can squeeze through gaps less than 2cm (¾″) high and can chew their own holes through wood, so securing your home against them is a very difficult task.

Once rats have moved in they can be destroyed with poisons—those containing Warfarin or the more severe Bromadiolone are effective. Another approach is the trusty rat trap, but to use it effectively you have to be sneakier than the rats. When first sighting something new lying around, rats will inspect it and in the process knock it and jump on it. If the rat trap goes off during this time the fright will scare them right away, and they will avoid the trap for some time. To fool the rats, you will need to put bait in the trap without setting it for a few days—bread, cheese and chocolate are commonly used, but nuts and pumpkin seeds, which are harder to dislodge, are even more successful. Only when the bait is disappearing regularly should you set the trap.

If you don't want to hurt the rat, there is a special trap which is a box with a one-way trapdoor, inside which the food bait is placed. This is called an Elliott trap and is manufactured by Elliott Scientific Equipment, Sayers Road, Upwey, VIC 3158. Telephone (03) 754 2171. The cost of this device is $16, plus freight charges. The only problem is working out what to do with the rat once you have caught it. This sort of trap is ideal if you suspect that the rat may be a native species.

REMOVALISTS

Moving is difficult at the best of times, and it is important to look around to find a company that will meet your requirements at a reasonable price. Before contacting a removalist it is a good idea to estimate your household goods in cubic metres. Seven average moving cartons will fit in a cubic metre (35 cubic ft) and the average household has 25–35 cubic metres (880–1230 cubic ft) of goods. It is also a good idea to measure up the spaces in your new house, so that you avoid problems when trying to fit things in.

It is essential to obtain a number of quotes, as prices vary enormously. However, a low price does not necessarily mean a poor job. A small company may move your goods as safely and carefully as a large company. The important consideration is how professional a company is and if their employees have been to removalist school.

The removalist school shown on 'Burke's Backyard' is run by the New South Wales Road Transport Industry Training Committee. There are branches of the Road Transport Industry Training Committee in every state, and they train removalists in all aspects of moving house, office, and so on. At the end of a five-day course the students are required to pass an examination.

If you plan to do your own packing, there are recommended methods for safety. Plates can be packed together with paper between them, up to six in a bundle, and then wrapped strongly. Stand them on their sides in the box. Glasses should be wrapped and stood on their rims.

Proper planning will help to make your move run smoothly. Start planning as early as possible, preferably a month in advance.

RISING DAMP

Rising damp is one of the most common and misunderstood problems around the house.

The symptoms of rising damp are musty, mouldy smells, bubbling, peeling paint or plaster, and badly stained walls. The cause of these problems is the damp-proof course—it is usually made of slate, lead, bitumen or aluminium covered with bitumen, and runs the length of the wall right through the brickwork just above ground level. It is designed to prevent the moisture in the ground from rising up into the walls. The damp-proof course should cover the entire width of the bricks.

Before spending a great deal of money on replacing a damp-proof course, check that there is nothing else making it ineffective. A concrete path alongside the house, particularly if it slopes towards the house, would collect rainwater at the base of the wall and prevent the wall from drying out. If you must have a path alongside the house wall, make sure it is laid on gravel or brick, and that it is set below the level of the damp-proof course.

Another problem is poor subsoil ventilation. Many houses have had alterations carried out that either completely or partially block vents. It is important to check every vent to make sure that nothing is obstructing the air flow. Another main cause of damp is inadequate stormwater drainage, for example, a downpipe discharging into an open gully that often overflows. Make sure the drainage runs into a proper drain, and if in doubt call a plumber.

The outside walls should not be painted with heavy sealers or suchlike; it is far better to use a good acrylic paint or a lime wash so that the walls can breathe.

If all of these preventive measures are carried out and there is still a problem with damp, it will be necessary to call a professional. Contact either the local Master Builders Association or your state branch of the Architects Advisory Service of the Royal Australian Institute of Architects.

SEPTIC OUTFLOWS

One of the great killers of Australian native plants is the urban septic tank. Many of us dream of having a wonderful home among the gum trees, but as soon as we set it up we start to destroy the natural environment. One of the ways in which we achieve this is through permitting septic outflow to run unchecked into the bushland, where it creates a corridor of death.

Septic outflows create problems for bushland in several ways.

They dramatically increase the nutrient levels in their paths. Large quantities of nitrogen and phosphorus flow in a 'plume' away from the septic tank. Australian soils are naturally quite low in nutrient content and most of our native flora has adapted to, and consequently grows best in, these conditions. High nutrient levels place the plants under great stress, as their roots cannot tolerate or handle these excessive amounts.

The soil in the outflow area becomes waterlogged, which again stresses plants not suited to these conditions.

Exotic weed species tend to flourish in the outflow area, and their seeds can spread throughout the neighbouring bushland.

Close examination of plants, such as gum trees, in the path of the outflow commonly reveals severe infestations of borers in the trunk and branches, as well as problems such as mistletoe and leaf eating insects in the crown. These infestations are merely symptoms of the tree's inability to cope with excessive amounts of nutrients. Similarly, waterlogging in the outflow area commonly results in root disease. While the tree is attempting to deal with these major changes in its environment, its natural defences are lowered and it becomes prone to attacks which it is too run down to resist.

Many plants can cope with conditions in septic outflows, but they are mostly exotic plants (that is, plants from other countries). One of the telltale signs of a septic outflow is a rich green sward of kikuyu grass. Kikuyu thrives on the conditions in the outflow area, and by utilising the nutrients and moisture for its own growth it prevents them from running into and damaging the bushland.

Most regular garden plants from other countries will also grow well in the outflow zone, and trees such as willows and poplars will flourish there. Suitable native plants are much fewer in number, but you can certainly grow most of the paperbarks and bottlebrushes. Some of the rainforest plants such as coachwood and lilly pilly may also manage these conditions.

Growing plants which will intercept the outflow is only one way of minimising the problem. Another technique is to construct earth contour banks running at right angles to the fall of the land. These will help to catch and contain the water, thereby limiting its distribution and effects. Rubble-filled absorption trenches dug along the contours and planted, after refilling, with water and nutrient-loving plants will control the outflow even more thoroughly.

One last method, and probably the most satisfactory of all, is to install one of the newer, more efficient types of septic systems (such as Biocycle or Envirocycle). These systems process the effluent from your home much more thoroughly, and then pump it into an irrigation system which can be used to water the best of your garden plants.

Ultimately it is the homeowner's responsibility to minimise the outflow from septic systems; this is especially important where it flows into bushland and damages the environment.

Biocycle is a compact, fully automatic water treatment system for household waste water. The unit treats the water with anaerobic and aerobic bacteria, clarifies it, disinfects it, and pumps it out via irrigation lines to an automatic spray watering system for lawns and gardens. A brochure is available direct from Biocycle.

Head Office
Biocycle Pty Ltd
56a Old Barrenjoey Road
Avalon NSW 2107
Telephone (02) 918 6188, (02) 918 9933

New South Wales
Biocycle North Coast
PO Box 12
Urunga NSW 2455
Telephone (066) 55 6666

Biocycle Great Lakes
Pacific Palms
Via Forster NSW 2428
Telephone (065) 54 4056

Queensland
Biocycle (QLD) Pty Ltd
4/98 Whitmore Street
Taringa QLD 4068
Telephone (07) 371 4630

South Australia/Northern Territory
Biocycle (SA) Pty Ltd
22 Greenhill Road
Wayville SA 5034
Telephone (08) 272 2577

Tasmania
Biocycle (TAS) Pty Ltd
1a Upper McEwans Road
Legana TAS 7251
Telephone (003) 30 1844

SKYLIGHTS

Skydome Industries Pty Ltd (Roofdome Industries in Queensland) produce a full range of skylights. They have factories in Sydney, Melbourne and Brisbane and installers 'in every major town from Cairns to Hobart'. Their comprehensive brochure is available from all of the following offices.

New South Wales
Cnr Queens Road and William Street
Five Dock NSW 2046
Telephone (02) 745 1522

79 Hillcrest Avenue
Hurstville NSW 2220
Telephone (02) 570 1777

3/493 Anzac Parade
Kingsford NSW 2032
Telephone (02) 344 0100

11 Hassall Street
Westmead NSW 2145
Telephone (02) 689 2699

3/21 Governor Macquarie Drive
Chipping Norton NSW 2170
Telephone (02) 727 0788

Victoria
412 Heidelberg Road
Fairfield VIC 3078
Telephone (03) 481 7055

Queensland
Cnr Wellington Road and Overend Street
East Brisbane QLD 4169
Telephone (07) 391 5599

18 Madden Street
Aitkenvale QLD 4814
Telephone (077) 79 6100

1920 Gold Coast Highway
Miami QLD 4220
Telephone (075) 35 5166

9 Brisbane Street
Ipswich QLD 4305
Telephone (07) 812 1788

SNEAKER CLEANING

The deep tread of sneakers, the popularity of walking and running, and the large dog population all combine to present obvious leisure-shoe cleaning problems.

As there isn't a doormat in existence that is equal to the problem, handyman Peter Harris has come up with a possible solution. Peter suggests that a few dollars' worth of plastic brushes be screwed in an appropriate outdoor spot; one with its bristles exposed upward for the sole, and the other to deal with the side of the tread of your sneakers.

It is important to choose a position where the brushes can be cleaned from time to time by being hosed down.

STORMWATER DRAINAGE

As the entry to a home is the most used area, and of course the part that makes the first impression, most people take pride in a neat, trim concrete or tarsealed driveway. But a sealed driveway automatically results in a large watershed, producing 100% runoff when it rains—which is, incidentally, the ideal time to witness problems the runoff may be causing as it heads for lower ground. Obviously driveways aren't the only areas subject to these considerations; patios, terraces and even lawns need to be assessed in terms of their ability to cope with stormwater satisfactorily.

In one 'Burke's Backyard' segment, Don Burke examined a large tarsealed and gravelled driveway, which was producing sufficient stormwater runoff to erode garden beds below it. During heavy rain the point at which maximum water gathered and ran off the drive could easily be located, and at this point a silt trap was constructed. A silt trap is simply a pit made of bricks with a grille across the top for safety, a pipe leaving the pit on the outlet side, and a reservoir below the level of the pipe to catch the dirt and gravel that may be washed into the silt trap. Maintenance of the silt trap involves shovelling out the reservoir and flushing the outlet pipe through with a fast running hose from time to time.

The key factor that determines whether the drain works or not is the size of the pipe. The only time a drainage system is going to be critically important is during a really severe storm that occurs maybe once every five years or so and floods the backyard. Frankly, if the drainage system won't carry all the water away then, there was no point in installing it in the first place.

Commonly available sizes of plastic drainpipes are 100mm (4″) diameter and 150mm (6″) diameter. At first glance the 150mm pipe may appear to be only slightly larger in capacity than the 100mm. In reality, the capacity of a pipe is proportional to the square of its radius. The radius of the 100mm pipe is 50mm, and 50 squared is 2500. The radius of the 150mm pipe is 75, and 75 squared equals 5625. 5625 is more than twice as much as 2500, so clearly an apparently small increase in the size of the pipe represents a considerable increase in its capacity to carry away stormwater.

While the diameter of solid drainpipes is critical in determining what size to install, there are other types of drains to consider as well. Another form of stormwater drainpipe is the spoon drain. This is made up of a series of half-pipes lowered into the soil to form a shallow, open, surface drain. Often these drains are more effective than solid, underground drainpipes because they are very easy to clean and unclog—any obstructions can be seen immediately and removed.

Other types of drainage pipes are designed to remove seepage water rather than stormwater. This is called agricultural pipe and it is usually flexible, with fine slots cut into the sides. The pipe is laid into a trench and surrounded by gravel, the purpose of which is to prevent the slots from becoming blocked by soil. Nylex also produces a completely different sort of seepage water drain, called a strip drain, which works in exactly the same way as the traditional agricultural pipe, despite its odd appearance. It comprises moulded plastic, patterned similarly to an egg carton, in a long strip surrounded by rockwool. The rockwool remains on the product; it serves a similar purpose to the gravel around agricultural pipe.

UNWANTED FAUNA IN THE HOME

If your worst nightmare involves a spider or snake, there are a few precautions you can take to avoid encountering one.

Spiders The first thing to remember with spiders is not to leave your gumboots or work boots outside to provide an easy hiding space for the spider. If you must leave them at the back door, give them a really good shake before putting them on.

> *Dogs may react severely to bites and stings of snakes, wasps and bees, but they are usually unaffected by funnel web spider bites.*

Gardening gloves are another favourite hiding spot. Just put the gloves on the ground and step on them. Make sure you're wearing solid-soled shoes. Then, if there is a spider inside, it won't be in a condition to hurt you. It's also a good idea not to leave clothes lying on the floor.

If there is a gap between the bottom of the door and the floor, spiders can enter your home. Weatherstrips can prevent this.

There are three main factors which increase the chance of spiders coming into your house: rain, earthworks, and pesticide spraying. While there's not much that can be done about rain and earthworks, you should be aware that spraying often doesn't kill spiders in their burrows, and instead they receive a sub-lethal dose which increases their activity, *and* the chance of them blundering into your home. If they do get inside, damp spots like bathrooms and laundries are attractive.

If you do want to remove a spider from your home, a safe way is to use a wide-mouthed jar and a piece of cardboard or a birthday card. Gently place the jar mouth-down over the spider, then slide the card between the spider and the wall or floor. Lift the jar, holding the card against the top of the jar, and turn it over so that the spider falls into the jar. If the spider is a Huntsman, put the lid on the jar as they can walk on glass.

If you're going to keep the spider for any length of time, get a little cottonwool, wet it and put it into the jar. Spiders need to drink just as we do. After you've had a good look at the spider, take it outside and let it go.

If you want to know what type of spider it is, a museum can usually identify it for you.

Lizards can also wander into the home unexpectedly. The first thing to do is to make sure it is a lizard and not to assume it's a snake. Blue-tongue lizards are often mistaken for death adders and needlessly killed. Just have a good look for legs or the distinctive blue tongue. If it is a blue-tongue then it can be picked up and carried out to a bushy area where it can eat up your garden snails and slugs. Blue-tongue lizards are harmless, but wear gardening or rubber gloves if you prefer.

Snakes however, are a totally different proposition. If you have a creature in your home, and after carefully looking at it you are convinced it is a snake, then the safest action is to call someone who knows about them. In most states the National Parks and Wildlife Service can help with identification and may be able to pass on a contact number for amateur herpetologists (reptile enthusiasts) who could come and remove the snake.

Preventing the problem is most important. Make sure there are no piles of rubbish, which may provide shelter for snakes, as well as breeding places for mice which attract snakes.

Bird aviaries with spilt bird seed also attract mice, and

consequently snakes. Keep them clear of rubbish and check for access holes in the aviary floor. If you are going to tidy the yard for summer, wear gumboots or strong shoes and long, heavy trousers so if the worst does occur and you find a snake, you have less chance of being bitten.

New South Wales On weekdays contact the National Parks and Wildlife Service in your town, or Head Office on (02) 585 6444. At weekends most NSW police stations will have a contact name of a local member of the amateur herpetological society who can help. A small fee may be involved to cover travelling costs. The Australian Museum can assist with advice on weekdays.

Victoria On weekdays telephone the National Parks and Wildlife Division—(03) 651 4011. Several local councils in 'problem' areas can help with rangers trained in removing reptiles. Many of these are on call at weekends. Also try the Melbourne Zoo—(03) 347 1522.

South Australia There is an organised group called the 'Adelaide Snakecatchers' who have trained volunteers in regions around the city who will come and collect the snake. The co-ordinator this summer is Mr Rudy Della Flora who can be contacted on (08) 332 6737, or leave a message on pager (08) 378 9147 if the case is urgent. The group can also be contacted through police, ambulance, RSPCA and other similar groups.

Western Australia The Western Australian Department of Conservation and Land Management's Wildlife Protection Unit can offer advice and descriptions—(09) 367 0333. They may also be able to refer callers for further assistance. Rentokil in Western Australia remove snakes in homes, but this is a chargeable service.

Queensland On weekdays and weekends the National Parks and Wildlife Service offices have rangers operating who can assist. Their head office number is (07) 227 4111. They may also be able to assist with contacts for local herpetologists.

For further information

If you are interested in finding out more about our Australian reptiles, write to:

Australian Herpetological Society
PO Box R79
Royal Exchange
Sydney NSW 2000

WOOD FOR OPEN FIRES

The romance, warmth and aroma of an open fire is something many of us enjoy during the cooler months. To help you make the most of your fireplace this winter, here are some guidelines.

The best time to collect your firewood is in summer. It can then be stored in a dry place for the next six months. If you get your firewood from the roadside, beware—this could be illegal in your state. If you are visiting a state forest you will need a permit to gather wood. Purchasing your firewood from a fuel merchant is probably the easiest method.

How much? We would suggest that you buy by volume and not by weight. How do you know how much a tonne of firewood is? A cubic metre (35 cubic ft) will more than fill your average box trailer. This will cost $75–$100, and for the weekend-only fire this quantity should see you through winter. However, if you enjoy an open fire on most winter days, you can expect to pay about $600 for the season. It is slightly cheaper to buy your wood unsplit, but that means hard work, and for an extra $10–$15 it is all done for you.

Which wood to buy? Wood that is still green contains up to 50% moisture, and most of the fire's heat will be used to vaporise this moisture. The denser the firewood, the more heat it will produce and the longer it will burn. Good hardwoods are mallee roots and box ironbarks like grey box and yellow box. You will need to double the volume of softer woods like radiata pine to provide the same heat.

Railway sleepers and telegraph poles that have been coated with substances like Creosote should not be burnt. Painted or other treated timbers could also give off dangerous fumes. Some cypress pines will crackle or explode, and the sparks may harm children or furnishings, so make sure a screen surrounds your open fire this winter.

CHAPTER 2
The Home Workshop

ANGLE GRINDERS

An angle grinder can cut through concrete, brick and steel with the greatest of ease.

But before you begin, take note:

1 A smaller, lighter machine will do the job almost as well as a large model and will be a lot easier to handle.
2 Wear the right safety equipment:
    protective clear goggles
    leather gloves
    a long sleeved shirt
    long trousers
    sturdy shoes
    This is to protect yourself from red-hot fragments.

3 Tie long hair back or tuck it up into a hat; don't wear loose clothing.
4 Check the switches; ensure that they are easily accessible and can be turned off readily during operation. Sliding switches can jam; toggle or rocker switches can be difficult to reach in a hurry.
5 Fit the blade correctly.
6 Make sure the object you are cutting is firmly clamped or held.
7 Ensure that the work site is clear so that you have plenty of room to operate.

Remember—although an angle grinder is one of the most effective tools, it is also one of the most dangerous.

CHAINSAWS

Many accidents are caused by people using chainsaws incorrectly or for the first time. They are available for hire for between $30–$50 per day. When collecting the chainsaw, ask for full details, that is, a complete rundown on how it operates and its safety features, and get some extra chains.

There are two different types of chainsaws, electric and petrol-driven. *Electric 12"* is suitable for cutting saplings, firewood, brush-cutting, hedges, and so on. While the *Electric 18"* is suitable for lopping trees, but is not as powerful as the petrol-driven chainsaw. A *power chainsaw* is fuel-driven and is suitable for large established trees. It has a very high noise level.

If you own a chainsaw it is essential to keep it clean and well-maintained.

Whether you buy or hire a chainsaw, you will need to wear ear muffs, and goggles to protect your eyes, while you are using it. It is also a good idea to wear a solid pair of boots.

Always start electric or petrol chainsaws on the ground. One of the greatest dangers when using them is kick back, which is why they are fitted with a chain brake.

CORDLESS TOOLS

In the adult toy department, cordless tools are the best inventions since Trivial Pursuit. Cordless tools can convert drilling and screwing from hard work into fun.

If you already have an electric drill, you might need only an electric screwdriver. Makita sells a cordless screwdriver for about $45. It is a compact, well-designed tool that drives in approximately one hundred average-sized screws before the battery needs a three-hour recharge.

The Black & Decker cordless screwdriver is also quite well designed, with the advantage of a metal gearbox. It is a little bit more expensive at about $56, and its drawback is that it takes about 12 hours to recharge.

When power is a long way off or even non-existent, the only really effective way to get that screwing and drilling job done is by using a battery powered, cordless screwdriver or drill. Greater versatility is afforded by using a tool that not only drives screws but also drills holes. Black & Decker produces a model with forward and reverse actions as well as a two-speed setting through the trigger. Unfortunately, the battery takes three hours to charge and cannot be removed from the machine. This cordless drill costs about $140.

The Makita version costs about $200. It is basically a heavy duty machine with the big advantage that the battery is removable, which means you can have a fully charged spare ready to take over.

If you have major building work in mind, the top-of-the-range Makita will screw and drill for about half a day on a one-hour battery charge. Additionally, it has the advantage of a clutch that adjusts for different density materials. It costs about $290.

The Rolls Royce of the range is the Metabo, which costs about $355. It will do just about anything that the others will do, and has the advantage of a burnout-proof motor and a hammer action that makes for really effective masonry drilling. This is the model preferred by many professional builders.

Hints When you are using these tools and you want the battery to last a little longer, drill pilot holes for screws before you drive them home and lubricate the screws with a touch of soap or liquid detergent.

Slotted head screws cause the screwdriver bit to slip. Use Phillips head screws wherever you can.

HAMMERING

The most basic tool in the home workshop is the hammer, but it is surprising how many people do not know how to use it correctly. Here are some helpful hints.

Firstly, to hold the hammer correctly, grab it low down on the handle and have your thumb running along the top of it. This gives a more accurate swing.

To help the nail penetrate the wood, lubricate the tip of the nail by rubbing it in a bar of soap.

Make a slow swing.

Make sure the hammer head is free of oil, grease or soap, or anything that is likely to cause the nail head to slip. For tricky situations, such as nailing around a corner, bend the nail first. This is a skill which requires a little practise.

For a neat finish on good timbers, always use a nail punch to finish driving the nail home. When nailing close to the edge of a piece of timber, give the pointed end of a nail a few sharp taps with the hammer. This will blunt it and prevent it from acting like a splitting wedge. It will also make a little countersunk hole in the wood that will take the nail head.

For the average home workshop, a medium claw hammer is all that is really necessary. The claw is very

useful for pulling nails out. When using the claw to pull out a nail, it is a good idea to place a block of wood under the hammer head. It not only protects the surface of the wood, but it also provides greater leverage, making the job a lot easier. For pulling out small nails, a pair of round-shouldered pincers is a must.

HEX HEAD SCREWS

Hex headed self-drilling screws are used for attaching steel roofing or cladding to timber or steel frames. They are a new development, saving a lot of time and making the job easier.

You will need a cordless driver drill to screw them in. An ordinary electric drill runs too fast. Use a chalk line or straight edge to indicate where the screws should be positioned. Then it is just a simple matter of putting the screw in the drill, pressing firmly on the spot and driving it home.

JAWS WRENCH

The Jaws wrench is one of the most useful and versatile tools around. Its design is superb. No more turn-screw adjusters; just flip the wrench backwards and its jaws open fully. Fit the jaws over the object to be turned and press them together, and they immediately lock tight to give a secure grip.

Use the wrench at any angle for nuts or bolts of any shape, or use it on corroded or rounded nuts. It's great in confined areas, such as under the sink or the car bonnet; in fact, it does the job of any spanner, wrench or multi-grip.

The Jaws wrench is available from leading hardware stores and plumbing supply outlets in all states in two sizes: with a 25cm (10″) handle and 3.7cm (1½″) jaw maximum opening for around $35; and with a 35.5cm (14″) handle and 6.2cm (2½″) jaw maximum opening for around $45.

LADDERS

There is nothing as frustrating or dangerous as carrying a load of tools up a ladder and trying to balance them.

A pouch to hold the tools, which is worn around the waist, can be purchased for around $50, or you can modify the top of your ladder for around $5.

Modifying the top of a stepladder is easy. All you have to do is drill the right sized holes across the top step of the ladder to hold the sort of tools that you want to use.

Three or four holes are usually plenty, as it is important not to weaken the ladder. If you have an aluminium stepladder, be extra careful, unless it is a really good quality one.

Another good idea is fitting a bracket to the side of the ladder to hold large tools like hammers and power drills. The brackets can be made of pre-drilled strap iron, which is available by the roll at most good hardware stores.

It is not advisable to carry large cans of paint up a ladder: transfer the paint to a smaller can which can be hung from a cup hook screwed to the side of the ladder.

To stop the ladder slipping, buy some rubber feet at your hardware store and attach them securely with screws.

Check that the support ropes are securely knotted, and that they are of the same length and in good condition.

Ladders are one of the single biggest causes of accidents around the home, so a little attention to these details will ensure your safety.

MITRE BOX

If you have ever tried to cut a small piece of timber off a longer length you will know how difficult it is to cut it with a handsaw.

There is an easy way, using a mitre box, which can be utilised not only for cutting mitres and 45° angles but also for cutting at 90° angles. This is perfect for cutting off small pieces of timber.

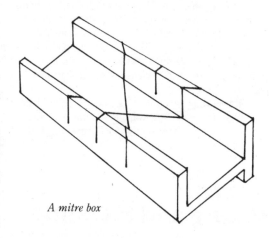

A mitre box

RECOMMENDED TOOLS

Some useful items for the home workshop are:

The *Bosch All Purpose Saw* is claimed to cut just about anything and get into the most difficult corners.

It has some good safety features, such as a double action on-off switch. It's comfortable and well-balanced, and a large number of blades are available to cut most materials. It will cut through PVC, make holes in walls and make pruning easy. Cost is $198.

The *Metabo Hedge Cutter* is light and manoeuvreable, which is important if it is to be used for long periods. Machine safety is good—if you stumble and fall, the machine stops operating as soon as it falls out of your hands. There is good spacing between the teeth, and both blades move at the same time. It retails for about

$350–$380 and is available from power tool specialists in all states.

ElectreSafe 5000 is an extension cord with a special automatic cutout device, which measures imbalances in electrical currents. It will cut out immediately there is any danger of electrocution. This device is useful wherever electricity is used, but is particularly valuable when using power tools, saws, hedge trimmers and lawnmowers, especially anywhere near water, such as around pools or on boats.

The ElectreSafe 5000 is available from hardware stores for around $90.

TOOL CARE

Check garden implements with wooden handles, such as rakes and forks, for drying out of the wood, and splinters. Also check to see if the head is firm or the wood has degenerated, resulting in a loose and unsafe head.

The handles should be rubbed with linseed oil, which is available at hardware stores. If linseed oil is used straight it sits on the surface and is sticky to touch, but if you add two parts mineral turpentine to the oil, mix them together and paint the mixture on, it will soak rapidly and easily into the wood to preserve it.

Shovels and spades Shovels are shaped for moving soil from one place to another. Spades (distinguishable from shovels because they are flat with a sharp edge) are cutting implements, for cutting holes in the ground and the roots of trees. Spades need to have their bottom edge sharpened every so often. It is very easy to use a bench grinder to put an edge on the spade (making sure that you wear goggles to protect your eyes).

If you don't have a bench grinder, you can use a sharpening stone. In general a hand stone will not do as good a job as a bench grinder, however. For about $100, a bench grinder is worth the investment.

If your spade is rusty, rub it with steel wool to remove surface rust and then oil it well.

Mattocks The mattock, another cutting implement, needs regular sharpening or it will not cut trenches effectively. The mattock can also be sharpened on the bench grinder to get a chisel edge, not a razor sharp finish.

Secateurs If you have blunt secateurs that are not cutting well, it is quite easy to improve them. Take them apart, removing first the spring and then the bolt so that the blade can be sharpened on a grinder. When sharpening a pair of secateurs, the aim is to bevel one side of the blade while keeping the other side absolutely flat. The second blade is left squared off. Join the blades back together—put the bolt through, place the second blade in place, put the washer on, screw on the nut and tighten. Put the spring back into the handle and the secateurs should be in excellent working order.

Saws Every so often a saw needs sharpening. To do this, use a metal triangular file. The basic principle is fairly simple—go along every second tooth in one direction filing out a nice sharp V, then turn the saw around and go back in the other direction. Even this will not have properly sharpened the saw—you need to bend the teeth as well. It is very important for cutting that the teeth bend in opposite ways. This gives a broad cut so that the body of the saw blade doesn't jam in the timber that is being cut. It is probably a good idea to take saws to the local hardware store to be sharpened professionally; or better still, when buying a new saw for the garden, choose a bow saw, which has replaceable blades. It will work out cheaper to buy new blades than to have ordinary saws sharpened. Bow saws will cut through timber very easily.

Screwdrivers Check your screwdrivers to see if tips have become rounded with their corners missing, as this will make them impossible to use. They can be fixed using a bench grinder. In reworking a screwdriver, the first thing to do is to grind off the tip so that it is no longer rounded— it needs a square end. Then it can be thinned down so that it is not too thick to fit into the slot of a screw.

Hammer heads often become loose and this is potentially dangerous. You can buy various types of wedges to hammer in to secure the head. Usually, it is easy to open up a split with a chisel and then hammer the wedge in to make sure it is anchored well.

Before putting away the repaired implements, rub oil into the metal parts to prevent rusting. It is essential to care for your tools. Never leave them out in the rain, keep them oiled and they will last forever.

THE WORKSHOP

Everybody has seen a handyperson's work area in which the only work that ever takes place is trying to sort out some of the mess and clearing a space. Getting things organised once and for all may take a little time, but will save hours and hours of your weekend time in the future.

One of the worst activities is sifting through a box of odds and ends trying to find matching screws. The cheapest alternative for storing small hardware items is the good old Vegemite jar, which can be attached to the underside of a shelf by its lid, or simply stored on top of a shelf. But be wary of using jars in workshops—tools and glass don't mix well and can represent a danger to your safety.

Metal cabinets with plastic drawers are not a bad buy for around $15-$25. The only drawbacks are that it's hard to see what is inside the drawers unless you actually open

them up, and this sort of unit is not easily portable.

For about the same price, a tackle box could be a better investment. With one movement the contents are visible and accessible, and portability is a big plus when 90% of the time you'll be using hardware that would fit in the box for odd jobs around the home.

When it comes to storing larger tools, a set of shelves can work well if you have enough space. An old filing cabinet can also give ready access to a wide variety of tools. Large buckets or bins stored under the bench can make handy portable containers for small power tools and other items.

Every home handyperson's dream is probably to own a workbench which is ready to use as soon as you enter the workshop, but in reality they usually end up as a giant storage area for everybody's junk, because the shelves are too few or too hard to get at, and the bench is the next best place to leave something. It might be advisable to consider using a smaller fixed workbench that can be kept completely free of tools and hardware, which could be kept on shelves overhead or on a small rack on the wall. Be innovative with materials; you could even make the rack out of an old leather belt. But be careful—don't put sharp tools into a rack because you could easily cut yourself.

If you find using a fixed bench vice irritating because it is always in the wrong position, try using a portable bench vice, which can make the workshop much more versatile. It will also go with you to wherever you're working around the house.

Remember, when you are using your workshop, safety should be your number one consideration. An uncluttered work area will help to prevent accidents and you will get the job done a great deal faster.

CHAPTER 3
Making and Mending

ALL WEATHER TAPE

A very handy product with a multitude of functions, Sellotape's All Weather Tape is available from major supermarkets, Mitre 10 stores and larger newsagents for around $5.70.

It can be used to patch up garden hoses, tarpaulins, fibreglass, roof guttering and gumboots; it can hold most things together until you have a chance to repair or replace them. Even emergency windscreen or radiator hose repairs are possible if you carry a roll in the glovebox.

It is important to ensure that the surface under repair is completely clean and dry, to allow the aggressive adhesive to perform properly, and make an effective seal. The tape is clear, will not yellow over time, and has inbuilt UV inhibitors so sunlight won't cause it to age.

BIRD AVIARY

There is nothing more pleasant to look at in a backyard than a bird aviary. These can be bought from a nursery or hardware store, but are usually metallic, look like a garden shed and add nothing to the garden. You can build one yourself that will enhance the landscape.

When building your bird aviary there are a few things to keep in mind. The first thing to consider is the door. It should not go right to the top of the aviary, as the birds will flutter around the top and try to escape. If the door is a bit lower in the wall, they won't fly down to exit the aviary. A tight fitting door, which opens internally and has a spring to ensure quick closure, is recommended.

The open side of the aviary should face north to northeast so that it gets the sun in the early morning and almost all day. Plants can be grown in an aviary, but with a dirt floor there is more chance of disease. Plants suitable for growing within an aviary are native grasses, grevilleas, coastal rosemary and ferns.

One suggestion is to make the aviary out of treated pine logs with a weld-mesh wire. The seed should be hung up off the ground to stop mice eating it. A protected corner should be provided by using fibreglass on the sides and roof of the southwest corner.

A nesting basket can be made by shaping chicken wire into a cylinder and stuffing it with straw or native grasses.

Other suggestions: a hollow log for quails, bare branches for extra perches, thick tea-tree branches for nesting sites.

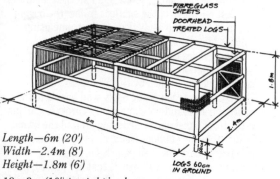

Length—6m (20')
Width—2.4m (8')
Height—1.8m (6')

12 × 3m (10') treated pine logs
18 × 2.4m (8') treated pine logs

Wire: 1cm square weld mesh aviary wire
Corrugated fibreglass for weather protection

CHILD'S SWING

What child hasn't dreamed of possessing the ability to fly? Many a climb to the top of the garden fence or the roof of the tool shed has been undertaken in an effort to achieve this elusive power, and many a limb has suffered grazes, fractures or even a break in the attempt.

The closest most children come to safe and sustainable self-propelled flight is on a swing; perhaps this is why swings hold such an attraction for children and provide so many hours of fun. But when it comes to fitting a swing to a tree in the backyard most people are too uncertain about how to secure it to bother with the project.

The first rule is *not* to tie anything (rope, chain or whatever) around a branch; the odds are that this will eventually kill the branch. The correct way to secure the swing safely is to put a big bolt through the middle of the branch. Many people would assume that to be the worst possible thing to do to a branch: in fact, this does not hurt the branch at all, and provides excellent anchorage.

Use an electric drill and a wood bit to drill a hole all the way through the branch. Then insert a galvanised eye bolt, which has a ring on the end, and, of course, a nut. Buy two washers as well. Assemble it through the hole you've drilled in the branch in this order; eye, washer, branch, washer, nut, then tighten it up very firmly.

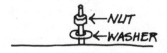

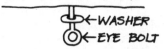

To make the washers fit snugly and tightly into the branch you will probably need to chisel a little of the bark away. This will do no harm to the tree. Next, attach your rope—nylon rope is best as it doesn't rot away—and hang a tyre or a swing at the bottom. If you choose to make a swing, you will need to attach two eye bolts and ropes to hold the seat.

There is one last very important step. Hop onto the tyre or swing and test it yourself. If it will take an adult's weight it is certainly safe for children.

CONCRETE

There are many ways to use cement. If you want to lay bricks, you will need a good mortar mix consisting of one part cement to four parts of brickie's sand. This sand has a greasy quality about it that makes the mortar more plastic and workable, so that you can line the bricks up in the mortar without disturbing the rest of the wall. Lime was once used, and still is sometimes, to give the same plastic effect, but it is harder to work and has to be soaked overnight. Most bricklayers use brickie's sand on ordinary domestic jobs, because it is much more convenient.

To prepare the mortar, first measure in the dry ingredients. If you are not sure of shovelfulls, use a bucket to measure out the ingredients. Mix the dry ingredients well before adding the water and *do not* use a hose—use a bucket, and then you can add a plasticiser to the water, which will increase the workability of the mortar even further. If you don't want to spend money on a whole bottle of plasticiser, use some ordinary liquid household detergent and it will do the job just as well. Add enough water to mix the mortar to a good workable consistency. Now you are ready to start bricklaying.

Another popular use for cement around the house is to make concrete for paving, driveways, paths or patios. A good concrete mix is one part cement, five parts gravel and three parts sand. This sand is not the normal brickie's sand, but a clean, sharp variety which you will find at most good building suppliers. Don't bring home a bucket of sand from the beach—it will ruin good concrete. Mix up all the dry ingredients and then add water to make a good stiff mix. Don't make it too sloppy, as it will weaken the concrete.

Now you are ready to put the concrete in the formwork or frame. Once this is done, compact it with a shovel, level it and leave for a couple of hours until the surface water is gone; you can then trowel it off to get the finish required.

Concrete paving is usually finished off with a wooden trowel, but if you want a really smooth finish, use a steel trowel. If you want a non-slip surface, once you have gone over it with a wooden trowel, work it over again with a stiff broom.

If you would like more details, contact your local office of the Cement and Concrete Association of Australia, as they have hundreds of brochures covering just about every use of cement or concrete.

DOG KENNELS

We looked at the range of dog kennel kits on the market, and while a couple were satisfactory, none met the high standards required by the RSPCA. We also checked a widely circulated plan for building a kennel, and found that it too was unsatisfactory. After lengthy consultations with the RSPCA, we decided to design our own, which was submitted to the RSPCA and received their approval and recommendation.

The kennel features include the following:

1   The floor of the kennel must be at least 10cm (4″) off the ground to allow air circulation and to keep the kennel dry. We recommend using treated pine for the base because it is rot-proof.
2   All materials must be durable and waterproof. We used resin-bonded ply for the walls, floor and roof. Metal kennels are unsuitable; they are cold in winter and too hot in summer.
3   The roof must be able to be opened to allow for easy cleaning and airing. The roof corners should be rounded to reduce the possibility of injury. A wide

overhang is needed at the front to keep rain out. The roof is also lined for insulation and to reduce noise from rain and hailstorms.
4   There must be as few joins as possible, because fleas seek shelter in them. All joins should be sealed with silicone to deter fleas and prevent draughts. We had the corners mitred for easy glueing, but if that seems like too much trouble then just overlap the corners, nail together and seal with Dow Corning sealant on the inside and outside joins.
5   The dog must be able to turn around and stand up inside the kennel.
6   Accessories include a tying ring for training pups in kennel use; a tin bracket to ensure that the water bowl remains upright; the hinged roof needs to be clipped down so it cannot fly up in the wind.

Sizes The *small* kennel is suitable for toy breeds and most small terriers.

The *medium* kennel is suitable for labradors, Irish setters, corgis, cocker spaniels and German shepherds.

The *large* kennel is suitable for afghans, borzois, old English sheepdogs, great danes, St Bernards or smaller dogs sharing the kennel.

Building instructions

1   On a flat, firm surface, lay out the treated pine subfloor frame and screw or nail it together. Position the centre subfloor member and screw or nail it to the outer frame. Similarly, screw and nail the remaining smallest members of the subfloor frame (the noggings).
2   Glue and screw the 5-ply floor to the frame using Fuller's Max Bond or similar.
3   Drill large holes through the subfloor frame to ensure cross-ventilation and water runoff to the 'compartments' formed by the frame.
4   Glue and screw each of the 5-ply wall panels to the subfloor frame, and to each other at corners, starting at the front panel and progressing around the frame. Ensure that the subfloor frame and ventilation holes are visible below the wall panels. Our drawing indicates corners of wall panels that are mitred, in preference to butt-joints, but either method is possible. Adjustments will need to be made to panel dimensions shown if butt-joints are used.
5   Use Dow Corning silicone seal on all internal joints while they are accessible, before fixing roof panels.
6   Tack the triangular ends that form the 'pitch' of the roof to the front and back panels (with waste ply or surplus timber), from the inside of the kennel, to position ends to receive roof panels.
7   Fix one side of the roof panels to line up with the apex of the roof, ensuring that you provide the overhangs shown on the drawing. It might be useful to mark the overhangs on the underside of the panel before

positioning. The apex (ridge) should preferably be mitred for strength and maximum glueing surface. Tack the first roof panel in place with small nails after glueing all edges that contact the panel, then screw the panel in place, ensuring that the 'box' of the floor and wall panels is not distorted.

8 Fix hinges and roof lock, as shown on the drawing, with small galvanised bolts.

9 Remove temporary cleats that are holding the roof down and raise the roof on its hinges to silicone the internal joints.

10 Fix Colorbond metal roof covering with Max Bond (or similar), with small 12mm (½″) clouts or self-tapping screws, ensuring that the bonding is directly under nail or screw holes.

11 Paint with exterior acrylic gloss or semi-gloss paint. Do not paint the interior.

12 Fix the tying ring and metal bracket for water bowl.

THE BURKE'S BACKYARD KENNEL

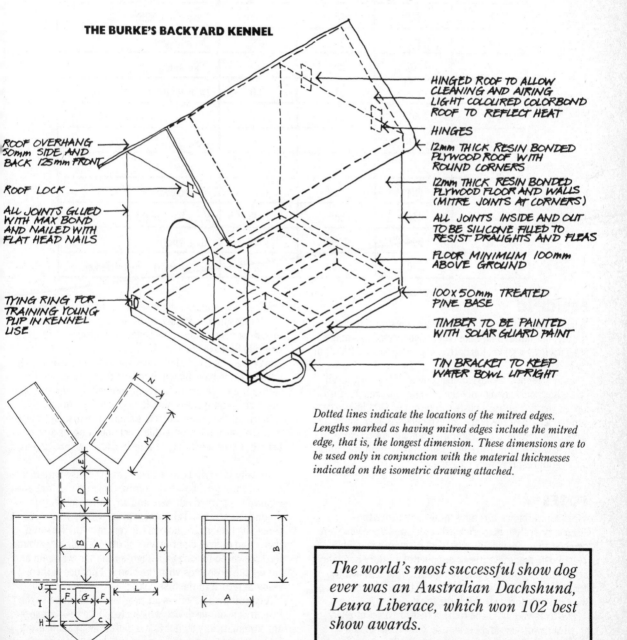

Dotted lines indicate the locations of the mitred edges. Lengths marked as having mitred edges include the mitred edge, that is, the longest dimension. These dimensions are to be used only in conjunction with the material thicknesses indicated on the isometric drawing attached.

The world's most successful show dog ever was an Australian Dachshund, Leura Liberace, which won 102 best show awards.

BURKE'S BACKYARD KENNEL CUTTING LIST (mm)				
LENGTH	SMALL	MEDIUM	LARGE	COMMENTS
A	480	800	1200	Floor width
B	600	1000	1500	Floor length
C	504	824	1224	Mitred edges
D	440	680	1080	Base box height
E	177	289	429	Peak height
F	162	257	412	Door side panel
G	180	310	400	Door width
H	50	50	50	
I	340	580	980	Door height
J	50	50	50	
K	624	1024	1524	Mitred edges
L	440	680	1080	Base box height
M	799	1199	1699	Roof length
N	370	565	809	½ roof width/one mitred edge

FENCING

When it comes to replacing the fence, most people use timber, but handyman Peter Harris suggested galvanised steel posts as a good alternative, especially on a difficult or rocky site.

If the steel post is buried in a cement-filled hole, it will last a lifetime, leaving only the palings to be replaced in say 20 years. The steel posts can be cut so that lattice can run the length of the fence, and the householder could have them trimmed to height by a fencing contractor.

After weathering, the entire fence takes stain well and the overall result is very pleasing.

FUSES

When a fuse blows it is a warning that either the electricity system is overloaded or the appliance you were using at the time is faulty. In most cases you should consult the manufacturer or supplier of a faulty appliance before making any attempt to repair it yourself, but you *can* check the fuses yourself. Unplug the appliance you were using before you check the fuses.

The tools you will need to fix a fuse are a set of pliers, a small screwdriver, and some fuse wire—this should always be kept handy to your fuse box.

When you examine the fuse box, it may have just two or three fuses in it or it may be quite large with separate groups of fuses. Some fuse boxes have groups of fuses to one side that are specifically designed to cater for the power loads of fixed appliances such as the stove. If these specific fuses have blown, it is best to call in an electrician rather than attempt to fix them yourself. Power and light fuses are usually quite simple to repair, however.

Turn off the power switch. Remove the fuse by grasping it at the top and bottom—don't get your fingers around behind it because it may still be live and you are risking a shock.

Usually you will be able to see that the fuse wire has burned through. Loosen the screws holding the wire and remove the burned out wire and any other debris from around the screws. Take a new piece of fuse wire and thread it through the hole in the centre of the fuse and then wind each end of the wire clockwise halfway around the screwhead to each end. Tighten the screws again and cut off the loose ends with the pliers. The fuse is then ready to return to the fuse box.

A circuit breaker offers an excellent alternative to the fuse. It is a simple device which plugs into the fuse socket and automatically switches itself off if an appliance is faulty or if the system is overloaded. All you need to do is switch the circuit breaker on again after the overload, or after the faulty appliance has been removed, thereby saving yourself the inconvenience of fixing the fuse.

Keep a small torch in the fuse box, in case a fuse blows at night.

Be sure to select the correct fuse wire as shown on the packet. Don't use other sorts of wire because problems could easily result from this and you could jeopardise insurance claims.

GATES

Garden gates are a frequently neglected backyard fixture—probably because they tend to be out of sight and out of mind. A sturdy, lockable gate is vital for home security however, (it acts as a deterrent, if nothing else) and for the safety of small children and pets. Repairing a sagging or crumbling garden gate can cost as little as $30 in hardware items and is a relatively simple operation.

First, chocks should be inserted under the sagging gate so that it is resting in the correct position. Then fit a decent set of hinges, using at least two or three nuts and bolts as well as screws. Gates are usually kicked around, slammed, and generally treated badly, and nuts and bolts are far less likely to work loose than screws.

Heavy gates tend to sag, and horizontal bars usually provide inadequate support. The gate can be greatly strengthened and made to keep its shape by fitting a diagonal brace to it. A piece of strap iron is cheap to buy and easy to fit. It has pre-drilled holes, so simply cut it to length and screw it on to the gate.

The gate post itself can be made more rigid by driving in a star stake next to it and attaching it to the post through the pre-drilled holes.

The best and cheapest form of security is provided by a decent sized pad bolt screwed and bolted to the gate. You can cut a hole in the gate for your hand just above the pad bolt, so it can be reached from the other side.

Your garden gate should now be safe and secure, and ready to soldier on for many more years.

HANGING A DOOR

Corinthian Doors publish a pamphlet which details the seven-step procedure for hanging a door. They also produce labour-saving pre-hung door systems.

For further information

Sydney (02) 597 0111
Melbourne (03) 794 1122
Brisbane (07) 277 6466
Adelaide (08) 243 0888
Perth (09) 455 1333

LATTICE

It is important to select the lattice that best suits your needs. Lattice with small holes has a great screening effect and is best used around outdoor living areas. Lattice with larger holes is fine for general use around the garden.

Lattice is not difficult to erect. Most suppliers will frame the lattice to the size you require, or you can do it yourself. However it might be worthwhile spending the extra money on having the job done professionally if you are not competent at using a mitre saw. If you are going to do it yourself, you can hire a mitre saw and save between $40 and $60 a frame. If it's a square frame, then the angle of cut will be 45°.

Next, fix the frame around the lattice. You will notice that the framing timber has a trench for the lattice to slot into. Then nail it all together. It is now ready to erect and become an attractive screen that will give you a degree of privacy and still allow the light and air to circulate freely.

With the advent of modern treated pine, pine lattice has really become a much more practical alternative than it was before, because it can last 10–20 years or more.

LEAKING TAPS

A leaking tap can waste 100 litres (22 gallons) of water per day. If the leak is bad, the waste can be as much as 700 litres (154 gallons) per day.

The part that usually needs replacement is the washer on the jumper valve. This is tightened and opened every time the tap is used, and becomes worn or chewed away, especially if the valve seating is rough.

New washers (or jumper valves complete with washers) can be bought from hardware stores. If the thread holding the washer nut is burred, buy a complete new valve. Make sure that the new washer is the right size for the tap. Most are 13mm (½″), but garden taps may have 20mm (¾″) washers.

Locate the water meter and turn off the main tap. It is also a good idea to turn on cold taps inside the house to relieve the pressure in the pipes.

With an adjustable spanner, remove the spindle revealing the jumper washer and the valve. Replace the washer on the spindle and put it back in the tap and screw in place. Make sure, when you are screwing it back, that the tap is fully on—otherwise you will put too much pressure on the washer as you screw it in. Finally, tighten with a wrench.

MOWER MAINTENANCE

If you haven't driven your mower for a long time, and the thought of getting it running again sends you into a flat spin, take the mower to a shop which belongs to the Mower Specialists Association of Australia (MSAA). A safety check on your mower will cost about $30 and the service will check the blades, bolts, air filter and spark plugs. A mechanical check involving a look at all the electrics could cost as much as $80.

If you want to buy a new lawnmower, the MSAA will advise you as to which mower they feel best suits the area you'll be using it in, and will completely service the mower after five hours' use, free of charge.

One important tip: when you are replacing a part, ensure that you take the old part with you, so that you get the correctly fitting replacement.

If you would like to tackle the running repairs yourself, you may like to follow our guidelines.

Petrol When purchasing petrol for the mower, never buy more than 4 litres (1 gallon) at any one time. This amount should last between three to six cuts of the lawn, depending on the size of the area. As alcohol is now added to the petrol mixture, and attracts moisture, never fill the mower with the last drops of petrol in the tin, as this fuel is not pure.

Spark plugs Always remove the spark plugs before you start playing around with your mower; this prevents you from injuring yourself with the blades or electrics. If a spark plug gets wet, remove and replace it. We would advise that a spare spark plug be kept on hand so that the old ones can be replaced immediately.

Air filter This should be checked and cleaned regularly, especially if the mower is stored in a dusty area.

Blades will generally last about 12 months. When you are replacing a set of blades, it is always wise to buy a spare set. Like an emery board, the blades suffer wear and tear and will lose their efficiency after a year.

Handles If you have a lawnmower with chrome handles, rub with Vaseline or spray with WD40 to keep them in top condition.

Pull cords These should not need replacing, but may wear out if you pull on the cord with greater strength than is necessary.

Tyres The tyres are generally semi-pneumatic and don't need pumping. The wheels should be lubricated every 12 months.

Catcher This is a part of the mower which is often forgotten. After emptying the catcher and rinsing it out with water, store it hanging up under a shelter. Do not leave it outside or on the floor as it will become brittle and crack and, at about $80, they are expensive to replace.

Storage If well maintained and stored, your mower should last between eight and ten years, given normal usage. Store the mower in a dry, sheltered area. If your garage or garden shed is prone to dampness it is better to sit the mower on a platform so that it will not deteriorate. This should also prevent insects from nesting in the mower.

OUTDOOR FURNITURE REPAIR

Garden furniture that is rickety and unsafe quickly becomes garden rubbish if not repaired correctly.

When wooden furniture is exposed to the elements for an extended period, the joints eventually loosen. Most people try to repair the furniture by belting it full of nails. Unfortunately, this just doesn't work—as the wood moves apart, it simple prises out the nails.

Nuts, washers and bolts, and coarse-threaded self-drilling screws are the best fasteners. Return the weakened joint to its original position, and clamp it if necessary. Insert a couple of screws or bolts. Make sure all the nuts and bolts are tight, so that they make the furniture rigid.

After tightening up all the joints in this fashion, the furniture is ready for a light sanding down to remove flaky pieces from its surface. Then you can add a finish. If you don't think the furniture is worth sanding too far back because all the gaps and cavities might show too much colour variation, and you don't want to spend a week dismantling it and sanding it down to get into all the nooks and crannies, it is better to use something like a decking stain that will mask all the colour variations. If the piece of furniture is going to live in a damp or shady spot, paint on a couple of coats of a good wood preservative before you put the stain on.

Of course, your old outdoor furniture will not look brand new, but should give you another three or four years of active service, and save you at least $300.

PICTURE HANGING

To hang a picture or a mirror on a wall, or to attach brackets for shelves, you need to locate the stud. You can do this by knocking along the wall and listening for a change in sound or better still, use an Electronic Stud Finder. These are readily available at hardware stores. When it locates the stud, mark the spot, and you can screw the fitting to the wall using ordinary wood screws.

If it is not a heavy object, it can be hung anywhere on the wall using any one of a number of wall fixings available at most hardware stores.

Metal anchors are designed for fibro or villaboard, and come with their own hooks for hanging pictures, mirrors, and so on.

Plastic toggles are for use on general purpose fixing to plasterboard. With these you have to drill the hole first.

A metal Wallmate is the easiest fitting to use. Fix it to the end of an electric screwdriver and push it into the wall—it is self-threading. The Wallmate forms the cylinder, and the self-tapping screw provides the mounting.

RE-GLAZING A WINDOW

The home handyperson will find the following tips useful for window re-glazing.

1 Remove all loose broken glass from the damaged window. For safety, wear a pair of thick leather gloves, safety spectacles, and heavy leather shoes—jagged glass can easily pierce a sneaker or sandshoe. Place a cloth drop sheet on the floor both inside and outside the window to catch the falling glass.

2 Run a glasscutter around all the remaining pieces of glass close to the putty. This will make the glass easier and safer to tap out with a hammer.

3 After breaking out as much material as possible, remove the rest of the glass and putty using an old chisel and a hammer. You will probably come across glazing nails or pins, which can be removed quite easily with a pair of pincers.

4 Once you have removed all the putty and have cleaned the frame with a stiff brush, the exposed timber of the frame should be treated with something such as linseed oil. This primes the wood and helps the putty stick to it. If you wish, a timber primer can be used for an extra protective finish.

5 It is important to select the right sort of glass for your application, so take a piece of the broken glass, together with the measurements of the window pane, to the local glass supplier. Remember, when taking measurements for the window, there is a possibility that the frame may not be square. You can check this quite easily by measuring the diagonals (from one inside corner to the opposite inside corner)—if they are equal, the window is even; if not, you should measure all four sides and give the four measurements to the glass supplier.

   To be sure that the new pane of glass is a good fit, take your measurements from the outside of the rebates (the grooves into which the pane of glass will fit) and subtract about 2mm ($1/16''$) from that measurement.

6 When the new pane of glass has arrived, knead putty until it is soft and pliable, and then put a bed of it, about 3mm (⅛") thick, into the entire frame.

7 Press the glass firmly but carefully into the putty and fix it in place with push pins or glazing pins placed every 250mm (10") or so.

8 Clean up the inside edge by wiping off the excess putty with a putty knife. Apply extra putty around the edges of the glass on the outside and smooth it off with the knife, making a nice, neat, triangular joint that covers the glazing pins, but is in line with the inside window frame.

   If you are having trouble getting the putty to a smooth consistency, a touch of linseed oil wiped onto the putty knife will help. Also, if your hand is a little unsteady, then a cross stick, used in the manner of an artist, will give you something to rest your hand on and make it more stable.

9 Let the putty harden for a couple of weeks before painting it. When you do apply the paint, let it flow over the putty onto the glass for just 2-3mm ($1/16$-⅛") all the way around to provide an extra weather seal.

RUSTY ARCH BARS

Arch bars are the steel supports that hold bricks above your windows and doors. When an arch bar rusts it forces the bricks apart, causing cracks which can seriously weaken the structure.

There is only one course of action, and that is to replace the bar. This job should not be attempted unless you are a competent handyperson. To start you will need a plugging chisel and a brickie's hammer.

Carefully remove the mortar around the arch bar, then loosen the bricks that support this bar. Remove the bricks, holding the bar in place, and the bar should slide out quite easily.

If the bricks above the bar have settled, jamming the bar in place, they will have to be removed. Also, if the window top is close to the top of the wall, this section will need to be supported, as all the bricks above the window are likely to be loose. If this is the case you will probably need to call in a professional to do the job.

However, if everything goes smoothly the new bar should slide into place. Remember that you need about 10cm (4") of overhang on either side of the bar. The supporting bricks can be put back and then wedged in place with pieces of fibro or something similar, and it is then ready to be mortared. To pack mortar into these joints, use a small trowel.

If the window or door is in a prominent position it might be worthwhile having the arch bar curved to match the existing shape. A steel fabricator can help you to do this.

Use a galvanised arch bar because they last longer—if not you will have to do the same replacement job in a few years' time.

SCREEN DOORS

The good old wooden flyscreen door is almost as Australian as a Hills Hoist. Modern aluminium screen doors with fibreglass flyscreen certainly do the same job, keeping the flies out and letting the breeze in, but they can be fairly easily damaged by children or dogs and cats. Fortunately, they can be repaired.

If your cats are damaging your screen door, it might be time to think of replacing the fibreglass mesh with aluminium flyscreen. It's a little more expensive—about $8 for the average door compared with $6 for fibreglass—but the aluminium is much stronger.

If you live near the ocean, corrosion could be a problem and the best weapon against this is bronze mesh. It's the toughest and most durable of the meshes but will cost you about $36 for the average door.

When the screen has to be replaced and you've decided what mesh you want to use, the procedure for changing the screen is quite straightforward. Simply remove the plastic tubing that holds the screen in place. Then remove the old mesh and place the new piece over the door. Using a spline-roller (available for about $3 from your local hardware store) run the tubing back into the groove around the door frame. Trim off the excess mesh with a sharp knife and the job is done.

Remember not to throw away the flyscreen offcuts; they are ideal for placing over drainage holes in the bottom of pots to stop the potting mix from falling out. They are also great for patching large holes in Gyprock walls.

TIMBER

Choosing timber from the wide selection at a timber yard can be a confusing experience, but if you know what you are looking for, the task is much easier.

If you want wood for an inside job, for example, building bookshelves or panelling a wall, softwoods are the most suitable. One of the most popular and cheapest timbers for inside use is radiata pine. A piece of shelving will cost about $5 per metre.

A more expensive alternative is maple or western red cedar—ideal for staining or varnishing—and this will cost about twice as much as pine. These timbers are fine for other inside jobs, such as skirting boards, architraves and wall panelling. Another timber for panelling walls is brush box, which is a rosy colour and is more durable than softwoods.

If the job is outside; for use on a carport, garden shed or deck, you will need to use hardwood or treated pine. Hardwood is cheaper, but it is harder to work with and tends to shrink. Treated pine costs a little more than other hardwoods. A word of warning about treated pine: the preservative used in the wood can be hazardous, so don't burn the offcuts.

Another versatile timber for both inside and outside use is Oregon. However, if it is to be exposed to the weather it should be treated with a good preservative.

Remember, plan and measure carefully before you buy and don't hesitate to ask for assistance. Good timber yards provide brochures which will make the task of ordering the correct timber a lot easier.

WINDOW SASHES

A box-frame window has an upper and lower sash, each counterbalanced by a weight at each side of the window. The weights run up and down inside the box sections as the windows are opened or closed. If one of the cords supporting the weights breaks, it is a good idea to replace the others at the same time.

First, use a broad chisel to remove the stop beading

fitted at both sides of the window. Prise it off in a few places and don't worry if it breaks—you can always buy more beading.

Lift out the bottom sash to expose the concealed panel that gives access to the inside of the window. This panel may be identified only by a small join in the wood. Ease the parting bead off—just push it to one side—and then prise the panel out with a broad chisel: it will expose the weight that the rope was tied to. This weight does not need to be removed.

The next step is to replace the sash cord into the frame with the aid of a 'mouse', which is a sinker attached to a piece of string. Push the window down the frame to expose the pulley. Feed the 'mouse' over the pulley and drop it down so that it appears at the bottom; feed through the top of the weight, pull the sash cord through, remove the 'mouse' and tie a figure of eight knot so that the sash cord doesn't get pulled back through the top of the weight. Before nailing the new sash cord to the side of the window, make sure it is the correct length. Put the panel and beading back in place and the window should be as good as new.

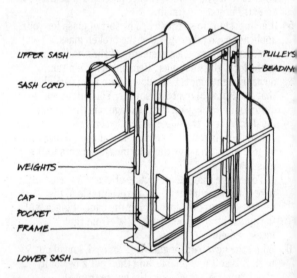

CHAPTER 4
Crafts and Kitchen

BASKET WEAVING

The following information was given to us by Audrey Simpson of Natural Fibre Basketry, 12 Nash Place, North Ryde, NSW 2113. Telephone (02) 887 2626. Audrey conducts basketry workshops in both the Sydney and New South Wales country areas.

Materials Vines and creepers, such as morning glory, ivy, honeysuckle, grapevine, wisteria, jasmine, virginia creeper and so on. Select long runners—trim off leaves—for storage, bundle into skeins or rounds and tie in several places to prevent breakage.

Flexible branches such as weeping willow, poplar, jacaranda leaf stems and so on. Choose the pliable ends of branches—pick those that are long, thin and straight.

New Zealand flax—cut the long leaves at any time—these can be used green, or the dried leaf at the base of the plant can also be used.

Watsonia, day lily, canna lily, red hot poker leaves (usually collected when they have dried—clean off any dirt before storing). A mixture of any of these leaves looks very effective.

Leaf sheaths such as philodendron—pick when dry and separated from plant.

Pine needles—may be gathered during any season—select long fallen needles or needle clusters. These are usually beige or reddish brown in colour. Separate clusters and tie into bundles until ready to use.

River reeds, rushes, long grasses, wheat, corn husks, fruiting bodies from palm trees, palm leaves, twigs, banana 'trash'.

When collecting fresh (green) materials, be careful not to interfere with the plant's appearance or growth process. Gently cut or pull materials from the plant, taking care to leave more than you remove. Make sure you use sharp cutting tools, and never rip or tear materials.

Generally materials are best cut after flowering—about 7-10 days. Non-flowerers may be cut just after their prime.

Storage Store materials in a dry, cool, airy place. Tie in bundles or skeins, removing leaves where necessary. Air must be allowed to circulate at all times, so don't use plastic containers or garbage bags. Don't store materials if they are wet, as they will mildew and rot.

Preparation Dry materials need soaking before working. The length of time depends on the density of the material; dry red hot poker leaves may only take minutes to become suitable, whereas very woody materials may require several hours of soaking.

Test all materials by gently bending—when the material is *flexible* and will not *crack* it is ready for use.

Try not to dampen more than you need for a project, otherwise you will need to start the whole drying process over again. In the dampening process never allow your materials to become waterlogged. Extra water tends to swell the natural fibres, causing extra shrinkage to your finished basket, and resultant loss of shape.

Collect as much material as you can—you always need much more than you think.

Making a coiled basket Use morning glory vines and wild grasses.

Tools required: scissors, large eyed darning needle.

Make a small loop in the middle of two or three vines. Thread the needle with some very thin vine. Insert needle through loop, pull through, concealing the end of thread by placing it between the loose ends.

Hold the loose ends in your left hand and wrap the thread around the loop, from the inside of the loop out. Do this about six times, or until you reach the starting point.

For the second row, coil the vines around the centre circle, stitching from inside the loop, over the vines and back up the loop—about 12 times. Add new vines and grasses to make a thicker bunch as necessary.

For the third row, wrap bundle around again. Insert needle into previous row, and stitch as before. Do this about 12 times.

Continue in this fashion until you reach the desired diameter. Until now you have been coiling rows side by side. To shape the basket, form the sides by working the coiled rows up and on top of the previous rows. The angle at which the rows are placed determines the shape. For example if rows are stitched directly on top of each other the shape will rise at a right angle with the base.

To finish—stitch off vines and grasses one by one until no coiling material is left. Conceal the last bit of stitching material within the finished coil.

Suggested reading

Basketry Today with Materials from Nature, Dona Z. Meilach and Dee Menagh, Crown Publishers, 1979.

The Techniques of Basketry, Virginia I. Harvey, Van Nostrand Reinhold, 1978.

Contemporary Basketry, Sharon Robinson, Davis Publications, 1978.

Baskets and Basketry, Dorothy Wright, A.M. & A.W. Reed Publishers, 1978.

Indian Basket Weaving, Navajo School of Indian Basketry, Dover Publications, 1971.

The New Basketry, Rossbach (Ed), Van Nostrand Reinhold, 1980.

A Book About Grass: Its Beauty and Uses, Mary Hunt Kahlenberg and Mark Schwartz, E.P. Dutton, 1983.

Basketry: Projects from Baskets to Grass Slippers, Hisako Sekijima, Kodansha International, 1986.

Splint Woven Basketry Robin Taylor Daugherty, Interweave Press, 1986.

CHRISTMAS DECORATIONS AND GIFTS FROM THE GARDEN

You'd be surprised at the Christmas gifts you can make from your very own garden!

These suggestions were prepared with the assistance of: Susan Avery, Floral Decorator, 122 Jersey Road, Woollahra, NSW 2025. Telephone (02) 328 7415 or (02) 32 1168.

Christmas wreaths The wreath can either be bought ready-made from a florist, or made with grape vine twisted or plaited into a circle.

To decorate the wreath with fresh flowers from the garden, take flowers and foliage and place them in small clumps. Wire them together leaving a tail of wire to thread into the wreath. Place each clump close together on the wreath and wind the tail around the wreath. As the flowers die off, they can be easily removed and replaced with a fresh clump.

Dried flowers and foliage, sprays of any of the Australian natives, grevilleas, gum leaves, bottlebrush or foliage with nuts and seed pods look wonderful. You may like to spray-paint some of the dried foliage with Christmas colours, and add bows and small decorations to the wreath.

Clumps of fresh flowers can be wired together to make a garland which can be placed on a hat.

Wire can be purchased from a florist, or many hardware stores stock a wire covered in plastic, which may be more practical if a child is making the gift.

Christmas cards Sheets of cardboard, in any colour, can be purchased from a newsagent, and cut to the desired size and shape. Ribbons tied into small bows, gumnuts and leaves can be glued onto the corner of the card, and your Christmas message written in green and red pencils.

Christmas bell A small, cheap terracotta pot can be transformed into a bell by using ribbons, gumnuts and leaves or flowers.

Take a length of ribbon, loop it at the top, thread it through the base of the pot, and knot just beneath the loop to secure the ribbon.

Gumnuts or similar can be glued to the end of the ribbons; and bows, seed pods and other foliage to the top.

Animals By using a little imagination, and gumnuts and jacaranda pods, all sorts of animals can be made. You may even like to dress up the animal with a ribbon around its neck.

Decorations Pinecones, gumnuts, seed pods, flowers and dried foliage can all be used to make your very own Christmas decorations. You may like to spray these with silver or gold. Make a loop with a ribbon and glue it to the top of the decoration, then hang it on your tree.

Christmas trees Almost any large pot plant will look terrific with some decorations and ribbons added. Some of the more unusual include a standard bay tree or ivy trained up a conical pyramid. Or you might like to decorate a Norfolk Island pine, Himalayan cedar or Norwegian spruce. Your local nursery may have some other suggestions.

Keep these pots indoors for only a few weeks, then place in semi-shade for a few days so the plant can reacclimatise to the outdoors.

For further information

Patricia Flannery
Shalimar Protea
3 Gondola Road
North Narrabeen NSW 2101
Telephone (02) 913 2498

Patricia conducts lessons in dried-flower arranging, and supplies dried flowers and foliage Australia-wide.

Ronald O'Shea
The Sydney Gardener
314 Willoughby Road
Naremburn NSW 2065
Telephone (02) 438 3224

CITRUS RECIPES AND HINTS

These recipes and hints are reprinted here courtesy of Tess Mallos, cooking expert and author.

The Australian Standard 250ml cup and standard spoon measures have been used in these recipes. Level dry ingredients when measuring.

Mandarin Cointreau marmalade (This recipe may also be used for kumquats)

1kg (2lb) firm mandarins
2 litres (8 cups) cold water
Juice of 2 lemons
About 2kg (4lb) sugar
4 tablespoons Cointreau or Grand Marnier

Wash mandarins in warm water. Halve or quarter them lengthwise and slice them thinly, reserving pips. Put fruit, water and lemon juice into a preserving pan, tie pips in a piece of muslin and add to pan. Bring to the boil, cover and simmer for 50–60 minutes until rinds are soft. Discard pips, measure fruit mixture and return to pan, adding a cup of sugar for each cup of fruit. Stir over heat, without boiling, until sugar is dissolved. Bring to the boil, uncovered, and boil rapidly, without stirring, for 30–40 minutes, until setting point is reached. Test by putting a little of the jam on a cold saucer; if a skin forms or the surface wrinkles when touched, the marmalade is ready. Let stand for 5 minutes. Stir in Cointreau and bottle in hot, sterilised jars. When cold, seal with sterilised lids.

Microwave method Use half the above quantities. Prepare as above, placing fruit and so on in a 3-litre (5 pint) microwave-proof casserole dish or bowl. *Do not use a plastic microwave container.* Cover and microwave on 'high' for 30 minutes or until rinds are tender. Measure and add a cup of sugar for each cup of fruit. Stir well until sugar dissolves; heat as necessary in microwave on 'high', and take care that the sugar is completely dissolved *before* the marmalade boils. When boiling, reduce to 'medium high' and boil, uncovered, for 30–40 minutes. If mixture threatens to boil over, open the door to stop cooking, then close and continue cooking. Test for gelling, finish and bottle as above.

Note: After the sugar is added to the cooked fruit, the container used should be less than half-filled, as the marmalade boils up considerably during the microwave cooking. Keep a close watch as it cooks.

Pectin test Most citrus fruits except for mandarins, kumquats and navel oranges, do not require this test. Use for other fruit, too.

After fruit has cooked, and before sugar is added, pour a teaspoon of the cooked fruit extract into a small bowl or jar. Add 3 teaspoons methylated spirits and gently shake container back and forth. If a thick clot forms, there is sufficient pectin in the fruit to ensure gelling; if small, soft clots form, remedial action is necessary. *Carry out this test away from heat or flame, and wash the test sample with spirits down the laundry tub.*

Remedial action For mandarins, kumquats and navel oranges, sweet apples, figs and peaches, add the juice of a lemon or a teaspoon of citric or tartaric acid for each kilo of fruit. Apricots will need extra pectin; strawberries, blackberries, sweet cherries and pears will require both an acid and pectin. Pectin or Jamsetta (a pectin–citric acid product) can be purchased from health food stores—follow packet directions.

Spiced orange slices

6 oranges
2 cups white wine vinegar
3 cups sugar
10cm (4″) cinnamon stick
4 blades mace (see *Note* below)
8 whole cloves
6 black peppercorns

Wash oranges with warm water. Place in a large pan, cover with water and bring to the boil. Simmer, covered, for 40–45 minutes until a fine skewer pierces the skins easily. Drain, reserve 1¼ cups of liquid, and cool the oranges quickly in cold water. Drain the oranges and cut into 4–5mm (¼″) slices, discarding ends.

Put vinegar, orange water and sugar into a large pan. Tie spices in muslin and add to pan. Stir occasionally over heat until sugar is dissolved, bring to the boil and boil 10 minutes. Add orange slices, bring to a simmer and simmer 30 minutes. Remove pan contents carefully to a bowl, invert a small plate on top of slices to keep them submerged, cover with a cloth and leave 24 hours.

Next day drain syrup into a clean pan and discard the bag of spices. Boil syrup for 15–20 minutes until thick (when bubbles begin to cover the entire surface). While syrup boils, pack orange slices in warm, sterilised jars (add a few spices from the bag for effect). Pour boiling syrup over the orange slices. Seal jars when the spiced oranges are cold, using glass or plastic lids, or use a doubled piece of plastic wrap under metal lids. Ensure the seal is good, as vinegar syrups evaporate. Label and date, and keep for at least six weeks before using. Use to decorate a leg of ham; serve with ham, corned beef of smoked lamb leg; use with hot or cold chicken, duck, turkey or pork.

Note: Mace is the husk of the nutmeg. It can be in pieces called 'blades', or ground to a powder. Ground mace is unsuitable for this recipe, and blade mace is difficult to obtain (better kitchenware shops often stock it). As a substitute for blade mace, break up a whole nutmeg with a mallet and use a quarter of the pieces.

Candied citrus peel

500–600g (1–1¹/₃lb) peels from oranges, lemons and grapefruit
3 cups sugar
2½ cups water

Use squeezed-out citrus halves. The peels from Valencia oranges are thicker and a little firmer, and are preferable to navel orange peels. Remove the remains of pulp and membrane from peels, leaving pith intact. Cut each half into quarters. Place peel in a plastic bag, seal and freeze overnight, or for days or weeks if necessary.

Put the frozen peels in a large stainless steel or enamel pan, cover with water and bring to the boil. Boil 10 minutes, drain, repeat once more. Cover again with water and boil 40–50 minutes until tender, then drain.

Put 2 cups of the sugar in the same pan with the 2½ cups of water and heat, stirring occasionally, until sugar is dissolved. Bring to the boil, add peels and return to boil. Boil gently for 10 minutes, invert a plate over peels to keep them submerged, cover and leave 24 hours.

Remove the plate and transfer peels to a bowl with a slotted spoon. Add the remaining cup of sugar to the syrup and heat, stirring occasionally, until dissolved. Bring to the boil, add peels, remove from heat and put aside again, submerging peels as before. Cover and leave 2 days.

Remove plate, return pan to heat, bring to the boil and boil gently until peels are almost transparent—about 20 minutes. Leave in syrup for further 24 hours.

Drain off syrup and place peels on a wire rack set on a tray. Leave to dry at room temperature for several days until fine sugar crystals form. To speed drying and crystal formation, peels may be dried in the sun (not the oven). Store in sealed jars in the pantry. When candied peel is required, chop or slice according to needs. Use in cakes, sweet buns or biscuits, to decorate iced cakes or as a confection.

Glacé Citrus Peel As above with the addition of 2 tablespoons lemon juice added to the sugar syrup when it is first made. This prevents crystallisation of the sugar. Use as for candied peel.

Lemonade flan (Recipe courtesy of the Dural Country Club—limes can be used in place of lemonade fruit)

3 whole eggs
200g (1 scant cup) caster sugar
300mls (½ pint) cream
Grated rind and juice of 4 fruit from lemonade tree

Cream eggs and sugar using a wooden spoon—do not beat, as air should not be introduced into the mixture. Stir in cream, lemonade rind and juice. Pour into a cooked 23cm (9″) pie shell and bake in a moderate oven, 175°C (350°F), for 30–35 minutes until set like a custard. Cool the flan and dust with icing sugar. The quantity of filling is sufficient for three 15cm (6″) cooked flan cases from the supermarket; these will take 20 minutes to cook.

Burke's Shortcut Wash the lemonade fruit well and chop roughly. Place in juice extractor and process. Do not use a citrus juicer.

Lemon hair rinse Pick about 100g (¼lb) lemon leaves and wash them well. Place in a large pan and add 2 litres (8 cups) water. Bring to the boil and continue to boil, uncovered, for 30 minutes until liquid is reduced by a third. Cool and strain through a sieve into a jug. Store in a clean bottle in a cool place. Use one part hair rinse to four parts hot water and pour through hair as a final rinse. Excellent for adding highlights to hair.

Citrus hints

Drying mandarin peels Place peels on a wire rack set on a baking tray and dry for an hour in a very slow oven—100°C (200°F). Leave in turned-off oven until cool, and store in a sealed jar. Use in Chinese recipes in place of dried tangerine peel; use a piece or two in the body cavity of chicken or duck when roasting, particularly if it is to be served with an orange sauce.

Orange skins Chop skins after squeezing and toss onto the garden to keep stray cats away.

Lemon skins Rub hands with squeezed-out lemon skin to soften or to remove stains. Also use to soften rough elbows.

To deodorise your garbage disposal unit, roughly chop lemon skin and put it through the unit. This also adds a lemon-fresh fragrance to the kitchen.

Storing Lemons Cut lemons from the tree with secateurs, leaving about 5mm (¼″) of stem. Purchase some builder's sand (free-flowing sand that has had the salt washed out) and make sure it is dry. Place a layer of sand in wooden boxes (line the base and sides with doubled hessian if there are gaps), or use polystyrene fruit boxes. Put lemons in, stem end up, leaving space between them. Cover with sand and add more lemons and sand as necessary. Store in a cool place and keep dry. Lemons should keep for 4–5 months—longer in a cool, dry climate (12°C–54°F—is the ideal storage temperature). Lemons should be dry and in good condition before storing; if slightly green, they will keep longer.

Lemon juice can be frozen in ice-cube trays—remove from trays, wrap each cube in plastic wrap to prevent cubes sticking together and store in a plastic freezer container in the freezer.

Storing citrus fruit for marmalade Freezing is a good method for storing citrus fruits, providing you have the space. Wash fruit with warm water, scrubbing gently with a soft brush if necessary. Dry and store in sealed freezer bags until required. Any citrus fruit can be stored in this way. Partly thaw the fruit before slicing. The freezing process causes some breakdown in the fruit, shortening cooking time. Because citrus fruits are high in vitamin C, an antioxidant, there is no loss of flavour during freezer storage; they can be stored for 8–10 months. By the way, frozen oranges are a healthy snack for children in hot weather.

COLOURED CORN

Coloured corn can be eaten, but it is not sweet like the usual corn. With its shades of earthy brown and gold colours, it is very useful as a decoration to hang in a rustic kitchen. It can be sliced into segments and threaded to make all sorts of decorations, and is great for children's projects.

The seed should be sown in spring and cultivated in the

...ame way as normal corn. When mature, it can be picked ...nd the leaves folded back and hung in an airy position to ...ry.

The coloured variety of corn is quite difficult to obtain ...rom shops or nurseries, but seeds for coloured corn are ...vailable Australia-wide through Thompson & Morgan.

HOME BREWING

...ome brewing is growing more popular every day, with ...uality full-bodied beer being produced at around a fifth of ...he cost of commercial beer, that is, 35c for a 750ml (1¹/₃ ...int) bottle. Home brew can be made in summer, requiring ...bout one week's fermentation and a further two to three ...weeks in the bottle, a little longer in winter. Home ...rewing is much simpler and much quicker than people ...magine—gone are the days when you would buy grain ...nd hops and boil it up in a stocking to extract the juices. ...t is all formulated in a can now, just open it, mix the ...ontents with warm water and sugar, add yeast and leave ...t to ferment. It is always wise to purchase home brew kits ...rom a specialty store, as there are a few do's and don'ts ...associated with brewing that the instructions don't ...always give you.

Another advantage with home brewing is that you can ...vary it to suit your taste. If the beer is not full-bodied ...enough, you can add more malt; if it is not bitter enough, ...you can add more hops, and so on. The alcohol content can ...be increased or decreased to suit your taste.

Home brewing kits can be purchased from any Mitre 10 ...store, most health food shops, some supermarkets and ...from New South Wales Home Brewing Supplies Pty Ltd, ...524 Pacific Highway, Chatswood, NSW 2067. Telephone ...(02) 413 3900; or 36 Stoddart Road, Prospect, NSW 2149. ...Telephone (02) 896 1211 or (02) 411 5844.

JENNY KEE KNITS

Jenny Kee Winter Knits is published by Simon & Schuster. It's available from bookstores and large newsagents. The recommended retail price is $19.95.

LILLY PILLY JELLY

Ingredients
Lilly pilly fruit—we used *Syzygium paniculatum*, commonly known as the Brush Cherry or Magenta Lilly Pilly. Many species of lilly pilly are edible but if you are in doubt have the plant identified by a plant identification service such as those provided by botanic gardens in capital cities.
One whole lemon
Sugar
Tartaric acid
Cheesecloth
Sterile jars
China marbles—not readily available. Glass marbles are

not suitable. China marbles can sometimes be purchased from second-hand stores.

Pick the fruit before it has fully ripened. Remove stalks and wash fruit well.

Cover with water, add one whole lemon, and boil for 20 minutes or until the fruit is discoloured and soft. Do not chop or mash the fruit.

Take a piece of cheesecloth or similar material, which has been rinsed in boiling water, and tip the boiled mixture into it. Tie the ends of the material together and suspend the bag of fruit above a pan to strain overnight. Never squeeze the bag, or the jelly will cloud.

The next day pour the strained juice into a saucepan and add half a dozen china marbles. These will stop the jelly from burning.

Add one cup of sugar per cup of liquid. Boil rapidly for 20–30 minutes until it thickens. If the fruit is fairly ripe it will be difficult to make it gel; in this case add one teaspoon of tartaric acid to six cups of liquid after the liquid has been brought to the boil.

Test whether the jelly is ready by putting a teaspoonful onto a saucer and placing it in the refrigerator to cool. When cooled press a finger against the dollop of jelly—if the surface crinkles or the jelly sticks to your finger, it is ready to bottle.

Bottle the thickened liquid in sterile jars.

This recipe was provided by amateur jam and jelly maker, Mr Owen Bennett of Sydney.

POTTERY IN THE BACKYARD

As well as being an entertaining and absorbing hobby, converting lumps of shapeless clay into pottery can provide a small-scale income. You can operate from a corner of your garden shed, garage or laundry. Initially, learning to pot can be a frustrating exercise, as unskilled hands attempt to force an uncompromising blob of clay to become something smooth and beautiful, as well as practical. Usually just a handful of lessons and you will start to produce the desired results, however. At this point the craft can swiftly develop into a relaxing, absorbing and relatively inexpensive hobby.

Having learned the principles and basic techniques of the craft, the next step is to gather materials. There are two main types of clay: earthenware, which is porous unless it is glazed (the most popular form is terracotta), and stoneware, which is far more durable. They both come in different colours depending on the mineral content. Good clays that are easy to work and handle range in price from $6 to $8 for a 12kg (26lb) pack. Obviously the more exotic or exclusive clays are more expensive.

The main difference between the two clays is that the stoneware is fired at much higher temperatures, which results in significant changes in the colour and texture of the finished product. It is very important to know what type of clay you are dealing with, as earthenware clay fired at stoneware temperatures can melt all over the kiln and ruin the pot beyond repair.

The next requirement is a sturdy bench with a sheet of chipboard or fibro on top. It has to be a surface that absorbs moisture so the clay doesn't stick and the board is easy to clean.

If you wish to make 'thrown' pots, as opposed to hand-built ones, you will need a wheel. Until you are sure the hobby is going to suit you, it may be best to hire a wheel from one of the big craft suppliers (for as little as $20 a month), or you could buy a second-hand wheel for a couple of hundred dollars. Most people prefer electric wheels to kick wheels—the average electric models range in price from $500 to $600 brand new.

It is an advantage, but not vital, to have a tap in your workroom. A bowl full of water and a bucket for the excess clay should be positioned near the wheel. The essential tools are very basic: a sponge, a needle tool for cutting edges, a flat piece of wood for trimming, some chamois for smoothing the rim, and a cutting wire made from some fishing line tied to two wooden toggles.

After the pot is thrown it takes a week or more to dry out before it is fired the first time. Then it can be glazed and decorated before being returned to the kiln for a second firing, which takes five to ten hours. Cooling takes about the same length of time. Gas and electric kilns are quite expensive—prices start at about $1800—but it is not necessary to have your own. You can get your pots fired at a local school or craft supply shop for just a couple of dollars per kilogram, which amounts to four or five small pots.

In fact, you don't even need a wheel to take up potting at home. You can mould pots and small sculptures using nothing more than a pack of clay and a little imagination. This is a great way to make inexpensive gifts for your friends.

For further information
Potters Society of Australia
68 Alexander Street
Crows Nest NSW 2065
Telephone (02) 436 1184

Victorian Ceramics Group
7 Blackwood Street
North Melbourne VIC 3051
Telephone (03) 329 1919

Potters Guild of SA
PO Box 234
Stepney SA 5069
Telephone (08) 326 0806

Queensland Potters Association
483 Brunswick Street
Fortitude Valley QLD 4006
Telephone (07) 358 5121

PRESSED FLOWERS
The age-old tradition and art of pressing flowers has come back into fashion. What better way to preserve your beautiful garden blooms, for use in bookmarks, pictures, greeting cards, and as gifts?

Suitable flowers

Flower	Colour	Method
Alyssum	Purple/white	Presses
Candytuft	All colours	Presses
Carnation	Dark-edged	Petals in books
Clematis	Small dark varieties	Books
Cosmos	All colours	Books
Daisies	Small	Presses
Freesias	All colours	Books
Fuchsia	Small outdoor	Presses
Honeysuckle	All varieties	Books
Hydrangeas	Red/green	Books
Narcissus	Yellow	Books
Pansy (viola)	All colours	Books
Phlox	Red/pink	Books
Primula	Red/orange	Books
Verbena	Red/pink	Presses
Floribunda rose	All colours	Petals in books
Hybrid tea rose	All colours	Petals in books
Miniature rose	Yellow/red	Presses

Suitable foliage, leaves and herbs

Plant	Method	Comment
Acacia	Heavy press	Use flowers, too
Bay leaves	Books	Small leaves are best
Clematis	Books	Use tendrils, too
Conifer	Presses	Small pieces
Elder	Presses	With flowers
Ferns	Presses	Brown/green
Holly	Heavy press	
Japanese maple	Books	
Maple	Presses	
Oak	Presses	Use the smallest leaves

The important point to remember when pressing flowers is that they should be fairly flat and open faced. You can't use something with a very complicated petal structure.

Tools Old books, telephone books, flower presses, blotting paper and newspaper. If you buy a flower press, we would advise you to throw the corrugated card away and substitute some newspaper.

Method Separate flowers and foliage into small pieces and lay them between blotting paper, then newspaper, and place between heavy books or in the flower press, whichever is recommended for the type of flower or foliage you have chosen. Layers of flowers-and-foliage, blotting paper and newspaper can fit in a flower press.

The requisite time for pressing flowers is six to eight weeks. The process can be speeded up somewhat by changing the blotting paper several times while the flowers are being pressed, although you must be extremely careful, as the plants will be exceptionally fragile at this point and it may do more harm than good to disturb them.

To retain the best colour in your flowers, they should be picked as they are coming into bloom.

Making pictures First arrange your foliage, leaves or herbs on cardboard, or hardboard for a picture. Add the flowers around the design in layers. If you are making cards or bookmarks, just carefully place a sheet of clear Contact over your design and trim with scissors. If you want to place it in a frame to hang on a wall, a light glue can be used to secure the flowers onto the surface (which could also be fabric), then carefully place the glass on top.

For further information

Your local library should have some craft publications with pictures to assist you.

You may like to seek out the book we used in filming our story:

Pressed Flowers, by Joanna Sheen, published by Merehurst Press, 1988.

ROCKING HORSES

Our story on rocking horses was filmed with Justin Oldfield, who would be delighted to provide further information about the reconstruction and restoration of rocking horses.

Justin may be contacted at:

34 Ryde Road
Hunters Hill NSW 2110
Telephone (02) 816 3820

NATIVE FAUNA

CHAPTER 1
Bees

Most of the bees seen around gardens during late autumn are ordinary honey bees or hive bees, which come from wild hives. They are feral rather than commercial bees. These bees often feed on wildflowers but the heavily laden, traditional garden flowers provide them with their richest source of pollen and nectar.

Lots of our little native bees have discovered exotic garden flowers too. Bees are particularly attracted to blue flowers, although generally the honey bees tend to be indiscriminate.

Like the honey bees, most of the native bees collect their pollen in pollen baskets on their legs. But while the honey bees take their pollen home to communal nests or hives, nearly all native bees are solitary. They don't live together in large nests, they don't make honeycombs and they don't have queens. There are no sterile workers, just males and females.

Trigona Bees There is one group of native bees that is social. Their scientific name is Trigona and most of them live in the tropics. All these bees are much smaller than honey bees and they don't have stings—one of their common names is Stingless Bees.

The bees construct their nests in tree holes using resin. They go out and collect the resin from trees and bring it home in blobs on their hind legs.

Resin has some other important uses for these bees. In the tropics the most common ants are the Weaver ants, locally known as Green Tree ants. They are extremely aggressive and ferocious hunters and, like most ants, they love honey. The little bees are constantly on the alert against these ants and they have devised a clever way of foiling them. They put a barrier of resin around the nest entrance. This sticky, unpleasant mixture seems to be a chemical as well as a physical barrier.

But ants do sometimes get past the resin barrier and in response the bee uses a very unusual and effective deterrent. Remember, it doesn't have a sting or any other kind of weapon. It smears a dollop of diluted resin, which it carries in its mouth, on to the ant as it goes past. The resin is tacky enough to immobilise the ant, and takes its mind off the honey it was seeking.

The resin also appears to have an unpleasant smell. Even the approach of a bee with resin in its mouth seems to disconcert the ants. When touched with even a small trace of resin, the ants try desperately to rid themselves of it. Once an ant is stuck down, other bees approach and add their dollops.

There is some cost to the bees—some of them are killed by the attacking ants—but with just a few sacrifices the raiders are repelled and the nest, its brood chambers, and most of its inhabitants survive.

CHAPTER 2
Birds

BIRD INJURIES
Unfortunately it is not uncommon to find or be given an injured bird, but there are a number of steps which should be taken to assist the bird in its recovery until you can take it to a veterinarian. Awareness of these steps may help you to preserve some of Australia's beautiful bird life.

The bird will need to be kept warm to help it overcome shock. It is no good simply wrapping a blanket around it. Put the bird in a box of a suitable size, or a cage if you have one, and then attach a 35 or 40-W light globe to the side of the box or cage. Cover the cage loosely with a towel.

The next step is to restore energy to the bird, and this is done by giving it some sort of food. The ideal ingredients are readily available in most households. You will need some canned cat or dog food and a little high protein baby cereal. Mix equal portions of these two ingredients together in a dish and then add a little water to make it runny. Feed the mixture to the bird using a small spoon or a paddle pop stick. This food ration is suitable for most injured birds, such as pigeons or magpies.

Add a little honey to the bird's drinking water as well—this is very important as it provides instant energy.

Having helped the bird over its shock and after giving it something to eat, the next step is to do something about strapping the injured limb until you are able to take the bird to a vet.

For a *broken wing*, take three strips of Elastoplast, two long and one short. Wrap one long one around the base of the wings near the tips. Do not obstruct the vent. Wrap the second long one around the shoulders or wing butts. Stick the third down the centre of the back to balance the bird.

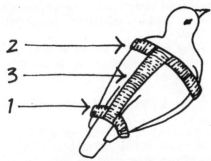

For a *broken leg*, make a butterfly splint using three layers of Elastoplast one on top of the other. Pinch them in the centre so that the two halves stick together for about 2cm. Stick the sides around the bird's leg and then back together again, making a sandwich around the leg. Cut off the excess.

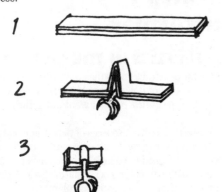

DUCKS AT NARRABEEN LAGOON

Sydney's Narrabeen Lagoon has a duck problem. The problem birds are various domestic breeds, such as the muscovy, the introduced North American mallard duck and mallard/black duck hybrids.

The mallards are of particular concern, as they interbreed with the native black duck (*Anas superciliosa*).

This interbreeding has the potential to cause the extinction of the black duck.

Narrabeen Lagoon, like many New South Wales coastal lagoons, is a drought refuge for native ducks. At times large numbers of native ducks use the lagoon when preferred areas, such as inland lakes and flood plains, are dry. There is a small resident population which includes black ducks and grey teals (*Anas gibberifrons*) and wood ducks (*Chenonette jubata*). Other wetland birds such as spoonbills, black swans, egrets, herons, pelicans, darters, cormorants and moorhens can also be found at Narrabeen throughout the year.

The domestic and feral ducks are resident at Narrabeen all year. Their population is reaching a level that is reducing the value of Narrabeen lagoon for native ducks. The problem ducks are occupying the habitat or 'living zone' of the native ducks. They are generally larger than the natives and therefore successfully compete with them for food, nesting sites and space.

The domestic ducks are quite tame and are readily fed by humans. This causes another problem, in that the duck population is not restricted by the availability of resources, which is often the case for the more timid native ducks. Therefore, as the domestic duck population increases (as more are able to breed) overall resources are reduced and the native duck numbers decline.

The domestic ducks congregate in a few areas, which is resulting in overgrazing of aquatic vegetation and a reduction in water quality. The high number of ducks results in a large amount of duck dung, which could cause many problems, such as disease and parasites (swimmer's itch) that can affect humans.

Organisations such as The Australian Museum, the Division of Wildlife Research, CSIRO and the New South Wales National Parks and Wildlife Service have advised Warringah Shire Council that this is of significant concern for native duck conservation.

Solution? Get rid of the offending domestic ducks (humanely).

This information was supplied by Peter Smith, Environmental Officer, Reserves Branch, Warringah Shire Council, Dee Why, NSW 2099. Telephone (02) 982 0333.

LEONARD AND LIZ TEALE'S LORIKEET MIX

3 slices of multigrain bread
1 heaped teaspoon of budgie seed
¼ teaspoon of powdered calcium carbonate
3 drops of Pentavite (infant's vitamin formula, available from chemists for about $5 for 20ml)
6 tablespoons of sugar
2 tablespoons of water

Roughly chop multigrain bread and place it in a food

processor. Gradually add ingredients. Dissolve the Pentavite drops in water before adding. Blend all the ingredients together until well mixed.

Stone fruit or apple peels can be added, as well as chopped apple, grapes and chopped banana. Do not use any citrus fruit or citrus peel.

SEAGULLS

One of the most adaptable and well-known of all birds is the great urban survivor, the seagull. The species which commonly populates beaches, bays, parks, cricket grounds, airports and rubbish dumps is the Silver Gull. Primarily a bird of the seashore, the silver gull is making its way further and further inland following the waterways.

The reason seagulls are often seen in large numbers at cricket grounds and airports is that they like to settle or roost in open places where they have a clear view of any predators that may approach them.

Seagulls vary in appearance at different times of the year and at different stages of maturity. Baby chicks are covered with mottled brown down. Immature birds up to one year old have mottled brown and grey plumage on their backs and black-brown eyes, bill and legs. Mature birds have white plumage with a grey back and black wing tips, bright red bill and legs, and white eyes with a red ring around them. In the breeding season the red of the beak and legs intensifies and the white feathers have a pearly sheen about them—birds in this condition are normally seen only in breeding colonies.

The tremendous adaptability of seagulls and their tendency to make use of rubbish dumps as a source of food has meant that the population has increased over the last 20 years at an alarming rate.

Seagulls nest in colonies in isolated places such as on islands with low vegetation which gives them good visibility. They prefer to nest on the ground, where they lay two to four eggs, which both parents help to incubate. When very young the chicks are extremely vulnerable, but they become independent at just six weeks of age.

Seagulls are migratory birds and have the long thin wings that make ocean birds masters of the air. One young bird found in Wollongong was later recaptured in Alice Springs.

WILD BIRDS IN THE GARDEN

Australia is regarded as having the world's most extensive and varied range of bird species for its land area. Of the more than 700 resident species, over half occur only in Australia.

Hand-feeding birds in the garden affords both the excitement and edification of viewing wild creatures at close quarters, and the longer term amusement and fascination of observing behaviour patterns and learning

to identify individual birds by their appearance or antics.

Proffered food should always be nutritious and should merely supplement, not replace, the birds' natural diet. A simple recipe for a dry lorikeet supplement is: 3 cups baby rice cereal, 1 cup rice flour, 1 cup glucose powder, 1 cup egg and biscuit mixture, available from pet shops, and (optional) 1 teaspoon dry multi-vitamin mixture, also from the pet shop.

This mixture is neither too strong nor too weak for lorikeets of all sizes. Honey should not be included in food mixtures as exposed honey can lead to the spread of diseases among local bees. Excessive amounts of sunflower or safflower seeds should also be avoided, as this can upset the diet of the local birds.

Plants to attract birds To attract nectar-feeding birds, plant grevilleas, banksias, callistemons (bottlebrush) and kangaroo paws.

Cotoneasters, pyracanthas and crataegus will provide edible berries for many parrots as well as gang-gang cockatoos; most nut trees will attract various other cockatoo species.

She-oaks provide edible seeds for red-headed finches as well as black cockatoos.

Unmown grass which is allowed to seed will provide excellent food for double bar and red-headed finches, eastern rosellas and other ground-feeding birds.

All bird species appreciate a shallow bird-bath, and most smaller birds require some dense shrubs (especially thorny ones) in which to take refuge when cats or hawks appear.

CHAPTER 3
Butterflies

BUTTERFLIES IN THE GARDEN

If you want to attract butterflies to your garden, you have to grow the kind of flowers that butterflies like to visit, that is, the type of flowers that want butterflies to visit them.

All butterflies require sources of nectar and suitable places to lay their eggs. A butterfly garden can be designed by examining a good handbook on butterflies in Australia to determine which species occur naturally in the region, and then planting appropriate host plants.

Although generalisations are difficult, some plants tend to be widely attractive to butterflies. Wattles, westringias (coastal rosemary) and kunzias are good nectar sources, as are banksias, some lantanas and the bauhinias with their butterfly-like leaves. Many of the old cottage garden perennials are attractive to butterflies; allysum, ageratum, bluebells, buddleias (the butterfly bush), numerous daisies, foxgloves, honeysuckle, lilac, lavender, polyanthus, petunias, phlox, verbena and wallflowers, to name but a few. Purple and red flowers and those with sweet scents are often strong attractants. Thistles, dandelion, clover and rough, unmown grasses also tend to draw butterflies.

But caterpillars don't feed on nectar, so the other thing you have to do is provide food for their offspring. Caterpillars of native Australian butterflies rarely damage garden plants, but one exception is the caterpillar of the Blue Triangle Butterfly.

If you live on the east coast, there is one certain way to encourage the exquisitely beautiful Blue Triangle Butterflies to stay around year after year. Blue triangle caterpillars feed on a number of native shrubs and trees, most of them belonging to the laurel family. Strangely enough, when they can get it they prefer the introduced camphor laurel tree.

Camphor laurels seem to spring up in gardens everywhere. You may not want a big tree, but it is worthwhile letting one or two seedlings grow to shrub size. If you cut them back hard you will get lots of lovely, tender new growth, where the blue triangle butterfly will lay eggs.

The big, velvety green caterpillars are quite hard to find. When they are not resting, usually on a pad of silk on the upper surface of a leaf, the caterpillars go through leaves as though every meal was their last. You can hear their mandibles nipping away from quite a distance. When a caterpillar is ready to pupate, it moves right away from where it has been feeding. A silk girdle will hold the caterpillar safely on the back of a leaf while it casts off its last caterpillar skin. The pupa is camouflaged with a pattern of veins to match those of the leaf. When the butterfly is ready to emerge, you can see its colours through the transparent skin of the pupa.

So if you want butterflies in your garden, give them flowers with plenty of nectar and be kind to their caterpillars.

ORCHARD BUTTERFLY

If you have an orange or lemon tree in your backyard you might find one or two of the big Orchard Swallowtail (*Papilio aegeus aegeus*) caterpillars feeding on the leaves. A few chewed citrus leaves are probably a small price to pay for the pleasure of having such magnificent black velvety butterflies sharing your backyard.

First noted in 1805, the Orchard Butterfly is distributed from throughout the southern Torres Strait Islands and Cape York to Victoria and South Australia. Its range has been extended by the cultivation of citrus plants. It is rare in Victoria south of the Murrumbidgee irrigation area.

The large, pale yellow *eggs* are laid singly, usually on the underside leaf edge of a food plant; eggs hatch in a little over a week.

The *larva* or *caterpillar* grows at an enormous rate.

When young, it resembles bird droppings; when older, it is handsome green with oblique brown and white markings. When disturbed, a red Y-shaped organ (an osmaterium) protrudes from behind its head and emits an odour of rotten oranges. Moulting occurs frequently as the caterpillar grows.

Three to four weeks after hatching the larva attaches itself to a support by a silken pad, and makes a silk sling to cradle its body. The last moult then occurs, and is quite hazardous as the insect must unhook its tail for a moment and is suspended only by its sling. The *pupa* or *chrysalis* then settles into its final shape. The colour may be brown or green, depending on the support. Camouflage is important as this pupal stage lasts a minimum of 13 days in warmer weather, or several months in winter.

The *mature butterfly* emerges in spring. The predominantly black and white wing pattern is surprisingly good camouflage. The female has lighter forewings and more red patches on the upper side of the hind wings and, overall, appears the more vivid. Males compete for the females' attention, and they may fly around for some time before mating occurs. The male beats his wings to shower the female with pheromones (sex scents).

WANDERER BUTTERFLY

The Wanderer Butterfly discovered Australia about 100 years after European settlement. These butterflies are native to America, where they are called Monarch Butterflies.

Our name for them is very appropriate, considering their journey to Australia. Over a few generations they hopped from one island to another right across the Pacific.

It is quite possible that some Wanderers reached Australia before European settlement. But if they did they couldn't have survived here, because the caterpillars of Wanderers won't feed on any other plant but Milkweed. Milkweed, sometimes called Cotton-bush, comes in two forms that are food sources for Wanderers and was introduced to this country after European settlement.

Milkweed also gives Wanderers protection from insect-eating birds; the milky fluid in the stem is poisonous to vertebrate animals.

Milkweed seeds have little parachutes and are readily dispersed in the wind. One form has red and orange flowers; the other, which is common along roadsides, has creamy-white flowers. The milky sap of milkweed is very irritating if it enters human eyes, and some people find it causes a rash on their skin, so take care if you are collecting any of the weed.

CHAPTER 4
Cane Toads

Cane toads were introduced to Australia in 1935 from Hawaii, having been brought there from South America. The deliberate introduction of cane toads to Australia was designed to achieve biological control of two species of cane beetle, the Grey-back and the Frenchi beetles, which were causing extensive damage to Queensland cane fields. The toads were bred in captivity and then released in their tens of thousands.

The introduction of the cane toad was a terrible mistake for several reasons. Firstly, it was not a specific predator of cane beetles so it would not die out as it ate out its food supply. While cane toads do love beetles, they also eat just about any other animal they can catch and fit in their mouths.

Secondly, frenchi beetle flights occur when the cane fields offer no ground cover to cane toads, and the grey-back beetle is only very rarely in contact with the ground where the toads live. Consequently the toad had no impact as a control. In the 1940s the advent of modern insecticides made the role of the toad redundant.

Thirdly, there is no toad-eating predator in Australia which is immune to the toxins in the toad's body, so a toad always kills its predators.

It is possible that cane toads will be in every state of Australia within the next 30 years. They are moving south along the coast of NSW at a rapid rate and ecological predictions say they should find Victoria to their liking as well. They could then move into South Australia along the coast, and if they found their way into the southwest of Western Australia and into the western areas of Tasmania they should do well there. The move southwards is just part of a natural progression but the toads have probably also had a lot of unwitting help from humans, being carried in loads of soil or timber, garden products and so on.

Now that the cane toad is so thoroughly established in Australia there is nothing much we can do to stop it. We are dealing with an animal that produces 20 000 to 40 000 eggs per female in a season. In areas at the forefront of their invasion a large proportion of those eggs will become tadpoles and metamorphose into toads.

Cane toads are the largest members of the toad family, and females may grow to 26cm (10″) long and weigh nearly 2.5kg (6lb). Cane toads have parotid glands on the sides of their necks which seep a thick white venom as a form of defence. When under violent attack cane toads can spray the venom over a distance of several metres. Human fatalities have occurred but only after the victims ate cane toad material (such as the eggs). Children are not at risk from cane toads unless they actually suck them. If cane toad venom makes contact with the eyes it causes a sharp pain. The eyes should be bathed thoroughly with water to relieve the discomfort. Under normal circumstances cane toads rarely exude venom, and can be handled without risk.

Pets are in much greater danger from cane toads than people, because they tend to mouth the toads and so absorb the poison. Fatal poisoning of cats and dogs is quite a common occurrence. The venom causes an effect similar to that of strychnine. The pet might convulse, and will probably produce huge amounts of saliva. It should be taken to a vet as quickly as possible because effective treatment is available, and without such treatment a small animal can die in as little as twenty minutes.

If you find cane toads in your backyard it is advisable to try to kill them quickly and painlessly.

CHAPTER 5
Caterpillars

CUP MOTH CATERPILLAR

Cup Moth Caterpillars are not as bad as they are often believed to be. Densey Clyne gives the following information in their favour.

They feed only on gum leaves, so you do not need to worry about them attacking your other garden plants. The damage they do to gum trees is usually fairly minor and, unless it is a particularly small tree they are attacking, you may as well leave them alone.

There are several kinds of cup moth. The caterpillars are sometimes called Chinese Junks, partly because of their shape and partly because of the smooth way they glide along. They move in this way because they don't have all the extra legs that most caterpillars have—but they move just as fast when they're in a hurry.

They all have a battery of very effective stinging spines. The spines can be raised and lowered at will, but they are used only in defence if the caterpillar is accidentally touched or deliberately attacked. The spines cause only minor irritation to most humans, no worse than a stinging nettle. But for a bird, even a very hungry bird, cup moths would be rather too much of a nasty mouthful. When they are not being used, the spines fall down out of the way into a kind of pocket.

After spending some time grazing the gum trees, the caterpillars begin to weave their cocoons. The first stage is like a flimsy string bag. The silk thread comes out of the front of the caterpillar from a spinneret, just below its mouth. The caterpillar uses its head as a shuttle, weaving the silk from side to side.

The bag is then closed off and the caterpillar seems to turn itself inside out, bringing head and tail together over its back. Now the caterpillar can rotate smoothly inside its string bag, laying down silk as it goes. It continually changes the axis of its rotation so that the whole surface of the bag gets covered. In this way the open mesh soon becomes a dense, tough fabric, hiding the caterpillar from view as it works. The finished cocoon is soaked with a fluid that dyes it brown and makes it as tough to crack as the gum nut, which it resembles as a disguise upon completion.

Eventually the lid of the cocoon is pushed up and what emerges is a very ordinary little brown moth.

HAIRY CATERPILLAR

Densey Clyne is fascinated by hairy caterpillars—she even keeps the occasional one in her kitchen so that she can find out what kind of moth it will be.

The name caterpillar actually means 'furry cat'. In the close up photography of Jim Frazier, which many people have seen on 'Burke's Backyard', the amazingly beautiful forms and colours of furry caterpillars can be appreciated. Perhaps we should all go around with magnifying glasses!

The hairs and bristles are not just decorative. They are a defence mechanism against predators, usually birds, but humans too are susceptible to the intensely irritating effect of the caterpillar hairs.

Most caterpillars are solitary, but many of the furry ones prefer to stick together. The common processionary caterpillars that feed on acacia trees spend the day in a huddle at the base of the tree, then every night link up head to tail to travel up the branches to feed. They eat leaves all night, then trundle down again before dawn.

When you see them in procession—rather like a series of fur-covered railway carriages—they are usually on their way to burrow underground and pupate.

TWITCHY TAIL CATERPILLAR

A plant which has become increasingly popular in gardens is balsam or impatiens. It pops up everywhere and scatters its seed about, and this has given rise to another name for it, 'Busy Lizzy'. An interesting caterpillar which feeds on the leaves of these plants is one of the Hawk Moth caterpillars. It doesn't have a common name, but Densey Clyne has named it 'Twitchy Tail' because, for some as yet unknown reason, the caterpillar wags its tail as it walks.

As this caterpillar grows and moults, its colour patterns will change several times until the caterpillar finally reaches its full size.

Nearly all hawk moth caterpillars have a spike or tail at the rear end. It is a good way of distinguishing hawk moths from other caterpillars. The only one which doesn't have this pointed tail is the Double Headed Hawk Moth. At the rear end of this caterpillar are found what appear to be prominent black eyes, which are probably there to frighten birds away. What appears to be a pointed tail on this caterpillar is in fact the head.

The Convolvulus Hawk Moth feeds on the morning glory vine and its relatives. It is an enormous caterpillar which is rarely seen in the garden.

Unless these caterpillars are in plague proportions, they do no harm and are really best left alone—or enjoyed for their antics.

WHITE-STEMMED GUM MOTH CATERPILLAR

One of the ways to track down the wildlife that might be living in your backyard is to look for clues such as footprints, nests, burrows and droppings. The droppings of the White-stemmed Gum Moth caterpillar (*Chelepteryx collesi*) are seemingly enormous for an insect and so are relatively easy to find on the ground under gum trees occupied by these creatures. The droppings have small ridges along them, and when broken open can be seen to contain plant material. Climbing the tree above will confirm their origin.

The caterpillars of the white-stemmed gum moth are very large, about 150mm (6″) in length, and have a fearsome appearance, being orange and black and covered in dense hairs and bristles. They are quite harmless, however, and can be handled gently without risk, although if they are squeezed the hairs will come off in your skin and cause an itchy rash. You can clearly see a lot of the interesting features of caterpillars on their bodies. These include big, fat prolegs, which are the sucker-like feet along the body of the caterpillar that are used for clinging on to trees (the six true legs are just behind the head), and spiracles, which are little air holes along the side of the caterpillar, one per segment, through which it breathes.

After the caterpillar forms its cocoon it is no longer harmless. All the little black hairs which used to lie safely against the caterpillar's skin work their way out through the walls of the cocoon to form a protective armour of spikes. If you touch the cocoon the tiny black hairs will penetrate the skin and cause a painful itching which can last for days. If this happens you can either shave off the hairs with a razor, or stick a piece of tape over the top of them and quickly pull it off—the spikes should come away with the tape.

These caterpillars feed on gum trees and do no significant damage in the garden. So don't reach for the pesticide or the shovel when you see one, just admire it and leave it to go about its business unharmed.

Strangler figs germinate in the forks of rainforest trees, then slowly choke them to death.

CHAPTER 6
Feral Cats

The following information is reprinted with
the kind permission of the National Parks
and Wildlife Service of New South Wales.

Feral animals are animals and their progeny, that were
domesticated but have escaped and survived in the wild.
Many animals become feral because they are dumped in
the bush or released from enclosures when they are no
longer wanted.

Feral animals in Australia include cats, dogs, pigs,
horses, goats, donkeys and camels. Many have bred so
successfully that they are major agricultural pests and are
declared noxious animals under the Pastures Protection
Act; all property owners must destroy these animals in
areas where they are declared noxious.

Feral animals also have a major detrimental impact on
native animals and plants. Some introduced species prey
on native animals or compete with them for food or
shelter. Others may browse an area so completely that the
vegetation structure is substantially changed. Serious soil
erosion can occur when the ground cover is removed by
feral animals. Feral animals can become reservoirs and
vectors for diseases of domestic stock and humans.

Cats Shortly after European settlement in Australia,
domestic cats became established in the wild. They found
ample food and faced little competition from native
predators. Feral cats are now established throughout
Australia from the Great Sandy Desert to sub-Antarctic
Macquarie Island.

Initially the feral cat population was composed of strays
and unwanted pets abandoned by people who believed they
were being kind to the animals by releasing them in the
bush. The population was given a boost in the 1880s with
the introduction of the New South Wales Rabbit Nuisance
Bill (1883), which advocated using cats to control the
exploding rabbit population. Thousands of cats were
released onto rural properties, particularly in the Riverina,
in an attempt to control rabbits, rats and mice. They
proved ineffective in curbing the expansion of rabbit
populations, and seem to have had little effect on the
frequent rodent plagues in rural areas.

When properly trained and supervised most domestic
cats are delightful pets. But when roaming wild in the
bush they become extremely cunning, ferocious and shy of
people. Feral cats are opportunistic scavengers and
hunters, and will prey on the most available and easily
caught species. They eat a variety of small animals,
including rabbits, birds, reptiles, amphibians, small
mammals and insects. Near towns and farm buildings
they will scrounge garbage scraps and will also eat
carrion. In rural areas their prey is primarily rabbits and

rodents. Studies of their food habits in the eastern
highlands show that in these areas feral cats rely heavily
on marsupial mice, native rats and possums. The effects
of predation by feral cats on these species is unknown.

Because they are difficult to catch, birds are usually a
minor part of the diet of feral cats, except on islands
where sea birds nest, and migratory birds rest and breed
in large numbers. Birds that nest in burrows are the most
vulnerable, and significant declines in populations of these
birds have been reported on islands infested with feral
cats.

It is open to question whether the feral cat has been
responsible for the decline of some native mammals
through predation or direct competition for food. The once
common eastern native quoll, *Dasyurus viverrinus*, is now
either rare or extinct over much of its former range, and
the feral cat has been at least partly responsible for this
animal's decline. Cats may now be doing little more than
filling a vacant ecological niche left by the disappearance
of this native predator.

Feral cats are not the only threat to wildlife. Even the
most lovable of our house cats can prey upon wildlife if
allowed to roam in bushland areas. Below is the record of
one well-fed domestic cat from Wahroonga, a bushland
suburb of Sydney. This list, of course, is incomplete, as a
large amount of prey would not be returned to be seen by
the owner.

Year—Animals Captured
1969—1 skink, 3 frogs, 1 tiger snake and 1 house mouse
1970—4 magpie larks, 5 red wattle birds, 1 lesser long-
   eared bat, 1 common mynah
1971—2 magpie larks, 1 red wattle bird, 1 rat
1972—2 fan-tailed cuckoos, 1 common mynah, 1 grey
   thrush, 1 bluetongue skink, 3 red wattle birds, 1
   magpie lark, 3 yellow-winged honeyeaters, 1
   eastern spinebill
1973—6 red wattle birds, 2 rats, 2 white-eared honeyeaters
1974—2 rats (different species), 3 red wattle birds, 2 little
   wattle birds, winged termites, 3 skinks
1975—2 mynahs, 1 small bluetongue skink, 1 skink, 1
   little wattle bird, 4 red wattle birds, 1 grey thrush,
   1 grey butcher-bird, 1 white eared honeyeater, 1
   king cricket, 1 longicorn beetle (Based on A.B. Rose,
   1976).

Feral cats are also known to have introduced diseases
such as sarcoptic mange and toxoplasmosis into native
populations. The latter is a disease which can be
transmitted to humans and can cause spontaneous
abortion, ulcerations and blindness.

Control of feral cats Feral cats are extremely difficult
to control because they are shy and generally wary of
traps and baits, and they often frequent inaccessible areas.
The feral cat problem must be tackled on two fronts. Feral

cats living in natural and agricultural areas must be eradicated, and the release of more domestic cats into bushland areas must be prevented.

Eradicating feral cats from the wild is difficult; many landholders still believe the cats keep down rabbit, rat and mouse numbers. This is true only if these animals are present in small numbers already and are not widespread. Only a few, unco-ordinated attempts to control feral cats have been made. Shooting and poisoning are highly selective methods of feral cat control but are labour intensive. Trapping is difficult, but if successful the animal should be taken to a veterinarian or the RSPCA to be destroyed. Do not attempt to remove the cat from the trap yourself or it may cause you serious injury by slashing with its claws. Reseach is being undertaken by the Vermin and Noxious Weed Destruction Board of Victoria into the biology and control of feral cats.

Under the National Parks and Wildlife Act, 1974, anyone who releases or dumps a domestic cat in the bush is liable to a fine of up to $1000. Unwanted cats or kittens should be taken to a veterinarian or the RSPCA to be killed humanely.

While sterilisation of existing feral cat populations is not feasible, sterilisation of domestic cats will reduce the number of unwanted kittens which could be dumped, and ensures that any cats that do escape into the bush will not be able to reproduce.

Perhaps the most important approach to be taken in attempting to solve the feral cat problem is to educate the community about the dangers to wildlife, and the health of domestic stock in releasing domestic cats in the bush. Your support is needed to make this programme work.

Books and articles

Anonymous — 'Domestic Animals Gone Bush', in *Ecos*, 13, 1977, pp 10–18.

Frith, H.J. — *Wildlife Conservation*, Angus & Robertson, Sydney, 1973, p 414. (Price, $37.95).

Rolls, E.C. — *They All Ran Wild*, Angus & Robertson, Sydney, 1969. (Price, $29.95).

Rose, A.B. — 'Cats', in *Parks and Wildlife*, 1(5), 1976, p 170.

CHAPTER 7
Fruit Bats

The following information is reprinted with the kind permission of the National Parks and Wildlife Service of New South Wales.

Bats are mammals—warm-blooded, furred animals that suckle their young. They are the only mammals that can truly fly and not just glide. Bats make up about 25% of Australia's land mammals, and form 20% of all known mammal species, second only to rodents (40%). Some species of bats can live for more than 30 years.

Bats occur on every continent except Antarctica and they are found across the Australian continent and on offshore islands. Sixty species of bat occur in Australia. About half of the species are endemic (occur only in Australia). About 30 species are found in New South Wales. They reach their greatest diversity in the tropics.

The distribution of bats is affected by the availability of roosting sites, food and climate. Primarily nocturnal, many species roost in large colonies in trees, mines and caves to keep warm and avoid predators. Most species produce one young each year, and may not breed until aged two years.

Bats are classified as Chiroptera, meaning 'hand-winged'. Their wings have the same structure as the human arm, but the fingers are greatly elongated and covered by a thin membrane. This membrane is an extension of the body skin and, in some species, acts as a blanket. In a fruit bat the wing is used as a fan when it is hot.

To dispel some myths:

* Bats do not attack people, although they may accidentally bump into people when disturbed. Bats never deliberately frighten people, although some species look ugly because of the highly developed flaps of skin around their noses and mouths.
* There are no vampire bats in Australia. They occur in tropical America and transfer the rabies virus to cattle and humans.
* Not all bats hibernate. Only some of the small 'insectivorous' species (Microchiroptera) hibernate in temperate climates.
* Bats do not spread disease, although, like all wild animals, they have parasites such as ticks and mites on their skin. You should wash your hands after handling bats.
* All bats have eyes, although they may be very small.

Fruit and blossom eating bats (Megachiropterans) Fruit bats are mostly large, weighing up to 1kg (2¼lb) and with a wing span of up to 1.6m (5¼′). They eat flowers, fruit and nectar. Eight species occur in Australia. Fruit bats have large eyes, simple oval ears, foxlike muzzles and a claw on the first and second digit of each wing. Unlike some smaller insectivorous bats, they do not hibernate during winter, but migrate or disperse to warmer areas. They do not use echolocation as a means of navigation. They have excellent night vision and an acute sense of smell.

The grey-headed and little red fruit bats are both common in New South Wales. The grey-headed fruit bat is mainly coastal, but the little red fruit bat is highly nomadic, following the flowering of eucalypts along the coast and inland rivers.

Camps are established over the summer period in shady secluded areas such as swamps, mangroves, rainforests and thick creek-bank vegetation. Tens of thousands of both species may camp together.

Both species feed on native figs and the flowers of eucalypts such as blackbutt, spotted gum, bloodwood tallow-wood and river red gum.

Due to varying climatic conditions, the bats' food supply is sometimes irregular and they will raid orchards, eating peaches, pears, apples, mandarins and other fleshy fruits. Both species follow regular routes on their nightly flights.

Breeding After mating in March and April, pregnant females form camps in October and show reluctance to fly if disturbed. Usually a single young is born in October. Most female bats give birth when hanging upside down, with the claws of their wings gripping the branch. The baby is licked clean and enclosed by one wing to keep it warm. The young bat clings to its mother and grips a nipple with its mouth. Its thumbs and feet also help it to hold on tightly as it is carried each night on its mother's feeding flights for about two months. It is then left in the camp, where the mother regularly returns to feed it. During this time young bats may fall victim to predatory animals such as goannas, carpet snakes, wedge-tailed eagles, white-bellied sea eagles and tiger quolls (native cats).

Unusually high mortality in adults may be due to scarcity of food, extremes of heat, heavy hail or the actions of man (for example, electrocution by power lines, particularly after windy nights). The Aborigines relished them as food.

Seed dispersal and pollination Fruit bats are important seed dispersers of native trees and shrubs. When fruit is eaten the seeds are discarded in the faeces, or they fall while the fruit is being eaten. They then germinate when conditions are suitable. Fruit bats have been observed eating privet berries, which may help explain the spread of this weed.

The rapid passage of seeds and food through their digestive system, and their habit of defecating while flying, makes fruit bats a very efficient seed dispersal mechanism.

Many cultivated tropical fruits like banana, avocado and figs have been developed from plants which were originally bat pollinated.

Protection of fruit Traditional control methods (such as shooting bats in camps or using flame throwers) are ineffective and inhumane methods of killing fruit bats.

Local protection of commercial crops and garden trees has centred on frightening the fruit bats away using bright lights, and noises made by bells, tins dangling in trees, firing gas scare-guns, electronic sound generators and recorded distress calls. Most of these methods are ineffective once the bats have settled onto the trees and started eating, or have become familiar with the deterrent. Acetylene gas guns have been found to be useful in small orchards.

In some cases, nets have been placed over individual trees, but fruit bats learned to crawl up the trunks and branches of these trees and bypassed the nets. Stringing barbed-wire around fruit trees has also been tried, but this is extremely inhumane because the thin membranous wings torn by barbed wire will not regrow, and the grounded bats provide easy prey for dogs and cats.

Strobe lights and stringing wire covered with sarlon across planted fruit crops have had some effect in deterring fruit bats from landing among fruit crops. However, there is no single method of preventing fruit damage, which peaks when the fruit is just ripe.

Protecting the whole fruit crop by erecting a frame and covering it with 'bat netting' is the best long-term method of reducing fruit damage by fruit bats. The netting, available from Sarlon Industries, Federal Irrigation Service and Jeff Frogley Agencies, has been treated to prevent disintegration in sunlight and will last up to five years. The cost of materials is about $2000 per hectare (2½ acres), but this should be recouped within the first few years from the extra amount of fruit produced for sale.

Unfortunately, other animals may become entangled in these nets and it is wise to inspect them regularly.

You should check with your state wildlife authority (see 'National Parks and Wildlife Authorities') before destroying or trapping fruit bats causing damage to fruit trees and crops.

Research into the behaviour of fruit bats is necessary to yield information useful in deterring them from fruit crops.

Threats to survival The major threats to the continued survival of fruit bats are: tree clearing for agricultural production; the use of pesticides; domestic and feral cats catching bats when they have fallen injured to the ground; foxes and other predators; urban expansion into existing fruit bat camps; and clearing and draining of mangrove swamps.

CHAPTER 8
Geckos

Most people are familiar with blue-tongue lizards and bearded dragons, but the little lizard called the Gecko is nocturnal and not often seen.

If you do find one it is important to be very careful when

handling it because geckos are notorious for dropping their tails when they're handled roughly. The tail will regrow in time. Geckos also regularly shed their skins as they grow.

Eyes Geckos have beautiful eyes. It is one of their peculiarities that they can't blink. Instead of moveable eyelids they have a transparent membrane over their eyes, rather like a contact lens. It keeps moisture in and dirt out. Of course, the lens itself has to be cleaned and this is achieved by sliding the long tongue over the surface of the lens.

Variations You can find geckos of one kind or another everywhere in Australia, particularly in the outback. They eat mostly arthropods (insects, spiders and so on) but some larger specimens include smaller geckos in their diet.

Leaf-tailed geckos are common around Sydney and live among rocks and under houses.

The Knob-tailed gecko is a strange little creature which is found in rocky places in the outback in far northern Australia. You couldn't find a greater contrast in tail than between the knob-tailed and the leaf-tailed geckos. The knob-tailed's true tail is a tiny little protuberance—it hasn't been broken off, that is its normal size.

CHAPTER 9
Koalas

The following information is reprinted with the kind permission of the National Parks and Wildlife Service of New South Wales.

Soft, ashen fur, a docile nature and a 'teddy-bear' expression give the koala its cuddly appearance. But those huge claws, which sink so easily into the bark of trees, can make a frightened koala quite a handful.

Of course, koalas are not really bears at all. True bears don't have pouches and their young arc well developed at birth. A newborn koala, however, would fit on your thumbnail.

Wombats are koalas' closest relatives and like them, have a pouch which opens towards the rear. This is fine for a wombat, but koalas need strong muscles ringing the pouch to keep the young one from falling out.

The largest koalas, over 10kg (22lb), are found in Victoria while the smallest, a mere 5.5kg (12lb) live in North Queensland. Koalas are found between these two areas, but only where enough suitable trees still remain.

Female koalas are fully grown at four years, while males take five to mature. Their maximum life span is between 10 and 20 years.

One of the koalas' more unusual features is the fact that they have two thumbs but only three fingers on each front paw. This arrangement makes their grip more even on

each side of a branch. Coupled with their huge claws and powerful muscles, it helps them to hold on very securely. The clawless big toes on their hind legs work against the other toes, so koalas can grip with their hind feet as well.

Like many other marsupials, koalas have two of their hind toes joined together to form a handy two-toothed comb for grooming the fur and removing ticks.

Breeding Female koalas can breed from about two years of age, and are able to produce one offspring each year.

Like other marsupials, newborn koalas are tiny and poorly developed; about the size of a two-cent coin. The blind, hairless young is born about a month after mating. Unaided, it drags itself into the mother's pouch and attaches to one of the two teats.

By about seven months, it has outgrown the pouch and rides on the mother's back, or rests cuddled against her chest as she drowses in the fork of a tree. During this time, the young one samples gum leaves and also the mother's faeces, possibly as a source of microbes which can help digest the tough leaves.

When the young koala is about a year old, its mother is ready to mate again. This usually happens between September and January when lovesick koalas serenade each other with a collection of indescribable noises: the piglike grunts and growls of the males mingling with the high pitched tremolo of the females.

Not surprisingly, these noisy and sometimes violent activities result in the young koala being driven off to start life on its own. The young ones can survive only if they find a suitable area, not already occupied by other koalas.

Feeding A koala eats about 0.5kg (1lb) of leaves each day, generally those growing on the tops and sides of branches. Although they are known to take over 40 varieties of leaves, they are fussy eaters, choosing most of their food from a few varieties of eucalypt: *Eucalyptus viminalis, E. ovata, E. obliqua, E. punctata, E. tereticornis, E. camaldulensis, E. microcorys, E. populnea, E. rudis.*

Smell seems to be important in choosing leaves as koalas sniff them before eating; if the right eucalypt oils have been added, they will even chew on a piece of blotting paper!

Around Sydney, grey gums and mahoganies are the most favoured trees. In northern areas of New South Wales tallow wood and forest red gum are important, while manna gum tops the bill in the south. These trees are all eucalypts, but koalas have been seen eating paperbark, she-oaks, brush box and acacias. They also use a variety of other trees for daytime shelter.

Koalas have individual preferences, and each animal will tend to favour particular trees within the range of suitable species. They also change from one type to another as the seasons progress. For instance, around

February, when tallow woods are sprouting new shoots, Port Macquarie's koalas leave them alone, favouring blackbutt instead. These changes may be caused by variations in the food value of the leaves.

Gum leaves are not the easiest things in the world to digest. They are tough, they contain oils which can be poisonous and they can even produce cyanide. To cope with such an unusual diet koalas have a long thin tube, like an appendix, branching out from their intestines. This tube, or caecum, grows to a world record length of 2 metres (6½ft). Although it probably helps with digestion, its exact function still remains a mystery.

Habitat Trees help protect koalas from predators and harsh weather, but most importantly they provide them with food. Virtually the only item you'll find at an Australian teddy-bears' picnic will be gum leaves.

Where forest areas are limited by man-made changes, life can be very hard for young koalas. They leave their mothers after about a year, and if the forest is fully occupied they have to leave the area. If this involves crossing open spaces, the young ones can be killed by cars or dogs, or attacked by ticks. A lack of suitable food may make them more liable to disease.

The only solution to these problems is to plant and retain trees for food and shelter in areas where the animals have access to them. It is especially useful if trees can form corridors between the different areas where koalas now live. Such corridors make the population much more viable, by allowing juvenile koalas to colonise new areas.

The National Parks and Wildlife Service, together with voluntary conservation bodies, has been active in planting koala food trees in several areas of New South Wales, including Port Macquarie and Lismore.

One area of the Service's current concern about koalas is disease. There have been epidemics affecting koalas since the 1880s. Low fertility caused by cystic ovary disease is one of the main problems facing koalas at present. A recent theory is that the population became overcrowded as Aboriginal hunting declined, causing diseases to spread more rapidly.

All in all, koalas are fascinating creatures, and we can look forward to their continued company as long as their forests remain.

CHAPTER 10
Mosquitoes

Mosquitoes are flies (insects with two wings)—the word 'mosquito' is Spanish and means 'little fly'. There are more than 3000 species of mosquitoes. They are found in all parts of the world, even the Arctic. They belong to the fly order Diptera and make up the family Culicidae. There are about 230 members in Australia, including three introduced types. The most important are Culex, Aedes and Anopheles.

Female mosquitoes may live for up to 30 days, while the males live for only seven to ten days. During their lifetime, female mosquitoes could lay as many as 3000 eggs, 100 to 300 at a time.

The life cycle of these insects has four stages:

Eggs The elliptical eggs float on water, usually joined together in 'rafts'.

Larvae Only about 1mm long when they emerge the larvae ('wrigglers') are legless and are equipped with a breathing tube ('siphon') on the abdominal tip which is brought to the water surface where the larvae hang upside down; they feed by fanning minute fragments from the water into their mouths with brushlike mouth parts. In order to grow, larvae must split their skin and shed it.

Pupae After four months they become pupae. They have a swollen head and thorax, a sharply curved abdomen, and dark spots for eyes; they breathe through two tubes just behind their head. They are active, propelling themselves jerkily like minute lobsters, but they do not eat. The pupal stage can be as short as 34 days.

Adults emerge from the pupal skin at the water's surface in such a way that they don't get wet; surface tension supports their tiny weight. The adult mouth parts are elongated into stylets enclosed in a sheath, to form a proboscis.

Males feed on plant juices such as nectar and decomposition liquids and sap. Females need vertebrate blood to mature their eggs, and feed on man, birds, reptiles, frogs, and so on.

Only female mosquitoes 'bite' and only the females of a few species attack humans and animals. They sip the victim's blood, which they need for the development of the eggs inside their bodies. The amount of blood taken varies greatly among individual mosquitoes. Some may sip as much as 1½ times their own weight at a 'sitting'.

The mosquitoes' hum results from the high frequency of its wingbeats; the female's slightly lower frequency may serve as a means of sex recognition. Breeding habits vary, but the female's chief aim in life is to mate and lay her eggs.

Most species of mosquito spend their entire lives within 1.6km (1 mile) of the place they hatched. A few kinds may travel as far as 32km (20 miles) to find food or mates. Mosquitoes lay their eggs in marshes, swamps and pools of still water, as well as tree holes, tyres and tin cans that contain standing water. Such places should be drained, or the surface of the water covered with a thin layer of light oil, if you wish to prevent mosquitoes breeding there.

Some people have quite a severe reaction to mosquito bites. This may be due to a reaction to the mosquito's saliva. Mosquitoes transmit serious diseases such as malaria, yellow fever, filariasis, dengue, encephalitis as well as heartworm in dogs and myxomatosis in rabbits.

The head of the Entomology Unit at Sydney's Westmead Hospital, and Senior Lecturer in Medical Entomology, Dr Richard Russell, says that mosquitoes are attracted to humans by the carbon dioxide they breathe out. Body odours and body heat may also attract mosquitoes to a lesser extent.

Insect-repelling candles contain citronella, a yellow oil which repels insects, as do products containing pyrethrum, an insecticide. Such products include the old mosquito coils and the modern-day equivalents, Mozzie Zappers and Clean Dead.

The Australian Consumers Association has repeatedly advised consumers against electronic insect electrocutors and ultrasonic repellents, which have been shown to be quite ineffective against biting insects.

Wet weather through much of 1989 has been very favourable to mosquitoes. On 'Burke's Backyard', Densey Clyne took the opportunity to study a fascinating 'puddleful' of them.

CHAPTER 11
Parma Wallabies

These marsupials were first described in 1831 by ornithologist John Gould, who named them Parma Wallabies or the White-throated Wallaby. By the turn of the century, they were noted to be extremely rare, and by 1930 were thought to be extinct.

Dr David Ride, an Australian scientist, found that there were some parma wallabies on Kawau, an island 32km (20 miles) off the coast of northeast New Zealand. They had been taken there by Sir George Grey when he was appointed Governor of New Zealand in 1870.

In 1971, Peter Piggott, along with representatives from the New South Wales National Parks and Wildlife Service, Taronga Zoo and Macquarie University, brought forty parma wallabies to Australia, where they were shared by the various parties. Only the wallabies kept by Peter Piggott at Mount Wilson survived, although some of these were taken by foxes. Peter built a special enclosure for the wallabies, and later returned to Kawau to bring back another nine parmas. Since then the animals have thrived, and Peter has supplied them to many Australian zoos. At present he has between 300 and 400.

In May 1988, 50 parma wallabies were released in bushland on the Illawarra escarpment. Twelve of them were equipped with radio collars so that their movements

can be tracked. At the site of the release, the wallabies were placed in a hessian yard for an acclimatisation period. The chances of survival for a group of less than 30 is only slight, as they are very susceptible to being killed by foxes, and therefore another 50 were released very soon after the first group.

This experiment was the largest release of an endangered species into the wild anywhere in the world, and is the result of years of planning by Peter Piggott and the National Parks and Wildlife Service. Tragically, none of the released wallabies survived. Different methods of increasing their chances of survival will be examined before future releases are attempted.

CHAPTER 12
Parrot Videos

A range of visually absorbing and informative videos about Australian parrots is currently available. The titles in the series are:

1 Lorikeets
2 Black cockatoos
3 White cockatoos
4 New arrivals
5 Specialists
6 Rosellas
7 Grass parrots

The videos are distributed by:

Documentaries of Australasia Pty Ltd
PO Box 206
Turramurra NSW 2074
Telephone (02) 44 1496

CHAPTER 13
Possums

BRUSH-TAILED POSSUM

The following information is reprinted with the kind permission of the National Parks and Wildlife Service of New South Wales.

The brush-tailed possum, *Trichosurus vulpecula*, is the most widely distributed possum in Australia. It is most common in the forests and woodlands of the east coast, but also occurs in inland areas, usually along tree-lined rivers and creeks. It is an arboreal animal, well adapted to tree climbing, with sharp claws which are also used for combing its fur.

This possum is nocturnal and usually spends the day sleeping in a hollow tree limb. A brush-tailed possum is about the size of a domestic cat and has a pointed snout, pink nose, long whiskers and large ears. The tail is thick and bushy but towards the end, on the underside, it is hairless. The strip of hairless skin probably helps the possum grip branches with its tail. The colour of the fur varies: in northern Australia it is pale grey, while in Tasmania it is dark brown. Size also varies, and while southern animals may weigh as much as 4kg (9lb), those in the north may be as light as 1kg (2¼lb).

Food In the wild, brush-tailed possums feed on a wide variety of leaves, buds, flowers and fruits. The possums have strong teeth and often use their front paws to hold their food while eating.

Range and territory Brush-tailed possums lead a solitary life, except when breeding, and in the wild both males and females apparently have their own territories. The female's territory is about 1 ha (2.5 acres) and that of the male about 3 ha (7.5 acres). These territories overlap so that a number of females occur in each male's home range. In urban areas males are territorial, but females appear to wander freely.

Each possum has its own sleeping place, in which it stays during the day. When it comes out to feed at night it usually stays in its own home range. Scent glands on the chest and chin produce a smelly substance that is rubbed onto branches to mark this range. If two possums meet at night, they try to avoid close contact. Fights between adult possums are rare, but juveniles may be attacked if they attempt to take over an adult's home range.

Breeding Brush-tailed possums are marsupials. The young are born in May and June after a gestation period of 17 days. The young possum weighs only 20–22g (less than 1oz) but it crawls unaided to the forward-opening pouch, where it attaches itself to a teat. The young possum spends about five months in the pouch and a further two months clinging to its mother's back as she moves about. Usually only one young is born at a time but the female may give birth to a second offspring during the two months when the first is carried on her back. Approximately 50% of female possums would give birth to a second offspring in September or October each year. Males are not involved in rearing the young.

Young possums become independent of their mothers when seven months old and are fully grown by about ten months of age. Females usually breed for the first time when they are twelve months old.

Possums and people Unlike many other native animals, brush-tailed possums have adapted well to life in close contact with people. They will readily take up residence in the roofs of houses or other buildings, where their

nocturnal activities can be a noisy and messy nuisance. They can also create havoc in the garden by pruning shrubs, flowers and fruit trees and disturbing your own or neighbouring dogs.

Trapping a possum Before you attempt to remove a possum from your property you must check with your state's wildlife authority whether you need to obtain a licence to do so. (See 'National Parks and Wildlife Authorities')

Once you have obtained a licence you will need a trap. A simple but effective trap design is shown here. The dimensions are approximate only: any large box will serve as a trap.

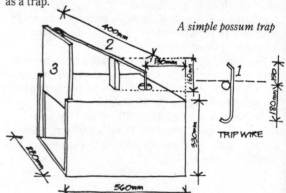

A simple possum trap

A suitable bait (for example, bread and honey or ripe fruit) is placed inside the trap on a hooked trip wire (1). When the possum removes the bait the movement of the trip wire releases the support stake (2), allowing the trap door (3) to fall.

A trapped possum will bite and scratch anyone attempting to handle it, so it should be removed carefully, using heavy gloves, and placed in a hessian bag. The possum should then be released, preferably at dusk or in the early evening, into a natural bush area. Once a possum is removed from a roof all possible points of entry should be barricaded to prevent another possum taking up residence.

Possum repellent If possums are a problem because of damaging flowers, vegetables, shrubs or fruit trees, a simple but effective mixture can be sprayed on the plants to repel the possums. The basic ingredient of the mixture, quassia chips, can be purchased from chemists in 100g (¼lb) packets.

Gently boil the chips for two hours in 9–10 litres (16–17½ pints) of water. Strain to remove the chips, then add more water to make the mixture up to 18–20 litres (31–35 pints).

The mixture should be sprayed over plants affected by the possums. The mixture has a foul taste which discourages further consumption of the plants by possums, but it is totally harmless to both possums and plants.

Make friends with a possum When you remove a possum from your property it is very likely that another will move in and take its place. However, because possums are territorial, if you already have a possum in residence it is unlikely that others will attempt to establish residence rights in the same territory. Therefore you can reduce your possum problems by making friends with one possum, which will then discourage others.

Barricade all entry points to your roof and supply the possum with suitable shelter, such as a large box, in a safe place where it will not be disturbed by dogs or people. Feeding it regularly with soft fresh fruit will minimise its attacks on your garden.

GLIDING POSSUMS

The following information is reprinted with the kind permission of the National Parks and Wildlife Service of New South Wales.

Have you ever seen a flying carpet? If you're lucky you might catch a glimpse of one in the Australian bush at night. Of course, flying carpets don't really exist, but Gliding Possums can certainly resemble them, with their flaplike folds of loose skin stretched taut during flight.

There are several gliding possum species: the feathertail glider (also known as the pygmy glider), the sugar glider, squirrel glider, yellow-bellied glider (also known as the fluffy glider) and the greater glider.

There are three groups of gliding possums, and each group is more closely related to non-gliding possums than to other groups of gliders. For example the greater glider is a type of ringtail possum, while the feathertail glider (pictured on the one-cent piece) is a gliding pygmy possum.

Distribution Generally gliders live in the tall wet or dry sclerophyll forests that line the east coast of Australia. Sugar gliders have the widest distribution, as they can tolerate a greater climatic range. They extend from the tropical parts of the Northern Territory into the cooler areas of Tasmania.

Features Gliders move about the treetops by means of a flying membrane. This usually stretches between the outer side of the hand and the ankle, but in the case of the greater glider it stretches from the elbow to the ankle and they glide with their front paws tucked under their chest.

When the animal leaps from a branch, the outspread limbs extend the membrane, enabling it to glide from tree to tree. The long, well-furred tail also helps, acting as a rudder to steer the flight. This feature is most highly specialised in the feathertail glider—all of the hairs are arranged like the filaments of a feather.

Gliding possums differ considerably in body length. The smallest of the group, the pygmy glider, measures a mere 70mm (2½″) while the largest, the greater glider, is almost cat-sized at 400mm (16″).

Gliding The yellow-bellied glider is the most capable flyer. Measuring 280mm (11″) in body length, it can cover distances of over 100m (330′) in one leap. The sugar glider and squirrel glider share a similar ability, with distances of 50m (165′) being average.

The beginning of the glide is steeply downwards, but as the animal gathers speed it flattens out. Just before reaching the desired landing spot, the glider uses its tail to bring it into a nose-up position with the four feet in front, ready to grasp the tree. It may then feed, or run up the tree to launch off on another glide.

With the exception of the greater glider, which is silent, most jumps are accompanied by a series of yowls or yaps.

Nesting Gliders usually make their nests in tree hollows, which they line with dry leaves. Some of the smaller varieties are more opportunistic—sugar gliders will move into the abandoned nests of ringtails, while one family of feathertail gliders was found to have built their nest in the lining of an old coat hanging from a tree.

Some species, particularly the greater glider, mark out territories using scent glands. They rub the gland against trees to warn off intruders. For instance, the sugar glider will use odour to distinguish or identify members of the family group. Any sugar glider from another group who wanders into foreign territory is quickly chased out.

Food Gliders feed at night, moving among their favourite food trees by using regular pathways. In most species the diet includes nectar, pollen, insects and the sap of certain eucalypt or wattle trees. The greater glider is very restricted in its diet: it feeds almost exclusively on eucalypt leaves.

Baby gliders The greater glider is the only gliding possum that doesn't live in a family or social group. These solitary animals come together only for mating, from which one young is usually born. Other gliders produce one or two young at a time, although the feathertail glider can have litters of up to four.

Like all baby marsupials, the naked, new born young would fit on your thumbnail. From the birth canal it must find its way to the mother's pouch and attach itself to a teat. Here it is kept warm and nourished with milk. After about three or four months it will venture out into the nest, eventually joining the adults in searching for food— young greater gliders hitch a ride on their mother's back for the first few months after they leave the pouch. When the young are big enough to fend for themselves, they will usually leave the family and establish a group or territory of their own. Some females may remain within the original group, but male offspring are often forced to leave by the adult males.

Protection All gliders are protected in New South Wales, but the squirrel glider and the yellow-bellied glider are quite rare, and are in need of special protection.

Although gliders do have natural predators, such as the powerful owl, the greatest threat to them comes from the destruction of the forests in which they live. When a forest is cleared, not only do they lose their homes, but they also become prey to additional species. Some gliders may be taken by foxes or wedge-tailed eagles when there are no trees to climb. They are easy targets in cleared areas during daylight.

The National Parks and Wildlife Service is protecting forests in national parks, but these form only a small proportion of the state and the future of gliders living outside national parks is far less secure.

Glider house If you are lucky enough to have any of these interesting marsupials in your area, you may be able to encourage them to stay by building a glider house. The house should be made from a thick wood, at least 2cm (¾") thick. All joins should be light-tight. Gliders prefer a dark enclosure. Make sure that you secure the house high up in a tree—the higher up the better. The house should be secured with either wire or strong nails—we'd hate to see it fall on anyone.

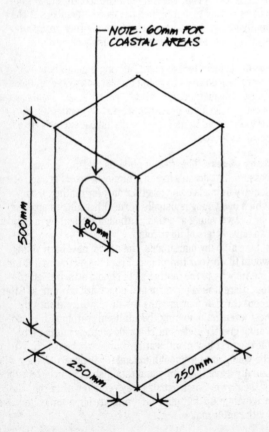

NOTE: 60mm FOR COASTAL AREAS
80mm
500mm
250mm
250mm

CHAPTER 14
Quolls

Quolls are carnivorous native marsupials. They are Australia's native cats and do much the same job in this country as cats used to do in the forests of Europe. The common name 'quoll' was derived by Captain Cook from the Aboriginal term for these animals and, although it was replaced by 'native cat' for some time, it is now back in use.

The quoll was the second Australian mammal to be described in scientific literature, after the kangaroo. It is an inquisitive, fearless little animal, apparently well able to defend itself against domestic cats and dogs, although some species in certain areas have undergone a drastic decline in numbers this century. Habitat destruction, trapping and shooting, and competitive pressure from introduced carnivorous animals, are all thought to be among the reasons. Even so, the quoll has proven itself to be adaptable and capable of living in close proximity to people and their dwellings. Nowadays quolls are seldom seen in the bush and are an extremely rare sight in urban areas.

There are four closely related species of native cats. The western native cat or chuditch (*Dasyurinus geoffroyi*) is believed to be distributed across the southwest and centre of Australia. Its length is 55-75cm (21½-29½") or more. The little northern native cat (*Satanellus hallucatus*) inhabits the tropical regions across the north of the continent. This is the smallest of the four species and is less than 55cm (21½") in length. The eastern native cat or quoll (*Dasyurus quoll* or *Dasyurus viverrinus*) is unfortunately now common only in Tasmania, although just 100 years ago it was equally common in the southeast of the mainland. This species is 55-75cm (21½-29½") in length. The tiger cat or tiger quoll (*Dasyurops maculatus*) inhabits eastern Australia and Tasmania and, although quite common in some areas, is rarely seen due to its nocturnal habits. Its body is 40-75cm (15½-29½") in length and its tail is 35-55cm (13½-21½") long.

Native cats have pale spots on the body but only the tiger quoll has spots on the tail as well. The base colour ranges from yellowish brown to grey or even black. The tiger quoll is reddish brown with white spots. Quolls have a powerful, crouching, catlike body, a bushy tail and sharp canine teeth. They eat rats, mice, birds, snakes and, in some cases, poultry—which made native cats unpopular in colonial times.

Quolls can take up to eight hours to mate and sometimes produce up to three times as many young as can be fed by the mother's six teats. Those which don't find a teat to attach to simply die. Such production of surplus young (superfetation) is extremely rare in Australian marsupials.

If a quoll is found in an urban area it should not be approached, as it could cause nasty injuries while attempting to defend itself. Contact a Wildlife Information and Rescue Service Volunteer, the National Parks and Wildlife Service, or a museum, for assistance in capturing and relocating the animal safely.

CHAPTER 15
Slugs

LEOPARD SLUG

Leopard Slugs (*Limax maximus*), at first glance, are simply squishy, sticky nuisances that slime their way around the garden after dark. But leopard slugs are actually helpful in the garden, and an important part of the food chain, because they are scavengers rather than herbivores. They feed on waste material such as bird droppings or rotting leaves, and pose little threat to living plants.

But undoubtedly the most astonishing thing about leopard slugs is the way they mate. Slugs are hermaphrodites, which means that each slug has both male and female sexual organs in its body.

The mating procedure begins when two slugs that are ready to mate locate each other and travel in single file towards a vertical object—usually a tree trunk, but sometimes the side of a house or a fence. Still moving in single file, the slugs slide up the tree. They choose a spot and begin to circle around each other in a small patch, over which they deposit a thick layer of mucus. After a while (about one hour) the slugs drop from the tree trunk twined around each other, and dangle by a strand of mucus from the patch on the tree.

The mating organs gradually emerge from a hole close to the head of each slug. These organs are strange, white, tubelike structures, which fan out at the ends as they enlarge and become entwined together. Inside these organs sperm is exchanged between the two slugs. This process takes about half an hour, during which the mucus thread connecting the slugs to the tree lengthens.

When mating is complete, the slugs drop the remaining distance to the ground and move off separately, although often one slug will climb back up the mucus strand (eating it as it goes) and return to the ground via the tree. Both slugs will later find separate damp crevices, such as under a rock or log, in which to lay their eggs.

This remarkable spectacle is most likely to be witnessed in summer on a warm, damp night.

RED TRIANGLE SLUG

Out in the bush you will often come across mysterious patterns on tree trunks. These are caused by a particular group of slugs known as the Red Triangle Slugs; the marks are their feeding tracks.

Feeding habits The red triangle slug is not one of your garden pests. Red triangles feed on microscopic plants that grow on moist surfaces such as rock and smooth bark tree-trunks. As they move along they leave marks where the food has been scraped away.

Description and habitat We don't usually think of slugs as being attractive, but the red triangles come close to it. They live in damp places all along the east coast of Australia, and come in a variety of colours. Some are said to rival the very beautiful marine slugs. The name comes from a bright triangular marking around the slug's breathing hole.

Slugs and snails don't have noses and use their mouths only for eating. They have a remarkable organ called a radula inside their mouths. This is rather like a tongue, but is covered with thousands of tiny teeth that scrape the food off the surface of things mouthful by mouthful.

Slugs are snails that have discarded their shells to give them greater mobility. Some kinds of slugs are still in the transition stage and carry a tiny shell that is too small to be of much use, except as part of the slug's camouflage.

Useful qualities Both slugs and snails have adapted quite successfully to life on dry land. Not all of them are herbivores. One rather flat little native snail can be welcomed by all gardeners: it is a carnivore and actually feeds on other snails, particularly the introduced ones that damage our gardens.

Remember that one sort of introduced slug, the Giant European Leopard Slug, should always be welcome in the garden because it is a scavenger. These slugs don't attack your vegies but they do take care of the mess. They will clean up rubbish such as bird droppings and fallen fruit.

CHAPTER 16
Snakes

The following information is reprinted with the kind permission of the National Parks and Wildlife Service of New South Wales.

Many people fear, or at least dislike, snakes. These reactions are generally based on ignorance of the animals and their habits. Contrary to popular belief, snakes are not slimy, nor are they all dangerous and aggressive.

Snakes are shy animals and, if threatened, will nearly always attempt to escape rather than fight. In general a snake will only attack if it is suddenly aroused or prevented from retreating. Most snake bites occur because the animal has been inadvertently stepped on or handled.

There is little likelihood of being bitten by a snake if a few common sense rules are followed.

* If you see a snake, retreat, giving it plenty of room to do the same.
* When bushwalking, wear appropriate clothes, including heavy shoes or boots and thick socks.
* Step carefully over logs and rocks and don't put your hands into hollow logs or other nooks and crannies.
* Wear thick gloves when gardening to prevent bites from snakes, spiders and insects.
* Keep piles of rubbish, thick bush and rocks away from the house so that snakes are not encouraged to become close neighbours.
* Most snakes are active on summer nights, so always carry a torch in the garden and around campsites and farmhouses.
* Keep sheds and farm buildings free of rats and mice, as these will attract snakes.
* Never let children collect or handle snakes.
* If you do find a snake in your garden or house, leave it alone, irrespective of whether or not you think it is venomous. Contact a pest exterminator or the local police, or seek advice from the National Parks and Wildlife Service.

Snakebite No matter how careful you are, you or a companion may be unfortunate enough to be bitten by a snake. Although only 20 species of Australian snakes are capable of inflicting a dangerous wound in a human, it is wise to treat all snakebites as potentially dangerous.

Most snakebites occur on the arms or legs, particularly the lower parts of the limbs.

The first aid treatment for snakebite is:
1 Keep the victim still and calm.
2 Immediately apply a firm, broad bandage over the bite and as much of the limb as possible. A flexible material, such as a crepe bandage or torn towel or clothing, should be used and the bandage should be wound as tightly as for a sprained wrist or ankle.

The limb should be kept as still as possible. Roll up clothing, but do not attempt to remove it as the movement will speed the flow of venom into the blood-stream. Bind the limb with some type of splint to further restrict movement and, if the bite is on an arm, place the limb in a sling. If snakebite occurs on the trunk, apply firm pressure over the bitten area if possible, but do not restrict chest movement. Do not apply pressure to the head or neck area.
3 If possible bring transport to the victim or carry him or her to transport. Do not remove the bandages or splint until medical care is reached.
4 If possible notify the hospital or doctor that you have a snakebite victim and try to reach medical attention within two hours.
5 If it can be done with safety, kill the snake responsible for the bite and take it to the hospital or doctor for identification.

Do not excise or incise the bitten area. Venom is injected quite deeply into the wound and very little is removed by cutting and sucking the wound.

Do not apply an arterial tourniquet.

Do not wash the bite area—drops of venom left on the skin may assist in the identification of the snake responsible for the bite.

For further information

If you find an unwanted snake in your backyard, it is advised that you phone the police, National Parks and Wildlife or your local council.

If you wish to obtain a snake as a pet, however, be aware that there are a number of regulations which apply, and which include such activities as obtaining permits and licences as well as keeping record books of transactions. These regulations vary from state to state, and you *must* check on the laws with the relevant wildlife authority (see 'National Parks and Wildlife Authorities').

Amateur Associations
Herpetological Society
PO Box R79
Royal Exchange NSW 2000

Reptile Keepers' Association
PO Box 98
Gosford NSW 2250

In *Victoria*, hobbyists generally must obtain reptiles from existing legally held collections or from interstate—not from the wild.

SA Herpetological Group
c/- SA Museum
North Terrace
Adelaide SA 5000

Western Herpetology Group
18 Creber Street
Whyalla Playford SA 5600

North Queensland Herpetological Society
c/- 1 Faraday Street
Wulguru QLD 4810

Southeast Queensland Herpetologists
c/- 9 Grey Street
Ipswich QLD 4305

Cape York Herpetological Society
c/- Wild World
PO Box 88
Cairns QLD 4870

It is a serious offence to keep any reptile for hobbyist purposes in *WA*. One individual per wildlife region holds specimen reptiles for public education.

ACT Herpetological Group
c/- ACT Parks and Conservation
PO Box 158
Canberra City ACT 2601

In *Tasmania*, any non-endangered species may be collected (not from national parks). Reptiles may not be imported from other states without a permit.

Regulations are undergoing change in the *Northern Territory*. It is likely that a list of species for collection will result.

CHAPTER 17
Spiders

SPIDERS COURTING

Densey Clyne presented the following intriguing information about the courting habits of some garden spiders.

When a male garden spider goes courting, he takes his life in his hands. This is because spiders generally are very short-sighted and anything of the right size that moves is likely to be a potential meal.

Male *Orb-weaver spiders* are among those at great risk because they have to approach the female when she is in her web. The safe approach for a male orb-weaver spider is to stay at the edge of the female's web and tap the web to let her know he is there. The female feels the vibrations through her feet, just as she does when she catches an insect in her web. She recognises that this is a different kind of movement and responds by coming out to meet him. The male strokes and taps the female to put her into a sort of trance so that she won't think that he is a meal.

The *St Andrews Cross Spider* is less cautious. He goes right onto the female's web and attracts her attention. He makes a hole in the web so he can slip behind it for safety.

Spiders that don't make a web must confront their potential mate face to face. *Lynx spiders* will pounce on anything that moves, so the male identifies himself clearly by flashing conspicuous black-tipped palps or mating organs. Females which are not ready to mate or have already mated will rebuff approaches.

Jumping spiders have good short range eyesight, so the male's approach is highly visual. Ritualised body language ensures that only the females of the same species will respond.

Male spiders of some other species tie the female down with strands of silk. This does not represent force, it is simply the means by which the male spider identifies himself. The female can easily break the strands at any time.

While these courtship strategies may seem strange, they are simply the rituals by which male spiders identify themselves in order to prevent mistakes and save time and their lives.

SPIDERS MATING

Densey Clyne is fascinated by spiders but even she will admit that some of their habits are rather strange.

Spiders' sex life is extraordinary. Take the process called 'sperm induction', which is unique to spiders. Before even going near a female, the male produces a drop of sperm fluid. He picks up the droplet with the male mating organs; specially modified palps which look like an extra pair of legs at the front of his body. The sperm is drawn inside and stored in the palps. The male then goes in search of a female.

A male spider's mating apparatus is suited only for his own kind of female. He locks the palp into a structure in the centre underside of the female and injects the sperm fluid—rather like artificial insemination.

The sperm is stored in the female's sperm bank and released every time she produces a batch of eggs.

WHITE-TAIL SPIDER

The White-tail Spider is cylindrical in shape and dark grey in colour with an obvious white spot on the end of its body (abdomen). It scurries around on the ground, and is found in the bush in leaf litter and logs, under bark and rocks, in crevices in the wild and in the house. At night they wander about looking for food. The female is approximately 1.5cm (¾″) long.

Dr Mike Grey, arachnologist from the Australian Museum, says that it is a misconception that the bite of the white-tail spider causes large dead areas (necrotic lesions) covering a large part of the skin's surface. The white-tail spider and other spiders are known to cause small necrotic lesions around the site of the bite, between the size of a 10 and a 20-cent piece. The main problem with the necrotic lesion, if it develops, is that it takes a long time to heal and it can be unpleasant and tender. There is no evidence that the spiders cause large weeping wounds.

These spiders have been in Australia since European settlement and have bitten many people. Most victims just get severe pain and an inflamed area around the site of the bite, and sometimes a necrotic lesion. If you see a white-tail spider in the house or yard, kill it. And always wear gardening gloves when working outdoors.

Spiders were the first 'balloonists' and have been found at 2000 metres.

CHAPTER 18
Water Wildlife

CREEK CREATURES

One of the most interesting places in the bush is under water. All you need, to observe the animals there, are a little bit of common sense so you don't fall in and drown, and something to catch the animals with—a net.

You can either buy a net, for about $5, or make one. To make a net, take a wire coathanger, bend it until it is more or less round and then tape it to a stick with masking tape. Then obtain some mosquito net. You can buy this at shops that sell fabric, or use the nets used for fruit bags, although these can be a little coarse. Drape your net over the wire, push down in the middle and then sew it to the wire all around the edge. This is a quick way of making a fairly cheap net.

Once you've got your net you need to find the animals. Under rocks and logs and on the edges of things are the best places to put your net to catch all the little animals. The easiest way to find out what you have caught is to tip the contents into a container, such as an icecream tub.

You might find little prawns or shrimps, back swimmers and water boatmen which are able, when they dive, to take down an air bubble over virtually their whole body because of their special hairs—rather like having their own scuba tank.

The damsel fly larva breathes through three gills at the back, and the water scorpion breathes through its tail, which actually punches through the surface film and gets oxygen that way.

Other things you might find in ponds include yabbies, tadpoles, and little frogs with sucker feet. There are also water striders that have special water repellent hairs on their legs which enable them to walk around on top of the water.

Ponds can be a fantastic place to spend a few hours on the weekend or in the school holidays. The important thing to remember is, when you finish with the little creatures, let them go. They're so much better off in the water than anywhere else.

ROCK POOL CREATURES

Rock pools around the edge of the ocean are among the most hostile environments on earth. For half the day they get belted by the waves and drowned by sea water, and for the other half they bake in the sun. Animals that can handle one of those extremes usually can't handle the other, yet if you take a look into a rock pool you will find a fantastic variety of life there.

Simple rules to follow before you start are: make sure you wear sneakers, keep an eye on the waves, don't put your fingers into crevices where you can't see what is inside, and leave the environment the way you found it.

Make sure you place any animals back where they belong after you've had a look, and gently replace any rocks you move so that the creatures underneath won't be damaged.

One of the first things you will see in pools further away from the ocean edge are little blue periwinkles or nodilittorina. The most interesting thing about them is that they are water snails but they never get wet. They do get some spray on them but they don't become submerged. You might also wonder what they eat in such a barren location. The rocks certainly look to be devoid of any source of food, but a layer of algae, which we can't see, grows on their surface. The snails have teeth on their tongues and at night crawl all over the rock rasping away at the algae with these unusual tongues.

Further down towards the water you will find rocks which are really worth turning over to see what is underneath. As long as you can see your hands it is safe to do this. Animals you may find include the sea hare and the elephant snail. They are both snails which have virtually lost their shells but the elephant snail still has a remnant of shell. They both eat plants by grazing over the rocks.

Crabs are also rock pool dwellers. Most crabs have two different claws. The smaller one is a very sharp, slicing claw and the larger is much blunter and is used for squashing. You could call them the carving knife and the meat tenderiser.

Sometimes you might find a crab referred to as a rubber crab. It will look like rubber, and when touched it will bend. This happens to crabs when they have just moulted their skins and the new shells haven't yet hardened.

Starfish are amazing creatures and are often found in rock pools. Four hundred million years ago these little animals invented hydraulics. Like all hydraulic systems they need very clean hydraulic fluid and that is why every starfish you see has a little spot in the middle on the top. That is a sieve plate, or the hydraulic fluid intake point, and it acts as a very fine filter. The hydraulics run all the little tubed feet that the starfish has on its underside and when it is feeling hungry it uses those feet to get hold of food and move it to the mouth. The mouth is in the middle of the underside. A starfish can actually turn its stomach inside out through its mouth and digest things outside its own body.

CHAPTER 19
Wildlife Warnings

Although Australia's native fauna is fascinating, some creatures are best avoided!

European wasps are introduced members of the paper wasp family and can be distinguished from the native species by their shorter, thicker bodies with sharply defined bands of yellow on black. Only female wasps are capable of stinging repeatedly. European wasps are attracted to meat which is being cooked and sweet drinks, and have recently become a serious problem, particularly in Victoria and Tasmania. Sightings of these wasps should be reported to the local Department of Agriculture or Primary Industries for extermination.

Redback spiders are common in urban areas throughout Australia. An effective antivenom was introduced in 1956, before which the spider was responsible for 13 deaths in Australia. The male spiders are not large enough to bite effectively, so only the females represent a threat. The venom is slow-acting and victims should be transported quickly but calmly to medical aid. Many colour variations occur in this species, including black, brown or even pale yellow-brown bodies and red, pink, orange, cream and white stripes in a variety of patterns.

Funnel-webs The funnel-web family of spiders includes numerous harmless species but is best known for the notorious Sydney Funnel-web, which is possibly the world's deadliest spider. Children living in the coastal area of New South Wales, where the spider occurs, should be taught to recognise the spider from pictures. It usually inhabits holes in posts, rock crevices and the areas underneath houses. Males have more toxic venom and are more frequently encountered, as they are vagrants. An antivenom is available.

Snakes A remarkably high proportion of Australian land snakes (about 70%) are venomous. The most widely distributed are the death adders, brown snakes, and the black and mulga snakes—tiger snakes and copperheads are other poisonous varieties. Carpet snakes, found in most parts of Australia, are large but non-venomous. The diamond python of the southeast coastal areas of Australia is closely related to the carpet snake—it can bite, but it has neither venom nor fangs, just small, solid, sharp teeth.

Most snakes are shy and retiring and unlikely to attack unless threatened, and all are protected by wildlife authorities (exceptions are usually made where human lives are under threat). Effective antivenoms are usually available and fatalities from snake bite are rare.

For further information

A detailed and comprehensive publication, *Toxic Plants and Animals: A Guide for Australia* was published by the Queensland Museum in 1987 and is available from most museum bookshops for about $25.

CHAPTER 20
Wombats

The following information is reprinted with the kind permission of the National Parks and Wildlife Service of New South Wales.

Wombats are stout, sturdy and strong, and their physical power is matched by a determination to go where they want by the most direct route—often through or under a farmer's fence.

The wombat is built like a small army tank—the head is large and blunt with small eyes and ears; the neck very muscular and short; the tail a mere stump. The stubby, powerful legs, combined with sharp claws, are great digging equipment. Wombats grow to about 1.3m (51"), can weigh up to 36kg (79lb) and have been known to live for up to 27 years in captivity.

There are two types of wombats: one well adapted to very dry open country—the hairy-nosed wombat, *Lasiorhinus sp*—the other to wetter, forest-covered areas. As the name suggests, the snout of the hairy-nosed wombat is covered with fine, silky hair, which reduces water evaporation in the desert. The common wombat, *Vombatus ursinus*, has a large, naked snout with granular skin. Hairy-nosed wombats are extinct in New South Wales and extremely rare in Queensland. In other parts of Australia, their distribution is very limited

Habitat A wombat must have well-drained soils to dig its burrows, as well as favourable conditions to keep its body temperature regulated. Its main habitat is the forest-covered, often mountainous, areas of south-eastern Australia.

Wombats live in burrows and keep cool by camping underground during the day. Burrows keep wombats cool in summer and warm in winter. They may extend 30m (33 yards) underground and are regularly enlarged, particularly after heavy rain. The most popular spot to build a burrow is on the sides of gullies.

At night a wombat may wander distances of up to 3km (1¾ miles) looking for food, but there is no problem of accommodation, as wombats share their homes. They use several burrows, crawling into any convenient one before sunrise. If alarmed, a wombat will scoot into the nearest hole and remain there.

Feeding Wombats spend from three to eight hours a night grazing on their favourite food—native grasses such as the tussocky 'snow grass', wallaby grass and kangaroo grass. They will even eat sedges and the roots or leaves of shrubs and trees. They cut their food with sharp, chisel-like front teeth, which grow continuously through life.

Although they will share burrows, wombats are possessive about their particular feeding grounds. They mark out these areas by leaving smells and droppings around the boundaries. If an intruder encroaches on their territory, a series of snorts, screeches and even a chase by the occupier discourages this invasion.

As each animal has a feeding ground, it follows that the population of an area is controlled by the number of feeding grounds available. A young wombat is usually forced to move to another area to find its own place, or else take the place of a wombat that has died.

Mating A wombat can start to mate after it reaches two years of age. Mating occurs between September and December and usually results in one offspring.

The newborn wombat is less than 3cm (1½″) long and weighs only one gram when it crawls from the birth canal into the mother's pouch. This pouch faces backwards to prevent dirt and twigs getting caught in it when the mother digs or climbs. Once safely tucked away, the young wombat sucks milk from a teat until it has developed enough to leave the pouch, seven to ten months later. Even then the young wombat stays close to its mother until the aggressive behaviour of other wombats forces it to find new feeding grounds for itself.

Wombats and people Humans have pushed the wombat into the rugged hills and mountains through settlement and agricultural land use. As long as the animal remains in these areas, wild dogs and collisions with cars provide more of a threat to wombats than landowners. However, because of their habit of romping down to the flats to enjoy the tasty morsels growing there—destroying fences on the way—they are sometimes killed by farmers.

Competition for food from introduced grazing animals, such as cattle, sheep, and especially rabbits, is also a problem—there appears to be little doubt that this has been a major factor in the rapid decline of the Southern Hairy-nosed Wombat.

Since 1970 wombats have been protected in New South Wales, and areas of wombat habitat are being preserved in the national park and nature reserve system.

WILDLIFE BOOK

Densey Clyne's Wildlife of Australia, by Densey Clyne, is published by Reed Books Pty Ltd, and distributed by Gordon and Gotch, Melbourne. Telephone (03) 805 1700.

NATIVE FLORA

CHAPTER I
Bush Tucker

The Australian bush is full of interesting edible plants and trees.

Port Jackson fig, *Ficus rubiginosa*. The fruit is ripe when it is red, and tastes like a normal, really sweet fig.

Kurrajong tree (*Brachychiton populneum*)—the Aborigines use different parts of this tree for all kinds of purposes and the seeds for food. Inside the pods are small seeds with prickly coverings. These can be crushed to make a coarse flour for making damper; or the seeds can be roasted first, then crushed and mixed with boiling water to make coffee.

The Lilly pilly (*Syzygium paniculatum*) is sometimes called the brush cherry. The small fruits are quite astringent but good to eat, and will make a very nice jam. See 'Lilly pilly jelly'.

Scattered throughout Australia are many relatives of the quandong tree, (*Santalum acuminatum*). These trees have fruit that, when fallen and dried, can be easily cracked to reveal the seed inside, which tastes like a walnut. Sandalwood (*Santalum spicatum*) was cut and exported from Western Australia for many years.

The grass tree (*Xanthorrhoea preissii*) can be used as food, but the tree has to be destroyed to get at the edible white leaf base—it is not something you would try to eat unless you were in dire straits. The flower stems are used as fire sticks or fishing spears. The gum at the base of these grass trees was melted and used as glue by the Aborigines, for example, to stick stones to spears.

It is important not to eat just anything you see in the bush, because some of the plants are poisonous.

We are reluctant to recommend native plants to eat, in case incorrect identification should lead to someone being poisoned.

For further information

If you are interested in this topic, we suggest that you either go on a bush tucker tour with Vic Cherikoff, Telephone (02) 816 3381, or purchase a book on the subject, such as *Bush Food*, by Jennifer Isaacs, published by Weldons Pty Ltd. Another book, which will be available in December 1989 is, *The Bush Food Handbook*, by Vic Cherikoff and Jennifer Isaacs, published by Titree.

CHAPTER 2
Indigenous Plants

To retain the character of a local area, it is important that old and dying trees and shrubs are replaced by plants indigenous to the area.

People often replace large gums with any sort of gum, or even with deciduous trees, so that in time the whole character of an area is lost. In Britain there are areas where the indigenous trees have completely disappeared. It is important that we do not allow a similar situation to arise in Australia.

The good news is that there are a number of nurseries which specialise in local plants. These range from spectacular gums, the types on which koalas once fed (and may still feed on in some areas), to shrubs and grasses.

Some nurseries even have kits of plants suitable for the regeneration of local areas. They are inexpensive and particularly suitable for schools or other organisations that are trying to protect indigenous plants.

CHAPTER 3
Jarrah Dieback

Throughout Australia our gum trees are dying. Western Australia in particular is badly affected by Jarrah dieback, caused by a fungus organism called phytophthora, which is eating away at the roots of the trees.

Root rot is spread in a number of ways. Construction

equipment carries it in the soil that sticks to wheels and tyres. It can also be spread by careless gardeners, incorrect watering and by nursery stock. Nurseries have not been able to completely eradicate phytophthora from their stock, and unfortunately it is likely to keep on spreading.

Australian wildflowers, particularly members of the Proteaceae family (dryandras, grevilleas and banksias) have little resistance to phytophthora. The southwestern corner of Australia is regarded by many people as being one of the richest areas of wildflowers in the world, and it is at risk from this disease.

Root rot is very difficult to identify and it can take you two to six months to become aware that your plants are suffering from it. Identification of phytophthora entails taking a sample of plant tissue, putting it in agar and growing it in a laboratory for a couple of weeks and then examining the fungal mycelium that is growing.

The Western Australian Nurseryman's Association is proposing that there should be a registration system that would start in the nurseries and hopefully give greater control of the disease. The WA Department of Agriculture does not support this idea, as it would be difficult, expensive and another government control. Registration of nurseries is either being carried out or legislated for in the other states in Australia.

CHAPTER 4
Mangroves

Until quite recently, waterlogged mangrove forests were commonly regarded as swamps which restricted the water view; or as smelly and mosquito-laden areas suitable only for reclamation to make desirable waterfront property.

Scientific research has forced us to reassess our attitude to mangroves. Along with sea grasses and salt marshes, mangroves have been shown to play an important role in the healthy functioning of an estuary. They are major producers of organic material used in the food web of the estuary, producing about 10 tonnes (9½ tons) per hectare (2½ acres) every year. They are also involved in the recycling of nutrients broken down by bacteria in the mud; and help reduce water pollution. They provide habitat (shelter, refuge, food) for many forms of wildlife, especially molluscs, crabs and birds; they act as silt traps, stabilising the foreshore and helping prevent bank erosion; they provide protection from storm surge; they can act as visual screens along industrial foreshores; and they form vital nursery areas for many commercially important fish species (including bream, blackfish, mullet, flathead, silver biddy and whiting), which shelter among the mangrove peg roots. The health of such areas is also important to oyster farmers.

To cope with the estuarine environment, mangroves

have special structures and tissues. They have the ability to excrete salt (you can taste it on their leaves); they can concentrate salt in older tissues and then discard them; and some have barriers to keep salt out.

The waterlogged soil in which they grow is frequently anaerobic, so the mangroves have peg roots called *pneumatophores*, which obtain atmospheric oxygen.

The mangrove food chain is one of the most productive in the world: mangroves photosynthesise and produce plant tissue; litter falls from the mangroves (fragments of leaves, bark and fruit); soluble nutrients are leached out and the litter is colonised by fungi and bacteria. The decomposed fragments are eaten by prawns and crabs; their excrement is recolonised by bacteria and fungi; and the detritus feeders are eaten by larger estuary fish and birds.

In many parts of Australia people are realising the economic and environmental value of mangroves and are starting to regenerate mangrove forests.

Mangroves are hardy trees. The word 'mangrove' is applied to at least 90 species of trees, few of which are related, but they are alike in that they survive on the fringe of intertidal shallows between the land and the sea. You can grow a mangrove seed in washed beach sand, topped up by sea water.

CHAPTER 5
Mistletoe

Mistletoe is a parasitic plant that grows in trees. It is easy to see if it is in a deciduous tree, but more difficult if in a gum tree. It sucks nutrients out of whatever tree it is growing on, and produces, after the flowers, gooey fruit that look a little bit like grapes.

The red and black mistletoe bird, *Dicaeum hirundinaceum*, is about 100mm (4") long and is found all over Australia, except in Tasmania. It makes the mistletoe its staple food. The mistletoe fruit is digested by the birds but the seeds are unchanged. The birds drop them on branches, rather than on the ground, and the seeds adhere to the branches because of their gelatinous outer covering. Not all germinate, but those that do quickly tap into the tree's sap flow. Thus the bird depends on the plant for survival and the plant depends on the bird for distribution.

Also dependent on mistletoe is the caterpillar of the Jezabel butterfly. The mistletoes survive their annual pruning by these caterpillars.

There are more than 70 kinds of mistletoes in Australia: they grow on rainforest trees, she-oaks, wattles, eucalypts and even other mistletoes.

Myths In ancient times, mistletoe was surrounded by myths and folklore. It was regarded as magical and medicinal and was used by the Druids. Later the custom of kissing under the mistletoe developed, which was believed to lead inevitably to marriage.

The modern myth about mistletoe, which Densey Clyne wishes to dispel, is that it kills gum trees. Out in the bush, eucalypts and mistletoes have been co-existing for millions of years. Mistletoes contain chlorophyll and can make some of their own food. In a natural situation, mistletoes don't kill gum trees but actually form the nucleus of a fascinating community of interdependent species.

It is important to note however, that in areas where the balance of nature has been disturbed by man, mistletoes can reproduce in large numbers and extensively damage trees.

If you have mistletoe on a gum tree in your backyard, it usually means the gum tree is sick, so it's worth having a close look at it to see what is wrong.

CHAPTER 6
Queensland Stinging Tree

Sometimes plants can pose a significant danger to domestic animals.

A rainforest tree, *Dendrocnide excelsa* (known as the stinging tree or the stinging nettle tree), causes injury to people and animals unfortunate enough to touch it.

The tree has huge leaves, which are covered by vicious stinging hairs. Stinging can occur when a person or animal brushes against any part of the leaf, and the pain is not only excruciating but usually persists for three to four weeks. It may recur for some months after that, especially when the affected part is washed.

CHAPTER 7
Stinkhorns

Among the weird and wonderful things to come up in the garden is a fungus called 'Stinkhorn'. One stinkhorn has the botanic name of *Phallus impudicus*, which might tell you why some little boys have coined the name 'doodles' when referring to these organisms.

Out of sight, beneath the soil's surface, reproductive spores ripen, and are borne aloft at the tip of a rapidly growing, stout stalk. The slimy mass of spores exudes a fetid odour so attractive to flies that they eat both spores and slime.

The spores pass unharmed through the fly, and, as up to 20 million spores can be passed in each piece of fly excrement, the potential for dispersal is enormous. Other fungi, such as the star shaped fungus, use the slime to attract flies.

Different methods of spore dispersal are employed by other fungi. Puffballs, for example, contain many bright yellow ochre spores, which are released on the slightest touch, even by a raindrop, and spread by air currents.

Most fungi consist of a network of threads or hyphae, which grow on dead plant matter. The part we see is the fruiting body or sexual organ, so perhaps the little boys are not too far out in their references to 'doodles'.

CHAPTER 8
Sundews

Carnivorous plants, such as venus fly traps and pitcher plants have become a familiar novelty at plant nurseries. Most are imported, but we have the same kind of plant growing in Australia—maybe in your own backyard. These are small plants called Sundews (Drosera). Like other carnivorous plants, they usually grow in such poor soil that they have to look elsewhere for some of their essential nutrients.

The sundew's leaf blade is covered with sensitive tentacles, which close over its insect prey. Each tentacle is tipped with a reddish gland which produces the sticky 'dew'-drop that traps the insect, secretes the enzymes to break down all but the insect's shell, and absorbs much of the resultant fluid into the plant's system.

Sundews themselves can be food for insects such as caterpillars, and one particular kind of insect which lives inside the sundew and 'shares' its catches.

For further information A suggested book is: *Carnivorous Plants*, by Adrian Slack, published by A.H. & A.W. Reed.

THE ENVIRONMENT

CHAPTER I
Australian Trust for Conservation Volunteers

The Australian Trust for Conservation Volunteers (ATCV) is an organisation that enables concerned individuals to do something practical to conserve the quality of our environment. It was established after the concept achieved great success and popularity in Britain.

Participants work in groups for up to a week at a time on a wide range of activities in local and national parks, at National Trust properties, on farms, and anywhere else where voluntary labour can make a contribution towards reducing an environmental problem. Activities undertaken include tree planting and maintenance, weeding, and building walking trails and fences. There is no prerequisite level of skill; any necessary training is provided by a task supervisor. However, minimum and maximum age limits do apply.

Further information about the hands-on approach of the ATCV and the work it has achieved, may be obtained from:

ATCV National Headquarters
(ATCV Victorian Division,
Ballarat Regional Office)
PO Box 423
Ballarat VIC 3350
Telephone (053) 33 1483

Albury Wodonga Regional Office
PO Box 17,
Wodonga VIC 3690
Telephone (060) 59 1398

Bendigo Regional Office
PO Box 879
Bendigo VIC 3550
Telephone (054) 41 6666

Melbourne Regional Office
PO Box 507
Cheltenham VIC 3192
Telephone (03) 583 3388

Western District Regional Office
PO Box 35,
Port Fairy VIC 3284
Telephone (055) 68 2468

ATCV Western Australian Division
PO Box 75
Bassendean WA 6054
Telephone (09) 27 9464

ATCV (NSW) Inc
PO Box Q397
Queen Victoria Building Post Office
Sydney NSW 2000
Telephone (02) 451 4028

CHAPTER 2
Bush Regeneration

Bushfires can pose a threat to houses, but their effects on the bush are a different matter. Every year we hear that thousands of hectares of bushland have been destroyed by bushfires, but do they really *destroy* the bush? Outward appearances suggest that they do, but on close examination the amazing ways in which plants can handle bushfires are clearly seen.

For example, hakeas have woody cones which are 'fire-proof'. After the fire passes, even though the hakea may be dead, the cones open, the seeds fall to the ground and the seedlings grow. They are very drought resistant and will continue to grow even without rain.

Wattles also use seeds as a bushfire survival mechanism. They don't have cones, but the seed itself is extremely resistant to various environmental pressures. It requires a trigger mechanism such as a bushfire to stimulate the seeds to sprout.

Eucalypts use other methods for survival. They have lignotubers, which are like underground food storage organs. If a tree dies in a bushfire, buds in the lignotuber develop and produce new stems, which continue the life of that tree. If the damage to the tree is not too severe, the epicormic buds found under the bark of most gum trees will shoot. These buds will sprout in large numbers as soon as the leaves of the tree are killed.

Even with all the adaptations for fire that plants have, bushfires can still cause many problems. They not only kill animals but also wipe out food supplies for animals that may survive. They also allow invasive weeds, such as bracken, a chance to establish quickly and, in many cases, actually replace the native vegetation that existed there before the fire. It is therefore very important that we all exercise extreme care with fire.

CHAPTER 3
Bushwalkers and The Environment

Bushwalking is a popular outdoor activity, enjoyed by people from all areas of life. A bushwalk can range from a short stroll after a family picnic to an expedition lasting several weeks.

Bushwalking is most enjoyable in a natural bush setting with pleasant company. Suitable country for bushwalking has declined over the years due to developments such as mining, logging and dam construction. The majority of those areas remaining are in some form of Crown ownership, such as national park, state forest or local council reserve.

Bushwalkers have a moral obligation to prevent damage to remaining bushland and wildlife through their activities, and to respect the wishes of other people, both private landholders and fellow bushwalkers.

In the natural environment, bushwalkers are visitors who should not leave any substantial trace of their presence.

At all times, bushwalkers should consider the safety of their own party and other users of the area, and remain considerate of other people.

The following guidelines are typical of those supplied to intending bushwalkers by bushwalking clubs.

Preservation of the natural environment All visitors to the natural environment should be self-sufficient. They should not use any form of mechanised transport, or rely on air-drops for food supplies. They should always provide their own overnight accommodation—a fly or tent.

In popular areas, only previously used campsites should be occupied. Camping on fragile vegetation should be avoided. Construction of tent platforms and bed sites, digging of trenches and the use of vegetation for bedding are unnecessary and unacceptable. Living or dead trees are part of the natural environment and should not be cut. Only fallen, dead wood should be used.

In areas where wood is scarce, stoves should be used for cooking, particularly in rainforests and alpine areas. In periods of extreme bushfire risk, only food that doesn't require cooking should be taken.

In well-walked areas, only existing fireplaces should be used. In less visited places, a space should be cleared of litter. When leaving, ashes should be spread, and leaf litter scattered over the fireplace, only after having ensured that the fire is completely extinguished. Firewood should be used sparingly. The use of rocks around the fire is unnecessary and disruptive to the environment; many creatures use rocks for shelter. A party should not light multiple fires but should use only one fire for cooking and warmth.

Toilet waste should be buried away from present and potential campsites, tracks and streams. Toilet paper should be well buried or burnt.

Water supplies should not be polluted by soap, waste or excreta. Swimming and washing should take place downstream of the campsite.

All rubbish must be carried out, especially aluminium foil, plastics and metal cans. Many packets have a layer of aluminium foil under paper and plastic—these must not be burnt. Do not burn food scraps whilst others are cooking.

Marked or formed routes should be used where they exist. Making of parallel tracks should be avoided. Blazes, cairns, tin tags and so on have no place in the natural environment.

Bushwalkers should never rely on huts for accommodation. Due to the scarcity of firewood around huts, stoves should be used in preference to fires. Supplies of wood should not be left for future parties, as this encourages overuse.

Large parties should not be taken into fragile areas such as alpine country.

Safety Written details of your walk should be left with a responsible person. Walkers should always carry a map and compass and be competent in their use. Walkers should carry a first aid kit suited to their needs and be familiar with basic first aid treatment. Matches should always be carried in a waterproof container.

Each member of the party should keep in contact with other party members. Any member who is unable to keep up should inform other party members at the earliest opportunity. A reliable person should bring up the rear in large parties, or parties with inexperienced members. All members should be kept informed of party progress and route planning. At major creek junctions, track junctions or ridge divisions the party should re-group to avoid separation.

Courtesy The sounds of the natural environment should predominate; conflict from radios and other devices is unacceptable.

Fires should be lit well away from any tent or fly.

Each member of the party should provide their own share of wood and water.

Stepping over uncovered food should be avoided.

Parties should avoid camping near others except where campsites are scarce. Rights of private landholders should be respected; permission should be obtained before crossing or camping on private property. Fences and gates are to be left as found.

For further information on bushwalking, contact the nearest bushwalking club in your major town.

New South Wales
NSW Federation of Bushwalking Clubs
GPO Box 2090
Sydney NSW 2001
Telephone (02) 548 1228

Victoria
Federation of Victorian Walking Clubs
GPO Box 815F
Melbourne VIC 3001

Queensland
Queensland Federation of Bushwalking Clubs
GPO Box 1573
Brisbane QLD 4001

Brisbane Bushwalkers
GPO Box 1949
Brisbane QLD 4001
Telephone (07) 856 4050

South Australia
Adelaide Bushwalkers Inc
PO Box 178
Unley SA 5061

Western Australia
Perth Bushwalkers
GPO Box 8321
Perth WA 6000
Telephone (09) 362 1614

Tasmania
Federation of Tasmanian Bushwalking Clubs
PO Box 1190
Launceston TAS 7250

Northern Territory
Darwin Bushwalking Club
PO Box 41568
Casuarina NT 0811
Telephone (089) 81 7629

NATIONAL PARKS AND WILDLIFE AUTHORITIES

The following government departments can provide information on national parks, wildlife and native flora.

NSW National Parks and Wildlife Service
Cnr Bridge Road and Forest Road
Hurstville NSW 2220
Telephone (02) 585 6444

National Parks and Wildlife Division (Victoria)
123 Brown Street
Heidelberg VIC 3084
Telephone (03) 450 8600

Department of Environment and Conservation
(Queensland)
PO Box 155
North Quay QLD 4002
Telephone (07) 202 0200

SA National Parks and Wildlife Service
GPO Box 667
Adelaide SA 5001
Telephone (08) 216 7777

WA Department of Conservation and Land Management
PO Box 104
Como WA 6152
Telephone (09) 367 0333

Department of Parks, Wildlife and Heritage (Tasmania)
GPO Box 44A
Hobart TAS 7001
Telephone (002) 30 2610

ACT Parks and Conservation Service
PO Box 1119
Tuggeranong ACT 2900
Telephone (062) 46 2849

Conservation Commission of the NT
(National Parks Enquiries)
PO Box 496
Palmerston NT 0831
Telephone (089) 89 4423

PEOPLE AND PLACES

CHAPTER I
Ashcombe Maze

The maze or labyrinth has always fascinated mankind. The green maze was very popular in Southern Europe during the 1600s, but the popularity of mazes later waned, and with modern day labour costs, they have nearly disappeared.

The Ashcombe Maze is the first major commercial maze to be constructed in Australia. It is on Victoria's Mornington Peninsula, just south of Melbourne. John Daly planted the hedge only four years ago. The maze was designed by Sally Daly after studying mazes as far back as the twelfth century.

The plant used in this maze is *Cupressus macrocarpa*, which is a fairly common plant in Australia. This variety is often sold as 'Lambertiana'. It is a good conifer for southern and inland areas of Australia; as it is extremely resilient to cold and drying out. It is not as good through the middle and northern areas of Australia; in fact, its golden form, 'Brunniana' was featured on 'Burke's Backyard' as having all sorts of disease problems.

A new maze of 1200 roses has recently been completed. The hedge is watered by a drip irrigation system, and with hand clippers.

Ashcombe Maze is open to the public from 10 am to 5 pm every weekend, and during public and school holiday periods. It is situated in Red Hill Road, Shoreham, VIC 3916. Telephone (059) 89 8387.

The type of tree used in the hedge has been named the 'Amazing Tree' and it is available at the maze.

CHAPTER 2
Botanic Golf

Just north of Wanneroo in Western Australia is Perth's golf course with a difference—'Botanic Golf'. It is an 18-hole mini-golf course, set in 2ha (5 acres) of landscaped gardens with rockeries, watercourses, waterfalls, ornamental ponds, exotic plants and fountains.

Originally the area was made up of white, desert-like sand dunes. To create this new landscape, 10 000 cubic metres of sand were removed and 700 tonnes of rock and 1000 tonnes of sewage sludge added.

It was first laid out in 1974, and most of the plants are not much more than ten years old. One of the interesting things about the garden is that Australian native plants were initially used, but after a few years they were replaced with conifers and other exotics. The garden was designed by Theo Puik, one of the best landscape designers in Australia.

The water features are created out of local limestone and cement with mosses and lichens growing over them. This is achieved by having a sprinkler system among the ground covers adjacent to the rocks.

Approximately 80 000 people a year pass through the garden and it stands up to this well. The lawns are a mixture of seaside bent grass and saltine. Couch is not used, as it tends to invade the garden beds.

CHAPTER 3
Canberra
Cork Tree Plantation

Cork, the familiar substance which is used to plug bottles, is made from the bark of a tree—an evergreen variety of oak, which has typical oak leaves and acorns.

The only cork oak plantation in Australia is situated in the Australian Capital Territory, just on the outskirts of Canberra. Walter Burley Griffin, who designed Canberra, commissioned a well-known botanist, Thomas Western, to create a European arboretum. The cork oak plantation is the only section of the arboretum that remains to this day.

About 4000 cork oak trees have survived. The plantation

is a success, in that the cork oak trees have grown, but it would not be a successful commercial plantation, because the trees have never been tended in the appropriate manner. They have not been thinned and the lower branches have not been removed.

Despite this, cork of commercial quality can be harvested from the trees by slicing through the bark and splitting it away from the trunk. Care is required; too deep a cut will kill the tree.

The Canberra cork oak plantation is a site of significance in the ACT. It is on the register of the National Estate, and the staff who tend the plantation are most careful to preserve it as it is, and to encourage people to see it as part of their cultural heritage.

There are very few people in Australia who have much experience at removing cork from trees. But in Portugal, where cork is grown commercially, people are trained during long apprenticeships to harvest cork correctly.

Cork trees could well be a viable commercial proposition somewhere in Australia if grown in rich soils in a region receiving higher rainfall than Canberra. However, there is a small trap. You don't harvest your first cork from a tree until it is about 25 years old, and harvesting then takes place every nine years after that. It is not until the third crop that the cork is of a high quality. That adds up to over 50 years before you cut your first really good cork to put in the top of a bottle.

So, while there is a good argument for more plantations to be established in Australia, the number of years involved means this is probably not very likely.

CHAPTER 4
Diane Cilento

Information about Diane Cilento's far north Queensland property, 'Karnak', the self awareness courses conducted there, and her recently completed open air theatre, may be obtained by writing to:

Miss Diane Cilento
PO Box 167
Mossman QLD 4873

CHAPTER 5
Dunk Island

One 'Burke's Backyard' programme featured Dunk Island Resort's interesting tropical gardens. The plants Don mentioned in the segment were:

Red-edged dracaena (*Dracaena marginata* 'Tricolor')
Crotons (*Codiaeum* sp)

Ixoras (*Ixora coccinea*)
Devil's ivy (*Raphidophora aurea*)
Parrot's beak flower (*Heliconia* sp)
Golden allamanda (*Allamanda neriifolia*)
Poinciana tree (*Delonix regia*)
Golden rain tree (*Cassia fistula*)
Torch ginger (*Hedychium* sp)

CHAPTER 6
The Forest of Tranquillity

The Forest of Tranquillity is located on Ourimbah Creek Road, Ourimbah, about an hour's drive north of Sydney, New South Wales, in the Gosford area, and is open daily except Monday and Tuesday.

For further information and the park's opening hours please ring (043) 62 1855, or write to the park:

The Forest of Tranquillity
Ourimbah NSW 2258

CHAPTER 7
Gumnut Village

The giant gumnut shown on one segment of 'Burke's Backyard' is part of Gumnut Village at Montrose in Victoria.

The two-storey gumnut includes a gift shop and gallery. The gift shop stocks an unusual range of souvenirs, including household goods, jewellery, clothing, books, stationery, and edibles. The gallery contains a large collection of paintings of Australian flora and fauna, and an extensive range of ceramic works. All items sold from the gumnut are Australian made.

A 270m² (323sq yd) mural adorns the upper walls and ceilings of the giant gumnut. It depicts characters from May Gibbs's stories, including Snuggle Pot and Cuddle Pie and the Big Bad Banksia Man.

The giant gumnut is situated at Gumnut Village, Austraflora Nursery, Belfast Road (PO Box 201), Montrose, VIC 3765. Telephone (03) 728 1222.

> *Trees can count. After perhaps 40 really cold days, they decide that spring is due and produce new leaves.*

CHAPTER 8
Healesville Sanctuary's White Kookaburra

The white (albino) kookaburra shown on 'Burke's Backyard' can be seen at:

Healesville Sanctuary
Badger Creek Road
Healesville VIC 3777

CHAPTER 9
Kings Cross—Sydney

John Byrell, author of *Up the Cross*, invited 'Burke's Backyard' to tour Sydney's infamous Kings Cross. His hope was to show the more pleasant aspects of the area, instead of the usual seamy scenes favoured by the media.

First stop was the local police station. This normally spartan-looking community building has, in this instance, been beautifully landscaped and virtually disappears into a green jungle. The surroundings are not only enjoyed by the local law enforcers but also by a group of thieves— ibises who have made Kings Cross their home and spend their days foraging through bins; stealing leftovers deposited by customers of the nearby fast food outlets.

Another item of interest is an avocado tree. Planted 50 years ago by a long time resident of the Cross, it has survived the demolition of many nearby buildings, the construction of a car park virtually on top of its roots, and many other attacks on its attempts to eke out an existence. The lady who planted this tree—long before avocados were fashionable—protected her crop by spreading a rumour that the tree's produce was actually a poison fruit from South Africa. These days the tree is maintained and protected by a group of Kings Cross bouncers.

John also showed us Victoria Street, which used to be filled with dilapidated tenements infested with rats and other vermin. According to John, people such as Jack Mundy and Juanita Neilson, through their 'Green Bans' and concern for the Cross, ensured that these areas were cleaned up. This street now has a green canopy over a Parisian-style area, full of restaurants (many with balconies overlooking the trees), beautiful outdoor eating places and numerous coffee shops.

The final character we met was John O'Leary who, in spite of finding both locals and visitors 'sleeping it off' from time to time amongst his shrubberies, has created a beautiful native garden in one of the busiest areas of the Cross.

Next time you visit Kings Cross, you might consider looking at it from a different perspective.

CHAPTER 10
Kings Park and Botanic Garden—Perth

Kings Park in Perth, Western Australia, is open daily and contains many historical memorials as well as the Western Australian Botanic Garden. Of the garden's 17ha (42 acres), 14ha (34½ acres) are devoted to a display of more than 1200 Western Australian native species. A detailed brochure is available on request.

Kings Park Board
West Perth WA 6005

For general enquiries, fire reports and horticultural advice on the cultivation of native plants, telephone (09) 321 4801, (09) 321 5065 or (09) 321 5228.

CHAPTER 11
Leyland Brothers' World

'Burke's Backyard' visited the Leyland Brothers' home and theme park—Leyland Brothers' World, which will be open to the public early in 1990. For further information, please contact:

Leyland Brothers' World
Pacific Highway
Tea Gardens NSW 2324
Telephone (049) 97 3103

CHAPTER 12
Reg Livermore's Garden

Reg Livermore's garden is situated at Wentworth Falls in the Blue Mountains of New South Wales.

Covering an area of 1.8ha (4½ acres), the garden contains an astonishing collection of cold-climate trees and shrubs, most of which have been assembled in the ten years since Reg went to live there.

The land was previously somewhat rural in character, and had been attached to a kiosk and tea room that serviced the lookout at Wentworth Falls. Sometimes people took picnics there, and it was also available for overnight caravan parking.

The land's character was interesting in its own right, and lent itself to imaginative landscaping and planting.

Reg confesses that his own early attempts were far from ideal, and eventually he enlisted the services of John Gaibor to undertake the serious landscaping that now attracts many visitors to the garden during spring and autumn.

It is due to both men that the result is so pleasing; John's eye for the shape and form of things, and Reg's love of colour and the plants that thrive there, complement each other perfectly. What was essentially a wilderness surrounded on all sides by tall old pine trees and a handful of mature silver poplars has been transformed into an imaginative park of great beauty and tranquillity.

The garden is called 'Pirramimma', a lilting Aboriginal word meaning the stars and the moon; it is open to visitors on weekends during September, October, April, and early May.

Coach trips may be arranged on weekdays during those times by writing to the address below. There is a small entrance fee.

The garden is well worth a visit, and has become one of the most popular tourist attractions of the Blue Mountains.

The garden is located at 168 Falls Road, Wentworth Falls, NSW 2782.

CHAPTER 13
Milton Park—Bowral

Milton Park is a superbly landscaped hilltop garden just east of Bowral in the Southern Highlands of New South Wales. It was inspired by the English school of landscape design, which prevailed until early this century, and is arguably the greatest garden in Australia. A fortuitous combination of mild summers and cool winters, rich volcanic soil and a regular rainfall has created an environment that is compatible with imported species of beech, ash, elm and maple trees.

The garden covers an area of 109ha (270 acres) and, with over 10 million plants, offers a spectacular vista. The flowering dogwoods in white, pink and ruby tones flank an emerald lawn, which leads past wide, curving beds packed with highly scented white, mauve and purple lilacs. The garden beds house over 100 000 forget-me-nots and 200 000 bulbs. A timber pergola supports a magnificent double, deep-purple wisteria, leading to a sparkling waterfall and, beside it, a towering rhododendron which is studded with pink-red flowers.

There is even a parterre garden; one which contains topiarised plants. The rose bushes are contained by a great wall, and box hedging in circular and triangular shapes trims the rose beds. Showing the wonderful sense of humour that is so typical of this style of garden, there is even a chicken, lovingly carved out of English box.

Everything at Milton Park is on a grand scale. The park itself is huge, and so are many of the plants—giant Californian redwoods, huge pines, giant grafted Japanese maples and giant tulip trees.

Milton Park also offers accommodation in a villa-style homestead, which is surrounded by lawns and curving garden beds. It is an exceptional garden, which preserves a fine tradition of English landscape design.

Milton Park
Horderns Road
Bowral NSW 2576
Telephone (048) 61 1522

CHAPTER 14
Mt Coot-tha Botanic Gardens—Toowong, Queensland

The botanic gardens on the Mt Coot-tha Road at Toowong in Queensland are open every day of the year. Special features of the gardens include a planetarium and lagoon; a fragrant plants and herbs garden; an exotic rainforest; a tropical display dome and temperate region plants; an arid zone and cacti/epiphyte display house, and also a demonstration garden. A brochure is available on request.

Mt Coot-tha Botanic Gardens
Mt Coot-tha Road
Toowong QLD 4066
Telephone (07) 377 8891, (07) 377 8893

CHAPTER 15
Replica Aircraft

Mr Eddie Matthews, builder of the replica planes that appeared in one segment of 'Burke's Backyard', has sold the aircraft to the Oakey Army Aviation Museum in Queensland. He intends to continue with his hobby, however, and plans for the construction of further models are underway.

Anyone wishing to see the replica planes can do so at the Oakey Army Aviation Museum, Oakey, 20 minutes south of Toowoomba, Queensland. The opening hours are: Wednesday, Thursday, Friday: 8 am–4 pm. Saturday, Sunday: 10 am–5 pm. All other times by appointment only. Telephone (076) 91 7011 and ask to speak to the museum staff.

For further information regarding construction of the

aircraft, Mr Eddie (Biggles) Matthews may be contacted at:

30 Coombabah Road
Biggera Waters QLD 4216
Telephone (075) 37 4628

CHAPTER 16
William Ricketts Sanctuary

Mr William Ricketts is a sculptor, who has lived and worked in his rainforest sanctuary at Mt Dandenong, Victoria for 57 years. He is now aged 91. Mr Ricketts has a great love of the Aboriginal people and their culture and Dreamtime, as well as Australia's native fauna. He dedicated the sanctuary to this culture, and has filled the rainforest with his sculptures of Aboriginal people and their Dreamtime imagery.

Entry fees are $3 per adult; $2 for pensioners, the unemployed and people holding a concession card; $1 for children 10-14 years old; children under 10 years gain free admission. The Sanctuary is open every day—from 10 am to 4.30 pm.

There is a wheelchair path through most of the Sanctuary; a few of the more remote sections may be inaccessible to disabled people, however. Sanctuary supervisors advise that park officers, if available, will assist with wheelchairs. There is no entry fee for people confined to a wheelchair.

The William Ricketts Sanctuary is located on the Mt Dandenong Tourist Road, Mt Dandenong, VIC 3767. Telephone (03) 751 1300. The Melways Directory reference is Map 66, G1.

CHAPTER 17
Royal National Park— Deer

The Royal National Park is just south of Sydney. Although the park was named only in 1954, it is in fact very old, having been dedicated as the Sutherland National Park on 28 April 1879, just five years after Yellowstone, making it the second oldest national park in the world.

In those days, acclimatisation was favoured over conservation so various creatures were released into the park, including five species of deer and one of antelope. When Rusa deer were introduced in 1904, they thrived at the expense of other species.

Cervus timorensis russa from Java is a large (110cm—43"—shoulder height) and aggressive deer, and has been so successful that it has caused problems such as the clearing of forest (by chewing up seedlings), pruning of older plants, track erosion and the forcing out of native species such as the grey kangaroo.

But the Javan deer have a positive side: they are visible during the daylight hours, unlike our nocturnal natives; they are attractive to look at, and provide a tourist attraction. The herd also has some heritage and historic value.

National Park authorities monitor the numbers of deer and when competition becomes intense, such as after bushfires, remove some of them to the deer farm. This prevents excessive park damage and protects the deer from illegal culling.

CHAPTER 18
Shortland Wetlands

The Shortland Wetlands Centre is an education, research and recreation facility based on wetlands and focusing on the valuable wetlands of the Hunter Estuary.

The centre is located on 65ha of wetland off Sandgate Road, Shortland (near Newcastle, New South Wales) on the edge of the 2500ha Hexham Swamp. The Centre was officially opened late in 1988. It is open to the public from 9 am to 5 pm seven days a week and at some times of the year for extended hours. Thousands of students of all ages, including many from overseas, visit the Centre each year.

The history of the Shortland Wetlands is unusual. The natural wetlands were used as a council rubbish dump for many years before the dump was converted into a football field. The football club was unsuccessful, and eventually a proposal was made to the Newcastle City Council, by members of the local community, to rehabilitate the degraded environment and restore the site to its original status as a wetland. The area would then become a reserve for the purposes of education, research and recreation. BHP and Brambles were major sponsors who helped to reconstruct ponds at the site.

Shortland Wetlands includes a visitors' centre with educational displays such as mounted bird specimens, live water plants and animals, walking trails, canoe trails, an observation tower, guided tours and explanatory talks (these should be prearranged), marshes, swamps, ponds and creeks. The egret rookery is unique in Australia because it is within a city boundary, close to residences, and one of very few colonies where all four egret species breed together. About 150 bird species, several very rare and more than 30 of these breeding, have been recorded at Shortland Wetlands.

For further information

Shortland Wetlands Centre
PO Box 130
Wallsend NSW 2287
Telephone (049) 51 6466

CHAPTER 19
Surry Hills—McElhone Street

In one segment of 'Burke's Backyard' we visited an old, inner-city Sydney street, transformed by the co-operation of its residents over the last 10 or 12 years, into one long garden.

Long-time resident and initiator of the greening, Johnny Costello, recalled that after initial opposition, the local council provided soil and plants to help with the project.

The surprise is that a splendid effect has been achieved, using quite ordinary, tough and readily available plants, such as:

Umbrella trees
Impatiens
Tibouchinas (Lasiandra)
Lavender
Rosemary
Azaleas
Kumquats
Willows
Viburnum
Geraniums
Variegated New Zealand Christmas bush
Philodendron selloum
Cassia bicapularis

These are all grown in containers such as laundry tubs.

Thanks to the neighbours' co-operation and the abundance of greenery, McElhone Street is now a leafy, friendly place, where people sit and chat, drink coffee and read the papers. They even hold champagne breakfast parties. Their efforts have not only built a beautiful garden, but a sense of community.

CHAPTER 20
Sydney Tropical Butterfly House

Many people are fascinated by butterflies, but with the increasing use of chemicals these magnificent creatures are becoming rarer. This has led to the establishment of a number of butterfly houses, where live butterflies are kept in special enclosures.

The latest is the Sydney Tropical Butterfly House at Dural, which was established by Ken Hargraves. It may seem a simple thing to have a few butterflies fluttering around, but a lot of modern technology is involved in maintaining suitable conditions for all phases of the butterfly life cycle.

The temperature in the butterfly house is kept at about 30°C (86°F), while the humidity is 71%. The interior has the appearance of a lush forest scene, with rock waterfalls, ponds and abundant greenery. The plants have been carefully selected to include those that are the special food plants of the caterpillars. The adult butterflies feed on a complex nectar formula, which they sip from artificial flowers comprised of silk petals around a small plastic tube that holds the nectar.

Without this special environment it would be difficult to encourage the butterflies to breed. The eggs are laid on plants in the main enclosure but are later collected and removed to a special 'growing room' until the next generation of butterflies is ready to emerge.

Some of the butterflies that can be seen in the Sydney Tropical Butterfly House (and the plants on which their caterpillars feed) are:

Orchard butterfly (citrus)
Cruiser (*Adenia heterophylla*, native passion vine)
Wanderer or Monarch (swan plant, milkweed)
Cairns Bird Wing (*Aristolochia tagala*)
Common Australian Crow (oleander)
Blue Triangle (camphor laurel)
Red Lacewing (*Adenia heterophylla*)

By growing caterpillar food plants you may be able to encourage some of these butterfly species to live in your own backyard.

For further information

Australian Tropical Butterflies, by Peter Valentine, published by Tropical Australia Graphics, 1988, is available for about $12.

CHAPTER 21
Unusual Putting Green

In most areas of Australia when you're chipping up towards the hole on a golf course, you are praying that your ball is going to land on the green. That is not the case in Moonta, South Australia.

At Moonta you're hoping that it lands on the black. It is too hot for the soft, tender grasses that are normally grown on golf courses. Instead, they use crushed slag from the nearby Wallaroo mines to spread over the putting green.

CHAPTER 22
Edna Walling and Bickleigh Vale Village

Edna Walling was probably Australia's best known landscape designer. She was born in England in 1896 and moved to Australia with her family as a teenager. Edna Walling was one of the first three women to study at the Burnley Horticultural College, and then worked as a gardener until she began to design gardens for architects. She worked continuously from the 1920s to the 1960s and eventually became a writer on the subject of her designs. In the latter years of her life Edna Walling became very unhappy with the urban sprawl of Melbourne. She moved to Queensland, and died there in 1973.

Edna Walling was passionate about the principles of the garden design she espoused. She did not like the garishness and regimentality of the suburban gardens of her time. She believed in subtle, free-form use of colour and line. Moss, lichen and foliage plants held greater appeal for her than a bed of bright annuals.

Edna liked to see trees planted in groups (their positions determined by the fall of potatoes thrown from a bucket) rather than in rows. She approved of secret, winding paths leading to wild nooks and crannies that combined the textures of stone walls and paths, water features and, of course, foliage.

Towards the end of her career Edna Walling became interested in Australian native plants, and helped popularise their use in suburban gardens.

Edna Walling designed a small housing estate, Bickleigh Vale Village, in the outer Melbourne suburb of Mooroolbark. It is now a National Heritage property. Her purpose in designing the estate was to demonstrate her theories of completely integrating all aspects of the environment; the homes and gardens all blending together to create a harmonious whole.

Edna Walling's books include: *Gardens in Australia: Their Design and Care*, *Cottage and Garden in Australia*, *A Gardener's Log* and *The Australian Roadside*. She also wrote a regular column for *Australian Home Beautiful*.

A play based on the life of Edna Walling, was recently performed in Melbourne's Fitzroy Gardens, titled *Edna for the Garden*. It was written by Suzanne Spunner and performed by The Home Cooking Theatre Company.

INDEX

"I hope you have enjoyed the first edition of 'Burke's Backyard Information Guide'. We're busily building up Fact Sheets from new segments for the second edition. Till then . . . Hooroo."

P.S. Just for fun, here's one more 'amazing fact'—the word backyard appears in this book 423 times.

NOTES

NOTES